BUSINESS ASSOCIATIONS

Copyright © 2013 Marcia Johnson

Published in USA by Aten Group, LLC

No part of this publication may be reproduced or transmitted in any form or by any means, electronic or mechanical, including photocopy, recording, or utilized by any information storage or retrieval system, without written permission from the publisher

Printed in the United States of America

ISBN-10: 0989693600

ISBN-13: 9780989693608

Acknowledgements

The authors wish to acknowledge and thank the following persons:

Dean Dannye Holley for supporting this effort to provide an effective learning resource for our students,

Professor Docia Rudley for her assistance in this effort,

To Stanley Love Tate, TMSL class 2013, an outstanding student, who insisted that this project be completed and who lead student researchers to assure it was.

To Tarishawn Morton, TMSL class 2014, who worked with us as a research assistant and who made herself available for tasks as needed.

To our editors:

Danyel Norris, Tanya Terry, Christopher Ogolla, A'Kiesha C. White, Business Editor, Thurgood Marshall Law Review, TMSL class 2014, and Andreience Hines, who provided her expert paralegal skills and who helped ensure consistency of format and style.

Our special acknowledgement, appreciation and attribution to Luckett Anthony Johnson who played a crucial role throughout the process conducting research, writing, compiling and editing.

"Any intelligent fool can make things bigger and more complex... It takes a touch of genius - and a lot of courage to move in the opposite direction."   Albert Einstein

INTRODUCTION

This book is designed to provide an introduction to Texas Business Organizations. Texas adopted its Business Organizations Code in 2006. Prior to that time the Texas legislature enacted several different statutes that addressed each form of recognized business entity. For example, The Texas Revised Partnership Act provided the legal principles for general partnerships, the Texas Business Corporations Act covered corporations law, The Texas Revised Limited Partnership Act covered the law of limited partnerships and the Texas Limited Liability Company Act provided the law for Texas limited liability companies. In an effort to codify and simplify these laws of business organizations in Texas, the legislature adopted the Texas Business Organizations Code.

Organizations are associations of persons who act together to reach one or more goals. The study of businesss organizations is principally about relationships discussed in the context of an organization structure. This basic course seeks to help you define and clarify the various relationships that occur between people and entities in the business arena.

Structure provides opportunity for a relationship to define roles to ensure optimum performance. Roles, functions, authority and systems of operation help to ensure that a business runs efficiently and properly. As an attorney, you may be called upon to advise persons and or businesses about a wide range of matters from pre-formation to termination. Minimally, you should be conversant in the areas to be able to provide competent representation.

In this book, we seek to present the subject of business organizations clearly and concisely and in a way that is easily understood. We begin with a discussion of Agency which is the foundation of business organizations. Next, we address five business organizations, the (1) general partnership, (2) the limited liability partnership, (3) limited partnership, (4) the corporation, and the (5) limited liability company. For each organization we examine how the entity is formed or created, how it is governed, liability of entity and governing persons including for breaches of fiduciary duties, financing and dissolution and termination.

Following each section, we include a quick reference guide to the pertinent Texas Business Organization Code provisions. That is followed by practice questions which seek to engage the student to employ his or her knowledge to solve practical situations.

Marcia Johnson Emeka
Duruigbo

Table of Contents

AGENCY 1
  Creating the Agency 1
  What is agency? 1
    §1.01 Agency defined. 1
    §1.02 Parties Labeling and Popular Usage Not Controlling. 1
  Establishing the elements 1
  Types of Agency Relationships 3
    §7.07 Employee Acting Within Scope of Employment… 3
  Establishing Agency 4
    Boyd v. Eikenberry 4
  Employee as Agent 7
    Del Carmen Flores v. Summit Hotel Group 7
  Employee vs. Independent Contractors 10
    Coleman v. Klöckner & Co. et.al. 10
    New Terminal Warehouse Corp. v. Wilson 19
  Capacity 22
    § 3.04 Capacity To Act As Principal 22
    § 3.05 Capacity To Act As Agent. 22
    May v. Ken-Rad Corporation, Inc. 22
    § 2.01 Actual Authority. 25
    § 2.02 Scope of Actual Authority.. 25
    § 2.03 Apparent Authority. 26
  Actual and Apparent Authority 27
    Sociedad De Solaridad Social "El Estillero" v. J.S. Mcmanus Produce Co. 27
    Streetman v. Benchmark Bank 29
    Nationsbank v. Dilling 33
  Scope of Employment 36
    Biggs v. U.S. Fire Ins. Co. 36
    Suarez v. Jordan 40

- § 2.05 Estoppel To Deny Existence Of Agency Relationship. 45
  - Wyndham Hotel Co. v. Self 45
- Doctrine of respondeat superior 52
  - Baptist Mem'l Hosp. Sys. v. Sampson 52
  - § 4.01 Ratification Defined 56
  - § 4.02 Effect Of Ratification 56
  - § 4.03 Acts That May Be Ratified. 57
  - § 4.04 Capacity To Ratify 57
  - § 4.05 Timing Of Ratification. 57
  - § 4.06 Knowledge Requisite To Ratification. 57
  - § 4.07 No Partial Ratification. 57
  - § 4.08 Estoppel To Deny Ratification. 57
  - Disney Enterprises, Inc. v. Esprit Finance, Inc., ... 58
- Fiduciary Duty: Rights, duties, and liabilities between principal and agent 63
- Principal to agent 63
  - § 8.13 Duty Created By Contract. 63
  - § 8.14 Duty To Indemnify. 63
  - § 8.15 Principal's Duty To Deal Fairly And In Good Faith. 63
- Agent to principal 64
- The Duty of Loyalty 64
  - § 8.01 General Fiduciary Principle. 64
  - § 8.02 Material Benefit Arising Out Of Position. 64
  - § 8.03 Acting As Or On Behalf Of An Adverse Party. 64
  - § 8.04 Competition. 64
  - § 8.05 Use Of Principal's Property; Use Of Confidential Information. 64
  - § 8.06 Principal's Consent. 65
  - § 8.07 Duty Created By Contract. 65
- Duty of Care 65
  - § 8.08 Duties Of Care, Competence, And Diligence. 65
  - § 8.09 Duty To Act Only Within Scope Of Actual Authority And To Comply With Principal's Lawful Instructions. 66

§ 8.10 Duty Of Good Conduct. 66
§ 8.11 Duty To Provide Information. 66
§ 8.12 Duties Regarding Principal's Property--Segregation, Record-Keeping, And Accounting. 66
§ 8.13 Duty Created By Contract. 66

Duties of Loyalty and Care 66
    West v. Touchstone 66
    Laredo Med. Grp. v. Lightner 70

Liability: Disclosed, Partially Disclosed and Undisclosed Principals 74

Agent's Liability 74
§ 6.01 Agent For Disclosed Principal. 75
§ 6.08 Other Subsequent Dealings Between Third Party And Agent. 75
§ 6.11 Agent's Representations. 75
§ 7.01 Agent's Liability To Third Party. 76
§ 7.02 Duty To Principal; Duty To Third Party. 76
§ 6.02 Agent For Unidentified Principal. 76
§ 6.03 Agent For Undisclosed Principal. 76
§ 6.06 Setoff. 76
§ 6.04 Principal Does Not Exist Or Lacks Capacity. 77
§ 6.07 Settlement With Agent By Principal Or Third Party 77

Principal's Liability 78
§ 7.03 Principal's Liability--In General 78
§ 7.04 Agent Acts With Actual Authority. 79
§ 7.05 Principal's Negligence In Conducting Activity Through Agent; Principal's Special Relationship With Another Person 79
§ 7.06 Failure In Performance Of Principal's Duty Of Protection 79
§ 7.07 Employee Acting Within Scope Of Employment 79
§ 6.09 Effect Of Judgment Against Agent Or Principal. 80
§ 6.10 Agent's Implied Warranty Of Authority. 80
§ 2.04 Respondeat Superior. An employer is subject to liability for torts committed by employees while acting within the scope of their employment. 80
§ 3.02 Formal Requirements 80

Liability – Disclosure of Principal 81
    Southwestern Bell Media, Inc. v. Trepper 81
Terminating the agency relationship 85
    § 3.07 Death, Cessation Of Existence, And Suspension Of Powers. 85
    § 3.06 Termination Of Actual Authority--In General 86
    § 3.08 Loss Of Capacity 86
    § 3.09 Termination By Agreement Or By Occurrence Of changed Circumstances. 86
    § 3.10 Manifestation Terminating Actual Authority 87
    § 3.11 Termination Of Apparent Authority 87
    § 3.12 Power Given As Security; Irrevocable Proxy 87
    § 3.13 Termination Of Power Given As Security Or Irrevocable Proxy 87
    Hartford v. McGillicuddy 88

Agency Problem Set 91

GENERAL PARTNERSHIPS 96
Core Concepts 97
Nature and Formation 97
    Exception: 97
Texas 97
    Exception: 97
Default Entity 97
Five Advantages of establishing the General Partnership: 98
Five Disadvantages of the General Partnership structure: 98
Texas General Partnership Statutes 98
    §152.051. Partnership Defined… 98
    Exxon Corporation v. Breezevale Ltd 99
    § 152.002. Effect Of Partnership Agreement; Nonwaivable And Variable Provisions 103
    § 152.208. Amendment To Partnership Agreement. 104
    § 152.052. Rules For Determining If Partnership Is Created 104
    Ingram and Behavioral Psychology Clinic, P.C. v. Deere et.al. 105
Partnership by estoppel 114
    §152.054. False Representation of Partnership or Partner 114

§152.307. 114

CCR, INC., et al., v. Chamberlain, et al., ... 115

United States of America, Ex Rel., v. Integrated Coast Guard Systems, et.al. 121

The Nature of the General Partnership 125

§152.056. Partnership As Entity. 125

§152.101. Nature Of Partnership Property. 125

§152.102. Classification As Partnership Property. 125

exceptions 126

§152.053. Qualifications To Be Partner; Nonpartner's Liability To Third Person. 126

§152.054. False Representation Of Partnership Or Partner. 126

Destec Energy, Inc., v. Houston Lighting & Power Company 127

Siller v. LPP Mortgage Ltd. 131

GOVERNANCE 134

Subchapter D: Relationship Between Partners and Between Partnership 134

§152.201. Admission As Partner 134

§152.203. Rights And Duties Of Partner. 134

§152.204. General Standards Of Partner's Conduct. 134

§152.205. Partner's Duty Of Loyalty. 135

§152.206. Partner's Duty Of Care. 135

§152.207. Standards Of Conduct Applicable To Person Winding Up Partnership Business. 135

§152.208. Amendment To Partnership Agreement 135

§152.209. Decision-Making Requirement. 136

§ 152.211. Remedies Of Partnership And Partners. 136

§152.212. Books And Records Of Partnership. 136

§152.213. Information Regarding Partnership. 137

§152.214. Certain Third-Party Obligations Not Affected. 137

§152.301. Partner As Agent 137

§152.302. Binding Effect Of Partner's Action. 137

Long v. Lopez 138

FINANCE 144

§152.202. Credits Of And Charges To Partner. 144

§152.308. Partner's Partnership Interest Subject To Charging Order. 144

Subchapter F. Transfer Of Partnership Interests 145

§152.401. Transfer Of Partnership Interest. 145

§152.402. General Effect Of Transfer. 145

§152.403. Effect Of Transfer On Transferor. 145

§152.404. Rights And Duties Of Transferee. 145

§152.405. Power To Effect Transfer Or Grant Of Security Interest. 146

§152.406. Effect Of Death Or Divorce On Partnership Interest. 146

Von Hohn, and in the Interest of H.B.V.H. and A.S.V.H., Minor Children 146

LIABILITY 153

§152.053. Qualifications To Be Partner; Nonpartner's Liability To Third Person. 153

§152.054. False Representation Of Partnership Or Partner. 153

§152.210. Partner's Liability To Partnership And Other Partners. 153

§152.304. Nature Of Partner's Liability. 154

§152.305. Remedy 154

§152.306. Enforcement Of Remedy. 154

§152.307. Extension Of Credit In Reliance On False Representation. 155

§152.204. General Standards Of Partner's Conduct. 155

§152.207. Standards Of Conduct Applicable To Person Winding Up Partnership Business 155

§152.303. Liability Of Partnership For Conduct Of Partner. 156

Howell v. Hilton Hotels Corp. 156

fiduciary Duties 159

Texas Business Organization Code provisions 160

§ 152.204. General Standards of Partner's Conduct 160

§ 152.205. Partner's Duty of Loyalty. 160

§ 152.206. Partner's Duty of Care 160

§ 152.207. Standards of Conduct Applicable to Person Winding up Partnership Business. 161

§ 154.201. Business Transactions Between Partner and Partnership 161

§ 152.213. Information Regarding Partnership 161

§ 152.002. Effect of Partnership Agreement; Nonwaivable and Variable Provisions 161

Champion v. Mizell 162

    Wilson v. Contwell 164

    Bohatch v. Butler & Binion 166

WINDING UP AND TERMINATION 175

Core Concepts 175

Winding Up the Business 175

    § 152.001. Definitions. 176

    § 152.207. Standards Of Conduct Applicable To Person Winding Up Partnership Business. 176

Subchapter G: Withdrawal of Partner 176

    § 152.501. Events Of Withdrawal. 176

    § 152.502. Effect Of Event Of Withdrawal On Partnership And Other Partners. 178

    § 152.503. Wrongful Withdrawal; Liability. 178

    § 152.504. Withdrawn Partner's Power To Bind Partnership. 179

    § 152.505. Effect Of Withdrawal On Partner's Existing Liability. 179

    § 152.506. Liability Of Withdrawn Partner To Third Party. 179

Subchapter H. Redemption Of Withdrawing Partner's Or Transferee's Interest 180

§ 152.602. Redemption Price. 180

§ 152.603. Contribution Obligation 180

§ 152.604. Setoff For Certain Damages 180

§ 152.605. Accrual Of Interest. 180

§ 152.606. Indemnification For Certain Liability 180

§ 152.607. Demand Or Payment Of Estimated Redemption. 181

§ 152.608. Deferred Payment On Wrongful Withdrawal. 182

§ 152.609. Action To Determine Terms Of Redemption. 182

§ 152.610. Deferred Payment On Winding Up Partnership. 182

§ 152.611. Redemption Of Transferee's Partnership Interest. 183

§ 152.612. Action To Determine Transferee's Redemption Price. 183

Subchapter I. Supplemental Winding Up And Termination Provisions 184

§ 152.701. Effect Of Event Requiring Winding Up. 184

§ 152.702. Persons Eligible To Wind Up Partnership Business. 184

§ 152.703. Rights And Duties Of Person Winding Up Partnership Business. 184

§ 152.704. Binding Effect Of Partner's Action After Event Requiring Winding Up 185

§ 152.705. Partner's Liability To Other Partners After Event Requiring Winding Up. 185

§ 152.706. Disposition Of Assets. 185

§ 152.707. Settlement Of Accounts. 185

§ 152.708. Contributions To Discharge Obligations. 186

§ 152.709. Cancellation Or Revocation Of Event Requiring Winding Up; Continuation Of Partnership. 186

§ 152.710. Reinstatement. 187

In re Leal v. Mokhabery 187

Coleman v. Coleman 196

Farnsworth v. Deaver 202

Table 1 207

General Partnership Problem Set 211

LIMITED LIABILITY PARTNERSHIPS 217

Core Concepts 217

Formation 217

§152.803. Name. 218

§152.805. Limited Partnership. 218

§ 152.802. Registration. 218

Apcar Investment Partners VI, Ltd. v. Gaus 220

Governance 223

Liability 224

§152.801. Liability Of Partner. 224

Evanston Insurance Company v. Dillard Department Stores, Inc., v. Chargois et.al. 225

FINANCE 231

Termination 231

Tabel 2 233

Limited Liability Partnerships Problem Set 236

LIMITED PARTNERSHIPS 241

Core Concepts 241

Nature of the Limited Partnership: The Nature and Structure 241

§ 153.002. Construction 242

§ 153.003. Applicability of Other Laws 242

§ 153.004. Nonwaivable Title 1 Provisions 242

§ 153.005. Waiver or Modification of Rights of Third Parties 243

Limited Partnership: Advantages and Disadvantages 243

Limited Partnership: Formation 244

§ 3.005. Certificate of Formation 245

§ 3.011. Supplemental Provisions Regarding Certificate of Formation of Limited Partnership 246

§ 5.055. Name of Limited Partnership or Foreign Limited Partnership 246

§ 2.003. General Prohibited Purposes. A domestic entity may not: 246

Entity Status 247

In Re Allcat Claims Serv., L.P. 247

Limited Partnership: Governance 250

Bradford Partners II, L.P. v. Fahning 250

Limited Partnership: Authority of General Partner 253

§ 153.152. General Powers and Liabilities of General Partner 253

§ 153.153. Powers and Liabilities of Person Who is Both General Partner and Limited Partner. 254

Limited Partnership: Authority of Limited Partner 254

§ 153.401. Right to Bring Action. 254

§ 153.402. Proper Plaintiff. 254

§ 153.403. Pleading. 255

7547 Corp. v. Parker & Parsley Development Partners, L.P. 255

Limited Partnership: Admission of Partners 260

§ 153.101. Admission of Limited Partners 260

§ 153.253 261

§ 153.151. Admission of General Partners 261

Limited Partnership: Right to Information 262

§ 153.552. Examination of Records and Information 262

Limited Partnership: Nature of a Partner's Ownership Interests 262

§ 154.001. Nature of Partner's Partnership Interest 262
Limited Partnership: Assignment of Ownership Interests 263
    § 153.251. Assignment of Partnership Interest 263
    § 153.252. Rights of Assignor 263
    § 153.253. Rights of Assignee 263
    § 153.254. Liability of Assignee 264
    § 153.255. Liability of Assignor 264
    § 153.256. Partner's Partnership Interest Subject to Charging Order 264
    § 153.552. Examination of Records and Information 265
Limited Partnership: Transfer of Partnership Property 265
    § 154.002. Transfer of Interest in Partnership Property Prohibited. 265
    North Cypress Med. Ctr. Oper. Co. v. St. Laurent 266
Limited Partnership: Financial Matters 267
    § 153.201. Form of Contribution. 267
    § 153.202. Enforceability of Promise to Make Contribution 268
    § 153.203. Release of Obligation to Partnership. 269
    § 153.204. Enforceability of Obligation 269
Limited Partnership: Allocation of Profits and Losses 269
    § 153.206. Allocation of Profits and Losses 269
    § 153.154. Contributions by and Distributions to General Partner. 270
    § 154.203. Distributions in Kind 270
Limited Partnership: Pass-through Taxation 270
Limited Partnership: Imposition of Franchise Tax 270
Limited Partnership: Liability 270
    § 153.152. General Powers and Liabilities of General Partner 271
    § 153.153. Powers and Liabilities of Person Who is Both General Partner and Limited Partner. 271
    Shawell v. Pend Oreille Oil & Gas Co. 271
    Shaw v. Kennedy, Ltd. 273
Limited Partnership: Indemnification 275
    § 8.003. Limitations in Governing Documents 276

- § 8.051. Mandatory Indemnification 276
- § 8.101. Permissive Indemnification 276
- § 8.102. General Scope of Permissive Indemnification.. 277
- Limited Partnership: Liability of Limited Partners... 278
- § 153.102. Liability to Third Parties.. 278
- Safe Harbor.. 278
  - § 153.103. Actions Not Constituting Participation in Business for Liability Purposes....... 279
  - § 153.104. Enumeration of Actions Not Exclusive. 281
  - § 153.105. Creation of Rights. 281
  - Delaney v. Fidelity Lease Limited... 281
  - § 153.106. Erroneous Belief of Contributor Being Limited Partner. 285
  - § 153.107. Statement Required for Liability Protection 285
  - § 153.108. Requirements for Liability Protection Following Expiration of Statement....... 285
  - § 153.109. Liability of Erroneous Contributor. 286
- Limited Partnership: Fiduciary Duties 286
- General Partner... 286
- Limited Partnership: Officers or Managers of Entity General Partner................. 287
  - Huges v. St. David's Support Corp... 288
  - In Re Harwood.. 290
  - Crenshaw v. Swenson 294
- Limited Partner... 296
  - Strebel v. Wimberly... 296
  - § 11.051. Event Requiring Winding Up of Domestic Entity................................. 302
  - § 11.058. Supplemental Provision for Limited Partnership................................. 303
  - § 11.314. Involuntary Winding Up and Termination of Partnership or Limited Liability Company... 303
- Withdrawal of General Partner.. 303
  - § 153.155. Withdrawal of General Partner... 303
  - § 153.156. Notice of Event of Withdrawal. 304
  - § 153.157. Withdrawal of General Partner in Violation of Partnership Agreement.. 304
  - § 153.158. Effect of Withdrawal 304

§ 11.058. Supplemental Provision for Limited Partnership 305

§ 11.152. Continuation of Business Without Winding Up 305

§ 153.501. Cancellation or Revocation of Event Requiring Winding Up; Continuation of Business 306

§ 153.161. Liability of General Partner for Debt Incurred After Event of Withdrawal 307

§ 153.162. Liability for Wrongful Withdrawal 307

Withdrawal of Limited Partner 308

§ 153.110. Withdrawal of Limited Partner. 308

§ 153.111. Distribution on Withdrawal.. 308

Forfeiture 308

§ 153.301. Periodic Report. 308

§ 153.307. Effect of Failure to File Report 308

§ 153.309. Effect of Forfeiture of Right to Transact Business 309

§ 153.310. Revival of Right to Transact Business 309

§ 153.311. Termination of Certificate or Revocation of Registration After Forfeiture 309

§ 153.312. Reinstatement of Certificate of Formation or Registration 310

Table 3 311

Limited Partnerships Problem Set 314

LIMITED LIABILITY LIMITED PARTNERSHIPS 318

Governance 319

Liability 319

Finance 319

Termination 319

Table 4 320

THE CORPORATION 323

Choosing the for-profit corporation entity 323

Nature of the Corporation 323

Citizens United v. Federal Election Commission 324

Perpetual existence 328

Centralized management 328

§21.401. Management By Board Of Directors. 328

§21.101. Shareholders' Agreement. 329
Limited liability 330
 §21.223. Limitation Of Liability For Obligations. 330
 §7.001. Limitation Of Liability Of Governing Person. 331
Free transferability of rights and ownership interests 332
 §21.209. Transfer Of Shares And Other Securities. 332
 §21.210. Restriction On Transfer Of Shares And Other Securities. 332
 §21.211. Valid Restrictions On Transfer. 332
 § 21.212. Bylaw Or Agreement Restricting Transfer Of Shares Or Other Securities. 334
 § 21.213. Enforceability Of Restriction On Transfer Of Certain Securities 334
Prior to forming the for-profit corporation 335
The Corporation's Name 335
Selecting a name 335
Reserving a name 335
Forming the Corporation 336
The corporation by estoppel 336
 §4.101. Correction Of Filings. 337
 American Vending Services, Inc. v. Durbano et.al. 337
Forming the Texas Corporation.. 344
Certificate of Formation 344
 §3.001. Formation And Existence Of Filing Entities. 344
Filing the Certificate 346
 §4.002. Action By Secretary Of State... 346
 §4.101. Correction Of Filings. 347
corporate Governance 347
The Corporation's Bylaws... 348
Appointing the Corporation's Directors 348
Introducing the parties to a corporation... 348
Shareholders 348
Distributions 350
Shareholder agreements 351

Directors 351
Role/Operational duties 352
   §21.302. Authority For Distributions. 352
   §21.303. Limitations On Distributions. 352
   §21.316. Liability Of Directors For Wrongful Distributions. 352
Fiduciary Duties and the Business Judgment Rule 353
Duty of Loyalty 354
   §21.418. Contracts Or Transactions Involving Interested Directors And Officers. 355
Duty of Care 356
   § 3.102. Rights Of Governing Persons In Certain Cases. 356
   §7.001. Limitation Of Liability Of Governing Person. 357
Good faith 358
§20.002. Ultra Vires Acts. 359
Derivative proceedings 360
Standing 360
Demand letter 360
Overcoming the business judgment rule 361
   Pace v. Houston Industries, Inc. et.al. 361
   Elloway, et.al. v. Pate, et.al. 368
   Sinclair Oil Corporation v. Levien 375
Corporate Officers 380
Express actual authority..380
Implied actual authority 380
Apparent authority 381
Ratification 381
   Templeton v. Nocona Hills Owners Association, Inc. 381
   Almar-York Company, Inc. v. The Fort Worth National Bank 384
   Redmon v. Griffith 386
   Boehringer v. Konkel 397
   Background 397
Corporate Liability 410

Ultra Vires Doctrine 411

Piercing the corporate veil 411

    The Texas Rule 412

    Allied Chemical Carriers, Inc. v. National Biofuels LP, et al. 413

    Walkovszky v. Carlton 417

Indemnification 422

The corporation's capital structure 423

Equity and Debt 423

Winding up and terminating the corporation 424

    §21.364. Vote Required To Approve Fundamental Action. 426

    §21.365. Changes In Vote Required For Certain Matters. 428

    §21.455. Approval Of Sale Of All Or Substantially All Of Assets. 429

    § 21.456. General Procedure For Submission To Shareholders Of Fundamental Business Transaction. 429

    §21.457. General Vote Requirement For Approval Of Fundamental Business Transaction. 430

Mergers 431

    § 10.002. Plan Of Merger: Required Provisions. 431

    §10.003. Contents Of Plan Of Merger: More Than One Successor. 432

    §10.004. Plan Of Merger: Permissive Provisions. 433

    §10.352. Definitions. 433

    §10.353. Form And Validity Of Notice. 434

    §10.354. Rights Of Dissent And Appraisal. 434

    § 10.355. Notice Of Right Of Dissent And Appraisal. 436

    § 10.356. Procedure For Dissent By Owners As To Actions; Perfection Of Right Of Dissent And Appraisal. 437

    §10.357. Withdrawal Of Demand For Fair Value Of Ownership Interest. 438

    § 10.358. Response By Organization To Notice Of Dissent And Demand For Fair Value By Dissenting Owner. 439

Involuntary winding up and termination of the corporation 440

Administrative termination 440

Judicial termination 441

    §11.301. Involuntary Winding Up And Termination Of Filing Entity By Court Action. ... 441

- §11.302. Notification Of Cause By Secretary Of State. 441
- §11.303. Filing Of Action By Attorney General. 442
- §11.304. Cure Before Final Judgment. 442
- §11.305. Judgment Requiring Winding Up And Termination...442
- Failure to pay franchise taxes 443
- Bringing judicial action 443
- Administrative forfeiture 444
- Shareholder or creditor request for termination 444
- Table 5 445
- Corporations Problem Set 451
- LIMITED LIABILITY COMPANIES..455
  - Core Concepts...455
  - Nature and Structure 455
  - Advantages and Disadvantages of the LLC 456
  - LLC Advantages...457
  - LLC Disadvantages 458
    - § 101.101. Members Required...458
  - Entity Status..458
    - § 101.113. Parties to Actions...459
    - Ingalls v. Standard Gypsum, L.L.C. 459
  - formation 462
  - Filing of Certificate 462
    - § 3.001. Formation and Existence of Filing Entities 463
    - § 3.005. Certificate of Formation..463
    - § 3.010. Supplemental Provisions Required in Certificate of Formation of Limited Liability Company. 464
    - § 4.002. Action by Secretary of State 464
    - § 4.051. General Rule. 464
    - § 4.052. Delayed Effectiveness of Certain Filings...465
    - § 101.051. Certain Provisions Contained in Certificate of Formation 465
    - § 101.001. Definitions...465

§ 101.052. Company Agreement 465

§ 101.053. Amendment of Company Agreement. 466

Pinnacle Data Services, Inc. v. Gillen 466

Formation of Series LLC 468

§ 101.601. Series of Members, Managers, Membership Interests, or Assets 468

§ 101.602. Enforceability of Obligations and Expenses of Series Against Assets 469

§ 101.605. General Powers of Series. 469

Pre-formation Contracts 469

Lentz Engineering, L.L.C. v. Brown, ... 470

Kahn v. Imperial Airport, L.P., ... 473

governance 476

Management Structure 476

§ 3.010. Supplemental Provisions Required in Certificate of Formation of Limited Liability Company. 477

§ 1.002. Definitions 477

§ 101.251. Governing Authority. 477

§ 101.252. Management by Governing Authority. 478

§ 101.302. Number and Qualifications 478

§ 101.254. Designation of Agents; Binding Acts 478

§ 3.103. Officers 479

EZ Auto, L.L.C. v. H.M. JR. Auto Sales, ... 479

Decision-Making 482

§ 101.353. Quorum. 482

§ 101.354. Equal Voting Rights 482

§ 101.355. Act of Governing Authority, Members, or Committee. 483

§ 101.356. Votes Required to Approve Certain Actions 483

§ 101.552. Approval of Voluntary Winding Up, Revocation, Cancellation, or Reinstatement 483

§ 101.053. Amendment of Company Agreement. 484

§ 101.105. Issuance of Membership Interests After Formation of Company 484

§ 101.357. Manner of Voting 484

§ 101.358. Action by Less Than Unanimous Written Consent 484

§ 101.359. Effective Action by Members or Managers With or Without Meeting. 485

§ 6.052. Waiver of Notice 485

Admission 486

Transfer of interests 486

§ 101.102. Qualification for Membership 487

§ 101.103. Effective Date of Membership 487

§ 101.105. Issuance of Membership Interests After Formation of Company. 487

§ 1.002. Definitions 488

§ 101.106. Nature of Membership Interest 488

§ 101.108. Assignment of Membership Interest 488

§ 101.109. Rights and Duties of Assignee of Membership Interest Before Membership ... 489

§ 101.110. Rights and Liabilities of Assignee of Membership Interest After Becoming Member 489

§ 101.111. Rights and Duties of Assignor of Membership Interest 489

§ 101.1115. Effect of Death or Divorce on Membership Interest 490

Membership Interest and Admission of Members 490

Faulkner v. Kornman 490

No. 10-301, 2012 WL 1066736 1 (Bankr. S.D. Tex. 2012) 490

Interest Transfer Restrictions 492

Ramco Oil & Gas LTD. v. Anglo–Dutch (Tenge) L.L.C. 492

Eikon King Street Manager, L.L.C. v. LSF King Street Manager, L.L.C. 496

Withdrawal of Membership 500

Ownership and Transfer of property 500

§ 101.106. Nature of Membership Interest 501

§ 101.112. Member's Membership Interest Subject to Charging Order 501

Record-keeping and Right to Information 501

§ 3.153. Right of Examination by Owner or Member. 502

§ 101.502. Right to Examine Records and Certain Other Information 502

§ 101.054. Waiver or Modification of Certain Statutory Provisions Prohibited; Exceptions 502

financial Matters 502

Raising Capital 502
    § 1.002. Definitions 503
    § 101.102. Qualification for Membership 503
    § 101.104. Classes or Groups of Members or Membership Interests 503
Pass-through Taxation 504
Franchise and other Taxes 504
Allocation of Profits and Losses 504
    § 101.201. Allocation of Profits and Losses. 505
Distributions 505
    § 101.202. Distribution in Kind. 505
    § 101.203. Sharing of Distributions. 505
    § 101.204. Interim Distributions. 505
    § 101.205. Distribution on Withdrawal. 506
    § 101.206. Prohibited Distribution; Duty to Return 506
LIABILITY 506
    § 101.114. Liability for Obligations. 507
    § 101.151. Requirements for Enforceable Promise. 507
    § 101.153. Failure to Perform Enforceable Promise; Consequences 508
    § 101.154. Consent Required to Release Enforceable Obligation. 508
    § 101.155. Creditor's Right to Enforce Certain Obligations. 508
Limited Liability 509
    Black v. Bruner 509
    Phillip Alexander Hajdasz v. Chase Merritt West Loop, L.L.C. 510
Direct Liability 512
    LJ Charter, L.L.C., v. Air America Jet Charter, Inc., ... 512
    Sanchezv. Mulvaney D/B/A Freestone Equipment Co. and Hypersonic Construction, LLC 516
Piercing the Company Veil 519
    McCarthy v. Wani Venture, A.S., ... 519
    Ward Family Foundation V. Arnette (In re Arnette) 527
    Pinebrook Properties, LTD. v Brookhaven Lake Property Owners Association 533
Derivative Suits 536

§ 101.452. Standing to Bring Proceeding. 536

§ 101.453. Demand 537

§ 101.454. Determination by Governing or Independent Persons 537

§ 101.455. Stay of Proceeding 538

§ 101.458. Dismissal of Derivative Proceeding 538

§ 101.461. Payment of Expenses 539

§ 101.463. Closely Held Limited Liability Company 539

Rogers v. Alexander 540

Holly v. Deason 543

2005 WL 770595 (N.D. Tex. 2005). 543

Indemnification 547

§ 101.402. Permissive Indemnification, Advancement of Expenses, and Insurance or Other Arrangements 547

fiduciary Duties 548

§ 101.255. Contracts or Transactions Involving Interested Governing Persons or Officers 548

§ 101.401. Expansion or Restriction of Duties and Liabilities. 549

Gadin v. Societe Captrade 550

Entertainment Merchandising Technology, L.L.C. v. Houchin 552

merger, Dissolution And Term Of Existence 556

§ 11.051. Event Requiring Winding Up of Domestic Entity. 557

§ 11.056. Supplemental Provisions for Limited Liability Company 557

§ 11.052. Winding Up Procedures 557

§ 11.053. Property Applied to Discharge Liabilities and Obligations 558

§ 11.055. Court Action or Proceeding During Winding Up. 558

§ 11.314. Involuntary Winding Up and Termination of Partnership or Limited Liability Company. 558

§ 11.151. Revocation of Voluntary Winding Up 559

§ 11.152. Continuation of Business Without Winding Up 559

§ 101.552. Approval of Voluntary Winding Up, Revocation, Cancellation, or Reinstatement 560

§ 11.102. Effectiveness of Termination of Filing Entity. 560

§ 11.356. Limited Survival After Termination 560

§ 11.201. Conditions for Reinstatement 561

§ 11.202. Procedures for Reinstatement 562

§ 11.205. Effectiveness of Reinstatement of Filing Entity. 562

§ 11.206. Effect of Reinstatement. When the reinstatement of a terminated entity takes effect: 562

Table 6 563

Limited Liability Company Problem Set 566

Appendix 570

Sample Certificate of Formation* 571

Table Of Cases 1

Table Of Statutes..587

AGENCY

AGENCY

Creating the Agency

Agency

The law of agency is based on the doctrine that a principal who has an agent do his bidding, incurs the same liability as if he, the principal, had done the bidding himself. For example, assume Patricia hires Alex to mow her lawn subject to her control. Alex, while mowing the lawn, mistakenly runs the mower across a bush of roses belonging to Thelma, Patricia's next-door neighbor. Since Alex was Patricia's agent, Patricia may be liable to Thelma for the damage to her roses. This concept of liability is the bedrock of agency law.

What is agency?

Generally, agency is a broad term that includes every relationship in which one person agrees to act for, or represent another by that person's authority. But in the law of principal and agent, the term is used in a more restricted sense. In that sense, "agency" is the fiduciary relationship resulting from the manifestation of consent by one person (principal) to another (agent) that the agent is to act on the principal's behalf and subject to the principal's control in dealings with third persons, and consent by the agent to so act.

Restatement of Agency, 3rd edition, defines agency as:

> **§1.01 Agency defined.** *Agency is the fiduciary relationship that arises when one person (a "principal") manifests assent to another person (an "agent") that the agent shall act on the principal's behalf and subject to the principal's control, and the agent manifests assent or otherwise consents so to act.*

And goes on to state:

> **§1.02 Parties Labeling and Popular Usage Not Controlling.** *An agency relationship arises only when the elements stated in § 1.01 are present. Whether a relationship is characterized as agency in an agreement between parties or in the context of industry or popular usage is not controlling.*

This definition describes three elements of the agency relationship, (1) mutual *consent* by parties for the agent to act (2) for the *benefit* of the principal (3) subject to the principal's *control*.

Establishing the elements

Consent

Two parties can create an agency relationship either through express or implied terms. The two can agree that the agent will carry out any act that the principal is able to do lawfully himself. In forming the agreement, if the two either orally agreed or wrote the agreement down on paper, then it is likely that the duo formed an agency relationship. It is also true, that where the parties had not entered any such formal agreement, the two still could form an agency relationship through their conduct. The restatement provides that "a person manifests assent or intention through written or spoken words *or other conduct.*" §1.03

On the other hand, the mere fact that the parties call a written or oral agreement an agency agreement is not determinative. The Restatement of Agency, 3rd edition, provides at §1.02 that *"whether a relationship is characterized as agency in an agreement between parties or in the context of industry or popular usage is not controlling".* The legal effect of such an agreement is determined by looking at the facts surrounding the agreement and its provisions.

In some instances, consent will be found in equity. That is, a court, by employing the doctrine of estoppels, may bind a principal (or agent) as if an agency existed in law, even though no such relationship was ever established. Estoppel is an equitable remedy available when no agency exists in law but will be considered to have existed to ensure fairness to a harmed third party.

Benefit

Generally, to establish an agency relationship, there must be a benefit to the principal. In other words, the agency exists to provide value to the principal. Value can be extrinsic (e.g. money, goods or services) or intrinsic (e.g. good will, love and affection, prestige). Another way of expressing the 'benefit' element is to say that the agent is acting *on behalf* of the principal. Viewed from that angle, even when the principal does not benefit from the service or even suffers a loss as a result, an agency relationship, nonetheless, may be found to exist. For example, X bought a ranch for $25,000. X asked Y to sell the land, even though X had initially planned to leave the land in the family. The instruction to Y did not include a recommended sale price. Y sold the land for $15,000 even though similarly situated properties were selling at much higher prices. X cannot renounce the agency by claiming that he derived no benefit from the transaction.

Control

The key element to determine if an agency was created is whether the principal retains some degree of control over the conduct and activities of the agent. To determine whether an agency relationship exists, courts look to the purported principal's right to control the purported agent's actions.

The right to control is commonly determined in two ways. First, consider whether the purported principal retained the right to control the details of the agent's work. Second, consider whether the purported principal retained the right to control the means and details of the process by which an agent will accomplish the task. If the principal retains both these types of control, then he has retained a right of control, and the relationship of a principal and agency can exist—even if the principal never exercises the right. Control is such a significant element of the agency relationship that even if a person consents to act for the benefit of another, without a principal's control, an agency relationship will not exist.

Types of Agency Relationships

Agency relationships are generally described as employer-employee, independent contractor or other agency.

The Restatement of Agency, 3rd edition, describes an employee as:

§7.07 *Employee Acting Within Scope of Employment...(3)(a) ... an agent whose principal controls or has the right to control the manner and means of the agent's performance of work...*

When the agent is the employee, then her principal, who is the employer, has the right to assert maximum control over <u>how</u> the work is to be performed, <u>where</u> the work is to be performed as well the <u>result</u> of the performance. Facts often considered by courts in determining whether the agent is an employee include the principal's:

1. Determination of the work hours of the agent
2. Whether the agent is paid hourly or receives a salary
3. Whether the principal provides the work place, supplies and or equipment the agent uses to perform the work
4. The agreement and intent of the parties

Contract Liability of Employer

An employer is liable for all contracts executed by the agent within his/her actual and or apparent authority. Non-public limitations on the agent's authority which are communicated by the employer to the agent, do not limit the agent's apparent authority from the perspective of third parties who deal with the agent in relation to the employer's business.

Tort Liability of Employer

Generally, employers are vicariously liable under the theory of respondeat superior for the torts committed by their employees. Such liability exists so long as the employee commits the tort "while acting within the scope of employment". The injured person may sue employee alone, employer alone, or both in one action (joint and several tort liability). An employee is considered acting within the scope of his or her employment when the employee's act was authorized by the employer; when the primary reason for the employee's actions at the time of the tort was to advance the employer's interest; if the employer furnished the instrumentality that caused the injury; and when it was foreseeable to the employer that an injury of that type would have occurred.

Independent Contractors

The Restatement of Agency, 3rd edition, no longer recognizes the traditional type of agency called the independent contractor. Instead, the restatement only speaks of employees and agents. However, some state jurisdictions, including Texas, continue to recognize the independent contractor as a type of agent.

An independent contractor is a person or entity that contracts with an employer or client but who performs the work according to his/her/its own methods, where the employer only controls the outcome of the work, not the manner in which the work is done. An independent contractor is generally not paid hourly or on salary, but on a fee for service basis.

There are cases where the employer authorizes an independent contractor to enter into contracts for the employer; thereby resembling an agent. However, if the independent contractor retains substantial control over how and when the work is done, then the employer will likely not be liable for the acts of the independent contractor.

Moreover, the employer is generally not liable for the torts committed by the independent contractor even when those torts were committed while the independent contractor was acting in the course and scope of his/her relationship with the employer. The most common exception to this rule is when the independent contractor is performing "inherently dangerous" work for the employer or where the employer's responsibility is non-delegable.

It should be noted also that some independent contractors are not agents. Thus, there are independent contractor agents and independent contractor non-agents. The distinguishing factor is the level of control exercised by the person engaging the services of the independent contractor. For example, a surgeon hired to undertake a tonsillectomy is an independent contractor, but not an agent of the patient. An attorney hired to settle a vehicular accident claim with an insurance company is an independent contractor and an agent of the client, because the client retains control over the outcome of the settlement.

Establishing Agency

Boyd v. Eikenberry
132 Tex. 408, 122 S.W.2d 1045 (1939)

Action by Mae N. Eikenberry and another against H. B. Boyd and another. From a judgment for plaintiff, the named defendant appealed to the Court of Civil Appeals at San Antonio which affirmed the judgment, 99 S.W.2d 701, and the named defendant brings error.

Reversed and remanded.

In the trial court Mae N. Eikenberry and Eloisa LeLievre were awarded judgment against H. B. Boyd and A. J. McColl, jointly and severally, in the sum of $6,773.50 as actual damages and against McColl individually in the sum of $1,500 as exemplary damages on account of fraudulent representations found to have been made to them by McColl in connection with the sale by him to them of certain land in Hidalgo County. J. L. Erwin and A. J. McColl Land Company, a corporation, were defendants in the trial court, but a verdict was returned in their favor pursuant to a peremptory instruction. Defendants in error did not appeal from that portion of the judgment denying them recovery against Erwin and the Land Company. Neither did McColl appeal. Boyd unsuccessfully prosecuted an appeal to the Court of Civil Appeals at San Antonio. 99 S.W.2d 701.

The opinion of the Court of Civil Appeals sets out the findings of the jury as follows:

"1. The land in question was not first class citrus land.
"2. There was no conspiracy between Boyd and McColl.
"3. McColl was Boyd's agent in selling the land.
"4. There was no partnership between McColl and Boyd.
"5. Boyd did not receive a benefit out of a sale of the land.
"6. The reasonable market value of the land at the time of the sale, had the same been as represented, would have been $1000 per acre.
"7. The actual reasonable market value of the land at the time it was delivered to appellees was $225 per acre.
"8. McColl wilfully misrepresented the land.
"9. Appellees were entitled to $1500 exemplary damages.
"10. McColl did not honestly believe the land was good land when he sold it.
"11. Boyd held the legal title to the land as collateral security for a debt owed to him by McColl."

The particular finding upon which liability was adjudged against Boyd was that McColl was his agent in selling the land. After the verdict was returned Boyd filed in the trial court a motion for judgment thereon or, alternatively, for judgment non obstante veredicto. In his motion he prayed the court to disregard the jury's finding that McColl was acting as his agent, because the issue was not pleaded, had no support in the evidence, and because the jury's answer thereto was rendered immaterial by its answers to the other issues submitted. This motion was overruled....

It was the view of the Honorable Court of Civil Appeals, as we understand its opinion, that it is a legal possibility for a mortgagor to become the agent of a mortgagee in the sale of the mortgaged property; that a principal may be bound by the fraud of his agent, even though he derives no benefit therefrom; and that, since the assignments of error presented no question for decision except the question of the character of judgment to be rendered on the verdict, it could not be held, as a matter of law, that the finding of agency either conflicted with, or was rendered immaterial by the other findings. Two cases from other jurisdictions were cited on the proposition that a mortgagor may become the agent of a mortgagee in the sale of the mortgaged property. National Citizens' Bank v. Ertz, 83 Minn. 12, 85 N.W. 821, 53 L.R.A. 174, 85 Am.St.Rep. 438; People's Savings Bank v. Smith, 114 Ga. 185, 39 S.E. 920. The Minnesota case did hold a mortgagee bound by the fraud of a mortgagor in the sale of the mortgaged property on the doctrine of agency, but placed its holding upon the ground that the mortgagee himself had the right to sell it, and could, therefore, employ another, even the mortgagor, to sell it for him. Whether or not we would reach the same conclusions upon corresponding facts we need not consider. In this State under the finding that Boyd held the legal title as security for a debt owed to him by McColl he, Boyd, did not have the legal right to sell the land. Doubtless an innocent purchaser from him would have been protected, but, as between him and McColl, the true owner, Boyd did not have the right to sell it. It is doubtless true that Boyd could have appointed an agent to sell whatever interest, if any, he had in the land. He could have appointed an agent to sell his mortgage. We know of no principle of law which would preclude McColl from becoming such agent, but liability upon that theory was neither pleaded nor submitted to the jury.

The petition did allege that McColl was Boyd's agent, but such allegations, when considered in their settings, related either to the plea of conspiracy, found by the jury not to exist, to the plea of partnership, likewise found by the jury not to exist, or to the theory, rejected by the jury, that Boyd was the owner of the land. We have decided that the case must be retried for the reason hereinafter assigned, and, since the pleadings will doubtless be recast before another trial, a fuller discussion thereof is not deemed advisable.

The issue submitted to the jury was not whether McColl was Boyd's agent in the sale of the latter's mortgage or other interest, if any he had, in the land, but was whether he was his agent in selling the land. To guide the jury in answering that issue the charge contained this definition of an agent: "You are instructed that an agent is one who undertakes to transact some business, or to manage some affair for another, by the authority and on account of the latter, and to render an account of it."

That definition is in substantially the same language as the one approved in Reed v. Hester, Tex.Com.App., 44 S.W.2d 1107. Other definitions embodying the same essential elements have been approved by this Court. In Thompson v. Schmitt, 115 Tex. 53, 274 S.W. 554, this definition was given …: "One who acts in my behalf, for my advantage, by my authority, is my agent."

In selling his own land McColl could not have been acting by Boyd's authority, for Boyd had no authority to sell it himself and could not, therefore, authorize another to do so. Neither was he acting in Boyd's behalf, and for his benefit. He was acting in his own behalf and for his own benefit. On the issue of fact as to who owned the land the jury found that Boyd did not own it. It could with reason be concluded that, in the light of that finding, the further finding of agency was but an erroneous finding of law, which should have been disregarded in rendering judgment; but, since it was a fact issue as to who owned the land, it seems to us that the better reasoning leads to the conclusion that the two findings conflict to such an extent that it is impossible to determine just what the jury did find. The verdict affords no sure basis upon which a judgment for either party may rest. The finding that McColl acted by authority of, and was accountable to Boyd is a finding that he sold Boyd's property and cannot be reconciled with the finding that Boyd did not own it.

Those portions of the judgment of the trial court denying defendants in error any recovery against Erwin and A. J. McColl Land Company and awarding them a recovery against McColl will not be disturbed. The judgment of the Court of Civil Appeals and that portion of the judgment of the trial court which awarded recovery against Boyd will be reversed and the cause, as between defendants in error and Boyd, will be remanded.

Opinion adopted by the Supreme Court.

****

Employee as Agent

Del Carmen Flores v. Summit Hotel Group
492 F. Supp. 2d 640 (W.D. Tex. 2006)

Plaintiffs are former employees of the Hampton Inn and Suites in El Paso, Texas ("the hotel"). Ayub was the general manager of the hotel. On July 29, 2005, Ayub informed all current hotel employees whether they would be eligible for employment with the hotel's new owner. Plaintiffs were specifically informed that they were not eligible for rehire, and their employment was terminated. On approximately August 1, 2005, Summit completed its purchase of the hotel.

On June 12, 2006, Plaintiffs filed their Original Petition in County Court at Law Number 3 in El Paso County, Texas. Plaintiffs allege that they were not rehired because Summit unlawfully retaliated against them and because Ayub and Hampton Inns, Inc. interfered with their prospective employment contracts with Summit. On July 24, 2006, Defendants removed the case from the Texas state court to the United States District Court for the Western District of Texas based on diversity jurisdiction.

Plaintiffs are all citizens of Texas. Summit is a South Dakota corporation with its principal place of business in South Dakota. Defendants contend that Hampton Inns, Inc. does not exist. However, Ayub is a citizen of Texas. Thus diversity of citizenship only exists if the Court disregards the citizenship of Ayub. Defendants contend that Ayub's citizenship can be ignored because he was improperly joined as a party, as "there is no possibility the Plaintiffs will be able to establish a cause of action against him." Plaintiffs argue that a valid claim lies against Ayub for tortious interference with a contract, and that the case should therefore be remanded to state court. Accordingly, the issue presently before the Court is whether Plaintiffs improperly joined Ayub to defeat removal and diversity jurisdiction.

Standard

When plaintiffs choose to file suit in state court, defendants may remove the case to federal court if there is complete diversity of citizenship among the parties involved and the amount in controversy exceeds $75,000. 28 U.S.C. §§ 1332, 1441(a). However, federal jurisdiction based on diversity is improper if "any party, by assignment or otherwise, has been improperly or collusively made or joined to invoke the jurisdiction of such court." 28 U.S.C. §

7

1359. Therefore, where defendants seek removal on the basis of diversity but non-diverse defendants are present in the case, the defendants must show that complete diversity exists by demonstrating that the plaintiff has improperly joined the non-diverse defendants. A removing party can establish improper joinder by showing either (1) actual fraud in a plaintiff's pleading of jurisdictional facts, or (2) inability of the plaintiff to establish a cause of action against the non-diverse defendants in state court. *Travis v. Irby*, 326 F.3d 644, 647 (5th Cir.2003). Because Defendants have not alleged actual fraud in Plaintiffs' pleading of jurisdictional facts, only the latter method of establishing improper joinder is before the Court.

In determining whether Plaintiffs are able to establish a cause of action against Ayub, the Court must determine whether the defendant has demonstrated that "there is no reasonable basis for the district court to predict that the plaintiff might be able to recover against an in-state defendant." *Smallwood v. Ill. Cent. R.R. Co.*, 385 F.3d 568, 574 (5th Cir.2004) (en banc). "The party seeking removal bears a heavy burden of proving that the joinder of the in-state party was improper." *Id.* at 573. The removing party must prove improper joinder by clear and convincing evidence, *Grassi v. Ciba-Geigy, Ltd.*, 894 F.2d 181, 186 (5th Cir.1990), and "all disputed questions of fact and all ambiguities in state law must be resolved in favor of the plaintiff," *Gray ex rel. Rudd v. Beverly Enters.-Miss., Inc.*, 390 F.3d 400, 405 (5th Cir.2004).

Analysis

To prevail on a claim for tortious interference with a contract under Texas law, a plaintiff must establish: "(1) the existence of a contract subject to interference; (2) willful and intentional interference; (3) interference that proximately caused damage; and (4) actual damage or loss." *Powell Indus., Inc. v. Allen*, 985 S.W.2d 455, 456 (Tex.1998). But it is clear that a party cannot tortiously interfere with its own contract. *Holloway v. Skinner*, 898 S.W.2d 793, 795 (Tex.1995). This rule extends to preclude agents from being held liable for tortiously interfering with their principal's contracts, as actions of the agent are deemed to be the principal's acts. An exception exists to this general preclusion from liability where a plaintiff establishes that the agent's actions were *solely* in furtherance of his own personal interests. *See Holloway*, 898 S.W.2d at 796; *COC Servs., Ltd. v. CompUSA, Inc.*, 150 S.W.3d 654, 675 (Tex.App.-Dallas 2004, pet. denied). The Court does not address this exception as no party has suggested that it applies to the present case. Accordingly, a showing that Ayub was acting as an agent of Summit when he took the actions underlying this cause would preclude him from personal liability for tortious interference.

"An 'agent' is one who is authorized by another to transact business or manage some affair." *Grace Cmty. Church v. Gonzales*, 853 S.W.2d 678, 680 (Tex.App.-Houston [14th Dist.] 1993, no writ). In assessing the existence of an agency relationship, Texas courts generally apply the "right to control" test. *See Royal Mortgage Corp. v. Montague*, 41 S.W.3d 721, 733 (Tex.App.-Fort Worth 2001, pet. denied). Under this test, "[t]he defining feature of the agency relationship is the principal's right to control the actions of the agent." *Schott Glas v. Adame*, 178

S.W.3d 307, 315 (Tex.App.-Houston [14th Dist.] 2005, pet. denied). An agency relationship exists when the principal can control "the end sought to be accomplished" as well as "the means and details of the accomplishment." *Schott Glas,* 178 S.W.3d at 315. Without such complete control, Ayub may have been an independent contractor, but he would not have been an agent.

"Whether an agency relationship exists is generally a question of fact," *id.,* and in a motion to dismiss for improper joinder "all disputed facts ... must be resolved in favor of the plaintiff," *Gray ex rel. Rudd,* 390 F.3d at 405. It is far from clear that Summit possessed the requisite degree of control over Ayub's actions. While Ayub may not have been acting purely in his own interests, a party is not an agent simply because he acts on behalf of another. *Happy Indus. Corp. v. Am. Specialties, Inc.,* 983 S.W.2d 844, 852 (Tex.App.-Corpus Christi 1998, pet. dism'd w.o.j.); *Walker v. Fed. Kemper Life Assurance Co.,* 828 S.W.2d 442, 452 (Tex.App.-San Antonio 1992, writ denied). Defendant indicates that it is Summit's custom in purchasing hotels to work with the seller and its managerial staff, and that the seller's managerial staff obtains employment applications and reviews them according to guidelines provided by Summit. Managers are then authorized to make employment offers on Summit's behalf. *Id.* Summit essentially asks the Court to infer from the parties' conduct that Ayub was acting at Summit's direction and on its behalf when he informed individual employees, including Plaintiffs, of their employment status. While an agency relationship need not be expressed or contractual, but may instead be implied from the parties' conduct, *Orozco v. Sander,* 824 S.W.2d 555, 556 (Tex.1992), the Court nonetheless is not prepared to infer an agency relationship here.

Texas law indicates that "[a]n agency relationship can arise only at the will and by the act of the principal, and its existence is always a fact to be proved by tracing it to some act of the alleged principal." *Thermo Prods. Co. v. Chilton Indep. Sch.,* 647 S.W.2d 726, 732 (Tex.App.-Waco 1983, writ ref'd n.r.e.). Defendant has produced evidence indicating Summit's general practice of working with a seller's managerial staff, and a statement that Ayub was acting as Summit's agent and in its interests. But it is uncontroverted that on July 29, 2005, Ayub was not yet Summit's employee, but rather he was still an employee of the seller's. Ayub was apparently acting on Summit's behalf, but Defendants merely indicate that it was Summit's custom in purchasing a hotel to provide the current manager with "guidelines" by which to evaluate employment applications. Summit may have had some control over "the end to be accomplished," but it is not clear that Summit exercised the requisite degree of control over Ayub through their control of "the means and details of the accomplishment." *See Schott Glas,* 178 S.W.3d at 315.

Having reviewed the evidence and arguments presented by the parties, the Court finds that the existence of an agency relationship between Ayub and Summit remains a disputed question of fact. While the evidence before the Court does not conclusively establish whether Ayub was acting as Summit's agent, the Court's "inability to make the requisite decision in a summary manner itself points to an inability of the removing party to carry its burden."

Smallwood, 385 F.3d at 574. The Court need not pretry the entire cause to resolve this issue, as such disputed questions must be resolved in favor of the plaintiff in a motion to dismiss for improper joinder. *Gray ex rel. Rudd,* 390 F.3d at 405; *Hart v. Bayer Corp.,* 199 F.3d 239, 246 (5th Cir.2000). Thus, for the purposes of Defendant's Motion to Dismiss, the Court assumes that Ayub was not acting as an agent of Summit on July 29, 2005 when he informed Plaintiffs that they would not be rehired by Summit. A claim for tortious interference with contract *may* lie against Ayub, and thus there exists a reasonable basis by which Plaintiffs could recover from him. The Court concludes that Defendants have not met the heavy burden of demonstrating that Ayub was improperly joined. Accordingly, Defendants having failed to prove improper joinder, "diversity is not complete, the diverse defendant is not entitled to remove, and remand is mandated." *See Smallwood,* 385 F.3d at 575.

[handwritten: Can recover personal from Ayub.]

Conclusion

Based on the foregoing legal principles and analysis, the Court concludes that Defendant Gabriel Ayub was properly joined as a party. Since complete diversity does not exist between Plaintiffs and Defendants, removal from the Texas state court was improper, and Plaintiffs' "Motion to Remand" should be granted pursuant to 28 U.S.C. § 1447. Accordingly, **IT IS ORDERED** that Defendant Gabriel Ayub's "Motion to Dismiss as Improperly Joined" (Docket No. 3) is DENIED....

****

Employee vs. Independent Contractors

Coleman v. Klöckner & Co. et.al.
180 S.W.3d 577 (Tex. App.— Houston [14th Dist.] 2005)

Background: Veterans of the Persian Gulf War and their family members brought action against entities that allegedly sold material and equipment to Iraq used to create biological and chemical weapons. The case was removed to federal court. The United States District Court, Southern District Texas, Galveston Division, 888 F. Supp. 1388, dismissed for lack of jurisdiction and remanded. Subsequent to remand, a German engineering company and holding company that owned it were added as defendants. The 23rd District Court, Brazoria County, Ben Hardin, J., granted the special appearances of the German companies, and plaintiffs appealed.

Holdings: The Court of Appeals, Charles W. Seymore, J., held that:
> (1) veterans waived contention that subsidiary corporations of nonresident German companies operated as a single business enterprise with German companies, for purposes of deciding whether subsidiaries' contacts with Texas could be attributed to nonresident German companies;

(2) evidence was sufficient to establish that subsidiary corporation was not an agent of nonresident German companies such that subsidiary's contacts with Texas could be attributed to German companies; and

(3) general jurisdiction over German companies could not be asserted based on single visit to Texas by former chief executive officer (CEO) of German engineering company.

Affirmed.

Appellants bring this interlocutory appeal from an order granting the special appearances of Klöckner & Co. AG ("Klöckner & Co.") and Klöckner Industrie–Anlagen GmbH INA ("Klöckner INA"). We affirm the trial court's judgment.

Appellants are veterans of the 1991 Persian Gulf War and some of their family members. In 1994, appellants filed suit against approximately eighty defendants alleging that the defendants sold to Iraq the material, equipment, and technology used to create biological and chemical weapons used in the war. The case was removed to federal court, which dismissed for lack of subject matter jurisdiction. *Coleman v. Alcolac,* 888 F.Supp. 1388, 1404 (S.D.Tex.1995) (order granting motion to dismiss for lack of subject-matter jurisdiction and remanding cause to state court).

Subsequent to remand, Klöckner & Co. and Klöckner INA (collectively, the "Klöckner defendants"), were added as defendants. The Klöckner defendants filed special appearances pursuant to Texas Rule of Civil Procedure 120a, challenging personal jurisdiction. On October 7, 2003, the trial court granted both special appearances, and appellants filed this interlocutory appeal from the trial court's order. *See* TEX. CIV. PRAC. & REM.CODE ANN. § 51.014(a)(7) (Vernon Supp.2004–05).

Single Business Enterprise Theory

In their first issue, appellants contend that Klöckner & Co., Klöckner INA, Klöckner Industrial, and UAT (collectively "the German entities") operate as a single business enterprise under Texas law. Therefore, appellants contend that the Texas contacts of UAT and Klöckner Industrial should be imputed to the Klöckner defendants for personal jurisdiction purposes.

The "single business enterprise" theory is an equitable doctrine used to disregard the separate existence of corporations when the corporations are not operated as separate entities, but rather integrate their resources to achieve a common business purpose. *Old Republic Ins. Co. v. Ex–Im Servs. Corp.,* 920 S.W.2d 393, 395–96 (Tex.App.-Houston [1st Dist.] 1996, no writ). Factors to be considered in determining whether corporations operate as a single business enterprise include, but are not limited to, the following: (1) common employees; (2) common offices; (3) centralized accounting; (4) payment of wages by one corporation to another corporation's employees; (5) common business name; (6) services rendered by the employees of

11

one corporation on behalf of another corporation; (7) undocumented transfers of funds between corporations; and (8) unclear allocation of profits and losses between corporations. *Paramount Petroleum Corp. v. Taylor Rental Ctr.,* 712 S.W.2d 534, 536 (Tex.App.-Houston [14th Dist.] 1986, writ ref'd n.r.e.).

Appellants did not plead the "single business enterprise" theory as a basis for imputing the contacts of Klöckner Industrial and UAT to the German defendants. Instead, appellants alleged that the German defendants should be subject to liability based on theories of agency and alter ego.... Furthermore, appellants did not present the "single business enterprise" theory at the special appearance hearing. Accordingly, the Klöckner defendants argue that appellants have waived their contention that the German entities operate as a single business enterprise.

Appellants respond that the "single business enterprise" theory has just recently begun to emerge in Texas appellate courts, and that a litigant cannot waive a previously undeveloped legal doctrine. Appellants also point out that in *Southern Union Co. v. City of Edinburg,* the Texas Supreme Court recently declined to decide whether "a theory of 'single business enterprise' is a necessary addition to Texas law" for purposes of disregarding corporate structure. 129 S.W.3d 74, 87 (Tex.2003). Nevertheless, before appellants filed the operative pleadings in this case, several Texas appellate courts previously recognized the "single business enterprise" theory as a method by which to disregard the corporate structure of related entities. *See, e.g., Hall v. Timmons,* 987 S.W.2d 248, 252 (Tex.App.-Beaumont 1999, no pet.); *Beneficial Personnel Servs. of Tex., Inc. v. Rey,* 927 S.W.2d 157, 165 (Tex.App.-El Paso 1996), *vacated by agreement,* 938 S.W.2d 717 (Tex.1997); *Old Republic Ins. Co.,* 920 S.W.2d at 395–96; *Paramount Petroleum Corp.,* 712 S.W.2d at 536. Accordingly, we conclude that appellants had notice of the "single business enterprise" theory, and thus had the opportunity to assert this theory in order to persuade the trial court to disregard the corporate structure of the German entities....

Agency Theory

In their second issue, appellants contend that Klöckner Industrial's contacts with Texas should be imputed to Klöckner INA for jurisdictional purposes because Klöckner Industrial served as an agent of Klöckner INA.

Standard of Review

The question of whether an agency relationship exists is generally a question of fact. *Lyons v. Lindsey Morden Claims Management, Inc.,* 985 S.W.2d 86, 90 (Tex.App.-El Paso 1998, no pet.); *Jorgensen v. Stuart Place Water Supply Corp.,* 676 S.W.2d 191, 194 (Tex.App.-Corpus Christi 1984, no writ). Here, the trial court did not expressly find the absence of an agency relationship between Klöckner INA and Klöckner Industrial. Nevertheless, all the facts necessary to support the trial court's judgment and supported by the evidence are implied. *Marchand,* 83 S.W.3d at 795. Accordingly, we construe appellants' argument that an agency relationship exists between Klöckner INA and Klöckner Industrial as a challenge to the legal and factual sufficiency of the evidence to support the trial court's implied finding that no such agency relationship exists. *See SITQ E.U., Inc. v. Reata Rests., Inc.,* 111 S.W.3d 638, 652 (Tex.App.-Fort Worth 2003, pet. denied) (noting that agency is generally a question of fact and holding that the evidence was legally and factually sufficient to support trial court's implied finding that an agency relationship existed); *Townsend v. Univ. Hospital-University of Colo.,* 83 S.W.3d 913, 921 (Tex.App.-Texarkana 2002, pet. denied) (holding that evidence was factually sufficient to support trial court's implied finding that there was no agency relationship between the parties)....

Review of Agency Principles

Because the parties dispute whether Klöckner Industrial is an agent of Klöckner INA—an issue which affects our minimum contacts analysis—we turn to the applicable agency principles to resolve the issue. An agent's contacts can be imputed to the principal for purposes of the jurisdictional inquiry. *Walker Ins. Servs. v. Bottle Rock Power Corp.,* 108 S.W.3d 538, 549 n. 4 (Tex.App.-Houston [14th Dist.] 2003, no pet.). However, agency will not be presumed, and the party asserting the relationship has the burden of proving it. *Schultz v. Rural/Metro Corp.,* 956 S.W.2d 757, 760 (Tex.App.-Houston [14th Dist.] 1997, no writ). An agency relationship may be found from the underlying facts or direct and circumstantial evidence showing the relationship of the parties. *Id.*

An agent is one who is authorized by a person or entity to transact business or manage some affair for the person or entity. *Townsend,* 83 S.W.3d at 921. The critical element of an agency relationship is the right to control, and the principal must have control of both the means and details of the process by which the agent is to accomplish his task in order for an agency relationship to exist. *Id.* Absent proof of the right to control the means and details of the work performed, only an independent contractor relationship is established. *Happy Indus. Corp. v. Am. Specialties, Inc.,* 983 S.W.2d 844, 852 (Tex.App.-Corpus Christi 1998, pet. dism'd w.o.j.). The distinction between an independent contractor and an agent is important to the jurisdictional inquiry because the actions of an independent contractor by themselves are not sufficient to subject a non-resident corporation to the jurisdiction of the forum state. *O'Quinn v. World Indus. Constructors, Inc.,* 874 F.Supp. 143, 145 (E.D.Tex.), *aff'd,* 68 F.3d 471 (5th Cir.1995).

Application of Agency Principles to Klöckner INA and Klöckner Industrial

Appellants contend that Klöckner Industrial is an agent of Klöckner INA, and therefore, all of Klöckner Industrial's contacts with the Texas engineering firms should be imputed to Klöckner INA for jurisdictional purposes. In support of their argument, appellants contend (1) Brosig acted as agent of Klöckner INA when he visited and corresponded with the Texas engineering firms because he solicited the firms to participate in foreign projects with Klöckner INA, (2) the fact that Klöckner Industrial consisted of only three employees demonstrates that it was merely an agent of Klöckner INA, (3) Brosig made representations to the Texas engineering firms that prove an agency relationship between Klöckner Industrial and Klöckner INA, and (4)

Klöckner Industrial is an "indispensable" agent of Klöckner INA because, without Klöckner Industrial, Klöckner INA could not (a) legally export U.S.-manufactured machinery and equipment abroad, or (b) obtain financing from the U.S. government-backed Exim Bank to ship U.S. manufactured goods overseas for use on Klöckner INA projects.

Solicitation of Business for Klöckner INA

Appellants contend that Brosig acted as an agent of Klöckner INA when he visited and corresponded with the Texas engineering firms because he solicited the firms to participate in foreign projects in which Klöckner INA was involved in the construction. In his deposition, Brosig testified that Klöckner Industrial would sometimes serve as "exporter of record" for U.S.-manufactured goods for projects on which Klöckner INA was involved in construction of the project, but that, on other occasions, Klöckner INA was not involved in the project. The record also reflects that Klöckner Industrial entered into contracts with Klöckner INA whereby Klöckner Industrial agreed to identify "qualified U.S. firms, which can assume the role of technical partners in [Klöckner INA's] international projects." This constitutes some evidence from which it can be inferred that Brosig visited the Texas engineering firms, in part, to promote the business of Klöckner INA.

However, the Klöckner defendants argue there is insufficient evidence that Klöckner Industrial was acting as the agent of Klöckner INA when it contacted the Texas engineering firms because appellants failed to prove the critical element of "control." The Klöckner defendants cite *Williamson v. Petrosakh Joint Stock Co.*, 952 F.Supp. 495 (S.D.Tex.1997) and *Dickson Marine, Inc. v. Panalpina, Inc.*, 179 F.3d 331 (5th Cir.1999) to support their position that the evidence fails to establish the "control" element that is requisite to an agency relationship.

In *Williamson*, the plaintiffs filed a wrongful death lawsuit against Petrosakh, a Russian corporation. 952 F.Supp. at 496. Petrosakh was owned 95% by Nimir Petroleum Petrosakh Limited ("Nimir Cyprus"), a Cyprus company. *Id.* Nimir Cyprus' sister company, Nimir Petroleum Company U.S.A., Inc. ("Nimir USA"), which was based in Texas, had a technical services contract with Petrosakh under which Nimir USA would recruit and hire independent contractor consultants to work at the Petrosakh refinery in Russia. *Id.*

Pursuant to the contract, Nimir USA located and hired Williamson, a Texas resident, to work at the Petrosakh refinery in Russia. *Id.* After Williamson died in an incident at the refinery, the plaintiffs filed the wrongful death suit against Petrosakh in a Texas court. *Id.* The plaintiffs asserted that jurisdiction over Petrosakh was proper based on the Texas contacts of Nimir USA. *Id.* The plaintiffs argued that Nimir USA was Petrosakh's agent because Nimir USA had recruited and hired Williamson on behalf of Petrosakh. *Id.* at 498. The court, however, held there was insufficient evidence to establish an agency relationship, despite the close corporate relationship between the entities. *Id.* The court concluded there was no evidence to show that

Petrosakh had the right to control the details of Nimir USA's work, even though Nimir USA acted on behalf of Petrosakh in fulfillment of the technical services contract. *Id.* Therefore, the court found there was only an independent contractor relationship between the entities and declined to impute the Texas contacts of Nimir USA to Petrosakh. *Id.*

The same issue of control was also present in *Dickson Marine,* which involved the Louisiana long-arm statute. Similar to Texas, the Louisiana long-arm statute extends to the limits of due process. *See* 179 F.3d at 336. In *Dickson Marine,* a vessel owned and operated by Dickson Marine, Inc. ("Dickson") needed repair work while operating off the coast of West Africa. *Id.* at 335. Dickson contacted Air Sea Broker, Ltd. ("Air Sea"), a Swiss corporation, to arrange for the repairs. *Id.* Air Sea referred Dickson to Panalpina Transports Mondiaux Gabon S.A. ("Panalpina Gabon"), a sister company, to handle the repairs. *Id. [footnote omitted]* During the repair work, the vessel capsized. *Id.* Dickson filed suit against Panalpina Gabon and Air Sea in a Louisiana court to recover for property damage to the vessel. *Id.* Dickson asserted that jurisdiction over Panalpina Gabon was proper based on the Louisiana contacts of Air Sea because Air Sea acted as Panalpina Gabon's agent. *Id.* at 338.

The court, however, found that there was insufficient evidence to show that Panalpina Gabon asserted sufficient control over Air Sea to establish an agency relationship. *Id.* The court noted it was undisputed that Air Sea had frequently benefitted Panalpina Gabon by assisting maritime companies in contracting with Panalpina Gabon for services to be performed in Gabon. *Id.* While the evidence showed that Air Sea was a "middleman" who assisted vessel owners in contracting with the Panalpina Worldwide Subsidiaries for maritime services, the court held that those facts alone were not sufficient to establish the control required to prove an agency relationship. *Id.* at 338.

Similarly, in this case, we find there is insufficient evidence in the record to show that Klöckner INA controlled Klöckner Industrial, or its president, Klaus Brosig. We find no evidence that Klöckner INA directed Brosig to travel to Texas to meet with the Texas engineering firms, nor do we find any evidence that Klöckner INA controlled the means and details of Brosig's work. Moreover, we find no evidence that Klöckner Industrial had actual authority to negotiate or enter into contracts on behalf of Klöckner INA. *Cf. Orozco v. Sander,* 824 S.W.2d 555, 556 (Tex.1992) (holding that under the facts and circumstances of the case, it could be implied that the alleged agent entered into the contract at the direction of and on behalf of the principal).

Although Brosig may have contacted the Texas engineering firms for the mutual benefit of both Klöckner Industrial and Klöckner INA, we find that such evidence alone is insufficient to establish an agency relationship. The missing element is Klöckner INA's right to control the means and details of Klöckner Industrial's work. *See Gutierrez v. Cayman Islands Firm of Deloitte & Touche,* 100 S.W.3d 261, 271 (Tex.App.-San Antonio 2002, pet. dism'd) (finding that evidence failed to establish an agency relationship between related accounting firms, even though one accounting firm performed auditing work for the other, because there was no evidence that one had the right to control the other's work).

2. Limited Size of Klöckner Industrial

Although appellants cite no direct evidence of control, they contend that the fact that Klöckner Industrial consisted of only three employees demonstrates that it was merely an agent of Klöckner INA. Appellants contend that Klöckner Industrial lacked any in-house engineering capabilities and assert that such a small company could not physically implement the construction projects in which it solicited the Texas engineering firms to participate. Therefore, appellants assert that any actual construction contracts Klöckner Industrial obtained were performed by and through Klöckner INA.

However, Brosig testified that Klöckner Industrial's work is not restricted to projects in which Klöckner INA was involved in the project. Brosig further testified that Klöckner Industrial does not need financial support from Klöckner INA in order to serve as "exporter of record" or to export U.S. equipment and material. The record further indicates that Klöckner Industrial was able to independently generate revenues, operate with sufficient capital, pay its own salaries and expenses, and maintain separate property. Under these circumstances, we will not presume that an agency relationship existed merely because of Klöckner Industrial's limited resources and personnel.

3. Representations Made by Brosig

Appellants also rely on Brosig's testimony concerning representations he made to the Texas engineering firms. In his deposition, Brosig testified as follows:

Q: Now, I take it when you would go [to] the various businesses, like Brown & Root or Haliburton or Hudson Engineering, and solicit their business to represent them in order to be the prime contractor for major projects overseas that you wouldn't come in and represent that you were asking them to contract with [Klöckner Industrial] that had total assets of $1.7 million for one hundred million dollar projects overseas, were you?

A: [Witness nodded head].

Q: You were representing that you were coming in as the representative of Klöckner INA Germany, weren't you?

A: Yes.

Q: And I would think that if I, Joe Blow, with an office in Garden City, New York and one secretary walked into M.W. Kellog and said, I want you to use me as prime contractor on a one hundred million dollar project, they would laugh me out of the door. But now when you walk in, they see you, and what you tell them is that, I'm a representative of Klöckner INA Germany, don't you?

A: No. I represented I'm a member of Klöckner INA in New York.

Q: Isn't true that you represented to those customers that you were there to speak on behalf of Klöckner INA Germany?

A: [No audible answer].

Q: Mr. Brosig, you're under oath to tell the truth.

A: Yes.

Q: The truth is the truth.

A: Can you please phrase this question again?

Q: When you were in Houston during '92 and '93, and at any other time, soliciting customers, didn't you represent to those potential customers that you were representing the interests of Klöckner INA Germany?

A: I represented interests of Klöckner INA international group.

Q: Which includes Klöckner INA Germany, doesn't it?

A: Yes.

An alleged agent may testify to facts concerning his authority to act on behalf of the principal. *See Cook v. Hamer,* 158 Tex. 164, 309 S.W.2d 54, 58 (1958). However, we find that Brosig's broad assertion that he represented the interests of Klöckner INA international group does not establish a sufficient factual basis to prove an agency relationship. Moreover, to the extent that appellants' argument can be construed as an assertion that Brosig's representations to the Texas engineering firms gave him apparent authority to act on behalf of Klöckner INA, we note that only an alleged principal's words or conduct that are represented to the third party can clothe an alleged agent with apparent authority. *BML Stage Lighting, Inc. v. Mayflower Transit, Inc.,* 14 S.W.3d 395, 401 (Tex.App.-Houston [14th Dist.] 2000, pet. denied). Therefore, an agency relationship cannot be established through any representations that Brosig made to the Texas engineering firms.

"Indispensable" Agent Theory

In further support of their claim of agency, appellants contend that Klöckner Industrial was an "indispensable" agent of Klöckner INA because, without Klöckner Industrial, Klöckner INA could not (1) legally export U.S.—manufactured machinery and equipment abroad, or (2) obtain financing from the U.S. government—backed Exim Bank to ship U.S. manufactured goods overseas for use on Klöckner INA projects.

Brosig testified that on certain projects in which Klöckner INA was involved in construction of the project, Klöckner Industrial would assist Klöckner INA's foreign customer in obtaining U.S. financing so that the foreign customer could purchase U.S. machinery and equipment to be used during construction. On these projects, Klöckner Industrial would also serve as "exporter of record." Brosig testified that United States law requires the "exporter of record" to be an American company, and that Exim Bank financing is only available when the "expert of record" is an American company. Therefore, appellants contend that Klöckner Industrial, as an American company, performed an "indispensable" function for Klöckner INA.

The record clearly establishes that on certain occasions, Klöckner Industrial performed a beneficial function for Klöckner INA. But the mere existence of a subsidiary corporation that performs a beneficial function for the parent does not automatically establish the existence of an agency relationship. Where, as here, there is an absence of any evidence to show that the parent controls the subsidiary's work, we do not presume the existence of an agency relationship. *See Schultz*, 956 S.W.2d at 760 (stating that an agency relationship will not be presumed).

After reviewing all of the evidence, we conclude that there is some evidence supporting the trial court's implied finding that Klöckner Industrial was not acting as the agent of Klöckner INA when it contacted the Texas engineering firms. *See Lee Lewis Constr.*, 70 S.W.3d at 782–83. Moreover, we conclude that the trial court's implied finding that Klöckner Industrial was not the agent of Klöckner INA with respect to these contacts is not manifestly unjust. *See Pool*, 715 S.W.2d at 635. Therefore, we find that the evidence is legally and factually sufficient to support the trial court's implied finding that no agency relationship existed with respect to Klöckner Industrial's contacts with the Texas engineering firms. Accordingly, we overrule appellants' second issue....

Conclusion

We hold that because appellants failed to present the "single business enterprise" theory to the trial court, they have waived their contention that the German entities operate as a single business enterprise. We further hold that there is some evidence to support the trial court's implied finding that Klöckner Industrial is not the agent of Klöckner INA, and that this finding is not against the great weight and preponderance of the evidence. Accordingly, we conclude that the Texas contacts of Klöckner Industrial and UAT cannot be imputed to the Klöckner defendants under either a single business enterprise theory or an agency theory.

Having concluded that the Texas contacts of Klöckner Industrial and UAT cannot be imputed to the Klöckner defendants, the only relevant Texas contact for jurisdictional purposes is the single visit to Texas by Klöckner INA's former CEO. We hold that this single contact is insufficient to support general jurisdiction over the Klöckner defendants. Accordingly, we affirm the trial court's judgment granting the special appearances of the Klöckner defendants.

New Terminal Warehouse Corp. v. Wilson
589 S.W.2d 465 (Tex. App. – Houston [14th Dist.] 1979)

This wrongful death suit involves an accident on a dock in which plaintiff's husband, a longshoreman, was struck and killed by a truck backing up to a crane. New Terminal Warehouse Corporation (appellant or New Terminal), is in the business of warehousing goods shipped by water, and provides docks for loading or unloading operations. On the morning of January 22, 1978, New Terminal had docked at its facilities a barge of fertilizer grain to be unloaded and stored. New Terminal arranged for Southern Stevedoring Company, Inc. (Southern) to provide a crane and a crew of longshoremen to unload the material onto trucks. New Terminal provides no trucks for such operations and it called Norman & Son, Inc. (Norman), a trucking company, to arrange for the necessary vehicles. Norman, having no available trucks, contacted Galena Park Trucking Company (Galena Park). Galena Park agreed to furnish the required transportation and sent three trucks, two of which were owned by Leon Stephens (Stephens) but leased to Galena Park. Of the two trucks owned by Stephens, one was driven by Stephens himself, and the other by an employee of Stephens, Myrko Balaban (Balaban). For that day, the unloading proceeded without significant problem. While one truck was backed up to the crane and being loaded, a second would be stopped some distance off waiting to back into position for loading. The third would be enroute to or from the warehouse.

While the barge was being unloaded, a second crew of longshoremen were engaged in a cleaning operation on a larger ocean-going vessel, the MALLORY LYKES, also docked at the New Terminal facilities approximately 100 feet from the barge. On the second day of unloading, Balaban, having dumped one load of fertilizer, stopped alongside the MALLORY LYKES to wait for the truck under the crane to be filled. Unknown to Balaban, Willie Wilson, the husband of the plaintiff, Minnie E. Wilson (Wilson), was enroute from a parking lot on the New Terminal property to the MALLORY LYKES where he was to be a foreman of the cleaning party. Willie Wilson had stopped some four feet behind Balaban's truck and was in conversation with another longshoreman when Balaban, seeing through his outside rearview mirror that the crane was ready to load his truck, started backing toward the crane. Willie Wilson was killed by the impact of the truck.

Wilson filed a wrongful death suit and, in her second amended petition, claimed that New Terminal, Southern, Norman, Galena Park, Stephens and Balaban were all guilty of specific acts of negligence culminating in the death of her husband. At the close of plaintiff's evidence, the trial court granted Norman's and Southern's motions for instructed verdict, and dismissed those parties from the case. The jury found New Terminal negligent in failing to provide a reasonably safe place for Willie Wilson to work, and that such negligence was a proximate cause of the accident. The jury found that either Galena Park's, Stephen's, or Balaban's negligence was a proximate cause of the death and further that Willie Wilson's failure to keep a proper lookout was a proximate cause of the accident. Asked to apportion the percentage of fault in causing the accident, the jury found that Willie Wilson contributed 10%, that Galena Park "and/or" Stephens "and/or" Balaban contributed 40%, and that New Terminal contributed 50%. Damages were found to be $700,000.00. but were reduced to $630,000.00 based on the findings of contributory negligence. Based on the jury finding that New Terminal failed to provide Balaban a reasonably safe place to work, the trial court granted complete indemnity to Galena Park, Stephens, and Balaban against New Terminal. New Terminal brings this appeal.

New Terminal asserts as error the trial court's granting of instructed verdicts for Southern and Norman. In an instructed verdict case, the controlling determination is "whether there is any evidence of probative force to raise fact issues on the material questions presented." Henderson v. Travelers Ins. Co., 544 S.W.2d 649, 650 (Tex.Sup.1976). New Terminal's position is that there was evidence in the record that Southern had a duty to control the trucks during the backing procedure on the dock. For support, New Terminal looks to the testimony of Kingcaid, a representative of Southern, who testified that New Terminal had no supervisors on the dock; that Southern controlled the "spacing" of the trucks; and that employees of Southern were under the control of Southern during the unloading operation. This testimony provides no direct evidence that Southern had any duty to control the backing of the trucks. The reference to spacing was limited to Southern's activities in informing the truck drivers when the truck was properly positioned to accept the load. New Terminal points to the Southern manpower on the barge and crane as evidence of control. The fact that Southern may have had sufficient personnel to control trucks is not direct evidence of a right to control the details of the work. Nor is there any direct evidence of probative force that Southern actually exercised control over the trucks. Balaban and Stephens testified that their cue to back the trucks came from their sighting of the preceding truck as it drove away from the crane and from their past experience in such operations, but not from any signal by the crane operator, as asserted by New Terminal. Cumulatively, the above evidence amounts to no more than a surmise or suspicion that Southern had a duty to control backing procedures of the truck, and therefore fails to constitute any evidence of probative force. Seideneck v. Cal Bayreuther Associates, 451 S.W.2d 752 (Tex.Sup.1970); Joske v. Irvine, 91 Tex. 574, 44 S.W. 1059, 1063 (1898). The instructed verdict was properly granted for Southern.

New Terminal seeks to have Norman held liable as a matter of law under the doctrine of respondeat superior on the ground that Galena Park and its employees, Balaban and Stephens, were agents acting on behalf of Norman and subject to its authority. Norman takes the position that Galena Park and its employees were independent contractors. The test recognized in Texas to determine if a principal/agent relationship exists "is whether the employer has the right of control in directing, not merely the end sought to be accomplished by the employment, but as well the means and details of its accomplishment; not only what shall be done, but how it shall be done." e. g., W. D. Haden Company v. Ryman, 362 S.W.2d 133, 135 (Tex.Civ.App.-Houston 1962, writ ref'd). In applying that rule to the case at bar, we find no evidence that Norman was anything more than a conduit furnishing independent contractors and trucks to New Terminal. New Terminal, desiring trucks, contacted Norman, who had no trucks available. Norman agreed to contact other trucking companies to provide the trucks. Norman called Galena Park, and it was Galena Park, through Stephens, Balaban, and a third truck driver, who fulfilled the order of New Terminal for three trucks. There is no evidence that Norman was present at the dock, or that it had the authority to control the details of the trucking on the dock. In the absence of such right of control, the doctrine of respondeat superior is not applicable....

In addition to finding that New Terminal had failed to provide a reasonably safe place for Willie Wilson to work, the jury also found New Terminal failed to provide Balaban with a safe place to work and that such negligence was a proximate cause of the accident. Based on that finding, the trial court granted complete indemnity to Galena Park, Stephens, and Balaban against New Terminal. See generally, Austin Road Co. v. Pope, 147 Tex. 430, 216 S.W.2d 563 (1949)....

We believe that the common law doctrine of indemnity between joint tort-feasors in negligence cases should be reconsidered in light of article 2212a. In particular, where there are negligent joint tort-feasors the statute provides:

> (b) In a case in which there is more than one defendant, and the claimant's negligence does not exceed the total negligence of all defendants, contribution to the damages awarded to the claimant shall be in proportion to the percentage of negligence attributable to each defendant.

> (c) Each defendant is jointly and severally liable for the entire amount of the judgment awarded the claimant, except that a defendant whose negligence is less than that of the claimant is liable to the claimant only for that portion of the judgment which represents the percentage of negligence attributable to him.

Tex.Rev.Civ.Stat.Ann. art. 2212a, §§2(b) and (c) (Supp.1978). The language of the statute applies here. Appellant New Terminal had a duty to exercise ordinary care to provide a reasonably safe place to work for both Willie Wilson and Balaban, employees of independent contractors. Balaban, and, vicariously, Galena Park and Stephens, had a duty to exercise reasonable care in the operation of the truck regardless of the fact that he was caused, perhaps negligently, to operate the truck in an area unsafe for pedestrian traffic. The jury was requested to apportion percentages of fault and in doing so was allowed to consider that, at least in part, the accident was proximately caused by New Terminal's failure to provide a reasonably safe place for Balaban to work. Under the jury finding assessing 50% fault to New Terminal, it would be and was improper to grant indemnity to Galena Park, Stephens, and Balaban, who were assessed 40% Fault....

Having reversed and rendered the indemnity portion of the judgment, and having ordered contribution in accordance with article 2212a, we affirm the remainder of the judgment. Reversed and rendered in part, and affirmed in part.

Capacity

The Restatement of Agency, 3rd edition, generally provides that any person may be empowered to act as an agent. Any person who has capacity to act in their own name for themselves has the capacity to serve as principal. This is commonly interpreted as allowing any person to serve as principal or as an agent of another, including one with a legal disability that makes contracts non-binding.

§ 3.04 Capacity To Act As Principal

(1) An individual has capacity to act as principal in a relationship of agency as defined in § 1.01 if, at the time the agent takes action, the individual would have capacity if acting in person.

(2) The law applicable to a person that is not an individual governs whether the person has capacity to be a principal in a relationship of agency as defined in § 1.01, as well as the effect of the person's lack or loss of capacity on those who interact with it.

(3) If performance of an act is not delegable, its performance by an agent does not constitute performance by the principal.

§ 3.05 Capacity To Act As Agent. *Any person may ordinarily be empowered to act so as to affect the legal relations of another. The actor's capacity governs the extent to which, by so acting, the actor becomes subject to duties and liabilities to the person whose legal relations are affected or to third parties.*

May v. Ken-Rad Corporation, Inc.
279 Ky. 601, 131 S.W.2d 490 (1939)

Action by George Oliver May and others, as partners doing business under the firm name and style of Price Waterhouse & Co., against the Ken-Rad Corporation, Incorporated, to recover for an audit. Judgment for defendant, and plaintiffs appeal. Reversed for new trial.

George Oliver May and a number of others, as partners doing business under the firm name and style of Price Waterhouse & Company, brought this action to recover of the Ken-Rad Corporation the sum of $2,506.40 for an audit made in circumstances presently set out. Trial before the court without intervention of a jury resulted in a judgment for the defendant and the plaintiffs are appealing.

Briefly stated the facts are: Appellee made application to the National Recovery Administration, which is commonly known and hereinafter referred to as the N R A, for a wage differential under the Electrical Code promulgated by the N R A. Since 1922 appellee has been engaged in the manufacture of radio tubes in Owensboro and was the only manufacturer of radio tubes located in the south. Northern and eastern competitors of appellee including the Hygrade-Sylvania Corporation filed answers and protests against the granting of the differential. It is unnecessary to go into detail concerning a hearing had on the application. It is sufficient to say that after evidence had been submitted representatives of N R A were sent to appellee's plant and to the plants of the Hygrade-Sylvania Corporation located at Salem, Massachusetts, and Emporium, Pennsylvania, to verify and possibly to augment the evidence by personal inspection and examination. After this was done the assistant deputy administrator advised representatives of appellee that figures and information obtained with respect to the relative costs of production at various plants did not justify the granting of a wage differential to it. Representatives of appellee, however, insisted that data furnished or obtained from its competitors was erroneous and subsequent conferences resulted in an agreement between the representatives of N R A and appellee to have an audit made of appellee and of the Hygrade Sylvania Corporation, the lowest cost producer of radio tubes, by a firm of reputable accountants selected by representatives of the N R A, the cost of the audit to be borne by appellee. This agreement was later confirmed by letter from appellee to N R A which contained suggestions as to the nature and character of the audit which should be made. Appellants were selected by N R A to make the audit. The Hygrade-Sylvania Corporation consented to an audit of its books under an agreement with N R A that it would be confidential and open only to the inspection of representatives of N R A. While a representative of appellant was making the audit of appellee's plant he told representatives of appellee that the audit was confidential and would not be divulged to their competitors and requested that appellee write a letter to appellants confirming the agreement to pay for the audit which was done. After the audit had been completed and appellants had filed their report with N R A the application for differential was at first denied but later an order was entered granting appellee 12 1/2 per cent wage differential. It is stated in brief for appellee that this latter action was brought about as a result of pressure brought to bear by a delegation from Owensboro and senators and congressmen from Kentucky and apparently for political reasons but this statement is not altogether borne out by the record.

Appellee demanded that it be furnished a copy of or that it at least be permitted to inspect the audit but this was denied by both N R A and appellants. It refused to pay and defended on the ground that the audit was not of the type and character it had authorized N R A to have made and that it did not agree to pay for an audit which it was not allowed to see and which was solely for the confidential consideration of N R A. The court's finding and judgment was in full accord with the contentions of appellee.

As grounds for reversal it is argued (1) that the court erred in holding N R A's refusal to reveal to appellee the result of the audit barred appellant's right to recover therefor; (2) that the audit was of the type, kind and character which appellee authorized N R A to have made; (3) that the court erred in refusing to consider appellant's evidence that the audit complied with all of N R A's instructions and (4) that the court erred in admitting incompetent evidence.

The record discloses beyond question or doubt that appellee made N R A its agent to select and employ a reputable firm of accountants to make the proposed audit and that it agreed to pay for same. There was no specific agreement as to the nature or character of the audit to be made nor did appellee's letter to N R A confirming the agreement specify the nature or character of audit which it expected or for which it would pay. It contained suggestions as to the character of audit that should be made. Representatives of appellee testified that they did not presume to dictate to N R A in that matter. Representatives of appellants testified that the audit covered everything suggested by appellee and the evidence of representatives of N R A indicates that the audit was satisfactory and furnished all information necessary or desired by it. There was no agreement that appellee would be furnished a copy of the audit and no suggestion in its letter that payment for the audit was conditioned upon it receiving a copy or having the privilege of inspecting it. The representative of appellants said enough to the representatives of appellee while the audit was being made to bring notice to appellee that the audit would be kept confidential. Appellee gave N R A full authority to employ accountants to make the audit without any conditions, restrictions or reservations or anything more than mere suggestions. There was nothing in appellee's letter which was seen by representatives of appellant that would indicate that N R A was acting under specific instructions or limited powers.

A principal is bound by the contract of his agent within the scope of the latter's apparent authority although not authorized in expressed terms. Columbia Land & Mining Company v. Tinsley, 60 S. W. 10, 22 Ky.Law.Rep. 1082; White Plains Coal Company v. Teague, 163 Ky. 110, 173 S.W. 360. It has been held that a principal is bound by the acts of the agent within the apparent scope of authority although the authority may be in fact limited, if one dealing with the agent is ignorant of limitations upon his authority. Hurst Home Insurance Company v. Ledford, 207 Ky. 212, 268 S.W. 1090. In the latter case it is further held that where one of two parties must suffer loss through acts of an agent the loss should fall upon the one who authorized the agent to act rather than the innocent third party unless the agent is acting beyond the scope of his apparent authority.

Appellee insists that N R A could not act as agent for anyone because the National Industrial Recovery Act was unconstitutional as was later held. In Talbot v. Bowen, 8 Ky. 436, 1 A.K. Marsh. 436, 10 Am.Dec. 747, it is held in effect that one under legal disability, whose contracts may not be binding upon him, may nevertheless as agent, by contract otherwise unexceptional, bind their principal. See also 21 R.C.L. 819, section 4. Furthermore, appellee fully recognized the agency by its letter confirming the agreement to pay for the audit; and it has been held by this court that one cannot act through another and then insist that the other is not his agent. Roesener v. Burdette, 208 Ky. 137, 270 S.W. 731….

It is our conclusion that the findings of the court are not sufficiently supported by the evidence; that appellants were entitled to recover the sum sued for and the court erred in adjudging otherwise. What we have already said sufficiently covers grounds 1 and 2 argued by counsel for appellants and renders it unnecessary to discuss the other grounds.

Wherefore, the judgment is reversed for a new trial and proceedings consistent with this opinion….

Agent's power and authority under the agency relationship

Under the agency relationship, the agent's authority encompasses all powers, whether actual or apparent, with which he has been granted by the principal. The agent's authority is his power to affect the legal relations of the principal by acts done in accord with the powers granted him. Thus, the agent's authority must flow from some word, act, or omission by the principal. When the agent acts within the scope of her authority, the general rule is that the principal will be liable for any damages resulting from such actions. On the other hand, if the principal has not granted the agent the authority to act, then the agent is acting outside of his authority and may be personally liable for his acts.

Actual Authority

An agent's actual authority comes from the powers the principal directly confers upon him, say from an agreement, as well as those that the principal either causes or permits him to believe that he possesses. The principal expressly grants the agent this authority either by written or spoken words (express actual authority) or by conduct which, reasonably interpreted, causes the agent to believe that the principal wants him to act on the principal's behalf (implied actual authority).

The Restatement of Agency, 3rd edition, describes actual authority in §§2.01 and 2.02

§ 2.01 Actual Authority. *An agent acts with actual authority when, at the time of taking action that has legal consequences for the principal, the agent reasonably believes, in accordance with the* principal's manifestations to the agent, *that the principal wishes the agent so to act.* [Emphasis added]

§ 2.02 Scope of Actual Authority. *An agent has actual authority to take action designated or implied in the principal's manifestations to the agent and acts necessary or incidental to achieving the principal's objectives, as the agent reasonably understands the principal's manifestations and objectives when the agent determines how to act.*

> *(1) An agent's interpretation of the principal's manifestations is reasonable if it reflects any meaning known by the agent to be ascribed by the principal and, in the absence of any meaning known to the agent, as a reasonable person in the agent's position would interpret the manifestations in light of the context, including circumstances of which the agent has notice and the agent's fiduciary duty to the principal.*

> *(2) An agent's understanding of the principal's objectives is reasonable if it accords with the principal's manifestations and the inferences that a reasonable person in the agent's position would draw from the circumstances creating the agency.*

Additionally, a principal may also implicitly grant an agent actual authority. The principal may grant the agent the authority to achieve a particular objective. Implicit in this authority is that the agent may have to engage in certain business practices, customs, or enter into certain agreements in order to achieve said objective. In those instances, although the principal may not have expressly granted the agent that authority, or impliedly acted in a manner on which the agent would have reasonably relied, where the agent is right to believe that his actual authority includes the ability to engage in these objective achieving actions, his authority will be implicit. For example, a principal might expressly grant actual authority to a real estate broker to sell principal's house by executing a listing agreement. If the contract states that broker is hired to sell the house without identifying specific methods the broker is to use, it may be implied that the broker would list the property on the multiple listing service (MLS) or otherwise promote the house. The broker would have implicit authority to actually show the house to prospective buyers.

An agent who has neither actual express authority nor actual implied authority may have what is known as apparent authority.

Apparent Authority

Apparent authority exists where the acts or conduct of the principal, caused a third-party to reasonably rely on those acts or conduct and to change her position to her detriment. Through his conduct, the principal is said to have granted the agent the apparent authority to engage in certain actions. Apparent authority is granted when the principal knowingly or negligently represents to third-persons that the agent has the authority to act. In those instances, if a reasonably prudent person, using diligence and discretion, would believe that the agent possessed those apparent powers, then the principal is estopped from denying the agent's authority. The extent of an agent's apparent authority is what a third-party reasonably believes the agent's powers to be.

> *§ 2.03 Apparent Authority. Apparent authority is the power held by an agent or other actor to affect a principal's legal relations with third parties when a third party reasonably believes the actor has authority to act on behalf of the principal and that belief is traceable to the principal's manifestations.*

Actual and Apparent Authority

Sociedad De Solaridad Social "El Estillero" v. J.S. Mcmanus Produce Co.
964 S.W.2d 332 (Tex. App. – Corpus Christi 1998)

This is a suit filed by Sociedad De Solaridad Social, "El Estillero" against J.S. McManus Produce Company to recover damages for breach of contract. Trial was to a jury, and after Sociedad presented its evidence, the trial court granted McManus's motion for a directed verdict. Sociedad appeals by five points of error. We affirm.

Moises Munoz Ortega formed an association in the State of Morelos, Mexico called Sociedad De Solaridad Social "El Estillero." It was comprised of fifteen individuals and five families. He formed it as a vehicle to pool resources and export agricultural produce abroad. At issue in this appeal is an alleged contract between Sociedad and J.S. McManus Produce Company in which McManus agreed to sell Sociedad's onion production on a consignment basis. Sociedad began planting the onions in July or August 1990. While Sociedad grew and produced the onions, it dealt with two purported agents of McManus, Gilberto Santos and Amadeo Zarate. The evidence also showed in December 1990, Moises allegedly received a telephone call from a "Roberto" from McManus. During this conversation, the alleged contract was confirmed. On January 11, 1991, Sociedad turned over its onions to Santos and began shipping thirty-three truckloads of sacked onions to the United States. The onions were shipped in sacks marked "S & S." The initials stood for Santos and Santos. The onions were *not* shipped in sacks bearing McManus's logo. Sociedad received about $120,000 or $124,000 for the onions. Sociedad maintains McManus still owes it money for the onions. At the close of Sociedad's evidence, the trial court granted a directed verdict for McManus.

The chief issue in this case, as expressed in Sociedad's second point of error, is whether an agency relationship existed between McManus and either Zarate, Santos, or "Roberto."

A principal is liable for his agent's acts which the agent has actual or apparent authority from the principal to do, and for acts which the principal ratifies. *Cameron County Sav. Ass'n v. Stewart Title Guar. Co.*, 819 S.W.2d 600, 602 (Tex.App.—Corpus Christi 1991, writ denied). *See Currey v. Lone Star Steel Co.*, 676 S.W.2d 205, 209 (Tex.App.—Fort Worth 1984, no writ) (actual and apparent authority); *Little v. Clark*, 592 S.W.2d 61, 64 (Tex.Civ.App.—Fort Worth 1979, writ ref'd n.r.e.) (ratification). "Actual" authority includes both express and implied authority and usually denotes the authority which a principal (1) intentionally confers upon an agent, (2) intentionally allows the agent to believe he possesses, or (3) by want of due care allows the agent to believe he possesses. *Cameron County Sav. Ass'n*, 819 S.W.2d at 603; *Currey*, 676 S.W.2d at 209–10; *Behring Int'l, Inc. v. Greater Houston Bank*, 662 S.W.2d 642, 649 (Tex.App.—Houston [1st Dist.] 1983, writ dism'd). Implied actual authority can exist only with express actual authority. *Behring*, 662 S.W.2d at 649. This is so because implied authority is authority which is proper, usual, and necessary to the exercise of the authority the principal expressly delegates. *Employers Casualty Co. v. Winslow*, 356 S.W.2d 160, 168 (Tex.Civ.App.—El Paso 1962, writ ref'd n.r.e.). *See Behring*, 662 S.W.2d at 649.

While actual authority is created by written or spoken words or conduct by the principal to the agent, apparent authority is created by written or spoken words or conduct by the principal to a third party. *Cameron County Sav. Ass'n*, 819 S.W.2d at 603. To establish apparent authority, one must show a principal either knowingly permitted an agent to hold itself out as having authority or showed a lack of ordinary care in order to clothe the agent with indicia of authority. *NationsBank v. Dilling*, 922 S.W.2d 950, 952–53 (Tex.1996) (per curiam); *Ames v. Great S. Bank*, 672 S.W.2d 447, 450 (Tex.1984). A court may consider only the conduct of the principal leading a third party to believe the agent has authority in determining whether an agent has apparent authority. *NationsBank*, 922 S.W.2d at 953; *Southwest Title Ins. Co. v. Northland Bldg. Corp.*, 552 S.W.2d 425, 428 (Tex.1977). A party seeking to charge a principal through the apparent authority of its agent must establish conduct by the principal which would lead a reasonably prudent person to believe the agent has the authority it purports to exercise. *Biggs v. United States Fire Ins. Co.*, 611 S.W.2d 624, 629 (Tex.1981). The principal must have affirmatively held out the agent as possessing the authority or must have knowingly and voluntarily permitted the agent to act in an unauthorized manner. *NationsBank*, 922 S.W.2d at 953. See *Douglass v. Panama, Inc.*, 504 S.W.2d 776, 778–79 (Tex.1974)....

Evidence of Agency

Due to Moises's death in May 1991, his son, Conrado, became Sociedad's leader and testified extensively about the growth and shipment of the onions. Santos and Zarate represented to Conrado they worked for McManus. He said Sociedad received some advances from McManus to help grow and produce the onions. However, he could produce no evidence to support this contention. He further testified Sociedad received all of its money by check. But, in 1990, Sociedad never received a check drawn on McManus's bank account. In 1991, when Sociedad began shipping the onions, the only payments it received came from Zarate.

Concerning actual authority, there is no evidence that McManus intentionally conferred authority on any agent, intentionally allowed any agent to believe he possessed authority, or by want of due care allowed the agent to believe he possessed authority. Similarly as to apparent authority, there is no evidence that McManus either knowingly permitted an agent to hold itself out as having authority or showed a lack of ordinary care in order to clothe the agent with indicia of authority. There is nothing in the record showing any knowledge by McManus of the representation of Santos and Zarate.

Accordingly, Sociedad did not meet its burden to propound some evidence showing Zarate, "Roberto," or Santos had authority, actual or apparent, to act as McManus's agents. We hold the trial court did not err by granting an instructed verdict on the ground of no agency relationship. We overrule point two.

By point one, Sociedad asserts the trial court erred in granting the directed verdict because the evidence showed there was an agreement between itself and McManus. Even assuming a contract existed between Sociedad and McManus, Sociedad turned over the onions to Santos, who was not McManus's agent. There is no evidence that Sociedad delivered onions to McManus. We affirm the trial court's judgment.

Streetman v. Benchmark Bank
890 S.W.2d 212 (Tex. App. – Eastland 1994)

Benchmark Bank sued Michael W. Streetman and his wife, Laura E. Streetman, for the balance due on delinquent promissory notes. The Streetmans filed a counterclaim for breach of contract, for breach of warranty, and for deceptive trade practices. The trial court entered a partial summary judgment for the Bank for $440,770.47 (the amount due on the promissory notes). The Streetmans' counterclaims were tried by a jury which found for the Streetmans on some of their claims and which assessed damages at $2,000,000.00. The trial court entered judgment notwithstanding the verdict that the Streetmans take nothing, and the Streetmans appeal. We affirm.

The Jury's Findings

The questions which were submitted to the jury and the jury's answers read in relevant part as shown:

QUESTION 1A: Do you find from a preponderance of the evidence that Don Watts had the authority or the *apparent authority* of Benchmark Bank to promise Michael Streetman and/or Laura Streetman that *Benchmark Bank would pay all overdrafts* drawn on the M & L Distributing deposit account with Benchmark Bank?

ANSWER: YES

QUESTION 1B: Did the Streetmans and Benchmark Bank agree that Benchmark would cover *all overdraft checks* drawn on Benchmark by the Streetmans for checks written relating to the M & L Distributing Nintendo Cartridge Business?

ANSWER: YES

QUESTION 2: Did Benchmark Bank breach its agreement with the Streetmans?

ANSWER: YES

QUESTION 3: Did Benchmark Bank engage in any false, misleading or deceptive act or practice in its course of dealings with the Streetmans which was a producing cause of damages, if any, to the Streetmans?

ANSWER: YES

QUESTION 4: Did Benchmark Bank make an express warranty that it would *cover all overdrafts* by the Streetmans?

ANSWER: YES

QUESTION 5: Did Benchmark Bank breach an express warranty which breach if any was a producing cause of damage, if any, suffered by the Streetmans?

ANSWER: YES

QUESTION 6: Did Benchmark Bank engage in any unconscionable action or course of action, which was a producing cause of damages to the Streetmans?

ANSWER: NO

QUESTION 7: Did Benchmark Bank engage in any such conduct knowingly?

ANSWER: NO

QUESTION 8: Do you find that there was a special relationship between the Bank and the Streetmans?

ANSWER: YES

QUESTION 9: Do you find that the Bank engaged in conduct, in the course of dealings with the Streetmans, which breached its duty of good faith and fair dealing and which was a proximate cause of the damages, if any, to the Streetmans?

ANSWER: YES

QUESTION 10: Do you find the breach of duty, if any, by the Bank was accompanied by malice on the part of the Bank?

ANSWER: NO

QUESTION 11: What sum of money, if any, if paid now in cash, do you find would fairly and reasonably compensate the Streetmans for their actual damages, if any?

ANSWER: $2,000,000.00

(Questions and Answers 12 and 13 omittted here)

QUESTION 14: Do you find from a preponderance of the evidence that Benchmark Bank's failure to comply with the *agreement, if any, to pay all overdrafts* drawn on the M & L Distributing deposit account with Benchmark Bank was excused?

ANSWER: NO

Under the instructions of the trial court, because of the negative answers to Questions 7 and 10, the jury was not required to answer Questions 12. Question 12 asked: "What sum of money, if any, in addition to actual damages should be awarded." or 13. Question 13 asked about "exemplary damages" caused by malice.

Appellants briefed four points of error in which they argue that the trial court erred: (Point No. 1) in granting the Bank's motion to disregard the jury's answers to questions concerning breach of contract, breach of warranty, and deceptive trade practices because there was evidence that the Bank's officer acted within the scope of his agency; (Point No. 2) in granting the Bank's motion to disregard the jury's answer concerning deceptive trade practices because Donald Gene Watts was an agent for the Bank and had authority to negotiate loans and approve the payment of overdrafts; (Point No. 3) in granting the Bank's motion to disregard the finding that the foreseeable result of the Bank's actions was the lost profits of $2,000,000.00; and (Point No. 4) in rendering judgment notwithstanding the verdict.

Background Facts

The Streetmans had been in the video rental business. In 1988, Mr. Streetman began to sell Nintendo cartridges out of the back of his pickup. The Nintendo business flourished, and the Streetmans decided to expand. In order to expand, they needed more financing than their original bank could authorize. They approached Benchmark Bank to ask for a loan and for assurance that their "overdraft" checks would be honored. Watts, the senior credit officer at the Bank, assisted the Streetmans with their loan. They opened a checking account for their business, M & L Distributing, in December of 1988.

Over the next several months, the Streetmans wrote approximately 500 overdraft checks. The Bank collected service charges on a majority of these checks. At one point in time, their checking account was overdrawn $204,863.10. On June 8, 1989, the Streetmans bought a Nintendo distributorship.

All of the overdrafts were honored until August 28, 1989, when the Bank suddenly stopped honoring their overdraft checks. Because of their lack of cash, the Streetmans were unable to purchase the Nintendo cartridges as soon as they became available, and they lost the valuable Nintendo distributorship which they had acquired. Their business failed.

Standard of Review

A judgment notwithstanding the verdict can only be upheld when a directed verdict would have been proper. *Dodd v. Texas Farm Products Company*, 576 S.W.2d 812 at 815 (Tex.1979). In order to uphold the trial court's judgment notwithstanding the verdict, we must determine that no evidence supports at least one essential element of the jury's findings. TEX.R.CIV.P. 301; *Mancorp, Inc. v. Culpepper*, 802 S.W.2d 226 (Tex.1990); *Williams v. Bennett*, 610 S.W.2d 144 (Tex.1980).

In determining a "no evidence" question, we must consider only the evidence and reasonable inferences therefrom that tend to support the jury findings, disregarding all evidence and inferences to the contrary. *Best v. Ryan Auto Group, Inc.*, 786 S.W.2d 670 (Tex.1990).

Authority of Bank Officer

The issue that controls this case is whether there is any evidence to support the jury's finding that Watts had the authority to bind the Bank by promising to pay "all" of the Streetmans' overdrafts. There is evidence that Watts said that the Bank would never return a check unpaid. However, in order to show that the Bank is liable for Watts' promise, there must be some evidence that Watts had the actual or apparent authority to make this agreement for the Bank. We overrule the first, second, and fourth points of error because there is no competent evidence of Watts' actual or apparent authority to [bind his principal to] pay "all overdrafts."

In order to show that Watts had actual authority, there must be some evidence that the Bank intentionally conferred the authority upon him; intentionally allowed him to believe that he possessed the authority; or, by want of care, allowed him to believe that he possessed the authority. *Cameron County Savings Association v. Stewart Title Guaranty Company*, 819 S.W.2d 600 at 603 (Tex.App.—Corpus Christi 1991, writ den'd). Actual authority may be express or implied. There is no evidence that the Bank gave Watts the authority or that the Bank allowed Watts to believe that he had the authority to promise to pay all overdrafts drawn on the Streetmans' account. Watts testified that he did not have such authority. Further, the evidence conclusively establishes that banks have federally mandated lending limits and that both Watts and the Bank were aware that the Bank could not exceed this limit. Although the evidence is undisputed that Watts, as the senior credit officer of the Bank, had the authority to loan money and to approve the payment of overdrafts up to the Bank's lending limit, there is no evidence that Watts had the actual authority to promise to pay "all overdrafts" drawn on the account.

There is also no competent evidence that Watts had the apparent authority to make such a promise. Apparent authority is based upon the doctrine of estoppel and is created when the principal's conduct would lead a reasonably prudent person to believe that the agent has the authority he purports to exercise. *Biggs v. United States Fire Insurance Company*, 611 S.W.2d 624 at 629 (Tex.1981); *Southwest Title Insurance Company v. Northland Building Corporation*, 552 S.W.2d 425 (Tex.1977); *Cameron County Savings Association v. Stewart Title Guaranty Company*, supra. Apparent authority is not available where the other party has notice of the limitations of the agent's power. *Douglass v. Panama, Inc.*, 504 S.W.2d 776 at 779 (Tex.1974). The undisputed evidence clearly shows that the Streetmans knew from dealing with their previous bank that banks have lending limits; consequently, they knew that Watts' authority was limited and that he could not agree to pay "all overdrafts" drawn on their account.

Moreover, a reasonably prudent person would not believe that Watts was acting within the scope of his authority by promising to pay "all overdrafts" drawn on the account. We hold that there is no evidence that Watts was acting within the scope of his authority by promising to pay "all overdrafts" or that the Bank engaged in any false, misleading, or deceptive acts in its course of dealings with the Streetmans. The trial court properly disregarded Jury Questions 1A, 1B, 2, 3, 4, and 5. The first, second, and fourth points of error are overruled. The third point becomes moot and need not be discussed. The judgment of the trial court is affirmed.

Nationsbank v. Dilling
922 S.W.2d 950 (Tex. 1996)

PER CURIAM

We must determine whether a bank is vicariously liable for the fraudulent acts of a bank teller whose participation in an investment scheme caused damages to a third party. We also must decide whether the bank is directly liable to the third party for negligently employing the teller, who improperly issued cashier's checks that the bank honored.

We hold that vicarious liability does not attach to an employer in the absence of evidence that its employee was acting within the scope of her actual or apparent authority, and that a bank owes no duty to protect a third party from making investment decisions in reliance on cashier's checks that were improperly issued by a bank teller but were honored by the bank. We reverse the judgment of the court of appeals, 897 S.W.2d 451, and render judgment for NationsBank.

After serving time in federal prison for bank fraud, Fritz McMillon formed McMillon Enterprises, Ltd. (MEL), a business purportedly organized to buy and sell rental cars. Carolyn Price, a NationsBank teller, was also involved in MEL's operations. Price herself had previous criminal convictions for theft and welfare fraud.

McMillon met Harry Dilling and offered Dilling an opportunity to invest in MEL. This "opportunity" was nothing but a scheme concocted by McMillon, Price, and others to defraud Dilling. Although Dilling knew that McMillon had served time in federal prison for bank fraud, he nevertheless made an initial investment in MEL.

In furtherance of the scheme to defraud Dilling, Price took a number of actions that her employer NationsBank did not authorize. Price accepted an MEL check from McMillon against which she issued several cashier's checks in amounts exceeding the value of the MEL check. NationsBank's internal policy required employees to obtain supervisory approval before issuing cashier's checks in amounts greater than $2,500. Although the value of the cashier's checks Price issued exceeded $2,500, Price did not seek approval. Price also fabricated deposit slips reflecting amounts deposited in MEL's account.

McMillon showed Dilling the deposit slips as evidence that MEL was a legitimate company with assets. In an effort to gain Dilling's confidence, McMillon repaid Dilling's initial investment plus a return on that investment with the cashier's checks issued by NationsBank. Satisfied by his initial "profit," Dilling made several larger investments in MEL. Dilling was not a NationsBank customer and never met with Price or any other NationsBank representative.

The fraudulent investment scheme succeeded for a time: Dilling invested an additional $595,000 in MEL. None of this amount was repaid. Dilling ultimately realized that he had been deceived and filed suit against McMillon, Price, and MEL for fraud and conspiracy, and against NationsBank for fraud, conspiracy, and negligence. The trial court rendered judgment against Price, McMillon, and MEL, but rendered a take-nothing summary judgment in favor of NationsBank. Dilling appealed the judgment for NationsBank on two grounds, arguing that (1)

NationsBank, as Price's employer, is vicariously liable for Price's fraudulent acts under an agency theory based on apparent authority and (2) NationsBank is liable for negligently employing Price as a teller because she had prior criminal convictions. The court of appeals agreed, reversed the trial court's judgment, and remanded these issues for disposition. 897 S.W.2d at 458.

NationsBank contends that the court of appeals erred in holding it vicariously liable for Price's fraudulent conduct because NationsBank did nothing that would allow Dilling to conclude that Price was acting with NationsBank's apparent authority in committing her fraudulent acts. NationsBank also argues that it owed no duty to Dilling as a matter of law because Dilling was not a NationsBank customer and it was not foreseeable that Dilling would rely on cashier's checks issued by NationsBank in making an investment decision.

The court of appeals incorrectly framed the issue of vicarious liability as whether Price, "clothed with [NationsBank's] apparent authority," could bind NationsBank for her fraudulent acts committed within the scope of her employment. 897 S.W.2d at 454. This question presupposes that Price, by issuing cashier's checks, had apparent authority to make representations about the soundness of Dilling's investment.

To establish apparent authority, one must show that a principal either knowingly permitted an agent to hold itself out as having authority or showed such lack of ordinary care as to clothe the agent with indicia of authority. *Ames v. Great S. Bank*, 672 S.W.2d 447, 450 (Tex.1984). A court may consider only the conduct of the principal leading a third party to believe that the agent has authority in determining whether an agent has apparent authority. *Southwest Title Ins. Co. v. Northland Bldg. Corp.*, 552 S.W.2d 425, 428 (Tex.1977). *See also Trahan v. Southland Life Ins. Co.*, 155 Tex. 548, 289 S.W.2d 753, 755 (1956) (holding that it is the principal's conduct, attitude, and knowledge that determines whether an agent had apparent authority).

NationsBank correctly argues that it cannot be held vicariously liable for Price's fraud on a theory of apparent authority because it established that it never took any action that would lead a reasonably prudent person to conclude that it had authorized Price to make representations regarding an investment in MEL. One seeking to charge a principal through the apparent authority of its agent must establish conduct by the principal that would lead a reasonably prudent person to believe that the agent has the authority that it purports to exercise. *Biggs v. United States Fire Ins. Co.*, 611 S.W.2d 624, 629 (Tex.1981). The principal must have affirmatively held out the agent as possessing the authority or must have knowingly and voluntarily permitted the agent to act in an unauthorized manner. *See Douglass v. Panama, Inc.*, 504 S.W.2d 776, 778–79 (Tex.1974).

Under these facts, the issuance of cashier's checks by NationsBank could not, as a matter of law, have led Dilling to believe that Price was clothed with Nationsbank's authority to make representations about the soundness of an investment in MEL. The only representation that Dilling could glean from NationsBank's issuance of cashier's checks is that NationsBank would honor those checks. The court of appeals incorrectly assumed that because Price was "clothed with [NationsBank's] apparent authority" to issue cashier's checks, her actions of improperly issuing checks imputed a representation about the risks of investing in the business of a NationsBank customer who received these checks. 897 S.W.2d at 454–56.

Nor did NationsBank make any representations about the soundness of an investment in MEL when Price manufactured deposit slips. A receipt from a bank indicating a deposit into an account is not a representation by the bank as to the soundness of a particular investment.

We disagree with the court of appeals that this case is similar to *Bankers Life Insurance Co. v. Scurlock Oil Co.*, 447 F.2d 997, 1005–07 (5th Cir.1971), because the fraudulent actions committed by the agent in *Bankers Life*, unlike those of the agent in this case, were done within the scope of its apparent authority. The court in *Bankers Life* noted that a principal may be held liable for the fraudulent misrepresentations of its agent "so long as the third person reasonably believed the agent was acting within the scope of his authority." *Bankers Life*, 447 F.2d at 1005 n. 12. The *Bankers Life* court went on to conclude that the agent in that case "undisputedly" possessed the principal's authority to deliver and sell oil and that the agent committed fraud in the delivery and sale of that oil. *Id.* at 1004–05. In this case, as already noted, Price was without the apparent authority to make representations regarding Dilling's investment in MEL.

We turn now to Dilling's negligent hiring claim. In the trial court, Dilling asserted both negligent hiring and negligent supervision claims against NationsBank. However, in its appeal of the trial court's summary judgment in favor of NationsBank, Dilling asserted only that NationsBank was negligent or reckless in employing Price, who had a criminal record. NationsBank correctly argues that it cannot be liable to Dilling under a theory of negligent hiring on these facts. In a negligence case, the threshold inquiry is whether a duty exists as a matter of law. *Greater Houston Transp. Co. v. Phillips*, 801 S.W.2d 523, 525 (Tex.1990). In making this determination, the court considers risk, foreseeability, and likelihood of injury, weighed against the social utility of the actor's conduct. *Id.* The court also considers the magnitude of the burden of guarding against the injury, and the consequences of placing this burden with the defendant. *Id.* In the absence of foreseeability, there is no duty. *See id.*

Dilling argues that NationsBank was negligent in hiring Price because it was foreseeable that Price would abuse her position as a bank teller to issue cashier's checks in a scheme to defraud innocent third parties. While it may have been reasonably foreseeable to NationsBank that a teller might exceed her actual authority by issuing a cashier's check in excess of $2,500 without obtaining supervisory approval, this means only that NationsBank would have no defense against payment of the check. Here, however, Dilling does not allege that NationsBank failed to honor the cashier's checks. The fact that it may have been foreseeable that a negligently employed teller would improperly issue checks does not make it foreseeable that a third party who never came into direct contact with the teller would rely on the issuance of cashier's checks to make investment decisions. We therefore hold that NationsBank established as a matter of law that it owed no duty to Dilling.

Accordingly, pursuant to TEX.R.APP.P. 170, this Court grants the application for writ of error, and, without hearing oral argument, reverses the judgment of the court of appeals and renders judgment for NationsBank.

Scope of Employment

Biggs v. U.S. Fire Ins. Co.
611 S.W.2d 624, Tex., 1981

This action for workers' compensation presents the sole question of whether James D. Biggs was injured in the course of employment within the meaning of the Texas Workers' Compensation Act. The trial court rendered judgment for Biggs on a jury verdict. The court of civil appeals reversed the judgment of the trial court and rendered a take-nothing judgment. 601 S.W.2d 132. We reverse the judgment of the court of civil appeals and remand the cause to that court.

James D. Biggs, a law clerk employed by Tom Upchurch, Jr., brought this workers' compensation suit against his employer's insurance carrier, United States Fire Insurance Company, to recover for accidental injuries allegedly sustained in the course of employment. On Saturday, December 6, 1975, Biggs fell and was seriously injured during working hours while attempting to repair the roof on a two-story apartment unit owned by, and at the direction of, John Lesly, an associate of the law firm. Trial was to a jury. In answer to special issue No. 1, the jury found that Biggs' injuries occurred in the course of employment with Upchurch; whereupon, the trial court rendered judgment for Biggs based on a favorable jury verdict.

On appeal, the court of civil appeals expressly sustained points of error presented by United States Fire Insurance Company asserting that there is no evidence to support the jury's finding that Biggs was in the course of his employment at the time of his injuries. It is this holding of the court of civil appeals that we are now called on to review. In doing so, we must consider only that evidence and the reasonable inferences that can be drawn therefrom, in their most favorable light, to support the jury's finding while disregarding all others. East Texas Theatres, Inc. v. Rutledge, 453 S.W.2d 466 (Tex.1970); Garza v. Alviar, 395 S.W.2d 821 (Tex.1965).

The evidence developed at trial on this point was sharply disputed. But, viewed in its most favorable light to support the jury's finding, the material evidence is as follows: In January 1974, James D. Biggs was employed as a law clerk by Tom Upchurch, Jr., who practiced law under the name of Tom Upchurch, Jr. and Associates. At his principal office in Amarillo, Upchurch also employed two attorneys as associates, …Steven F. Scott and John Lesly, a bookkeeper, and several secretaries. While employed by Upchurch, Biggs performed a wide variety of duties, consisting primarily of running errands for Upchurch and the employees in the law office. Many of these errands were related to Upchurch's law practice and many were personal errands for Upchurch, the associates, and the secretaries.

Personal errands that Biggs performed at the direction of Upchurch included babysitting for Upchurch's children, taking his children to dinner at Six Flags Over Texas, driving Upchurch's automobiles to and from Fort Worth for repairs, delivering packages and liquor to Upchurch's home, changing tires and repairing Upchurch's automobile, and acting as a night watchman at a warehouse owned by one of Upchurch's friends.

In addition, Biggs performed personal errands for the associates, Scott and Lesly. Biggs testified that he changed a flat tire on Scott's car and a battery in the car of Scott's wife. Once, Scott directed him to pick up and deliver packages to Scott's wife. Biggs testified that on separate occasions Scott required him to pick up liquor, ammunition, and sporting equipment. For Lesly, Biggs also changed a flat tire and a battery. One weekend, Lesly directed Biggs to water plants at Lesly's home while his wife was out of town. Routinely, Lesly directed Biggs to pick up rents from the manager of an apartment unit that Lesly owned several blocks from the law office. In fact, Lesly even instructed Biggs to pick up these rents after Biggs returned to work after his injuries of December 6, 1975. On other occasions, Biggs also delivered screens and made repairs on Lesly's apartment unit.

Biggs was certain that Upchurch knew of these personal errands because Upchurch often made passing remarks about it. For instance, Biggs testified that Upchurch once commented, "I guess you have been to Lesly's picking up rents on those apartments," and on another occasion, "I guess you have been out to Scott's working on that car again." Scott also testified that he informed Upchurch of these personal errands that Biggs was being required to perform for Lesly and that he, Upchurch, and Lesly discussed the matter. According to Lesly, however, Upchurch only discussed not using Biggs and other law clerks for changing tires. Nevertheless, Biggs was never told of the discussion nor was he ever instructed by anyone not to perform these personal errands. To Biggs, everyone was the boss; he thought his job was to do whatever anyone told him, and he was never told otherwise.

For all these personal errands, Biggs turned in his time and was paid by the bookkeeper from the account of Tom Upchurch, Jr. There is testimony, although Upchurch denies it, that Upchurch knew that he was paying Biggs for all these personal errands. In fact, the Monday following Biggs' accident he was paid by Upchurch's office for his Saturday's work.

An essential element that an employee must prove in order to recover workers' compensation benefits is that the injury was sustained in the course of employment. Article 8306 s 1. Unless this is shown, the employee can only seek relief for his injury through his common law causes of action and in such instances the employer retains all common law defenses. As a general rule an injury sustained in the course of employment (1) must be of a kind or character originating in or having to do with the employer's work, and (2) must have occurred while engaged in the furtherance of the employer's business or affairs. Article 8309 s 1; Texas Employers Insurance Ass'n v. Page, 553 S.W.2d 98 (Tex.1977); Shelton v. Standard Insurance Co., 389 S.W.2d 290 (Tex.1965); Texas General Indemnity Co. v. Bottom, 365 S.W.2d 350 (Tex.1963).

There are exceptions to this general rule. One exception applicable to this case is that:

"(A)n employee who is employed in the usual course of the trade, business, profession or occupation of an employer and who is temporarily directed or instructed by his employer to perform service outside of the usual course of trade, business, profession or occupation of his employer is also an employee while performing such services pursuant to such instructions or directions; ..."

37

Under this so-called "temporary direction" exception, if an employee is directed by his employer and is then injured, his injury is sustained in the course of his employment. In other words, an employee does not forfeit his workers' compensation coverage while acting in obedience to his employer's orders. See Traders & General Insurance Co. v. Ihlenburg, 243 S.W.2d 250 (Tex.Civ.App. San Antonio 1951, writ ref'd). The purpose underlying the enactment of the exception was to eliminate a dilemma that would otherwise face an employee when instructed to perform a task outside his employer's usual business, to-wit: either obey his employer and lose his compensation coverage or disobey his employer and lose his job. 1 Larson, Workmen's Compensation Law, s 27.40 (1972); see generally, Traders & General Insurance Co. v. Powell, 82 S.W.2d 747, 750 (Tex.Civ.App. Beaumont 1935), rev'd on other grounds, 130 Tex. 375, 110 S.W.2d 559 (1937).

The court of civil appeals considered this exception and concluded that it is inapplicable to the case at hand. It reached this conclusion on two grounds: (1) the exception only applies to directions given by employers and the evidence is undisputed that Biggs was directed by Lesly, and not Upchurch, his employer; and (2) there is no testimony or testimonial inference that Lesly's directions to Biggs to repair the roof in question were given with Upchurch's authority.

It should be recognized at the outset that, in line with the express terms of the "temporary direction" exception, compensation has generally been allowed whenever the employer directs or instructs any work done. Texas General Indemnity Co. v. Luce, 491 S.W.2d 767 (Tex.Civ.App. Beaumont 1973, writ ref'd n.r.e.); Texas Employers Insurance Ass'n v. Weber, 386 S.W.2d 835 (Tex.Civ.App. Austin 1965, writ ref'd n.r.e.); Texas Employers' Insurance Ass'n v. Davidson, 295 S.W.2d 482 (Tex.Civ.App. Fort Worth 1956, writ ref'd n.r.e.); Traders & General Indemnity Co. v. Ihlenburg, supra; Texas Employers' Insurance Ass'n v. Harrison, 207 S.W.2d 168 (Tex.Civ.App. Fort Worth 1947, writ ref'd n.r.e.). Only a few cases, however, have been decided in this State involving the exact point presented herein; that is, where directions are given by one of the employer's supervisory personnel as opposed to the employer himself. See Federal Underwriters Exchange v. Lehers, 132 Tex. 140, 120 S.W.2d 791 (1938); Great American Indemnity Co. v. Kingsbery, 201 S.W.2d 611 (Tex.Civ.App. Amarillo 1947, writ ref'd n.r.e.), and St. Paul Insurance Co. v. Van Hook, 533 S.W.2d 472 (Tex.Civ.App. Beaumont 1976, no writ). A survey of these cases reveals that the exception also applies to work ordered by a supervisor so long as the order is authorized by the employer, regardless of whether the order benefits the employer's business or is personal in nature.

The case of Great American Indemnity Co. v. Kingsbery, 201 S.W.2d 611 (Tex.Civ.App. Amarillo 1947, writ ref'd n.r.e.), is illustrative. In that case, Breedlove, the employer, owned an airport and employed Williams as his general manager to operate services for powered airplanes. Kingsbery was employed by Breedlove as a pilot, instructor, and salesman of powered aircraft. Hall, who owned a glider and stored it in one of Breedlove's hangars, and Williams discussed inaugurating a private venture to instruct courses in glider training. On the day finally agreed on to begin the glider service, Hall decided to make a flight. Williams instructed Kingsbery to enter the glider to acquaint himself with its operation so he could act as a glider pilot. When descending to the runway, the glider crashed and Kingsbery was injured.

38

Kingsbery sued Breedlove's insurer for workers' compensation benefits, alleging his injury was sustained in the course of employment. In holding that there was no evidence that Kingsbery was injured in the course of employment, the court of civil appeals stated:

> "It is not shown that (Breedlove) gave Williams any authority to direct (Kingsbery) to make the flight nor does the testimony connect him in any way with the arrangement between Williams and Hall to inaugurate the glider service.... It does not appear that Williams purported to represent Breedlove or to bind him to the agreement with Hall but even if he had purported to represent Breedlove, the testimony reveals no authority from Breedlove under which he was authorized to do so.... There is no testimony to the effect that Williams had authority beyond that which was designated by Breedlove and perhaps implied from his designation as manager. The implication goes no further, however, than Breedlove's testimony, that is, that he had no further authority than to manage the airport and conduct the business that was then being operated by Breedlove. There is no testimony to the effect that he had authority as Breedlove's agent to add to the business that was then being carried on and take into it the additional glider service, nor to arrange for any sort of a partnership between Breedlove and Hall in connection with it." Id. at 615, 616.

Implicit in the Kingsbery decision is the fact that had Williams been given authority from Breedlove to instruct Kingsbery to make the glider flight, the "temporary direction" exception would have placed Kingsbery's injury within the scope of employment with Breedlove. And, since the only authority that Williams had from Breedlove was that implied from his position as general manager, he was only authorized to give orders that benefited Breedlove's airplane business.

Biggs contends that the court of civil appeals erred in reversing the judgment of the trial court, because there is some evidence that Biggs was injured in the course of employment with Upchurch. More specifically, he urges that the court of civil appeals erred in disregarding evidence of Lesly's apparent authority from Upchurch to use him for personal errands and, as a result of this authority, he remained in the course of employment with Upchurch under the "temporary direction" exception while performing such errands at Lesly's direction. We agree.

Apparent authority is based on the doctrine of estoppel, and one seeking to charge the principal through apparent authority of an agent must establish conduct by the principal that would lead a reasonably prudent person to believe that the agent has the authority that he purports to exercise. Southwest Title Insurance Co. v. Northland Building Corp., 552 S.W.2d 425 (Tex.1977); Douglass v. Panama, Inc., 504 S.W.2d 776 (Tex.1974); Chastain v. Cooper and Reed, 152 Tex. 322, 257 S.W.2d 422 (1953). When an agent acts within the scope of this apparent authority, the acts bind the principal as though the agent actually possessed such authority. See Cox, Inc. v. Humble Oil and Refining Co., 16 S.W.2d 285 (Tex.Comm'n App. 1929, judgmt adopted). Apparent authority provides authorization where the actual authority of the agent is lacking. Likewise, an employee should be allowed to rely on apparent authority to establish a supervisor's authority from the employer in order to bring his injury under the "temporary direction" exception, when actual authority on the part of the supervisor is lacking.

Conclusion

In this case, there is some evidence that Lesly had the apparent authority from Upchurch to use Biggs for personal errands including repairing the roof on the apartment unit on the date in question. There is evidence that Upchurch knew and acquiesced in the use of Biggs by Lesly and other employees for personal errands. In fact, Biggs was never told by anyone not to perform such errands. There is also evidence that Upchurch's office paid Biggs for the time spent on these errands and that Upchurch knew of these payments. From this evidence, the jury could have concluded that Upchurch's conduct induced Biggs to believe that Lesly had the authority to use him for personal errands. Because there is some evidence that Lesly's use of Biggs for personal errands was within the limits of his apparent authority, we hold that the "temporary direction" exception applied to bring Biggs' injury within the scope of employment with Upchurch….

The judgment of the court of civil appeals is reversed and the cause is remanded to that court for further proceedings consistent with this opinion.

****

Suarez v. Jordan
35 S.W.3d 268 (Tex. App. — Houston [14 Dist.] 2000)

This appeal concerns the alleged creation of a prescriptive easement and its implications for a bona fide purchaser for value of real estate. Appellant Roberto Suarez ("Roberto") appeals the trial court's grant of appellee Marjorie Jordan's motion for summary judgment and the trial court's rendition of a final judgment based upon the interlocutory summary judgment and upon an alleged settlement agreement. In four issues presented, Roberto asserts: (1) that the trial court erred by granting Jordan's motion because Jordan did not conclusively establish her right to a prescriptive easement on his property; and (2) that the trial court erred by enforcing the Settlement Agreement against Roberto even though Roberto never agreed to be bound by the Settlement Agreement. We reverse and remand this case to the trial court for further proceedings consistent with this opinion.

Background

Roberto purchased a home from Santiago Flores, Jr. and Martha Flores. At the time of the sale, Roberto did not know that Mr. and Mrs. Flores were defendants in this lawsuit. In her original petition in this case, Jordan sued Mr. and Mrs. Flores, seeking to establish that a ten inch strip of the Flores' property was subject to a prescriptive easement in favor of Jordan. After moving into his new home, Roberto began building a fence, at which time his neighbor, Jordan, told him that he could not fence this property as it was the subject of litigation. Jordan amended her petition to add Roberto as a defendant. Jordan served Roberto with the following requests for admissions:

> 1. Admit that the Defendant as designated in this lawsuit is a proper party to this suit involving the existence of a user right upon and across 15334 Elgin, Channelview, Harris County, Texas.

2. Admit that you were in the process of building a fence, fencing off an area involving a driveway to which Plaintiff utilizes as access to some buildings upon her property located in the rear of her property.

3. Admit that you knew about the "right-of-way" that was established by the Plaintiff as result of her tenants going back and forth to the rear portions of her lot.

4. Admit that Plaintiff has tenants living on or about her property.

5. Admit that Plaintiff has tenants living in the rear of her property.

6. Admit that Plaintiff occupied her property prior to your purchasing the house and lot upon which your property is located next door.

7. Admit that you purchased the property from a relative.

Roberto did not respond to these requests for admissions, so Jordan filed a Motion for Imposition of Sanctions and for Summary Judgment Based Upon Admissions Deemed. Jordan's motion appeared to seek $750 as attorney's fees for the prosecution of this suit and $150 as a discovery sanction. The trial court granted Jordan's motion in part, signing an interlocutory summary judgment. The judgment that the trial court signed is entitled "Order Granting Sanctions and Summary Judgment." The trial court, however, only awarded $750.00. It is not clear whether the $750 was intended as a discovery sanction or as attorney's fees for prosecuting the suit. Reading the motion and the interlocutory judgment together indicates that no sanctions were awarded, only attorney fees for prosecuting the suit. *[footnote omitted]* ...."

After the trial court signed the interlocutory summary judgment, a court-ordered mediation was scheduled. Jordan and Mr. and Mrs. Flores appeared for the mediation in person, along with their respective counsel. Roberto's attorney, Neal Pickett, did not appear. Roberto did not appear in person either. Roberto had a job out of town that day. Roberto sent his son, Gilberto Suarez ("Gilberto"), *[footnote omitted]* to the mediation because of this job and because Gilberto speaks English more fluently than his father. Gilberto, without assistance of counsel and acting against his father's wishes, signed a Settlement Agreement that admitted the existence of the disputed ten-inch easement on Roberto's property and that required Roberto to move his fence poles.

After the mediation, Roberto filed a motion for new trial and requested a hearing. At the hearing, Gilberto testified that he had no authority to sign the Settlement Agreement on behalf of his father, that he signed the Settlement Agreement under pressure from Mr. and Mrs. Flores and their attorney, and that, at the time he signed the Settlement Agreement, he knew that his father would probably not have signed this agreement. After Gilberto signed the Settlement Agreement, the words "for 3rd Party Defendant" were added after his name. This notation apparently was meant to refer to Roberto. Although Roberto was added by Jordan as a defendant—not a third

41

party defendant—in her First Amended Original Petition, and although Mr. and Mrs. Flores never filed third party claims against Roberto, Jordan did obtain an order from the trial court granting her leave to add Roberto as a "third party defendant." This designation appears to be a misnomer.

There was no testimony in the trial court below that Gilberto was authorized to sign the Settlement Agreement on behalf of his father, and there was no testimony that Gilberto told any of the people at the mediation that he was authorized to sign the Settlement Agreement on behalf of his father. The trial court indicated that it did not wish to hear testimony from Roberto. The trial court further stated that Roberto was "obviously" not a party to the Settlement Agreement since his son signed it. The trial court, however, denied Roberto's motion for new trial and signed a final judgment. This final judgment incorporated the interlocutory summary judgment against Roberto, awarded Jordan an easement over Roberto's property, required Roberto to move his fence ten inches closer to his home, and bound Roberto to the terms of the Settlement Agreement.

Summary Judgment

In Roberto's first issue, he contends the trial court erred in granting summary judgment based on deemed admissions which fail to establish the essential elements of a prescriptive easement. The standards for review of a summary judgment are well established: (1) the movant must show there is no genuine issue of material fact and that movant is entitled to a judgment as a matter of law; (2) in deciding whether there is a disputed material fact issue precluding summary judgment, the court must take evidence favorable to the nonmovant as true; and (3) the court must indulge every reasonable inference in favor of the nonmovant and resolve any doubts in the nonmovant's favor. *See Nixon v. Mr. Property Management Co.,* 690 S.W.2d 546, 548–49 (Tex.1985). Because the propriety of a summary judgment is a question of law, we review the trial court's decision *de novo. See Natividad v. Alexsis, Inc.,* 875 S.W.2d 695, 699 (Tex.1994).

A person acquires a prescriptive easement by the open, notorious, continuous, exclusive, and adverse use of someone else's land for ten years. *See Brooks v. Jones,* 578 S.W.2d 669, 673 (Tex.1979); *Stallman v. Newman,* 9 S.W.3d 243, 248 (Tex.App.—Houston [14th Dist.] 1999, pet. denied). The "adverse use" element of a prescriptive easement requires that the claimant's use of the alleged easement be of such a nature and character as to notify the true owner that the claimant is asserting a hostile claim to the land. *See Stallman,* 9 S.W.3d at 248. In order to obtain a summary judgment on her prescriptive easement claim, Jordan was required to present evidence establishing each of the elements of a prescriptive easement as a matter of law. *See Nixon,* 690 S.W.2d at 548; *Boyter v. MCR Const. Co.,* 673 S.W.2d 938, 940–41 (Tex.App.—Dallas 1984, writ ref'd n.r.e.)(summary judgment reversed because deemed admissions did not prove up all essential elements of plaintiff's case as a matter of law).

In this case, the trial court granted summary judgment based on the seven deemed admissions that we recited above. These deemed admissions address, among other things, whether Roberto "knew about the 'right-of-way' that was established by the Plaintiff as a result of her tenants going back and forth to the rear portions of her lot." These deemed admissions do not establish any of the following: (1) when Roberto obtained this alleged knowledge; (2) the nature and extent of the alleged "right-of-way"; (3) that Jordan made use of an easement upon Roberto's land in an exclusive, open and adverse manner; or (4) that Jordan's use of this easement was continuous for at least ten years. The deemed admissions upon which the trial court based its summary judgment do not establish the essential elements for a prescriptive easement. *See Stallman,* 9 S.W.3d at 248 (noting essential elements of prescriptive easement are: open, notorious, continuous, exclusive, and adverse use of someone else's land for ten years). Therefore, granting a summary judgment based on these admissions was error. *[footnote omitted]* Accordingly, we sustain Roberto's first issue.

Settlement Agreement

Roberto's three remaining issues challenge the final judgment enforcing the Settlement Agreement. Roberto asserts that the Settlement Agreement does not bind him because he did not sign it and because Gilberto was not authorized to sign the agreement on his behalf. We sustain these issues and hold that Roberto is not bound by the Settlement Agreement as a matter of law.

The law does not presume agency. *Buchoz v. Klein,* 143 Tex. 284, 184 S.W.2d 271, 271 (1944). Absent actual or apparent authority, an agent cannot bind a principal. *See Currey v. Lone Star Steel Co.,* 676 S.W.2d 205, 209 (Tex.App.—Fort Worth 1984, no writ). Both actual and apparent authority are created through conduct of the principal communicated either to the agent (actual authority) or to a third party (apparent authority). *See Currey,* 676 S.W.2d at 210.

Actual authority denotes that authority which the principal intentionally confers upon the agent, or intentionally allows the agent to believe he has, or by want of ordinary care allows the agent to believe himself to possess. *See Spring Garden 79U, Inc. v. Stewart Title Co.,* 874 S.W.2d 945, 948 (Tex.App.—Houston [1st Dist.] 1994, no writ). There is no power of attorney in the record or anything in the Settlement Agreement itself to demonstrate that Roberto gave Gilberto actual authority to act as his agent. In fact, Roberto introduced uncontradicted evidence establishing that his son did not have actual authority to act as his agent.

Certain limitations apply in determining whether apparent authority exists. *Humble Nat. Bank v. DCV, Inc.,* 933 S.W.2d 224, 237 (Tex.App.—Houston [14th Dist.] 1996, writ denied). First, apparent authority is determined by looking to the acts of the principal and ascertaining whether those acts would lead a reasonably prudent person using diligence and discretion to suppose the agent had the authority to act on behalf of the principal. *See NationsBank, N.A. v. Dilling,* 922 S.W.2d 950, 953 (Tex.1996); *Humble Nat. Bank,* 933 S.W.2d at 237. Only the conduct of the principal may be considered; representations made by the agent of his authority have no effect. *Southwest Title Ins. Co. v. Northland Bldg. Corp.,* 552 S.W.2d 425, 428 (Tex.1977); *Humble Nat. Bank,* 933 S.W.2d at 237. Second, the principal must either have affirmatively held the agent out as possessing the authority or the principal must have knowingly and voluntarily permitted the agent to act in an unauthorized manner. *NationsBank,* 922 S.W.2d at 952, 953; *Humble Nat. Bank,* 933 S.W.2d at 237. Finally, a party dealing with an agent must ascertain both the fact and the scope of the agent's authority, and if the party deals with the agent without having made such a determination, she does so at her own risk. *Humble Nat. Bank,* 933 S.W.2d at 237.

The fact that Gilberto signed the Settlement Agreement does not bind Roberto because there is nothing in the Settlement Agreement or elsewhere in the record which would indicate Gilberto was acting as the authorized agent of Roberto. The mere fact of a father-son relationship does not clothe Gilberto with authority to act on behalf of his father. Gilberto testified that he had no authority to sign the Settlement Agreement on behalf of his father, that he signed the Settlement Agreement under pressure from Mr. and Mrs. Flores and their attorney, and that, at the time he signed the Settlement Agreement, he knew that his father would probably not have signed this agreement. The Settlement Agreement does not explicitly state that Gilberto signed it on behalf of his father. After Gilberto signed the Settlement Agreement, the words "for 3rd Party Defendant" were added after his name. Apparently this was meant to refer to Roberto, although Roberto was a defendant in the trial court; he was not a third party defendant.

There was no testimony in the trial court that Gilberto was authorized to sign the Settlement Agreement on behalf of his father, and there was no testimony that Gilberto told any of the people at the mediation that he was authorized to sign the Settlement Agreement on behalf of his father. There is no evidence of any words or conduct of Roberto that would lead a reasonably prudent person to believe that Gilberto had the authority to enter into the Settlement Agreement on behalf of Roberto. *See NationsBank,* 922 S.W.2d at 953. The Settlement Agreement recites that "[e]ach signatory… warrants and represents ... [t]hat such person has authority to bind the party or parties for whom such person acts." Gilberto signed the document; Roberto did not. Therefore, Gilberto—not Roberto—made this representation. Without acts of the purported principal (Roberto), acts of a purported agent (Gilberto) which may mislead persons into false inferences of authority, however reasonable, will not serve as predicate for apparent authority. *See Southwest Land Title Co. v. Gemini Financial Co.,* 752 S.W.2d 5, 7 (Tex.App.—Dallas 1988, no writ).

It is a fundamental tenet of contract law that in order to be bound by an agreement, one must be a party to it. The Settlement Agreement does not identify Roberto as a party or a signatory to the contract. Neither Roberto nor his counsel signed the Settlement Agreement. The trial court correctly stated at the hearing that Roberto was "obviously" not a party to the Settlement Agreement. Roberto can only be affected by the Settlement Agreement if Gilberto's signature on the agreement binds Roberto under agency principles. The record in this case, however, is barren of any evidence which would suggest that Roberto clothed Gilberto with either actual or apparent authority to bind Roberto to the Settlement Agreement. Therefore, Gilberto's signing of the Settlement Agreement cannot be deemed the act of Roberto and cannot bind Roberto as a matter of law. *See Southwest Land Title Co.*, 752 S.W.2d at 7. It was error for the trial court to enter final judgment based on the Settlement Agreement. Accordingly, we sustain Roberto's remaining issues and reverse and remand this case to the trial court for further proceedings consistent with this opinion.

Ostensible Agency/Agency By Estoppel

> **§ 2.05 Estoppel To Deny Existence Of Agency Relationship.** *A person who has not made a manifestation that an actor has authority as an agent and who is not otherwise liable as a party to a transaction purportedly done by the actor on that person's account is subject to liability to a third party who justifiably is induced to make a detrimental change in position because the transaction is believed to be on the person's account, if*
>
> *(1) the person intentionally or carelessly caused such belief, or*
>
> *(2) having notice of such belief and that it might induce others to change their positions, the person did not take reasonable steps to notify them of the facts.*

Wyndham Hotel Co. v. Self
893 S.W.2d 630 (Tex. App. — Corpus Christi 1994)

This is an appeal from a judgment in favor of the plaintiff in a personal injury lawsuit tried before a jury. In the trial below, Opal Self sued the Wyndham Hotel Company under theories of recovery involving negligence, *respondeat superior*, ostensible agency, and negligent entrustment. In six points of error, Wyndham challenges the trial court's charge to the jury, the sufficiency of the evidence, the rendition of judgment based on the verdict, and the award of prejudgment interest. We affirm.

Facts

Over the Thanksgiving holiday of 1986, Self visited the Bahamas with her daughter, Linda Paul, and grandson, Daniel. Self and her family stayed at the Wyndham Cable Beach Hotel, which is run by Wyndham but ultimately owned by the Bahamian government. As part of the comprehensive vacation package, Wyndham provided transportation between the airport and hotel. Some guests travelled to the hotel in the Wyndham Hotel van, but others were transported by unmarked taxis.

Once at the hotel, Self saw Wyndham advertisements that described the water sports facilities among the other activities offered by the hotel. These advertisements were located both in the hotel lobby and in a brochure left in Self's hotel room. A rating card that invited Wyndham guests to evaluate and comment on the hotel's various facilities also mentioned the water sports activities as a feature of the Wyndham Hotel.

Because Daniel was interested in snorkeling, which was an activity advertised in the brochure, Linda went to the front desk of the Wyndham Hotel to inquire about the water sport offerings. The clerk at the front desk told Linda that snorkeling was included in the glass-bottomed boat tour, which departed from the hotel's private pier. The clerk also explained that Linda could get tickets for the boat tour from the Watersports Center in the hotel courtyard and that Linda could charge the ticket price to her hotel bill.

Self spent part of the next morning by the pool with her family. Whenever they wanted another Wyndham Hotel insignia towel or an additional deck chair, they were required to sign for the item at the Watersports Center, which itself bore the Wyndham logo. All the Wyndham employees working in the courtyard wore tan pants with brown and orange tropical print shirts; the persons working at the Watersports Center were dressed identically.

Later that morning, a man dressed in tan pants with an orange and brown tropical print shirt approached several of the Wyndham Hotel guests. This man, Basil Palmer, asked if any of the guests were interested in the glass-bottomed boat tour. When Self explained that she and Daniel wished to join the tour, Palmer led Self to the Watersports Center to purchase tickets. With Palmer standing right beside her, Self gave her hotel room number and received a receipt from the woman behind the counter at the Watersports Center. Palmer explained that the boat tour would depart from the Wyndham Hotel's private pier.

After Self, Daniel, and several other Wyndham Hotel guests had congregated at the hotel's pier, Palmer arrived to say that there had been a change in plans. Palmer explained that the tour group would have to leave from a pier in town, but that he had arranged transportation, which would be included in the original price for the tour. Palmer led the group to the Watersports Center so that they could sign for snorkeling equipment and towels, and then he led them through the Wyndham Hotel lobby to his waiting car. Like some of the taxis that Wyndham used to transport guests from the airport to the hotel, Palmer's car was not marked. As Palmer ushered the guests into his car, there was some dispute regarding the driver, Clifford Stubbs. Stubbs's lack of a current driver's license and the possibility that Stubbs had been drinking were specifically discussed. In any event Palmer's car crashed through Stubbs's negligence, and Self was injured.

Self asserted that Palmer was negligent in entrusting Stubbs with the car; under theories of ostensible agency and *respondeat superior*, Self attributed this negligence to Wyndham. As part of its defense to this cause of action, Wyndham countered that Palmer was working as a freelance operator when he approached Self and the other guests. In response to this defense, Self amended her petition to allege Wyndham's more general negligence in failing to keep such freelance solicitors from preying on Wyndham's guests. Self also pursued Wyndham under the Deceptive Trade Practices—Consumer Protection Act, but the trial court granted Wyndham's pretrial motion for summary judgment on this claim.

The jury found that Palmer was not a Wyndham employee, but that he was acting as an agent of Wyndham on the occasion in question. The jury also found that Palmer was negligent in entrusting Stubbs with the car. Significantly, the jury was not asked whether Palmer was acting within the apparent scope of the ostensible agency when he entrusted Stubbs with the car. This omission is notable in light of the jury finding that absolved Wyndham of negligence in failing to prevent Palmer from entrusting Stubbs with the car. Finally, when asked to apportion the responsibility for Self's injuries, the jury assigned 50% of the negligence to Wyndham, 20% each to Palmer and Stubbs, and 10% to Self. Based on these findings, the trial court ordered that Wyndham pay 90% of Self's damage award; 10% was deducted to account for Self's comparative negligence.

Jury Charge

In its second and fourth points of error, Wyndham complains of jury question two, which asked if there was an agency relationship between Palmer and Wyndham at the time of Self's injury. Wyndham's second point concerns the omission of an instruction on the scope of any ostensible agency, and Wyndham's fourth point argues that the question misstates the law. Wyndham contends that we are obliged to render a take-nothing judgment as a result of these errors. We disagree.

The Law of Agency by Estoppel

The court submitted the issue as follows:

On the occasion in question, was there an agency relationship between Basil Palmer and Wyndham Hotel Company?

You are instructed that an agency relationship existed if either of the following circumstances occurred:

A. If the Wyndham Hotel Company, acting through its employees and agents, represented by act, conduct or statement that Basil Palmer was its employee or agent, and there was a reliance by Opal Self on the representation, if any, and the representation caused a change of position by Opal Self.

OR

B. If Opal Self consented to the boat ride in question on the reasonable belief that Basil Palmer was the employee or agent of Wyndham Hotel Company, and the Wyndham Hotel Company intentionally or negligently caused such belief, or the Wyndham Hotel Company knew of such belief but failed to notify Opal Self that her belief was mistaken.

ANSWER "yes" or "no."

During the charge conference, Wyndham objected that this question was incomplete without a definition to explain the course and scope of any ostensible agency. Wyndham also complained that the question, as submitted, did not allow the jury to consider whether Palmer's negligent actions exceeded his apparent authority.

In Texas, the leading case on apparent authority explains the theory of recovery as follows:

> The doctrine of apparent authority is based on estoppel, and one seeking to charge a principal through the apparent authority of an agent to bind the principal must prove such conduct on the part of the principal as would lead a reasonably prudent person, using diligence and discretion, to suppose that the agent has the authority he purports to exercise. *Chastain v. Cooper & Reed*, 152 Tex. 322, 257 S.W.2d 422, 427 (1953); *see also Ames v. Great S. Bank*, 672 S.W.2d 447, 450 (Tex.1984) (apparent authority may also rise from principal's actions that are so careless as to clothe the ostensible agent with indicia of authority that led the plaintiff to reasonably believe in the agent's authority); *Rourke v. Garza*, 530 S.W.2d 794, 803 (Tex.1975) (principals may be estopped from denying apparent authority when they fail to act in light of facts sufficient to put them upon inquiry that would have revealed plaintiff's reasonable belief in the ostensible agency).
>
> Nevertheless, a cause of action based on agency by estoppel does not necessarily require a separate finding that the ostensible agent was acting within the scope of apparent authority. Instead, Texas law allows the plaintiff to prove the following three elements: (1) the party must have a reasonable belief in the agent's authority, (2) that belief must derive from some representation by act or omission of the principal, and (3) the party's detrimental reliance on this representation of authority must be justifiable. *Nicholson v. Memorial Hosp. Sys.*, 722 S.W.2d 746, 750 (Tex.App.—Houston [14th Dist.] 1986, writ ref'd n.r.e.) (citing *Ames*, 672 S.W.2d at 450 and *Brownsville Medical Ctr. v. Gracia*, 704 S.W.2d 68, 74–75 (Tex.App.—Corpus Christi 1985, writ ref'd n.r.e.)).
>
> The jury's determinations of whether the party's belief in the agency was reasonable and whether the party's reliance on that belief was justifiable subsumes the scope-of-agency issue. *Cf. Biggs v. United States Fire Ins. Co.*, 611 S.W.2d 624, 629 (Tex.1981) (discussing the relationship between the basis for agency by estoppel and the apparent scope of such ostensible authority). This approach to agency by estoppel reflects the fact that an *ostensible* agency relationship is not a *true* agency relationship with a predefined scope. *See Id.* ("Apparent authority provides authorization where the actual authority of the agent is lacking.") In Texas, the plaintiff may dispense with the fiction of defining the terms of a relationship that does not exist in reality. Under this formulation of the theory, actions beyond the scope of any hypothetical agency are addressed in terms of whether the party's belief and consequent reliance were reasonable and justified.
>
> By agreement, however, this issue was tried with reference to the law of the Bahamas, which is English common law for all purposes relevant to the suit. The English law of agency by estoppel was recently revisited by the Court of Appeal, Civil Division, which reiterated the long-held principle:
>
>> An "apparent" or "ostensible" authority ... is a legal relationship between the principal and the contractor created by a representation, made by the principal to the contractor, intended to be and in fact acted upon by the contractor, that the agent has the authority to enter on behalf of the principal into a contract of a kind within the scope of the "apparent" authority, so as to

48

render the principal liable to perform any obligations imposed on him by such contract. *[citations omitted]*

As applied to facts similar to the facts of the instant case, this principle of law underlies the decision in *Soanes v. London & S.W. Rail Co.,* 88 L.J.K.B. 524 (Eng.C.A.) (1919....

In *Soanes,* the plaintiff sued the rail company for the loss of his suitcase. The plaintiff, who was on crutches at the time, went to Waterloo train station at the location designated for arriving passengers. A man dressed in the rail company porter's uniform took the plaintiff's baggage and accompanied the plaintiff past the point where only ticketed passengers and company employees were allowed. When the plaintiff learned that he would have to catch a later train, the man in the porter's uniform agreed to hold the suitcases while the plaintiff waited in the cafe. The man in the porter's uniform left the baggage unattended just outside the ticketing office. By the time of the later train's departure, one of the plaintiff's two bags was stolen. The rail company denied responsibility on grounds that the man in the porter's uniform was a porter at the company's Hampton station and not authorized to work at Waterloo. The rail company claimed that the porter was off duty and outside the scope of employment and, therefore, working freelance either because of sympathy for the plaintiff on crutches or in hope of a tip.

Because the man in the porter's uniform was outside the scope of his authority, the county court judge ruled in favor of the rail company. On appeal, the divisional court reversed this judgment because the porter was a general agent of the rail company and the company had not prohibited the disputed exercise of the porter's authority. The Court of Appeal affirmed the divisional court judgment but offered a different rationale. The high court held that the company's careless failure to prevent the actions of the man in the porter's uniform amounted to a representation that the man was a porter.

As evidence of this negligent representation, the Court of Appeal looked to the fact that the porter was not questioned by the company employees as he accompanied the plaintiff onto the train. The court also considered that the company allowed the porter to present himself in uniform at the place where porters were employed in the very manner that the plaintiff employed the disputed porter....

Under Texas law, ...the issue of whether the party's belief in the ostensible agency was reasonable subsumes much of the issue regarding the apparent nature of the agency. ...

In the instant case, all the evidence indicates that Palmer was acting within the *apparent* scope of the ostensible agency when he negligently entrusted his car and the passengers to Stubbs. In addition to testimony from Self and her daughter, the jury heard testimony from two other Wyndham Hotel guests who were solicited by Palmer to join the glass-bottomed boat tour. Each witness who testified regarding Palmer's conduct confirmed that Palmer *appeared* to be an agent of the hotel responsible for coordinating water sports activities. Wyndham presented nothing to controvert this convincing evidence from the disinterested witnesses who testified about the scope of Palmer's *apparent* authority.

Certainly, Wyndham presented evidence that Palmer was not a Wyndham employee and that Palmer's actions were beyond the scope of any *actual* relationship with Wyndham. But evidence regarding the scope and existence of the actual relationship between Palmer and Wyndham has no bearing on the *apparent* scope of the *ostensible* agency relationship. *See, e.g., Soanes*, 88 L.J.K.B. 524 (the English Court of Appeal implicitly found that the ostensible porter was acting within the scope of apparent authority after explicitly noting that "there can be no appeal from that question of fact that the porter was acting outside the scope of his authority").

Because Wyndham presented no evidence to rebut the unanimous testimony from every witness who addressed the issue of Palmer's apparent authority, submission of this issue was unnecessary. *See* Tex.R.Civ.P. 279; *Washington*, 581 S.W.2d at 157. As a result, the faulty submission of the issue to inquire whether Self's belief in the ostensible agency was reasonable instead of asking about the scope of Palmer's apparent authority was harmless error. *See Island Recreational Dev.*, 710 S.W.2d at 555 (error in the jury charge is not reversible unless the error probably caused the rendition of an improper judgment).

The question submitted by the court was flawed under both Texas and Bahamian law, but the omission of an instruction on the apparent scope of agency cannot serve as grounds for reversal. Accordingly, we overrule Wyndham's second point of error....

Sufficiency Of The Evidence

In its third point of error, Wyndham contests the legal and factual sufficiency of the evidence that Palmer's acts fell within the apparent scope of the ostensible agency. But much of the evidence regarding the apparent scope and nature of Palmer's ostensible relationship with Wyndham was not effectively contested.

Wyndham advertised a boat tour that left from the hotel's private pier. The clerk working at the front desk in the hotel lobby explained that boating tickets were for sale at the Watersports Center in the courtyard and that the tickets could be charged to the guest's hotel bill. While dressed in a manner similar to the Wyndham employees, Palmer approached several Wyndham guests and asked if they would care to join the boat tour. Palmer led Self to the Watersports Center so that she could purchase tickets for the boat tour that was scheduled to leave from Wyndham's private pier, as advertised. When circumstances prevented the boat tour from leaving from Wyndham's private pier, Palmer explained that he had arranged for transportation to a pier in downtown Nassau. The tour participants were not charged for this transportation, which was included in the price for the boat tour. Palmer led the tour participants to the Watersports Center to sign for equipment, and then led the participants through the Wyndham lobby to the waiting car. In addition to Self, several other Wyndham guests believed that Palmer was an agent of Wyndham.

Under *Soanes*, these circumstances are some evidence to support a finding that Palmer was an ostensible agent of Wyndham with the authority to book and organize activities for Wyndham guests. *See Soanes*, 88 L.J.K.B. 524 (agency by estoppel established by the fact that the rail company allowed the ostensible agent to present himself as a porter plus the fact that the rail company's employees treated the ostensible agent as a porter plus the fact that the plaintiff employed the ostensible agent in the manner that porters are usually employed). Accordingly, we cannot sustain Wyndham's contention that Self adduced no evidence on this issue. *See Browning–Ferris, Inc. v Reyna*, 865 S.W.2d 925, 928 (Tex.1993) (discussing review of "no evidence" arguments); *Housing Auth. of Corpus Christi v. Massey,* 878 S.W.2d 624, 627 (Tex.App.—Corpus Christi 1994, n.w.h.) (citing *Weirich v. Weirich,* 833 S.W.2d 942, 945–46 (Tex.1992) for requirements of legal sufficiency review).

Under Wyndham's factual sufficiency contest, we review this evidence in light of the entire record to see if it is so weak that a proper finding of agency would have been clearly wrong. *See Cain v. Bain,* 709 S.W.2d 175, 176 (Tex.1986) (per curiam); *Twenty–Four Thousand One Hundred Eighty Dollars in U.S. Currency v. State,* 865 S.W.2d 181, 185 (Tex.App.—Corpus Christi 1993, writ denied). Under this standard, Wyndham's factual sufficiency challenge also fails.

Each of the Wyndham guests who testified said that Palmer appeared to be a Wyndham agent with authority to organize water sports activities. Wyndham alleged that it warned guests about freelance tour operators, but this was wholly unsupported by the testimony of Self, her daughter, and both disinterested witnesses. While dressed in a manner nearly identical to the Wyndham employees, Palmer approached Wyndham's guests in Wyndham's courtyard to solicit for participants in the glass-bottomed boat tour. Still dressed in this misleading manner, Palmer paraded the tour participants down the hotel's private pier and through the hotel's courtyard and lobby. During this whole time, Palmer was never questioned by any Wyndham employee. In fact, when one of the Wyndham guests subsequently sought to complain to Palmer about the accident, the guest was directed to the Wyndham employee lounge where he found Palmer.

All of these facts are persuasive evidence that provides a sufficient basis from which the jury could conclude that Wyndham's inaction created the ostensible agency. Furthermore, the fact that transportation to the downtown pier was included in the price of the tour implies that Palmer's negligent act fell within the apparent scope of his ostensible authority. Even if the jury had been properly charged on the issue of ostensible agency, these facts would preclude any challenge to the factual sufficiency of the evidence. *Cain,* 709 S.W.2d at 176; *Twenty–Four Thousand One Hundred Eighty Dollars,* 865 S.W.2d at 185. Accordingly, we overrule Wyndham's third point of error....

The pleadings and evidence in this case clearly support the finding that Wyndham negligently created the appearance of agency by failing to take any action to prevent such a misunderstanding. ...

Having considered and overruled each of Wyndham's six points of error, we affirm the judgment of the trial court.

Doctrine of respondeat superior

Baptist Mem'l Hosp. Sys. v. Sampson
969 S.W.2d 945 (Tex. 1998)

In this case, we decide whether the plaintiff raised a genuine issue of material fact that defendant Hospital was vicariously liable under the theory of ostensible agency for an emergency room physician's negligence. We granted Baptist Memorial Hospital System's application for writ of error to resolve a conflict in the holdings of our courts of appeals regarding the elements required to establish liability against a hospital for the acts of an independent contractor emergency room physician. We hold that the plaintiff has not met her burden to raise a fact issue on each element of this theory. Accordingly, we reverse the judgment of the court of appeals, 940 S.W.2d 128, and render judgment that the plaintiff take nothing.

On March 23, 1990, Rhea Sampson was bitten on the arm by an unidentified creature that was later identified as a brown recluse spider. By that evening, her arm was swollen and painful, and a friend took her to the Southeast Baptist Hospital emergency room. Dr. Susan Howle, an emergency room physician, examined Sampson, diagnosed an allergic reaction, administered Benadryl and a shot of painkiller, prescribed medication for pain and swelling, and sent her home. Her condition grew worse, and she returned to the Hospital's emergency room by ambulance a little over a day later. This time Dr. Mark Zakula, another emergency room physician, treated her. He administered additional pain medication and released her with instructions to continue the treatment Dr. Howle prescribed. About fourteen hours later, with her condition rapidly deteriorating, Sampson went to another hospital and was admitted to the intensive care ward in septic shock. There, her bite was diagnosed as that of a brown recluse spider, and the proper treatment was administered to save her life. Sampson allegedly continues to have recurrent pain and sensitivity where she was bitten, respiratory difficulties, and extensive scarring.

Sampson sued Drs. Howle and Zakula for medical malpractice. She also sued Baptist Memorial Hospital System ("BMHS"), of which Southeast Baptist Hospital is a member, for negligence in failing to properly diagnose and treat her, failing to properly instruct medical personnel in the diagnosis and treatment of brown recluse spider bites, failing to maintain policies regarding review of diagnoses, and in credentialing Dr. Zakula. Sampson also alleged that the Hospital was vicariously liable for Dr. Zakula's alleged negligence under an ostensible agency theory. Sampson nonsuited Dr. Howle early in the discovery process. The trial court granted BMHS summary judgment on Sampson's claims of vicarious liability and negligent treatment. The trial court severed those claims from her negligent credentialing claim against BMHS and her malpractice claim against Dr. Zakula. Sampson appealed only on the vicarious liability theory.

Both parties agree that BMHS established as a matter of law that Dr. Zakula was not its agent or employee. Thus the burden shifted to Sampson to raise a fact issue on each element of her ostensible agency theory, which Texas courts have held to be in the nature of an affirmative defense. *See Brownlee v. Brownlee*, 665 S.W.2d 111, 112 (Tex.1984); *Smith v. Baptist Mem'l*

Hosp. Sys., 720 S.W.2d 618, 622 (Tex.App.—San Antonio 1986, writ ref'd n.r.e.), *disapproved on other grounds by St. Luke's Episcopal Hosp. v. Agbor*, 952 S.W.2d 503, 509 n. 1 (Tex.1997). Sampson contended that she raised a material fact issue on whether Dr. Zakula was BMHS's ostensible agent. The court of appeals, with one justice dissenting, agreed and reversed the summary judgment. 940 S.W.2d 128. In our review, we must first determine the proper elements of ostensible agency, then decide whether Sampson raised a genuine issue of material fact on each of these elements.

Under the doctrine of respondeat superior, an employer is vicariously liable for the negligence of an agent or employee acting within the scope of his or her agency or employment, although the principal or employer has not personally committed a wrong. *See DeWitt v. Harris County*, 904 S.W.2d 650, 654 (Tex.1995); RESTATEMENT (SECOND) OF AGENCY § 219 (1958). The most frequently proffered justification for imposing such liability is that the principal or employer has the right to control the means and methods of the agent or employee's work. *See Newspapers, Inc. v. Love*, 380 S.W.2d 582, 585–86 (Tex.1964); RESTATEMENT (SECOND) OF AGENCY § 220, cmt. d. Because an independent contractor has sole control over the means and methods of the work to be accomplished, however, the individual or entity that hires the independent contractor is generally not vicariously liable for the tort or negligence of that person. *See Enserch Corp. v. Parker*, 794 S.W.2d 2, 6 (Tex.1990); *Redinger v. Living, Inc.*, 689 S.W.2d 415, 418 (Tex.1985). Nevertheless, an individual or entity may act in a manner that makes it liable for the conduct of one who is not its agent at all or who, although an agent, has acted outside the scope of his or her authority. Liability may be imposed in this manner under the doctrine of ostensible agency in circumstances when the principal's conduct should equitably prevent it from denying the existence of an agency. *See, e.g., Marble Falls Hous. Auth. v. McKinley*, 474 S.W.2d 292, 294 (Tex.Civ.App.—Austin 1971, writ ref'd n.r.e.). Ostensible agency in Texas is based on the notion of estoppel, that is, a representation by the principal causing justifiable reliance and resulting harm. *See Ames v. Great S. Bank*, 672 S.W.2d 447, 450 (Tex.1984); RESTATEMENT (SECOND) OF AGENCY § 267; KEETON ET AL., PROSSER AND KEETON ON THE LAW OF TORTS § 105, at 733–34 (5th ed.1984).

Many courts use the terms ostensible agency, apparent agency, apparent authority, and agency by estoppel interchangeably. As a practical matter, there is no distinction among them. *[citations omitted]* Regardless of the term used, the purpose of the doctrine is to prevent injustice and protect those who have been misled. *See Roberts v. Haltom City*, 543 S.W.2d 75, 80 (Tex.1976).

Texas courts have applied these basic agency concepts to many kinds of principals, including hospitals. *See Sparger v. Worley Hosp., Inc.*, 547 S.W.2d 582, 585 (Tex.1977) (explaining that "[h]ospitals are subject to the principles of agency law which apply to others"). A hospital is ordinarily not liable for the negligence of a physician who is an independent contractor. *[citations omitted]* On the other hand, a hospital may be vicariously liable for the medical malpractice of independent contractor physicians when plaintiffs can establish the elements of ostensible agency. *[citations omitted]*

In this case, the court of appeals held that two distinct theories of vicarious liability with different elements are available in Texas to impose liability on a hospital for emergency room physician negligence: agency by estoppel (referred to in this opinion as ostensible agency), based on the Restatement (Second) of Agency section 267, and apparent agency, based on the Restatement (Second) of Torts section 429. Under section 267, the party asserting ostensible agency must demonstrate that (1) the principal, by its conduct, (2) caused him or her to reasonably believe that the putative agent was an employee or agent of the principal, and (3) that he or she justifiably relied on the appearance of agency. RESTATEMENT (SECOND) OF AGENCY § 267 (1958). Although neither party mentioned section 429 in the trial court or in their briefs to the court of appeals, the court of appeals then proceeded to adopt section 429 and hold that under that section, plaintiff had only to raise a fact issue on two elements: (1) the patient looked to the hospital, rather than the individual physician, for treatment; and (2) the hospital held out the physician as its employee. *See* 940 S.W.2d at 132. Holding that the plaintiff had established a genuine issue of material fact on each element of this latter affirmative defense, the court reversed and remanded to the trial court for trial on the merits. The court of appeals further suggested that a hospital could do nothing to avoid holding out a physician in its emergency room as its employee because notification to prospective patients in any form would be ineffectual:

> [W]e take an additional step in our analysis to consider whether notice provided in consent forms and posted in emergency rooms can ever be sufficient to negate a hospital's "holding out"....
>
> ...Because we do not believe hospitals should be allowed to avoid such responsibility, we encourage the full leap—imposing a nondelegable duty on hospitals for the negligence of emergency room physicians.
>
> Thus, the court of appeals would create a nondelegable duty on a hospital solely because it opens its doors for business.

We first reject the court of appeals' conclusion that there are two methods, one "more difficult to prove" than the other, to establish the liability of a hospital for the malpractice of an emergency room physician. 940 S.W.2d at 132. Our courts have uniformly required proof of all three elements of section 267 to invoke the fiction that one should be responsible for the acts of another who is not in fact an agent acting within his or her scope of authority. As we have explained:

> Apparent authority in Texas is based on estoppel. It may arise either from a principal knowingly permitting an agent to hold herself out as having authority or by a principal's actions which lack such ordinary care as to clothe an agent with the indicia of authority, thus leading a reasonably prudent person to believe that the agent has the authority she purports to exercise....
>
> A prerequisite to a proper finding of apparent authority is evidence of conduct by the principal relied upon by the party asserting the estoppel defense which would lead a reasonably prudent person to believe an agent had authority to so act.

Thus, to establish a hospital's liability for an independent contractor's medical malpractice based on ostensible agency, a plaintiff must show that (1) he or she had a reasonable belief that the physician was the agent or employee of the hospital, (2) such belief was generated by the hospital affirmatively holding out the physician as its agent or employee or knowingly permitting the physician to hold herself out as the hospital's agent or employee, and (3) he or she justifiably relied on the representation of authority. To the extent that the Restatement (Second) of Torts section 429 proposes a conflicting standard for establishing liability, we expressly decline to adopt it in Texas. *[citations omitted]*

Next, we reject the suggestion of the court of appeals quoted above that we disregard the traditional rules and take "the full leap" of imposing a nondelegable duty on Texas hospitals for the malpractice of emergency room physicians. 940 S.W.2d at 136. Imposing such a duty is not necessary to safeguard patients in hospital emergency rooms. A patient injured by a physician's malpractice is not without a remedy. The injured patient ordinarily has a cause of action against the negligent physician, and may retain a direct cause of action against the hospital if the hospital was negligent in the performance of a duty owed directly to the patient. *[citations omitted]*

We now examine the record below in light of the appropriate standard. The Hospital may be held liable for the negligence of Dr. Zakula if Sampson can demonstrate that (1) she held a reasonable belief that Dr. Zakula was an employee or agent of the Hospital, (2) her belief was generated by some conduct on the part of the Hospital, and (3) she justifiably relied on the appearance that Dr. Zakula was an agent or employee of the Hospital. *[citation omitted]*

As summary judgment evidence, BMHS offered the affidavit of Dr. Potyka, an emergency room physician, which established that the emergency room doctors are not the actual agents, servants, or employees of the Hospital, and are not subject to the supervision, management, direction, or control of the Hospital when treating patients. Dr. Potyka further stated that when Dr. Zakula treated Sampson, signs were posted in the emergency room notifying patients that the emergency room physicians were independent contractors. Dr. Potyka's affidavit also established that the Hospital did not collect any fees for emergency room physician services and that the physicians billed the patients directly. BMHS presented copies of signed consent forms as additional summary judgment evidence. During both of Sampson's visits to the Hospital emergency room, before being examined or treated, Sampson signed a "Consent for Diagnosis, Treatment and Hospital Care" form explaining that all physicians at the Hospital are independent contractors who exercise their own professional judgment without control by the Hospital. The consent forms read in part:

> I acknowledge and agree that ..., Southeast Baptist Hospital, ... and any Hospital operated as a part of Baptist Memorial Hospital System, is not responsible for the judgment or conduct of any physician who treats or provides a professional service to me, but rather each physician is an independent contractor who is self-employed and is not the agent, servant or employee of the hospital.

To establish her claim of ostensible agency, Sampson offered her own affidavits. In her original affidavit, she stated that although the Hospital directed her to sign several pieces of paper before she was examined, she did not read them and no one explained their contents to her. Her supplemental affidavit stated that she did not recall signing the documents and that she did

55

not, at any time during her visit to the emergency room, see any signs stating that the doctors who work in the emergency room are not employees of the Hospital. Both affidavits state that she did not choose which doctor would treat her and that, at all times, she believed that a physician employed by the hospital was treating her. Based on this record we must determine if Sampson produced sufficient summary judgment evidence to raise a genuine issue of material fact on each element of ostensible agency, thereby defeating BMHS's summary judgment motion.

Even if Sampson's belief that Dr. Zakula was a hospital employee were reasonable, that belief, as we have seen, must be based on or generated by some conduct on the part of the Hospital. "No one should be denied the right to set up the truth unless it is in plain contradiction of his former allegations or acts." *Gulbenkian v. Penn*, 151 Tex. 412, 252 S.W.2d 929, 932 (1952). The summary judgment proof establishes that the Hospital took no affirmative act to make actual or prospective patients think the emergency room physicians were its agents or employees, and did not fail to take reasonable efforts to disabuse them of such a notion. As a matter of law, on this record, no conduct by the Hospital would lead a reasonable patient to believe that the treating emergency room physicians were hospital employees.

Sampson has failed to raise a fact issue on at least one essential element of her claim. Accordingly, we reverse the judgment of the court of appeals and render judgment that Sampson take nothing.

Ratification

§ 4.01 Ratification Defined

(1) Ratification is the affirmance of a prior act done by another, whereby the act is given effect as if done by an agent acting with actual authority.

(2) A person ratifies an act by
 (a) manifesting assent that the act shall affect the person's legal relations, or
 (b) conduct that justifies a reasonable assumption that the person so consents.

(3) Ratification does not occur unless
 (a) the act is ratifiable as stated in § 4.03,
 (b) the person ratifying has capacity as stated in § 4.04,
 (c) the ratification is timely as stated in § 4.05, and
 (d) the ratification encompasses the act in its entirety as stated in § 4.07.

§ 4.02 Effect Of Ratification

(1) Subject to the exceptions stated in subsection (2), ratification retroactively creates the effects of actual authority.

(2) Ratification is not effective:
 (a) in favor of a person who causes it by misrepresentation or other conduct that would make a contract voidable;
 (b) in favor of an agent against a principal when the principal ratifies to avoid a loss; or

(c) to diminish the rights or other interests of persons, not parties to the transaction, that were acquired in the subject matter prior to the ratification.

§ 4.03 Acts That May Be Ratified. *A person may ratify an act if the actor acted or purported to act as an agent on the person's behalf.*

§ 4.04 Capacity To Ratify

(1) A person may ratify an act if
    (a) the person existed at the time of the act, and
    (b) the person had capacity as defined in § 3.04 at the time of ratifying the act.

(2) At a later time, a principal may avoid a ratification made earlier when the principal lacked capacity as defined in § 3.04.

§ 4.05 Timing Of Ratification. *A ratification of a transaction is not effective unless it precedes the occurrence of circumstances that would cause the ratification to have adverse and inequitable effects on the rights of third parties. These circumstances include:*

(1) any manifestation of intention to withdraw from the transaction made by the third party;

(2) any material change in circumstances that would make it inequitable to bind the third party, unless the third party chooses to be bound; and

(3) a specific time that determines whether a third party is deprived of a right or subjected to a liability.

§ 4.06 Knowledge Requisite To Ratification. *A person is not bound by a ratification made without knowledge of material facts involved in the original act when the person was unaware of such lack of knowledge.*

§ 4.07 No Partial Ratification. *A ratification is not effective unless it encompasses the entirety of an act, contract, or other single transaction.*

§ 4.08 Estoppel To Deny Ratification. *If a person makes a manifestation that the person has ratified another's act and the manifestation, as reasonably understood by a third party, induces the third party to make a detrimental change in position, the person may be estopped to deny the ratification.*

Disney Enterprises, Inc. v. Esprit Finance, Inc.,
981 S.W.2d 25 (Tex. App. – San Antonio 1998)

This is an accelerated appeal from an interlocutory order denying Disney Enterprises, Inc.'s ("Disney") Rule 120a special appearance. *See* TEX. CIV. PRAC. & REM. CODE ANN. §51.014(a)(7) (Vernon Supp.1998). Because we find that Disney is not amenable to suit in Texas, we reverse the trial court's order and order the cause dismissed for lack of personal jurisdiction.

Factual & Procedural Background

On June 6, 1995, Esprit Finance, Inc. ("Esprit") filed suit in Texas against Disney Enterprises, Inc., and several other defendants for fraud and negligent misrepresentation arising out of a failed business transaction. Howard D. Pollack, Cesar Morales, Mussari S.A. de C.V. and Rene Mijares Reyes were also named defendants. All parties to the lawsuit, including Esprit, are nonresidents of Texas. Esprit is a British Virgin Islands corporation; Disney is a Delaware corporation; Global is a Florida corporation; and Mussari S.A. de C.V. is a Mexican corporation.

In August 1993, Sergio Trevino Sada ("Trevino"), an agent of Esprit, was contacted in Mexico by Rene Mijares of Mussari S.A. de C.V. on behalf of Global Talent Group, Inc., a Florida corporation with its principal office in Oklahoma, about sponsoring and promoting the Disney Symphonic Fantasy Tour in Mexico. Trevino and Mijares traveled to Norman, Oklahoma and met with Global representatives Howard Pollack and Cesar Morales to discuss the business venture. Trevino claims that a contract was produced at this meeting, and that Pollack and Morales represented that they were negotiating on behalf of Disney. Trevino states that in the contract rider, Disney was defined as "The Walt Disney Company and its related and affiliated companies." Trevino was informed that the tour was scheduled to run from August 31, 1993 through September 18, 1993, at a cost of one million dollars. The total cost would be financed through advanced ticket sales, except that Esprit would need to contribute $250,000. Of this $250,000 contribution, $30,000 was needed up front to cover rehearsal expenses, and $220,000 was to be placed in an escrow account in Florida. Trevino was told the escrow account would remain untouched unless ticket sales failed to cover expenses. Trevino was also assured that the performers would be able to obtain the necessary visas.

On August 13, 1993, Trevino and Morales flew from Oklahoma to McAllen, Texas. From McAllen, the men drove to Mission, Texas to withdraw $30,000. Trevino states that in Texas Morales reiterated that Global represented Disney and the $30,000 was needed as a good faith gesture to lock in the contract. Based on these representations, Trevino gave Morales $30,000 in cash and had $220,000 wire transferred to a Florida bank account.

On August 24, 1993, Esprit was notified the tour performances in Mexico were canceled. Esprit contacted the Florida bank for the return of the escrow funds only to learn the account had been liquidated. Esprit's attorney, John Harmon, contacted Disney's general counsel office in California to inquire about the missing funds. Harmon states he spoke with Disney attorney Sandy Litvak who explained, "Global had negotiated with an agent of the Walt Disney Company for the performance of the Disney Symphonic Fantasy in Guadalajara and Monterrey, Mexico....

Global was to make payment of $400,000 by August 24, 1993.[T]hat payment was not made.... Disney had incurred $250,000 in expenses and demanded that amount.... Disney eventually received $220,000 for expenses from its agents that had negotiated with Global."

Esprit attributes the tour's cancellation to Disney's difficulties in obtaining visas for the performers. Evidence introduced by Disney offers a different explanation for the cancellation. BCLF, a Canadian corporation, schedules the world-wide promotions of the Disney Symphonic Fantasy Tour for Walt Disney Special Events Company, a subsidiary of Disney. Once a location is selected, BCLF arranges a promotion package for the show. It appears that Global and BCLF had entered into a deal for the promotions of the August–September 1993 Mexico tour. As part of the contract, Global was required to make a payment of $400,000 to BCLF by August 24, 1993. BCLF did not receive the money, and consequently the tour was canceled. The record indicates that John Meglen, BCLF's touring division director, informed Global on August 24, 1993 that the show was canceled due to Global's failure to remit the final deposit. Meglen also informed Global that due to its breach, it was retaining Global's "deposit."

Esprit filed suit in Webb County for fraud/negligent representation. Disney filed a special appearance pursuant to Rule 120a challenging personal jurisdiction. The trial court had two hearings on the matter. Following the first hearing, the trial court granted Disney's special appearance and dismissed Esprit's claims against Disney for lack of jurisdiction. Esprit filed a motion for reconsideration, and following a hearing on this motion, the trial court reversed itself. The trial court set aside and vacated its earlier order and findings of fact and conclusions of law and entered findings of fact and conclusions of law in support of its denial of Disney's special appearance.

Personal Jurisdiction Over Nonresident

A Texas court may exercise jurisdiction over a nonresident if: (1) the Texas long-arm statute authorizes the exercise of jurisdiction, and (2) the exercise of jurisdiction comports with state and federal constitutional guarantees of due process. *See Guardian Royal Exch. Assur., Ltd. v. English China,* 815 S.W.2d 223, 226 (Tex.1991). The Texas long-arm statute authorizes the exercise of jurisdiction over nonresident defendants "doing business" in Texas. *See* TEX. CIV. PRAC. & REM.CODE ANN. § 17.042 (Vernon 1997). The statute expressly identifies several acts that constitute "doing business," and states that such list is not an exhaustive list. The "broad language" of the long-arm statute permits an expansive reach, limited only by federal constitutional requirements of due process. *Schlobohm v. Schapiro,* 784 S.W.2d 355, 357 (Tex.1990). Thus, we need only consider whether it is consistent with federal constitutional requirements of due process for Texas to assert personal jurisdiction over Disney.

Under the federal constitutional test of due process, a state may assert personal jurisdiction over a nonresident defendant if: (1) the defendant has purposely established minimum contacts with the forum state, and (2) the exercise of jurisdiction comports with fair play and substantial justice. *Burger King Corp. v. Rudzewicz,* 471 U.S. 462, 475–76, 105 S.Ct. 2174, 85 L.Ed.2d 528 (1985).

Minimum Contacts

Under the minimum contacts analysis, we focus on the defendant's intentional activities and expectations in deciding whether it is proper to call him before the forum state's courts. *World–Wide Volkswagen Corp. v. Woodson,* 444 U.S. 286, 291–92, 100 S.Ct. 559, 62 L Ed.2d 490 (1980). The minimum contacts requirement may be satisfied if either specific or general jurisdiction exists. Specific jurisdiction attaches if the cause of action arises out of or relates to the nonresident defendant's contact with the forum state. *Guardian Royal,* 815 S.W.2d at 227. The contact between the defendant and the forum state must have occurred as a result of the defendant's purposeful conduct. *Id.*

At the second hearing and on appeal, Esprit approached this case as a specific jurisdiction case. Specifically, Esprit argued that the minimum contacts requirement was satisfied through the alleged tortious conduct of Disney's agents, Pollack and Morales. Esprit contends Pollack and Morales, acting as Disney's agents, defrauded Esprit in Texas. Esprit further asserts that Disney later ratified Global's conduct by retaining the fruit of the fraud, confirming that Global was acting as Disney's agent, and thereby subjecting Disney to jurisdiction in Texas. Esprit's contention that Disney is amenable to suit in Texas under an agency theory of vicarious liability does not find support in the record.

We begin with the general proposition that the law does not presume agency. *Buchoz v. Klein,* 143 Tex. 284, 184 S.W.2d 271, 271 (1944). The individual alleging agency has the burden to prove its existence. *Id.* Further, absent actual or apparent authority, an agent cannot bind a principal. *Currey v. Lone Star Steel Co.,* 676 S.W.2d 205, 209 (Tex.App.—Fort Worth 1984, no writ). Actual authority denotes that authority which the principal intentionally confers upon the agent, or intentionally allows the agent to believe he has, or by want of ordinary care allows the agent to believe himself to possess. *Spring Garden 79U, Inc. v. Stewart Title Co.,* 874 S.W.2d 945, 948 (Tex.App.—Houston [1st Dist.] 1994, no writ). Apparent agency exists where the principal's conduct would lead a reasonably prudent person to believe that the agent possessed the authority to act on behalf of the principal. *See Maccabees Mut. Life Ins. Co. v. McNiel,* 836 S.W.2d 229, 232–33 (Tex.App.—Dallas 1992, no writ). Apparent authority is determined by looking to the acts of the principal and ascertaining whether those acts would lead a reasonably prudent person using diligence and discretion to suppose the agent had the authority the agent purported to exercise. *NationsBank, N.A. v. Dilling,* 922 S.W.2d 950, 953 (Tex.1996). Only the acts of the principal may be considered; representations made by the purported agent of his authority have no effect. *Southwest Title Ins. Co. v. Northland Bldg. Corp.,* 552 S.W.2d 425, 428 (Tex.1977). Both actual and apparent authority are created through conduct of the principal communicated either to the agent (actual authority) or to a third party (apparent authority). *Currey,* 676 S.W.2d at 210 (citing *Product Promotions, Inc. v. Cousteau,* 495 F.2d 483 (5th Cir.1974)). Finally, a party dealing with an agent must ascertain both the fact and the scope of the agent's authority, and if the party deals with the agent without having made such a determination, he does so at his own risk. *Elliot Valve Repair Co. v. B.J. Valve & Fitting Co.,* 675 S.W.2d 555, 561 (Tex.App.—Houston [1st Dist.]), *rev'd on other grounds,* 679 S.W.2d 1 (Tex.1984).

In the instant case, there is no evidence demonstrating that Disney, the purported principal, gave Global actual authority to act as its agent, or that Disney negligently allowed

Global to believe it had been given actual authority to represent Disney. In fact, Disney introduced uncontradicted evidence to the contrary. Disney's evidence established that Global did not have actual authority to act as its agent. With respect to apparent authority, Esprit points only to the conduct of Pollack and Morales, which consists of presenting a contract containing a reference to Disney, and Pollack and Morales' oral assurances of their authority, as evidence that Global was authorized to act as Disney's agent. As noted, in order to charge the principal through apparent authority of his agent, the third party must establish conduct by the principal or written or spoken words by the principal that would lead a reasonably prudent person to believe the agent had the authority to act. *See NationsBank*, 922 S.W.2d at 953. Here, Global did allegedly present Esprit with a "package" and a contract rider that identified Disney, and Global repeatedly stated that it was authorized to negotiate for Disney. These representations were unilaterally orchestrated by Global. Without acts of the purported principal, acts of a purported agent which may mislead persons into false inferences of authority, however reasonable, will not serve as predicate for apparent authority. *Southwest Land Title Co. v. Gemini Financial Co.*, 752 S.W.2d 5, 7 (Tex.App.—Dallas 1988, no writ). Moreover, the fact that Global may have had a contract with one of Disney's agents does not improve Esprit's position. That is, Global's contractual relationship with BCLF would not, by itself, empower Global to act as Disney's agent absent written or oral manifestations from Disney that it intended to have Global act on its behalf.

Esprit further asserts that an agency relationship between Global and Disney has been demonstrated because Disney ratified Global's alleged tortious conduct by retaining the fruit of the fraud, thereby confirming that Global was acting as Disney's agent. Disney counters that because ratification is a doctrine of agency, it is inapplicable when no underlying agency is proved. *See Southwestern Inv. Co. v. Neeley*, 412 S.W.2d 925, 932 (Tex.Civ.App.—Fort Worth 1967), *modified on other grounds*, 430 S.W.2d 465 (Tex.1968); *see also Lynn v. United Technologies Corp., Inc.*, 916 F.Supp. 1217, 1220 (M.D.La.1996); *Shapiro v. American Home Assur. Co.*, 584 F.Supp. 1245, 1251 (D.Mass.1984); *E.P. Dobson, Inc. v. Richard*, 17 Ark.App. 155, 705 S.W.2d 893, 894 (1986). Disney further argues that without evidence of a pre-existing agency relationship, the doctrine of ratification cannot create one. *See Neeley*, 412 S.W.2d at 932.

Ratification is the affirmance by a person of a prior act which when performed did not bind him, but which was professedly done on his account, whereby the act is given effect as if originally authorized by him. RESTATEMENT (SECOND) OF AGENCY §82 (1958). Ratification, in this context, is not a form of authorization, but a legal concept in agency law describing the relations between parties after affirmance by a person of a transaction done or purported to be done for him. RESTATEMENT (SECOND) OF AGENCY §82 cmt. a, b (1958). A ratification will lie when the individual for whom an act was done retains the benefits of the transaction after acquiring full knowledge of the transaction. *See Land Title Co. of Dallas v. F.M. Stigler, Inc.*, 609 S.W.2d 754, 756 (Tex.1980). Most case law interpreting the doctrine of ratification couches its discussion in the context of an existing agency relationship where the agent exceeds the scope of her authority and the principal later accepts the benefits of such act after acquiring full knowledge. *See e.g., id.; Humble Nat'l Bank v. DCV, Inc.*, 933 S.W.2d 224, 237 (Tex.App.—Houston [14th Dist.] 1996, writ denied); *Old Republic Ins. Co., Inc. v. Fuller*, 919 S.W.2d 726, 728 (Tex.App.—Texarkana 1996, writ denied). Ratification, however, can occur outside this general paradigm. *See* RESTATEMENT (SECOND) OF AGENCY § 85 cmt d of (1) (1958). While most cases will fall within the context of an agency relationship, such a relation is not necessary to cause the ratification to be effective. *See id.* It is true, however, that because ratification is not a form of authorization, the ratification of an act of a stranger will not create an agency relationship, it will only bind the ratifier to the specific transaction that is ratified. *See* RESTATEMENT (SECOND) OF AGENCY § 82 cmt d, § 85 cmt d of (1) (1958).

As applied to the instant case, however, the doctrine of ratification does not aid Esprit's position. Esprit relies upon Harmon and Litvak's conversation as evidence that Disney knowingly retained the benefits of a fraud after acquiring full knowledge of the fraudulent transaction. We disagree. First, the record does not contain documentation regarding the whereabouts of Esprit's money. In fact, there is no documentation regarding either the initial deposit of money into the escrow account, or the liquidation of the account. Moreover, the Harmon/Litvak conversation merely confirms that Disney is in possession of Global's money, which may or may not in actuality be Esprit's money. Second, the evidence suggests that any money acquired by Disney or the Disney Special Events Company was acquired lawfully through a contract between Global and BCLF. The record indicates that Global had a contract with BCLF in which Global was required to pay BCLF a final down payment on August 24, 1993 for the tour. Global allegedly failed to pay, thereby breaching its contract. In response to the breach, BCLF retained Global's "deposit." Thus, because there is no evidence that Disney retained Esprit's money after acquiring full knowledge of an alleged fraudulent transaction, the doctrine of ratification is inapplicable to the instant case. Because the record does not affirmatively establish that Global had actual or apparent authority to bind Disney, it was error for the trial court to conclude that the minimum contacts requirement had been met. *See Koch Graphics, Inc. v. Avantech, Inc.,* 803 S.W.2d 432, 434–35 (Tex.App.—Dallas 1991, no writ).

Fair Play and Substantial Justice

Even if there was some evidence upon which to conclude that Disney had established minimum contacts with Texas, the assertion of jurisdiction is proper only if such exercise of jurisdiction comports with fair play and substantial justice. *International Shoe Co. v. Washington,* 326 U.S. 310, 316, 66 S.Ct. 154, 90 L.Ed. 95 (1945). In determining this second prong, courts consider: (1) the burden on the defendant, (2) the interest of the forum state in adjudicating the dispute, (3) the plaintiff's interest in obtaining convenient and effective relief, (4) the interstate judicial system's interest in obtaining the most efficient resolution of controversies, and (5) the shared interest of the several states in furthering fundamental substantive social policies. *Burger King,* 471 U.S. at 476–77, 105 S.Ct. 2174. We find that there is no evidence to support the trial court's conclusion that the exercise of jurisdiction in the instant case comports with fair play and substantial justice. First, Disney will probably incur substantial travel and litigation costs defending the case in South Texas. Second, Texas has no recognizable interest in the suit. No Texas residents are directly or indirectly involved in the suit; no Texas residents have been harmed by the alleged transactions; there are no witnesses residing in Texas; and there is no evidence to be gathered in Texas. Third, Esprit's interest in obtaining relief would not be impaired if it had to litigate the case in Oklahoma or California. Fourth, Oklahoma seemingly has an interest in litigating the case because Global is operating out of Oklahoma, Global brought Esprit to Oklahoma, and the alleged fraudulent negotiations began in Oklahoma.

Conclusion

Esprit, the apparent victim of a business scam, is a sympathetic plaintiff attempting to recover a substantial sum of money it gave to a company in good faith during a business transaction. It is well settled, however, that a nonresident defendant will not be made to answer to a suit in a jurisdiction based upon the unilateral activity of third party. *See Guardian Royal*, 815 S.W.2d at 227. The record demonstrates that Global was not authorized either by actual or apparent authority to act on Disney's behalf. The record further demonstrates that Disney did not ratify Global's alleged fraudulent activity, but rather that Disney lawfully obtained money from Global through a contract between Global and one of Disney's agents. Because the record establishes that Disney has no contacts with Texas, the trial court erred in denying Disney's special appearance. Point of error number one is sustained.

Accordingly, the judgment of the trial court is reversed and the cause is dismissed for lack of personal jurisdiction over Disney. *See* TEX.R.APP. P. 43.2(c).

FIDUCIARY DUTY: Rights, duties, and liabilities between principal and agent

Principal to agent

An agency is a fiduciary relationship, wherein the "principal has a duty to deal with the agent fairly and in good faith, including a duty to provide the agent with information about risks of physical harm or pecuniary loss that the principal knows, has reason to know, or should know are present in the agent's work but unknown to the agent." *See Restatement of Agency*, 3rd edition, §8.15.

> **§ 8.13 Duty Created By Contract.** *A principal has a duty to act in accordance with the express and implied terms of any contract between the principal and the agent.*
>
> **§ 8.14 Duty To Indemnify.** *A principal has a duty to indemnify an agent*
>
> *(1) in accordance with the terms of any contract between them; and*
>
> *(2) unless otherwise agreed,*
>   *(a) when the agent makes a payment*
>   *(i)   within the scope of the agent's actual authority, or*
>   *(ii) that is beneficial to the principal, unless the agent acts officiously in making the payment; or*
>
>   *(b) when the agent suffers a loss that fairly should be borne by the principal in light of their relationship.*
>
> **§ 8.15 Principal's Duty To Deal Fairly And In Good Faith.** *A principal has a duty to deal with the agent fairly and in good faith, including a duty to provide the agent with information about risks of physical harm or pecuniary loss that the principal knows, has*

reason to know, or should know are present in the agent's work but unknown to the agent.

Agent to principal

The agent's fiduciary duties to the principal are generally limited to actions occurring within the scope of its agency. Customarily, the duties that an agent owes to its principal are in two categories; the duty of loyalty and the duty of care.

The Duty of Loyalty

The duty of loyalty requires the agent to place the principal's interest first—that is, the agent is prohibited from acting in any manner inconsistent with the agency and is at all times bound to exercise the utmost good faith and loyalty in the performance of his duties. Examples of loyalty include informing a principal of every and all material facts of which the agent knows that concerns, in any manner, either the purpose of the agency relationship; and avoiding self-dealing in the principal's property without the principal's knowledge. Under the Restatement, the duty of loyalty is discussed as encapsulating numerous duties, each of which requires the agent to act in the best interest of the principal and at all times to exercise the duty of loyalty in good faith.

The Restatement of Agency, 3rd edition, provides:

> *§ 8.01 General Fiduciary Principle. An agent has a fiduciary duty to act loyally for the principal's benefit in all matters connected with the agency relationship.*
>
> *§ 8.02 Material Benefit Arising Out Of Position. An agent has a duty not to acquire a material benefit from a third party in connection with transactions conducted or other actions taken on behalf of the principal or otherwise through the agent's use of the agent's position.*
>
> *§ 8.03 Acting As Or On Behalf Of An Adverse Party. An agent has a duty not to deal with the principal as or on behalf of an adverse party in a transaction connected with the agency relationship.*
>
> *§ 8.04 Competition. Throughout the duration of an agency relationship, an agent has a duty to refrain from competing with the principal and from taking action on behalf of or otherwise assisting the principal's competitors. During that time, an agent may take action, not otherwise wrongful, to prepare for competition following termination of the agency relationship.*
>
> *§ 8.05 Use Of Principal's Property; Use Of Confidential Information. An agent has a duty*
>> *(1) not to use property of the principal for the agent's own purposes or those of a third party; and*
>>
>> *(2) not to use or communicate confidential information of the principal for the agent's own purposes or those of a third party.*

§ 8.06 Principal's Consent.

(1) Conduct by an agent that would otherwise constitute a breach of duty as stated in §§ 8.01, 8.02, 8.03, 8.04, and 8.05 does not constitute a breach of duty if the principal consents to the conduct, provided that

(a) in obtaining the principal's consent, the agent

(i) acts in good faith,

(ii) discloses all material facts that the agent knows, has reason to know, or should know would reasonably affect the principal's judgment unless the principal has manifested that such facts are already known by the principal or that the principal does not wish to know them, and

(iii) otherwise deals fairly with the principal; and

(b) the principal's consent concerns either a specific act or transaction, or acts or transactions of a specified type that could reasonably be expected to occur in the ordinary course of the agency relationship.

(2) An agent who acts for more than one principal in a transaction between or among them has a duty

(a) to deal in good faith with each principal,

(b) to disclose to each principal

(i) the fact that the agent acts for the other principal or principals, and

(ii) all other facts that the agent knows, has reason to know, or should know would reasonably affect the principal's judgment unless the principal has manifested that such facts are already known by the principal or that the principal does not wish to know them, and

(c) otherwise to deal fairly with each principal.

§ 8.07 Duty Created By Contract.
An agent has a duty to act in accordance with the express and implied terms of any contract between the agent and the principal.

Duty of Care

The agent is also required to perform its duties employing due care and diligence. The agent is required to follow the terms and conditions expressed in applicable contracts, regulations and laws. The agent is held to ordinary care unless they have special skills and or knowledge which will generally require the agent to act with the care required of one with such expertise.

§ 8.08 Duties Of Care, Competence, And Diligence.
Subject to any agreement with the principal, an agent has a duty to the principal to act with the care, competence, and diligence normally exercised by agents in similar circumstances. Special skills or knowledge possessed by an agent are circumstances to be taken into account in determining whether the agent acted with due care and diligence. If an agent claims to

possess special skills or knowledge, the agent has a duty to the principal to act with the care, competence, and diligence normally exercised by agents with such skills or knowledge.

§ 8.09 Duty To Act Only Within Scope Of Actual Authority And To Comply With Principal's Lawful Instructions. *An agent has a duty to take action only within the scope of the agent's actual authority.*

> *(1) An agent has a duty to comply with all lawful instructions received from the principal and persons designated by the principal concerning the agent's actions on behalf of the principal.*

§ 8.10 Duty Of Good Conduct. *An agent has a duty, within the scope of the agency relationship, to act reasonably and to refrain from conduct that is likely to damage the principal's enterprise.*

§ 8.11 Duty To Provide Information. *An agent has a duty to use reasonable effort to provide the principal with facts that the agent knows, has reason to know, or should know when:*

> *(1) subject to any manifestation by the principal, the agent knows or has reason to know that the principal would wish to have the facts or the facts are material to the agent's duties to the principal; and*

> *(2) the facts can be provided to the principal without violating a superior duty owed by the agent to another person.*

§ 8.12 Duties Regarding Principal's Property--Segregation, Record-Keeping, And Accounting. *An agent has a duty, subject to any agreement with the principal,*

> *(1) not to deal with the principal's property so that it appears to be the agent's property;*

> *(2) not to mingle the principal's property with anyone else's; and*

> *(3) to keep and render accounts to the principal of money or other property received or paid out on the principal's account.*

§ 8.13 Duty Created By Contract. *A principal has a duty to act in accordance with the express and implied terms of any contract between the principal and the agent.*

Duties of Loyalty and Care

West v. Touchstone
620 S.W.2d 687 (Tex. App. — Dallas 1981)

Suit was brought alleging that defendant, while acting as plaintiffs' real estate agent, communicated with a prospective purchaser in such manner as to cause said purchaser to refrain from purchasing plaintiffs' property. The 162nd District Court, Dallas County, Dee Brown Walker, J., entered summary judgment for defendant, and plaintiffs appealed. The Court of Civil Appeals, Akin, J., held that defendant failed to negate his agency as a matter of law at the time the communications occurred; that is, a fact issue existed, precluding entry of summary judgment, as to whether defendant was the agent of plaintiffs and thus owed them fiduciary duties when he advised prospective purchaser that tentative purchase price was excessive and that the market value for comparable land was far less than the price discussed by plaintiffs and the prospective purchaser. Reversed and remanded.

The principal question presented by this appeal is whether Touchstone established, as a matter of law, that he was not the agent of appellants. We hold that Touchstone failed to negate his agency as a matter of law. Accordingly, we reverse and remand.

Appellants (West) are the owners of certain real property. In May 1975, they entered into an exclusive listing agreement with Touchstone to sell the property. In August 1976, West informed Touchstone by letter that the exclusive listing agreement was terminated. In 1977, Touchstone was contacted by a party who expressed an interest in purchasing West's property. Touchstone had previously shown the property in question to this prospective purchaser in 1975 when he was acting as West's exclusive agent. Touchstone advised West of the prospective purchaser's interest in the property and agreed to assist in bringing the parties together. During this period, West was attempting to negotiate a sale of the property with the Dallas Housing Authority (DHA). Touchstone wrote a letter to the Dallas City Manager, which was subsequently forwarded to the DHA, stating that the tentative purchase price which West and the DHA were discussing was excessive and that the market value for comparable land in the area was far less than the discussed purchase price. West alleges that Touchstone's letter and subsequent contacts with officials at the DHA resulted in the DHA's failure to purchase the property.

West's second amended petition alleged causes of action against Touchstone for breach of fiduciary duties, failure to disclose amounting to fraud, deceptive trade practices, and violation of the Real Estate Brokers' Canons of Ethics amounting to negligence. *[footnote omitted]* The gravamen of West's complaints is that Touchstone was acting as their agent at the time he wrote the letter in question and that his communications with Dallas officials constituted violation of his duty of loyalty as their agent, actionable under the four broad causes of action alleged. In response, Touchstone filed a motion for summary judgment which the trial court sustained.

Touchstone's motion for summary judgment specifically alleged that he was not, at the relevant times, West's agent and that he owed no fiduciary duty to West. The summary judgment evidence shows that on May 30, 1975, John R. West Co. and Gifford Touchstone & Co. entered into an exclusive listing agreement with respect to the property the subject of the instant action. *[footnote omitted]* The exclusive listing agreement provided that it would be in effect for twelve months and thereafter from month to month until either party gave the other one month's prior written notice of termination.

On August 12, 1976, John R. West wrote Touchstone to inform him that "the Sales Agency Agreement between Gifford Touchstone & Co. and the John R. West Co. ceased to exist as of May 20, 1976." The letter further stated that: "As a result of our desire to promote our property through you or others, we made a sales agreement with Moser Co. for the sale of a portion of the John R. West Co. property on June 4, 1976."

Touchstone argues that this letter terminated any agency relationship between him and West. He further asserts that, after receiving the letter, he did not enter into any other agency agreement with West. Thus, he contends that, at the time relevant in this lawsuit, he was not West's agent and owed no duty of loyalty to West as his principal.

We need not address the question of whether the letter from John R. West to Touchstone completely terminated the agency relationship between them, as Touchstone contends, or whether the letter terminated only the exclusive feature of the relationship, as West argues. This is so because the summary judgment evidence does not negate, as a matter of law, the existence of an agency relationship, apart from the exclusive listing agreement, which West maintains existed between them at the time of Touchstone's alleged communications to the DHA.

In this respect, Robert H. West's affidavit states:

> In late July or early August 1977 Gifford Touchstone had contacted me and had informed me that Roy Millican, through his agent Zettie Bozeman, was again interested in purchasing the property from us. Since this was the same property which we had been negotiating to sell to the Dallas Housing Authority, I relayed the information concerning the price and the details of the transaction to Gifford Touchstone and told him that, while we would be willing to discuss the matter with Millican and his agent, we would have to have entirely different terms than were proposed approximately one year earlier. Following that conversation Mr. Touchstone assured me that he would work to convince Millican to increase his price, and a meeting for this purpose was established in Gifford Touchstone's office approximately October 1, 1977. (Emphasis added.)

Touchstone contends that, as a matter of law, he has established that he was a mere middleman between West and Millican and, as such, owed West no fiduciary duties. We disagree. An agent is one who consents to act on behalf of and subject to the control of another, the principal, who has manifested consent that the agent shall so act. The relationship between agent and principal is a fiduciary relationship. RESTATEMENT (SECOND) OF AGENCY §1 (1958). Applying this definition of an agent to the facts of this case, we hold that a fact issue exists as to whether Touchstone was the agent of West and, therefore, owed him fiduciary duties. The fact issue is presented by the affidavit of Robert H. West which states that Touchstone agreed to negotiate with Millican in order to get Millican to increase the amount of his offer. Additionally, the information obtained by Touchstone with respect to the proposed sale to DHA was obtained during his discussions with West as to the proposed Millican negotiations. Taken as true, this testimony indicates that Touchstone was acting on behalf of, and with the consent of, West and that Touchstone was thus West's agent. If Touchstone was West's agent, Touchstone owed West a fiduciary duty of loyalty, that is, to act solely for the benefit of his principal in all matters connected with his agency. RESTATEMENT (SECOND) OF AGENCY §387 (1958). It follows that Touchstone's communications with the DHA, if made by him while acting as West's agent or if the information communicated to the DHA was obtained by him while acting as West's agent, would be in violation of his duty of loyalty to West.

In contending that, as a matter of law, he was a mere middleman between West and Millican and, therefore, owed West no fiduciary duties, Touchstone relies primarily on Peters v. Lerew, 139 S.W.2d 321 (Tex.Civ.App. Galveston 1940, writ dism'd judgmt cor.). We do not construe Peters as standing for the proposition that a "middleman" owes no fiduciary duties even though he is acting on behalf of another. We conclude that even though a broker may be a "middleman," he may nevertheless be an agent, as defined by the Restatement, if he undertakes to perform services on behalf of an owner.

Nevertheless Touchstone maintains that any communication he may have had with the DHA constituted a privileged exercise of his right to question the expenditure of public funds and was in protection of his rights as a taxpayer and a citizen. We hold that such a right as a citizen does not extend to excuse a violation of an agent's duty of loyalty to his principal. In other words, if Touchstone was the agent of West at the time of his communication or communications to the DHA, he was not privileged to make such communication or communications in derogation of West's interest. The cases cited to us by Touchstone in this respect are distinguishable in that they do not deal with communications made by an agent in violation of a duty of loyalty to his principal.

Touchstone further contends that any communication he had with the DHA was true. We hold, however, that if Touchstone was West's agent at the time of his communication with the DHA, whether the statement was true is no defense in a suit by a principal against a disloyal agent.

Touchstone next argues that West did not have a binding contract of sale with the DHA and that any possible expectation of West with respect to the DHA's purchase of the land in question was too remote and speculative to form the basis of a recovery against Touchstone. We cannot agree that this is a ground for affirmance of this summary judgment. This but raises a fact issue as to whether Touchstone's communication with the DHA caused the body not to enter into a contract of sale with West. Proof of such causation, along with proof of the other elements of West's claims, may entitle West to recover from Touchstone.

Finally, Touchstone contends that the reasons for the DHA's decision not to purchase West's land are fully set forth in a letter from William H. Darnall, Executive Director of the Housing Authority of the City of Dallas, to John R. McDowell, Area Director of the Department of Housing and Urban Development, and that this letter fails to make any mention of Touchstone's communication with the DHA. The letter is attached to Touchstone's motion for summary judgment as an exhibit. Even assuming that the letter is properly in evidence before us, it raises no more than a fact issue as to whether Touchstone's communication with the DHA caused the DHA to refrain from purchasing West's Property.

In summary, we hold that Touchstone has not negated, as a matter of law, one or more essential elements of West's causes of action. Accordingly, we reverse the judgment of the trial court and remand this cause for further proceedings.

Laredo Med. Grp. v. Lightner

153 S.W.3d 70 (Tex. App. — San Antonio 2004)

This case involves a salary dispute between Laredo Medical Group ("LMG") and its employee, Dr. Oscar Lightner. Lightner claims his employment agreement with LMG created a duty of good faith and fair dealing between the parties that LMG breached. He also claims he was not bound by the agreement's covenant not to compete. We disagree and reverse the trial court's judgment.

In October 1995, Lightner sold his medical practice to LMG and became one of its employees. Under Lightner's employment agreement, LMG guaranteed Lightner's income for the first three years of his employment, but after that time Lightner's income would be based on a percentage of the total revenue LMG collected from his practice. The agreement also included a non-compete provision. During the course of Lightner's employment, LMG did not collect all of his accounts receivable. Lightner claimed this resulted in an income shortfall of approximately one-half million dollars over the four-year term of his employment.

In June 1999, Lightner filed suit against LMG claiming LMG breached its duty of good faith and fair dealing by failing to adequately collect his accounts receivable. Four months later, Lightner resigned from his position at LMG. LMG filed a counterclaim against Lightner seeking to enforce the non-compete provision in Lightner's employment agreement and to recover damages.

Based on jury findings that LMG maliciously breached its duty of good faith and fair dealing to Lightner, *[footnote omitted]* the trial court rendered judgment for Lightner for actual and punitive damages. Lightner's claim for attorney's fees was denied. The court further ordered that LMG take nothing on its counterclaim.

LMG challenges the jury's findings claiming: (1) it owed no duty of good faith and fair dealing; (2) there is insufficient evidence that any duty of good faith and fair dealing was breached; (3) there is insufficient evidence to support the award of actual or punitive damages; (4) there is insufficient evidence to prove it acted with malice; (5) the amount of post-judgment interest should be reduced; and (6) there is no evidence to support the jury's finding regarding the covenant not to compete.

Duty of Good Faith & Fair Dealing

Texas does not recognize a cause of action for breach of a duty of good faith and fair dealing in the context of an employer/employee relationship. *See City of Midland v. O'Bryant*, 18 S.W.3d 209, 216 (Tex.2000). No distinction is made for employment governed by an express agreement. *Id.* However, Lightner claims LMG nevertheless owed him a duty of good faith and fair dealing because the power of attorney provisions within the parties' employment and asset-purchase agreements created an agency relationship. *See Crim Truck & Tractor Co. v. Navistar*

Int'l Transp. Corp., 823 S.W.2d 591, 593–94 (Tex.1992) (recognizing principal-agent relationship gives rise to fiduciary duty encompassing duty of good faith and fair dealing). It is essential to an agency relationship, however, that the principal have the right to "assign the agent's task and to control the means and details of the process by which the agent will accomplish the task." *Walker v. Fed. Kemper Life Assurance Co.*, 828 S.W.2d 442, 452 (Tex.App.-San Antonio 1992, writ denied). Thus, even if a person acts for and on behalf of another, if he is not under the other person's control, an agency relationship does not exist. *Id.* The agreements between the parties contain provisions that make LMG Lightner's attorney-in-fact for the collection of fees. Although the appointment of an attorney-in-fact ordinarily creates an agency relationship, there is no agency relationship here because there is no evidence LMG was under Lightner's control. *See Walker*, 828 S.W.2d at 452.

Lightner also argues LMG owed him a duty of good faith and fair dealing because he trusted LMG with his property interest in his accounts receivable, citing *Manges v. Guerra*, 673 S.W.2d 180 (Tex.1984). We find Lightner's argument unpersuasive for two reasons. First, the *Manges* court recognized that a holder of executive rights to a mineral estate owes a fiduciary duty to the non-executive interest. *Manges*, 673 S.W.2d at 183. This case is not comparable to that situation. Second, Lightner's argument is based on the premise that the fees generated by his work belonged to him. This is simply not true. The parties' employment agreement specifically provides that "all fees and other revenues attributable to [Lightner's] services ... belong to [LMG]."

Finally, Lightner argues that a "special relationship," implicating a duty of good faith and fair dealing, existed between the parties by virtue of an imbalance of bargaining power. A "special relationship" has been recognized where there is unequal bargaining power between the parties and a risk exists that one of the parties may take advantage of the other based upon the imbalance of power, *e.g.*, insurer-insured. *See Arnold v. Nat'l County Mut. Fire Ins. Co.*, 725 S.W.2d 165, 167 (Tex.1987). But the supreme court has ruled that the elements which make a relationship special are absent in the relationship between an employer and an employee. *See City of Midland v. O'Bryant*, 18 S.W.3d at 215.

We hold that LMG owed no duty of good faith and fair dealing to Lightner.

Covenant Not To Compete

The employment contract that Lightner actually signed failed to include a page that contained provisions addressing the restrictions placed on Lightner by his non-compete agreement with LMG. *[footnote omitted]* An earlier unsigned draft of the document that included the omitted provisions was reviewed by Lightner's attorney. When the final document was prepared for signatures, one of the pages was included twice and an apparent gap in the text from one of the pages to the next indicated a skipped page. Even so, all the pages were numbered consecutively. LMG claims the page was omitted from the final document by an inadvertent mistake, that Lightner knew of the non-compete agreement and its terms, and that he even accepted $100,000 in exchange for it. *[footnote omitted] Ac*cordingly, LMG says either Lightner is bound by the non-compete agreement, or in the alternative it is entitled to the return of its $100,000.

> *The omitted language provided: (1) Recognition and acknowledgment that time, effort and expense has been devoted by LMG to establish its patient base and hiring staff to treat the patients; that the patient base is a valuable asset of LMG; that Physician is given access to the patient base under the agreement; and that Physician's solicitation of the patient base outside of the agreement would be highly damaging to LMG. (2) The agreement's geographical limitation of a twenty-five mile radius. (3) The liquidated damages provision in the event of violation. (4) Physician's acknowledgment that the restrictions are reasonable in scope and essential to LMG's business interests. (5) Provision for Physician's voluntary termination of non-compete restrictions upon payment to LMG of $200,000.*

The signed agreement included the following non-compete provisions:

ARTICLE VIII

COVENANT NOT TO COMPETE

A. Covenant Not to Compete. For and in consideration of Physician's agreement to the terms and conditions of the covenant not to compete and other covenants set forth in this Article VIII, Medical Group shall pay to the Physician a one-time amount of $100,000, which shall be paid on or before the Commencement Date. Physician hereby agrees that, for the duration of Physician's employment with Medical Group, and for a period of two (2) years (twenty-four (24) months) after termination of employment with Medical Group for any reason at any time, Physician shall not in any manner directly or indirectly:

> 1. Disclose or divulge to any other person, partnership, corporation, business organization, firm, or other entity whatsoever, or use for Physician's own benefit or for the benefit of any other person, partnership, corporation, business organization, firm, or other entity directly or indirectly in competition with Medical Group, any knowledge, information, business methods, techniques, or patient lists, letters, files, records, or other information, of Medical Group other than as may be required by a court with jurisdiction over Physician and Medical Group.

> 2. Solicit, divert, or otherwise interfere with the patients or their immediate family members, patronage, employees, or agents of Medical.... ....

.... (omitted provisions)

E. Waiver of Practice Restriction. *The practice restriction in subparagraph 3 of paragraph A of this Article shall be waived only in the following circumstances:*

> *1. If Medical Group elects to waive the restriction upon an affirmative recommendation of not less than seventy-five percent (75%) of the Board, or*
>
> *2. If Medical Group elects to terminate Physician's employment for any reason other than one or more of the reasons listed in subparagraphs 1 through 6 paragraph A of Article VII.*

The jury found the omission of the page was not a mutual mistake, and the trial court thereupon refused to enforce the non-compete agreement. LMG challenges this jury finding claiming that mutual mistake was established as a matter of law and that the finding should be disregarded.

We see the question as being whether the parties had a mutual understanding and intent that Lightner was to be bound by a non-compete agreement when he signed the employment contract with LMG. That question can be resolved in the affirmative simply by considering Lightner's testimony and by examining the document Lightner actually signed.

Lightner testified he was aware his employment agreement included a covenant not to compete, but he disclaimed any interest in it and denied knowing its terms. He said "It was not an important issue for me in signing [the agreement]." Moreover, the document Lightner signed clearly contains a promise not to compete against LMG for two years after termination. And the agreement expressly acknowledges that he was to be paid $100,000 "[f]or and in consideration of [Lightner's] agreement to the terms and conditions of the covenant not to compete."

Lightner says he was "completely unaware" of the omitted provisions, which he says destroys any mutual understanding and intent that would support an agreement. We disagree. The evidence conclusively establishes Lightner's intent to be bound by the covenant not to compete. Lightner's claim not to know all the terms of the covenant does not avoid his responsibilities under the agreement he made. *See Roland v. McCullough,* 561 S.W.2d 207, 213 (Tex.Civ.App.-San Antonio 1978, writ ref'd n.r.e.) ("A contract may not be avoided on the ground of mistake of fact where it appears that ignorance of the facts was the result of carelessness, indifference, or inattention.").

"Reformation is a proper remedy when the parties have reached a definite and explicit agreement, understood in the same sense by both, but, by their mutual or common mistake, the written contract fails to express this agreement." *Champlin Oil & Ref. Co. v. Chastain,* 403 S.W.2d 376, 377 (Tex.1965). Because it is clear the parties had a non-compete agreement, but it is unclear from the signed document what all the terms of the agreement were, the matter must be remanded to the trial court to reform the written contract to conform to the terms of the agreement.

Conclusion

Because we hold LMG owed Lightner no duty of good faith and fair dealing, we reverse and render judgment that Lightner take nothing from LMG. We further hold that the omission of the page from the written employment contract was a mistake that did not invalidate Lightner's explicit agreement not to compete. Accordingly, the matter is remanded to the trial court to reform the written contract to conform to the actual agreement of the parties, and to determine the reasonableness and enforceability of the covenant not to compete. *[concurring and dissenting opinions omitted]*

LIABILITY: Disclosed, Partially Disclosed and Undisclosed Principals

Whether an agent fully discloses, partially discloses or fails to disclose the existence and or identity of the principal can impact whether the principal or agent would be liable to a third party. A disclosed or partially disclosed principal is generally liable to a third party for a contract made by an agent who is acting within the scope of his or her authority.

A Disclosed Principal is a principal whose existence and identity are known to the third party at the time the agent makes a contract for the principal with the third party. A partially disclosed principal (also known as an "unidentified principal" under the Third Restatement) is a principal whose identity is not known to the third party, but the third party does know that the agent is representing some principal at the time the agent makes a contract with the third party. In many states, the agent is also liable on a contract with a partially disclosed principal. An undisclosed principal is one whose identity nor the fact that the agency exists is disclosed by an agent to the third party at the time a contract is made, the agent is presumed to be acting on his or her own behalf, and thus, will be liable as a party to the contract. If the agent is acting within the scope of his authority in acting on behalf of the undisclosed principal, the principal will be liable to the agent and subject to indemnifying the agent for any damages he/she/it incurs. In cases where the agent has *actual* authority but the principal is undisclosed, the principal is also generally liable to a third party under any contract entered by the agent acting within the scope of that authority.

Agent's Liability

Contracts

In those instances where an agent discloses to the third-party that he is (1) working for a principal and (2) the principal's identity, then the agent is not a party to the authorized contract. However, the agent will become a party to the contract, if he and the third-party so agree. After an agent enters into an authorized contract on behalf of an unidentified principal, the agent is a party to the contract and may be liable to the third-party. He does not become a party to the contract if he and the third-party so agree, however. And, finally, where the agent enters into an authorized contract with a third-party without disclosing that he is working for a principal, then both the agent and the principal are liable to the third-party.

Torts

Although the agent acts with either actual or apparent authority or within the scope of his employment, he may still be liable to a third-party who is harmed by his tortious conduct.

Third-parties to principal

Where a principal is undisclosed to a third-party, the principal typically has the right to receive the benefit the agent got from the third-party. After the undisclosed principal reveals his identity to the third-party who contracted with the agent, the principal then has the right to bring suit to enforce the contract.

> **§ 6.01 Agent For Disclosed Principal.** *When an agent acting with actual or apparent authority makes a contract on behalf of a disclosed principal,*
>
> > *(1) the principal and the third party are parties to the contract; and*
> >
> > *(2) the agent is not a party to the contract unless the agent and third party agree otherwise.*
>
> **§ 6.08 Other Subsequent Dealings Between Third Party And Agent.** *When an agent has made a contract with a third party on behalf of a disclosed or unidentified principal, subsequent dealings between the agent and the third party may increase or diminish the principal's rights or liabilities to the third party if the agent acts with actual or apparent authority or the principal ratifies the agent's action.*
>
> > *(1) When an agent has made a contract with a third party on behalf of an undisclosed principal,*
> >
> > > *(a) until the third party has notice of the principal's existence, subsequent dealings between the third party and the agent may increase or diminish the rights or liabilities of the principal to the third party if the agent acts with actual authority, or the principal ratifies the agent's action; and*
> > >
> > > *(b) after the third party has notice of the principal's existence, subsequent dealings between the third party and the agent may increase or diminish the principal's rights or liabilities to the third party if the agent acts with actual or apparent authority or the principal ratifies the agent's action.*

§ 6.11 Agent's Representations.

> *(1) When an agent for a disclosed or unidentified principal makes a false representation about the agent's authority to a third party, the principal is not subject to liability unless the agent acted with actual or apparent authority in making the representation and the third party does not have notice that the agent's representation is false.*
>
> *(2) A representation by an agent made incident to a contract or conveyance is attributed to a disclosed or unidentified principal as if the principal made the representation*

directly when the agent had actual or apparent authority to make the contract or conveyance unless the third party knew or had reason to know that the representation was untrue or that the agent acted without actual authority in making it.

(3) A representation by an agent made incident to a contract or conveyance is attributed to an undisclosed principal as if the principal made the representation directly when

> *(a) the agent acted with actual authority in making the representation, or*
>
> *(b) the agent acted without actual authority in making the representation but had actual authority to make true representations about the same matter. The agent's representation is not attributed to the principal when the third party knew or had reason to know it was untrue.*

(4) When an agent who makes a contract or conveyance on behalf of an undisclosed principal falsely represents to the third party that the agent does not act on behalf of a principal, the third party may avoid the contract or conveyance if the principal or agent had notice that the third party would not have dealt with the principal.

§ 7.01 Agent's Liability To Third Party. *An agent is subject to liability to a third party harmed by the agent's tortious conduct. Unless an applicable statute provides otherwise, an actor remains subject to liability although the actor acts as an agent or an employee, with actual or apparent authority, or within the scope of employment.*

§ 7.02 Duty To Principal; Duty To Third Party. *An agent's breach of a duty owed to the principal is not an independent basis for the agent's tort liability to a third party. An agent is subject to tort liability to a third party harmed by the agent's conduct only when the agent's conduct breaches a duty that the agent owes to the third party.*

§ 6.02 Agent For Unidentified Principal. *When an agent acting with actual or apparent authority makes a contract on behalf of an unidentified principal,*

> *(1) the principal and the third party are parties to the contract; and*
>
> *(2) the agent is a party to the contract unless the agent and the third party agree otherwise.*

§ 6.03 Agent For Undisclosed Principal. *When an agent acting with actual authority makes a contract on behalf of an undisclosed principal,*

> *(1) unless excluded by the contract, the principal is a party to the contract;*
>
> *(2) the agent and the third party are parties to the contract; and*
>
> *(3) the principal, if a party to the contract, and the third party have the same rights, liabilities, and defenses against each other as if the principal made the contract personally, subject to §§ 6.05-6.09.*

§ 6.06 Setoff

> *(1) When an agent makes a contract on behalf of a disclosed or unidentified principal, unless the principal and the third party agree otherwise,*
>
> *(2) the third party may not set off any amount that the agent independently owes*

the third party against an amount the third party owes the principal under the contract; and

(3) *the principal may not set off any amount that the third party independently owes the agent against an amount the principal owes the third party under the contract.*

(4) *When an agent makes a contract on behalf of an undisclosed principal,*
- (a) *the third party may set off*
  - (i) *any amount that the agent independently owed the third party at the time the agent made the contract and*
  - (ii) *any amount that the agent thereafter independently comes to owe the third party until the third party has notice that the agent acts on behalf of a principal against an amount the third party owes the principal under the contract;*
- (b) *after the third party has notice that the agent acts on behalf of a principal, the third party may not set off any amount that the agent thereafter independently comes to owe the third party against an amount the third party owes the principal under the contract unless the principal consents; and*
- (c) *the principal may not set off any amount that the third party independently owes the agent against an amount that the principal owes the third party under the contract, unless the principal and the third party agree otherwise.*

(3) *Unless otherwise agreed, an agent who is a party to a contract may not set off any amount that the principal independently owes the agent against an amount that the agent owes the third party under the contract. However, with the principal's consent, the agent may set off any amount that the principal could set off against an amount that the principal owes the third party under the contract.*

§ 6.04 Principal Does Not Exist Or Lacks Capacity.

Unless the third party agrees otherwise, a person who makes a contract with a third party purportedly as an agent on behalf of a principal becomes a party to the contract if the purported agent knows or has reason to know that the purported principal does not exist or lacks capacity to be a party to a contract.

§ 6.07 Settlement With Agent By Principal Or Third Party

(1) *A principal's payment to or settlement of accounts with an agent discharges the principal's liability to a third party with whom the agent has made a contract on the principal's behalf only when the principal acts in reasonable reliance on a manifestation by the third party, not induced by misrepresentation by the agent, that the agent has settled the account with the third party.*

(2) *A third party's payment to or settlement of accounts with an agent discharges the third party's liability to the principal if the agent acts with actual or apparent authority in accepting the payment or settlement.*

(3) *When an agent has made a contract on behalf of an undisclosed principal,*

(a) until the third party has notice of the principal's existence, the third party's payment to or settlement of accounts with the agent discharges the third party's liability to the principal;

(b) after the third party has notice of the principal's existence, the third party's payment to or settlement of accounts with the agent discharges the third party's liability to the principal if the agent acts with actual or apparent authority in accepting the payment or settlement; and

(c) after receiving notice of the principal's existence, the third party may demand reasonable proof of the principal's identity and relationship to the agent. Until such proof is received, the third party's payment to or settlement of accounts in good faith with the agent discharges the third party's liability to the principal.

Principal's Liability

Contracts

When an agent acts within the powers the principal conferred to him (actual or apparent), the principal is bound to third-parties by the agent's acts. The principal's liability does not change if the agent is also liable, or even if he receives no benefit from the action. Whether the principal was disclosed (identified or unidentified) or undisclosed also does not change his liability to third persons for authorized acts by his agent. If the agent engages in an unauthorized act, however, then the principal will generally not be liable for the unauthorized act, but may be liable for any authorized act that can be separated from the tainted action.

§ 7.03 Principal's Liability--In General

(1) A principal is subject to direct liability to a third party harmed by an agent's conduct when

(a) as stated in § 7.04, the agent acts with actual authority or the principal ratifies the agent's conduct

(i) the agent's conduct is tortious, or

(ii) the agent's conduct, if that of the principal, would subject the principal to tort liability; or

(b) as stated in § 7.05, the principal is negligent in selecting, supervising, or otherwise controlling the agent; or

(c) as stated in § 7.06, the principal delegates performance of a duty to use care to protect other persons or their property to an agent who fails to perform the duty.

(2) A principal is subject to vicarious liability to a third party harmed by an agent's conduct when

(a) as stated in § 7.07, the agent is an employee who commits a tort while acting within the scope of employment; or

(b) as stated in § 7.08, the agent commits a tort when acting with apparent authority in dealing with a third party on or purportedly on behalf of the principal.

§ 7.04 Agent Acts With Actual Authority. *A principal is subject to liability to a third party harmed by an agent's conduct when the agent's conduct is within the scope of the agent's actual authority or ratified by the principal; and*

(1) the agent's conduct is tortious, or

(2) the agent's conduct, if that of the principal, would subject the principal to tort liability.

§ 7.05 Principal's Negligence In Conducting Activity Through Agent; Principal's Special Relationship With Another Person

(1) A principal who conducts an activity through an agent is subject to liability for harm to a third party caused by the agent's conduct if the harm was caused by the principal's negligence in selecting, training, retaining, supervising, or otherwise controlling the agent.

(2) When a principal has a special relationship with another person, the principal owes that person a duty of reasonable care with regard to risks arising out of the relationship, including the risk that agents of the principal will harm the person with whom the principal has such a special relationship.

§ 7.06 Failure In Performance Of Principal's Duty Of Protection. *A principal required by contract or otherwise by law to protect another cannot avoid liability by delegating performance of the duty, whether or not the delegate is an agent.*

§ 7.07 Employee Acting Within Scope Of Employment

(1) An employer is subject to vicarious liability for a tort committed by its employee acting within the scope of employment.

(2) An employee acts within the scope of employment when performing work assigned by the employer or engaging in a course of conduct subject to the employer's control. An employee's act is not within the scope of employment when it occurs within an independent course of conduct not intended by the employee to serve any purpose of the employer.

(3) For purposes of this section,

(a) an employee is an agent whose principal controls or has the right to control the manner and means of the agent's performance of work, and

(b) the fact that work is performed gratuitously does not relieve a principal of liability.

§ 7.08 Agent Acts With Apparent Authority. *A principal is subject to vicarious liability for a tort committed by an agent in dealing or communicating with a third party on or purportedly on behalf of the principal when actions taken by the* *agent with apparent authority constitute the tort or enable the agent to conceal its commission.*

§ 6.09 Effect Of Judgment Against Agent Or Principal. *When an agent has made a contract with a third party on behalf of a principal, unless the contract provides otherwise,*

>   (1) *the liability, if any, of the principal or the agent to the third party is not discharged if the third party obtains a judgment against the other; and*

>   (2) *the liability, if any, of the principal or the agent to the third party is discharged to the extent a judgment against the other is satisfied.*

§ 6.10 Agent's Implied Warranty Of Authority. *A person who purports to make a contract, representation, or conveyance to or with a third party on behalf of another person, lacking power to bind that person, gives an implied warranty of authority to the third party and is subject to liability to the third party for damages for loss caused by breach of that warranty, including loss of the benefit expected from performance by the principal, unless*

>   (1) *the principal or purported principal ratifies the act as stated in § 4.01; or*

>   (2) *the person who purports to make the contract, representation, or conveyance gives notice to the third party that no warranty of authority is given; or*

>   (3) *the third party knows that the person who purports to make the contract, representation, or conveyance acts without actual authority.*

Torts

A principal may be directly liable to a third-party for his agent's tortious conduct. Situations giving rise to the principal's liability include (1) the agent engaged in the tortious conduct while acting with actual authority; (2) the principal was negligent in selecting, supervising, or otherwise controlling the agent; or (3) the principal told the agent to use due care in protecting another person's property and the agent failed to perform that duty. Of course, the principal is directly liable to the third-party for his own tortious conduct.

The principal may be vicariously liable for the agent's conduct where (1) the agent is an employee of the principal and commits a tort within the scope of his employment; or (2) the agent commits a tort while acting with apparent authority when dealing with a third-party.

§ 2.04 Respondeat Superior. *An employer is subject to liability for torts committed by employees while acting within the scope of their employment.*

§ 3.02 Formal Requirements. *If the law requires a writing or record signed by the principal to evidence an agent's authority to bind a principal to a contract or other transaction, the principal is not bound in the absence of such a writing or record. A* *principal may be estopped to assert the lack of such a writing or record when a third party has been induced to make a detrimental change in position by the reasonable belief that an agent has authority to bind the principal that is traceable to a manifestation made by the principal.*

Liability – *Disclosure of Principal*

Southwestern Bell Media, Inc. v. Trepper
784 S.W.2d 68 (Tex. App. — Dallas 1989)

Southwestern Bell Media, Inc. (Bell) sued Elliot L. Trepper, doing business as Dallas Building Systems, for breach of contract. Trepper attempted to avoid liability on the contract by claiming that he was the agent for Innovative Metal Building Concepts, Inc., doing business as Dallas Building Systems. Bell now appeals an adverse judgment and raises six points of error. We sustain Bell's first two points of error.

Prior to the making of the contract in question, Southwestern Bell Telephone Company entered into at least one written Yellow Pages advertising contract with "Dallas Building Systems." That contract was dated January 23, 1984, and was signed by Michael Irvin on the line marked "Applicant (Customer or Authorized Agent)." Irvin showed his title to be "P. Owner," as appears underneath the signature line marked "Title" beside Irvin's signature. Above the line marked "Title" and next to the preprinted word "Contract" appeared the typed words "J. Gonzales & M. Irvin." Near the top of the contract appear the words "Dallas Building Systems, 2511 N. Walton Walker, Steel Fabricators" alongside a telephone number "688–1698."

The two contracts on which Bell sued Trepper contained the wording "Dallas Building Systems, 2511 N. Walton Walker, Steel Fabricators" alongside a telephone number "688–1698" near the top of the contracts. The first of the two contracts was dated May 8, 1985, and the second was dated April 15, 1986. Trepper signed his name on the two contracts on the line marked "Advertiser," showing his title to be "President." Below Trepper's signature on both contracts appears preprinted language stating that the "advertiser warrants that he personally or as agent has the authority to request and agree to pay for such advertising." At trial, Bell judicially admitted that this contract language was an acknowledgement by Bell that the person signing the contract form in the space above the word "advertiser" could sign the contract solely as an agent for the advertiser without agreeing to be personally liable for the cost of the advertising.

At the time of the execution of the two contracts on which Bell sued, Dallas Building Systems was a name being used by a corporation called Innovative Metal Building Concepts, Inc. Innovative Metal Building Concepts, Inc. also did business under the name Dallas Building Systems Co., as evidenced by an assumed name certificate filed in the Dallas County assumed name records on January 27, 1986. Innovative Metal Building Concepts, Inc. was incorporated on October 29, 1984. Mike Irvin was president of Innovative Metal Building Concepts, Inc. Dallas Building Systems was also a name being used by a partnership calling itself both Dallas Building Systems Company and Dallas Building Systems Co. Its partners included Mike Irvin.

Trepper was part owner and president of Pebcor Corporation. In approximately March 1985, Dallas Building Systems, through Michael Irvin, requested Pebcor Corporation, a company of which Trepper was part owner and president, to act as a consultant to Dallas Building Systems. It was through this consulting relationship between Dallas Building Systems and Pebcor that Michael Irvin, the president of Innovative Metal Building Concepts, Inc., gave authority to Trepper to sign the Yellow Pages contracts as President of Dallas Building Systems. Trepper testified at trial that he believed he was signing the contracts on behalf of Innovative Metal Building Concepts, Inc. doing business as Dallas Building Systems.

At trial, Trepper further testified that he indicated he was signing on behalf of Dallas Building Systems by writing the word "President" above the line marked "Title" alongside his signature. Trepper stated that he did not intend to be personally bound when he signed the contracts for Dallas Building Systems and signified that to Tom Gilmour, the sales representative of Bell, by signing the contracts as "President." Trepper testified that he signed the contracts in question and designated his title on the contracts as "President" in the presence of Gilmour. At the time the contracts were executed, Gilmour met with Trepper at Pebcor's office at 2002 Quincy in Dallas, which was a different address than Dallas Building Systems' office at 2511 N. Walton Walker. Trepper stated that at the time of the signing of the first contract in May 1985, Gilmour asked why the meeting was at Pebcor's office and that he explained to Gilmour Pebcor's consulting relationship with Dallas Building Systems.

Gilmour testified that he did not know that Trepper was an agent for Innovative Metal Building Systems, Inc. He stated that he understood that Dallas Building Systems was buying the advertising but that he did not consider whether Trepper was agreeing to be personally liable because "it's not something that a sales rep usually worries about when he's out in the field." Gilmour testified that although Trepper wrote his title on the contracts as "President," Gilmour thought that Dallas Building Systems was probably incorporated, but that it was also possible that Dallas Building Systems was a partnership or a sole proprietorship. Gilmour stated that if Trepper had written "Owner" on the line used to identify the signing party's "title", he would have thought that Trepper was personally responsible. Gilmour further testified that in connection with the first contract Trepper signed, Bell must have obtained a credit application which asked whether the advertiser was a sole proprietorship, partnership, or corporation because the contract represented a substantial increase in the cost of advertising over the previous year's contract; however, Bell did not produce a credit application in response to a request for production calling for such documents.

Bell's billing records show that the billing account for the Dallas Building Systems' advertising charges was maintained by Bell under the name and address "J. Gonzales & M. Irvin, Ptnrs dba Dls Bldg Sys, 2511 N. Walton Walker, Dallas, TX 75212." The wording "Ptnrs dba Dls Bldg Sys" meant partners doing business as Dallas Building Systems. Bell never sent any bill or invoice to Trepper for the Dallas Building Systems Yellow Pages advertisements, and Trepper's name does not appear in Bell's billing records for the Dallas Building Systems' advertising. During several meetings between Trepper and the Bell representative in approximately May or June 1987 about the 1987–1988 Yellow Pages advertisement for Pebcor Corporation, the Bell representative inquired of Trepper about the Dallas Building Systems account (which was almost a year delinquent) but neither asked nor demanded that Trepper pay the account nor suggested to Trepper that Bell considered Trepper to be liable for the account.

In its first two points of error, Bell asserts that the trial court erred in overruling its objection to the submission of jury question number one because it improperly placed upon Bell the burden to negate Trepper's affirmative defense of agency and because it omitted material elements of that defense. Specifically, Bell maintains that Trepper, to avoid liability for his signature on a contract, must have disclosed to the other contracting party both his intent to sign as a representative and the identity of his principal. Bell also contends that the use of a trade name is not a sufficient disclosure of the identity of the principal or of the fact of agency. *See Lachmann v. Houston Chronicle Publishing Co.*, 375 S.W.2d 783, 785 (Tex.Civ.App.—Austin 1964, writ ref'd n.r.e.). Thus, Bell argues that because Trepper filed an answer alleging that he signed the contracts in a representative capacity only, Trepper had the burden of proving his affirmative defense of agency and of obtaining jury findings that the agency existed and that the agency was disclosed. *See Glendon Invs., Inc. v. Brooks*, 748 S.W.2d 465, 467 (Tex.App.—Houston [1st Dist.] 1988, writ denied). …

…Bell requested that the jury be instructed "that a person signing a contract is liable unless an agency is disclosed," and that an "[a]gency relationship is a relationship in which there is consent by one person to another to act on the former's behalf." We conclude that Bell properly preserved error regarding the submission of jury question number one and Trepper's failure to submit an issue on disclosure. *See Morris v. Holt*, 714 S.W.2d 311, 312 (Tex.1986); *Clarostat Mfg., Inc. v. Alcor Aviation, Inc.*, 544 S.W.2d 788, 795 (Tex.Civ.App.—San Antonio 1976, writ ref'd n.r.e.); TEX.R.CIV.P. 278. Trepper waived his affirmative defense of agency. *See* TEX.R.CIV.P. 279.

Before addressing Bell's points of error, we note that it is well settled that the law does not presume agency. *Lachmann*, 375 S.W.2d at 785. As explained in *Mahoney v. Pitman*, 43 S.W.2d 143, 146 (Tex.Civ.App.—Amarillo 1931, writ ref'd):

> *It is the duty of the agent, if he would avoid personal liability on a contract entered into by him on behalf of the principal, to disclose not only the fact that he is acting in a representative capacity but also the identity of his principal, as the person dealt with is not bound to inquire whether or not the agent is acting as such for another.*

Thus, an agent, who fails to disclose the fact of his agency to a third party with whom he contracts, may be held personally liable on the contract. *Glendon*, 748 S.W.2d at 467, citing *Heinrichs v. Evins Personnel Consultants, Inc. Number One*, 486 S.W.2d 935, 937 (Tex.1972); *see also Bayoud v. Shank, Irwin & Conant*, 774 S.W.2d 22, 24 (Tex.App.—Dallas 1989, no writ). This is true even though the agent has disclosed *a* principal but has failed to disclose the *true* principal. *See Wynne v. Adcock Pipe & Supply*, 761 S.W.2d 67, 69 (Tex.App.—San Antonio 1988, writ denied); *A To Z Rental Center v. Burris*, 714 S.W.2d 433, 436–37 (Tex.App.—Austin 1986, writ ref'd n.r.e.); *Carter v. Walton*, 469 S.W.2d 462, 470–71 (Tex.Civ.App.—Corpus Christi 1971, writ ref'd n.r.e.); *Lachmann*, 375 S.W.2d at 785. Therefore, disclosure is an essential element of the affirmative defense of agency in order to avoid personal liability on a contract. *Glendon*, 748 S.W.2d at 467. Moreover, the agent is not relieved from personal liability merely because the person with whom he dealt had a means of discovering that the agent was acting in a representative capacity, and "knowledge" of the real principal, irrespective of the source, is the test, which does mean actual knowledge, not suspicion. *See Anderson v. Smith*, 398 S.W.2d 635, 637 (Tex.Civ.App.—Dallas 1965, no writ); *Burris*, 714 S.W.2d at 435. In this instance, it is undisputed that Trepper signed the two contracts on which Bell sued. It is also undisputed that Trepper signed in a representative capacity as evidenced by his signature on the contract.

However, a question arises as to whether Trepper accurately communicated his representative capacity since he was not the president of Dallas Building Systems. In fact, he was signing on behalf of the president of Dallas Building Systems.

The rule concerning the burden of proof on the agency defense is as follows:

> [W]here one is sought to be held personally liable on a contract, and his defense rests on the ground that he made the agreement as the agent of another, that person has the burden of proving all material facts necessary to exonerate him from personal responsibility. More specifically, he must show that he was, in fact, acting as the agent of his principal in making the contract, that he had *informed the other party to* the agreement of his true legal status in the matter, and that he had also *disclosed to that other party the name* of the *alleged principal for whom he was purportedly acting*. *Id.*, citing 3 TEX.JUR.3d § 226, p. 310 (1980) (emphasis original).

Trepper argues that he, in fact, did not have to assert an affirmative defense since Bell failed to present a prima facie case. Trepper maintains that the contracts themselves unambiguously show that because he signed in a representative capacity and disclosed his principal, Dallas Building Systems, he is not individually liable. Thus, Trepper asserts that the issue of liability is to be decided as a matter of law. In the alternative, Trepper contends that if the contracts are ambiguous, he is, nevertheless, free of individual liability because all of the evidence established that both Bell and Trepper understood and intended that Trepper would not be individually liable.

…To avoid personal liability, an agent has two duties. He must: (1) disclose his representative capacity, and (2) identify his true principal. *A to Z Rental*, 714 S.W.2d at 435. A trade name inadequately discloses the fact of agency or the identification of the true principal. *See Lachmann* at 785. Even though by signing as president, Trepper may have fulfilled his first duty, he, nevertheless, failed in his second duty because he did not disclose his true principal. Failing to fulfill both of his duties necessary to avoid personal liability, Trepper assumed personal liability when he signed the contract. Furthermore, Trepper failed to submit a jury question on the issue of disclosure….

Because we hold that the trial court improperly refused to submit an issue on disclosure, and, thus, reversible error was committed, it is not necessary to the disposition of this appeal that we address all of Bell's remaining points of error.

Based on the record before us, we conclude, as a matter of law, that the parties did enter into a contract for advertising and that Trepper agreed to pay for the advertising. Because

Trepper failed to obtain affirmative jury findings on his defense of disclosed agency, he is individually liable. Accordingly, the judgment of the trial court is reversed, and judgment is rendered against appellee Elliot Trepper, individually and d/b/a Dallas Building Systems.

Terminating the agency relationship

The principal and agent can only terminate the relationship either by an act, an agreement, or by operation of law. Until one of those three things occurs, an agency relationship is presumed to continue. The parties can mutually agree to terminate the relationship. Absent express agreement, the duo's conduct can show mutual assent to terminate the relationship through their conduct. Or the parties could have limited the agency relationship to a certain time or date certain or upon the accomplishment of a certain act. Once the date or time occurs or the agent completes the act, then the agency relationship is terminated.

In forming the agreement, one of the parties may have reserved the right to terminate the relationship. If so, upon the happening of the termination-causing event the person with the right to terminate generally must notify the other party that he is terminating the relationship.

In general, an agency relationship may be terminated by operation of law e.g. where one of the parties dies. The Third Restatement of Agency provides that the death of an individual principal terminates the agent's actual authority, but that termination is effective only when the agent has notice of the principal's death. Where the agent's position or authority is coupled with an interest, it does not, as a general rule, terminate with the act or death of the principal. It is thus the case that "[a] A power of attorney coupled with an interest, whether durable or not, cannot be revoked, even by death of the principal. A power coupled with an interest arises when the agent receives an interest in the property that is the subject of the agency contemporaneously with the power of attorney." (Aloysius A. Leopold, 3A Tex. Prac., Land Titles And Title Examination § 11.9 (3d ed. 2013)).

§ 3.07 Death, Cessation Of Existence, And Suspension Of Powers.

(1) The death of an individual agent terminates the agent's actual authority.

(2) The death of an individual principal terminates the agent's actual authority. The termination is effective only when the agent has notice of the principal's death. The termination is also effective as against a third party with whom the agent deals when the third party has notice of the principal's death.

(3) When an agent that is not an individual ceases to exist or commences a process that will lead to cessation of existence or when its powers are suspended, the agent's actual authority terminates except as provided by law.

(4) When a principal that is not an individual ceases to exist or commences a process that will lead to cessation of its existence or when its powers are suspended, the agent's actual authority terminates except as provided by law.

Similarly, where the principal loses the capacity to become a party to a transaction (e.g., the principal becomes mentally incompetent), then the relationship is suspended until the principal regains capacity.

§ 3.06 Termination Of Actual Authority--In General

An agent's actual authority may be terminated by:

(1) the agent's death, cessation of existence, or suspension of powers as stated in § 3.07(1) and (3); or

(2) the principal's death, cessation of existence, or suspension of powers as stated in § 3.07(2) and (4); or

(3) the principal's loss of capacity, as stated in § 3.08(1) and (3); or

(4) an agreement between the agent and the principal or the occurrence of circumstances on the basis of which the agent should reasonably conclude that the principal no longer would assent to the agent's taking action on the principal's behalf, as stated in § 3.09; or

(5) a manifestation of revocation by the principal to the agent, or of renunciation by the agent to the principal, as stated in § 3.10(1); or

(6) the occurrence of circumstances specified by statute.

§ 3.08 Loss Of Capacity

(1) An individual principal's loss of capacity to do an act terminates the agent's actual authority to do the act. The termination is effective only when the agent has notice that the principal's loss of capacity is permanent or that the principal has been adjudicated to lack capacity. The termination is also effective as against a third party with whom the agent deals when the third party has notice that the principal's loss of capacity is permanent or that the principal has been adjudicated to lack capacity.

(2) A written instrument may make an agent's actual authority effective upon a principal's loss of capacity, or confer it irrevocably regardless of such loss.

(3) If a principal that is not an individual loses capacity to do an act, its agent's actual authority to do the act is terminated.

§ 3.09 Termination By Agreement Or By Occurrence Of changed Circumstances.

An agent's actual authority terminates (1) as agreed by the agent and the principal, subject to the provisions of § 3.10; or (2) upon the occurrence of circumstances on the basis of which the agent should reasonably conclude that the principal no longer would assent to the agent's taking action on the principal's behalf.

§ 3.10 Manifestation Terminating Actual Authority

(1) Notwithstanding any agreement between principal and agent, an agent's actual authority terminates if the agent renounces it by a manifestation to the principal or if the principal revokes the agent's actual authority by a manifestation to the agent. A revocation or a renunciation is effective when the other party has notice of it.

(2) A principal's manifestation of revocation is, unless otherwise agreed, ineffective to terminate a power given as security or to terminate a proxy to vote securities or other membership or ownership interests that is made irrevocable in compliance with applicable legislation. See §§ 3.12-3.13.

§ 3.11 Termination Of Apparent Authority

(1) The termination of actual authority does not by itself end any apparent authority held by an agent.

(2) Apparent authority ends when it is no longer reasonable for the third party with whom an agent deals to believe that the agent continues to act with actual authority.

§ 3.12 Power Given As Security; Irrevocable Proxy

(1) A power given as security is a power to affect the legal relations of its creator that is created in the form of a manifestation of actual authority and held for the benefit of the holder or a third person. This power is given to protect a legal or equitable title or to secure the performance of a duty apart from any duties owed the holder of the power by its creator that are incident to a relationship of agency under § 1.01. It is given upon the creation of the duty or title or for consideration. It is distinct from actual authority that the holder may exercise if the holder is an agent of the creator of the power.

(2) A power to exercise voting rights associated with securities or a membership interest may be conferred on a proxy through a manifestation of actual authority. The power may be given as security under (1) and may be made irrevocable in compliance with applicable legislation.

§ 3.13 Termination Of Power Given As Security Or Irrevocable Proxy

(1) A power given as security or an irrevocable proxy is terminated by an event that

    (a) discharges the obligation secured by the power or terminates the interest secured or supported by the proxy, or

    (b) makes its execution illegal or impossible, or

    (c) constitutes an effective surrender of the power or proxy by the person for whose benefit it was created or conferred.

(2) Unless otherwise agreed, neither a power given as security nor a proxy made irrevocable as provided in § 3.12(2) is terminated by:

    (a) a manifestation revoking the power or proxy made by the person who created it; or

    (b) surrender of the power or proxy by its holder if it is held for the benefit of another person, unless that person consents; or

(c) loss of capacity by the creator or the holder of the power or proxy; or

(d) death of the holder of the power or proxy, unless the holder's death terminates the interest secured or supported by the power or proxy; or

(e) death of the creator of the power or proxy, if the power or proxy is given as security for the performance of a duty that does not terminate with the death of its creator.

Hartford v. McGillicuddy
103 Me. 224, 68 A. 860 (1907)

This is an action of assumpsit brought by a real estate agent to recover a commission of 2 per cent on the price fixed by the owner for the sale of real estate, the plaintiff claiming that he procured a customer on the authorized terms, but that the defendant refused to make the conveyance.

The jury found for the plaintiff, and the defendant by motion asks to have the verdict set aside on two grounds-first, because whatever authority had been given by him to the agent to make a sale had been revoked by operation of law; and, second, because as a matter of fact the plaintiff did not procure the would-be purchaser. So far as material to the questions before us, the evidence shows the following facts:

The plaintiff is a real estate agent residing in Lewiston, where the defendant also resided up to the year 1896, when he moved with his family to North Jay, where he has since made his home. Just prior to his leaving Lewiston the defendant placed in the plaintiff's hands for sale certain vacant real estate in Lewiston, the price as claimed by the defendant to be $3,000, or, as claimed by the plaintiff, the asking price to be $3,000, but the lowest figure to be $2,800. The plaintiff at once placed his signs upon the land, where they remained for many years, and, as he says, until shortly after this suit began. From time to time he endeavored to sell the property to various parties, but without success. In 1901 or 1902 he wrote the defendant, suggesting the advisability of selling off the wood lot; but the defendant preferred to sell the whole together. In 1903 he had an interview with one Bridgham concerning a sale, but the latter wished only to purchase one portion, and negotiations therefore ceased for the time. In December, 1905, a Mr. Whitten, who was interested with Mr. Bridgham, wrote directly to the defendant, offering $2,000 for the property, and the defendant replied, declining that offer, but making a counter offer to sell for $2,800. Early in April, 1906, Mr. Whitten went to North Jay to interview the defendant, but the latter refused to stand by his offer. On April 19, 1906, Mr. Bridgham went again to the plaintiff, who knew nothing of the attempted trade between Mr. Whitten and the defendant, renewed the negotiations of some years before, and offered $2,800 for the entire property,

88

which the plaintiff accepted. A check for $100 was given on that day to bind the bargain, and within a week a tender of the remaining $2,700 was made to the plaintiff. The plaintiff notified the defendant of the sale as soon as it was made, and the defendant's wife, who held the title, replied, at first denying the plaintiff's authority to sell at any price, and later denying that he was authorized to sell for $2,800, and refusing to make the transfer. This suit resulted.

The defendant's first contention is that, where no time limit is agreed upon by the parties, a real estate broker is entitled to only a reasonable time in which to find a purchaser, and, if no purchaser is found within a reasonable time, the contract terminates by operation of law, that what is a reasonable time is a question of law, and that under the facts of this case the court must hold that the authority given to the plaintiff in 1896 was revoked by operation of law prior to 1906.

We are unable to reach that conclusion. The relation between these parties is that of principal and agent, and the rights and liabilities of a real estate agent under such circumstances are well settled. The principal in 1896 conferred upon the agent the authority to sell the real estate at a given price. It is true that no definite period of time was expressly agreed upon during which the agency was to continue. That was unnecessary. Its duration was fixed in another way. It was established for a particular purpose, and was therefore in the contemplation of the parties to continue until that purpose was accomplished, unless sooner terminated by revocation or otherwise. 1 Clark and Skyles, Agency, § 154. The plaintiff was appointed to sell this land, and his agency, once established, was presumed to continue until the sale was effected, and the burden was on the defendant to rebut the presumption. Bourke v. Van Keuren, 20 Colo. 95, 36 Pac. 882. That burden the defendant has not sustained. Such termination may be proved by express revocation on the part of the principal (Sibbald v. Bethlehem Iron Co., 83 N. Y. 378, 38 Am. Rep. 441), or by such conduct of the parties or such circumstances as would justify the conclusion that there had been in fact a termination. But that is a question of fact for the jury, and not of law for the court. The only evidence in this case tending to prove such termination by implication was the lapse of a period of 10 years between the creation of the agency and the accomplishment of its purpose. That was simply one fact to be considered by the jury, and over against it was other evidence tending strongly to negative such a termination. The plaintiff's signs remained on the premises, and more or less correspondence passed between the parties during all these years. The defendant had never returned to Lewiston to attend to the sale of the property himself, nor had he withdrawn it from the plaintiff's hands and placed it in the charge of any other agent. Of striking significance too is his admission that in his interview with Mr. Whitten he asked the latter if the plaintiff had anything to do with the sale, and that the reason for this inquiry was to ascertain whether the plaintiff was instrumental in making the sale. He doubtless had in mind the question of commissions, but that could only arise in case the plaintiff were still his agent. It is evident that the continuance of the agency was recognized by the defendant as well as by the plaintiff and the purchaser.

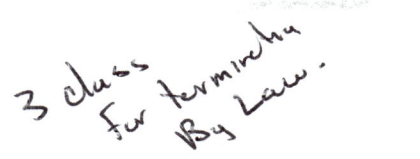

Contracts of agency may be terminated by operation of law, but such cases fall within one of three classes: a change in the law, making the required acts illegal; a change in the subject-matter of the contract, as the destruction of the property by fire; or a change in the condition of the parties, as by death or insanity. 1 Clark and Skyles, Agency, § 181. Within none of these classes does the present case fall.

The authorities cited by the defendant as to the reasonable time within which an offer of reward is held to continue are not analogous. In those cases the proposal is made to all the world, and the courts properly hold that such proposal as a mere offer must be accepted by performance within a reasonable time, or, in the absence of other facts, the law will presume a revocation after a reasonable time. Mitchell v. Abbott, 86 Me. 338, 29 Atl. 1118, 25 L. R. A. 503, 41 Am. St. Rep. 559.

But in the case at bar there was a complete contract of agency for a special purpose, and it was presumed to continue until that purpose was accomplished, unless revoked in fact. There was no evidence of revocation in this case other than the mere lapse of time, and the jury have found that not to be sufficient, in which conclusion we concur.

The second point raised by the defendant is that the evidence does not sustain the finding of the jury that the plaintiff procured a purchaser for the land in 1906 for $2,800. The rule as laid down in recent decisions in this state requires that the agent shall procure and produce to the principal a customer willing and prepared to purchase and pay for the property at the price and on the terms given by the principal to the agent. Garcelon v. Tibbetts, 84 Me. 148, 24 Atl. 797; Smith v. Lawrence, 98 Me. 92, 56 Atl. 455.

In the case at bar the jury returned special findings that the defendant in 1896 authorized the plaintiff to sell the land in question for $2,800, and that he procured a purchaser for the land for the price of $2,800. The precise point was therefore brought sharply to their attention. These special findings as well as the general verdict are sustained by the evidence. The plaintiff's negotiations with the purchaser Bridgham began three years before the sale, and then were broken off. The plaintiff alone brought the matter to Mr. Bridgham's attention. These negotiations were renewed and completed in April, 1906. The fact that in the meantime Mr. Bridgham's partner had also unsuccessfully negotiated with the owner ought not to destroy the plaintiff's claim, as the plaintiff was in entire ignorance of that fact, and acted in the utmost good faith in making the sale. To hold otherwise would be to afford too great temptation to owners of property to repudiate the commissions of their agents after a sale had been consummated.

If a real estate broker procures and produces a purchaser ready and willing and able to complete the purchase on the authorized terms, and through the fault of the owner the sale is not consummated, the commission is due. McGavock v. Woodlief, 20 How. (U. S.) 221, 15 L. Ed. 884; Garcelon v. Tibbetts, 84 Me. 148, 24 Atl. 797. The jury have found that state of facts in this case, and the evidence does not warrant the reversal of the verdict. Motion overruled.

Agency Problem Set

1. John opened the doors of St. John's convenience store to the public in 1985. After 25 years of hard work as the owner and manager and experiencing tremendous success, he sold the stores to Chen in October 2010. Chen retained John as manager and kept the store name, thus leading the public to believe that ownership had not changed hands. Two years later, John fully retired. Chen asked John to come back to work only for Black Friday 2012 . Chen told John not to sign any new contracts for the supply of cigarettes since Chen was traveling to China that weekend and was going to explore new supply sources in China. Rothman Cigarettes, Inc. called John on Black Friday and offered him a new 2-year contract for the supply of cigarettes. The offer was the juiciest he has ever received and John accepted, believing that Chen would be pleased. Rothman faxed the contract that same day and John signed in his capacity as manager. It was undisputed that convenience store managers routinely enter into such contracts. Chen found an even better deal in China and rejected the Rothman deal. Rothman successfully sued Chen, with the judge noting that principals are bound by contracts concluded by agents acting with authority.

    What type of authority did John have?

2. Abby, an orthodontist in Pearland, asked the office receptionist, Van Buren, to purchase an iPad on her behalf from Best Buy. Abby wrote a check for $500 to cover the cost of a particular version she saw at a Best Buy store in Houston. Van Buren forgot to take the check with him on his way to the store. He opted to pay with his personal credit card and to seek reimbursement later. Van Buren informed the cashier that his boss, Dr. Abby, really needed the iPad that day for her business and that he would bring the check the next morning. Due to a sudden power surge, the store lost the ability, momentarily, to process credit card transactions. The cashier took the credit card information with Van Buren's signature and allowed Van Buren to take the iPad but he misplaced the iPad in a taxi cab. The credit card was declined when the cashier entered the information into the system after Van Buren's departure. Abby collected the check from Van Buren and refused to release it, arguing that since she never saw the iPad, she bears no responsibility for paying for it. The court agreed with her and held that only Van Buren is responsible. Unfortunately, Van Buren has no money. Believing that it has no legal recourse, Best Buy is considering appealing to Abby's "good conscience" to secure the payment.

    Does Best Buy have a viable case to pursue in court?

3. In the hospital, and eager to raise funds for additional treatment, Solis told his daughter, Avon, to sell his land in the city. A few weeks after the instruction, Solis slipped into a coma. Solis's first son, Junior, who would inherit the land, does not want the property sold. As Avon was about to close a deal, Junior challenged the proposed sale on the basis

that Avon could not validly transfer the title, having not been properly appointed. Two other patients heard Solis when he gave the instruction to Avon and testified accordingly in court afterwards. The court dismissed the challenge, stating that no formality is required to create an agency and that under Agency Law, an agent steps into the shoes of the principal, hence the maxim *qui facit per alium facit per se*.

Will Junior prevail on appeal?

4. Ibrahim and Muhammad are twin brothers who jointly purchased some land in Provo Canyon, Utah. In September 2011, they approached Lawyer about selling the land to him for $6 million. Lawyer performed a title search to verify that the property was owned by the twins and was accurately valued. In October 2011, to settle a debt owed to their cousin, Suleiman, the brothers agreed to transfer equal parts of their interest to the cousin. Thus, each of them owned one-third interest in the property. Suleiman was opposed to selling the land to Lawyer for $6 million and preferred a sale to the Coast Guard. Lawyer neither knew of Suleiman's interest in the property nor of his objection. The brothers continued negotiations without informing Lawyer of these facts, because they felt it could delay or jeopardize the transaction. Nevertheless, they made sure that title to the property was properly changed (to include Suleiman) and recorded in the appropriate government office. In December 2011, Ibrahim and Muhammad deeded the property to Lawyer as required by the contract of sale. Obviously, Suleiman did not sign as his name did not appear anywhere on the deed. Lawyer paid through two $3 million checks made out separately to Ibrahim and Muhammad. The brothers sent a check of $2 million to Suleiman for his share of the proceeds along with a note informing him of the sale price and the manner in which the proceeds were distributed. Suleiman cashed the check and made no objection until six months after the sale and three months after he received his share of the proceeds. He had discovered that the Coast Guard would have paid up to $7 million for the land. At that point, Suleiman brought a suit to set aside the sale. Lawyer moved for summary judgment, contending that by keeping silent after collecting his share of the proceeds and by accepting the benefits, Suleiman impliedly ratified the transaction. The court granted the motion, holding that "acquiescence may be evidence of ratification." Suleiman has appealed.

Does he have a good chance of success?

5. Jamie worked for Global Haulers, Inc. in Dallas as a delivery truck driver for eleven years and resigned in 2011. Immediately thereafter, he set up business for himself, hauling goods from and to the Houston area. Jamie did not sign a non-compete contract while employed with Global Haulers. He solicited business from some customers of his erstwhile employer, whose names and addresses he was fortunate to remember. He also used written lists of customers that he compiled during the course of his employment, a copy of which he took with him as he departed. Global Haulers noticed a major drop in

business volume and believed that Jamie was responsible for diverting some business that would have come to the company. Accordingly, Global Haulers brought a lawsuit seeking a disgorgement of all the profits earned by Jamie from doing business with its former customers. The court held that Jamie had not done anything wrong since his duties to Global Haulers ended upon his departure. Global Haulers has appealed the decision.

Who wins?

6. Singh, a celebrated movie producer in Hollywood, recently and secretly converted from the Sikh religion and became a Christian. Nevertheless, Singh decided to make a movie about the history and principles of Christianity. He approached another well-known producer, Sly Lewis, and signed a contract with him to produce the movie. The contract stated that Sly would be paid a monthly salary and 20% of the movie's gross earnings. If for any reason the movie production is discontinued before any profit is made, Sly would be paid $50,000. Also Sly would be free to do whatever he would do as if he were the sole producer but should not let anyone know that Singh is involved in the movie in any way. Singh also told Sly orally not to use Mirafacts studios for any of the shoots because his past relationships with the studio were not good. Sly searched for suitable studios but unable to find one, rented on credit for 12 months an ultra-modern studio owned by Mirafacts, paying a 10% deposit. The studio lease agreement obligated Sly as the lessee to pay for a whole year's rent of $250,000, regardless of usage. A little while later, Singh changed his mind about making the movie and paid off Sly, who then left the US for an undisclosed location. The studio owners discovered the contract between Singh and Sly and sued Singh for the $225,000 outstanding rent on the studio lease. The trial court held that Sly had implied actual authority to rent the studio, since that was necessary to accomplish Singh's express directives and ordered Singh to pay the outstanding amount plus attorney fees. Singh appealed. The court of appeals held that Sly had apparent authority and not implied authority but ruled that the studio was not entitled to the full rent since that would be a windfall that it was not expecting.

Which of the courts had a better understanding of agency law?

7. Houston-based Agro Corporation sells, purchases, and brokers deals between sellers and purchasers of agricultural commodities. In January 2010, because of price volatility, the company's president directed the purchasing manager, Bob, who reports directly to him, not to deal in two commodities: barley and wheat. Bob ignored the directive and ordered some barley at a very good price from a farmer in Chicago who had never done business with Agro Corporation, with payment due 30 days later. His intention was to convince his boss of the wisdom of his action when the products arrive. The products arrived, his boss agreed it was a good deal, sold a small portion thereof, but when Agro's sales clerks could not sell the rest, returned them to Bob. Bob tried returning the products to the

farmer as well as payment for the quantity collected by Agro but the farmer rejected the money and the goods, demanding the full purchase price. Upon discovering that Bob acted on behalf of Agro, the farmer decided to sue both Bob and Agro.

Will the farmer succeed in holding Agro liable for the remaining amount?

8. Clint is a great actor, filmmaker and philanthropist who is highly regarded for his enormous financial contributions to social causes in the Houston area. In March 2009, he was successfully represented in a lawsuit by famed civil defense attorney, Rusty Softing. Shortly thereafter, Softing, seeking to burnish Clint's image after the bruising court battle, approached the president of a local university informing her that Clint would contribute $10 million to the school if it would name its art studio and movie theater complex after him. The ecstatic president quickly presented the matter to the Board of Regents, which readily approved the naming of the complex after Clint. The letter informing Clint of the honor did not mention anything about the name change being conditioned on a $10 million donation. Clint replied to the letter accepting the honor. Upon receipt of Clint's letter, the president called him to ascertain when he would be releasing the check. Clint replied that he was not responsible for the promised donation. The university went to court, seeking to make Clint honor the agreement Rusty had signed on his behalf. The court held that since the position of an attorney is that of an independent contractor agent, and since apparent authority may arise by position, the agreement with the university was binding on Clint.

Do you agree with the court?

9. Miranda is a broker with Quantum Mechanics, Inc., a manufacturing company in San Antonio, Texas. Miranda sells goods on behalf of the manufacturer and receives a salary and commission. She uses her own automobile in the performance of her business tasks, has discretion as to how to conduct the business, which city to visit and who to contact. In rushing to deliver some Quantum products to a valuable customer, her van hit a pedestrian trying to cross the road. The pedestrian brought a personal injury action against both Miranda and Quantum Mechanics. The court awarded compensatory damages of $250,000 to the plaintiff. The court based its ruling, in part, on the reasoning that Quantum was liable for the tort of an agent acting within the scope of employment. Quantum is considering an appeal.

Would you advise Quantum to proceed?

10. Anthony, Baker and Clay are the only directors of Angel Capital, Inc, a Texas corporation. In exonerating them from a claim seeking to attach liability to them as agents of the corporation, the court ruled they were not agents, relying on the following statement from a famous business law casebook: "Because all corporate power is vested

in the board of directors (under corporation law), the board is not subject to the corporation's control." The Texas Supreme Court recently overturned the decision, noting that since a corporation is an inanimate being that could only act through agents, the directors acted on behalf of the corporation and an agency relationship therefore existed.

Do you agree with the Supreme Court?

GENERAL PARTNERSHIPS

GENERAL PARTNERSHIPS

Core Concepts

A general partnership is an association of two or more persons (including entities) that carry on a business for profit. It is an entity distinct from the partners which means that it can own property, sue and be sued in the partnership name. Each partner is an agent of the partnership and each partner may be held personally liable for the debts and obligations of the partnership.

Nature and Formation

only intent to perform a biz as co-owners

General partnerships may be created by an oral agreement between the partners to conduct the business of the partnership. However, the partners need not have the intent to create a partnership so long as they have the intent to perform the business as co-owners for profit. All states have statutes that provide rules for operating a partnership, however, those rules are default and used only in the event that there is no written partnership agreement between the partners or when their partnership agreement is silent on the matter.

When the partners have an oral agreement and agree as to the terms of that agreement, their agreement stands. It is only when the partners have no agreement or disagree what the term of their partnership is that the statute governs.

illegal / public policy

Exception: Even when the partners agree to the term(s) of their partnership, any such term that is illegal or against public policy will be avoided and the statute (default rule) will apply in lieu of the partnership agreement.

Texas

no documentation needed.

General partnerships are not required to file any formation documents in Texas nor does Texas require the general partnership to adopt a formal written partnership agreement.

Exception: The limited liability partnership (LLP) is a general partnership that limits partner liability. The LLP is a filing entity in Texas and thus is required to register with the state in order to take advantage of limited liability.

must register

Default Entity

Generally, Texas does not recognize the de facto entity. The effect is that when an association of two or more persons desires to establish a corporation, LLC, LP or LLP but fails to meet the legal requisites for formation, the entity defaults to a general partnership. If it is a single owner of the to-be-formed business who fails to properly form a dejure entity, it will default to a sole proprietorship.

if only one   *Default*

Five Advantages of establishing the General Partnership:

1. Ease of formation, including cost
2. Flexible management structure with all partners having the right to manage
3. The general partnership is a flow through entity for purposes of taxes which means it is not taxed as a partnership
4. Shared risk
5. Limited disclosure requirements to governments and third parties

Five Disadvantages of the General Partnership structure:

1. Joint and several liability of partners
2. Limited capital
3. Risk of deadlock
4. Non-transferability of partnership shares
5. Risk of dissolution or termination on death, desire, or mental illness of a partner

From TEXAS BUSINESS ORGANIZATIONS CODE (TBOC)
NATURE AND FORMATION

§152.051. PARTNERSHIP DEFINED...

(b) Except as provided by Subsection (c) and Section 152.053(a), an association of two or more persons to carry on a business for profit as owners creates a partnership, regardless of whether:

(1) the persons intend to create a partnership; or

(2) the association is called a "partnership," "joint venture," or other name.

(c) An association or organization is not a partnership if it was created under a statute other than:

(1) this title and the provisions of Title 1 applicable to partnerships and limited partnerships;

(2) a predecessor to a statute referred to in Subdivision (1); or

(3) a comparable statute of another jurisdiction.

(d) The provisions of this chapter govern limited partnerships only to the extent provided by Sections 153.003 and 153.152 and Subchapter H, Chapter 153.

Exxon Corporation v. Breezevale Ltd
82 S.W.3d 429 (TexApp-Dallas, 2002)

OPINION

Exxon Corporation (Exxon) appeals the trial court's judgment following a jury verdict awarding Breezevale Limited (Breezevale) $34.3 million as damages for breach of an oral contract, $1 million for breach of a contract implied in law, and $3.495 million in attorneys' fees. In its first three issues, Exxon asserts (1) the evidence is legally and factually insufficient to support a finding that the parties reached an enforceable oral agreement, (2) the claimed agreement is not enforceable under the statute of frauds, and (3) the trial court incorrectly instructed the jury regarding the doctrine of promissory estoppel. In its final five issues, Exxon complains about the lost profits award, the attorneys' fees award, some of the trial court's evidentiary rulings, and the judgment being contrary to public policy.

Breezevale brings three issues in a cross appeal. Breezevale first contends the trial court erred in its calculation of interest on the breach of contract award. In two conditional cross-points, Breezevale complains of the trial court's dismissal of its breach of fiduciary duty claim by directed verdict and the trial court's exclusion of evidence.

For the reasons that follow, we reverse the trial court's award of $34.3 million on Breezevale's breach of contract claim, affirm the award of $3.495 million in attorneys' fees, and affirm the trial court's directed verdict on Breezevale's breach of fiduciary duty claim.

FACTUAL BACKGROUND

In the early 1990s, the Nigerian government opened its deepwater offshore to oil and gas exploration, inviting bids from international oil companies for deepwater blocks. Exxon submitted a bid requesting blocks 209 and 210. In June 1993, the Nigerian government formally awarded block 209 to Exxon. Exxon subsequently leveraged some of its interest in block 209, through trades and farm-ins, to acquire interests in other blocks that had been awarded to other companies.

This case arises from a dispute between Exxon and Breezevale, a company hired by Exxon to provide local assistance in its effort to procure exploration rights in Nigeria. Breezevale, a London-based corporation, operated in various countries in Europe, the Middle East, and Africa, including Nigeria. Exxon contacted Breezevale in 1990, requesting its assistance with services such as arranging appointments, conducting briefings, obtaining information and technical data on available blocks of interest to Exxon, and speaking with government officials on Exxon's behalf. Breezevale provided these types of services to Exxon over a period of approximately eighteen months, with no formal agreement in place as to Breezevale's compensation for its services. As the business relationship progressed, the parties began negotiating the terms of a contract to formalize their relationship. Although Exxon initially pursued only a short-term services agreement with Breezevale, Breezevale expressed an interest in a more involved, long-term relationship in which Breezevale would share the risk and rewards of Exxon's Nigerian exploration. Representatives of Exxon and Breezevale met several times to discuss their business relationship.

The last of these meetings occurred on April 3, 1992. In this and previous meetings, the parties discussed both a services contract and a participation agreement. The parties discussed different options that would provide Breezevale with a participation interest in Exxon's Nigerian exploration and production, including a 2 1/2 percent paid working interest, whereby Breezevale would pay 2 1/2 percent of the costs of production and receive 2 1/2 percent of the production profits. The parties' dispute as to whether an oral working interest agreement was reached at the April 3rd meeting became the basis for Breezevale's lawsuit against Exxon. Breezevale claimed Exxon offered, and it accepted, a 2 1/2 percent working interest in all of Exxon's Nigerian oil operations. Exxon claimed an agreement on essential terms was never reached and it terminated negotiations with Breezevale before a contract was formed. Neither party disputes an agreement on the services contract was never reached.

The day after the April 3, 1992 meeting, Exxon's main contact at Breezevale, Habib Bou–Habib, traveled to Nigeria to speak with the Ministry of Petroleum on Exxon's behalf. Breezevale contends the trip was made at the request of Exxon; Exxon asserts it never requested nor authorized the visit. On April 9, 1992, Habib contacted Gerald Mudd, an Exxon representative, telling him to "[g]o open the champagne," because Exxon had been awarded a block. Block 209 was formally awarded to Exxon by the Nigerian government in June 1993.

On April 13, 1992, Exxon sent Breezevale a letter terminating its relationship with Breezevale and enclosing a $30,000 check to cover Breezevale's services. According to Mudd, Exxon had begun to have concerns about Habib's actions in Nigeria; consequently, Exxon decided to terminate the business relationship. Habib returned the check.

Breezevale sued Exxon, claiming, among other things, that Exxon breached its oral contract with Breezevale and its fiduciary duty to Breezevale. The case was tried to a jury. After Breezevale rested its case, Exxon moved for a directed verdict on all counts. The trial court granted Exxon's motion for a directed verdict with regard to Breezevale's breach of fiduciary duty claim, but denied the remainder of the motion. The jury found the parties had entered into an oral agreement that Breezevale would acquire a 2 1/2 percent working interest in "any deepwater blocks awarded to Exxon by the government of Nigeria" and "any deepwater blocks in which Exxon obtains a farm-in from a private company by trading any interest awarded to Exxon by the government of Nigeria." The jury valued the working interest at $34.3 million and additionally awarded Breezevale $1 million for services on an implied contract in law, and $3.495 million for attorneys' fees. The trial court entered judgment on the jury verdict. Exxon appealed.

EXXON'S APPEAL

In its first three issues, Exxon attacks the jury's findings that an enforceable contract existed between the parties. Specifically, Exxon claims there is no or insufficient evidence to support the jury's finding that the parties reached an agreement on all the material terms necessary to the formation of an enforceable agreement. Additionally, Exxon contends that, as a matter of law, the claimed oral agreement is unenforceable under the statute of frauds. Finally, Exxon argues the trial court erred in its submission of the jury question on promissory estoppel. Because we agree with Exxon that the statute of frauds applies, we assume, without deciding, [that] the parties reached an oral agreement, and address Exxon's second issue regarding the applicability of the statute of frauds.

Statute of Frauds

The statute of frauds, in section 26.01 of the Texas Business and Commerce Code, provides in pertinent part:

> (a) A promise or agreement described in subsection (b) of this section is not enforceable unless the promise or agreement, or a memorandum of it, is
>
> > (1) in writing; and
> >
> > (2) signed by the person to be charged with the promise or agreement or by someone lawfully authorized to sign for him....
>
> (b) Subsection (a) of this section applies to:
>
> > (4) a contract for the sale of real estate; ...

There are two types of fiduciary relationships-formal and informal. Formal fiduciary relationships arise as a matter of law, and include the relationships between attorney and client, principal and agent, partners, and joint venturers. Informal fiduciary relationships arise from "a moral, social, domestic or purely personal relationship of trust and confidence, generally called a confidential relationship." Confidential relationships may arise when one party has dealt with another in a certain manner for a long period of time such that one party is justified in expecting the other to act in its best interest, and in cases where "influence has been acquired and abused, in which confidence has been reposed and betrayed." However, to give full force to contracts, we do not recognize such a relationship lightly. To impose such a relationship in a business transaction, the relationship must exist prior to, and apart from, the agreement made the basis of the suit. The fact that one businessman trusts another and relies on another to perform a contract does not give rise to a confidential relationship, because something apart from the transaction between the parties is required. Although the existence of a confidential relationship is ordinarily a question of fact, where there is no evidence to establish the relationship, it is a question of law.

Breezevale first asserts that a formal fiduciary relationship existed because it was partners with Exxon. However, we have held there was no working interest agreement between the parties because any oral agreement violated the statute of frauds. Therefore, there is no evidence the parties were working interest partners. *See Schlumberger*, 959 S.W.2d at 176 (partnership consists of express or implied agreement containing four required elements: (1) community of interest in venture, (2) agreement to share profits, (3) agreement to share losses, and mutual right of control or management of enterprise). Without an agreement, there is no evidence the parties were partners and no evidence to support Breezevale's argument that a formal fiduciary relationship existed arising from the partnership.

Breezevale also argues it submitted evidence that Breezevale and Exxon had developed a relationship of trust and confidence and there was some evidence of an informal fiduciary relationship between the parties. It relies on evidence that before Exxon and Breezevale began the dealings at issue in this suit, Breezevale had a ten-year distributorship relationship with Exxon Chemical in Nigeria. However, the evidence shows Exxon Chemical is a separate Exxon affiliate, and nothing in the record indicates this relationship was anything more than an arms-length business relationship.

Not a fiduciary relationship

Breezevale also relies on evidence it "trusted Exxon's numerous promises that an agreement ... would be forthcoming;" it clearly informed Exxon it wanted a long-term relationship; it shared with Exxon confidential information it learned from the Nigerian officials regarding the bidding process; and Exxon requested that Breezevale work exclusively for Exxon. Even if true, these facts are not evidence of an informal fiduciary relationship. Breezevale's claim that it subjectively trusted Exxon to provide it a working interest agreement is insufficient to impose fiduciary obligations on Exxon as a matter of law. Mere subjective trust does not transform arms-length dealing into a fiduciary relationship. "[T]he fact that one businessman trusts another, and relies upon his promise to carry out a contract, does not create a constructive trust ... [t]o hold otherwise would render the Statute of Frauds meaningless.") The record shows the parties had an arms-length relationship, with each party separately represented by its own counsel. There is no evidence of a long-term relationship apart from the parties' negotiations for the services contract and working interest agreement. We conclude that, because the record contains no evidence of a fiduciary relationship between the parties, the trial court did not err in granting Exxon's motion for directed verdict on Breezevale's breach of fiduciary duty claim. The trial court erred in denying Exxon's motion for directed verdict on Breezevale's claim that it had a "special relationship of trust and confidence" with Exxon. Consequently, we find no merit in Breezevale's second issue in its cross appeal.

We reverse the trial court's award of $34.3 million against Exxon for breach of contract and affirm the remaining portions of the trial court's judgment that are the subject of this appeal.

§ 152.002. EFFECT OF PARTNERSHIP AGREEMENT; NONWAIVABLE AND VARIABLE PROVISIONS.

(a) Except as provided by Subsection (b), a partnership agreement governs the relations of the partners and between the partners and the partnership. To the extent that the partnership agreement does not otherwise provide, this chapter and the other partnership provisions govern the relationship of the partners and between the partners and the partnership.

(b) A partnership agreement or the partners may not:

(1) unreasonably restrict a partner's right of access to books and records under Section 152.212;

(2) eliminate the duty of loyalty under Section 152.205, except that the partners by agreement may identify specific types of activities or categories of activities that do not violate the duty of loyalty if the types or categories are not manifestly unreasonable;

(3) eliminate the duty of care under Section 152.206, except that the partners by agreement may determine the standards by which the performance of the obligation is to be measured if the standards are not manifestly unreasonable;

(4) eliminate the obligation of good faith under Section 152.204(b), except that the partners by agreement may determine the standards by which the performance of the obligation is to be measured if the standards are not manifestly unreasonable;

(5) vary the power to withdraw as a partner under Section 152.501(b)(1), (7), or (8), except for the requirement that notice be in writing;

(6) vary the right to expel a partner by a court in an event specified by Section 152.501(b)(5);

(7) restrict rights of a third party under this chapter or the other partnership provisions, except for a limitation on an individual partner's liability in a limited liability partnership as provided by this chapter;

(8) select a governing law not permitted under Sections 1.103 and 1.002(43)(C); or

(9) except as provided in Subsections (c) and (d), waive or modify the following provisions of Title 1:

(A) Chapter 1, if the provision is used to interpret a provision or to define a word or phrase contained in a section listed in this subsection;

(B) Chapter 2, other than Sections 2.104(c)(2), 2.104(c)(3), and 2.113;

(C) Chapter 3, other than Subchapters C and E of that chapter; or

(D) Chapters 4, 5, 10, 11, and 12, other than Sections 11.057(a), (b), (c)(1), (c)(3), and (d).

(c) A provision listed in Subsection (b)(9) may be waived or modified in a partnership agreement if the provision that is waived or modified authorizes the partnership to waive or modify the provision in the partnership's governing documents.

(d) A provision listed in Subsection (b)(9) may be waived or modified in a partnership agreement if the provision that is modified specifies:

(1) the person or group of persons entitled to approve a modification; or

(2) the vote or other method by which a modification is required to be approved.

§ 152.208. AMENDMENT TO PARTNERSHIP AGREEMENT. *A partnership agreement may be amended only with the consent of all partners.*

§ 152.052. RULES FOR DETERMINING IF PARTNERSHIP IS CREATED.

(a) Factors indicating that persons have created a partnership include the persons':

(1) receipt or right to receive a share of profits of the business;

(2) expression of an intent to be partners in the business;

(3) participation or right to participate in control of the business;

(4) agreement to share or sharing:

(A) losses of the business; or

(B) liability for claims by third parties against the business; and

(5) agreement to contribute or contributing money or property to the business.

(b) One of the following circumstances, by itself, does not indicate that a person is a partner in the business:

(1) the receipt or right to receive a share of profits as payment:

(A) of a debt, including repayment by installments;

(B) of wages or other compensation to an employee or independent contractor;

(C) of rent;

(D) to a former partner, surviving spouse or representative of a deceased or disabled partner, or transferee of a partnership interest;

(E) of interest or other charge on a loan, regardless of whether the amount varies with the profits of the business, including a direct or indirect present or future ownership interest in collateral or rights to income, proceeds, or increase in value derived from collateral; or

(F) of consideration for the sale of a business or other property, including payment by installments;

(2) co-ownership of property, regardless of whether the co-ownership:

(A) is a joint tenancy, tenancy in common, tenancy by the entirety, joint property, community property, or part ownership; or

(B) is combined with sharing of profits from the property;

(3) the right to share or sharing gross returns or revenues, regardless of whether the persons sharing the gross returns or revenues have a common or joint interest in the property from which the returns or revenues are derived; or

(4) ownership of mineral property under a joint operating agreement.

(c) An agreement by the owners of a business to share losses is not necessary to create a partnership.

Ingram and Behavioral Psychology Clinic, P.C. v. Deere et.al.
288 S.W.3d 886 (Tex, 2009)

In this case, we review a court of appeals judgment reinstating a jury verdict finding that Louis Deere, D.O. and Jesse C. Ingram, Ph.D. formed a partnership pursuant to the Texas Revised Partnership Act (TRPA).

TRPA lists five factors to be considered in determining whether a partnership has been formed. This determination should be made by examining the totality of the circumstances in each case, with no single factor being either necessary or sufficient to prove the existence of a partnership. Here, the evidence is legally insufficient to establish that a partnership existed between Ingram and Deere. Because the evidence of the formation of a partnership is legally insufficient, we do not address the issue raised in Ingram's cross-petition challenging the court of appeals' decision that Ingram owed Deere a fiduciary duty. Accordingly, we reinstate the trial court's take-nothing judgment in favor of Ingram and reverse the court of appeals' judgment.

FACTUAL AND PROCEDURAL BACKGROUND

Ingram, a licensed psychologist, and Deere, a board certified psychiatrist, entered into an oral agreement in 1997, which provided that Deere would serve as the medical director for a multidisciplinary pain clinic. Deere contends that they agreed he would receive one-third of the clinic's revenues, Ingram would receive one-third, and the remaining one-third would be used to pay the clinic's expenses. Deere also claims that when he and Ingram began working together, Ingram told him their work "was a joint venture, or [they] were partners, or [they] were doing this together." Ingram contends that they only agreed Deere would receive one-third of the clinic's revenues and that there was no agreement as to the other two-thirds. Deere acknowledges that, during his time at the clinic, he never contributed money to the clinic, he did not participate in the hiring of any employees, he did not know any of the clinic staff's names, he never purchased any of the clinic's equipment, his name was not on the clinic's bank account, and his name was not on the lease agreement for the clinic space.

Fourteen months after Deere began working at the clinic, Ingram prepared a written agreement to memorialize their arrangement. The document was entitled "Physician Contractual Employment Agreement" and stated that Ingram was the "sole owner" of the clinic. Deere refused to sign the document, claiming that it contradicted their initial arrangement. Immediately after Deere received the document, he ceased working at the clinic.

Deere later sued Ingram, asserting claims of common law fraud, statutory fraud, fraudulent inducement, breach of contract, breach of fiduciary duty, and declaratory judgment and seeking specific performance, damages, and attorneys' fees. The jury found that Deere and Ingram entered into a partnership agreement and that Ingram breached the agreement and his fiduciary duty to Deere. The trial court entered judgment on the jury verdict awarding damages of (1) $34,249.68 for compensation owed Deere through March 1999, (2) $2,525,437.00 for Deere's share of the partnership's revenue from April 1999 through the time of trial, (3) $2,500,000.00 for Deere's share of revenue to accrue after trial, and (4) $27,500.00 in attorneys' fees for the trial stage with additional fees in the event of a motion for new trial and various appeals.

Ingram filed a motion for judgment non obstante veredicto (judgment n.o.v.). After a hearing, Judge David Evans signed a new judgment, eliminating a portion of the damages awarded by the jury and reducing the award of attorneys' fees. Following his decision, Judge Evans recused himself without explanation, and the case was assigned to Judge Merrill Hartman. Ingram then filed a second motion for judgment n.o.v. or, in the alternative, a motion for new trial. Judge Hartman signed a judgment n.o.v. and rendered a take-nothing judgment in Ingram's favor.

The court of appeals reversed the trial court's take-nothing judgment on the second motion for judgment n.o.v. and reinstated the trial court's judgment on the first motion for judgment n.o.v. The court held that Ingram waived his right to challenge the existence of a partnership because he failed to raise the issue in his second motion for judgment n.o.v. Without discussing whether Deere and Ingram created a partnership, the court held that there was legally sufficient evidence to support the jury's finding that the partnership continued to exist through the time of trial. However, the court affirmed the trial court's ruling that Ingram did not owe Deere a fiduciary duty, as there was no evidence of a confidential relationship between Deere and Ingram that would give rise to an informal fiduciary duty. On appeal to this Court, Ingram argues that the court of appeals erred in reinstating the trial court's judgment on the first motion for judgment n.o.v. because there is no evidence that Deere and Ingram created a partnership. Deere principally contends that Ingram waived all of the alleged errors in one way or another at the trial court. Deere also filed a cross-petition appealing the court of appeals' adverse ruling on his breach of fiduciary duty claim. Because we conclude there is no evidence of a partnership, we do not reach the other issues raised by Deere or Ingram.

Under the common law, the Court recognized that a partnership or joint enterprise "presupposes an agreement to that end," which could be either express or implied. We explained that the "intention of the parties to a contract is a prime element in determining whether or not a partnership or joint venture exists." The common law also considered that profit sharing was the most important factor shedding light on the intention to establish a partnership. A common interest in the profits is an essential element to constitute a partnership." These two elements were incorporated into a five-factor test that developed under the common law for partnership formation: (1) intent to form a partnership, (2) a community of interest in the venture, (3) an agreement to share profits, (4) an agreement to share losses, and (5) a mutual right of control or management of the enterprise. These factors continued to guide the question of partnership formation when Texas promulgated and later amended statutory regimes governing partnerships.

Prior case law discusses differences between joint ventures and partnerships. We see no legal or logical reason for distinguishing a joint venture from a partnership on the question of formation of the entity. In fact, a joint venture that satisfies the definition of "partnership" is a partnership subject to TRPA.

The partnership in this case was allegedly formed in 1997. It is uncontested that TRPA governs this dispute; rather, the parties contest whether Deere has proven the existence of a partnership under TRPA.

Three statutory regimes have governed partnerships formed in Texas—TUPA [Texas Uniform Partnership Act], TRPA [Texas Revised Partnership Act], and the Texas Business Organizations Code (TBOC). TRPA, enacted in 1993, replaced TUPA. TRPA governs partnerships formed on or after January 1, 1994, and other, existing partnerships that elected to be governed by it. In 2003, the TBOC replaced TRPA. The TBOC governs partnerships formed on or after January 1, 2006, and other partnerships that elect to be governed by the TBOC. In addition, TRPA and the TBOC contain transition rules, providing that the preceding law will apply to existing partnerships for a period of years after each act's effective date, unless the partnership elects to be governed by the new act immediately. On January 1, 2010, TRPA will expire, and the TBOC will apply to all partnerships, regardless of their formation date. TRPA and the TBOC's rules for determining partnership formation are substantially the same.

TRPA provides that "an association of two or more persons to carry on a business for profit as owners creates a partnership." Unlike TUPA, TRPA articulates five factors, similar to the common law factors, that indicate the creation of a partnership. They are: (1) receipt or right to receive a share of profits of the business; (2) expression of an intent to be partners in the business; (3) participation or right to participate in control of the business; (4) sharing or agreeing to share: (A) losses of the business; or (B) liability for claims by third parties against the business; and (5) contributing or agreeing to contribute money or property to the business.

Four years after TRPA was enacted, Oregon adopted factors almost verbatim to the factors listed in TRPA for determining whether a partnership exists. Oregon and Texas are the only states to enact a statute that deviates from the UPA's rules for determining the existence of a partnership.

The common law required proof of all five factors to establish the existence of a partnership. However, TRPA contemplates a less formalistic and more practical approach to recognizing the formation of a partnership.

First, TRPA does not require direct proof of the parties' intent to form a partnership. Formerly, the intent to be partners was a "prime," although not controlling, element in the creation of a partnership. Instead, TRPA lists the "expression of intent" to form a partnership as a factor to consider. Second, unlike the common law, TRPA does not require proof of *all* of the listed factors in order for a partnership to exist. Third, sharing of profits—deemed essential for establishing a partnership under the common law—is treated differently under TRPA because sharing of profits is not required. Still, TRPA comments note that the traditional import of sharing profits as well as control over the business will probably continue to be the most important factors. Additionally, TRPA recognizes that sharing of losses may be indicative of a partnership arrangement but states that such an arrangement is "not necessary to create a partnership." TRPA also restates and extends the list of circumstances in TUPA that do not by themselves indicate that a person is a partner.

According to TRPA, "[one] of the following circumstances, by itself, does not indicate that a person is a partner in the business":

(1) the receipt or right to receive a share of profits:

(A) as repayment of a debt, by installments or otherwise;
(B) as payment of wages or other compensation to an employee or independent contractor;
(C) as payment of rent;
(D) as payment to a former partner, surviving spouse or representative of a deceased or disabled partner, or transferee of a partnership interest;
(E) as payment of interest or other charge on a loan, regardless of whether the amount of payment varies with the profits of the business, and including a direct or indirect present or future ownership interest in collateral or rights to income, proceeds, or increase in value derived from collateral; or
(F) as payment of consideration for the sale of a business or other property by installments or otherwise;

(2) co-ownership of property, whether in the form of joint tenancy, tenancy in common, tenancy by the entireties, joint property, community property, or part ownership, whether combined with sharing of profits from the property;

(3) sharing or having a right to share gross returns or revenues, regardless of whether the persons sharing the gross returns or revenues have a common or joint interest in the property from which the returns or revenues are derived; or

(4) ownership of mineral property under a joint operating agreement.

The question of how many of the TRPA factors are required to form a partnership is a matter of first impression for this Court. The TRPA factors seem to serve as a proxy for the common law requirement of intent to form a partnership by identifying conduct that logically suggests a collaboration of a business's purpose and resources to make a profit as partners. After examining the statutory language and considering that TRPA abrogated the common law's requirement of proof of all five factors, we determine that the issue of whether a partnership exists should be decided considering all of the evidence bearing on the TRPA partnership factors. While proof of all five common law factors was a prerequisite to partnership formation under the common law, the totality-of-the-circumstances test was, in some respect, foreshadowed in Texas case law. As Justice Jack Pope wrote for the San Antonio Court of Appeals, no single fact may be stated as a complete and final test of partnership.

Each case must rest on its own particular facts and the presence or absence of the usual attributes of a partnership relation. The earlier Texas rule indicated that profit sharing was the controlling test. We think it is now generally held that such a test is not all-inclusive and controlling.... The absence of an express provision obligating the parties to share in the losses is also important and indicates that no partnership existed. But this feature too is not controlling.

We note the difficulty of uniformly applying a totality-of-the-circumstances test, but we cannot ignore the Legislature's decision to codify the essential common law partnership factors in TRPA without specifying that proof of all or some of the factors is required to establish a partnership. Yet, we can provide additional guidelines for this analysis. Of course, an absence of any evidence of the factors will preclude the recognition of a partnership under Texas law. Even conclusive evidence of only one factor normally will be insufficient to establish the existence of a partnership. To hold otherwise would create a probability that some business owners would be legally required to share profits with individuals or be held liable for the actions of individuals who were neither treated as nor intended to be partners. The Legislature does not indicate that it intended to spring surprise or accidental partnerships on independent business persons,…. On the other end of the spectrum, conclusive evidence of all of the TRPA factors will establish the existence of a partnership as a matter of law. The challenge of the totality-of-the-circumstances test will be its application between these two points on the continuum.

Existence of a Partnership

In this case, we consider whether more than a scintilla of evidence of any of the factors indicative of a partnership was introduced at trial.

Profit Sharing

Deere argues that he received or had the right to receive a share of the clinic's profits because he and Ingram had an agreement in which each of them would receive one-third of the clinic's "gross revenue" and the remainder would be used for expenses. It is true that the "receipt or right to receive a share of profits of the business" may be indicative of the existence of a partnership under TRPA, but a share of profits paid as "wages or other compensation to an employee or independent contractor" is not indicative of a partnership interest in the business.

The evidence does not establish that Deere received a share of profits as contemplated under TRPA for two reasons. First, the agreement between Ingram and Deere cannot constitute Deere's receipt of "profits," but rather of gross revenue. Because TRPA does not define the term "profits," we define it using its ordinary meaning. The ordinary meaning of "profits" is "[t]he excess of revenues over expenditures in a business transaction." Furthermore, this Court, interpreting similar language in TUPA, established that the receipt of gross revenue is not profit sharing. There is no evidence that the allocation for expenses was sufficient to satisfy all the clinic's expenses, leaving only profits to be split. Even if some funds may have been reserved for expenses, as Deere claims, there is no evidence that Deere's share would have decreased if expenses grew or increased if expenses shrank. Simply put, Deere's share depended on the clinic's receipts, not its excess of revenues over expenditures. Therefore, the evidence in this case leads to one conclusion: Deere did not share the clinic's profits but agreed to and received a percentage of the clinic's gross revenues.

Second, Ingram wrote twenty checks to Deere as compensation from January 1997 until March 1999. These checks referred to Deere as a "medical consultant" and the payments as "contract labor." Therefore, they contradict his argument that he received profits as a partner in the clinic. Under TRPA, receipt of profits as compensation for an employee's services or an independent contractor's work is not evidence that parties were partners. Because Deere cashed the checks without challenging the characterizations, this fact also does not support his argument.

Expression of Intent to Be Partners

"[E]xpression of an intent to be partners in the business" is one of five factors courts use in determining whether a partnership exists. This is different from the common law definition of a partnership that required proof that the parties intended to form a partnership at the outset of their agreement. Conversely, TRPA evaluates the parties' *expression* of intent to be partners as one factor, and it does not by its terms give the parties' intent or expression of intent any greater weight than the other factors.

When analyzing expression of intent under TRPA, courts should review the putative partners' speech, writings, and conduct. While under the common law, evidence probative on other factors is considered evidence of "intent," under TRPA, the "expression of intent" factor is an inquiry separate and apart from the other factors. Courts should only consider evidence not specifically probative of the other factors. In other words, evidence of profit or loss sharing, control, or contribution of money or property should not be considered evidence of an expression of intent to be partners. Otherwise, all evidence could be an "expression" of the parties' intent, making the intent factor a catch-all for evidence of any of the factors, and the separate "expression of intent" inquiry would be eviscerated. Such an interpretation would undermine the language of TRPA, which establishes five separate factors to be considered when determining the existence of a partnership.

Evidence of expressions of intent could include, for example, the parties' statements that they are partners, one party holding the other party out as a partner on the business' letterhead or name plate, or in a signed partnership agreement.

The terms used by the parties in referring to the arrangement do not control, and merely referring to another person as "partner" in a situation where the recipient of the message would not expect the declarant to make a statement of legal significance is not enough. The term "partner" is regularly used in common vernacular and may be used in a variety of ways. Referring to a friend, employee, spouse, teammate, or fishing companion as a "partner" in a colloquial sense is not legally sufficient evidence of expression of intent to form a business partnership. However, the same terms could constitute legally significant evidence of expression of intent when made in a circumstance that indicates significance to the business endeavor. Thus, courts should look to the terminology used by the putative partners, the context in which the statements were made, and the identity of the speaker and listener.

Deere argues that he expressed his intent to be a partner with Ingram by sharing the clinic's profits and losses and having access to the clinic's records. His evidence of other factors, sharing of profits and losses and control of the business, is insufficient to establish expression of intent. Deere's evidence is also insufficient because there must be evidence that both parties expressed their intent to be partners.

Control

Deere argues he had an equal right to control and manage the clinic's business because, although he was never allowed to see the books and records, he repeatedly requested to see them. He also points to Ingram's testimony that "maybe" Deere viewed the clinic's books on one occasion. Furthermore, Deere argues that he had control because Ingram discussed with him how much the clinic made, the amounts paid to the staff, and the need to hire Ingram's wife as personnel director. No other evidence supports these statements and proves he participated in or had the right to control the clinic's business.

The right to control a business is the right to make executive decisions. However, being sporadically provided information regarding the business does not indicate that Deere had control of or the right to control the business. At most, Deere's evidence demonstrates that Ingram talked with Deere about the business. But owners talk with consultants, employees, accountants, attorneys, spouses, and many others about their businesses, and these conversations do not establish that these people have control of the businesses. Likewise, those same classes of people may have the opportunity to look at the businesses' books, but once again, a review of the books itself is not evidence of control. Deere submitted no evidence that he made executive decisions or had the right to make executive decisions and has shown no evidence of this factor.

Sharing of Losses and Liability for Third Party Claims

Contrary to the common law, under TRPA an agreement to share losses is not necessary to create a partnership. Therefore, while under TRPA the absence of an agreement to share losses is not dispositive of the existence of a partnership, the existence of such an agreement could support Deere's argument that a partnership existed between him and Ingram.

According to Deere, he and Ingram agreed that Deere would receive one-third of the clinic's gross revenue, Ingram would receive one-third of the clinic's gross revenue, and the remainder would be used to pay clinic expenses. Deere argues that this agreement determined how losses would be shared, but he testified that there was never a discussion of how expenses in excess of one-third of the clinic's gross revenue would be divided between him and Ingram. The meaning of "net operating losses" is "the excess of operating expenses over revenues, the amount of which can be deducted from gross income if other deductions do not exceed gross income." Here, Ingram and Deere never discussed what would happen to the allocation if expenses exceeded one-third of the revenue or gross income. They never discussed losses, only expenses. There is no legally cognizable evidence to support the contention that Ingram and Deere agreed to share losses.

Contribution of Money or Property

Finally, there is no evidence that Deere "contribut[ed] or agree[d] to contribute money or property" to the clinic as a partner. Deere does not argue that there was any *agreement* that he contribute either money or property to the enterprise. Furthermore, Deere does not contend that he actually contributed money to the clinic. In fact, Deere acknowledged at trial that he did not contribute to clinic renovations or the purchase of medical equipment and supplies and that he did not agree to use his personal resources to pay for any expenses in the operation of the clinic. Rather, Deere's only argument regarding this factor is that he contributed his reputation as property to the alleged partnership.

TRPA defines "property" as "all property, real, personal, or mixed, tangible or intangible, or an interest in that property." Reputation is a type of goodwill and may be valuable intangible property. Therefore, an individual's reputation can be property that is contributed to the partnership. However, even if a person lends her good name to a business, she does not automatically become a de facto partner. At a minimum, the putative partner would have to prove that any such value can be distinguished from services rendered or property given as an employee.

Contribution of Valuable Property

Although Deere claims his reputation was a valuable contribution to the alleged partnership, the evidence does not support this assertion. Deere argues that the testimony of Ingram's expert, Ron McClellan, who stated that Deere's reputation was a "benefit to the clinic" and "added value" to the clinic, supports his claim. However, McClellan only testified generally that Deere's reputation could add value to the clinic, and he acknowledged that his statements were unsupported and mere assumptions, stating: "Not knowing Dr. Deere and his reputation, I can only assume." His opinion, therefore, was merely speculation. In order to show that Deere's reputation improved the goodwill of the clinic, McClellan, at a minimum, had to know Deere's reputation in the psychiatric or pain management fields. McClellan admitted he had no such knowledge.

Contribution as a Partner

Furthermore, there is no evidence that Deere added value to the clinic as a partner and not an employee. Even if we were to assume that Deere contributed quantifiable value and enjoyed a good reputation in the psychiatric or pain management fields, he cannot establish this factor without evidence that the contribution is distinguishable from the contributions of an employee. Employees may contribute to business endeavors by lending their time and reputation, but that is not a contribution to the venture indicative of a partnership interest. Even assuming Deere's reputation was impeccable, nothing indicates that Deere contributed or agreed to contribute to the clinic as a partner and not as an employee. In sum, there is no legally sufficient evidence that Deere contributed property to the multidisciplinary pain clinic that would establish a partnership interest.

CONCLUSION

Whether a partnership exists must be determined by an examination of the totality of the circumstances. Evidence of none of the factors under the Texas Revised Partnership Act will preclude the recognition of a partnership, and even conclusive evidence of only one factor will also normally be insufficient to establish the existence of a partnership under TRPA. However, conclusive evidence of all five factors establishes a partnership as a matter of law. In this case, Deere has not provided legally sufficient evidence of any of the five TRPA factors to prove the existence of a partnership. Accordingly, we reverse the court of appeals' judgment and reinstate the trial court's take-nothing judgment.

Partnership by estoppel

A partnership by estoppel is a legal concept courts in equity use to provide relief to a plaintiff, who has reasonably relied on representations that a person was a partner in an existing partnership or when no partnership existed. The plaintiff has the burden of proving that 'his or her injury occurred because a purported partner, by words spoken or written or by conduct, represented himself, or consented to another representing him to any one, as a partner in an existing partnership or with one or more persons not actual partners. He is liable to any such person to whom such representation has been made, who has, on the faith of such representation, given credit to the actual or apparent partnership, and if he has made such representation or consented to its being made in a public manner he is liable to such person, whether the representation has or has not been made or communicated to such person so giving credit by or with the knowledge of the apparent partner making the representation or consenting to its being made." Essentially, this doctrine requires a plaintiff to prove that a defendant's conduct caused him or her to believe that the defendant was in a partnership, which resulted in the plaintiff's damages.

A plaintiff has the burden of proving a partnership by estoppel. In most jurisdictions, he does this by showing that a defendant held himself out as a partner, that the defendant consented to others holding him out as a partner; that the plaintiff knew of the defendant holding himself out as a partner; that the plaintiff reasonably relied on the claimed partnership, and that plaintiff suffered damages. If a plaintiff proves these elements, a judge may rule in favor of the plaintiff, who is then likely to recover damages from a defendant.

§152.054. False Representation of Partnership or Partner

(a) A false representation or other conduct falsely indicating that a person is a partner with another person does not of itself create a partnership.

(b) A representation or other conduct indication that a person is a partner in an existing partnership, if that is not the case, does not of itself make that person a partner in the partnership.

§152.307.

(a) The rights of a person extending credit in reliance on a representation described in 152.054 are determined by applicable law other than this chapter and other partnership provisions, including the law of estoppel, agency, negligence, fraud, and unjust enrichment.

(b) The rights and duties of a person held liable under Subsection (a) are also determined by law other than the law described by Subsection (a).

CCR, INC., et al., v. Chamberlain, et al.,
Number 13-97-312-CV, Tex.Ct.App.-Corpus Christi (13th Dist)

Appellants, CCR, Inc., W.T. Young Construction Company, W.T. Young, and Glen Young, sued appellees, Chamberlain, Hrdlicka, White, Johnson, & Williams; Chamberlain, Hrdlicka, White, Williams & Martin; James J. Spring III; and numerous other entities and individuals affiliated with the Chamberlain law firm, alleging legal malpractice, breach of fiduciary duty, fraud, Deceptive Trade Practices Act violations, civil conspiracy and breach of contract. The trial court entered summary judgments against W.T. Young Construction Company, W.T. Young, and Glen Young ("the Youngs") on the ground they lacked standing to sue, against CCR as to its claims with a two-year limitations period, and in favor of seventeen individual defendants who claimed they were not partners of the firm. We reverse and remand in part, and affirm in part.

In August of 1989, Glen and W.T. Young had discussions with Keith Hudson and James J. Spring III, concerning raising substantial funds to finance the operation, expansion, and acquisition of various subsidiaries of CCR, a Utah corporation of which their families were controlling shareholders. Glen and W.T. were the chief operational and executive officers of CCR. The parties planned to have CCR form another subsidiary which would issue bonds to be sold in Europe. Approximately eighty-five percent of the proceeds of the bond sales would be invested in U.S. government securities and approximately fifteen percent would be put in "loan portfolios," *i.e.*, loaned to the Youngs to meet their objectives. The plan involved the formation of other entities, which would be involved in the handling of portions of the loan proceeds and the management of the loan portfolios. Apparently, such a plan would result in substantial residual fees to be paid to Glen and W.T. and their families personally, separate and apart from the corporate entities. Glen and W.T. discussed these residual fees on more than one occasion.

On August 30, 1989, W.T., as president of CCR, signed an engagement letter retaining the Chamberlain law firm to prepare the legal work for the bond offering. CCR forwarded $250,000 to appellees for the purpose of the investments. Hudson, who was not a Chamberlain firm lawyer, was responsible for selling the bonds. Hudson had been previously convicted of embezzlement, a fact which was known to some Chamberlain lawyers, but never revealed to the Youngs. The bond transactions never materialized. Spring represented to the Youngs that the bond offering failed because of the business climate.

Hudson was subsequently charged with, and convicted of, felony theft in connection with the proposed bond transaction. Appellants filed the instant lawsuit, complaining, in part, of the Chamberlain firm's failure to disclose Hudson's prior conviction and seeking to recover for losses associated with the failed investments.

After granting the summary judgments, the trial court severed the instant parties and claims, resulting in a final appealable order. By five points of error, appellants challenge the propriety of the summary judgments.

Standing

In point of error three, appellants assert the trial court erred in granting summary judgment on the basis the Youngs lacked standing to sue. The motions for summary judgment presented by appellees raise two grounds for summary judgment: (1) the Youngs' legal malpractice and related claims were barred by the "privity rule," *i.e.*, that persons outside of the attorney-client relationship have no standing to sue attorneys for negligence associated with the representation of another, and (2) the Youngs lacked standing to assert any claims for the corporation, CCR. Appellees conclude the motion by stating summary judgment should be granted because the only entity which "sought or acquired services from the firm was CCR."

Attorney-Client Relationship and Right to Sue

Persons outside the attorney-client relationship have no cause of action for injuries they might sustain due to the attorney's failure to perform a duty owed to his client. *Berry v. Dodson, Nunley & Taylor, P.C.*, 717 S.W.2d 716, 718 (Tex. App.--San Antonio 1986), *writ granted, judgment set aside by agr.*, 729 S.W.2d 690 (citations omitted).

Under the privity rule, only the actual client is entitled to sue for legal malpractice associated with the representation of a client; non-clients may not sue a lawyer for his negligence in representing a client, even if they are affected by the negligence. *Barcelo v. Elliott*, 923 S.W.2d 575, 577-78 (Tex. 1996). The privity rule ensures that an attorney's representation of a client will not be compromised by the threat of suit by third parties who also have an interest in the subject of the representation. *Id.* at 578-79 (attorney owes no duty to non-client third parties, even if third parties are damaged by the negligent representation).

When the defendant moves for summary judgment because no attorney-client relationship exists, the defendant takes on the burden of proving the absence of the relationship as a matter of law. *See Yaklin*, 875 S.W.2d at 383. Appellees rely primarily on the engagement letter and the deposition testimony of Glen Young. On August 28, 1989, Spring sent a letter to W.T. Young, Glen Young, and CCR, Inc., regarding a request to serve as counsel to CCR in the proposed sale of corporate bonds. The letter explains the types of services to be provided to CCR and the fee schedule. W.T. Young, as president of CCR, Inc., accepted the terms set forth in the letter by signing and returning it to Spring. While the letter evidences an express attorney-client relationship between CCR and the firm, it does not *negate* an attorney-client relationship between the Youngs and the firm. *See Yaklin*, 875 S.W.2d at 384 (summary judgment evidence establishing lawyer had an attorney-client relationship with bank in a transaction did not negate the possibility of attorney-client relationship with another party to the same transaction).

Appellees argue Glen Young's deposition testimony also establishes that no attorney-client relationship existed as a matter of law. Glen testified as follows:

Q: Are you claiming in this case that the Chamberlain law firm was the attorney for W.T. Young Construction Company?

A: I would assume that if they were the attorney for CCR, then it would be considered the attorney for the subsidiaries, too; but I'm not sure. I guess that's a legal question.

Appellees argue this testimony constitutes a judicial admission that no attorney-client relationship existed between the Youngs and the Chamberlain firm. A party's testimonial declarations which are contrary to his legal position are quasi-admissions. *Mendoza v. Fidelity & Guaranty Ins. Underwriter, Inc.*, 606 S.W.2d 692, 694 (Tex. 1980). Such statements are some evidence and the weight to be given them is decided by the trier of fact. *Id.* A party's quasi-admissions will be given conclusive effect only when they meet certain requirements, including that they are deliberate, clear, and unequivocal. *Id.* Moreover, when the testimony is modified or explained, admissions are not given conclusive effect. *Griffin v. Superior Ins. Co.*, 338 S.W.2d 415, 418 (Tex. 1960).

The summary judgment record contains other evidence which raises a material fact question about the existence of an attorney-client relationship between the Youngs and the firm. ...

<u>Corporate Standing and Shareholders' Right to Sue</u>

A shareholder may not recover damages for an injury done solely to the corporation, even though he may be injured by that wrong. *Wingate v. Hajdik*, 795 S.W.2d 717, 719 (Tex. 1990). This rule, however, does not prohibit a shareholder from recovering damages for wrongs done to him individually where the wrongdoer violates a duty owed directly to the shareholder. *Id.*; *Murphy v. Campbell*, 964 S.W.2d 265, 268 (Tex. 1998) (stockholders had standing to sue accountant for malpractice where he counseled not only corporation, but also stockholders). In other words, a shareholder may recover if he proves a personal cause of action and a personal injury. *Murphy*, 964 S.W.2d at 268; *Wingate*, 795 S.W.2d at 719. Point of error number three is sustained.

Statute of Limitations

By their fourth point of error, appellants complain the trial court erred in granting summary judgment on all claims governed by the two-year statute of limitations. The trial court ordered that "CCR take nothing against Movants on all causes of action governed by the two-year statute of limitations." The Chamberlain firm and Spring presented the affirmative defense of limitations as to the Youngs' claims in their summary judgment motions; however, because the trial court dismissed the Youngs' claims based on a lack of standing, it never considered the limitations issue.

An appellate court may, in the interest of judicial economy, consider whether summary judgment was proper on grounds upon which the trial court did not rule, if those issues were preserved for appellate review. *Cincinnati Life Ins. Co. v. Cates*, 927 S.W.2d 623, 624 (Tex. 1996). The statute of limitations was raised by appellees in the trial court and adequately argued in the briefs to preserve the matter for our review. Even though the trial court never ruled on limitations as to the Youngs, in the interest of judicial economy, we address whether the appellees conclusively established their limitations defense. ...

Because there is a material fact issue as to when the Youngs discovered, or in the exercise of reasonable diligence should have discovered, the nature of their injury, we hold appellees failed to establish their limitations defense as a matter of law. Based on our conclusion that appellees failed to establish when the Youngs discovered the nature of their injury as a matter of law, we need not address whether appellants have raised a fact question as to fraudulent concealment. Point of error number four is sustained.

No Partner Liability

In point of error two, appellants argue the trial court erred in dismissing seventeen appellees from the suit on the basis they had no partnership liability. Appellees alleged in separate summary judgment motions that they were not jointly and severally liable for the obligations of the firm because they were not partners. Appellees submitted affidavits stating they either had not been a partner during the relevant period, had never been a partner, or the corporate entity which had been a partner ceased to exist. They further stated they practiced law as a shareholder and employee of the firm, never represented to anyone that they were a partner and were not aware of any person representing them to be a partner, never communicated with the appellants or were involved in the legal services rendered to CCR, and received salary checks rather than partnership draws.

On appeal, appellants do not argue appellees failed to meet their summary judgment burden, but rather that the summary judgment evidence raises a material fact dispute. Appellants argue in their brief that the following summary judgment evidence controverts appellees' claims that they were not partners:

1. Verbal representations made by James Spring as to his own partner status and general references to other firm lawyers as "partners."

2. Representations in the August 28, 1989 engagement letter that "tax partners" and "securities partners" would perform certain legal services.

3. Hudson's and John Johnston's testimony that firm lawyers generally referred to themselves as partners or associates.

4. Spring's reference in Hudson's 1992 criminal trial that Shelley Cashion was one of his tax "partners."

5. Cashion's testimony in Hudson's 1992 criminal trial in which she refers to her relationship with her "partners."

6. Statements by appellees' lawyers in depositions, hearings, and in one motion in the present litigation identifying appellees collectively as the "former partners," "past and present partners," and the "Chamberlain, Hrdlicka partners."

Appellants argue this evidence creates a reasonable inference the firm was a partnership. The summary judgment record reflects, and appellants acknowledge, the firm was comprised of two primary partners, Chamberlain, Hrdlicka, White, Williams & Martin, a Georgia P.C., and Chamberlain, Hrdlicka, White, Williams & Martin, a Texas P.C., as well as several other partners which were individual professional corporations. The issue, however, is not whether appellants raised a fact issue as to the existence of a partnership, but whether appellants controverted appellees' evidence they were *not* partners in the firm from August of 1989 to fall of 1990, the time the firm is alleged to have represented the Youngs. The evidence appellants cite in their brief fails to raise a fact issue as to whether the appellees were partners during the relevant period.

Focusing on information presented in the Martindale-Hubbell Law Directory, appellants argue the summary judgment was improper because there is conflicting evidence as to whether appellees held themselves out as partners. Appellants' primary argument is not that they controverted the actual partner status of the appellees, but rather that the evidence raises a question as to partnership by estoppel.

If a party opposing a summary judgment relies on a defense such as a partnership by estoppel, he must come forward with summary judgment proof sufficient to raise an issue of fact on each element of the defense. *See Baptist Memorial Hosp. Sys. v. Sampson*, 969 S.W.2d 945, 947 (Tex. 1998) (where hospital met summary judgment burden in negligence case by establishing as a matter of law that treating doctor was not its agent or employee, burden shifted to plaintiff to raise a fact issue on each element of ostensible agency); *Ryland Group, Inc. v. Hood*, 924 S.W.2d 120, 121 (Tex. 1996) (once movant established entitlement to summary judgment based on limitations, nonmovants had burden to raise fact issue on their affirmative defenses of fraudulent concealment and willful misconduct); *Brownlee v. Brownlee*, 665 S.W.2d 111, 112 (Tex. 1984).

Partnership by estoppel consists of two elements: (1) a representation that the one sought to be bound is a partner; and (2) the one to whom the representation is made must rely on the representation. *Paramount Petroleum Corp. v. Taylor Rental Center*, 712 S.W.2d 534, 538 (Tex. App.--Houston [1st Dist.] 1986, writ ref'd n.r.e.). The representation may be made directly by the alleged partner, or by others, provided the alleged partner knowingly allows others to make the representation and fails to correct them. *Id.*

The summary judgment evidence fails to raise a fact issue as to both the representation and reliance elements of partnership by estoppel. There is some evidence Spring made broad references to "partners" in his communications with the Youngs; however, there is no evidence of specific representations made to the Youngs about the partner status of any appellee.

We also are unpersuaded that Martindale-Hubbell represents the appellees as "partners." The Martindale-Hubbell listings identify the Chamberlain firm as a "Partnership including Professional Corporations" and then categorize each lawyer in the firm under either the heading of "Members of Firm," "Of Counsel," or "Associates." The Martindale-Hubbell listings do not state the appellees are *partners* in the firm.

Even if the Martindale-Hubbell listing raises a fact question as to the element of representation, the evidence fails to raise a fact question on the element of reliance. As demonstrated by W.T. Young's deposition testimony, at the time the firm was retained, he did not know the identity of the lawyers, partners, or shareholders in the firm, with the obvious exception of Spring. It is also undisputed the Youngs never consulted Martindale-Hubbell, and therefore, never relied on this information.

In reply, appellants argue they are not required to raise a fact issue as to reliance. Appellants assert that when a partnership representation has been made in a "public manner," such as in Martindale-Hubbell, the alleged partner is estopped to deny liability, whether or not the representation has been communicated to the relying party. In support of this argument, appellants cite to the Texas Uniform Partnership Act, which provided in relevant part:

§16. Partner by Estoppel

> Sec. 16. (1) When a person, by words spoken or written or by conduct, represents himself, or consents to another representing him to any one, as a partner in an existing partnership or with one or more persons not actual partners, he is liable to any such person to whom such representation has been made, who has, on the faith of such representation, *given credit* to the actual or apparent partnership, and *if he has made such representation or consented to its being made in a public manner he is liable to such person, whether the representation has or has not been made or communication to such person so giving credit* by or with the knowledge of the apparent partner making the representation or consenting to its being made . . . .

Texas Uniform Partnership Act, May 16, 1961, 57th Leg., p. 289, ch. 158 (expired 1999)(emphasis supplied).

We have found no Texas cases interpreting this language; however, other jurisdictions construing the same provisions have held that even in public-manner representation cases, one must show reliance on the public representation to establish partnership by estoppel. *See National Premium Budget Plan Corp. v. National Fire Ins. Co.*, 97 N.J. Super. 149, 234 A.2d 683, 729-32 (1967), *aff'd* 106 N.J. Super. 238, 254 A.2d 819 (1969); *Reisen Lumber and Millwork Co. v. Simonelli*, 98 N.J. Super. 335, 237 A.2d 303, 306-08 (1967); *Pruitt v. Fetty*, 148 W. Va. 275, 134 S.E. 2d 713 (W. Va. Sup. Ct. 1964); *but see Gilbert v. Howard*, 64 N.M. 200, 326 P.2d 1085, 1087 (1958).

Additionally, the express language of the statute and Texas case law indicate this statute expressly applied to circumstances involving the extension of credit to a partnership. *Friedman v. West Newberry Village* Assoc., 787 S.W.2d 154, 158 (Tex. App.--Houston [1st Dist.] 1992, no writ) (loans obtained based on representation of partnership);*Gray v. West*, 608 S.W.2d 771, 777 (Tex. Civ. App.--Amarillo, 1980, writ ref'd n.r.e.) ("[T]he statute speaks specifically of the giving of credit to the actual or apparent partnership on the faith of a representation of partnership. . ."); *Cox Enterprises, Inc. v. Filip*, 538 S.W.2d 836, 838 (Tex. Civ. App.--Austin 1976, no writ) (applying section 16 in suit on a sworn account for unpaid advertising services). The Youngs never extended credit to the Chamberlain firm, and therefore, this statute is inapplicable under the facts of this case.

Because appellants failed to raise a material fact dispute as to appellees' actual partner status or as to each element of partnership by estoppel, the trial court did not err in granting summary judgment. Point of error number two is overruled.

The judgment of the trial court is AFFIRMED in part, and REVERSED and REMANDED, in part, to the trial court for proceedings consistent with this opinion.

United States of America, Ex Rel., v. Integrated Coast Guard Systems, et.al.
705 F.Supp.2d 519 (2010) U S Dist Ct, N.D. Texas, Dallas Division

MEMORANDUM OPINION AND ORDER

Relator's Factual Allegations and Procedural History

For purposes of deciding the pending motions to dismiss, the Court accepts as true the well-pleaded factual allegations of Relator Michael J. DeKort's ("Dekort's") Fifth Amended Complaint ("Complaint"), and views all facts in the light most favorable to DeKort. *See Sonnier v. State Farm Mutual Auto. Ins. Co.*, 509 F.3d 673, 675 (5th Cir.2007). The background facts recounted below are therefore based on the well-pleaded factual allegations of DeKort's Complaint.

The Coast Guard's Deepwater Program and the Deepwater Contract

Beginning in the late 1990s, the United States Coast Guard ("Coast Guard") began evaluating ways to modernize or replace its fleet of ships, planes and helicopters, an effort which became known as the Coast Guard's Integrated Deepwater System Program ("Deepwater"). (Compl., Exs. A, K and L). This modernization effort included conversion of forty-nine 110-foot patrol boats into 123-foot patrol boats. (*Id.*) In June 2002, following a lengthy proposal evaluation period, the Coast Guard awarded the Integrated Deepwater System Contract ("Deepwater Contract") to ICGS, a limited liability company created under Delaware law. (*Id.* ¶¶ 8, 10). Pursuant to the Deepwater Contract, ICGS was to design, construct, deploy, support and integrate Deepwater assets to meet Coast Guard requirements. (*Id.*, Ex. L at 3).

Defendants Lockheed and Northrop Grumman are members of ICGS, as well as first-tier subcontractors to ICGS on Deepwater, responsible for different portions of the Deepwater program work. (*Id.* ¶ 10). Lockheed was responsible for modernizing the patrol boats' "Command, Control, Communications, Computer, Intelligence, Surveillance, and Reconnaissance" ("C4ISR") systems. (*Id.*, Ex. K at 1). Northrop Grumman, through its subcontractor Bollinger Shipyards, was primarily responsible for ship design, including propeller shaft alignment and hull construction necessary to convert the 110-foot patrol boats into 123-foot patrol boats. (*Id.* ¶¶ 126-137, and Ex. K at 1).

Relator DeKort's Involvement with Deepwater

From July 2003 to February 2004, Lockheed employed DeKort as the Deepwater Lead Systems Engineer for the conversion of 110-foot patrol boats to 123-foot patrol boats. (*Id.* ¶ 27). DeKort is a C4ISR systems expert, and although he wanted to remain on the Deepwater program, Lockheed removed him as Lead Systems Engineer in February 2004 "because of apparent friction arising from his complaints to his direct management about ICGS's concealed defects and its improper and shoddy work." (*Id.*). Since his termination, DeKort has been "seeking a remedy for ICGS's corruption on the Integrated Deepwater System contract." (*Id.*).

During prior employment with Lockheed in or around 2001, DeKort was a member of ICGS's proposal-planning group for the Deepwater Contract. (*Id.* ¶ 154). In proposal-planning meetings, ICGS, primarily through Lockheed, developed a strategy of persuading the Coast Guard to delete its standard "will" or "shall" language from much of the requirements of the Deepwater Contract. ICGS's and Lockheed's expressed intention was to persuade the Coast Guard to replace "requirements" language with "guidance" language, allowing the ICGS joint venture nearly unlimited latitude in developing the Deepwater "system of systems." (*Id.*). "ICGS, by and through Lockheed, planned to promise the Coast Guard that ICGS, through both Lockheed and Northrop, would deliver superior design and products if the Coast Guard would 'untie the contractors hands' from inflexible requirements." (*Id.*). In the summer of 2003, in his role as Lockheed's Deepwater Lead Systems Engineer, DeKort "learned that ICGS, primarily through Lockheed, had succeeded with its 'guidance' pitch; the contractual project requirements included guidance language rather than firm 'shall' or 'will' requirements." (*Id.* ¶ 155).

Delivery of Flawed and Non-Compliant 123-Foot Patrol Boats to Coast Guard

Between March 1, 2004 and January 13, 2006, ICGS delivered eight 123-foot patrol boats to the Coast Guard, specifically: the Matagorda; the Vashon; the Metompkin; the Padre; the Attu; the Nunivak; the Monhegan; and the Manitou. (*Id., Exs. C-J*). The 123-foot patrol boats ICGS delivered to the Coast Guard had numerous flaws relating to both the C4ISR systems, and the hull, mechanical and electrical ("HM & E") work. ...

Even though Defendants were aware of the flaws, Defendants continued to invoice for the work completed and certified that the delivered assets met all requirements. ICGS certified and signed conformance documents falsely representing that all eight of the 123-foot patrol boats met contractual requirements. More specifically, with regard to the lead vessel, the Matagorda, on or about March 1, 2004, ICGS submitted to the Coast Guard a Certificate of Compliance (sometimes referred to as, "COC"), signed on behalf of ICGS by or for its Domain Program Manager, Quality Assurance Manager, and Director of Contracts, which provided:

Description: This [Delivery Task Order] provides the detailed design and construction for major modification of the 110-foot patrol boat Matagorda, including completion of all design, analyses, construction, and testing to deploy the lead vessel of the proposed 123-Ft Cutter Class, and to demonstrate compliance requirements. Included in the modifications was an extensive ultrasonic survey of the hull ... resulting in the replacement of over 800 square feet of wasted hull plate; a new deckhouse providing an enlarged, 360-degree bridge and berthing for a dual-gender crew; a stern extension with a stern ramp and door for launch and recovery of the Short-Range

Prosecutor; and upgraded C4ISR suite to ensure interoperability with the IDS; and all related logistics and training.

I certify that on 1 March 2004, the ICGS Deepwater Program furnished the supplies and/or services called for in accordance with all applicable requirements. I further certify that the supplies and/or services are of the quality specified and conform in all respects with the contract requirements, including specifications, drawings, preservation, packaging, packing, marking requirements, and physical item identification, and are in the quantity shown on the attached acceptance document. (*Id.,* Ex. D at 2). ICGS submitted nearly identical Certificates of Compliance with: the March 9, 2004 delivery of the Vashon (*id.,* Ex. C at 2); the May 13, 2004 delivery of the Metompkin (*id.,* Ex. E at 2); the June 24, 2004 delivery of the Padre (*id.,* Ex. F at 2); the August 2, 2004 delivery of the Attu (*id.,* Ex. G at 2); the February 14, 2005 delivery of the Nunivak (*id.,* Ex, H at 2); the October 3, 2005 delivery of the Monhegan (*id.,* Ex, I at 2); and the January 13, 2006 delivery of the Manitou (*id.,* Ex, J at 2).

In addition to a Certificate of Compliance, each delivery was accompanied by a "Material Inspections and Receiving Report," also knows as a "DD Form 250" ("DD-250"), signed by the Coast Guard's contracting officer. (*Id.,* Exs. C-J) (showing Contracting Officer's signature next to attestation that "[q]uantities shown ... were received in apparent good condition except as noted"); (*Id.,* Exs. H-J) (showing additional government signature next to attestation that "acceptance of listed items has been made by me or under my supervision and they conform to contract, except as noted herein or on supporting documents.").

Further, ICGS, primarily through Lockheed, was contractually required to enter certain information into an Action Item Database System. (*Id.* ¶ 173). ICGS, primarily through Lockheed, fraudulently omitted information and data. ... In addition to the fraudulent omissions from the Action Item Database System, ICGS, primarily through Lockheed, never advised the Coast Guard of the falsely incomplete information. (*Id.*). ICGS, primarily through Northrop, fraudulently omitted information and data regarding the shaft alignment and hull damages from the contractually mandated Action Item Database System, and failed to advise the Coast Guard of the incomplete information. (*Id.* ¶ 174). When DeKort entered some of this information himself in January 2004, Lockheed's Paul J. Messer removed the entries, stating that DeKort's entries lacked detail. (*Id.* ¶ 175). After deleting DeKort's entries, Defendants never re-entered any information regarding the ... defects, nor did they disclose the concealed facts. (*Id.*).

The Coast Guard eventually decommissioned all eight 123-foot patrol boats due to problems with the vessels, primarily associated with the hull, mechanical and electrical issues. (*Id.* ¶ 131). The total loss of the patrol boats due to Defendants' "shoddy and deceptive work" likely caused a loss of $11.75 million dollars per patrol boat, or $96 million dollars. (*Id.* ¶ 26).

"Joint Venture" and "Alter-Ego" Allegations

At various times, Lockheed and ICGS executives, as well as ICGS's website, have referred to ICGS, which is a limited liability company, as a "joint venture" between Lockheed and Northrop, and used the term "partners" to describe Lockheed and Northrop. (*Id.* ¶¶ 7-11, 18, and Exs. K and L). Further, ICGS operated as an alter-ego of Lockheed and of Northrop, and "[f]or all the purposes of the Deepwater program ICGS, Lockheed and Northrop are all one and the same." (*Id.* ¶ 11, and Ex. L). ICGS did not have any of its own employees, but was operated by Lockheed and Northrop employees, and its Board of Directors was dominated by members of Lockheed's and Northrop's Boards. (*Id.* ¶ 8). ICGS was funded by Lockheed and Northrop and ICGS had no business other than the Deepwater Contract, the tasks of which were carried out by Lockheed and Northrop employees using Lockheed and Northrop resources. (*Id.* ¶ 13). ICGS operated with grossly inadequate capital of its own, and the daily operations of ICGS were not kept separate and distinct from those of Lockheed and Northrop. (*Id.*). Lockheed and Northrop had common business departments and ICGS used Lockheed's and Northrop's engineering and development departments. (*Id.*). Lockheed and Northrop executed the actions that gave rise to the allegations of wrongdoing in this lawsuit. Because the controlling directors of ICGS are also the directors of Lockheed and Northrop, ICGS took orders from the participating Lockheed and Northrop directors, rather than the other way around. Lockheed's and Northrop's representatives were, simultaneously, duty-bound to act in Lockheed's and Northrop's best interests. (*Id.* ¶¶ 14-15).

On October 15, 2009, Defendants Lockheed and ICGS filed separate motions to dismiss, both arguing that DeKort has failed to plead a *qui tam* cause of action under § 3729(a) with the particularity required by Federal Rule of Civil Procedure 9(b), and that DeKort has failed to state a claim upon which relief may be granted under Rule 12(b)(6). Prior to addressing the pending motions to dismiss, the Court sets forth the applicable legal standards. ...

...Finally, Lockheed contends that it cannot be held liable for FCA violations stemming from deficiencies in the hull, mechanical and electrical work, since the Complaint alleges that Northrop Grumman, not Lockheed, was charged with the HM & E work under the Deepwater Contract. Lockheed Brief at 22-23; Lockheed Reply at 9-10. Relator, in opposition, argues that, nevertheless, Lockheed and Northrop Grumman are estopped from denying that they were partners in a joint venture, and are thus jointly liable. Relator Opp. at 2-5.

To reiterate, Relator alleged that at various times, Lockheed and ICGS executives, as well as ICGS's website, have referred to ICGS, a limited liability company, as a "joint venture" between Lockheed and Northrop, and used the term "partners" to describe Lockheed and Northrop. Compl. ¶¶ 7-11, 18, and Exs. K and L. From these allegations, Relator seeks to hold Lockheed and Northrop Grumman jointly liable. In support, Relator contends that Defendants, in light of these "repeated public admissions that they are a joint venture" (*id.* ¶ 7), should be estopped from denying they are a joint venture.

ICGS is a registered limited liability company under Delaware law, not a partnership or joint venture, and thus joint and several liability does not apply. *See* Del.Code Ann. tit. 6, § 18-303. Further, estoppel requires that the Coast Guard: (1) must have been unaware of ICGS's actual legal form, (2) must have acted in reliance on this misunderstanding; and (3) must have been harmed as a result. *See Bragg v. Johnson*, 229 A.2d 497, 498-99 (Del.Super.1966); *Wilson v. Am. Ins. Co.*, 209 A.2d 902, 903-04 (Del.1965). As Lockheed correctly notes, Relator makes no such allegations. Accordingly, the Court grants this portion of Lockheed's motion to dismiss Relator's false certification allegations, and dismiss the HM & E claims with respect to Lockheed.

ICGS moves to dismiss Relator's FCA allegations, arguing that: (i) it is a Delaware limited liability company and, therefore, cannot be held responsible for the actions of Lockheed and/or Northrop Grumman under either Relator's joint venture allegations or alter-ego allegations, and (ii) Relator's allegations of FCA violations should be dismissed pursuant to Rule 12(b)(6) for failure to state a claim, and Rule 9(b) for failure to allege fraud with particularity.

Joint Venture and Alter-Ego Allegations

The Court first addresses ICGS's argument that, as a limited liability company formed under Delaware law, it cannot be held responsible for Lockheed's actions under either Relator's joint venture allegations or alter-ego allegations. ...Relator alleges that, notwithstanding that ICGS is a limited liability company formed under Delaware law, and [that] Lockheed and Northrop are its members, based on Defendants' "repeated public admissions that they are a joint venture" (Compl.¶ 7), Defendants should be estopped from denying they are a joint venture. ...[T]he Court ... rejects Relator's attempts to hold all Defendants jointly liable based on his allegations that Defendants held themselves out as a joint venture and partnership, and are [therefore] estopped from denying the same. (See § I.C.2.b.i., *supra*). Accordingly, the Court ... grants ICGS's motion to dismiss Relator's joint venture allegations ....

The Nature of the General Partnership

§152.056. PARTNERSHIP AS ENTITY. A partnership is an entity distinct from its partners.

§152.101. NATURE OF PARTNERSHIP PROPERTY. Partnership property is not property of the partners. A partner or a partner's spouse does not have an interest in partnership property.

§152.102. CLASSIFICATION AS PARTNERSHIP PROPERTY.

(a) Property is partnership property if acquired in the name of:

(1) the partnership; or

(2) one or more partners, regardless of whether the name of the partnership is indicated, if the instrument transferring title to the property indicates:

(A) the person's capacity as a partner; or
(B) the existence of a partnership.

(b) Property is presumed to be partnership property if acquired with partnership property, regardless of whether the property is acquired as provided by Subsection (a).

(c) Property acquired in the name of one or more partners is presumed to be the partner's property, regardless of whether the property is used for partnership purposes, if the instrument transferring title to the property does not indicate the person's capacity as *a partner or the existence of a partnership, and if the property is not acquired with partnership property.*

(d) For purposes of this section, property is acquired in the name of the partnership by a transfer to:

> *(1) the partnership in its name; or*
>
> *(2) one or more partners in the partners' capacity as partners in the partnership, if the name of the partnership is indicated in the instrument transferring title to the property.*

EXCEPTIONS

§152.053. QUALIFICATIONS TO BE PARTNER; NONPARTNER'S LIABILITY TO THIRD PERSON.

(a) A person may be a partner unless the person lacks capacity apart from this chapter.

(b) Except as provided by Section 152.307, a person who is not a partner in a partnership under Section 152.051 is not a partner as to a third person and is not liable to a third person under this chapter.

§152.054. FALSE REPRESENTATION OF PARTNERSHIP OR PARTNER.

(a) A false representation or other conduct falsely indicating that a person is a partner with another person does not of itself create a partnership.

(b) A representation or other conduct indicating that a person is a partner in an existing partnership, if that is not the case, does not of itself make that person a partner in the partnership.

Destec Energy, Inc., v. Houston Lighting & Power Company
966 S.W.2d 792 (Tex.App.-Austin, 1998)

In 1994, Lyondell Petrochemical Company ("Lyondell") owned and operated a large petrochemical plant in Channelview, Texas on the Houston Ship Channel. Lyondell bought its electric power from Houston Lighting & Power Company (HL & P). Destec Energy, Inc. ("Destec") and its subsidiary Cogen Lyondell, Inc. ("CLI") owned and operated a nearby facility that generated electric power and sold it to various customers, including to utilities for resale. At that time, Lyondell began considering the possibility of utilizing statutory "self-use" and "cogeneration" exemptions by building an electric-power generation facility at its plant in an effort to reduce electricity costs. Lyondell received a number of proposals for constructing or leasing various facilities. In late 1994, Lyondell began negotiating with Destec for the acquisition of a portion of the existing facility under Destec's control. After much negotiation, Lyondell and CLI, a Destec subsidiary, formed the Channelview CoGen General Partnership (the "Partnership") to sublease a portion of the facility from CLI.

Unlike other proposals, this arrangement offered Lyondell an almost immediate source of electricity, a much smaller capital outlay, and cost certainty. Lyondell's only major capital expense was the acquisition of a right-of-way for, and construction of, a two-and-a-half-mile transmission line from the facility to the plant. Under the Partnership Agreement, CLI owned an 88% interest in the Partnership, while Lyondell owned a 12% interest. For all intents and purposes, CLI would manage the facility on behalf of the Partnership for a fixed monthly fee. The partners would make monthly payments to cover each partner's share of the fixed management fees and the variable operating, maintenance, and fuel costs. The Partnership would transfer electricity as an in-kind distribution to the partners Lyondell and CLI. CLI agreed to indemnify Lyondell from most third-party, environmental, and other claims. The only purpose of the Partnership was the generation of electricity for the partners. The only assets of the Partnership were the sublease of the facility and the electricity generated.

Shortly after the Partnership was formed, HL & P sued the Public Utility Commission ("PUC"), Destec, CLI, and Destec subsidiary Destec Operating Company for injunctive and declaratory relief that the Partnership was required to obtain a certificate of convenience and necessity (CCN) from the PUC before delivering electricity to Lyondell and CLI. Lyondell intervened seeking a declaratory judgment that a CCN was not required. Following a two-day bench trial, the court rendered judgment declaring that CLI and Lyondell were required to obtain a CCN before operating as planned. In essence, the trial court used two alternative theories in deciding that the arrangement did not qualify for a CCN exemption. First, it ruled that, under the circumstances, the transfer of electricity was in substance a retail sale of power, even if it took the apparent form of a partnership distribution. Second, the trial court ruled that even if this was not a retail sale, the transfer of electricity did not qualify under the self-use exception. Destec, Destec Operating Company, CLI, and Lyondell perfected this appeal.

DISCUSSION

The Code defines an "electric utility" as "a person ... that owns or operates for compensation in this state equipment or facilities to produce, generate, transmit, distribute, sell, or furnish electricity in this state." Under the Code, a "person" includes a partnership. The Code requires an electric utility to obtain a CCN before rendering any service to the public. However, a person or corporation that generates and furnishes electricity only to itself is not considered an electric utility. Therefore, a partnership furnishing electricity only to itself would not be required to obtain a CCN in order to operate.

Appellants' first, second, and fifth points of error challenge the trial court's conclusion that the arrangement in question does not qualify for the exemption from the requirement of obtaining a CCN from the PUC. We review conclusions of law *de novo*. The gist of appellants' argument is that the Partnership was a valid partnership and that the delivery of electricity to the partners was not a retail sale but merely a distribution of partnership assets to the partners. HL & P responds that, irrespective of the *form* of the transaction, its *substance* was a retail sale, asserting in its brief that:

> (1) CLI continues to control and operate an existing power plant, as it has for several years, and is responsible for providing all resources necessary for operations.
>
> (2) Lyondell has no role in the management of the power plant or the "partnership" and is indemnified from all liabilities arising from operation of the plant or from the "partnership."
>
> (3) During normal operations, Lyondell will receive and pay for only the power it needs, up to 61.4MW of power, no matter how much power the power plant is actually producing.
>
> (4) Lyondell's only contributions to the "partnership" are four monthly payments, none of which reflect the actual costs of operating the power plant.
>
> (5) If the actual cost of making Lyondell's power is more or less than Lyondell's payments, only CLI loses or gains.
>
> (6) If Lyondell defaults, it loses nothing except its right to receive power.
>
> (7) The "partnership" has no real assets or employees, does not accumulate assets or debts and will distribute nothing upon termination; it is simply a shell through which Lyondell's payments flow to CLI.

We agree that the substance of a transaction will generally control over its form for regulatory purposes. However, we need not address the intricacies of the present partnership arrangement because this appeal can be decided on a simpler, more direct basis.

In their fifth point of error, appellants contend the trial court erred by concluding that the Partnership's distribution of electric power to its partners constitutes a transfer of electricity between separate entities and therefore is not "self-use." Appellants support this contention by asserting that [the Code] expressly authorizes partnerships to utilize the self-use exemption and that the "aggregate theory" of partnership should apply to the distribution of power to the partners. Appellants argue that the transfer of electricity by a partnership to its partners is merely a distribution that partners have a right to receive as part of their ownership interest in the partnership.

A partnership interest includes the right to receive distributions. Distributions may be a transfer of cash or other property. Appellants contend that electricity is an allowable form of such a distribution of property. Appellants also contend that the "aggregate theory" of partnership is still utilized in TRPA in certain circumstances and should be utilized here to determine that the distribution of electricity is not a transfer between separate entities. We conclude, however, that appellants' argument does not overcome the clear language of TRPA.

TRPA declares that "a partnership is an entity distinct from its partners." TRPA unequivocally embraces the entity theory of partnership by specifically stating in this section that a partnership is an entity distinct from its partners. This clear statement is intended to allay previous concerns that stemmed from confusion as to whether a partnership was an entity or an aggregate of its members....

Despite this language, appellants suggest that the aggregate theory is still utilized when "explicitly needed."

Appellants also cite *Lawler v. Dallas Statler–Hilton Joint Venture,* 793 S.W.2d 27 (Tex.App.—Dallas 1990, writ denied), as an example of the type of case that demands use of the aggregate theory. In *Lawler,* the court refused to apply the entity theory to a workers' compensation case, holding instead that employees of a partnership could sue individual partners as employers in addition to the partnership itself. *Id.* at 34. That case, however, was decided under the now-repealed Texas Uniform Partnership Act rather than TRPA. Moreover, even in *Lawler,* the court noted that the entity theory of partnerships is followed for most purposes, being especially reflected in four areas: property, creditors' rights, responsibility, and continuity. *Id.* at 33. TRPA is even more direct in applying the entity theory.

In addition, TRPA unequivocally provides that partnership property is not owned by individual partners: "Partnership property is not property of the partners. Neither a partner nor a partner's spouse has an interest in partnership property." The self-use exception of the Code applies if a partnership furnishes electricity only to itself. Here, however, the Partnership is furnishing electricity to its partners, who are distinct from the Partnership. Appellants present no reason why we should ignore the entity theory to meet its suggested standard of "explicit need." We hold that, under the present circumstances, when electricity moves from the

Partnership to the partners, the electricity is not being furnished to the Partnership itself; rather, it is moving between distinct, separate entities. We overrule point of error five.

In their third point of error, appellants contend the trial court improperly considered the alleged adverse effect a decision that the Partnership was not regulated by the Code would have on HL & P and third parties. The findings of fact in question state:

> HL & P has numerous industrial customers, many of whom occupy sites in close proximity to each other along the Houston Ship Channel, in the Bayport area and near Freeport, Texas.
>
> Several of these customers have existing cogeneration plants and occupy sites that adjoin the plant sites of other HL & P industrial customers.
>
> If the transaction in this case were held to be exempt from PUC regulation under the self-service exception provided by Public Util. Regulatory Act (PURA), then any user of electricity, including other customers of HL & P, could enter into arrangements with owners of cogeneration facilities and obtain their power from these non-regulated entities. Such de facto deregulation, if it is to come, should be effected by the Legislature.

In the body of this point of error, appellants assert that the trial court improperly considered this adverse effect on HL & P in deciding whether the Partnership met the statutory requirements for formation. In reviewing the record, however, we find that consideration of this adverse effect goes to the interpretation of the Code provisions in question, not to whether the Partnership met the requirements of partnership formation under the TRPA. "In construing a statute, whether or not the statute is considered ambiguous on its face, a court may consider among other matters the: ... (5) consequences of a particular construction." The trial court was well within its discretion in considering the effect on third parties and HL & P as consequences of its construction of the self-use exception in the Code....

In point of error seven, appellants argue that the trial court erred by finding that CLI and Lyondell agreed to terminate the Partnership if a court determined that a CCN was required for the Partnership's distribution of electricity to its partners. Appellants contend there is no evidence that the parties made such an agreement. In the Partnership Agreement, CLI and Lyondell agreed that several events would require winding up, including a court determination that a CCN was required, *unless* both partners agree to appeal such order. Appellants argue that because they have appealed the trial court's decision, the admitted agreement to wind up the partnership has not yet become effective. We agree that the finding of fact is incomplete in that it does not state when the agreement to wind up becomes effective. Nonetheless, this defect is harmless in the present context. Despite even a wholly erroneous finding of fact, if a judgment is otherwise correct on the merits, the judgment will be upheld. Here, the finding of fact may be somewhat misleading in that the exception to the agreement to wind up was not noted therein, but even without the finding there is ample support for the judgment. Point of error seven is overruled.

CONCLUSION

Because the trial court's judgment is supported by the conclusion that an in-kind distribution of electricity from a partnership to its partners is not the same as a partnership's furnishing electricity to itself, we overrule appellants' points of error and affirm the trial court's judgment.

****

Siller v. LPP Mortgage Ltd.
Court of Appeals of Texas, San Antonio
Not Reported in S.W.3d, 2008 WL 5170251

Juan Jose Siller and Perfecta G. Siller appeal the trial court's order granting summary judgment in favor of LPP Mortgage Ltd. in a lawsuit in which Juan and Perfecta assert numerous claims against LPP arising from a dispute over the title to certain real property. Because the summary judgment evidence raised a genuine issue of material fact with regard to the ownership of the property, we reverse the trial court's order and remand the cause to the trial court for further proceedings.

BACKGROUND

In 1967, a 520 acre tract of land in Cotulla, Texas (the "Property") was conveyed by a deed to Abel Siller, Santiago Siller, Mario Siller, and Jose M. Siller, Jr., who were brothers. The brothers used the acreage for farming.

In 1981, the [Small Business Association] SBA entered into a loan agreement which listed the borrower as "Abel, Mario & Santiago Siller" and was signed by Abel, Mario and Santiago. The note that was signed to evidence the loan listed the borrower as Siller Brothers Farms. The note was signed on behalf of Siller Brothers Farms by Mario, Santiago, Abel, and their wives. The signatures of Mario, Santiago and Abel indicated they were signing in their capacities as individuals and partners. A Deed of Trust listing Siller Brothers Farms as grantor also was signed granting a lien against the Property to secure the note. The Deed of Trust was signed by Mario, Santiago, and Abel in their capacities as individuals and partners. Notably absent from the SBA loan agreement, promissory note and Deed of Trust was the signature of Jose M. Siller, Jr. Four months after the SBA loan was made, Mario Siller, Santiago Siller, and Abel Siller filed a certificate of partnership for Siller Brothers Farm with the Texas Secretary of State.

The SBA subsequently assigned the note to LPP. Jose died in July of 2001. Following a default by the borrowers, LPP foreclosed on the Property in August of 2001. In April of 2002,

Jose's wife, Perfecta, and son, Juan, sued LPP asserting title to a 1/4 interest in the Property. After the parties filed competing motions for summary judgment, the trial court granted summary judgment in favor of LPP.

DISCUSSION

In order to grant summary judgment in favor of LPP, the trial court necessarily concluded that the evidence established as a matter of law that the Property was purchased in 1967 by a partnership in which the four brothers were partners, and, as a result, the four brothers, as partners, held title on behalf of the partnership. Juan and Perfecta challenge this conclusion on several grounds....

Ownership of the Property

In order for LPP to have prevailed on its traditional summary judgment, the evidence had to conclusively establish as a matter of law that the Property was owned by the partnership at the time it was purchased in 1967. If the Property was purchased by the individuals, any oral transfer to the partnership would be barred by the statute of frauds. Moreover, Perfecta would not have any community property interest in the Property if it was purchased by the partnership.

Whether land taken in the name of one or more partners is partnership property depends on the parties' intent and the understanding and design under which they acted. An implied agreement that property will be owned by a partnership may be established by "the general purposes of the parties, the nature of their business, and the manner in which they have dealt with the property in question." Mere use of property in the operation of a partnership does not make it an asset of the partnership. Instead, whether property used in a partnership's operation is owned by the partnership is a question of intent.

In its brief, LPP relies on the following summary judgment evidence as conclusively establishing that the Property was owned by a partnership of the four brothers: (1) admissions by Santiago and Abel that the Property was partnership property; (2) partnership tax records listing the four brothers as partners and the Property as a partnership asset; (3) property taxes assessed against the partnership as record owner of the Property; (4) evidence that the partnership did not pay rent to the four brothers for the use of the Property; and (5) reporting of the condemnation award as partnership income. Although the evidence relied on by LPP does support the contention that the Property was owned by the partnership, in our review of a summary judgment, we must consider the evidence in the light most favorable to the non-movant and indulge all reasonable inferences and resolve any doubts in the non-movant's favor. Applying this standard to the evidence presented, we must consider Abel's deposition testimony that the partnership was not formed until after the Property was purchased since two of the brothers were in Vietnam fighting in the army at the time of purchase and one brother, Mario, did not return until two years later.

The manner in which the SBA loan was documented also raises fact issues as to whether the Property was owned by a partnership of all four brothers or whether the SBA only obtained a lien as to the interests in the Property owned by Abel, Santiago, and Mario. The original loan agreement listed the borrower as Abel, Santiago, and Mario, and the loan agreement was signed by the three brothers in their individual capacities. The Deed of Trust was signed by the three brothers both as partners and in their individual capacities. A title opinion obtained at the time of the loan listed the owner of the Property as the four brothers. The record contains an affidavit signed by Abel, Santiago, and Mario stating: (1) the Property was owned by the four brothers individually; (2) Abel, Santiago, and Mario only intended to encumber their interest in the Property as security for the SBA loan; and (3) Abel, Santiago, and Mario did not intend to encumber Jose's interest in the Property, and no one had authority to encumber Jose's interest. Santiago testified in his deposition that to his knowledge, Jose was unaware of the SBA loan. At the time of the loan from the SBA, Abel, Santiago, and Mario signed a document entitled "Certificate as to Partners" certifying that they were all of the partners of Siller Brothers Farms.

Finally, the record contains a memo to the senior loan committee at the time LPP was undertaking to foreclose the loan stating that the borrower is a general partnership established in 1985 and noting that if LPP was the successful bidder, LPP would jointly own the Property with Jose based on a title opinion in the file showing that the four brothers owned the Property.

Because the foregoing evidence raises a genuine issue of material fact with regard to whether: (1) the Property was purchased and owned by the four brothers individually; and (2) the Deed of Trust encumbered Jose's interest in the Property, the trial court erred in granting summary judgment in favor of LPP. The fact issue regarding ownership of the Property also precludes summary judgment as to whether the foreclosure notice was proper and whether Juan and Perfecta are entitled to a partition of the Property.

CONCLUSION

The trial court's judgment is reversed, and the cause is remanded to the trial court for further proceedings.

GOVERNANCE

General Partnerships are commonly managed by the partners. The general rule is that each partner has an equal say in the management of the affairs of the general partnership. However, the partners may agree to other forms of management that will provide more management authority in one or more partners than in the remaining partners. Under this governance model management of the partnership may by the managing partner, managing partners or management committee.

General partners act by voting, unless they otherwise agree. The partners can decide whether partner vote is based on their financial interest in the partnership or on a per capita basis. For example, a partnership may decide that a partner who has invested 65% of the partnership capital, may have 65% of the vote.

Subchapter D: Relationship Between Partners and Between Partnership

§152.201. ADMISSION AS PARTNER. A person may become a partner only with the consent of all partners.

§152.203. RIGHTS AND DUTIES OF PARTNER.

(a) Each partner has equal rights in the management and conduct of the business of a partnership. A partner's right to participate in the management and conduct of the business is not community property.

(b) A partner may use or possess partnership property only on behalf of the partnership.

(c) A partner is not entitled to receive compensation for services performed for a partnership other than reasonable compensation for services rendered in winding up the business of the partnership.

(d) A partner who, in the proper conduct of the business of the partnership or for the preservation of its business or property, reasonably makes a payment or advance beyond the amount the partner agreed to contribute, or who reasonably incurs a liability, is entitled to be repaid and to receive interest from the date of the:

   (1) payment or advance; or
   (2) incurrence of the liability.

§152.204. GENERAL STANDARDS OF PARTNER'S CONDUCT.

(a) A partner owes to the partnership, the other partners, and a transferee of a deceased partner's partnership interest as designated in Section 152.406(a)(2):

   (1) a duty of loyalty; and
   (2) a duty of care.

(b) A partner shall discharge the partner's duties to the partnership and the other partners under this code or under the partnership agreement and exercise any rights and powers in the conduct or winding up of the partnership business:

    (1) in good faith; and

    (2) in a manner the partner reasonably believes to be in the best interest of the partnership.

(c) A partner does not violate a duty or obligation under this chapter or under the partnership agreement merely because the partner's conduct furthers the partner's own interest.

(d) A partner, in the partner's capacity as partner, is not a trustee and is not held to the standards of a trustee.

§152.205. PARTNER'S DUTY OF LOYALTY.

A partner's duty of loyalty includes:

(1) accounting to and holding for the partnership property, profit, or benefit derived by the partner:

    (A) in the conduct and winding up of the partnership business; or

    (B) from use by the partner of partnership property;

(2) refraining from dealing with the partnership on behalf of a person who has an interest adverse to the partnership; and

(3) refraining from competing or dealing with the partnership in a manner adverse to the partnership.

§152.206. PARTNER'S DUTY OF CARE.

(a) A partner's duty of care to the partnership and the other partners is to act in the conduct and winding up of the partnership business with the care an ordinarily prudent person would exercise in similar circumstances.

(b) An error in judgment does not by itself constitute a breach of the duty of care.

(c) A partner is presumed to satisfy the duty of care if the partner acts on an informed basis and in compliance with Section 152.204(b).

§152.207. STANDARDS OF CONDUCT APPLICABLE TO PERSON WINDING UP PARTNERSHIP BUSINESS.

Sections 152.204-152.206 apply to a person winding up the partnership business as the personal or legal representative of the last surviving partner to the same extent that those sections apply to a partner.

§152.208. AMENDMENT TO PARTNERSHIP AGREEMENT.

A partnership agreement may be amended only with the consent of all partners.

§152.209. DECISION-MAKING REQUIREMENT.

(a) A difference arising in a matter in the ordinary course of the partnership business may be decided by a majority-in-interest of the partners.

(b) An act outside the ordinary course of business of a partnership may be undertaken only with the consent of all partners.

§ 152.211. REMEDIES OF PARTNERSHIP AND PARTNERS.

(a) A partnership may maintain an action against a partner for a breach of the partnership agreement or for the violation of a duty to the partnership causing harm to the partnership.

(b) A partner may maintain an action against the partnership or another partner for legal or equitable relief, including an accounting of partnership business, to:

(1) enforce a right under the partnership agreement;

(2) enforce a right under this chapter, including:

(A) the partner's rights under Sections 152.201-152.209, 152.212, and 152.213;

(B) the partner's right on withdrawal to have the partner's interest in the partnership redeemed under Subchapter H or to enforce any other right under Subchapters G and H; and

(C) the partner's rights under Subchapter I;

(3) enforce the rights and otherwise protect the interests of the partner, including rights and interests arising independently of the partnership relationship; or

(4) enforce a right under Chapter 11.

(c) The accrual of and a time limitation on a right of action for a remedy under this section is governed by other applicable law.

(d) A right to an accounting does not revive a claim barred by law.

§152.212. BOOKS AND RECORDS OF PARTNERSHIP.

(a) In this section, "access" includes the opportunity to inspect and copy books and records during ordinary business hours.

(b) A partnership shall keep its books and records, if any, at its chief executive office.

(c) A partnership shall provide access to its books and records to a partner or an agent or attorney of a partner.

(d) The partnership shall provide a former partner or an agent or attorney of a former partner access to books and records pertaining to the period during which the former partner was a partner or for any other proper purpose with respect to another period.

(e) A partnership may impose a reasonable charge, covering the costs of labor and material, for copies of documents furnished under this section.

§152.213. INFORMATION REGARDING PARTNERSHIP.

(a) On request and to the extent just and reasonable, each partner and the partnership shall furnish complete and accurate information concerning the partnership to:

(1) a partner;

(2) the legal representative of a deceased partner or a partner who has a legal disability; or

(3) an assignee.

(b) A legal representative of a deceased partner or a partner who has a legal disability and an assignee are subject to the duties of a partner with respect to information made available.

§152.214. CERTAIN THIRD-PARTY OBLIGATIONS NOT AFFECTED.
Sections 152.203, 152.208, and 152.209 do not limit a partnership's obligations to another person under Sections 152.301 and 152.302.

§152.301. PARTNER AS AGENT.
Each partner is an agent of the partnership for the purpose of its business.

§152.302. BINDING EFFECT OF PARTNER'S ACTION.

(a) Unless a partner does not have authority to act for the partnership in a particular matter and the person with whom the partner is dealing knows that the partner lacks authority, an act of a partner, including the execution of an instrument in the partnership name, binds the partnership if the act is apparently for carrying on in the ordinary course:

(1) the partnership business; or

(2) business of the kind carried on by the partnership.

(b) An act of a partner that is not apparently for carrying on in the ordinary course a business described by Subsection (a) binds the partnership only if authorized by the other partners.

(c) A conveyance of real property by a partner on behalf of the partnership not otherwise binding on the partnership binds the partnership if the property has been conveyed by the grantee or a person claiming through the grantee to a holder for value without knowledge that the partner exceeded that partner's authority in making the conveyance.

Long v. Lopez
115 S.W.3d 221 (Tex.Civ.App.-Ft. Worth, 2003)

Partner who entered into office equipment lease on behalf of partnership brought action against other partner, seeking reimbursement for money paid to settle lessor's claim against partnership for past due amounts. Following a bench trial, the 235th District Court, Cooke County, entered a take nothing judgment against plaintiff. Plaintiff appealed. The Court of Appeals, held that: (1) partner was authorized to settle lessor's action against partnership; (2) partner was not required to be joined in lessor's action against partnership; (3) partner was required to reimburse partner who paid to settle lessor's action against partnership, one-half of amount paid; (4) partner who incurred attorney fees to defend action by lessor was entitled to reimbursement from other partner of one-half of attorney fees paid; and (5) partner who brought action against other partner for reimbursement of amount paid to settle lessor's action against partnership was entitled to recover reasonable and necessary attorney fees incurred in bringing action. Reversed.

Appellant Wayne A. Long sued Appellee Sergio Lopez to recover from him, jointly and severally, his portion of a partnership debt that Appellant had paid. After a bench trial, the trial court ruled that Appellant take nothing from Appellee. We reverse and render, and remand for calculation of attorney's fees in this suit and pre- and post-judgment interest.

Formation and operation of the partnership

Appellant testified that in September 1996, Appellant, Appellee, and Don Bannister entered into an oral partnership agreement in which they agreed to be partners in Wood Relo ("the partnership"), a trucking business located in Gainesville, Texas. Wood Relo located loads for and dispatched approximately twenty trucks it leased from owner-operators.

Appellant said that in forming this partnership, the three individuals signed and filed with the county clerk on September 3, 1996 an assumed name certificate stating they were doing business as Wood Relo, a "General Partnership." This certificate was admitted into evidence at trial. Appellant testified that the three partners agreed to share equally one-third of the profits and losses of the partnership. All three partners were authorized to sign checks on Wood Relo's bank account. Appellee testified, however, that even though they signed the assumed name certificate and the bank ownership form, in his opinion there was no partnership agreement among the three men.

> It was noted at trial that the bank's "Business Account Agreement" states in the section designated "Ownership of Account" that Wood Relo is a "Corporation—For Profit," even though one of the possible boxes that could have been checked is "Partnership." Appellant testified that this was a mistake and that when the three partners signed the bank ownership card, they did not notice that the wrong box was checked; he stated that Wood Relo is definitely not a corporation

The trial court found that Appellant, Appellee, and Bannister formed a partnership, Wood Relo, without a written partnership agreement. In his brief on appeal, Appellee does not contest these findings. Appellant testified that to properly conduct the partnership's business, he entered into an office equipment lease with IKON Capital Corporation ("IKON") on behalf of the partnership. The lease was a thirty-month contract under which the partnership leased a telephone system, fax machine, and photocopier at a rate of $577.91 per month. The lease agreement was between IKON and Wood Relo; the "authorized signer" was listed as Wayne Long, who also signed as personal guarantor.

Appellant stated that all three partners were authorized to buy equipment for use by the partnership. He testified that the partners had agreed that it was necessary for the partnership to lease the equipment and that on the day the equipment was delivered to Wood Relo's office, Appellant was the only partner at the office; therefore, Appellant was the only one available to sign the lease and personal guaranty that IKON required.

Appellant and Appellee both acknowledged that around March of 1997, the disintegration of a key business relationship between Wood Relo and another company caused Wood Relo to become unable to carry out its business. Appellant testified that Bannister, the third partner, "decided to ... pull up stake and go home," quitting the partnership. Later, Bannister filed for personal bankruptcy. Appellant testified that when Bannister left Wood Relo, the partnership still had "quite a few" debts to pay, including the IKON lease.

The claim by IKON

In April 1997, when the partnership closed its Gainesville office due to decreased business, the IKON office equipment was moved to an office the parties were using in Sherman. Appellant testified that he and Appellee worked with IKON to negotiate a settlement for IKON to repossess the equipment, but IKON would not do so. Eventually, IKON did repossess all the leased equipment. Appellant testified that he received a demand letter from IKON, requesting payment by Wood Relo of overdue lease payments and accelerating payment of the remaining balance of the lease. IKON sought recovery of past due payments in the amount of $2,889.55 and accelerated future lease payments in the amount of $11,558.20, for a total of $14,447.75, plus interest, costs, and attorney's fees, with the total exceeding $16,000. Appellant testified that he advised Appellee that he had received the demand letter from IKON.

Ultimately, IKON filed a lawsuit against Appellant individually and d/b/a Wood Relo, but did not name Appellee or Bannister as parties to the suit. Through his counsel, Appellant negotiated a settlement with IKON for a total of $9,000. An agreed judgment was entered in conjunction with the settlement agreement providing that if Appellant did not pay the settlement, Wood Relo and Appellant would owe IKON $12,000.

After settling the IKON lawsuit, Appellant's counsel sent a letter to Appellee and Bannister regarding the settlement agreement, advising them that they were jointly and severally liable for the $9,000 that extinguished the partnership's debt to IKON, plus attorney's fees. At trial, Appellant said Appellee then called him, very upset, saying that he refused to pay anything. Appellant claimed that he told Appellee about the default on the IKON lease before the lawsuit was filed; however, Appellee testified he did not know of the default until Appellant sent a letter to him informing him that the settlement had already occurred.

In response to Appellant's original petition, Appellee filed a general denial, but did not file a verified plea denying the existence of the partnership.

FINDINGS OF FACT AND CONCLUSIONS OF LAW

After ruling that Appellant take nothing from Appellee, the trial court made the following findings of fact and conclusions of law:

FINDINGS OF FACT

1. Plaintiff and Defendant were two of the three partners in a partnership.
2. The third partner is in bankruptcy.
3. Plaintiff signed a contract with a third party for the partnership and individually as a guarantor.
4. The partnership did not have a written partnership agreement.
5. The partnership defaulted on the payments dues [sic] under the contract with the said third party.
6. The third party sued Plaintiff after the default.
7. Defendant was not sued by the third party, and was not brought into the lawsuit by the Plaintiff.
8. Defendant was not aware of the lawsuit by the third party.
9. Plaintiff settled the lawsuit with the third party without consulting Defendant or obtaining Defendant's agreement.
10. Plaintiff sued Defendant for 1/3 of the amount for which the Plaintiff settled the lawsuit brought by the third party.

CONCLUSIONS OF LAW

1. *A partner does not have authority to act for a partnership unless it is apparent authority* or authority granted to them by a written partnership agreement.
2. When Plaintiff settled the lawsuit with the third party, and without bringing Defendant into the lawsuit, or consulting the Defendant, *the Plaintiff was not acting for the partnership, because he had no apparent authority with respect to lawsuits.*
3. Plaintiff takes nothing as to Defendant in the present lawsuit. [Emphasis added.]

TEXAS REVISED PARTNERSHIP ACT

The trial court determined that Appellant was not entitled to reimbursement from Appellee because Appellant was not acting for the partnership when he settled IKON's claim against the partnership. The court based its conclusion on the fact that Appellant had no "apparent authority with respect to lawsuits" and had not notified Appellee of the IKON lawsuit.

Authority to act for partnership

To the extent that a partnership agreement does not otherwise specify, the provisions of the Texas Revised Partnership Act govern the relations of the partners and between the partners and the partnership. Under the Act, each partner has equal rights in the management and conduct of the business of a partnership. With certain inapplicable exceptions, all partners are liable jointly and severally for all debts and obligations of the partnership unless otherwise agreed by the claimant or provided by law. A partnership may be sued and may defend itself in its partnership name. Each partner is an agent of the partnership for the purpose of its business; unless the partner does not have authority to act for the partnership in a particular matter and the person with whom the partner is dealing knows that the partner lacks authority, an act of a partner, including the execution of an instrument in the partnership name, binds the partnership if "the act is for apparently carrying on in the ordinary course: (1) the partnership business." If the act of a partner is not apparently for carrying on the partnership business, an act of a partner binds the partnership only if authorized by the other partners.

The extent of authority of a partner is determined essentially by the same principles as those measuring the scope of the authority of an agent. As a general rule, each partner is an agent of the partnership and is empowered to bind the partnership in the normal conduct of its business. Generally, an agent's authority is presumed to be coextensive with the business entrusted to his care. An agent is limited in his authority to such contracts and acts as are incident to the management of the particular business with which he is entrusted.

Winding up the partnership

A partner's duty of care to the partnership and the other partners is to act in the conduct and winding up of the partnership business with the care an ordinarily prudent person would exercise in similar circumstances. During the winding up of a partnership's business, a partner's fiduciary duty to the other partners and the partnership is limited to matters relating to the winding up of the partnership's affairs.

Appellant testified that he entered into the settlement agreement with IKON to save the partnership a substantial amount of money. IKON's petition sought over $16,000 from the partnership, and the settlement agreement was for $9,000; therefore, Appellant settled IKON's claim for 43% less than the amount for which IKON sued the partnership.

Both Appellant and Appellee testified that the partnership "fell apart," "virtually was dead," and had to move elsewhere. Appellant testified that, because of the demise of the partnership operations, the company for which the partnership was acting as an agent had reworked its system, resulting in the partnership no longer being able to make any profit. The inability of the partnership to continue its trucking business was an event requiring the partners to wind up the affairs of the partnership. It was no longer capable of operating its business, and had moved its operations to Sherman, where the partners could begin to dispose of the partnership's property.

The Act provides that a partner winding up a partnership's business is authorized, to the extent appropriate for winding up, to perform the following in the name of and for and on behalf of the partnership:

(1) prosecute and defend civil, criminal, or administrative suits;
(2) settle and close the partnership's business;
(3) dispose of and convey the partnership's property;
(4) satisfy or provide for the satisfaction of the partnership's liabilities;
(5) distribute to the partners any remaining property of the partnership; and
(6) perform any other necessary act.

Appellant accrued the IKON debt on behalf of the partnership when he secured the office equipment for partnership operations, and he testified that he entered into the settlement with IKON when the partnership was in its final stages and the partners were going their separate ways. Accordingly, Appellant was authorized by the Act to settle the IKON lawsuit on behalf of the partnership.

In a suit brought against a partnership, it is not necessary to serve all the partners to support a judgment against the partnership. "Citation served on one member of a partnership authorizes a judgment against the partnership and the partner actually served. If a suit is against several partners who are jointly indebted under a contract and citation has been served on at least one but not all of the partners, the court may render judgment against the partnership and against the partners who were actually served, but may not award a personal judgment or execution against any partner who was not served. Any partnership may be sued in its partnership name for the purpose of enforcing against it a substantive right.

APPELLEE'S LIABILITY FOR THE IKON DEBT

If a partner reasonably incurs a liability in excess of the amount he agreed to contribute in properly conducting the business of the partnership or for preserving the partnership's business or property, he is entitled to be repaid by the partnership for that excess amount. A partner may sue another partner for reimbursement if the partner has made such an excessive payment.

With two exceptions not applicable to the facts of this case, all partners are liable jointly and severally for all debts and obligations of the partnership unless otherwise agreed by the claimant or provided by law. Because Wood Relo was sued for a partnership debt made in the proper conduct of the partnership business, and Appellant settled this claim in the course of winding up the partnership, he could maintain an action against Appellee for reimbursement of Appellant's disproportionate payment.

ATTORNEY'S FEES

Appellant sought to recover the attorney's fees expended in defending the IKON claim, and attorney's fees expended in the instant suit against Appellee. Testimony established that it was necessary for Appellant to employ an attorney to defend the action brought against the partnership by IKON; therefore, the attorney's fees related to defending the IKON lawsuit on behalf of Wood Relo are a partnership debt for which Appellee is jointly and severally liable. As such, Appellant is entitled to recover from Appellee one-half of the attorney's fees attributable to the IKON lawsuit. The evidence established that reasonable and necessary attorney's fees to defend the IKON lawsuit were $1725. Therefore, Appellant is entitled to recover from Appellee $862.50.

Appellant also seeks to recover the attorney's fees expended pursuing the instant lawsuit. We agree that Appellant is entitled to recover reasonable and necessary attorney's fees incurred in bringing the instant lawsuit. Because we are remanding this case so the trial court can determine the amount of pre- and post-judgment interest to be awarded to Appellant, we also remand to the trial court the issue of the amount of attorney's fees due to Appellant in pursuing this lawsuit against Appellee for collection of the amount paid to IKON on behalf of the partnership.

CONCLUSION

We hold the trial court erred in determining that Appellant did not have authority to act for Wood Relo in defending, settling, and paying the partnership debt owed by Wood Relo to IKON. Appellee is jointly and severally liable to IKON for $9,000, which represents the amount Appellant paid IKON to defend and extinguish the partnership debt. We hold that Appellee is jointly and severally liable to Appellant for $1725, which represents the amount of attorney's fees Appellant paid to defend against the IKON claim. We further hold that Appellant is entitled to recover from Appellee reasonable and necessary attorney's fees in pursuing the instant lawsuit.

We reverse the judgment of the trial court. We render judgment that Appellee owes Appellant $5362.50 (one-half of the partnership debt to IKON plus one-half of the corresponding attorney's fees). We remand the case to the trial court for calculation of the amount of attorney's fees owed by Appellee to Appellant in the instant lawsuit, and calculation of pre- and post-judgment interest.

FINANCE

General partnerships are usually financed by the partners through investment (equity) or debt. Partners often raise equity funds through their own capital contributions, by adding a new partner, or by restructuring the relative ownership interests of the existing partners to reflect new contributions. Debt financing for general partnerships is commonly dependent on the individual creditworthiness of the owners. But this is not always the case. Since a general partnership is an entity separate from its partners, the business itself may have and rely on its own creditworthiness to secure debt.

General partners customarily have a financial interest in the partnership. The interest represents their share of ownership in the partnership. A partner may transfer all or part of his interest in the partnership. However, such transfer does not create any management rights in the transferee.

§152.202. CREDITS OF AND CHARGES TO PARTNER.

(a) Each partner is credited with an amount equal to:

(1) the cash and the value of property the partner contributes to a partnership; and

(2) the partner's share of the partnership's profits.

(b) Each partner is charged with an amount equal to:

(1) the cash and the value of other property distributed by the partnership to the partner; and

(2) the partner's share of the partnership's losses.

(c) Each partner is entitled to be credited with an equal share of the partnership's profits and is chargeable with a share of the partnership's capital or operating losses in proportion to the partner's share of the profits.

§152.308. PARTNER'S PARTNERSHIP INTEREST SUBJECT TO CHARGING ORDER.

(a) On application by a judgment creditor of a partner or of any other owner of a partnership interest, a court having jurisdiction may charge the partnership interest of the judgment debtor to satisfy the judgment.

(b) To the extent that the partnership interest is charged in the manner provided by Subsection (a), the judgment creditor has only the right to receive any distribution to which the judgment debtor would otherwise be entitled in respect of the partnership interest.

(c) A charging order constitutes a lien on the judgment debtor's partnership interest. The charging order lien may not be foreclosed on under this code or any other law.

(d) The entry of a charging order is the exclusive remedy by which a judgment creditor of a partner or of any other owner of a partnership interest may satisfy a judgment out of the judgment debtor's partnership interest.

(e) This section does not deprive a partner or other owner of a partnership interest of a right under exemption laws with respect to the judgment debtor's partnership interest.

(f) A creditor of a partner or of any other owner of a partnership interest does not have the right to obtain possession of, or otherwise exercise legal or equitable remedies with respect to, the property of the partnership.

SUBCHAPTER F. TRANSFER OF PARTNERSHIP INTERESTS

§152.401. TRANSFER OF PARTNERSHIP INTEREST. A partner may transfer all or part of the partner's partnership interest.

§152.402. GENERAL EFFECT OF TRANSFER. A transfer of all or part of a partner's partnership interest:

> (1) is not an event of withdrawal;
>
> (2) does not by itself cause a winding up of the partnership business; and
>
> (3) against the other partners or the partnership, does not entitle the transferee, during the continuance of the partnership, to participate in the management or conduct of the partnership business.

§152.403. EFFECT OF TRANSFER ON TRANSFEROR. After transfer, the transferor continues to have the rights and duties of a partner other than the interest transferred.

§152.404. RIGHTS AND DUTIES OF TRANSFEREE.

(a) A transferee of a partner's partnership interest is entitled to receive, to the extent transferred, distributions to which the transferor otherwise would be entitled.

(b) If an event requires a winding up of partnership business under Subchapter I, a transferee is entitled to receive, to the extent transferred, the net amount otherwise distributable to the transferor.

(c) Until a transferee becomes a partner, the transferee does not have liability as a partner solely as a result of the transfer.

(d) For a proper purpose the transferee may require reasonable information or an account of a partnership transaction and make reasonable inspection of the partnership books. In a winding up of partnership business, a transferee may require an accounting only from the date of the latest account agreed to by all of the partners.

(e) Until receipt of notice of a transfer, a partnership is not required to give effect to a transferee's rights under this section and Sections 152.401-152.403.

§152.405. POWER TO EFFECT TRANSFER OR GRANT OF SECURITY INTEREST. A partnership is not required to give effect to a transfer prohibited by a partnership agreement.

§152.406. EFFECT OF DEATH OR DIVORCE ON PARTNERSHIP INTEREST.

(a) For purposes of this code:

(1) on the divorce of a partner, the partner's spouse, to the extent of the spouse's partnership interest, if any, is a transferee of the partnership interest;

(2) on the death of a partner:

(A) if the partnership interest of the deceased partner is subject to redemption under Subchapter H, the partner's surviving spouse, if any, and an heir, devisee, personal representative, or other successor of the partner, to the extent of their respective right to the redemption price, are creditors of the partnership until the redemption price is paid; or

(B) if the partnership interest of the deceased partner is not subject to redemption under Subchapter H, the partner's surviving spouse, if any, and an heir, devisee, personal representative, or other successor of the partner, to the extent of their respective partnership interest, are transferees of the partnership interest; and

(3) on the death of a partner's spouse, an heir, devisee, personal representative, or other successor of the spouse, other than the partner, to the extent of their respective partnership interest, if any, is a transferee of the partnership interest.

(b) An event of the type described by Section 152.501 occurring with respect to a partner's spouse is not an event of withdrawal.

(c) This chapter does not impair an agreement for the purchase or sale of a partnership interest at any time, including on the death or divorce of an owner of the partnership interest.

Von Hohn, and in the Interest of H.B.V.H. and A.S.V.H., Minor Children
260 S.W.3d 631(Tex App-Tyler, 2008)

BACKGROUND

Edward and Susan Joan Von Hohn were married on June 28, 1997 and are the parents of two children, H.B.V.H. and A.S.V.H. Susan filed for divorce in July 2004, and the parties agreed that Susan be appointed sole managing conservator of the children and that Edward be appointed possessory conservator. Edward was also ordered to pay child support. The parties could not agree on a division of their community property, particularly the community property interest, if any, in Edward's ownership interest in the law firm of Nix, Patterson & Roach (the "Nix Law Firm").

146

Edward and the other partners of the Nix Law Firm signed a partnership agreement. The partnership agreement allotted each partner a certain number of units of participation, assigned each partner an undivided profits account and a capital account, and included a formula for calculating a partner's interest in the partnership as of the date of his death and as of the effective date of his retirement, withdrawal, or expulsion. The partnership agreement did not provide a method of valuing a partner's interest in the event of his divorce. The trial court granted, in part, Edward's motion to exclude the expert testimony of James C. Penn, concluding that the proper measure of the value of the community property interest in the Nix Law Firm included methods other than those set forth in the partnership agreement. However, the trial court found that no more than two years of the Nix Law Firm's future earnings should be considered in valuing Edward's interest in the firm. Ultimately, a jury found that the value of Edward's interest in the Nix Law Firm was $4.5 million dollars, subject to taxes. This appeal followed.

Analysis

Before trial, Edward filed a motion to exclude Susan's expert, James C. Penn, who was to testify regarding Penn's valuation of the Nix Law Firm. The trial court held a hearing on Edward's motion, during which Penn testified. The trial court partially granted Edward's motion finding that the proper measure of the value of the community interest in the Nix Law Firm could include methods other than those set forth in the partnership agreement. The court allowed Penn to testify regarding his valuation based on withdrawal value, the asset approach, and/or the income approach. However, the court ordered that Penn limit any valuation utilizing the income approach to income reasonably expected to be collected within two years from the valuation date.

We will not disturb the trial court's decision to allow Penn to testify absent clear abuse. In his brief, Edward contends that Penn's methodology was unreliable and flawed and, as support, points to six statements made by Penn or matters taken into consideration by Penn in his valuation. These statements were not part of Penn's testimony at the *Daubert* hearing, but instead, were made by Penn at a prior hearing on Susan's motion for additional discovery. Edward complains that Penn could not recall a specific instance when he had taken specific cases, valued them, and then adjusted the assets of a law firm's balance sheet. He also points out that Penn testified he had never used information from patent cases in valuations of law firms. However, in the *Daubert* hearing, Penn stated that he had been performing business valuations for approximately fifteen years and had been an expert witness for a professional business valuation about seventy-five to one hundred times. According to his curriculum vitae, he had been a speaker at a variety of seminars on topics such as valuations, commercial and personal goodwill, and business valuation of a partner's interest in a law firm. Penn stated that he had previously testified in court regarding valuation of a partnership interest using the income approach and had relied on the types of projections used here in valuing a contingency fee practice in Dallas, Texas.

PARTNERSHIP AGREEMENT AND GOODWILL

As part of his first issue, Edward argues that the trial court erred in its interpretation and application of the law regarding the division of a community property interest in a professional partnership. He contends that his interest in the Nix Law Firm was defined by the partnership agreement and that the community estate was not entitled to a greater interest than that to which he was entitled in the firm's commercial goodwill.

Applicable Law

Professional goodwill attaches to the person of the professional man or woman as a result of confidence in his or her skill and ability, and would be extinguished in the event of the professional's death, retirement, or disablement. Such professional goodwill is not property in the estate of the parties and, therefore, not divisible upon divorce. To the extent that goodwill exists in the professional practice separate and apart from the professional's personal ability and reputation, that goodwill has a commercial value and is community property subject to division upon divorce. In order to determine whether goodwill attaches to a professional practice that is subject to division upon divorce, we apply a two prong test: (1) goodwill must be determined to exist independently of the personal ability of the professional spouse; and (2) if such goodwill is found to exist, then it must be determined whether that goodwill has a commercial value in which the community estate is entitled to share.

Analysis

In partially granting Edward's motion to exclude Penn, the court found that the proper measure of the value of the community interest in the Nix Law Firm could include methods other than those set forth in the partnership agreement. In the court's charge to the jury, the court stated that, although the jury could not consider personal goodwill or time and labor to be expended after the divorce, the jury could consider the commercial goodwill, if any, of the firm, the partnership agreement, and the amendments to the partnership agreement.

We must determine if the trial court erred in determining that the jury could consider the commercial goodwill, if any, of the Nix Law Firm. As to the two prong test for determining if commercial goodwill attaches to a professional practice, Edward does not dispute that the first prong has been met, i.e., that goodwill exists independently of the personal ability of the professional spouse. *See Finn*, 658 S.W.2d at 741. However, he argues that the goodwill does not have a commercial value in which the community estate is entitled to share and directs us to the facts and analysis in *Finn*. *See id.* In *Finn*, the trial court found that the husband's law firm had goodwill independent and apart from the professional ability of the husband. *Id.* at 741. However, the pertinent question was whether the community estate was entitled to share in the value of the law firm's commercial goodwill. *Id.* The court determined that the community estate was not entitled to a greater interest than that to which the husband was entitled in the firm's

148

goodwill. *Id.* According to the court, the extent of the husband's interest was governed by the partnership agreement. *Id.*

According to the partnership agreement, if the husband in *Finn* had died or withdrawn from the firm, he would have been entitled to certain amounts based on his capital account, undistributed earned income, and interest in the firm's reserve account. The court acknowledged that the partnership agreement did not provide any compensation for accrued goodwill to a partner who ceased to practice law with the firm, nor did it provide any mechanism to realize the value of the firm's goodwill. In *Finn,* the only mechanism through which the husband could realize the value of the accrued goodwill was through continuing to practice law as a member of the firm. Thus, the court found, such realization in the future is no more than an expectancy dependent on the husband's continued participation in the firm and, therefore, his interest in the firm's goodwill was not property of the community estate.

The decision in *Finn* was en banc with four justices joining the majority opinion, two justices concurring, and five justices dissenting. Justice Stewart wrote a concurring opinion, stating that the firm's goodwill is an asset of the partnership entity and, thus, does not belong to either the separate or community estate of the individual partners. According to Justice Stewart, the partnership agreement did not control the value of the individual partnership interests. The asset being divided was the husband's interest in the partnership as a going business, not his contractual death benefits or withdrawal rights. The formula in the partnership agreement may represent the present value of the husband's interest, but should not preclude a consideration of other facts. The value of the husband's interest, Justice Stewart concluded, should be based on the present value of the partnership entity as a going business, which would include consideration of partnership goodwill. Goodwill is property and, although intangible, is an integral part of a business.

The Fort Worth court of appeals agreed with the concurrence in *Finn,* concluding that because a partnership is not being terminated, the provision in the partnership agreement determining the value of the business in the event of the partner's withdrawal or death is not applicable. The court stated that the formula in a partnership agreement with respect to death or withdrawal is not necessarily determinative of the value of a spouse's interest in an ongoing partnership as of the time of divorce.

In this case, Edward became a partner in the Nix Law Firm in 1999 and signed the Fourth Amendment to the Nix Law Firm Partnership Agreement. The original partnership agreement specified the payment for a partner's interest in the partnership in the event of the partner's death, withdrawal, retirement, or expulsion. If a partner died or withdrew, he would be entitled to any unpaid draw, his capital account, and his undivided profit accounts, based upon his units of participation. At the time of trial, Edward testified that he was a partner in the Nix Law Firm, that he had not withdrawn, and that he had no plans to withdraw.

Based on these facts, we agree with the concurrence in *Finn* that the Nix Law Firm partnership agreement does not control the value of the individual partnership interests in the event of a divorce. Therefore, the trial court did not err when it determined that the proper measure of the value of the community interest in the Nix Law Firm could include methods other than those set forth in the partnership agreement.

FUTURE EARNINGS

As part of his first issue, Edward contends that the trial court erred in allowing future earnings to be used to determine the commercial goodwill of the Nix Law Firm. More particularly, he argues that neither case law nor current valuation methodology permits commercial goodwill to be valued using speculative future income streams.

Applicable Law

In a decree of divorce, a court shall order a division of the estate of the parties in a manner that the court deems just and right, having due regard for the rights of each party. We review a trial court's division of property under an abuse of discretion standard. A trial court does not abuse its discretion if there is some evidence of a substantive and probative character to support the decision. Moreover, we should reverse a court's division of property only if the error materially affects the court's just and right division of the property.

Similarly, errors in the valuation of property do not require reversal unless, because of such errors, the division made by the trial court is manifestly unjust. However, once reversible error affecting the "just and right" division of the community estate is found, an appellate court must remand the entire community estate for a new division.

A spouse is not entitled to a percentage of his or her spouse's future earnings. A spouse is only entitled to a division of property that the community owns at the time of divorce. All assets of the community estate are valued as of the time of dissolution of the marriage. Further, a jury must have an evidentiary basis for its findings.

Analysis

At trial, Penn testified regarding his valuation of Edward's interest in the Nix Law Firm using the income approach. He stated that he included the commercial goodwill of the firm, but excluded personal goodwill and future time, toil, and labor. According to the trial court's instructions, he considered income reasonably expected to be collected by the Nix Law Firm within the next two years. Penn valued Edward's interest in the general law firm at $1.5 million. He testified that in this analysis, he considered the general law firm's historical operations and attempted to normalize income that would occur in the future, but deducted nonrecurring events, any Data Treasury ("seminal type cases," analogous to the tobacco litigation) case income, and partner compensation. Penn testified that Edward's interest in the settled Data Treasury cases was

150

$400,000.00. He stated that the settlement agreements with these defendants have two types of payment terms. The first type of payment is fixed, and paid both "up front" in cash and over a specified number of years. The second type of payment is based on a royalty rate to be paid in the future. Consequently, he testified, some settlement money had been received while additional settlement money had yet to be received. For most of the settled defendants, he had a payment history based on their settlement and royalty agreements and was able to estimate payments to be received in the next two years. However, two defendants had not begun making payments and, without such history, Penn refused to speculate and valued Edward's interest in these settled defendants at zero.

Using a royalty rate based on the prior settlement agreements, he valued Edward's interest in the pending but unsettled Data Treasury cases at $4.1 million dollars. In this analysis, Penn focused on the four large defendants that would most likely settle in the next two years. He also testified that if all the pending Data Treasury cases, including all the smaller defendants, settled in the next two years, Edward's interest would increase by $2.2 million dollars. At the conclusion of the trial, the jury found that the value of Edward's interest in the Nix Law Firm was $4.5 million dollars, subject to taxes.

We must determine if there was some evidence to support the jury's valuation of Edward's interest. Penn's valuation of Edward's interest in the Nix Law Firm and the settled Data Treasury cases totaled $1.9 million. Edward's interest in the settled Data Treasury cases is based on settlement agreements that were executed before the date of divorce. According to Penn, Edward does not have to expend future time or labor to collect his interest in these proceeds. We agree, concluding that Edward's right to receive these proceeds is contractual and the amounts to be received are fixed or readily ascertainable. Further, because no future time or labor is necessary to receive these proceeds, Edward's income from the settled Data Treasury cases is not future earnings.

Penn valued Edward's interest in the pending Data Treasury cases at $4.1 million with an additional $2.2 million for the other pending cases. Susan is not entitled to Edward's future earnings, and all assets of the community estate must be valued as of the date of divorce. Penn admitted that no money had been received by the firm from the pending but unsettled Data Treasury cases. Revenue from these cases is no more than an expectancy interest and any money to be received constitutes future earnings to which Susan is not entitled. There was no other evidence from which the jury could have concluded that Edward's interest in the Nix Law Firm totaled $4.5 million dollars.

Because Edward's future earnings are his separate property, which the trial court may not divest, we conclude the property division is manifestly unjust. Accordingly, we sustain that portion of Edward's first issue contending that future earnings could not be used in valuing his interest in the Nix Law Firm.

DISPOSITION

Having sustained a portion of Edward's first issue, we *reverse* the portion of the final decree of divorce dividing the marital estate and *remand* to the trial court to determine a just and right division of community property. In all other respects, the trial court's judgment is *affirmed*.

LIABILITY

General partners are personally, jointly and severally liable for the debts and obligations of the partnership. One of the most significant features of a partnership is the *unlimited liability* of the partners. Each partner is personally liable for the entire amount of any partnership obligation. This means that a general partner who has a 10 percent interest in the partnership is not responsible for only 10 percent of partnership obligations. She is responsible for 100 percent of the obligation. If her other partners are unable to pay their respective shares, she must pay the entire amount. She likely has recourse against the other partners who may be unable to pay.

Each partner's personal liability for all of the debts of the partnership means that a partner's personal property and or wealth may be accessible to creditors. A partner's personal liability includes any debts incurred by any of the other partners on behalf of the partnership. Any general partner is able to bind the partnership by entering into a contract on behalf of the partnership whether the non-acting partner authorized the contract or whether she even knew of its existence.

Each partner is also liable for the other partner's negligence. For example, when two or more professionals practice together as a partnership, each partner is generally liable for the negligence or malpractice of any other partner. Subject to certain exceptions, a creditor of the partnership cannot recover from a partner personally without first seeking satisfaction from partnership property or exhausting partnership assets.

§152.053. QUALIFICATIONS TO BE PARTNER; NONPARTNER'S LIABILITY TO THIRD PERSON.

(a) A person may be a partner unless the person lacks capacity apart from this chapter.

(b) Except as provided by Section 152.307, a person who is not a partner in a partnership under Section 152.051 is not a partner as to a third person and is not liable to a third person under this chapter.

§152.054. FALSE REPRESENTATION OF PARTNERSHIP OR PARTNER.

(a) A false representation or other conduct falsely indicating that a person is a partner with another person does not of itself create a partnership.

(b) A representation or other conduct indicating that a person is a partner in an existing partnership, if that is not the case, does not of itself make that person a partner in the partnership.

§152.210. PARTNER'S LIABILITY TO PARTNERSHIP AND OTHER PARTNERS.

A partner is liable to a partnership and the other partners for:

(1) a breach of the partnership agreement; or

(2) a violation of a duty to the partnership or other partners under this chapter that causes harm to the partnership or the other partners.

§152.304. NATURE OF PARTNER'S LIABILITY.

(a) Except as provided by Subsection (b) or Section 152.801(a), all partners are jointly and severally liable for all obligations of the partnership unless otherwise:

(1) agreed by the claimant; or

(2) provided by law.

(b) A person who is admitted as a partner into an existing partnership does not have personal liability under Subsection (a) for an obligation of the partnership that:

(1) arises before the partner's admission to the partnership;

(2) relates to an action taken or omission occurring before the partner's admission to the partnership; or

(3) arises before or after the partner's admission to the partnership under a contract or commitment entered into before the partner's admission.

§152.305. REMEDY.
An action may be brought against a partnership and any or all of the partners in the same action or in separate actions.

§152.306. ENFORCEMENT OF REMEDY.

(a) A judgment against a partnership is not by itself a judgment against a partner. A judgment may be entered against a partner who has been served with process in a suit against the partnership.

(b) Except as provided by Subsection (c), a creditor may proceed against one or more partners or the property of the partners to satisfy a judgment based on a claim against the partnership only if a judgment:

(1) is also obtained against the partner; and

(2) based on the same claim:

(A) is obtained against the partnership;

(B) has not been reversed or vacated; and

(C) remains unsatisfied for 90 days after:

(i) the date on which the judgment is entered; or

(ii) the date on which the stay expires, if the judgment is contested by appropriate proceedings and execution on the judgment is stayed.

(c) Subsection (b) does not prohibit a creditor from proceeding directly against one or more partners or the property of the partners without first seeking satisfaction from partnership property if:

(1) the partnership is a debtor in bankruptcy;

(2) the creditor and the partnership agreed that the creditor is not required to comply with Subsection (b);

(3) a court orders otherwise, based on a finding that partnership property subject to execution in the state is clearly insufficient to satisfy the judgment or that compliance with Subsection (b) is excessively burdensome; or

(4) liability is imposed on the partner by law independently of the person's status as a partner.

(d) This section does not limit the effect of Section 152.801 with respect to a limited liability partnership.

§152.307. EXTENSION OF CREDIT IN RELIANCE ON FALSE REPRESENTATION.

(a) The rights of a person extending credit in reliance on a representation described by Section 152.054 are determined by applicable law other than this chapter and the other partnership provisions, including the law of estoppel, agency, negligence, fraud, and unjust enrichment.

(b) The rights and duties of a person held liable under Subsection (a) are also determined by law other than the law described by Subsection (a).

§152.204. GENERAL STANDARDS OF PARTNER'S CONDUCT.

(a) A partner owes to the partnership, the other partners, and a transferee of a deceased partner's partnership interest as designated in Section 152.406(a)(2):
  (1) a duty of loyalty; and
  (2) a duty of care.

(b) A partner shall discharge the partner's duties to the partnership and the other partners under this code or under the partnership agreement and exercise any rights and powers in the conduct or winding up of the partnership business:
  (1) in good faith; and
  (2) in a manner the partner reasonably believes to be in the best interest of the partnership.

(c) A partner does not violate a duty or obligation under this chapter or under the partnership agreement merely because the partner's conduct furthers the partner's own interest.

(d) A partner, in the partner's capacity as partner, is not a trustee and is not held to the standards of a trustee.

§152.207. STANDARDS OF CONDUCT APPLICABLE TO PERSON WINDING UP PARTNERSHIP BUSINESS.
Sections 152.204-152.206 apply to a person winding up the partnership business as the personal or legal representative of the last surviving partner to the same extent that those sections apply to a partner.

§152.303. LIABILITY OF PARTNERSHIP FOR CONDUCT OF PARTNER.

(a) A partnership is liable for loss or injury to a person, including a partner, or for a penalty caused by or incurred as a result of a wrongful act or omission or other actionable conduct of a partner acting:

(1) in the ordinary course of business of the partnership; or
(2) with the authority of the partnership.

(b) A partnership is liable for the loss of money or property of a person who is not a partner that is:

(1) received in the course of the partnership's business; and

(2) misapplied by a partner while in the custody of the partnership.

Howell v. Hilton Hotels Corp.
84 S.W.3d 708 Court of Appeals of Texas, Houston (1st Dist.), 2002

Appellants, Charles Ben Howell, individually, and as administrator of the estate of Frederick Lane Howell, deceased, and on behalf of Ted R. Howell, deceased, and J. Maxine Larson (collectively Plaintiffs) brought suit against Hilton Hotels Corporation (Hilton) and Stanley Wadsworth for the death of Frederick Howell. In eight points of error, Plaintiffs challenge a summary judgment rendered in favor of Hilton and Wadsworth. We affirm in part and reverse and remand in part.

BACKGROUND FACTS AND PROCEDURAL HISTORY

Frederick Howell, a Texas resident, died on September 15, 1986, in Durango, Colorado. He and his fellow employees went to Colorado on a business trip sponsored by their employer. On September 12, 1986, Howell and several co-workers took a sightseeing excursion on a bus provided by Tamarron Resort. During the excursion, the bus was struck by a runaway tractor trailer. Howell died three days later as a result of injuries he sustained in the accident.

On September 8, 1988, Frederick Howell's brothers, Charles Ben Howell and Ted Howell filed suit against Tamarron, Inc., owner of the resort, and R & D Harris Transportation, Inc., owner of the tractor-trailer. Eight and one-half years later, in April 1997, Plaintiffs filed their first amended petition which added J. Maxine Larson, "devoted companion of Frederick Howell," as a plaintiff and added Hilton as a defendant. Plaintiffs' first amended petition also named Golf Host Resorts, Inc. (Golf Host), the corporate successor of Tamarron, Inc., as a defendant.

In February 1998, Plaintiffs filed their second amended petition, which added Stanley Wadsworth, a shareholder and officer of the corporate resort owner, as a defendant. Plaintiffs' third amended petition, filed August 12, 1999, added two additional defendants, Brent

Wadsworth and C. James McCormick, who along with Stanley Wadsworth, were the majority shareholders of Tamarron, Inc. and its corporate successor.

Plaintiffs' third amended petition can be read to assert causes of action against Hilton based on negligence and breach of warranty. In their third amended petition, Plaintiffs seek to hold Hilton liable based on a management agreement entered into by Hilton and Golf Host in November 1995 relating to Tamarron Resort. Plaintiffs contend that the management agreement was actually a partnership agreement between Hilton and Golf Host.

With regard to Stanley Wadsworth, Plaintiffs allege claims of negligence and breach of warranty. Plaintiffs assert that Wadsworth is individually liable because the corporate resort owner was his alter ego. Plaintiffs also allege that in 1998, Wadsworth and the other two majority shareholders of Golf Host sold their stock to Starwood Capital. As part of this transaction, Plaintiffs state that Wadsworth agreed in writing to indemnify Starwood Capital for any liability it had to Plaintiffs relating to this case. Plaintiffs assert that they are entitled to judgment against Wadsworth based on the indemnity agreement.

Hilton and Wadsworth filed a motion for summary judgment and an amended motion for summary judgment. In the amended motion for summary judgment, Hilton alleges that: (1) it is not liable as a partner of Golf Host; (2) even assuming that there was such a partnership agreement, Hilton would not be liable for any partnership responsibilities that arose before Hilton entered into the partnership; (3) Plaintiffs' survival claims and breach of warranty claims are barred by the respective statutes of limitations; and (4) no evidence exists as to one or more elements of Plaintiffs' claims. In addition to asserting the third and fourth grounds asserted by Hilton, Wadsworth also moved for summary judgment on the basis that the corporate resort owner at the time of the accident—Tamarron, Inc.—was not his alter ego. Plaintiffs filed a response to the motion for summary judgment, but did not file a separate response to the amended motion for summary judgment.

Without stating the basis, the trial court granted Hilton's and Wadsworth's motions for summary judgment. Plaintiffs' claims against Hilton and Wadsworth were severed, which rendered the summary judgment final for purposes of this appeal.

DISCUSSION

Claims Against Hilton

In issue four, Plaintiffs assert that the trial court erred to the extent it granted summary judgment in favor of Hilton on the basis that Hilton cannot be liable for partnership obligations that arose before it became Golf Host's partner.

It is undisputed that Frederick Howell died in 1986 and that Hilton and the corporate resort owner—Tamarron, Inc.—were not partners at that time. However, the parties dispute whether Hilton and Golf Host became partners in 1995 when they signed the management agreement.

Hilton argues that, even if it entered into a partnership with Golf Host in 1995, its liability is precluded by the Texas Revised Partnership Act (TRPA), which provides:

A person admitted as a partner into an existing partnership does not have personal liability ... for an obligation of the partnership that:

(1) arose before the partner's admission to the partnership;
(2) relates to an action taken or omissions occurring before the partner's admission to the partnership; or
(3) arises before or after the partner's admission under a contract or commitment entered into before the partner's admission to the partnership.

Plaintiffs admit that Hilton may not have "personal liability"; however, they assert they can recover money that Hilton advanced to the partnership as well as profits received by Hilton from the operation of Tamarron Resort. Plaintiffs argue that such funds constitute "partnership property." In their appellate brief, Plaintiffs contend: "Although the statute prevents a general judgment or personal judgment against Hilton, it does not prevent Plaintiffs from suing for and recovering advances and profits, paid or payable to Hilton." In support of this contention, Plaintiffs rely on the 1993 Comment of Bar Committee to article 6132b–3.07, which states:

Although the language of this section is significantly different from that of TUPA [Texas Uniform Partnership Act] § 17, the result is not significantly different. This section continues the rule that a new partner has no personal liability for obligations of the partnership that arose before the partner's admission to the partnership or relate to actions taken or commitments entered into before the partner's admission to the partnership.... TUPA §17 purported to make the new partner liable, *but limited the new partner's liability to partnership property. This section reaches the same result in a more direct manner*.

"Parties admitted as partners into existing partnerships are bound by all partnership obligations then outstanding, the same as though they had been partners when such obligations were initially incurred, except that their liabilities as to unpaid obligations existing at the time of their admission could only be satisfied out of partnership property."

Plaintiffs also assert that, because Hilton offered no summary judgment evidence to refute them, the following assertions pled in their third amended petition must be taken as true: (1) Hilton advanced over $1 million to the partnership "in exchange for the right to share in profits for up to 20 years," and (2) "Hilton is liable to account to Plaintiffs for the profits from Tamarron Hilton Resort." However, even taking these allegations as true, Hilton is not liable to Plaintiffs as a partner. Any funds due Hilton that it advanced to the alleged partnership or that were paid to Hilton as profits, would be Hilton's property and not partnership property.

158

We hold that Hilton cannot be held personally liable for Plaintiffs' claims, as a matter of law, because (1) the claims arose nine years before Hilton executed the alleged partnership agreement with Golf Host, and (2) Hilton does not possess partnership property.

We overrule issue four.

CONCLUSION

We affirm the summary judgment rendered in favor of Hilton Hotels Corporation.

FIDUCIARY DUTIES

The TBOC provides that partners owe duties of care and loyalty to the partnership, fellow partners and transferees of deceased partners. However, the TBOC makes a deliberate choice not to refer to these duties as fiduciary duties, primarily in recognition of the fact that partners are not fiduciaries in the truest sense, as partners are free to advance their personal interests. Nevertheless, the courts are likely to continue to attach the "fiduciary" label to the duties of care and loyalty owed by partners. The duty of loyalty encompasses an obligation to refrain from competing with the firm, engaging in conflict of interest transactions or self-dealing that are not fair to the partnership, usurping partnership opportunities, or using partnership property for nonpartnership purposes. The duty of care imposes a requirement on the partner to act with the care expected of an ordinarily prudent person in similar circumstances.

The duties of care and loyalty do not apply during the formation of the partnership. Thus negotiations to form a partnership are considered arm's length negotiations. Instead, the duties of care and loyalty apply during the conduct and winding up of the partnership business. Apart from the duties of care and loyalty, partners also have an obligation to discharge their duties in good faith and in the best interests of the partnership as well as the duty to disclose and render information. Partners may not eliminate the duties of loyalty and care and the obligation to discharge duties in good faith by agreement. Moreover, the partnership agreement may not "unreasonably restrict" a partner's right to access to the partnership books and records. The partners are at liberty to contractually identify specific types or categories of activities that do not violate the duty of loyalty and determine the standards by which the performance of the duty of care and fulfillment of the obligation of good faith are to be measured so long as, in each case, the provisions are not manifestly unreasonable.

Texas Business Organization Code provisions

§ 152.204. General Standards of Partner's Conduct

(a) A partner owes to the partnership, the other partners, and a transferee of a deceased partner's partnership interest as designated in Section 152.406(a)(2):

(1) a duty of loyalty; and
(2) a duty of care.

(b) A partner shall discharge the partner's duties to the partnership and the other partners under this code or under the partnership agreement and exercise any rights and powers in the conduct or winding up of the partnership business:

(1) in good faith; and
(2) in a manner the partner reasonably believes to be in the best interest of the partnership.

(c) A partner does not violate a duty or obligation under this chapter or under the partnership agreement merely because the partner's conduct furthers the partner's own interest.

(d) A partner, in the partner's capacity as partner, is not a trustee and is not held to the standards of a trustee.

§ 152.205. Partner's Duty of Loyalty. A partner's duty of loyalty includes:

(1) accounting to and holding for the partnership property, profit, or benefit derived by the partner:

(A) in the conduct and winding up of the partnership business; or
(B) from use by the partner of partnership property;

(2) refraining from dealing with the partnership on behalf of a person who has an interest adverse to the partnership; and

(3) refraining from competing or dealing with the partnership in a manner adverse to the partnership.

§ 152.206. Partner's Duty of Care

(a) A partner's duty of care to the partnership and the other partners is to act in the conduct and winding up of the partnership business with the care an ordinarily prudent person would exercise in similar circumstances.

(b) An error in judgment does not by itself constitute a breach of the duty of care.

(c) A partner is presumed to satisfy the duty of care if the partner acts on an informed basis and in compliance with Section 152.204(b).

§ 152.207. Standards of Conduct Applicable to Person Winding up Partnership Business. Sections 152.204-152.206 apply to a person winding up the partnership business as the personal or legal representative of the last surviving partner to the same extent that those sections apply to a partner.

§ 154.201. Business Transactions Between Partner and Partnership. Except as otherwise provided by the partnership agreement, a partner may lend money to and transact other business with the partnership. Subject to other applicable law, a partner has the same rights and obligations with respect to those matters as a person who is not a partner.

§ 152.213. Information Regarding Partnership

(a) On request and to the extent just and reasonable, each partner and the partnership shall furnish complete and accurate information concerning the partnership to:

(1) a partner;
(2) the legal representative of a deceased partner or a partner who has a legal disability; or
(3) an assignee.

(b) A legal representative of a deceased partner or a partner who has a legal disability and an assignee are subject to the duties of a partner with respect to information made available.

§ 152.002. Effect of Partnership Agreement; Nonwaivable and Variable Provisions

(a) Except as provided by Subsection (b), a partnership agreement governs the relations of the partners and between the partners and the partnership. To the extent that the partnership agreement does not otherwise provide, this chapter and the other partnership provisions govern the relationship of the partners and between the partners and the partnership.

(b) A partnership agreement or the partners may not:

(1) unreasonably restrict a partner's right of access to books and records under Section 152.212;

(2) eliminate the duty of loyalty under Section 152.205, except that the partners by agreement may identify specific types of activities or categories of activities that do not violate the duty of loyalty if the types or categories are not manifestly unreasonable;

(3) eliminate the duty of care under Section 152.206, except that the partners by agreement may determine the standards by which the performance of the obligation is to be measured if the standards are not manifestly unreasonable;

(4) eliminate the obligation of good faith under Section 152.204(b), except that the partners by agreement may determine the standards by which the performance of the obligation is to be measured if the standards are not manifestly unreasonable . . . .

Champion v. Mizell
904 S.W.2d 617 (Texas) 1995

Partner sued defendant partner for terminating partnership. The District Court, Number 12, Leon County, entered judgment for defendant, and plaintiff appealed. The Waco Court of Appeals reversed, finding that jury finding that defendant breached duty to plaintiff included finding that partnership continued in existence until alleged breach of duty occurred. Defendant applied for writ of error to Supreme Court. The Supreme Court held that jury's finding that plaintiff breached partnership agreement when he was barred from entering customer property for theft of equipment controlled legal determination as to when partnership terminated, regardless of finding that defendant breached fiduciary duty. Application for writ of error granted, judgment of court of appeals reversed, judgment rendered for defendant.

This case involves a dispute between two former partners. The dispositive issue is whether the trial court correctly construed the jury verdict in rendering judgment. The court of appeals held it did not. We disagree.

Dennis Mizell and M.R. Champion, as partners, contracted to provide services to Northwestern Resources Company for a year beginning in January 1986. At the end of that year, Champion negotiated a second one-year contract with Northwestern under the name of M.R. Champion, Inc. ("MRCI"), assuring Mizell that they would still perform the contract as partners. In January 1987, Northwestern barred Mizell from its premises for taking some of its property. Champion continued to work for Northwestern throughout the year using equipment leased from Mizell. In December 1987, Champion negotiated a three-year contract with Northwestern covering 1988–1990, again in the name of MRCI. A month later Champion told Mizell the partnership was over.

Mizell sued Champion and MRCI. Before the case could be tried, Champion died and the independent executrix of his estate was added as a defendant. Although Mizell asserted a number of claims, he went to trial on only one: breach of fiduciary duty in not obtaining the three-year contract with Northwestern for the partnership. The law applicable to this claim is not disputed. Partners owe each other and their partnership a duty in the nature of a fiduciary duty in the conduct and winding up of partnership business, and are liable for a breach of that duty. After the partnership terminates, however, the duty is limited to matters relating to the winding up of the partnership's affairs. Specifically, a person has no duty to offer his former partners or partnership a business opportunity which arises after the partnership has terminated. The dispute centers on when the partnership terminated. Defendants contend that the partnership terminated in January 1987 as a result of Mizell's misconduct toward Northwestern, and that Champion had no duty to refer new business opportunities, like the three-year contract, to the partnership. Mizell asserted that the partnership was not dissolved until Champion withdrew in January 1988, and that Champion continued to be bound by his fiduciary duty when he obtained the three-year contract for MRCI.

The trial court instructed the jury that Champion owed Mizell and the partnership a fiduciary duty which the trial court defined. The definition did not describe how the duty was affected by termination of the partnership. The jury found that Champion breached his fiduciary duty to Mizell and the partnership, but it was not asked to find when the breach occurred. The jury also found that after Mizell was barred from Northwestern's premises in January 1987, he breached the partnership agreement and conducted himself in such a way that it was not reasonably practicable to carry on partnership business. Based upon this latter finding, the trial court found that the partnership terminated in January 1987, before the breach of fiduciary duty asserted by Mizell.

On motions of all parties for judgment on the verdict, the trial court rendered judgment for defendants. The court of appeals reversed and rendered judgment for Mizell. It reasoned that since no party complained of a lack of evidence to support any of the jury's findings, judgment must be based on those findings if possible. In the court of appeals' view, the jury's finding that Champion breached his fiduciary duty to Mizell necessarily included the finding that the partnership continued in existence until December 1987, when the only damages claimed by Mizell occurred. The court of appeals concluded that the breach finding left the trial court no alternative but to render judgment for Mizell.

We disagree with the court of appeals' analysis. Whether Champion still had a duty to Mizell in December 1987 was not a factual determination which the jury could, or was asked to, make. It was a legal determination, based on the jury's finding concerning Mizell's conduct in January 1987, and the trial court's finding that the partnership terminated. The jury was not instructed that the legal effect of Mizell's conduct was to terminate the partnership, and it may have believed otherwise. But that belief, if it existed, cannot change the legal effect of the jury's finding. The jury's finding that Champion breached his fiduciary duty does not control the legal determination of whether such duty existed; the finding concerning Mizell's conduct does.

We conclude that the trial court correctly rendered judgment for defendants. Accordingly, a majority of the court grants Champion's application for writ of error and, without hearing oral argument, reverses the judgment of the court of appeals and renders judgment that Mizell take nothing.

Wilson v. Contwell
2007 WL 2285947 N.D.Tex., 2007.

MEMORANDUM OPINION AND ORDER

Before the court is Defendants Jay S. Cantwell and Waterjet Tech, Inc.'s Rule 12(b)(6) Motion to Dismiss with Brief in Support, filed May 8, 2007. After careful review of the motion, response, record, and applicable authority, the court denies Defendants' ... Rule 12(b)(6) Motion to Dismiss.

Factual and Procedural Background

Plaintiff Frank Wilson, Jr. ("Plaintiff" or "Wilson") filed this diversity action for declaratory judgment, breach of fiduciary duty, breach of contract, injunctive relief, and quantum meruit on October 17, 2006, against Defendants Jay S. Cantwell ("Cantwell") and Waterjet Tech, Inc. ("Waterjet") (collectively, "Defendants"). This case arises from an alleged business arrangement to patent, produce, and market products incorporating Direct Part Marking ("DPM") technology. Compl. ¶ 6. Wilson asserts that, in the early 1990s, he and Cantwell orally established an enterprise or partnership, jointly owned and controlled by them, to patent, produce, and market products using DPM technology. *Id.* ¶¶ 6-7. Wilson also contends Defendant Waterjet was established in furtherance of these efforts. *Id.* ¶ 9. Wilson asserts Cantwell procured patents related to DPM technology in his name only when the alleged joint enterprise was the rightful patent owner. *Id.* ¶ 12. Wilson argues that he and Cantwell should co-own the DPM patents and Waterjet assets. *Id.* ¶ 16. Defendants deny Wilson's allegations and refuse to recognize his right to produce or sell products incorporating DPM technology. Neither party disputes that Cantwell is the named holder of the patents at issue: Patent Nos. 6666257, 6666255, and 6220333.

The parties agree Wilson provided funds to Cantwell at some unspecified time or times. Wilson asserts he provided over $500,000 working capital to the enterprise. *Id.* ¶ 8. Defendants contend Wilson simply loaned an unknown amount of money to Cantwell, but deny that any payment of money was pursuant to an agreement giving Wilson rights to the DPM patents or any related business or profits. Wilson contends Defendants' refusal to recognize his rights to the DPM patents and the alleged joint enterprise impedes him from proceeding with business opportunities and could allow Cantwell to improperly transfer or license the patents at issue. *Id.* ¶¶ 13, 31. On May 8, 2007, Defendants filed a motion to dismiss under Federal Rule of Civil Procedure 12(b)(6), arguing that Wilson failed to state a claim upon which relief could be granted. ...

Analysis

Declaratory Judgment

Wilson seeks a declaration of the following: he and Cantwell "entered into an oral partnership or joint venture;" he and Cantwell co-own all assets of WaterJet as property of the partnership or joint venture, or the property should be held in a constructive trust; and "the patents governing the DPM products are property of the partnership/joint venture or, in the alternative, are exclusively and perpetually licensed to [it]." Compl. ¶ 16. Defendants contend Wilson is not entitled to a declaratory judgment because he has not pleaded an actual, substantial controversy. . . .

Here, Wilson wishes to recover the funds he provided, receive profits, and produce and sell DPM products incorporating the patents at issue, and Defendants contest the circumstances surrounding the provision of funds and refuse to recognize Wilson's rights to receive profits and produce and sell the products. Compl. ¶ 13; Answer ¶ 13. Wilson alleges Defendants' refusal to recognize his rights related to the patents and partnership has resulted and continues to result in lost sales, profits, and business opportunities. Compl. ¶ 27. He also asserts that he faces a continuing risk of future harm because Defendants could sell or license the patents. *Id.* ¶ 31. Thus, Wilson has alleged more than a past injury; there is a continuing, real, and immediate controversy that creates a definite threat of future injury. Furthermore, the past wrongs alleged against Cantwell, such as denying Wilson's rights to the DPM patents and Waterjet assets, demonstrate a continuing harm and a real and immediate threat of repeated injury in the future because Wilson is unable to receive profits, protect his patent rights, and produce and sell DPM products. Therefore, Wilson has adequately pleaded that he will suffer injury in the future. Accordingly, dismissal of Wilson's claim for declaratory judgment is inappropriate at this time.

Breach of Fiduciary Duty

Wilson alleges that Cantwell, as a partner or joint venturer, owed Wilson a fiduciary duty and breached that duty by failing to transfer patents to the partnership or joint venture, hindering it from achieving its purpose, and mismanaging and wasting Wilson's financial investments. *Id.* ¶¶ 18-19. Defendants argue that Wilson's breach of fiduciary duty claim must be dismissed because no fiduciary relationship exists, as Wilson pleaded only that a "business relationship" amounting to a partnership or joint venture existed. Defendants also contend that Wilson did not allege sufficient facts to show breach of the purported fiduciary duty. In Texas, to prevail on a breach of fiduciary duty claim, a plaintiff must show the following: (i) the plaintiff and defendant had a fiduciary relationship; (ii) the defendant breached his fiduciary duty to the plaintiff; and (iii) that breach resulted in either injury to the plaintiff or benefit to the defendant. *Burrow v. Arce,* 997 S.W.2d 229, 237 (Tex.1999).

In his Complaint, Wilson alleges that a fiduciary relationship exists between him and Defendants based on the alleged partnership or joint venture. Compl. ¶ 18. Under Texas law, partners owe the partnership and partners the fiduciary duties of loyalty and care. Tex. Bus. Orgs.Code Ann. § 152.204(a) (Vernon 2006). Furthermore, partners must discharge their duties to partners and the partnership in good faith and in the best interests of the partnership. § 152.204(b). Thus, taking all well-pleaded facts as true, the partnership Wilson alleges in his Complaint would create a fiduciary relationship between Wilson and Defendants. Wilson further alleges that Cantwell breached his fiduciary duty to Wilson through numerous acts, including patenting DPM technology only in Cantwell's name. Compl. ¶¶ 19-20. Additionally, Wilson contends that he lost profits and incurred additional expenses, among other injuries, due to Cantwell's breach. *Id.* ¶ 20. The court determines that Wilson has alleged facts necessary to state a breach of fiduciary duty claim. . . .

Conclusion

For the reasons stated herein, the court determines that Wilson has stated valid claims upon which relief could be granted for declaratory judgment, breach of fiduciary duty, breach of contract, injunctive relief, and quantum meruit against Defendants Jay S. Cantwell and Waterjet Tech, Inc. Accordingly, the court denies Defendants Jay S. Cantwell and Waterjet Tech, Inc.'s Rule 12(b)(6) Motion to Dismiss.

It is so ordered.

****

Bohatch v. Butler & Binion
977 S.W.2d 543, 41 Tex. Sup. Ct. J. 308

Partnerships exist by the agreement of the partners; partners have no duty to remain partners. The issue in this case is whether we should create an exception to this rule by holding that a partnership has a duty not to expel a partner for reporting suspected overbilling by another partner. The trial court rendered judgment for Colette Bohatch on her breach of fiduciary duty claim against Butler & Binion and several of its partners (collectively, "the firm"). The court of appeals held that there was no evidence that the firm breached a fiduciary duty and reversed the trial court's tort judgment; however, the court of appeals found evidence of a breach of the partnership agreement and rendered judgment for Bohatch on this ground. 905 S.W.2d 597. We affirm the court of appeals' judgment.

I. FACTS

Bohatch became an associate in the Washington, D.C., office of Butler & Binion in 1986 after working for several years as Deputy Assistant General Counsel at the Federal Energy Regulatory Commission. John McDonald, the managing partner of the office, and Richard Powers, a partner, were the only other attorneys in the Washington office. The office did work for Pennzoil almost exclusively. Bohatch was made partner in February 1990. She then began receiving internal firm reports showing the number of hours each attorney worked, billed, and collected. From her review of these reports, Bohatch became concerned that McDonald was overbilling Pennzoil and discussed the matter with Powers. Together they reviewed and copied portions of McDonald's time diary. Bohatch's review of McDonald's time entries increased her concern. On July 15, 1990, Bohatch met with Louis Paine, the firm's managing partner, to report her concern that McDonald was overbilling Pennzoil. Paine said he would investigate. Later that day, Bohatch told Powers about her conversation with Paine.

The following day, McDonald met with Bohatch and informed her that Pennzoil was not satisfied with her work and wanted her work to be supervised. Bohatch testified that this was the first time she had ever heard criticism of her work for Pennzoil. The next day, Bohatch repeated her concerns to Paine and to R. Hayden Burns and Marion E. McDaniel, two other members of the firm's management committee, in a telephone conversation. Over the next month, Paine and Burns investigated Bohatch's complaint. They reviewed the Pennzoil bills and supporting computer print-outs for those bills. They then discussed the allegations with Pennzoil in-house counsel John Chapman, the firm's primary contact with Pennzoil. Chapman, who had a long-standing relationship with McDonald, responded that Pennzoil was satisfied that the bills were reasonable. In August, Paine met with Bohatch and told her that the firm's investigation revealed no basis for her contentions. He added that she should begin looking for other employment, but that the firm would continue to provide her a monthly draw, insurance coverage, office space, and a secretary. After this meeting, Bohatch received no further work assignments from the firm.

In January 1991, the firm denied Bohatch a year-end partnership distribution for 1990 and reduced her tentative distribution share for 1991 to zero. In June, the firm paid Bohatch her monthly draw and told her that this draw would be her last. Finally, in August, the firm gave Bohatch until November to vacate her office. By September, Bohatch had found new employment. She filed this suit on October 18, 1991, and the firm voted formally to expel her from the partnership three days later, October 21, 1991.

The trial court granted partial summary judgment for the firm on Bohatch's wrongful discharge claim, and also on her breach of fiduciary duty and breach of the duty of good faith and fair dealing claims for any conduct occurring after October 21, 1991 (the date Bohatch was formally expelled from the firm). The trial court denied the firm's summary judgment motion on Bohatch's breach of fiduciary duty and breach of the duty of good faith and fair dealing claims for conduct occurring before October 21, 1991. The breach of fiduciary duty claim and a breach of contract claim were tried to a jury. The jury found that the firm breached the partnership agreement and its fiduciary duty. It awarded Bohatch $57,000 for past lost wages, $250,000 for past mental anguish, $4,000,000 total in punitive damages (this amount was apportioned against several defendants), and attorney's fees.

The trial court rendered judgment for Bohatch in the amounts found by the jury, except it disallowed attorney's fees because the judgment was based in tort. After suggesting remittitur, which Bohatch accepted, the trial court reduced the punitive damages to around $237,000. All parties appealed. The court of appeals held that the firm's only duty to Bohatch was not to expel her in bad faith. 905 S.W.2d at 602. The court of appeals stated that " '[b]ad faith' in this context means only that partners cannot expel another partner for self-gain." *Id.* Finding no evidence that the firm expelled Bohatch for self-gain, the court concluded that Bohatch could not recover for breach of fiduciary duty. *Id.* at 604. However, the court concluded that the firm breached the partnership agreement when it reduced Bohatch's tentative partnership distribution for 1991 to zero without notice, and when it terminated her draw three months before she left. *Id.* at 606. The court concluded that Bohatch was entitled to recover $35,000 in lost earnings for 1991 but none for 1990, and no mental anguish damages. *Id.* at 606–07. Accordingly, the court rendered judgment for Bohatch for $35,000 plus $225,000 in attorney's fees. *Id.* at 608.

II. BREACH OF FIDUCIARY DUTY

We have long recognized as a matter of common law that "[t]he relationship between ... partners ... is fiduciary in character, and imposes upon all the participants the obligation of loyalty to the joint concern and of the utmost good faith, fairness, and honesty in their dealings with each other with respect to matters pertaining to the enterprise." *Fitz–Gerald v. Hull,* 150 Tex. 39, 237 S.W.2d 256, 264 (1951) (quotation omitted). Yet, partners have no obligation to remain partners; "at the heart of the partnership concept is the principle that partners may choose with whom they wish to be associated." *Gelder Med. Group v. Webber,* 41 N.Y.2d 680, 394 N.Y.S.2d 867, 870–71, 363 N.E.2d 573, 577 (1977). The issue presented, one of first impression, is whether the fiduciary relationship between and among partners creates an exception to the at-will nature of partnerships; that is, in this case, whether it gives rise to a duty not to expel a partner who reports suspected overbilling by another partner. At the outset, we note that no party questions that the obligations of lawyers licensed to practice in the District of Columbia—including McDonald and Bohatch—were prescribed by the District of Columbia Code of Professional Responsibility in effect in 1990, and that in all other respects Texas law applies. Further, neither statutory nor contract law principles answer the question of whether the firm owed Bohatch a duty not to expel her. The Texas Uniform Partnership Act, TEX.REV.CIV. STAT. ANN. art. 6701b, addresses expulsion of a partner only in the context of dissolution of the partnership. *See id.* §§ 31, 38.

In this case, as provided by the partnership agreement, Bohatch's expulsion did not dissolve the partnership. Additionally, the new Texas Revised Partnership Act, TEX.REV.CIV. STAT. ANN. art. 6701b–1.01 to –11.04, does not have retroactive effect and thus does not apply. *See id.* art. 6701b–11.03. Finally, the partnership agreement contemplates expulsion of a partner and prescribes procedures to be followed, but it does not specify or limit the grounds for expulsion. Thus, while Bohatch's claim that she was expelled in an *improper way* is governed by the partnership agreement, her claim that she was expelled for an *improper reason* is not. Therefore, we look to the common law to find the principles governing Bohatch's claim that the firm breached a duty when it expelled her.

Courts in other states have held that a partnership may expel a partner for purely business reasons. *See St. Joseph's Reg'l Health Ctr. v. Munos,* 326 Ark. 605, 934 S.W.2d 192, 197 (1996) (holding that partner's termination of another partner's contract to manage services performed by medical partnership was not breach of fiduciary duty because termination was for business purpose); *Waite v. Sylvester,* 131 N.H. 663, 560 A.2d 619, 622–23 (1989) (holding that removal of partner as managing partner of limited partnership was not breach of fiduciary duty because it was based on legitimate business purpose); *Leigh v. Crescent Square, Ltd.,* 80 Ohio App.3d 231, 608 N.E.2d 1166, 1170 (1992) ("Taking into account the general partners' past problems and the previous litigation wherein Leigh was found to have acted in contravention of the partnership's best interests, the ouster was instituted in good faith and for legitimate business purposes.").

Further, courts recognize that a law firm can expel a partner to protect relationships both within the firm and with clients. *See Lawlis v. Kightlinger & Gray,* 562 N.E.2d 435, 442 (Ind.App.1990) (holding that law firm did not breach fiduciary duty by expelling partner after partner's successful struggle against alcoholism because "if a partner's propensity toward alcohol has the potential to damage his firm's good will or reputation for astuteness in the practice of law, simple prudence dictates the exercise of corrective action ... since the survival of the partnership itself potentially is at stake"); *Holman v. Coie,* 11 Wash.App. 195, 522 P.2d 515, 523 (1974) (finding no breach of fiduciary duty where law firm expelled two partners because of their contentious behavior during executive committee meetings and because one, as state senator, made speech offensive to major client).

Finally, many courts have held that a partnership can expel a partner without breaching any duty in order to resolve a "fundamental schism." *See Waite,* 560 A.2d at 623 (concluding that in removing partner as managing partner "the partners acted in good faith to resolve the 'fundamental schism' between them"); *Heller v. Pillsbury Madison & Sutro,* 50 Cal.App.4th 1367, 58 Cal.Rptr.2d 336, 348 (1996) (holding that law firm did not breach fiduciary duty when it expelled partner who was not as productive as firm expected and who was offensive to some of firm's major clients); *Levy v. Nassau Queens Med. Group,* 102 A.D.2d 845, 476 N.Y.S.2d 613, 614 (1984) (concluding that expelling partner because of "[p]olicy disagreements" is not "bad faith").

The fiduciary duty that partners owe one another does not encompass a duty to remain partners or else answer in tort damages. Nonetheless, Bohatch and several distinguished legal scholars urge this Court to recognize that public policy requires a limited duty to remain partners— *i.e.,* a partnership must retain a whistleblower partner. They argue that such an extension of a partner's fiduciary duty is necessary because permitting a law firm to retaliate against a partner who in good faith reports suspected overbilling would discourage compliance with rules of professional conduct and thereby hurt clients. While this argument is not without some force, we must reject it.

A partnership exists solely because the partners choose to place personal confidence and trust in one another. *See Holman,* 522 P.2d at 524 ("The foundation of a professional relationship is personal confidence and trust."). Just as a partner can be expelled, without a breach of any common law duty, over disagreements about firm policy or to resolve some other "fundamental schism," a partner can be expelled for accusing another partner of overbilling without subjecting the partnership to tort damages. Such charges, whether true or not, may have a profound effect on the personal confidence and trust essential to the partner relationship. Once such charges are made, partners may find it impossible to continue to work together to their mutual benefit and the benefit of their clients.

We are sensitive to the concern expressed by the dissenting Justices that "retaliation against a partner who tries in good faith to correct or report perceived misconduct virtually assures that others will not take these appropriate steps in the future." 977 S.W.2d at 561 (Spector, J., dissenting). However, the dissenting Justices do not explain how the trust relationship necessary both for the firm's existence and for representing clients can survive such serious accusations by one partner against another. The threat of tort liability for expulsion would tend to force partners to remain in untenable circumstance—suspicious of and angry with each other—to their own detriment and that of their clients whose matters are neglected by lawyers distracted with intra-firm frictions.

Although concurring in the Court's judgment, Justice Hecht criticizes the Court for failing to "address amici's concerns that failing to impose liability will discourage attorneys from reporting unethical conduct." 977 S.W.2d at 556 (Hecht, J., concurring). To address the scholars' concerns, he proposes that a whistleblower be protected from expulsion, but only if the report, irrespective of being made in good faith, is proved to be correct. We fail to see how such an approach encourages compliance with ethical rules more than the approach we adopt today. Furthermore, the amici's position is that a reporting attorney must be in good faith, not that the attorney must be right. In short, Justice Hecht's approach ignores the question Bohatch presents, the amici write about, and the firm challenges—whether a partnership violates a fiduciary duty when it expels a partner who in good faith reports suspected ethical violations. The concerns of the amici are best addressed by a rule that clearly demarcates an attorney's ethical duties and the parameters of tort liability, rather than redefining "whistleblower." We emphasize that our refusal to create an exception to the at-will nature of partnerships in no way obviates the ethical duties of lawyers. Such duties sometimes necessitate difficult decisions, as when a lawyer suspects overbilling by a colleague. The fact that the ethical duty to report may create an irreparable schism between partners neither excuses failure to report nor transforms expulsion as a means of resolving that schism into a tort.

We hold that the firm did not owe Bohatch a duty not to expel her for reporting suspected overbilling by another partner.

III. BREACH OF THE PARTNERSHIP AGREEMENT

The court of appeals concluded that the firm breached the partnership agreement by reducing Bohatch's tentative distribution for 1991 to zero without the requisite notice. 905 S.W.2d at 606. The firm contests this finding on the ground that the management committee had the right to set tentative and year-end bonuses. However, the partnership agreement guarantees a monthly draw of $7,500 per month regardless of the tentative distribution. Moreover, the firm's right to reduce the bonus was contingent upon providing proper notice to Bohatch. The firm does not dispute that it did not give Bohatch notice that the firm was reducing her tentative distribution. Accordingly, the court of appeals did not err in finding the firm liable for breach of the partnership agreement. Moreover, because Bohatch's damages sound in contract, and because she sought attorney's fees at trial under section 38.001(8) of the Texas Civil Practice and Remedies Code, we affirm the court of appeals' award of Bohatch's attorney's fees.

We affirm the court of appeals' judgment. . . .

SPECTOR, joined by PHILLIPS, Chief Justice, dissenting

[W]hat's the use you learning to do right when it's troublesome to do right and ain't no trouble to do wrong, and the wages is just the same? — *The Adventures of Huckleberry Finn*

The issue in this appeal is whether law partners violate a fiduciary duty by retaliating against one partner for questioning the billing practices of another partner. I would hold that partners violate their fiduciary duty to one another by punishing compliance with the Disciplinary Rules of Professional Conduct. Accordingly, I dissent.

I.

This dispute arose after Colette Bohatch, a partner in Butler & Binion's Washington, D.C. office, expressed concerns to the firm's managing partner, Louis Paine, about possible overbilling by another partner, John McDonald. The firm had hired Bohatch to join McDonald as one of three attorneys in the firm's Washington office, which was devoted almost exclusively to Pennzoil matters. Bohatch had several years' experience working at the Federal Energy

Regulatory Commission, ending her tenure there as Deputy Assistant General Counsel for Gas and Oil Litigation. Once Bohatch became a partner in Butler & Binion, just over two years after being hired, she began receiving billing reports that indicated McDonald was charging Pennzoil for eight to twelve hours of work each day. Bohatch developed doubts about McDonald's billing practices after observing that he only worked an average of three to four hours per day. She first expressed her suspicions about McDonald's billing practices to Richard Powers, the other partner in the Washington office, when he approached her with similar concerns. Together, Powers and Bohatch examined McDonald's time diary. They saw many vague entries that did not comply with firm requirements for keeping time records; Bohatch thought the records might have been falsified in an attempt to conceal overbilling.

Powers told Bohatch that she should do something about her concerns. Before reporting her suspicions, Bohatch reviewed the District of Columbia's ethical rules and consulted counsel. She ultimately met with Louis Paine, the firm's managing partner, to report that she suspected McDonald was overbilling Pennzoil on the level of $20,000 to $25,000 each month. Paine told Bohatch that she was right to report her concerns to him. Within a few hours, Bohatch informed Powers, upon his inquiry, that she had made a report to Paine.

The *day after* Bohatch made her report and immediately after an hour-long conversation with Powers, McDonald, the partner whose billing was in question, told Bohatch that Pennzoil had been dissatisfied with her work and that he would be supervising her future work. Bohatch testified that McDonald delivered this criticism with "red-faced anger." She also maintained that she had never before heard any criticism of her work for Pennzoil. Bohatch phoned Paine that night and expressed fear that McDonald's criticism was a response to her report.

Within a few weeks, McDonald removed her from a pending Pennzoil case, reassigning it to an associate of one month's tenure, and barred her from taking on any new work for Pennzoil. Within six weeks of Bohatch's initial report, Paine met with her and told her she should look for a new position. But the firm continued to provide her with a monthly draw, office space, and a secretary. Later, Bohatch's share in the distribution of the firm's profits was reduced to zero, and ultimately, her monthly draw was cut off. Bohatch eventually found new employment and filed this suit. Butler & Binion's partners then formally voted to terminate her from the partnership. Bohatch contends that instead of properly investigating and responding to the allegations, McDonald, Paine, and the firm's management committee immediately began a retaliatory course of action that culminated in her expulsion from the partnership. The partners deny these claims.

Paine and another partner on the management committee, Hayden Burns, conducted an investigation of the overbilling allegations and testified at trial that they concluded the allegations were groundless. They maintain that Bohatch made her report for selfish or spiteful reasons, not out of a desire to fulfill her ethical responsibilities as a lawyer.

The jury heard Bohatch's and the firm's versions of the events and weighed the credibility of Bohatch, McDonald, Paine, and other witnesses. It returned a verdict in favor of Bohatch, finding that the defendants had failed to comply with the partnership agreement and had breached their fiduciary duty to Bohatch. The jury found that $57,000 would compensate Bohatch for lost earnings sustained before October 21, 1991 and $250,000 would compensate her for mental anguish suffered in the past. The jury also awarded $4 million in punitive damages against Paine, Burns, and McDonald. The punitive damages were substantially reduced on remittitur. The court of appeals held that under the Texas Uniform Partnership Act and the common law, partners violate a fiduciary duty in expelling another partner only if they act in bad faith for self-gain. 905 S.W.2d 597, 602. It concluded that the record in this suit contains no evidence of a breach of fiduciary duty because there was no evidence that the partners expelled Bohatch for self-gain. *Id.* at 604. This Court, however, has never limited claims for a breach of fiduciary duty to circumstances in which a partner acts for self-gain. *See, e.g., Crim Truck & Tractor Co. v. Navistar Int'l Transp. Corp.*, 823 S.W.2d 591, 594 (Tex.1992). Today, the Court should have followed the advice of several leading legal scholars and disapproved of the court of appeals' opinion. Instead, this Court, by affirming the court of appeals' judgment, discards the jury's conclusion that the partners violated their fiduciary duty.

II.

The majority views the partnership relationship among lawyers as strictly business. I disagree. The practice of law is a profession first, then a business. Moreover, it is a self-regulated profession subject to the Rules promulgated by this Court. As attorneys, we take an oath to "honestly demean [ourselves] in the practice of law; and ... discharge [our] duty to [our] *client[s]* to the best of [our] ability." TEX. GOV'T CODE § 82.037 (emphasis added). This oath of honesty and duty is not mere "self-adulatory bombast" but mandated by the Legislature. *See Schware v. Board of Bar Exam'rs*, 353 U.S. 232, 247, 77 S.Ct. 752, 760–761, 1 L.Ed.2d 796 (Frankfurter, J. concurring) (noting that the rhetoric used to describe the esteemed role of the legal profession has real meaning). As attorneys, we bear responsibilities to our clients and the bar itself that transcend ordinary business relationships.

Certain requirements imposed by the Rules have particular relevance in this case. Lawyers may not charge unconscionable fees. TEX. DISCIPLINARY R. PROF'L CONDUCT 1.04(a), *reprinted in* TEX. GOV'T CODE, tit. 2, subtit. G app. A (TEX. STATE BAR R. art. X, § 9); *see* D.C. R. PROF'L CONDUCT 1.5(a)(1) (West 1997). Partners and supervisory attorneys have a duty to take reasonable remedial action to avoid or mitigate the consequences of known violations by other lawyers in their firm. TEX. DISCIPLINARY R. PROF'L CONDUCT 5.01; *see* D.C. R. PROF'L CONDUCT 5.1. Lawyers who know that another lawyer has violated a rule of professional conduct in a way that raises a substantial question as to that lawyer's honesty or fitness as a lawyer must report that violation. TEX. DISCIPLINARY R. PROF'L CONDUCT 8.03(a); D.C. R. PROF'L CONDUCT 8.3. In Texas, Rules 5.01 and 8.03 are essential to the self-regulatory nature of the practice of law and the honor of our profession itself. This Court has the exclusive authority to issue licenses to practice law. TEX. GOV'T CODE § 82.021. This Court also has the jurisdiction to discipline errant attorneys and establish procedures for doing so. *Id.* §§ 81.071, 81.072(a)-(c).

Attorneys, whether they are sole practitioners, employees, or partners, are still "officers of the court." *In re Snyder*, 472 U.S. 634, 644, 105 S.Ct. 2874, 2880–2881, 86 L.Ed.2d 504 (1985) (quoting *People ex rel. Karlin v. Culkin*, 248 N.Y. 465, 162 N.E. 487, 489 (1928)); *Dow Chem. Co. v. Benton*, 163 Tex. 477, 357 S.W.2d 565, 567 (1962). In sum, attorneys organizing together to practice law are subject to a higher duty toward their clients and the public interest than those in other occupations. As a natural consequence, this duty affects the special relationship among lawyers who practice law together. It is true that no high court has considered the issue of whether expulsion of a partner for complying with ethical rules violates law partners' fiduciary duty. The dearth of authority in this area does not, however, diminish the significance of this case. Instead, the scarcity of guiding case law only heightens the importance of this Court's decision.

III.

The few cases that provide guidance here do so with conflicting results, but each case highlights the grave implications of those decisions for a self-regulated profession. Ultimately, agreements to practice law may not by their terms or effect circumvent the ethical obligations of attorneys established by law. *See Southwestern Bell Tel. Co. v. DeLanney,* 809 S.W.2d 493, 494 n. 1 (Tex.1991); *Central Educ. Agency v. George West Indep. Sch. Dist.,* 783 S.W.2d 200, 202 (Tex.1989).

A.

In *Wieder v. Skala,* the New York Court of Appeals held in an at-will employment context that an associate terminated for reporting another associate's misconduct had a valid claim for breach of contract against his law firm based on an implied-in-law obligation to comply with the rules of the profession. 80 N.Y.2d 628, 593 N.Y.S.2d 752, 757, 609 N.E.2d 105, 110 (1992). The court recognized that "[i]ntrinsic to [the hiring of an attorney to practice law] ... was the unstated but essential compact that in conducting the firm's legal practice both plaintiff and the firm would do so in compliance with the prevailing rules of conduct and ethical standards of the profession." *Id.* 593 N.Y.S.2d at 756–57, 609 N.E.2d at 109–10. To find otherwise would amount to "nothing less than a frustration of the only legitimate purpose of the employment relationship," *id.* 593 N.Y.S.2d at 757, 609 N.E.2d at 110, that is, "the lawful and ethical practice of law." *Id.* 593 N.Y.S.2d at 755, 609 N.E.2d at 108. *See also* Seymour Moskowitz, *Employment–at–Will and Codes of Ethics: The Professional's Dilemma,* 23 VAL. U.L.REV.. 33, 56–66 (1988) (arguing for a public policy exception to at-will employment for professional codes of ethics). The plaintiff was not just an employee, but also an "independent officer[ ] of the court responsible in a broader public sense for [his] professional obligations." *Wieder,* 593 N.Y.S.2d at 755, 609 N.E.2d at 108.

Only one reported case involves an attorney who was punished solely for failing to report another lawyer's misconduct. The case is more notable for its rarity and effect than for the holding itself. The Illinois Supreme Court suspended an attorney for one year for failing to report misconduct pursuant to a settlement agreement forbidding reporting of unprivileged information about the conversion of client funds by another attorney. *In re Himmel,* 125 Ill.2d 531, 127 Ill.Dec. 708, 713, 533 N.E.2d 790, 795 (1988). Aware of the possible practical effect of its holding in setting an ethical standard for attorneys, the court found that "public discipline is necessary in this case to carry out the purposes of attorney discipline." *Id.* 127 Ill.Dec. at 713, 533 N.E.2d at 795. Together these cases illustrate that lawyers, by their agreements, may not sidestep their ethical obligations.

B.

I believe that the fiduciary relationship among law partners should incorporate the rules of the profession promulgated by this Court. *See Central Educ. Agency,* 783 S.W.2d at 202 (noting that employment contracts incorporate existing law). Although the evidence put on by Bohatch is by no means conclusive, applying the proper presumptions of a no-evidence review, this trial testimony amounts to some evidence that Bohatch made a good-faith report of suspected overbilling in an effort to comply with her professional duty. Further, it provides some evidence that the partners of Butler & Binion began a retaliatory course of action *before* any investigation of the allegation had begun. In light of this Court's role in setting standards to govern attorneys' conduct, it is particularly inappropriate for the Court to deny recourse to attorneys wronged for adhering to the Disciplinary Rules. *See* Blackwell, *supra,* at 44–48. I would hold that in this case the law partners violated their fiduciary duty by retaliating against a fellow partner who made a good-faith effort to alert her partners to the possible overbilling of a client.

C.

The duty to prevent overbilling and other misconduct exists for the protection of the client. Even if a report turns out to be mistaken or a client ultimately consents to the behavior in question, as in this case, retaliation against a partner who tries in good faith to correct or report perceived misconduct virtually assures that others will not take these appropriate steps in the future. Although I agree with the majority that partners have a right not to continue a partnership with someone against their will, they may still be liable for damages directly resulting from terminating that relationship. *See Woodruff v. Bryant,* 558 S.W.2d 535, 539 (Tex.Civ.App.—Corpus Christi 1977, writ ref'd n.r.e.).

IV.

The Court's writing in this case sends an inappropriate signal to lawyers and to the public that the rules of professional responsibility are subordinate to a law firm's other interests. Under the majority opinion's vision for the legal profession, the wages would not even be the same for "doing right"; they diminish considerably and leave an attorney who acts ethically and in good faith without recourse. Accordingly, I respectfully dissent.

Winding Up and Termination

Core Concepts

Although partnerships may be established to last in perpetuity, they often have a specified time period or condition that will trigger dissolution, winding up and termination of the partnership. There are numerous conditions that may trigger the end of the partnership including the death of a partner, bankruptcy, the withdrawal of a partner, deadlock and so on. These conditions, including the death of a partner may dissolve the partnership unless the partners have expressly agreed to continue the partnership. If the partnership is not continued, the remaining partners must wind up the partnership. The partnership is terminated when no part of the business is carried on, and all debts and liabilities have been satisfied and all assets and profits distributed.

Winding Up the Business

A partnership does not terminate when it dissolves if the business still requires winding up. It continues until the liquidation is completed and the proceeds are distributed. However, if one partner buys out all the interests of the other partners, the partnership terminates at the time of the transaction. Although the business is not discontinued, it is no longer being carried on by a partnership. It has become a sole proprietorship.

The death of one partner in a two-person partnership will not terminate the entity if the partner's estate or successor in interest continues to share in the firm's profits or losses. In addition, if one partner in a two-person firm dies or retires, she is considered to be a partner if she continues to receive liquidating payments from the firm until her interest is completely liquidated.

After dissolution, any partner who has not wrongfully withdrawn has an equal right to possess the firm assets, to participate in the winding up process, and to dispose of the firm assets for the purpose of liquidating and winding up the firm affairs. If dissolution occurs because of the death of one partner, the surviving partners ordinarily have full power to control and dispose of the assets in order to terminate partnership business. The partners may, however, agree among themselves that one or more of them shall have exclusive authority to possess, control and dispose of the assets.

Even after dissolution, no one individual partner is entitled to exclusive possession for his own use of specific partnership property until the partnership has been liquidated, an accounting has been made, and the property has been applied to the payment of firm debts.

Some partners do not have the authority to wind up the partnership, including bankrupt or insolvent partners or partners who have wrongfully dissolved the partnership.

§ 152.001. DEFINITIONS. In this chapter:

(1) "Event of withdrawal" or "withdrawal" means an event specified by Section 152.501(b).

(2) "Event requiring a winding up" means an event specified by Section 11.051 or 11.057. ...

(5) "Transfer" includes:
- (A) an assignment;
- (B) a conveyance;
- (C) a lease;
- (D) a mortgage;
- (E) a deed;
- (F) an encumbrance; and
- (G) the creation of a security interest.

(6) "Withdrawn partner" means a partner with respect to whom an event of withdrawal has occurred.

§ 152.207. STANDARDS OF CONDUCT APPLICABLE TO PERSON WINDING UP PARTNERSHIP BUSINESS. Sections 152.204-152.206 apply to a person winding up the partnership business as the personal or legal representative of the last surviving partner to the same extent that those sections apply to a partner.

Subchapter G: Withdrawal of Partner

§ 152.501. EVENTS OF WITHDRAWAL.

(a) A person ceases to be a partner on the occurrence of an event of withdrawal.

(b) An event of withdrawal of a partner occurs on:

(1) receipt by the partnership of notice of the partner's express will to withdraw as a partner on:
- (A) the date on which the notice is received; or
- (B) a later date specified by the notice;

(2) an event specified in the partnership agreement as causing the partner's withdrawal;

(3) the partner's expulsion as provided by the partnership agreement;

(4) the partner's expulsion by vote of a majority-in-interest of the other partners if:
- (A) it is unlawful to carry on the partnership business with that partner;
- (B) there has been a transfer of all or substantially all of that partner's partnership interest, other than:

(i) a transfer for security purposes that has not been foreclosed; or

(ii) the substitution of a successor trustee or successor personal representative;

(C) not later than the 90th day after the date on which the partnership notifies an entity partner, other than a nonfiling entity or foreign nonfiling entity partner, that it will be expelled because it has filed a certificate of termination or the equivalent, its existence has been involuntarily terminated or its charter has been revoked, or its right to conduct business has been terminated or suspended by the jurisdiction of its formation, if the certificate of termination or the equivalent is not revoked or its existence, charter, or right to conduct business is not reinstated; or

(D) an event requiring a winding up has occurred with respect to a nonfiling entity or foreign nonfiling entity that is a partner;

(5) the partner's expulsion by judicial decree, on application by the partnership or another partner, if the judicial decree determines that the partner:

(A) engaged in wrongful conduct that adversely and materially affected the partnership business;

(B) wilfully or persistently committed a material breach of:
(i) the partnership agreement; or
(ii) a duty owed to the partnership or the other partners under Sections 152.204-152.206; or

(C) engaged in conduct relating to the partnership business that made it not reasonably practicable to carry on the business in partnership with that partner;

(6) the partner's:

(A) becoming a debtor in bankruptcy;

(B) executing an assignment for the benefit of a creditor;

(C) seeking, consenting to, or acquiescing in the appointment of a trustee, receiver, or liquidator of that partner or of all or substantially all of that partner's property; or

(D) failing, not later than the 90th day after the appointment, to have vacated or stayed the appointment of a trustee, receiver, or liquidator of the partner or of all or substantially all of the partner's property obtained without the partner's consent or acquiescence, or not later than the 90th day after the date of expiration of a stay, failing to have the appointment vacated;

(7) if a partner is an individual:

(A) the partner's death;

(B) the appointment of a guardian or general conservator for the partner; or

(C) a judicial determination that the partner has otherwise become incapable of performing the partner's duties under the partnership agreement;

(8) termination of a partner's existence;

(9) if a partner has transferred all of the partner's partnership interest, redemption of the transferee's interest under Section 152.611; or

(10) an agreement to continue the partnership under Section 11.057(d) if the partnership has received a notice from the partner under Section 11.057(d) requesting that the partnership be wound up.

§ 152.502. EFFECT OF EVENT OF WITHDRAWAL ON PARTNERSHIP AND OTHER PARTNERS.

A partnership continues after an event of withdrawal. The event of withdrawal affects the relationships among the withdrawn partner, the partnership, and the continuing partners as provided by Sections 152.503-152.506 and Subchapter H.

§ 152.503. WRONGFUL WITHDRAWAL; LIABILITY.

(a) At any time before the occurrence of an event requiring a winding up of partnership business, a partner may withdraw from the partnership and cease to be a partner as provided by Section 152.501.

(b) A partner's withdrawal is wrongful only if:

(1) the withdrawal breaches an express provision of the partnership agreement;

(2) in the case of a partnership that has a period of duration, is for a particular undertaking, or is required under its partnership agreement to wind up the partnership on occurrence of a specified event, before the expiration of the period of duration, the completion of the undertaking, or the occurrence of the event, as appropriate:

(A) the partner withdraws by express will;

(B) the partner withdraws by becoming a debtor in bankruptcy; or

(C) in the case of a partner that is not an individual, a trust other than a business trust, or an estate, the partner is expelled or otherwise withdraws because the partner wilfully dissolved or terminated; or

(3) the partner is expelled by judicial decree under Section 152.501(b)(5).

(c) In addition to other liability of the partner to the partnership or to the other partners, a wrongfully withdrawing partner is liable to the partnership and to the other partners for damages caused by the withdrawal.

§ 152.504. WITHDRAWN PARTNER'S POWER TO BIND PARTNERSHIP.

(a) The action of a withdrawn partner occurring not later than the first anniversary of the date of the person's withdrawal binds the partnership if the transaction would bind the partnership before the person's withdrawal and the other party to the transaction:

(1) does not have notice of the person's withdrawal as a partner;

(2) had done business with the partnership within one year preceding the date of withdrawal; and

(3) reasonably believed that the withdrawn partner was a partner at the time of the transaction.

(b) A withdrawn partner is liable to the partnership for loss caused to the partnership arising from an obligation incurred by the withdrawn partner after the withdrawal date and for which the partnership is liable under Subsection (a).

§ 152.505. EFFECT OF WITHDRAWAL ON PARTNER'S EXISTING LIABILITY.

(a) Withdrawal of a partner does not by itself discharge the partner's liability for an obligation of the partnership incurred before the date of withdrawal.

(b) The estate of a deceased partner is liable for an obligation of the partnership incurred while the deceased was a partner to the same extent that a withdrawn partner is liable for an obligation of the partnership incurred before the date of withdrawal.

(c) A withdrawn partner is discharged from liability incurred before the date of withdrawal by an agreement to that effect between the partner and a partnership creditor.

(d) If a creditor of a partnership has notice of a partner's withdrawal and without the consent of the withdrawn partner agrees to a material alteration in the nature or time of payment of an obligation of the partnership incurred before the date of withdrawal, the withdrawn partner is discharged from the obligation.

§ 152.506. LIABILITY OF WITHDRAWN PARTNER TO THIRD PARTY.

A person who withdraws as a partner in a circumstance that is not an event requiring a winding up of partnership business under Section 11.051 or 11.057 is liable to another party as a partner in a transaction entered into by the partnership or a surviving partnership under Section 10.001 not later than the second anniversary of the date of the partner's withdrawal only if the other party to the transaction:

(1) does not have notice of the partner's withdrawal; and

(2) reasonably believed that the withdrawn partner was a partner at the time of the transaction.

SUBCHAPTER H. REDEMPTION OF WITHDRAWING PARTNER'S OR TRANSFEREE'S INTEREST

§ 152.601. REDEMPTION IF PARTNERSHIP NOT WOUND UP.
The partnership interest of a withdrawn partner automatically is redeemed by the partnership as of the date of withdrawal in accordance with this subchapter if:

(1) the event of withdrawal occurs under Sections 152.501(b)(1)-(9) and an event requiring a winding up of partnership business does not occur before the 61st day after the date of the withdrawal; or

(2) the event of a withdrawal occurs under Section 152.501(b)(10).

§ 152.602. REDEMPTION PRICE.
(a) Except as provided by Subsection (b), the redemption price of a withdrawn partner's partnership interest is the fair value of the interest on the date of withdrawal.

(b) The redemption price of the partnership interest of a partner who wrongfully withdraws before the expiration of the partnership's period of duration, the completion of a particular undertaking, or the occurrence of a specified event requiring a winding up of partnership business is the lesser of:

(1) the fair value of the withdrawn partner's partnership interest on the date of withdrawal; or

(2) the amount that the withdrawn partner would have received if an event requiring a winding up of partnership business had occurred at the time of the partner's withdrawal.

(c) Interest is payable on the amount owed under this section.

§ 152.603. CONTRIBUTION OBLIGATION.
If a wrongfully withdrawing partner would have been required to make contributions to the partnership under Section 152.707 or 152.708 if an event requiring winding up of the partnership business had occurred at the time of withdrawal, the withdrawn partner is liable to the partnership to make contributions to the partnership in that amount and pay interest on the amount owed.

§ 152.604. SETOFF FOR CERTAIN DAMAGES.
The partnership may set off against the redemption price payable to the withdrawn partner the damages for wrongful withdrawal under Section 152.503(b) and all other amounts owed by the withdrawn partner to the partnership, whether currently due, including interest.

§ 152.605. ACCRUAL OF INTEREST.
Interest payable under Sections 152.602-152.604 accrues from the date of the withdrawal to the date of payment.

§ 152.606. INDEMNIFICATION FOR CERTAIN LIABILITY.
(a) A partnership shall indemnify a withdrawn partner against a partnership liability incurred before the date of withdrawal, except for a liability:

(1) that is unknown to the partnership *at the time*; or

(2) incurred by an act of the withdrawn partner under Section 152.504.

(b) For purposes of this section, a liability is unknown to the partnership if it is not known to a partner other than the withdrawn partner.

§ 152.607. DEMAND OR PAYMENT OF ESTIMATED REDEMPTION.

(a) If a deferred payment is not authorized under Section 152.608 and an agreement on the redemption price of a withdrawn partner's interest *is not reached* before the 121st day after the date *a written demand for payment is made by either party, not later than the 30th day after the expiration of the period, the partnership* shall:

(1) pay to the withdrawn partner in cash the amount the partnership estimates to be the redemption price and any accrued interest, reduced by any setoffs and accrued interest under Section 152.604; or

(2) make written demand for payment of its estimate of the amount owed by the withdrawn partner to the partnership, minus any amount owed to the withdrawn partner by the partnership.

(b) If a deferred payment is authorized under Section 152.608 or a contribution or other amount is owed by the withdrawn partner to the partnership, the partnership *may offer in writing to pay, or deliver a written statement of demand for,* the amount it estimates to be the net amount owed, stating the amount and other terms of the obligation.

(c) On request of the other party, the payment, tender, offer, or demand required or allowed by Subsection (a) or (b) must be accompanied or followed promptly by:

(1) if payment, tender, offer, or demand is made or delivered by the partnership, a statement of partnership property and liabilities from the date of the partner's withdrawal and the most recent available partnership balance sheet and income statement, if any; and

(2) an explanation of the computation of the estimated payment obligation.

(d) The terms of a payment, tender, offer, or demand under Subsection (a) or (b) govern a redemption if:

(1) accompanied by written notice that:

(A) the payment or tendered amount, if made, *fully satisfies a party's obligations relating to the redemption of the withdrawn partner's partnership interest;* and

(B) an action to determine the redemption price, a contribution obligation or setoff under Section 152.603 or 152.604, or other terms of the redemption obligation must be commenced not later than the first anniversary of the later of:

(i) the date on which the written notice is given; or

(ii) the date on which the information required by Subsection (c) is delivered; and

(2) the party receiving the payment, tender, offer, or demand does not commence an action in the period described by Subdivision (1)(B).

§ 152.608. DEFERRED PAYMENT ON WRONGFUL WITHDRAWAL.

(a) A partner who wrongfully withdraws before the expiration of the partnership's period of duration, the completion of a particular undertaking, or the occurrence of a specified event requiring a winding up of partnership business is not entitled to receive any portion of the redemption price until the expiration of the period, the completion of the undertaking, or the occurrence of the specified event, as appropriate, unless the partner establishes to the satisfaction of a court that earlier payment will not cause undue hardship to the partnership.

(b) A deferred payment accrues interest.

(c) The withdrawn partner may seek to demonstrate to the satisfaction of the court that security for a deferred payment is appropriate.

§ 152.609. ACTION TO DETERMINE TERMS OF REDEMPTION.

(a) A withdrawn partner or the partnership may maintain an action against the other party under Section 152.211 to determine:

(1) the terms of redemption of that partner's interest, including a contribution obligation or setoff under Section 152.603 or 152.604; or

(2) other terms of the redemption obligations of either party.

(b) The action must be commenced not later than the first anniversary of the later of:

(1) the date of delivery of information required by Section 152.607(c); or

(2) the date written notice is given under Section 152.607(d).

(c) The court shall determine the terms of the redemption of the withdrawn partner's interest, any contribution obligation or setoff due under Section 152.603 or 152.604, and accrued interest and shall enter judgment for an additional payment or refund.

(d) If deferred payment is authorized under Section 152.608, the court shall also determine the security for payment if requested to consider whether security is appropriate.

(e) If the court finds that a party failed to tender payment or make an offer to pay or to comply with the requirements of Section 152.607(c) or otherwise acted arbitrarily, vexatiously, or not in good faith, the court may assess damages against the party, including, if appropriate, in an amount the court finds equitable:

(1) a share of the profits of the continuing business;

(2) reasonable attorney's fees; and

(3) fees and expenses of appraisers or other experts for a party to the action.

§ 152.610. DEFERRED PAYMENT ON WINDING UP PARTNERSHIP.

If a partner withdraws under Section 152.501 and not later than the 60th day after the date of withdrawal an event requiring winding up occurs under Section 11.051 or 11.057:

(1) the partnership may defer paying the redemption price to the withdrawn partner until the partnership makes a winding up distribution to the remaining partners; and

(2) the redemption price or contribution obligation is the amount the withdrawn partner would have received or contributed if the event requiring winding up had occurred at the time of the partner's withdrawal.

§ 152.611. REDEMPTION OF TRANSFEREE'S PARTNERSHIP INTEREST.

(a) A partnership must redeem the partnership interest of a transferee for its fair value if:

(1) the interest was transferred when:

(A) the partnership had a period of duration that had not yet expired;

(B) the partnership was for a particular undertaking not yet completed; or

(C) the partnership agreement provided for winding up of the partnership business on a specified event that had not yet occurred;

(2) the partnership's period of duration has expired, the particular undertaking has been completed, or the specified event has occurred; and

(3) the transferee makes a written demand for redemption.

(b) If an agreement for the redemption price of a transferee's interest is not reached before the 121st day after the date a written demand for redemption is made, the partnership must pay to the transferee in cash the amount the partnership estimates to be the redemption price and any accrued interest from the date of demand not later than the 30th day after the expiration of the period.

(c) On request of the transferee, the payment required by Subsection (b) must be accompanied or followed by:

(1) a statement of partnership property and liabilities from the date of the demand for redemption;

(2) the most recent available partnership balance sheet and income statement, if any; and

(3) an explanation of the computation of the estimated payment obligation.

(d) If the payment required by Subsection (b) is accompanied by written notice that the payment is in full satisfaction of the partnership's obligations relating to the redemption of the transferee's interest, the payment, less interest, is the redemption price unless the transferee, not later than the first anniversary of the written notice, commences an action to determine the redemption price.

§ 152.612. ACTION TO DETERMINE TRANSFEREE'S REDEMPTION PRICE.

(a) A transferee may maintain an action against a partnership to determine the redemption price of the transferee's interest.

(b) The court shall determine the redemption price of the transferee's interest and accrued interest and enter judgment for payment or refund.

(c) If the court finds that the partnership failed to make payment or otherwise acted arbitrarily, vexatiously, or not in good faith, the court may assess against the partnership in an amount the court finds equitable:

    (1) reasonable attorney's fees; and

    (2) fees and expenses of appraisers or other experts for a party to the action.

(d) The redemption of a transferee's interest under Sections 152.611(a) and (b) may be deferred as determined by the court if the partnership establishes to the satisfaction of the court that failure to defer redemption will cause undue hardship to the partnership business.

SUBCHAPTER I. SUPPLEMENTAL WINDING UP AND TERMINATION PROVISIONS

§ 152.701. EFFECT OF EVENT REQUIRING WINDING UP.

On the occurrence of an event requiring winding up of a partnership business under Section 11.051 or 11.057:

    (1) the partnership continues until the winding up of its business is completed, at which time the partnership is terminated; and

    (2) the relationship among the partners is changed as provided by this subchapter.

§ 152.702. PERSONS ELIGIBLE TO WIND UP PARTNERSHIP BUSINESS.

(a) After the occurrence of an event requiring a winding up of a partnership business, the partnership business may be wound up by:

    (1) the partners who have not withdrawn;

    (2) the legal representative of the last surviving partner; or

    (3) a person appointed by the court to carry out the winding up under Subsection (b).

(b) On application of a partner, a partner's legal representative or transferee, or a withdrawn partner whose interest is not redeemed under Section 152.608, a court, for good cause, may appoint a person to carry out the winding up and may make an order, direction, or inquiry that the circumstances require.

§ 152.703. RIGHTS AND DUTIES OF PERSON WINDING UP PARTNERSHIP BUSINESS.

(a) To the extent appropriate for winding up, as soon as reasonably practicable, and in the name of and for and on behalf of the partnership, a person winding up a partnership's business may take the actions specified in Sections 11.052, 11.053, and 11.055.

(b) Section 11.052(a)(2) shall not be applicable to a partnership.

§ 152.704. BINDING EFFECT OF PARTNER'S ACTION AFTER EVENT REQUIRING WINDING UP.
After the occurrence of an event requiring winding up of the partnership business, a partnership is bound by a partner's act that:

(1) *is appropriate for winding up; or*

(2) *would bind the partnership under Sections 152.301 and 152.302 before the occurrence of the event requiring winding up, if the other party to the transaction does not have notice that an event requiring winding up has occurred.*

§ 152.705. PARTNER'S LIABILITY TO OTHER PARTNERS AFTER EVENT REQUIRING WINDING UP.

(a) *Except as provided by Subsection (b), after the occurrence of an event requiring winding up of the partnership business, the losses with respect to which a partner must contribute under Section 152.708(a) include losses from a liability incurred under Section 152.704.*

(b) *A partner who incurs, with notice that an event requiring a winding up of the partnership business has occurred, a partnership liability under Section 152.704(2) by an act that is not appropriate for winding up is liable to the partnership for a loss caused to the partnership arising from that liability.*

§ 152.706. DISPOSITION OF ASSETS.

(a) *In winding up the partnership business, the property of the partnership, including any required contributions of the partners under Sections 152.707 and 152.708, shall be applied to discharge its obligations to creditors, including partners who are creditors other than in the partners' capacities as partners.*

(b) *A surplus shall be applied to pay in cash the net amount distributable to partners in accordance with their right to distributions under Section 152.707.*

§ 152.707. SETTLEMENT OF ACCOUNTS.

(a) *Each partner is entitled to a settlement of all partnership accounts on winding up the partnership business.*

(b) *In settling accounts among the partners, the partnership interest of a withdrawn partner that is redeemed under Section 152.610 is credited with a share of any profits for the period after the partner's withdrawal but is charged with a share of losses for that period only to the extent of profits credited for that period.*

(c) *The profits and losses that result from the liquidation of the partnership property must be credited and charged to the partners' capital accounts.*

(d) *The partnership shall make a distribution to a partner in an amount equal to that partner's positive balance in the partner's capital account. Except as provided by Section 152.304(b) or 152.801, a partner shall contribute to the partnership an amount equal to that partner's negative balance in the partner's capital account.*

§ 152.708. CONTRIBUTIONS TO DISCHARGE OBLIGATIONS.

(a) Except as provided by Sections 152.304(b) and 152.801, to the extent not taken into account in settling the accounts among partners under Section 152.707:

(1) each partner shall contribute, in the proportion in which the partner shares partnership losses, the amount necessary to satisfy partnership obligations, excluding liabilities that creditors have agreed may be satisfied only with partnership property without recourse to individual partners;

(2) if a partner fails to contribute, the other partners shall contribute the additional amount necessary to satisfy the partnership obligations in the proportions in which the partners share partnership losses; and

(3) a partner or partner's legal representative may enforce or recover from the other partners, or from the estate of a deceased partner, contributions the partner or estate makes to the extent the amount contributed exceeds that partner's or the estate's share of the partnership obligations.

(b) The estate of a deceased partner is liable for the partner's obligation to contribute to the partnership.

(c) The following persons may enforce the obligation of a partner or the estate of a deceased partner to contribute to a partnership:

(1) the partnership;
(2) an assignee for the benefit of creditors of a partnership or a partner; or
(3) a person appointed by a court to represent creditors of a partnership or a partner.

§ 152.709. CANCELLATION OR REVOCATION OF EVENT REQUIRING WINDING UP; CONTINUATION OF PARTNERSHIP.

(a) If a partnership has a period of duration, is for a particular undertaking, or is required under its partnership agreement to wind up the partnership on occurrence of a specified event, all of the partners in the partnership may cancel under Section 11.152 an event requiring a winding up specified in Section 11.051(1) or (3), or Section 11.057(c)(1), by agreeing to continue the partnership business notwithstanding the expiration of the partnership's period of duration, the completion of the undertaking, or the occurrence of the event, as appropriate, other than the withdrawal of a partner. On reaching that agreement, the event requiring a winding up is canceled, the partnership is continued, and the partnership agreement is considered amended to provide that the expiration, the completion, or the occurrence of the event did not result in an event requiring winding up of the partnership.

(b) A continuation of the business for 90 days by the partners or those who habitually acted in the business during the partnership's period of duration or the undertaking or preceding the event, without a settlement or liquidation of the partnership business and without objection from a partner, is prima facie evidence of agreement by all partners to continue the business under Subsection (a).

(c) All of the partners of a partnership, by agreeing to continue the partnership, may cancel under Section 11.152 an event requiring winding up specified in Section 11.057(d) that arises from a request to wind up from a partner.

(d) To approve a revocation under Section 11.151 by a partnership of a voluntary decision to wind up pursuant to the express will of all the partners as specified in Section 11.057(b), prior to completion of the winding up process, all the partners must agree in writing to revoke the voluntary decision to wind up and to continue the business of the partnership.

(e) To approve a revocation under Section 11.151 by a partnership of a voluntary decision to wind up pursuant to the express will of a majority-in-interest of the partners as specified in Section 11.057(a), prior to completion of the winding up process, a majority-in-interest of the partners must agree in writing to revoke the voluntary decision to wind up and to continue the business of the partnership.

(f) All of the partners of a partnership, by agreeing to continue the partnership, may cancel under Section 11.152 an event requiring winding up specified in Section 11.057(c)(3) that arises from the sale of all or substantially all of the property of the partnership.

§ 152.710. REINSTATEMENT. *To approve a reinstatement of a partnership under Section 11.202, all remaining partners, or another group or percentage of partners as specified by the partnership agreement, must agree in writing to reinstate and continue the business of the partnership.*

In re Leal v. Mokhabery
360 B.R. 231, 2007

For the reasons set forth below, the Court finds that Plaintiff and Defendant have each engaged in wrongful conduct with respect to the business partnership formed by them. A separate judgment has been issued.

Background

On or around March 15, 2000, Omar Leal and Kevin Mokhabery entered into a general partnership doing business under the assumed name All American Auto Glass. The purpose of the business was the installation of automotive glass. Each party owned a 50% interest in the partnership. Mokhabery provided the capital for the business while Leal provided sweat equity and received a salary. The primary place of business was in McAllen, Texas.

On April 1, 2005, Leal filed suit against Mokhabery in the 206th Judicial District Court, Hidalgo County, Texas. Leal sought a temporary restraining order and damages due to Mokhabery's alleged waste of business assets, among other claims. On June 23, 2005, Mokhabery filed a counterclaim, alleging breach of fiduciary duty, conversion and unfair competition among other allegations.

On or around May 19, 2005, the state court entered an agreed order appointing a receiver.

On October 19, 2005, Leal filed a petition for relief under chapter 13 of the Bankruptcy Code. The Plaintiff filed a notice of removal on February 21, 2006. A two-day trial was held on October 23, 2006, and October 24, 2006. Upon conclusion of the trial, the Court took the matter under advisement.

Applicable Law

The Texas Revised Partnership Act ("TRPA") governs the relations between partners unless a partnership agreement provides otherwise. A partnership has the same powers as an individual or corporation to do all things necessary or convenient to carry out its business and affairs. Unless agreed otherwise, each partner has equal rights in the management and conduct of the partnership's business and a right to access the partnership books and records. Every partner is an agent of the partnership for the purpose of its business. Unless a partner does not have authority to act for the partnership, the act of each partner binds the partnership if the act is for apparently carrying on the partnership business or affairs.

Absent an express agreement that a partnership is for a particular term or specific undertaking, a partnership is at the will of each person who enters into the partnership. A partnership at will continues until the partnership is terminated.

Section 6.01(a) of the TRPA provides that a partner ceases to be a partner on the occurrence of an event of withdrawal. Section 6.01(b) identifies events of withdrawal that do not require a partnership to wind up. One such event includes the partnership's receipt of notice of a partner's express will to withdraw as a partner. In addition, § 8.01 sets forth additional events that require the winding up of a partnership. Such events include the express will of a majority-in-interest of the partners, the entry of certain judicial decrees, and a request for winding up the partnership from a partner, among other events.

Partners owe to the partnership and to each other fiduciary duties as a matter of law, including a duty of loyalty and care. Such duties include a duty to: (1) account to the partnership and hold for it all partnership profits and property; (2) refrain from dealing with the partnership on behalf of a party adverse to the partnership; and (3) refrain from competing with the partnership. As a fiduciary, a partner is under an obligation not to usurp opportunities for personal gain, and equity will hold a partner accountable to the partnership for his profits if he does so.

A partner's duties also include a strict duty of good faith and candor. Thus, the partnership relation imposes upon all partners an obligation of the utmost good faith, fairness and honesty in their dealings with each other with respect to matters pertaining to the partnership business.

When an event of withdrawal occurs, the remaining partners have the right to continue the business. If no event requiring a winding up occurs within 60 days after an event of withdrawal, the withdrawn partner is automatically entitled to redeem his interest as of the date of withdrawal. Where the withdrawal is not wrongful as defined by § 6.02, the redemption price is the fair value of the partner's interest as of the date of withdrawal. If an event requiring a winding up occurs, the partnership continues until the winding up of its business is completed, at which time the partnership is terminated. The rules governing distribution upon a winding up dictate that assets first be applied to pay debts held by creditors of the partnership. Any surplus will be paid in cash as distributions to a partner with a positive balance in the partner's capital account. A partner's capital account is determined by crediting the partner's account with the partner's contributions to the partnership (consisting of cash and the value of any other contributions) and the partner's share of profits subtracting any distributions to the partner and the partner's share of the partnership losses. Absent an agreement to the contrary, each partner is responsible for a share of the losses in proportion to the partner's share of the profits.

Analysis

It is undisputed that although Leal and Mokhabery entered into a partnership, they did not have a written partnership agreement. The parties' oral agreement addressed only a few matters. The parties agreed that each partner owned a 50% interest in the partnership, and that Mokhabery would provide some start-up capital and Leal would provide the day-to-day labor for the business. The parties did not provide that the partnership was for a particular term or discuss whether any events would result in a winding up of the partnership. Thus, the partnership was at the will of each partner. Upon creation of the partnership in 2000, each partner owed the partnership and each other fiduciary duties including the duty of loyalty and care with respect to the All American's affairs.

The evidence shows that Mokhabery provided the partnership with limited assets upon creation of the partnership, including a truck from Mokhabery's business in Dallas, Texas, Advantage DFW Auto Glass, Inc. Leal worked on site at All American's business premises during all relevant periods while Mokhabery lived in Dallas and oversaw the business from there. In 2002, Mokhabery handled the partnership's payroll tax bills using a certified public accountant in Dallas. However, in 2003, the parties changed their business arrangement and Leal began handling All American's bills and payroll taxes, in addition to the day-to-day operations that he already oversaw. Leal admits that prior to joining All American he had never operated an auto glass business and that his office management and organization skills were poor and needed much improvement.

On April 1, 2005, Leal filed this lawsuit seeking a temporary restraining order and damages. Leal alleged that Mokhabery wasted business assets, failed to pay business debts, used the partnership name to obtain personal loans, and improperly withdrew business assets. Mokhabery filed a counterclaim, alleging breach of fiduciary duty, conversion and unfair competition among other allegations. After reviewing all the evidence, it is clear that this dispute arose because neither Leal nor Mokhabery took his fiduciary duty seriously.

Leal's claim for damages

Leal asserts that in 2002 Mokhabery improperly used partnership assets for personal use. Partners do not have any interest in partnership property. Partnership property includes property acquired in the name of the partnership or in the name of one or more partners if the instrument transferring title indicates the grantee's capacity as a partner or the existence of the partnership. All American received capital and assets from Mokhabery when the business was started. All American purchased glass from sellers under its partnership name and held bank accounts under the partnership name.

Leal alleges that Mokhabery improperly withdrew business assets and failed to account for the withdrawals. Specifically, Leal contends that Mokhabery withdrew $34,000 from a partnership account for use in Mokhabery's Dallas business. Mokhabery admits that he took $34,000 from All American's account in 2003 without approval from Leal but argues he is owed at least this much in profits that should have been dispensed to him pursuant to his 50% interest in the partnership if Leal had properly managed the business. Mokhabery is an experienced businessman, and whether or not Mokhabery was entitled to partnership profits at the time he withdrew the money, he had a duty not to use partnership property for his own benefit and knew the withdrawal was wrong. Mokhabery breached his duty of loyalty when he arbitrarily removed the money and failed to hold it for the partnership or account to the partnership for the withdrawal. Accordingly, the partnership is entitled to recover $34,000 from Mokhabery.

Leal further asserts that Mokhabery improperly used All American's bank account to pay taxes for his Dallas business, Advantage DFW Auto Glass, Inc. The evidence shows that 14 checks totaling $23,656.91 were paid to Chase Bank from an All American bank account. In the Memo section on each check is typed "XX–XXXXXXX." Leal asserts that this number is the tax identification number for Advantage DFW Auto Glass. Mokhabery testified that his accountant paid All American's taxes for 2002 from Dallas and that these checks were used for this purpose, but were simply mislabeled by the accountant. Leal has presented no evidence that All American is liable for any outstanding tax debt for 2002, or any evidence that he paid All American's taxes himself in 2002. To the contrary, the evidence before the Court shows that Leal began handling the partnership's taxes in 2003 and that notices of federal tax liens have only been filed for the tax periods encompassing 2003 and 2004. Accordingly, Leal has failed to meet his burden of proof with respect to these alleged damages.

Leal also seeks damages in the amount of $7,150.59 based on rebates that Mokhabery allegedly received pursuant to purchases he made on behalf of glass for All American. The evidence shows that Mokhabery received these rebates between July 16, 2003, and March 11, 2004. Although Mokhabery admits that he received such rebates, he argues they were for purchases for his Dallas business in addition to All American's business, and that his negotiations with these sellers saved All American $30,000 in glass costs. The evidence is clear that the $7,150.59 was credited for purchases made on two accounts for All American. Partnership property includes property acquired in the name of one partner where the instrument transferring title to the property indicates the existence of a partnership regardless of whether the name of the partnership is indicated. There is no evidence that the partnership or Leal approved Mokhabery's personal receipt of the rebates. Accordingly, the partnership is entitled to recover $7,150.59 from Mokhabery.

With respect to Leal's other causes of action, Leal has failed to meet his burden of proof. Leal has not presented evidence concerning the alleged waste of business assets or use of the partnership name to obtain personal loans. Leal did present evidence of past due advertising bills and 2003 and 2004 taxes owed by the partnership. However, the evidence shows that in 2003 and subsequent years, Leal was in control of the partnership accounts and had accepted responsibility for paying the payroll and partnership bills. Although Leal demanded that Mokhabery contribute to the partnership's advertising debts due to the Yellow Pages, it is unclear what time period the bill for the Yellow Pages' advertisements encompassed. The evidence shows that Mokhabery refused to pay the bill since Leal was in possession of all of the advertised phone lines at the time the request to pay was made. Finally, Leal is not entitled to attorneys fees based on the total absence of evidence in support of a fee recovery.

Mokhabery's claim for damages

In his counter petition, Mokhabery argues that Leal breached his fiduciary duties. Mokhabery also asserted causes of action for conversion, unfair competition, an accounting and fraud, and sought a declaratory judgment and an injunction against Leal. Mokhabery also asserted claims against J.D. Garcia. No evidence imposing liability against Garcia was introduced.

The crux of Mokhabery's argument for damages based on the various causes of action is that Leal failed to properly run All American's business. Mokhabery's argument focuses on two claims: (1) that the partnership should have been more profitable, and (2) that Leal failed to keep proper accounting records. Mokhabery testified that based on his experience in the auto glass business, the average markup is approximately 300% so that for every $50 in glass purchases the business should generate sales of $150. Based on this, Mokhabery seeks damages. Mokhabery's argument is defective. First, the evidence shows that Mokhabery's personal businesses' cost-to-revenue ratio was higher than 33%. Mokhabery even admitted that his individual businesses lost money at times but defended his assertions regarding the proper cost-to-revenue figures by explaining that the businesses were dissimilar since he purchased glass in bulk from a wholesaler or dealt in other business areas in addition to auto glass. Essentially, Mokhabery is upset with Leal's management of the business and the fact that All American was not as profitable as he expected. Business ventures and partnerships involve risks, and absent a contractual guarantee or

191

tortuous conduct, there is no legal remedy available to a businessman who is later disappointed by the partnership's actual revenues or profits. Even if the Court assumes that Leal ran the business poorly, absent a showing of wrongful conduct, poor management performance is not actionable. At best, Mokhabery established that Leal was a poor manager.

Mokhabery further alleges that Leal was not depositing cash for the business or properly accounting for actual revenue as required and seeks damages for this fraud. Again, the basis of these arguments is that Leal did not handle the business as Mokhabery would have preferred. In particular, Mokhabery testified that he taught Leal the procedures to organize and manage the business. When a potential customer called, All American would offer a quote. If the customer agreed to have the work completed, All American would issue a work order showing that the work would be completed. Upon completion of the work, an invoice was to be issued. Although not all quotes would turn into work orders, ideally all work orders would become invoices and revenue for the partnership. Based on this model, Mokhabery presented evidence regarding the number of quotes made by All American and the number of work orders prepared and compared these numbers to the partnership's revenues. Mokhabery contends that Leal was either receiving unreported payments in cash or converting partnership assets because the revenue did not equal that shown on the work orders. However, Mokhabery admitted that some clients do not pay. Leal also testified that his organization and accounting skills are below par and therefore he often failed to create invoices or proper reports. In addition, the evidence shows that Leal paid many business operations expenses in cash before such revenues were ever deposited into the partnership's bank accounts. Although the Court recognizes that there were some discrepancies within the All American glass purchase and sales figures initially provided by Leal, Leal addressed the discrepancy and subsequently provided amended figures. While Leal's management of All American's business operations may have been sub par, the evidence is insufficient to prove damages.

On March 30, 2005, John D. Garcia, Leal's attorney, sent a letter to "All American Auto Glass, ATTN: Kevin Mokhabery." The letter stated that "Mr. Leal has decided to pull out in [sic] the general partnership agreement and purse [sic] a more singularity approach to his business model." This letter operated as an event of withdrawal when received by Mokhabery on or around April 1, 2005.

As a result, Leal ceased to be a partner of All American on April 1, 2005. Because a partnership requires two or more partners, Leal's letter expressing his will to withdraw from the partnership was effectively a request for a winding up of the partnership. Nonetheless, the partnership continues to exist at least for purposes of winding up the partnership business. [The Act] sets forth who is authorized to perform necessary acts with respect to the partnership business after the occurrence of an event requiring a winding up. A partner who has not withdrawn is one such person. Because Leal withdrew from the partnership and Mokhabery was the only remaining partner, Mokhabery was the only partner authorized to wind up All American's business and affairs.

However, the evidence is undisputed that after notifying Mokhabery that he wished to pull out of the partnership, Leal took cash from All American's bank accounts and customers, as well as All American's business equipment, to use in a new auto glass business, Starline Glass Distributors Inc., which Leal created. Leal admits that he operated Starline's business under the name of All American Auto Glass and that he changed the locks on the partnership premises and excluded Mokhabery, All–American's sole remaining partner, from any access to Starline or the partnership assets. Then Leal filed this action seeking a temporary restraining order against Mokhabery. When the state court appointed a receiver and Mokhabery sought to compel Leal's compliance with the court order, Leal filed bankruptcy.

Leal's conduct was clearly wrongful. Once he withdrew from the partnership, Leal did not have any right to control All American or to determine what was in All American's best interest. Leal's rights were then limited to the redemption price of his partnership interest. However, because the partnership consisted of only two partners, Leal's withdrawal effectively constituted an event requiring a winding up that left Mokhabery as the sole remaining partner authorized to wind up All American's business. Instead, Leal took the partnership assets and excluded Mokhabery from access to them. Leal then started a new auto glass business, Starline, using the partnership's assets. Conversion occurs when a person makes an unauthorized and wrongful assumption and exercise of dominion and control over the personal property of another, to the exclusion or inconsistent with the owner's rights. Here, Leal had no interest in the partnership property and was no longer a partner with the authority to act on behalf of the partnership or fiduciary duties owed to the partnership. However, as a former agent of the partnership and one who remained in possession of the partnership property subsequent to his notice of withdrawal, Leal still owed duties to the partnership that an agent owes its principal following termination of the agency. There is no dispute that the money was in the partnership's bank accounts or due to the partnership and Leal had no individual right to take the property. Accordingly, the Court finds that Leal is guilty of conversion.

Leal seeks to justify his wrongful conversion of All American's assets and argues that he took possession of the partnership assets only after Mokhabery improperly withdrew money from the partnership's accounts. He testified that he never intended that Starline be solely his business, but that he established Starline to continue the partnership's business and protect the partnership's assets from Mokhabery so that he could pay the partnership's debts. The Court does not find this testimony to be credible. Instead, the Court concludes that Leal intended to convert the partnership's remaining assets to his own use. Notwithstanding the complexity of the facts involved in this matter and the wrongdoing by both partners, the law is clear—if a partner withdraws, he ceases to be a partner. Leal may not tender his notice of withdrawal and then continue acting as a partner, exercising control over the business and claiming profits by reason of the partnership's business. Such acts violate Texas partnership law and subject Leal to liability for theft or conversion of All American's property. That is the path Leal chose to pursue in this matter. Subsequent to his withdrawal, Leal disregarded the law and treated All American's assets as his own. He is liable for his wrongful actions.

The Court finds that the fair market value of the assets was $145,000. Mokhabery testified that All American held approximately $30,000 in inventory at the time of Leal's withdrawal. He further testified that All American's accounts receivables for the partnership's business with insurance companies was approximately $20,000–$40,000 and that the partnership owned 12–13 phone numbers by which it received the majority of its business. Although the precise value of the telephone numbers is not known, there is no question that the rights to the phone numbers, and other intangibles including the business name, had substantial value. In addition, Leal's bankruptcy schedules disclose various assets of Starline. Schedule B lists Leal's personal property as including two bank accounts for Starline Glass Distributors Inc. in the amounts of $1,454.14 and $659.04, as well as 100% stock in Starline's assets valued at $13,950.00. Schedule B further lists four vehicles valued at $35,000.

The Court notes that Leal was the wrongdoer when he converted the assets. When he converted the assets, he held them in trust for the partnership. As the holder of assets in trust, he bore the burden to account for the assets. Leal failed on that burden. The Court will accept Mockhabery's values.

In addition, the Court finds that Leal is liable for damages caused by his wrongful conversion of the partnership name under which he admits he operated his new business, Starline. The evidence shows that in 2005, Starline's bank deposits totaled $322,536.26 and expenses totaled $381,289.94. These expenses, however, included $23,081.91 that Leal spent for legal and professional fees relating to his chapter 13 bankruptcy case and this litigation. Thus, Starline's actual business expenses were $358,208.03. The business operated at a loss. The Court declines to award additional damages based on those operations.

The Court is very troubled by the conduct of each partner in this case. When he took over the records and responsibility for paying the partnership bills in 2003, Leal had a responsibility to maintain the partnership records. Leal clearly failed at this and breached his fiduciary duties. Mokhabery is an experienced businessman and knew that he did not possess any interest in the partnership property that would allow him to arbitrarily withdraw funds when he wanted to do so. When Leal withdrew from the partnership, neither partner followed the law as to how to wind up the partnership. Texas law provides that a winding up should occur "as soon as reasonably practicable." Leal disregarded the legal effect of his withdrawal and Mokhabery failed to invoke his rights under Texas law. Once the parties appeared in court to resolve their issues, Leal refused to comply with the state court's orders. The conduct of both parties is inexcusable, however the conduct of Leal is much more atrocious. Accordingly, the Court denies Leal's request that the Court use its inherent powers to dissolve the All American partnership and award Starline to Leal.

Despite this ruling, the Court does not find that Mokhabery is innocent. As discussed above, Mokhabery breached his fiduciary duties and is liable to the partnership. In addition, Mokhabery started a competing business in April 2005. Mokhabery admits that he ran this business for approximately 15 months. Such conduct conflicts with Mokhabery's duties owed to the partnership. Even though Leal's withdrawal occurred prior to Mokhabery's creation of the business, Mokhabery remained a partner until the winding up of All American's affairs was complete and the partnership terminated. However, given the fact that Leal wrongfully continued to operate the partnership and has presented no evidence of damages due to the competing business, the Court denies this claim.

Under Texas law, Mokhabery is the only partner presently authorized to wind up All American's affairs. Based on the evidence before the Court, the Court finds that it is appropriate for Mokhabery to wind up the partnership's affairs. Within 10 days after entry of this order, Mokhabery shall establish a bank account in the partnership's name into which payments shall be deposited.

Because Leal has operated the business for nearly 22 months, the Court finds that it is appropriate to order Leal to pay the partnership the fair market value of the assets as of the date of his wrongful withdrawal, with interest from April 1, 2005. Prior to February 1, 2007, Leal shall deposit $145,000 into the partnership account.

Prior to February 1, 2007, Mokhabery shall deposit $41,150.59 into the partnership account, with prejudgment interest from April 1, 2005.

Upon receipt of these payments, Mokhabery is ordered to comply with the Texas Revised Partnership Act. Thus, Mokhabery is ordered to satisfy the debts of the partnership from the cash received from the liquidation of the partnership assets. To the extent a deficiency remains, the parties are each ordered to contribute 50% of the partnership's total deficiency to satisfy all partnership debts. To the extent any surplus remains, each partner shall be paid in cash in an amount equal to any positive balance in the partner's capital account.

The Court recognizes that either Mokhabery or Leal or both may fail to deposit the required amounts into the partnership account. The partnership may enforce its judgment against the partner failing to make the deposit into the partnership account. If Leal fails to deposit the $145,000 plus interest into the partnership account, Mokhabery may act in the name of the partnership to collect the $145,000 judgment from Leal. If Mokhabery fails to deposit $41,150.59 plus interest into the partnership account, Leal may act in the name of the partnership to collect the $41,159.59 from Mockhabery.

The Court notes that these amounts are due to the partnership. Leal and Mockhabery may not offset these amounts against amounts owed to each other.

****

Coleman v. Coleman
170 S.W.3d 231(Tex.App.-Dallas, 2005)

This case concerns the disposition of a business partnership between brothers after one of them died. Max Coleman, the surviving partner, appeals the judgment awarding the redemption value of his brother's partnership interest to his widow, Debbie Coleman. In five issues, Max asserts that (1) as a transferee of his brother's interest, Debbie is not entitled to receive the redemption value of the partnership interest; (2) the trial court erred in excluding evidence of an alleged oral "buy-sell" agreement whereby life-insurance proceeds would be used to buy out a deceased partner's interest; (3) the amount of setoff and credits the trial court awarded was not supported by the evidence; (4) the value of Robert's interest, held by Debbie as a transferee, was not supported by the evidence; and (5) the trial court erred in awarding Debbie attorney fees and costs. We affirm the trial court's judgment.

Facts

Brothers Max and Robert Coleman were equal partners in a business begun in 1980. Initially, they bought green plants in Florida and shipped them to Texas, but the business eventually evolved into a trucking firm that worked mostly for one client. The business operated principally under the partnership entitled Coleman Properties, using as well the beneficially owned corporation Green Foliage and Supply, Inc. for certain business purposes (collectively, the Partnership).

On December 1, 2001, Robert committed suicide. Max continued to operate the business, advancing Robert's salary to his widow, Debbie Coleman, and paying certain of her expenses after Robert's death. Debbie, the named beneficiary to a life insurance policy in Robert's name, collected the proceeds on the policy. Debbie sought recovery of the value of Robert's interest in the Partnership, demanding that Max wind up the business and distribute the proceeds. Max continued to operate the business and use the Partnership assets, operating under the newly registered name Coleman Logistics. Subsequently, Debbie sued Max, demanding the "redemption value" of Robert's interest in the Partnership.

After a bench trial, the trial court determined, among other things, that (1) Debbie gave notice to wind up but Max failed to do so, (2) Debbie was entitled to the redemption price for Robert's interest, and (3) Max never tendered the redemption price. The trial court rendered judgment against Max, discounting the redemption value of Robert's interest by 15% because of "lack of control," as Debbie was a transferee of the interest and not a partner. The court awarded Debbie the amount of $161,500, less certain amounts for a setoff and credit for payments made by Max, plus attorney fees for $20,000 and certain costs. Max's motion for new trial was overruled by operation of law, and he filed this appeal.

Redemption or Distribution of Capital Account

In his first issue, Max argues that under the relevant statute, Debbie is a transferee of Robert's interest, not a partner, and thus she is not entitled to receive the "redemption price" for Robert's partnership interest. Rather, Max argues, the statutory provision governing distribution upon the winding up of a partnership applies, thus affording Debbie only the positive balance in Robert's capital account at the time of his death.

The Texas Revised Partnership Act

It is undisputed that Max and Robert did not have a written partnership agreement. It is also undisputed that the partnership was not for a particular term, for a specified undertaking, nor was a winding up required upon the occurrence of a specified event. Thus, the parties agree that the Partnership was a "partnership at will."

The Texas Revised Partnership Act (TRPA) governs the relations between partners when the partners have not agreed otherwise. The structure of the TRPA provides two ways for a departing partner to recover the value of his or her partnership interest: (1) through disposition of the partnership assets upon the winding up of the partnership, under TRPA § 8.06, or (2) if the partnership business is continued, through the buyout of the withdrawing partner's interest by the remaining partners, under TRPA § 7.01.

Section 8.01 governs the winding up of a partnership. It provides that notice from a partner of a partnership at will constitutes an event requiring a winding up, but provides that a majority in interest may elect to continue the partnership. The rules for distribution upon a winding up require that assets first be applied to debts and next to "settle partnership accounts among the partners." Section 8.06(b) governs the settlement procedures and provides, among other things, that "the profits and losses that result from the liquidation of the partnership property must be credited and charged to the partners' capital accounts."

Section 8.01(g) states in pertinent part:

> *(f) Notice from Partner if No Term or Undertaking; Option to Continue. If a partnership is not for a definite term or a particular undertaking and its partnership agreement does not provide for a specified event requiring a winding up, a request for winding up the partnership from a partner ... requires a winding up 60 days after the date of the partnership's receipt of notice of the request or at a later date as specified by the notice, unless a majority-in-interest of the partners agree to continue the partnership.*

Section 8.06(a) states:

> *(a) **Application of Property to Obligations.** In winding up the partnership business, the property of the partnership, including the contributions of the partners required by this section, must be applied to discharge its obligations to creditors, including, to the extent permitted by other applicable law, partners who are creditors other than in their capacities as partners. Any surplus must be applied to pay in cash the net amount distributable to partners in accordance with their right to distributions under Subsection (b).*

Section 8.06(b) provides that:

> *(b) **Settlement of Accounts Among Partners.** Each partner is entitled to a settlement of all partnership accounts on winding up the partnership business. In settling accounts among the partners, the partnership interest of a withdrawn partner that is not redeemed under Section 7.01 is credited with a share of any profits for the period after the partner's withdrawal but is charged with a share of losses for that period only to the extent of profits credited for that period, and the profits and losses that result from the liquidation of the partnership property must be credited and charged to the partners' capital accounts. The partnership shall make a distribution to a partner in an amount equal to that partner's positive balance in the partners' capital accounts....*

Section 7.01, entitled "Redemption of Withdrawing Partner or Transferee's Interest if Partnership Not Wound Up," entitles a withdrawn partner to redeem his or her interest as follows:

> *(a) **Redemption.** If an event of withdrawal occurs ... and an event requiring a winding up does not occur within 60 days after the date of the withdrawal, ... the partnership interest of the withdrawn partner automatically is redeemed by the partnership as of the date of withdrawal in accordance with this section.*

The *"redemption price"* is the *"fair value"* of the interest as of the date of withdrawal. The Comment to that section refers to *"redemption" as a "buyout."*

One event of withdrawal that triggers redemption is a "partner's death." Upon the death of a partner, the partner's surviving spouse and his or her heirs become "transferees" of the partnership interest from the partner.

Max argues that Debbie is entitled at most to any positive balance in Robert's capital account, according to the provision governing distribution upon the winding up of a partnership. Specifically, he argues that Debbie is a "transferee" of Robert's interest, not a partner, and only partners are entitled to the redemption price under the literal terms of section 7.01(a). Further, he argues, section 7.01(n) is the *exclusive* provision for a transferee to redeem an interest, and Debbie does not qualify under that subsection. That is, section 7.01(n) provides a mechanism for redemption by a transferee of an interest in a partnership that is for a specific term or purpose, but not for a transferee of an interest in a partnership at will, as is the case here. Thus, Max argues, Debbie is entitled at most to any positive balance in Robert's capital account under the winding up provisions in section 8.06(b).

Section 7.01(n) deals with the obligation to redeem a transferee's interest in a partnership that is not a "partnership at will":

> (n) **Obligation to Redeem Transferee.** A partnership must redeem the partnership interest of a transferee for its fair value if:
>
> (1) the interest was transferred when:
>
> (A) the partnership was for a definite term not then expired or a particular undertaking not then completed; or
> (B) the partnership agreement provided for winding up on a specified event that has not yet occurred;
>
> (2) the definite term has expired, the particular undertaking has been completed, or the specified event has occurred; and
>
> (3) the transferee makes a written demand for redemption.

We cannot agree with the construction of TRPA urged by Max. Section 8.06(b) requires that "the profits and losses that result from the liquidation of the partnership property must be credited and charged to the partners' capital accounts." The trial court found that Max did not wind up the business. It is undisputed that Max did not liquidate the business but continued to use the Partnership assets to operate the same business. Nonetheless, with no liquidation, Max urges that the portion of section 8.06(b) entitling a partner to the positive balance in the capital account should apply.

Max also argues that section 7.01(n) is the *exclusive* means by which a transferee may realize a redemption, or buyout, of a partnership interest and Debbie does not meet the criteria of section 7.01(n). We note that, on its face, section 7.01(n) does not apply to a partnership at will. We look to the overall structure of the statute to ascertain legislative intent. The structure reveals the intent that a partnership interest be recoverable in one of two ways, through distribution upon a winding up of the partnership or through a buyout by the remaining partner(s) if the business continues. In the circumstances, the provision governing distribution upon a winding up does not apply because Max did not liquidate the business. Further, the legislative intent is clear that, under 7.01(a), had Robert elected when he was alive to withdraw voluntarily from the Partnership, he would have been entitled to receive the redemption value under section 7.01(a). We see no need to read the provisions governing redemption so narrowly as to deny his widow the right to receive the redemption price when the surviving partner uses partnership assets to continue the same business. We resolve Max's first issue against him.

Setoff and Credits

In his third issue, Max asserts that the evidence is legally and factually insufficient to support the amount of setoff and credits awarded Max against the redemption price. The trial court found that Max was entitled to a setoff in the amount of $17,800 for advances made to Robert in excess of those taken by Max, as well as a $28,000 credit for payments made to Debbie after Robert's death. Max argues he proved excess advances to Robert totaling some $27,006 and credits totaling $35,612.

Analysis and Conclusion

Max asserts he conclusively showed he was entitled to $27,006, not $17,800, for advances taken by Robert above those taken by Max. Max testified the partnership advanced Robert $7,046 for rent for Robert's daughter in college, $4,483 for his son's car, and $15,477 for funds expended on Robert's motorcycle. Although Max asserted these expenses exceeded those that he took, he produced no listing of monies he drew out in the same time period. Yet, he conceded that the Partnership had paid his daughter's tuition during the relevant time period.

Because Max had the burden of proof on this issue, in our legal-sufficiency review, we examine whether he conclusively established all vital facts in support of the amounts he asserts he was owed as a setoff. We cannot conclude that the evidence conclusively proves an amount larger than the $17,800 awarded. Neither can we conclude, after weighing all of the evidence, that the finding of $17,800 is so contrary to the overwhelming weight of the evidence as to be clearly wrong and unjust.

Max testified that he made over $35,612 in payments to Debbie after Robert's death, not merely $28,000 as found by the trial court. His testimony indicates he had a document itemizing those payments, but it is not in the record before us. Debbie testified that Max made post-death payments of about "thirty, thirty-five thousand." This included a documented $19,200 in continuing payments of Robert's salary. Debbie's testimony, however, indicated that the $30–35,000 figure also included payment of her daughter's rent while in college (about $7,000, accounted for in the setoff) and payment on the heating and air conditioning system at their residence. Debbie testified that the system was installed before her husband's death, that Max had a system installed in his home, and that both were being paid over time through the Partnership. Thus, the evidence supports the conclusion that Debbie's receipt of payments on the heating and air conditioning system does not represent a benefit above what Max received.

Accordingly, the evidence does not conclusively prove Max was entitled to a credit for $35,612. Weighing all the evidence, we cannot conclude the award of $28,000 in credit is against the great weight and preponderance of the evidence. Accordingly, we resolve Max's third issue against him.

Valuation of the 50% Interest Held by Debbie

In his fourth issue, Max challenges the legal and factual sufficiency of the evidence to support the valuation of Robert's 50% partnership interest, as held by Debbie as a transferee. The trial court found the value of the Partnership to be $380,000. Max challenges the valuation by Debbie's expert, Robert Dohmeyer, on a number of grounds. Because Max did not have the burden of proof on valuation, in reviewing for legal sufficiency, we examine the evidence to ascertain whether there is more than a scintilla of evidence to support the challenged finding.

Max complains that Dohmeyer valued the business as of December 31, not December 1, 2001, which was the date of death. We note that Dohmeyer testified, nonetheless, that the value as of December 1 was not materially different than the value as of December 31. This is more than a scintilla of evidence to support the conclusion that Dohmeyer's valuation was valid as of December 31.

Dohmeyer's report stated a going-concern value of $373,909. Max asserts that he used inaccurate values for assets and liabilities as a basis for the valuation. Max testified that the correct values are those he had obtained from valuations of the individual pieces of equipment and the liabilities against each. We note the evidence shows that Dohmeyer's figures came from the Partnership's 2001 tax return and conclude this constitutes more than a scintilla of evidence to support the use of that data.

Max asserts the evidence was legally and factually insufficient to support the trial court's finding that the value of the partnership was $380,000, as the maximum figure Dohmeyer testified to was $373,909. Our review of the evidence shows that there was evidence to support the higher value of $380,000. At trial, Max challenged certain data that Dohmeyer had used to attribute additional income to the partners. For her part, Debbie contended at trial that the Partnership owned two additional parcels of land, which had not been included in Dohmeyer's valuation for the business. In post-trial argument, Debbie adjusted the figures to correct for the income errors Max had asserted and added back value consistent with her evidence at trial. With these adjustments, Debbie's final valuation totaled $407,500. This constitutes more than a scintilla of evidence to support the value of $380,000.

In reviewing for factual sufficiency, we note that Max testified, based on the valuations of pieces of equipment he had obtained, that the debt was greater than the equipment was worth. Max, however, did not present an expert to value the business as a going concern. He testified that he originally thought the business was worth $120,000, but he now understood that "due to the offsets of long-term debt, the positives of receivables and things like that, there is a higher value to be ascertained." We cannot conclude that the trial court's finding that the Partnership was worth $380,000 is against the great weight and preponderance of the evidence.

Max also argued that Dohmeyer failed to evaluate the interest as a "transferee interest," failing to account for the lack of control and lack of a non-compete agreement by Max. Max also complained the use of 15% as a discount factor was unsupported. The record shows that Dohmeyer testified, "in all my prior work where I've had this come up," that a 10 to 15% discount was applied to a 50% interest. We note that Max did not object to Dohmeyer's qualification as an expert, nor did he raise a *Daubert* challenge to this testimony.

We conclude that there is more than a scintilla of evidence to support the trial court's discounting of the interest at 15%. Further, we cannot conclude that this finding is against the great weight and preponderance of the evidence. Accordingly, we resolve Max's fourth issue against him.

In his fifth issue, Max asserts that the trial court erred in awarding Debbie attorney fees and costs, because she was entitled to no recovery. Having concluded that Debbie is entitled to receive the redemption price, we resolve this issue against Max.

Accordingly, we **AFFIRM** the trial court's judgment.

****

Farnsworth v. Deaver
147 S.W.3d 662, Tex. App., Amarillo, 2004

Johnny and Janie R. Farnsworth (the Farnsworths) appeal from a final judgment entered in favor of John M. and Carol J. Deaver (the Deavers). Through the judgment, the trial court denied recovery by the Farnsworths against the Deavers but awarded the latter monetary relief and attorney's fees against the former. Furthermore, the dispute between the parties involved a partnership they had entered into, which partnership eventually fell upon hard times and had to be dissolved. The four issues before us concern the repayment of capital accounts, the removal of partnership property which the Deavers considered to be theft, the breach of fiduciary duties, and the award of attorney's fees. The judgment is modified and affirmed as modified.

Issue One–Repayment of Capital Account Imbalance

In their first issue, the Farnsworths contend the trial court erred when it ordered them to pay the Deavers $6,134.37. The latter purportedly represented one-half of the difference between the capital accounts of the Farnsworths and Deavers. According to the Farnsworths, "one partner does not have the right to recover the difference between positive partnership capital accounts from another partner." This is purportedly so because the Texas Revised Partnership Act simply obligates those partners with negative capital accounts to repay the negative balance and return the account to zero, and the Farnsworths had a positive balance in their account. We overrule the issue.

In arriving at our decision we must say that the reasoning of the Farnsworths is accurate in certain respects. When settling accounts between the partners, statute does prescribe that generally, a partner "shall contribute to the partnership an amount equal to that partner's negative balance in the partner's capital account." So, as suggested by the Farnsworths, a partner is required only to reimburse the partnership an amount equal to the negative balance. Yet, we disagree with the manner in which they determined whether they had a negative capital account.

In winding up the affairs of a partnership, creditors of the entity are not the only ones entitled to payment. So too "shall [the partnership] make a distribution to a partner in an amount equal to the partner's positive balance in the partner's capital account." Given this, capital accounts having a positive balance are debts of the partnership. Being debts, they must be included within the liabilities for which the partners are ultimately responsible. Of course, partners can affect the manner in which the partnership treats capital accounts by executing a partnership agreement touching upon the subject. However, no such agreement was executed at bar. Thus, the Texas Revised Partnership Act controls the treatment of those accounts here.

Next, if the debts of the partnership exceed its assets (which also include the value assigned to each capital account) it can be said that the partners have suffered a capital loss. And, these losses, like all other debts, must be satisfied by the partners in direct proportion to their share of the profits. For example, let us assume that three partners contributed $10,000, $5000, and $2000, respectively, to capitalize Partnership X and agreed to share profits equally. Let us also assume that upon dissolution of the partnership only $5000 remained after paying all creditors other than partners who are creditors in their capacity as partners. Since each partner is entitled to repayment of his capital, Partnership X has a loss of $12,000, *i.e.* the $17,000 representing the sum of the capital due each partner less the $5000 remaining after payment of all obligations other than those owed the partners as partners. Dividing the $12,000 loss between the partners in proportion to their share of the profits, *i.e.* one-third each, would result in each partner owing $4000 to the partnership. And, once this $4000 is offset against the sums due from the partners as reflected by their respective capital accounts, the partner who initially paid $10,000 in capital would have a positive balance of $6000 in his capital account. The one who paid $5000 would have a positive balance of $1000, while the one who paid $2000 would have a negative balance of $2000. Thus, the partner with the negative balance would be obligated to pay $2000 to the partnership to remove his capital account from its negative position.

Here, the jury found that the Deavers had a capital account of $34,349.73, while the Farnsworths had one of $22,080.68. Thus, the partnership owed a debt of $56,430.09, representing the total capital it was obligated to repay. Assuming that it had no assets left after satisfying all non-partner debt and because the partners agreed to split profits 50/50, the Farnsworths and Deavers would each owe $28,215.04 to cover the loss. And, when that sum is offset against the capital due each partner, the Deavers would have a positive capital balance of $6134.37 (*i.e.* $34,349.41 minus $28,215.04) while the Farnsworths would have a negative balance of $6134.36 (*i.e.* $22,080.68 minus $28,215.04). So, the latter would owe the partnership an additional $6134.36 to satisfy that negative balance, and that happens to be the approximate sum the trial court ordered them to pay the Deavers (*i.e.* $6,134.37).

Nevertheless, the uncontroverted testimony of Carol Deaver revealed that upon the liquidation of the partnership's assets and payment of all debt (other than that related to capital accounts) there remained $880 in cash. This sum was not taken into calculation by the trial court when computing the capital loss for which each partner was responsible. In other words, there was an additional $880 available to pay the capital accounts. Accordingly, the capital loss attributable to each partner is wrong. When the $880 is considered, the Farnsworths' negative capital balance is not $6134.36 but $5694.36.

Next, the Farnsworths also argued that if they owed the Deavers payment for their capital account, then the trial court erred in allowing prejudgment interest to accrue on that sum at 10% per annum "[b]ecause no prejudgment interest statute applies to this case." According to § 304.103 of the Texas Finance Code, prejudgment interest accrued at the same rate as post-judgment interest. Furthermore, post-judgment interest accrued, when the judgment was signed here (*i.e.* September 5, 2002), at the rate of 10% per year. So, if no statute applied, as argued by the Farnsworths, then the trial court was entitled to adopt a rate of 10%, and, again, that happens to be the rate ordered in the judgment.

Issue Two–Evidence of Civil Theft

In their second issue, the Farnsworths contend that there is no evidence or insufficient evidence to support the finding of civil theft because there is neither evidence of their intent to contribute their personal items to The Ivy Cottage nor evidence of any intent to deprive the partnership. We overrule the issue.

Specifically, the trial court asked the jury to determine whether "any of the items of property removed from the Ivy Cottage premises by the Farnsworths on August 6, 2000 were partnership property" and, if so, whether the "Farnsworths commit[ted] theft in removing the property...." To each question, the jury answered yes. Whether these answers are legally and factually supportable depends upon the application of pertinent standards of review. The standards are well-settled and need not be reiterated.

Next, to be found culpable of theft, it must be shown that the accused unlawfully appropriated the property of another with the intent to deprive the owner of it. Here, the allegation involved the theft of property belonging to the Ivy Cottage partnership. Furthermore, one of the items taken by the Farnsworths was a decorative elephant which Janie Farnsworth knew the partnership bought for resale. That alone comprises more than a scintilla of evidence permitting the jury to say "yes" not only to the question asking whether "any" property removed belonged to the partnership but also to that asking whether the Farnsworths appropriated property with the intent to deprive the owner of it. So, in perusing the record for only that evidence supporting the jury's answers to the questions as written and submitted by the trial court, we do encounter some which renders them legally sufficient.

As to the contention about the verdict lacking factually sufficient evidentiary support, we note that Janie Farnsworth testified to taking the elephant though knowing that it was the partnership's property. Nothing of record contradicts that. Given this, we cannot say, upon considering all evidence of record, that the evidence was factually insufficient to support the jury's answers to the questions at issue and as written.

Issue Four–Attorney's Fees

The fourth issue before us concerns attorney's fees. The Farnsworths contend that the trial court erred in awarding the Deavers $58,128 in such fees for trial preparation. This was purportedly so because the Deavers did not properly segregate fees which were recoverable from those which were not. Purportedly, the $58,000 sum included both. We overrule the issue.

Generally, attorney's fees incurred by one party are not recoverable from another unless allowed by statute or contract. Moreover, when a claimant pursues multiple causes of action, some of which permit the recovery of fees while others do not, he has the burden of distinguishing between those fees incurred while prosecuting claims for which fees may be awarded from all others. Yet, segregation is not required when the causes of action are dependent upon the same facts or circumstances and, consequently, are intertwined and inseparable. Should that situation arise, then all the fees incurred while prosecuting the intertwined claims may be awarded.

Here, and as itemized in appellants' brief, the Farnsworths sued for a breach of contract and a declaratory judgment. So too did they seek an accounting and the dissolution of the partnership. In turn, the Deavers filed a counterclaim asserting that the Farnsworths breached the partnership agreement and committed theft under the Texas Theft Liability Act.

According to the provisions of the Texas Theft Liability Act, one who prevails under it may recover reasonable and necessary attorney's fees from his opponent. As illustrated in issue two, the Deavers prevailed in their prosecution of their theft claim. Moreover, they did so by proving that the Farnsworths removed at least one item of partnership property without authorization of the partnership. That same allegation and evidence also comprised a basis on which the Deavers refused to fulfill their purported agreement to buy the Farnsworths' interest in the partnership. In short, they did not believe that they were getting the benefit for which they bargained. So, the facts pivotal to the cause upon which fees could be recovered, *i.e.* the theft claim, were also the same facts used to defend against the Farnsworths' claim of breached contract.

Additionally, it cannot be forgotten that the Farnsworths also sought a declaratory judgment from the trial court. Through that particular cause of action, the court was asked not only to declare that the Deavers had contracted to buy the Farnsworths' interest in the partnership and breached that contract but also to "determine the existence of the partnership, and the assets and liabilities of" it and "declar[e] and determin[e] the rights and obligations of the parties in such regard." More importantly, by making the request, the Farnsworths imbued the trial court with the discretion to award attorney's fees in any manner it deemed "equitable and just." That did not mean the trial court was restricted to simply awarding them fees. On the contrary, the blanket of authority arising from the demand for declaratory relief encompassed the discretion to award fees to any party, including the Deavers. So, to the extent that the Deavers incurred attorney's fees while addressing the declaratory judgment allegations, the trial court was permitted to award them those fees. And, those allegations, as worded by the Farnsworths, were all encompassing.

In short, of all the claims being asserted back and forth, we find none having facts or circumstances unrelated to those for which attorney's fees could be awarded in one way or another. Given this, we cannot say that the Deavers neglected to segregate recoverable from unrecoverable fees.

We modify that portion of the judgment awarding the Deavers $6134.37 against the Farnsworths and reduce the sum to $5694.36. As modified and having overruled each issue, we affirm the judgment of the trial court.

TBOC DECONSTRUCTED	
GENERAL PARTNERSHIPS	
FORMATION	
association	1.002
Partner defined	1.002(66)
partnership	1.002(67)
Filing entity defined	1.002(22)
Domestic entity	1.002(18)
Entity defined	1.002(21)
Person defined	1.002(69-b)
Signature defined	1.002(82)
Writing or written defined	1.002(89)
partnership is entity	152.056
no certificate of formation required	3.002
period of duration	3.003
CREATING/ESTABLISHING	
Effect of partnership agreement	152.002
Partnership defined	152.051
Rules for determining if partnership is created	152.052
False representation of partnership or partner	152.054
qualification of partner	152.053
Professional partnerships	152.055
Admission as partner	152.201
standards of partner conduct	152.204
FIDUCIARY DUTIES and PARTNER OBLIGATIONS	
duty of loyalty	152.205
duty of care	152.206
duties on winding up	152.207
access and obligation to maintain books and records	152.212
PARTNER RIGHT TO TRANSFER INTEREST	
right to transfer	152.401
effect of transfer generally	152.402
effect of transfer on transferor	152.403
rights and duties of transferee	152.404
partnership not bound by prohibited transfer	152.405
effect of death or divorce	152.406

PARTNER RIGHT TO CONTINUE PARTNERSHIP	
canceling revocation	152.709
reinstatement	152.71
GOVERNANCE	
GOVERNING DOCUMENT(S)	
partnership agreement is governance document	152.208
amending governance document	152.208
when TBOC controls	
GOVERNING PERSONS	
decisionmakers	152.209
binding effect of partner action generally	152.302
binding effect of partner action after event of winding up	152.704
who qualified to wind up	152.702
withdrawing partner's power to bind partnership	152.504
rights and duties generally	152.203
partner as agent	152.301
access to books and records	152.213
rights and duties of person winding up	152.703
standards of partner conduct	152.204
FIDUCIARY DUTIES and PARTNER OBLIGATIONS	
duty of loyalty	152.205
duty of care	152.206
duties on winding up	152.207
obligation to maintain books and records	152.212
PARTNER RIGHT TO TRANSFER INTEREST	
right to transfer	152.401
effect of transfer generally	152.402
effect of transfer on transferor	152.403
rights and duties of transferee	152.404
partnership not bound by prohibited transfer	152.405
effect of death or divorce	152.406

PARTNER RIGHT TO CONTINUE PARTNERSHIP	
canceling revocation	152.709
reinstatement	152.71
LIABILITY	
PARTNERSHIP LIABILITY	
generally	152.203
not bound by prohibited transfer	152.405
withdrawing partner's power to bind partnership	152.504
redemption upon withdrawal	152.601 et.seq.
redemption to transferee	152.611
binding effect of partner act after winding up	152.704
PARTNER LIABILITY	
generally	152.210-
nature of partner liability: joint and several	152.304
effect of withdrawing partner's existing liability	152.505
liability of withdrawing partner to third party	152.506
partner liability to other partners; event requiring winding up	152.705
contributions to discharge obligations	152.708
REMEDIES	
remedies of partnership and partners generally	152.211
remedy	152.305
enforcement of remedy	152.306
creditor's rights	152.307
charging order	152.308
FINANCING	
GENERAL RULE	152.202
PARTNERSHIP INTERESTS	
generally	1.002(68)
transfering pship interests	152.401
effect of partner death or divorce	152.406
WINDING UP/TERMINATION	
liquidation	152.706

settlement of accounts	152.707
contributions to discharge obligations	152.708

TERMINATION

WITHDRAWAL

events of withdrawal	152.501
effect of withdrawal	152.502
wrongful withdrawal	152.503
withdrawing partners power to bind partnership	152.504
withdrawing partners existing liability	152.505
liability of withdrawing partner to third parties	152.506
redemption	152.601
redemption price	152.602
contribution from wrongful withdrawer	152.603
set off	152.604
interest accrual	152.605
indemnification	152.606
demand of payment	152.607
deferring payment to wrongful withdrawer	152.608
civil action to determine redemption terms	152.609
effect of partner's death or divorce	152.406

WINDING UP

events requiring winding up	152.701
deferring payment	152.610-
rights and duties of transferee	152.404
redemption to transferee	152.611
civil action to determine transferee's redemption price	152.612
who qualified to wind up	152.702
rightd and duties of person winding up	152.703
binding effect of partner acts after winding up	152.704
partner liability to other partners; event of winding up	152.705
liquidation	152.706
settlement of accounts	152.707
contributions to discharge obligations	152.708

CONTINUING PARTNERSHIP

canceling revocation	152.709
reinstatement	152.710-

General Partnership Problem Set

1. Horizon Partners was established as a general partnership in 2003 to trade in foreign exchange. The forex business boomed in the early to mid-2000s and the partnership became quite successful. The management committee decided to make a huge speculative bet on the Euro in 2008, which coincided with the global financial crisis of that year. Horizon lost almost everything in the process and was also sued by a major competitor. While the lawsuit was pending, Horizon's partners, through a proper vote, admitted Kahn as a new partner on the following terms: Kahn conveyed to the partnership an office building in the city's financial district, in exchange for a 20% interest in the partnership and a preferential return of 10% on future profits. Kahn and all of Horizon's partners signed an agreement stipulating that the office building cannot be encumbered without Kahn's approval. Competitor won the suit but found that the partnership had insufficient cash to satisfy the multi-million dollar verdict. Competitor sought to take title to the property but Kahn refused to sign any transfer documents, prompting an application to the court for an order transferring it. The court ruled against Competitor, holding that Competitor cannot use the office building to satisfy the partnership's obligation, because Kahn is the de facto owner and based on the partners' agreement with him, the building cannot be encumbered without Kahn's approval. Competitor appealed and the appellate court held that Kahn is only a 20% owner of the property and the other 80% ownership interest could be used to satisfy the partnership's obligations. The court held, however, that the building cannot be used to satisfy obligations that occurred before Kahn joined the partnership because of the well-known rule that a partner is not liable for partnership obligations that were incurred prior to the partner's admission.

   Which of the court's opinions would the Supreme Court endorse?

2. Akeem and Bella formed AB Construction Company as a general partnership in 1999. The partnership has witnessed exponential growth in the volume of its business and number of partners. One of the new partners is Larry Page, co-founder of Goggle. To avoid excessive exposure to liability, Larry Page signed an agreement with the partnership and all of its partners that in the event of any liability incurred by the partnership, his liability shall not exceed $100,000. During a major construction project, Akeem negligently dropped some equipment that severely injured Temp, a temporary construction worker. Temp decided to sue only Larry Page because he has deep pockets. In court, Temp argued that since partnership liability is joint and several, he can choose to sue any partner to avoid the inconvenience and expense associated with numerous defendants or multiple lawsuits. The trial court agreed and awarded a $10 million verdict against Larry Page. Larry Page appealed and the appellate court reversed on the following grounds: (1) The plaintiff can only proceed at the first stage against the

partnership and not any of its partners for the accident; (2) Larry Page effectively limited his liability to $100,000 and cannot be made to pay an amount above that limit. The partnership and its partners should make up the difference.

Which of the courts got the law right?

3. Barbershop Partnership was established in 2008 with 4 partners, Randi, Nicki, Mariah and Keith. Because of family responsibilities, Randi and Mariah do not work on weekends. Keith and Nicki not only work on weekends but also manage the partnership's affairs. The partnership generated profits for the first time in 2010. Keith and Nicki distributed the entire profit of $80,000 as follows: $10,000 to each partner; $20,000 each as additional payment to Keith and Nicki to compensate for their extra work. In 2011, the partnership ran into a loss of $25,000. Keith and Nicki allocated the losses only to Randi and Mariah in equal amounts, reasoning that they incur losses daily by showing up everyday and carrying the additional burden of running the partnership. Randi and Mariah were not happy with the distributions and sought legal advice. A widely respected business lawyer informed them that they have no case because in the absence of an agreement on how to allocate profits and losses, the approach taken by Keith and Nicki accords with common sense and equity and thus would be upheld by the courts.

Are there grounds for challenging the distributions or do you instead agree with the legal advice?

4. Munoz, Estelle and Paul wanted to acquire and run a carpet cleaning business. Munoz and Estelle led Paul to believe that the cost of acquiring an existing carpet cleaning firm was $450,000. Paul agreed to participate and paid to them $150,000 for a 33.3% stake in the general partnership that the three would form to take over the carpet cleaning business. Munoz and Estelle then purchased the carpet cleaning business not for $450,000, but rather for $250,000 without disclosing it to Paul. The Partnership Agreement provides that the purpose of the partnership is to engage in the business of providing carpet cleaning services to commercial and industrial facilities. Munoz is the partner responsible for the Sugar Land area. The partnership provides a van for every partner to use for carrying cleaning equipment and transporting personnel to service sites. The partnership conducts business only on weekdays. To make extra money, Munoz provides carpet cleaning services to a few upscale private homes in Sugar Land on Sundays. He uses his own cleaning equipment, which he loads in the van assigned to him. Last year, Paul accidentally learned of the true facts surrounding the purchase of the business and that Munoz has earned thousands of dollars from his Sunday services. Filled with envy and rage, he sued to compel Munoz to share the profits with the rest of the partners and for Munoz and Estelle to return the approximately $66,666 excess he paid for his partnership interest. Regarding the claims against Munoz, the court ruled in

favor of Paul, ordering Munoz to disgorge the profits from his weekend business and moreover to refund Paul's overpayment for his partnership interest, holding that he breached his fiduciary duty to his fellow partners.

Do you agree with the court?

5. At a banquet celebrating last year's Law Week by the School of Law, Baruch, an alumnus of the law school falsely and publicly announced that he had joined the law firm of Baines & Hill as a partner. In fact, Baruch had no affiliation with the law firm whatsoever. Baines & Hill is a major tax and estate planning law firm in Houston with 23 partners. Two of the firm's partners – Jake and Laura – were present at the banquet but did not correct the false statement. They understood that Baruch made the statement in order to impress the university administrators. One student who had inherited some money was impressed by Baruch's speech and contacted him the following day about handling his tax-related matters. They met at a local restaurant and agreed on a fee of $50,000 which the student promptly paid. A professor who had not attended the banquet and did not know of the announcement saw the student coming out of the restaurant. The student introduced Baruch as his estate planning lawyer, adding that he had recently been made a partner at Baines & Hill. The professor engaged Baruch to handle a pending tax investigation and paid $25,000. Baruch spent the moneys received, provided no services and left town. Student and Professor sued Baines and Hill and all of its partners. The court ruled in the plaintiffs' favor, stating that Baruch's public announcement in the presence of some partners made him a partner of Baines & Hill, imposing personal liability on the 23 partners and the firm. The defendants have appealed.

Will the appeal succeed?

6. In 2003, Southwest International Traders Association (SITA) entered into an agreement with Jubilee Exposition Company, a Texas-based professional show producer and trade fair organizer, for future production of SITA shows and trade fairs in Houston. The preamble to the 2003 agreement announced that "SITA wishes to participate in such shows as sponsors and partners . . . ." However, in contemporaneous conversations relating to the meaning of the term "partners", Jubilee's president informed SITA's executive director that he understands the use of "partners" in the preamble to be in the colloquial sense of a cooperative joint effort, not a partnership in the strict legal sense. Under the agreement, SITA agreed to sponsor and endorse only shows produced by Jubilee; to persuade SITA members exhibit at those shows; and to permit Jubilee to use SITA's name for promotional purposes. On its part, Jubilee undertook to obtain all necessary leases, licenses, permits and insurance; assume all the show-related losses or any other loss resulting from the arrangement; accord SITA the right to accept or reject any exhibitor; audit show income; advance all the capital required to finance the shows.

Gross show receipts were to be shared: 55% to Jubilee; 45% to SITA. Cho, a college student who attended the fair in 2010, was injured when a stand that was improperly assembled by Jubilee's employees collapsed on him. Cho sued Jubilee and SITA seeking $50,000 in damages for his personal injury. Jubilee is almost judgment-proof, while SITA's finances are in robust shape. The court stated that since the parties expressly agreed to share profits on a 55-45 formula and because the Partnership Act "explicitly identifies profit sharing as a particularly probative indicium of partnership formation," a general partnership existed. The court further held that since Jubilee agreed to assume all the losses of the business, Jubilee alone was liable to Cho.

Did the court get it right?

7. Zenith Manufacturing Co. is a Texas general partnership devoted since inception to the manufacture of plastic products for industrial applications. Shaq, Kobe, Iverson and Zen are the partners. Zen has a solid reputation for integrity. In January 2009, a customer, Ms. Yokohama, brought stock certificates and gold bars to Zenith's offices and deposited them with Zen for safe-keeping. Zen issued a "receipt" acknowledging that he received the items and signed as partner of Zenith. Two weeks later, Ms. Yokohama brought silver coins worth half-a million dollars to Zen, but because the offices had closed, took them to Zen's house. Zen issued a similar receipt. Zen fraudulently converted the items. Ms. Yokohama sued Zenith and its partners as well as Zen for the conversion. The other partners argued that because they did not participate or have knowledge of the conversion, they were not liable. The trial court agreed. Instead, it held Zenith Manufacturing Co. and Mr. Zen liable to the customer but noted that since partnership assets need to be exhausted before recourse to an individual partner's assets, the suit was not properly brought against Mr. Zen. On appeal by the partnership, the court of appeals held that the defendants were jointly and severally liable (but *only* for the items brought to Zenith's offices since that transaction occurred in the ordinary course of business) and that the plaintiff could proceed against either or both of them at the same time.

Which of the courts do you agree with?

8. In 2005, Julie, Crystal, Erika, Edith and Tina established the Five Amigas Restaurant Company as a general partnership for an indefinite duration. In March 2010, Julie notified the other partners that she was withdrawing from the partnership, to tend to her ailing husband. Crystal and Erika believed that Julie's exit dissolved the partnership while Edith and Tina believed that the partnership continues in existence if at least 50% of the remaining partners vote to continue within 90 days of exit. Thus, Edith and Tina voted to continue. On June 19, 2010, Crystal, believing the partnership had dissolved, purchased for herself the building housing the restaurant. She expressed her willingness to retain the restaurant as a tenant on the same terms as the previous landlord, if Edith

and Tina wished to continue conducting the business there. Edith and Tina brought a suit to declare Crystal's purchase of the building and interest in becoming the restaurant's landlord as improper, unfair and illegal. The court disagreed, noting that since the rent did not change, the deal was fair; besides, the restaurant was free to move to another location. Edith and Tina are considering an appeal.

Will they prevail?

9. Amir, Blanche, Dennis and Rowland formed a law firm partnership in 2001. The partners did not enter into a written partnership agreement. Initially, partners made decisions jointly at weekly meetings. However, as each partner got busy with a heavier caseload, Blanche started functioning as a de facto managing partner, making all the day-to-day decisions regarding the partnership, including preparing employee paychecks for the administrative staff and attending outside meetings on behalf of the firm. The other partners welcomed Blanche's role because they respected her finance background. By 2011, it was obvious that the partnership had outgrown its facilities – an office building that it purchased at the start of the law practice. In January 2012, without consulting the other partners, Blanche mortgaged the office building and leased a bigger property on behalf of the partnership. Amir likes the new location because it is closer to his residence. Dennis is upset because he is the oldest partner in age and therefore felt he should have been consulted. Newlywed Rowland objects to the long commute created by the new location. The partners have sought an independent legal opinion from a retired judge and arbitrator who wrote, in part: "Partner Blanche's recent decisions and actions are without legal foundation because the law is clear that ordinary partnership decisions should be made by a majority of the partners." Blanche is adamant in maintaining her position. The other parties to the real estate transactions are nervous that the transactions may be voided.

Are their fears unfounded?

10. David, Gary, John, Keisha and Will formed David Enterprises as a general partnership in Texas. The partnership was formed in 1999 and was slated to last till 2019. The partners appointed Will as the managing partner. They also agreed on a buyout price of $1 million for each departing partner. In 2009, Keisha accepted a Cabinet position in the Obama administration and left the partnership. Will accepted the move and promptly paid Keisha $1 million as buyout payment at a time the partnership was feeling the effects of the recession badly. David, a strong opponent of President Obama, objected to Keisha's exit and had some choice words for Will. David sent a letter to Will, expressing his intent to leave the partnership and demanding an immediate buyout. Will noted that David was not entitled to a buyout until 2019 and warned him that he would be responsible for any expenses incurred by the partnership as a result of his premature exit. The matter wound up in court where the judge ruled that since the partnership bears David's name only and because he is the most important person in the business, coupled with his express will to leave, his exit is tantamount to dissolution of the partnership.

Did Will or the court get it right?

LIMITED LIABILITY PARTNERSHIPS

Limited Liability Partnerships

Core Concepts

The limited liability partnership is a partnership where the normally unlimited liability of the general partners are commuted to limited liability. A limited partnership may also become a limited liability partnership pursuant to the Texas Business Organizations Code. When a limited partnership becomes a limited liability partnership, the general partner (s) of the limited partnership is/are protected from personal liability generally attributable to a general partner.

Texas was the first state to permit Limited Liability Partnerships in 1996, however many states quickly followed. Many states have restricted use of the limited liability partnership to specific professions.

The Limited Liability Partnership (LLP) is a a filing entity that is created under state partnership laws. Accordingly, the distinction lies in that the limited liability partnership affords *every* partner with protections against personal liability for the debts and obligations of the partnership and for the actions of others. In sum, the LLP is a partnership in which all the general partners enjoy limited liability.

Formation

The Texas Business Organizations Code enumerates general provisions applicable to filing entities, i.e., (1) they must file a certificate of formation; (2) the filing instrument must be signed by an authorized person; and (3) forms must be properly delivered to the secretary of state, include all required fees, and be timely) that govern limited liability partnerships. Tex. Bus. Orgs. Code § 152.802.

In addition to the general filing requirements, in Texas, for a partnership to become a limited liability partnership, it must:

(1) set out the name of the partnership, the federal taxpayer identification number, the street address of the partnerships principal office, and the number of partners at the date of application; Tex. Bus. Orgs. Code § 152.802(a)

(2) Contain a brief statement of the partnerships business which must be signed by: (a) the majority-in-interest of the partners; or (b) one or more partners authorized by a majority-in- interest of the partners. Tex. Bus. Orgs. Code §§ 152.802(b).

A limited liability partnership becomes effective on the date on which a completed initial or renewal application is properly filed with the secretary of state or on a later date specified on the application. Thereafter, a limited partnership may engage in any lawful business unless a more limited purpose is stated in its partnership agreement. This is effective until the first anniversary of the effective, renewal, or later specified date; at which time the entity must renew its application or risk losing liability protection. Tex. Bus. Orgs. Code §§ 152.802(c)(1),(c)(2). An effective registration may be renewed by filing a renewal application before the expiration of the prior registration. Tex. Bus. Orgs. Code § 152.802(e).

Most states require entities with liability shields to put others on notice (actual or constructive) prior to commencing business. The certificate of formation on file with the secretary of state is notice that the partnership is a limited liability partnership and of all other facts contained in the certificate as required. Tex. Bus. Orgs. Code § 3.011(d). Thus, when operating, the name of the limited liability partnership must contain:

(1) the phrase "limited liability partnership", or

(2) An abbreviation of the phrase. (i.e. LLP, L.L.P.). Tex. Bus. Orgs. Code §152.803.

In Texas, (1) or (2) must be the last words or letters of its name.

§152.803. NAME. The name of a limited liability partnership must comply with Section 5.063.

§152.805. LIMITED PARTNERSHIP. A limited partnership may become a limited liability partnership by complying with applicable provisions of Chapter 153.

§ 152.802. REGISTRATION.

(a) In addition to complying with Section 152.803, a partnership, to become a limited liability partnership, must file an application with the secretary of state in accordance with Chapter 4 and this section. The application must:

(1) set out:

(A) the name of the partnership;

(B) the federal taxpayer identification number of the partnership;

(C) the street address of the partnership's principal office in this state or outside of this state, as applicable; and

(D) the number of partners at the date of application; and

(2) contain a brief statement of the partnership's business.

(b) The application must be signed by:
(1) a majority-in-interest of the partners; or
(2) one or more partners authorized by a majority-in-interest of the partners.

(c) A partnership is registered as a limited liability partnership by the secretary of state on:

(1) the date on which a completed initial or renewal application is filed in accordance with Chapter 4; or

(2) a later date specified in the application.

(d) A registration is not affected by subsequent changes in the partners of the partnership.

(e) The registration of a limited liability partnership is effective until the first anniversary of the date of registration or a later effective date, unless the application is:

(1) withdrawn or revoked at an earlier time; or

(2) renewed in accordance with Subsection (g).

(f) A registration may be withdrawn by filing a withdrawal notice with the secretary of state in accordance with Chapter 4. A certificate from the comptroller stating that all taxes administered by the comptroller under Title 2, Tax Code, have been paid must be filed with the notice of withdrawal. A withdrawal notice terminates the status of the partnership as a limited liability partnership from the date on which the notice is filed or a later date specified in the notice, but not later than the expiration date under Subsection (e). A withdrawal notice must:

(1) contain:

(A) the name of the partnership;

(B) the federal taxpayer identification number of the partnership;

(C) the date of registration of the partnership's last application under this subchapter; and

(D) the current street address of the partnership's principal office in this state and outside this state, if applicable; and

(2) be signed by:

(A) a majority-in-interest of the partners; or

(B) one or more partners authorized by a majority-in-interest of the partners.

(g) An effective registration may be renewed before its expiration by filing an application with the secretary of state in accordance with Chapter 4. A renewal application filed under this subsection continues an effective registration for one year after the date the registration would otherwise expire. The renewal application must contain:

(1) current information required for an initial application; and

(2) the most recent date of registration of the partnership.

(h) The secretary of state may remove from its active records the registration of a partnership the registration of which has:

(1) been withdrawn or revoked; or

(2) expired and not been renewed.

(i) Repealed by Acts 2011, 82nd Leg., R.S., Ch. 139, Sec. 66(2), eff. September 1, 2011.

(j) A document filed under this subchapter may be amended by filing an application for amendment of registration with the secretary of state in accordance with Chapter 4 and this subsection. The application for amendment must:

(1) contain:

(A) the name of the partnership;

  (B) the taxpayer identification number of the partnership;

  (C) the identity of the document being amended;

  (D) the date on which the document being amended was filed;

  (E) a reference to the part of the document being amended; and

  (F) the amendment or correction; and

(2) be signed by:

  (A) a majority-in-interest of the partners; or

  (B) one or more partners authorized by a majority-in-interest of the partners.

Apcar Investment Partners VI, Ltd. v. Gaus
161 S.W.3d 137 (Tex.App.-Eastland, 2005)

Apcar Investment Partners VI, Ltd. brought suit for breach of a lease agreement against Smith & West, L.L.P. Apcar also sought to recover for the alleged breach of the lease against Smith & West, L.L.P.'s partners, Michael L. Gaus and John C. West, in their individual capacities. The trial court granted summary judgment to Gaus and West. The trial court severed Apcar's claims against Gaus and West from the remainder of the suit. Thus, the judgment in favor of Gaus and West became final and appealable. We reverse the judgment of the trial court and remand this cause for further proceedings consistent with this opinion.

Background Facts

On March 6, 1995, Smith & West, L.L.P. registered as a domestic limited liability partnership under the Texas Revised Partnership Act. On August 11, 1999, MF Partners I, Ltd. and Smith & West, L.L.P. entered into the lease in question. Under the lease, Smith & West, L.L.P. leased office space from MF Partners I, Ltd. for a term of 60 months. In connection with the lease, Gaus and West signed a guaranty personally guaranteeing Smith & West, L.L.P.'s performance during the first 24 months of the lease.

MF Partners I, Ltd. assigned its interest in the lease to Apcar. Apcar claimed that, on October 31, 2002, Smith & West, L.L.P. stopped paying rent under the lease and abandoned the leased premises. Apcar filed suit for breach of lease against Smith & West, L.L.P.; Gaus; and West. Gaus and West moved for summary judgment on two grounds: (1) that, as partners in a registered limited liability partnership, they were not individually liable for the partnership's obligations under the lease and (2) that the guaranty they signed in connection with the lease limited their personal liability to the first two years of the lease term. Apcar moved for partial summary judgment, asserting that Gaus and West were individually liable for Smith & West, L.L.P.'s obligations under the lease because Smith & West, L.L.P. was not a registered limited liability partnership when it entered into the lease in question. The trial court granted Gaus and West's motion for summary judgment and denied Apcar's motion for partial summary judgment.

Issues Presented

Apcar presents four points of error for review. In its first point of error, Apcar argues that the trial court erred in granting Gaus and West's motion for summary judgment and in denying its motion for partial summary judgment. Because our holding in the first issue is dispositive of this appeal, we need not address Apcar's other issues.

Registered Limited Liability Partnership Statute

As one ground for summary judgment, Gaus and West argued that they were protected from individual liability under the Texas Revised Partnership Act. No Texas case has addressed the issue before this court.

"Liability in and Registration of Registered Limited Liability Partnership" provides that "a partner in a registered limited liability partnership is not individually liable ... for debts and obligations ... incurred while the partnership is a registered limited liability partnership." Apcar contends that the lease obligations were not incurred while Smith & West, L.L.P. was a registered limited liability partnership because Smith & West, L.L.P.'s status as a registered limited liability partnership expired in 1996–three years before the lease was executed. Therefore, Apcar asserts that Gaus and West are personally liable for the lease obligations. Gaus and West contend that Smith & West, L.L.P.'s initial registration as a registered limited liability partnership in 1995 protects them from individual liability in this case. To support their argument, Gaus and West rely on cases involving the statutory filing requirements for limited partnerships. They assert that, based on the reasoning of the limited partnership cases, Smith & West, L.L.P. did not need to comply with statutory renewal requirements for maintaining its status as a registered limited liability partnership in order to protect them from individual liability under the lease.

A partnership is registered as a registered limited liability partnership on filing a completed initial or renewal application, in duplicate with the required fee, or on a later date specified in the application. An initial application filed under this subsection and registered by the secretary of state expires one year after the date of registration or later effective date unless earlier withdrawn or revoked or unless renewed in accordance with Subdivision (7). An effective registration may be renewed before its expiration by filing in duplicate with the secretary of state an application containing current information of the kind required in an initial application and the most recent date of registration of the partnership. The renewal application must be accompanied by a fee of $200 for each partner on the date of renewal. A renewal application filed under this section continues an effective registration for one year after the date the effective registration would otherwise expire.

Smith & West, L.L.P. filed its initial application registering as a registered limited liability partnership on March 6, 1995. [The statute] provided that the initial registration would expire one year after the date of registration (on March 6, 1996) unless renewed in accordance with Subdivision (7). Smith & West, L.L.P. did not file a renewal application before the expiration date. Therefore, its status as a registered limited liability partnership expired on March 6, 1996.

Smith & West, L.L.P. entered into the lease three years after its status as a registered limited liability partnership expired. Article 6132b–3.08(a)(1) protects partners from individual liability for debts and obligations that are incurred while the partnership is a registered limited liability partnership. Smith & West, L.L.P. was not a registered limited liability partnership when it incurred the lease obligations. Thus, the clear language supports Apcar's position that Gaus and West are not protected from individual liability for the lease obligations.

Gaus and West argue that a limited liability partnership is not required to strictly comply with the registration requirements for its partners to be protected from individual liability. In the context of limited partnerships, courts have held that it is not necessary for limited partnerships to strictly comply with statutory filing requirements for its limited partners to receive limited liability protection. In each of th[o]se cases, the courts held that limited partners did not lose their limited liability status when the partnership failed to comply with filing requirements.

The Texas Revised Limited Partnership Act provides that, to form a limited partnership, the partners must execute a certificate of limited partnership and the partners shall file the certificate of limited partnership with the secretary of state.

The limited partnership cases are distinguishable from registered limited liability partnership cases for two reasons. First, the clear language of Article 6132b–3.08(a)(1) provides that partners are protected from individual liability only for debts and obligations that are incurred while the partnership is a registered limited liability partnership. Article 6132b–3.08(b)(5) and (b)(7) provides that registration expires in one year unless it is renewed prior to the expiration date. To apply the reasoning of the limited partnership cases would conflict with the clear language of Article 6132b–3.08. Second, the Texas Revised Limited Partnership Act (Article 6132a–1) contains a provision that is not present in Article 6132b–3.08. Article 6132a–1, section 2.01(b) provides in part as follows: [A] limited partnership is formed at the time of the filing of the initial certificate of limited partnership with the secretary of state or at a later date or time specified in the certificate if there has been substantial compliance with the requirements of this section. Article 6132b–3.08 does not contain a "substantial compliance" section, nor does it contain a grace period for filing a renewal application. We hold that a partnership must be in compliance with the registration requirements in Article 6132b–3.08(b) for its partners to receive protection from individual liability under Article 6132b–3.08(a)(1). Smith & West, L.L.P. was not a registered limited liability partnership when it incurred the lease obligations; therefore, Gaus and West are not protected from individual liability for the lease obligations under Article 6132b–3.08(a)(1).

The Guaranty

As an additional ground for summary judgment, Gaus and West argued that the guaranty they signed in connection with the lease limited their personal liability to the first two years of the lease term. The guaranty stated as follows:

> NOTWITHSTANDING ANYTHING TO THE CONTRARY HEREIN, PROVIDED LESSOR HAS NOT ASSERTED ANY CLAIM AGAINST THE UNDERSIGNED FOR PAYMENT UNDER THIS GUARANTY, THIS GUARANTY SHALL TERMINATE AND BE OF NO FURTHER FORCE OR EFFECT ON THE DATE THAT IS 24 MONTHS AFTER THE COMMENCEMENT DATE.

While Gaus's and West's liability under the guaranty may have been limited to the first two years of the lease, the issue of their liability under the guaranty is different from the issue of their liability under the lease itself. We have determined that Gaus and West, as partners in Smith and West, L.L.P., may be individually liable for Smith & West, L.L.P.'s lease obligations because Smith and West, L.L.P. was not a registered limited liability partnership when it incurred the lease obligations. The guaranty did not limit Gaus's and West's liability as partners for the partnership's lease obligations. Gaus and West failed to show that they were entitled to judgment as a matter of law. The trial court erred in granting summary judgment to Gaus and West. Apcar's first point of error is sustained insofar as it complains of the granting of summary judgment to Gaus and West.

This Court's Ruling

The judgment of the trial court is reversed, and this cause is remanded for further proceedings consistent with this order.

Governance

Limited liability partnerships are filing entities and are therefore intentionally created. For that reason, generally the roles and functions of the partners are defined in the paperwork filed with the secretary of state.

Typically, the designation of the entity as a LLP will not change the governance roles of the partners. If the LLP is comprised solely of general partners, then all partners have the right to freely participate in managing the affairs of the partnership. If the LLP is comprised of general and limited partners then the limited partners will continue to have a limited role in the management of the partnership, which responsibility lies in the general partners.

Liability

The Texas Business Organizations Code provides

§152.801. LIABILITY OF PARTNER.

(a) Except as provided by the partnership agreement, a partner is not personally liable to any person, including a partner, directly or indirectly, by contribution, indemnity, or otherwise, for any obligation of the partnership incurred while the partnership is a limited liability partnership.

(b) Sections 2.101(1), 152.305, and 152.306 do not limit the effect of Subsection (a) in a limited liability partnership.

(c) For purposes of this section, an obligation is incurred while a partnership is a limited liability partnership if:

(1) the obligation relates to an action or omission occurring while the partnership is a limited liability partnership; or

(2) the obligation arises under a contract or commitment entered into while the partnership is a limited liability partnership.

(d) Subsection (a) does not affect:

(1) the liability of a partnership to pay its obligations from partnership property;

(2) the liability of a partner, if any, imposed by law or contract independently of the partner's status as a partner; or

(3) the manner in which service of citation or other civil process may be served in an action against a partnership.

(e) This section controls over the other parts of this chapter and the other partnership provisions regarding the liability of partners of a limited liability partnership, the chargeability of the partners for the obligations of the partnership, and the obligations of the partners regarding contributions and indemnity.

This does not limit the effect of the entity:

a) Having the same powers as an individual to take action necessary or convenient to carry out its business and affairs. (Tex. Bus. Orgs. Code §2.101) Except as otherwise provided by this code, the powers of a domestic entity include the power to sue, be sued, and defend suit in the entity's business name. (Tex. Bus. Orgs. Code § 2.101(1));

b) An action may be brought against the partnership and any or all of the partners in the same action or in separate actions. (Tex. Bus. Orgs. Code § 152.305); or

c) Enforcement of Remedies (Tex. Bus. Orgs. Code § 152.306).

An obligation is incurred while a partnership is a limited liability partnership if: (1) the obligation relates to an act or omission occurring while the partnership is a limited liability partnership; or (2) the obligation arises under a contract or commitment entered into while the partnership is a limited liability partnership. Tex. Bus. Orgs. Code § § 152.801 (c)(1), (c)(2).

Liability protection does not protect partners from their own malpractice, tort, or contractual suits. Tex. Bus. Orgs. Code § 152.801(e)(2). Additionally, limitation of partner liability does not affect the liability of the partnership to pay its obligations out of partnership property or the manner in which service of citation or other civil process may be served in an action against a partnership. Tex. Bus. Orgs. Code § 152.801(e)(1). Recall, each general partner is an agent of the limited partnership on whom may be served any process, notice, or demand required or permitted by law to be served on the limited partnership.

In sum, liability protection of partners does not affect: (1) the liability of a partnership to pay its obligations from partnership property; (2) the liability of a partner, if any, imposed by law or contract independently of the partner's status as a partner; or (3) the manner in which service of citation or other civil process may be served in an action against a partnership. Tex. Bus. Orgs. Code § §152.801(d)(1)-(3).

Initially states mandated limited liability partnerships carry insurance or to have assets large enough to cover successful lawsuits. In Texas and in many other states, recent statutes do not have any such mandates, but instead leave the issue to insurance statutes governing the profession or occupation. Tex. Bus. Orgs. Code § 152.804.

Evanston Insurance Company v. Dillard Department Stores, Inc., v. Chargois et.al.
602 F.3d 610 (U.S.Ct.App-5th—2010)

PER CURIAM:

Damon Chargois and Cletus Ernster appeal the district court's judgment holding them personally liable to Dillard Department Stores, Inc. for a judgment originally entered against their law firm partnership. For the following reasons, we affirm the judgment of the district court.

Damon Chargois and Cletus Ernster formed a law partnership in 2002. They registered it as a limited liability partnership, known as Chargois & Ernster, L.L.P. (CELLP), with the State of Texas in 2002. CELLP prosecuted lawsuits against Dillard Department Stores, Inc. (Dillard's), alleging that Dillard's racially discriminated against its customers. In an attempt to solicit business, CELLP developed a website in June 2003 which included a link using the "Dillard's" name and logo. Clicking this link took visitors to dillardsalert.com, a separate website documenting acts of alleged racial profiling by the department stores.

On July 14, 2003, Dillard's sued CELLP in Texas state court for trademark infringement and various business torts. It sought damages and an injunction against CELLP's use of its trademark. On October 31, 2003, CELLP's professional liability insurer, Evanston Insurance Co., filed a declaratory judgment action in federal district court, seeking a declaration that its policy did not insure CELLP against Dillard's claims. On November 21, 2003, after voluntarily dismissing the state court lawsuit, Dillard's filed a cross-claim in the Evanston case against CELLP reasserting its allegations and adding federal cyberpiracy and trademark claims. On January 15, 2004, pursuant to the parties' agreement, the court dismissed Evanston's claims for declaratory relief. Dillard's third-party claims against CELLP were all that remained.

On February 9, 2004, while the litigation continued, Chargois and Ernster executed a separation agreement that provided for "dissolution" of the partnership on February 27, 2004. CELLP's registration as an LLP was not renewed and, on July 25, 2004, the registration expired under Texas law. Notwithstanding these facts, the defunct LLP remained a party to the Dillard's litigation, and no party was substituted on its behalf. On November 2, 2004, the court entered a final judgment ordering "Chargois & Ernster, L.L.P." to pay Dillard's $143,500.

Dillard's attempt to collect on the judgment did not succeed. On January 10, 2008, in the docket of the Evanston case, Dillard's filed a third-party complaint for a declaratory judgment against Chargois and Ernster in their individual capacities. Dillard's sought a declaration that the two were personally liable, jointly and severally, for the 2004 final judgment entered against CELLP. Both Chargois and Ernster were personally served with the third-party complaint, and each moved to dismiss. Dillard's then restyled its third-party complaint as a first amended complaint, which reasserted the allegations of personal liability against Chargois and Ernster (hereinafter, the "2008 action"). Dillard's filed a motion for summary judgment, to which both defendants responded with lengthy opposition briefs. The court granted judgment for Dillard's in the amount of $143,500 against Chargois and Ernster, jointly and severally, and each appealed.

STANDARD OF REVIEW

"We review a district court's grant of summary judgment *de novo*." *Goodman v. Harris County*, 571 F.3d 388, 393 (5th Cir.2009). "Summary judgment is appropriate 'if the pleadings, the discovery and disclosure materials on file, and any affidavits show that there is no genuine issue as to any material fact and that the movant is entitled to judgment as a matter of law.' " *Id.* (quoting FED.R.CIV.P. 56(c)). "We consider the evidence in a light most favorable to ... the non-movant, but [he] must point to evidence showing that there is a genuine fact issue for trial to survive summary judgment." *Id.* (quotation omitted).

DISCUSSION

Chargois and Ernster press four main arguments, two of which present issues of federal law and two of which present issues of Texas law. [The issues of federal law were subject matter jurisdiction and due process and are omitted]

It is undisputed that CELLP was formed in 2002 and ceased to exist as a registered LLP on July 25, 2004. Therefore, the Texas Revised Partnership Act (TRPA) applies to this dispute. See TRPA § 11.03(c) (codified at TEX.REV.CIV.STAT.ANN. art. 6132b–11.03(c)). Appellants advance two main arguments under state law. First, they contend that Texas partnership law confers immunity upon them as individual partners, whether of an LLP or general partnership. Second, they contend that the statute of limitations bars Dillard's 2008 action to hold them personally liable for the judgment against CELLP.

Immunity from Personal Liability (TRPA §§ 3.04 and 3.08)

As a general matter, the TRPA imposes joint and several liability on individual partners for all debts and obligations of a partnership. Section 3.04 of the TRPA provides:

> *Except as provided by Section 3.07 or 3.08(a), all partners are liable jointly and severally for all debts and obligations of the partnership unless otherwise agreed by the claimant or provided by law.* TEX.REV.CIV. STAT. ANN. art. 6132b–3.04.

Under this provision, appellants are liable for the debts and obligations of CELLP unless one of the enumerated exceptions applies. *See, e.g.,* ROBERT W. HAMILTON ET AL., 19 TEXAS PRACTICE § 8.5 (2d ed. 2009) ("In general, each partner is personally liable for all debts and obligations of the partnership."). The first exception, § 3.07, concerns the liability of incoming partners and is not relevant in this case.

As for the second exception, TRPA § 3.08(a) limits liability for partners of registered LLPs. It provides:

> *(a) Liability of Partner. (1) Except as provided in Subsection (a)(2), a partner in a registered limited liability partnership is not individually liable, directly or indirectly, by contribution, indemnity, or otherwise, for debts and obligations of the partnership incurred while the partnership is a registered limited liability partnership.*
>
> *(2) A partner in a registered limited liability partnership is not individually liable, directly or indirectly, by contribution, indemnity, or otherwise, for debts and obligations of the partnership arising from errors, omissions, negligence, incompetence, or malfeasance committed while the partnership is a registered limited liability partnership and in the course of the partnership business by another partner or a representative of the partnership not working under the supervision or direction of the first partner unless the first partner:*

(A) was directly involved in the specific activity in which the errors, omissions, negligence, incompetence, or malfeasance were committed by the other partner or representative; or

(B) had notice or knowledge of the errors, omissions, negligence, incompetence, or malfeasance by the other partner or representative at the time of occurrence and then failed to take reasonable steps to prevent or cure the errors, omissions, negligence, incompetence, or malfeasance.

Appellants argue that § 3.08(a)(1) insulates them from liability because CELLP's debt was incurred when the infringing website was created in June 2003, at which time CELLP was still a registered limited liability partnership. The parties characterize the 2004 judgment against CELLP as a "debt" rather than an "obligation." We assume, without deciding, that this characterization is correct. Dillard's, meanwhile, contends that the debt was incurred when the judgment was entered on November 2, 2004, at which time the erstwhile LLP had lost its liability-limiting attributes.

In Texas, "[t]he meaning of a statute is a legal question," which is reviewed "*de novo* to ascertain and give effect to the Legislature's intent." *Entergy Gulf States, Inc. v. Summers*, 282 S.W.3d 433, 437 (Tex.2009). "Where text is clear, text is determinative of that intent." *Id.* "We must interpret a statute according to its terms, giving meaning to the language consistent with other provisions in the statute." *Dallas County Cmty. Coll. Dist. v. Bolton*, 185 S.W.3d 868, 874 (Tex.2005). "Only when [the legislature's] words are ambiguous do we resort to rules of construction or extrinsic aids." *Entergy Gulf States*, 282 S.W.3d at 437 (quotation omitted).

Although the terms "debt" and "incurred" are not defined by the TRPA, a plain reading of the statute's text supports Dillard's proffered interpretation. Neither partner was necessarily aware in June 2003 that displaying the Dillard's mark on the law firm website would ultimately lead to a partnership debt. The underlying conduct gave rise to the *possibility* of a future debt, but to say that a debt was "incurred" at that time unrealistically distorts the meaning of the word. After all, CELLP's conduct may have gone undetected, it may have been adjudged perfectly innocent, or Dillard's may have opted not to sue. Under any of those scenarios, no debt would ever have been incurred, let alone incurred in June 2003. It was only when the district court entered judgment against CELLP in November 2004 that a payable debt came into existence. It was then that CELLP incurred the debt within the meaning of the provision.

Moreover, the neighboring language of § 3.08(a)(2) demonstrates that the Texas legislature, when it so chooses, is capable of drafting a provision that focuses on the commission of events that lead to liability, rather than the fixing of consequent liability from those events. In that provision, the legislature insulated an LLP partner from personal liability "arising from errors, omissions, negligence, incompetence, or malfeasance *committed*" by another partner "while the partnership is a registered limited liability partnership." TRPA § 3.08(a)(2) (emphasis added). Thus, to decide whether the first partner's liability is limited for the second partner's malfeasance under § 3.08(a)(2), a court must look to when the second partner committed the malfeasance. Had the legislature intended to enact the same "when committed" approach for § 3.08(a)(1), it could have used the language from § 3.08(a)(2). *See* 2A NORMAN J. SINGER ET AL., SUTHERLAND STATUTES AND STATUTORY CONSTRUCTION § 46:6 ("[W]hen the legislature uses certain language in one part of the statute and different language in another, the court assumes different meanings were intended."). It chose, however, to use different language, and created a regime in which partners could be held individually liable for debts and obligations incurred when the partnership was not a registered LLP [§ 3.08(a)(1)], but in which partners would not bear liability for one another's independent malfeasance committed while the LLP existed [§ 3.08(a)(2)].

Because CELLP's registration had expired, it was not a valid registered LLP at the time its debt was incurred. Therefore, § 3.08 does not foreclose individual liability and § 3.04's default rule operates to hold appellants personally liable for CELLP's debt.

TRPA § 3.05

Appellants further argue that in addition to suing CELLP in 2003, Dillard's was required to sue the partners themselves on the trademark and tort claims in order to later hold them individually liable. They rely on TRPA § 3.05(c), which provides:

> *A judgment against a partnership is not by itself a judgment against a partner, but a judgment may be entered against a partner who has been served with process in a suit against the partnership.*

This provision is unhelpful to appellants, however, because Dillard's does not rely on the 2004 judgment against the LLP "by itself" to support their individual liability. Instead, it relies on the 2008 judgment it obtained against them individually.

Appellants' reliance on *Kao Holdings, L.P. v. Young* is also unavailing. 261 S.W.3d 60 (Tex.2008). Construing § 3.05(c), the Texas Supreme Court held that its purpose appears to be to make clear that while partners are generally liable for the partnership's obligations, a judgment against the partnership is not automatically a judgment against the partner, and that judgment cannot be rendered against a partner who has not been served merely because judgment has been rendered against the partnership. *Id.* at 64 (footnote omitted). Here, the record belies any argument that judgment against the partners was entered "automatically"; instead, Chargois and Ernster were defendants in a different action that they lost after defending their individual interests vigorously on the merits.

229

Statute of Limitations

Finally, appellants assert that Dillard's 2008 action is barred by the statute of limitations. The inquiry depends on the nature of Dillard's cause of action. Dillard's contends that the cause of action is one for debt, that is, to enforce the 2004 judgment against the partners on the basis of their statutorily compelled individual liability. Appellants, meanwhile, argue that the causes of action are for tort and trademark infringement; appellants view the 2008 claims as identical to those contained in Dillard's 2003 cross-claim against CELLP.

Dillard's amended complaint does not contain any allegations of individual wrongdoing, nor does it identify the individual conduct of either appellant as a basis for personal liability. If, counterfactually, Dillard's were suing appellants for personal wrongdoing in June 2003—the same conduct for which it sued CELLP—then its cause of action would have accrued at that time and the tort or trademark limitations period would apply. Instead, Dillard's seeks to impose liability on Chargois and Ernster for partnership debt by operation of Texas law.

In Texas, a person must bring a suit for debt "not later than four years after the day the cause of action accrues." TEX. CIV. PRAC. & REMEDIES CODE ANN. § 16.004(a)(3). The cause of action accrued, at the earliest, upon entry of judgment against CELLP on November 2, 2004. Because Dillard's filed its third-party complaint (which was eventually replaced by its amended complaint) on January 10, 2008, its action fell within this four-year limitations period and is not time-barred.

CONCLUSION

For the foregoing reasons, the judgment of the district court is AFFIRMED.

Finance

Limited liability partner's capital contribution to the partnership varies by agreement. Like other partnerships, LLP partners' share in profits and losses and capital according to agreement.

A partner's partnership interest is personal property for all purposes. Tex. Bus. Orgs. Code § 152.001(a). A partner does not have an interest in specific partnership property.

LLPs are required to keep an accurate accounting of their finances and solvency. This information must be filed with the secretary of state annually. These records are subject to audit and may also be reviewed by persons with valid authority to do so.

The general partners owe fiduciary duties of care and loyalty in an LLP. The extent of the duties are governed by the agreement, where the agreement is silent, the courts will consider the historical conduct of the partners and where none, rely on the statutory language.

Termination

Limited liability partnerships are dissolved in accordance with their certificate or by the consent of all the members. Retirement, death, or mental incompetence of a general partnership does not result in automatic termination of the partnership. The business may continue and replace the general partners according to their agreement.

A withdrawal notice filed with the secretary of state, terminates the status of the partnership as a limited liability partnership from the date on which the notice is filed or later date specified in the notice, but not later than the expiration date. The filing must also include payment of applicable fees along with a certificate from the comptroller stating that all taxes administered by the comptroller are paid. Tex. Bus. Orgs. Code § 152.802 (f). Like the registration, the withdrawal must:

(1) Set out the name of the partnership, the federal taxpayer identification number, the street address of the partnerships principal office, and the number of partners at the date of application; and

(2) Contain a brief statement of the partnerships business which must be signed by: (a) the majority-in-interest of the partners; or (b) one or more partners authorized by a majority-in- interest of the partners.

A voluntary decision to "wind up" the affairs of a limited liability partnership requires written consent of all partners; unless otherwise provided by the partnership agreement. Tex. Bus. Orgs. Code § 11.058.

Alternatively, dissolution may be involuntarily mandated by the courts. Courts tend to intervene in such decisions only in instances where the partners cannot work together or where dissolution is necessary to prevent fraud, theft, or other egregious acts against the partnership.

Upon dissolution, creditors (i.e., banks, suppliers, former employees if owed money, landlords, tenants, guarantors and personal injury claimants, etc...) are first to be paid. Thereafter, partners and former partners receive unpaid distributions according to their agreement.

In the absence of a partnership agreement that provides the procedures for withdrawal, winding up, dissolving and or termination the process will be governed by the TBOC.

Tabel 2

TBOC DECONSTRUCTED	
LIMITED LIABILITY PARTNERSHIPS	
GOVERNANCE	
TOPIC	**RULE**
GOVERNING DOCUMENT(S)	
partnership agreement is governance document	152.208
amending governance document	152.208
when TBOC controls	152.002
GOVERNING PERSONS	
decisionmakers	152.209
binding effect of partner action generally	152.302
binding effect of partner action after event of winding up	152.704
who qualified to wind up	152.702
withdrawing partner's power to bind partnership	152.504
rights and duties generally	152.203
partner as agent	152.301
access to books and records	152.213
rights and duties of person winding up	152.703
standards of partner conduct	152.204
FIDUCIARY DUTIES and PARTNER OBLIGATIONS	
duty of loyalty	152.205
duty of care	152.206
duties on winding up	152.207
obligation to maintain books and records	152.212
PARTNER RIGHT TO TRANSFER INTEREST	
right to transfer	152.401
effect of transfer generally	152.402
effect of transfer on transferor	152.403
rights and duties of transferee	152.404
partnership not bound by prohibited transfer	152.405
effect of death or divorce	152.406
PARTNER RIGHT TO CONTINUE PARTNERSHIP	

canceling revocation	152.709
reinstatement	152.71
LIABILITY	
PARTNERSHIP LIABILITY	
generally	152.203
not bound by prohibited transfer	152.405
withdrawing partner's power to bind partnership	152.504
redemption upon withdrawal	152.601 et.seq.
redemption to transferee	152.611
binding effect of partner act after winding up	152.704
PARTNER LIABILITY	
generally	152.210-
nature of partner liability: joint and several	152.304
effect of withdrawing partner's existing liability	152.505
liability of withdrawing partner to third party	152.506
partner liability to other partners; event requiring winding up	152.705
contributions to discharge obligations	152.708
REMEDIES	
remedies of partnership and partners generally	152.211
remedy	152.305
enforcement of remedy	152.306
creditor's rights	152.307
charging order	152.308
FINANCING	
GENERAL RULE	152.202
PARTNERSHIP INTERESTS	
generally	1.002(68)
transfering pship interests	152.401
effect of partner death or divorce	152.406
WINDING UP/TERMINATION	
liquidation	152.706
settlement of accounts	152.707
contributions to discharge obligations	152.708

TERMINATION	
WITHDRAWAL	
events of withdrawal	152.501
effect of withdrawal	152.502
wrongful withdrawal	152.503
withdrawing partners power to bind partnership	152.504
withdrawing partners existing liability	152.505
liability of withdrawing partner to third parties	152.506
redemption	152.601
redemption price	152.602
contribution from wrongful withdrawer	152.603
set off	152.604
interest accrual	152.605
indemnification	152.606
demand of payment	152.607
deferring payment to wrongful withdrawer	152.608
civil action to determine redemption terms	152.609
effect of partner's death or divorce	152.406
WINDING UP	
events requiring winding up	152.701
deferring payment	152.610-
rights and duties of transferee	152.404
redemption to transferee	152.611
civil action to determine transferee's redemption price	152.612
who qualified to wind up	152.702
rights and duties of person winding up	152.703
binding effect of partner acts after winding up	152.704
partner liability to other partners; event of winding up	152.705
liquidation	152.706
settlement of accounts	152.707
contributions to discharge obligations	152.708
CONTINUING PARTNERSHIP	
canceling revocation	152.709
reinstatement	152.710-

Limited Liability Partnerships Problem Set

1. Gun Mastery, LLP was established as a Texas limited liability partnership in 2006. Its primary business is the organization of gun shows and related exhibitions. Henrique is the managing partner. In 2007, Henrique, using part of the initial contributions made by partners, purchased a ranch in Dallas, which the partnership uses for some of its exhibitions. In 2010, Marciano, a partner, took a personal loan from Heritage Bank, using as collateral his 20% ownership interest in the partnership. He defaulted on the loan and Heritage sued to foreclose on the ranch. The court held that the property can be foreclosed upon and sold but Heritage is only entitled to recover 20% of the proceeds or the amount owed, whichever is less. The court also ordered that none of the bank's expenses in pursuing the debt recovery can be paid from the proceeds of sale.

   Was the court's ruling correct?

2. Plato Coopers, LLP is an advertising agency than runs 6-month marketing campaigns for Texas businesses. Cheng is one of the five founding partners of the firm. In 2012, Cheng went through a painful divorce from his wife of many years. The court ordered that half of Cheng's stake in the LLP be transferred to his wife. Accordingly, the former wife becomes an additional partner with 10% interest in the company while Cheng's interest is reduced from 20% to 10%. Mrs. Cheng showed up for work last week, insisting that she be treated like a partner. The position of managing partner will be vacant in two weeks time. The position has always been occupied by a founding partner.

   Under what circumstances, if any, can Mrs. Cheng become the managing partner?

3. Amazon Distribution, LLP has grown to become the largest wholesaler of imported fabrics from the Mediterranean region. Sheikh became a partner in 2009. In 2012, Sheikh approached a long-standing customer informing him that the partnership decided to supply its products to him at a 10% discount, provided the purchase meets a minimum threshold of $75,000. The customer appreciated the fact that his loyalty over the years seemed to be paying off and immediately made a cash payment of $75,000 to Sheikh, for which Sheikh gave a written acknowledgment of receipt on behalf of Amazon. In fact, the partnership had made no such decision and no other partner knew of this transaction. Sheikh pocketed the money and used it to pay off some pressing personal debts. The customer sued the LLP and all of its partners to recover the money paid to Sheikh.

   Should Plaintiff be able to recover his payment from the LLP and or the partners, individually?

4. Caritas CPA & Allied Services, LLP was properly formed in 2005 as a Texas limited liability partnership. The Partnership Agreement identified the business purpose as "the

provision of accounting services" and provided that new partners may be admitted by a majority vote of the existing partners. The initial partners were Aisha, Bob, Jude, Lehman and Sanchez. The partners elected Aisha as the managing partner. Last year, Bob filed tax returns for a corporate client but some information was missing. The IRS notified Bob of the incomplete submission, informing him that if complete information was not received by April 15, 2010, it would be treated as non-filing, which would attract penalties unless the taxpayer applied for an extension. Through Caritas' internal network infrastructure, alerts from the IRS are automatically copied to the managing partner. Bob missed the deadline for filing the extension thereby attracting late filing penalty for the client that amounted to $50,000. The customer sued the LLP and its partners for the money paid to the IRS. The court held that only Aisha and Bob are liable. Both sides want to appeal.

Who wins?

5. Cannon, LLP provides language translation services for businesses across the world. When a business person is in a country to do business and does not understand the language of the place, he can contact Cannon who would arrange for a life translator that would speak with the business person. This is a premium service. Apart from this premium, Cannon also offers translation services through the internet, without any direct interaction with a human being. Acting contrary to the agreement of the partners not to order any software without unanimous authorization, Sanchez, one of the partners, bought a translation software at the New Technologies Conference for $12,000. Sanchez informed the merchant that he was a partner at Cannon, LLP and was making the purchase on the firm's behalf. He paid with his personal credit card, which was declined when the merchant tried to process payments the next day. Sadly, Sanchez misplaced the software while changing airplanes. The partners do not want to pay for the software.

Can the merchant successfully sue the LLP and its partners? Discuss fully.

6. Eagle Eye Accounting Partners, LLP was established in 2000 for the purpose of providing accounting services. Since its formation, the partnership has focused exclusively on private-sector accounting services. Pierre is a new partner in the firm. In 2011, after playing a round of golf, the city comptroller mentioned to his friend, Pierre that the city was planning to conduct an external audit of a recent public project. He asked if Pierre would be interested in doing the public-sector job on a personal basis since his firm exclusively worked on private-sector clients. Pierre, seeking to boost his retirement savings, jumped at the chance to earn extra income. He undertook the assignment in his spare time, worked at home, and used his own materials. In essence, no company time, personnel or resources were utilized in executing the task. Pierre's fellow partners demand that he surrender and share the profits earned from the city assignment.

Do you agree?

7. With the exception of the managing partner, Rolle, every partner in Rolle's Law Group, LLP ("RLG") is expressly forbidden to enter into contracts on behalf of the law firm. During a recent training workshop of the American Trial Lawyers Group, Gary, a senior partner of RLG was approached by a representative of Nexis, who introduced what was billed as "an indispensable electronic research tool for every trial lawyer in America." Gary did not want to place his firm at a competitive disadvantage and therefore decided to obligate RLG to a 2-year contract for the product. At the end of the workshop, he returned to the firm, but the rest of the partners voted against purchasing the tool, until they have had time to read reports of its effectiveness. Accordingly, Gary wrote a letter to Nexis, returning the material. Nexis has sued Gary and RLG for the full price of the product.

   Will Nexis recover and from whom?

8. Elite Landscaping, LLP was formed by three friends – Milo, Shamir and Tran, in 2004 as a Texas limited liability partnership. The partnership started out working with residential homes but as business boomed, the partners decided to create a commercial premises division under Tran's supervision. Working on the campus of Apple Computers, Inc., the lawnmower used by Julio, a new employee of Elite, malfunctioned injuring an Apple distributor. Shamir was also at work at the Apple campus on that day, working next to Julio, but did not direct Julio's work in any way. The distributor sued the LLP, its partners and Julio. The court held that under Texas LLP Law, only Shamir and Tran are liable.

   Did the court get the law right?

9. Chipsco, LLP is a partnership devoted to the distribution of computer chips. Joanna, one of the partners, decided to deliver some boxes of chips to an assembly plant in Austin. While executing the assignment, using her personal car, she lost control and ran into a vehicle in front of her. Since the car did not have Chipsco's name or logo, the victim did not know of any relationship Joanna had with the LLP at the time of the accident. Accordingly, when the accident victim sued, the court held that only Joanna was liable since she committed the tort and the victim was not aware of the LLP's existence. The appellate court overruled, holding that as a partner in an LLP, Joanna enjoys limited liability and is therefore not liable for work done in her capacity as a partner.

   Which of the courts got it right?

10. Portfolio Securities Dealers, LLP helps clients across the United States purchase and sell stocks, bonds and derivative securities. It has 50 partners. Because of the difficulty of assembling such a large group to make prompt decisions relating to regular operations, the partners decided to concentrate authority for making such decisions in the managing partner. Rajiv was elected the first managing partner last year. Tiffany, a founding

partner, lost the election to Rajiv and has since resented his overbearing attitude. In September 2010, noticing that one of the photocopiers had stopped functioning, Tiffany contacted and contracted with Office Land to replace the copier, which cost $1,800. Tiffany signed Office Land's work order: "Tiffany, Partner, Portfolio Securities Dealers, LLP." Tiffany did not consult with Rajiv or any of the other partners before having Office Land deliver and install a new copier.

Are Portfolio, Tiffany and the other partners liable to Office Land for the copier repair?

LIMITED PARTNERSHIPS

LIMITED PARTNERSHIPS

Core Concepts

Nature of the Limited Partnership: *The Nature and Structure*

A limited partnership is a partnership that consists of a minimum of one general partner and at least one limited partner. The general partner has responsibility for managing the business while the limited partner is a passive investor that enjoys limited liability in exchange for a lack of participation in management. Thus, as a form of business organization, the limited partnership is more structured than the general partnership. Similarly to the general partnership, the limited partnership comes into existence as a result of the agreement of the partners. Unlike the general partnership, the limited partnership may only be validly formed by the filing of a certificate with the State. Like every other business form, the suitability of the limited partnership as an investment vehicle depends on the station and aspirations of the investors. For example, an inventor in Silicon Valley with some bright ideas and products but without cash may team up with a Hollywood actor emerging with lots of cash from a successful movie. The inventor becomes the general partner while the actor becomes the limited partner. Some wealthy individuals or institutions, such as pension funds may also pool their money into a venture capital firm. The wealthy investors become limited partners while entrusting the management of the resources to experienced experts who become the general partners of the venture capital firm.

The provisions of the Texas Business Organizations Code applicable to limited partnerships may be cited as the Texas Limited Partnership Law ("TLPL"). *See* TBOC § 1.008(g). Texas Limited Partnership Law is primarily concentrated in chapter 153 of the Texas Business Organizations Code. Other pertinent provisions are Title 1 [§ 1.001 et seq.] and Chapters 151 and 154, to the extent applicable to limited partnerships. Of particular importance is the fact that, absent conflict, the rules governing general partnerships also apply to limited partnerships. *See* TBOC § 153.003(a).

The future of the limited partnership may lie with the limited liability limited partnership (LLLP). LLLPs are limited partnerships that grant limited liability to the general partners of the limited partnership. Instead of creating an additional structure through the entity general partner model in order to clothe general partners with limited liability, LLLPs provide this attractive feature without the extra layer by requiring only the filing of a certificate. In a limited partnership, this same result may be accomplished by forming another entity such as a corporation and making the entity the general partner. That way, the individual investors that manage the corporate general partner would still be afforded protection from personal liability, since the entity general partner would be the one personally liable for the limited partnership's obligations. The beauty of the LLLP is that it provides this attractive feature without the extra layer and burden of forming another entity. Instead, the benefits are received simply by filing a certificate.

Texas Business Organization Code provisions

§ 153.002. Construction

(a) This chapter and the other limited partnership provisions shall be applied and construed to effect its general purpose to make uniform the law with respect to limited partnerships among states that have similar laws.

(b) The rule that a statute in derogation of the common law is to be strictly construed does not apply to this chapter and the other limited partnership provisions.

§ 153.003. Applicability of Other Laws

(a) Except as provided by Subsection (b), in a case not provided for by this chapter and the other limited partnership provisions, the provisions of Chapter 152 governing partnerships that are not limited partnerships and the rules of law and equity govern.

(b) The powers and duties of a limited partner shall not be governed by a provision of Chapter 152 that would be inconsistent with the nature and role of a limited partner as contemplated by this chapter.

(c) A limited partner shall not have any obligation or duty of a general partner solely by reason of being a limited partner.

§ 153.004. Nonwaivable Title 1 Provisions

(a) Except as provided by this section, the following provisions of Title 1 may not be waived or modified in the partnership agreement of a limited partnership:

(1) Chapter 1, if the provision is used to interpret a provision or define a word or phrase contained in a section listed in this subsection;

(2) Chapter 2, other than Section 2.104(c)(2), 2.104(c)(3), or 2.113;

(3) Chapter 3, other than Subchapters C and E of that chapter and Section 3.151 (provided, that in all events a partnership agreement may not validly waive or modify Section 153.551 or unreasonably restrict a partner's right of access to books and records under Section 153.552); or

(4) Chapter 4, 5, 10, 11, or 12, other than Section 11.058.

(b) A provision listed in Subsection (a) may be waived or modified in the partnership agreement if the provision that is waived or modified authorizes the limited partnership to waive or modify the provision in the limited partnership's governing documents.

(c) A provision listed in Subsection (a) may be modified in the partnership agreement if the provision that is modified specifies:

(1) the person or group of persons who are entitled to approve a modification; or

(2) the vote or other method by which a modification is required to be approved.[1]

§ 153.005. Waiver or Modification of Rights of Third Parties. *A provision in this title or in that part of Title 1 applicable to a limited partnership that grants a right to a person, other than a general partner, a limited partner, or assignee of a partnership interest in a limited partnership, may be waived or modified in the partnership agreement of the limited partnership only if the person consents to the waiver or modification.*

Limited Partnership: Advantages and Disadvantages

The limited partnership retains force as the investment vehicle of choice for many entrepreneurs and investors because of the several advantages it possesses. However, its influence has also been reduced and it has lost some space or market share to newer entities such as the Limited Liability Company and Limited Liability Partnership because of the disadvantages that are associated with those business forms. Limited partnerships are now likely to be used in some specialized areas such as tax shelter investments, notably oil and gas and real estate ventures; venture capital and leveraged buy-out transactions; and estate planning through family limited partnerships. *See* JOSEPH SLADE, BUSINESS ASSOCIATIONS IN A NUTSHELL 43-44 (3d ed.2010).

Advantages

1. Provides limited liability protection to the limited partners.
2. Provides federal tax benefit as the entity is not subject to federal income taxation.
3. If it qualifies as a passive entity, it provides state tax benefit, as such limited partnerships are exempt from the state franchise tax, known as "margin" tax.
4. It is a valuable estate planning tool that enables families to transfer assets to the younger generation while the older generation retains management powers, while enjoying favorable tax treatment.
5. It allows for specialization in function where partners skilled in management are in control of the business while those that do not want to be saddled with the responsibility can contribute capital and still enjoy the gains of the business while sitting on the sidelines.

---

[1] It should be noted that "TBOC § 153.004(a) ... was clarified by S.B. 748 § 51 to indicate that a limited partnership agreement may reasonably restrict a partner's right to access to books and records under TBOC § 153.552" See Byron F. Egan, BUSINESS ENTITIES IN TEXAS AFTER 2011 TEXAS LEGISLATURE. LEGISLATIVE CHANGES AFFECTING BUSINESS ENTITIES, July 13, 2011.

Disadvantages

1. Does not afford limited liability protection to the general partners.
2. The limited liability shield afforded limited partners can be lost if the limited partners participate in control. This rule has been modified extensively, as will be shown later in this chapter.
3. It is generally subject to the state franchise or "margin" tax as only a small percentage of limited partnerships would qualify as passive entities, which are general partnerships, limited partnerships and trusts whose federal gross income consists of at least 90% of certain types of passive income, such as dividends, interest, capital gains, and royalties. Rental income is excluded from the definition of passive income.
4. Through the control rule, it deprives the business of the benefit of the skills and expertise of limited partners who could make valuable contribution to the management of the firm without being fully involved in the firm's operations.

Limited Partnership: Formation

Filing of Certificate

The valid formation of a limited partnership in Texas requires the filing of a certificate of formation with the Secretary of State, accompanied by the statutory filing fee. However, the filing of a certificate and payment of the filing fee are not sufficient. The partners are also required to have a partnership agreement, which could be oral or in writing, as part of the formation requirements. The absence of such agreement, even when a certificate has been filed, means that an essential condition for formation has not been met and thus, no limited partnership comes into existence.

A filed certificate of formation is constructive notice of the fact that the business is organized as a limited partnership and of all other facts required to be included in the certificate. Texas law no longer includes a "substantial compliance" standard. That standard protected limited partners where the putative limited partnership had substantially complied with the statutory requirements regarding formation, even though some steps had been omitted or delayed. Whether protection for a limited partner in a defectively formed limited partnership continues is an open question. See Robert W. Hamilton, Elizabeth S. Miller & Robert A. Ragazzo, 19 Tex. Prac., Business Organizations § 13:19 (3d ed. 2012). Some commentators believe that while "the filing of the certificate of limited partnership is necessary to put the public on notice of the liability limitations provided by law, if the party with whom the partnership is dealing is aware the partnership is a limited partnership, then the filing of the certificate is not necessary for the entity to be a limited partnership." Edward K. Esping, J.D. and Susan L. Thomas, J.D., 57 Tex. Jur. 3d Partnership § 176 (updated January 2013). Also, there is protection under procedures clearly specified by statute for those who erroneously believe they are limited partners, as discussed under the liability section of this chapter.

The law specifies the essential contents of the certificate of formation, including the name of the partnership, the name and address of each general partner, and the address of the principal office of the partnership in the United States where records are to be kept or made available. A limited partnership is required to include in its name the word "limited," the phrase "limited partnership," or an abbreviation of that word or phrase. Limited partnerships are prohibited from using the words "lotto" or "lottery" in their name. Grossly offensive names are also prohibited. Each general partner must sign the certificate of formation. The existence of the limited partnership commences when the filing of the certificate of formation takes effect. Often, the certificate takes effect on filing, but it may also take effect at a specified date and time or on the occurrence of a future event or fact, including an act of any person.

Texas Business Organization Code provisions

§ 3.005. Certificate of Formation

(a) The certificate of formation must state:

(1) the name of the filing entity being formed;

(2) the type of filing entity being formed;

(3) for filing entities other than limited partnerships, the purpose or purposes for which the filing entity is formed, which may be stated to be or include any lawful purpose for that type of entity;

(4) for filing entities other than limited partnerships, the period of duration, if the entity is not formed to exist perpetually and is intended to have a specific period of duration;

(5) the street address of the initial registered office of the filing entity and the name of the initial registered agent of the filing entity at the office;

(6) the name and address of each:

(A) organizer for the filing entity, unless the entity is formed under a plan of conversion or merger;

(B) general partner, if the filing entity is a limited partnership; or

(C) trust manager, if the filing entity is a real estate investment trust;

(7) if the filing entity is formed under a plan of conversion or merger, a statement to that effect and, if formed under a plan of conversion, the name, address, date of formation, prior form of organization, and jurisdiction of formation of the converting entity; and

(8) any other information required by this code to be included in the certificate of formation for the filing entity.

(b) The certificate of formation may contain other provisions not inconsistent with law relating to the organization, ownership, governance, business, or affairs of the filing entity.

(c) Except as provided by Section 3.004, Chapter 4 governs the signing and filing of a certificate of formation for a domestic entity.

§ 3.011. Supplemental Provisions Regarding Certificate of Formation of Limited Partnership

(a) To form a limited partnership, the partners must enter into a partnership agreement and file a certificate of formation.

(b) The partners of a limited partnership formed under Section 10.001 or 10.101 may include the partnership agreement required under Subsection (a) in the plan of merger or conversion.

(c) A certificate of formation for a limited partnership must include the address of the principal office of the partnership in the United States where records are to be kept or made available under Section 153.551.

(d) The fact that a certificate of formation is on file with the secretary of state is notice that the partnership is a limited partnership and of all other facts contained in the certificate as required by Section 3.005.

§ 5.055. Name of Limited Partnership or Foreign Limited Partnership

(a) The name of a limited partnership or foreign limited partnership must contain:

(1) the word "limited";

(2) the phrase "limited partnership"; or

(3) an abbreviation of that word or phrase.

(b) The name of a domestic or foreign limited partnership that is a limited liability limited partnership must also contain the phrase "limited liability partnership" or an abbreviation of that phrase.

(c) The name of a domestic or foreign limited partnership that is a limited liability limited partnership complies with the requirements of Subsections (a) and (b) if the name of the limited partnership contains the phrase "limited liability limited partnership" or an abbreviation of that phrase.

§ 2.003. General Prohibited Purposes. A domestic entity may not:

(1) engage in a business or activity that:

(A) is expressly unlawful or prohibited by a law of this state; or

(B) cannot lawfully be engaged in by that entity under state law; or

(2) operate as a:

(A) bank;

(B) *trust company;*

(C) *savings association;*

(D) *insurance company;*

(E) *cemetery organization*, except as authorized by Chapter 711, 712, or 715, Health and Safety Code; or

(F) *abstract or title company governed by* Title 11, Insurance Code.

****

Entity Status

A limited partnership, under Texas Law, is a separate entity from its partners, with the power to hold property and to sue and be sued in its name. (BOC § 152.056: "A partnership is an entity distinct from its partners."). Sometimes parties argue that the limited partnership is not a separate entity for particular purposes, including employment relations and income taxation.

In Re Allcat Claims Serv., L.P.
356 S.W.3d 455 (TEX. 2011)

In this original proceeding Allcat Claims Service, L.P., a limited partnership, and one of its limited partners seek an order directing the Comptroller to refund franchise taxes Allcat paid that were attributable to partnership income allocated, but not distributed, to its natural-person partners. Allcat claims it is entitled to a refund for two reasons. First, the tax facially violates Article VIII, Section 24 of the Texas Constitution because it is a tax on the net incomes of its natural-person partners that was not approved in a statewide referendum. Second, as applied by the Comptroller to Allcat and its partners, the franchise tax violates Article VIII, Section 1(a) of the Constitution, which requires taxation to be equal and uniform. We hold that: (1) the tax is not a tax imposed on the net incomes of the individual partners, thus it does not facially violate Article VIII, Section 24; and (2) we do not have jurisdiction to consider the equal and uniform challenge....

Is the Tax Constitutional?

As an initial matter, we note Allcat contends that only Texas law applies to the issues presented. We agree. The Bullock Amendment and Texas partnership law, not some other law such as the federal Internal Revenue Code (IRC), control whether the Act violates the Texas Constitution. Allcat insists that the franchise tax is, in effect, an income tax notwithstanding the Legislature's express statement to the contrary. *See* Act § 21 ("The franchise tax imposed by Chapter 171, Tax Code, as amended by this Act, is not an income tax...."). It reasons that because the income of a partnership is allocated to each partner according to the partner's partnership interest, the Act taxes each partner's allocated share of Allcat's income. Allcat asserts that, in this manner, the franchise tax is a tax on the net incomes of its partners and violates the Bullock Amendment as to partners who are natural persons. The Comptroller counters that the franchise tax is not an income tax because it can result in taxes due even if the entity loses money. She further argues that whether the tax is an income tax is irrelevant because Texas has adopted the entity theory for partnership law and a tax imposed on a limited partnership entity does not constitute a tax on the net incomes of the partnership's individual partners. Because it is dispositive, we begin with the Comptroller's second argument. Under the aggregate theory of partnership law a partnership is not an entity separate and distinct from its individual partners. Rather, the "partnership" name or label is a convenient way of referring to the partners as a group. *See* 1 ALAN R. BROMBERG & LARRY E. RIBSTEIN, BROMBERG AND RIBSTEIN ON PARTNERSHIP § 1.03(a)–(b) (Release No. 31, 2011–12 Supp.). In contrast, under the entity theory of partnership law the partnership is an entity separate and distinct from its partners. *Id.* Although it has not always been so, Texas adheres to the entity theory. In 1961 the Legislature adopted the Texas Uniform Partnership Act (TUPA), TEX. CIV. STAT. ANN. art. 6132(b) which "lean[ed] heavily toward the entity idea." *Id.*, § 1, cmt. This Court recognized that the aggregate theory had been abandoned for most purposes with the TUPA's adoption:

> [under the aggregate theory] a partnership was considered to be an aggregate of individuals acting under contract.... However, after the adoption of [TUPA], a partnership was recognized as an entity legally distinct from its partners for most purposes. The entity theory of partnership is consistent with other laws permitting suit in the partnership name and service on one partner.

Haney v. Fenley, Bate, Deaton & Porter, 618 S.W.2d 541, 542 (Tex.1981) (per curiam). Yet despite the TUPA, some courts continued to apply the aggregate theory in certain situations. *See, e.g., Lawler v. Dallas Statler–Hilton Joint Venture,* 793 S.W.2d 27, 33–34 (Tex.App.-Dallas 1990, writ denied) (recognizing that Texas is "predominantly an entity theory state" but determining that under the TUPA there were sufficient aggregate features to a partnership for the court to apply the aggregate theory to an employment relationship). Courts' application of the aggregate theory in certain contexts and the entity theory in others led to some confusion. So, "to allay previous concerns that stemmed from confusion as to whether a partnership was an entity or an aggregate of its members," the 73rd Legislature passed the Texas Revised Uniform Partnership Act (TRPA) in 1993 and thereby "unequivocally embrace[d] the entity theory of partnership by specifically stating ... that a partnership is an entity distinct from its partners." TEX.REV.CIV. STAT. ANN. art. 6132b–2.01, Comment of Bar Committee—1993. The TRPA, codified in the Texas Business Organizations Code, plainly provides that "[a] partnership is an entity distinct from its partners," and "[a] partner is not a co-owner of partnership property." TEX. BUS. ORGS.CODE §§ 152.056, 154.001(c). Further, it is the partnership interest that is a partner's "personal property for all purposes." *Id.* § 154.001(a); *see also Reid Road Mun. Util. Dist. No. 2 v. Speedy Stop Food Stores, Ltd.,* 337 S.W.3d 846, 855 (Tex.2011) (noting that the general partner of a limited partnership is not an owner of the limited partnership's property). . . .

Allcat urges that the separate entity concept applies only in contexts unrelated to net income, such as property ownership and enforcement of liability. Citing *Destec Energy, Inc. v. Houston Lighting & Power Co.,* 966 S.W.2d 792 (Tex.App.-Austin 1998, no pet.), it argues that

Texas has not adopted the entity approach for partnership income, thus partnership income is divided into shares essentially owned by the partners regardless of whether the income shares are actually distributed to the partners. We disagree with Allcat's position and its reading of *Destec.* In *Destec* the court of appeals rejected the aggregate theory of partnership law in deference to the Legislature's adoption of the entity theory in the TRPA. *Id.* at 795–96. That same court recently reviewed the nature of partnership income under the entity theory. *See Smith v. Grayson,* No. 03–10–00238–CV, 2011 WL 4924073, at *5–*6 (Tex.App.-Austin Oct. 12, 2011, no pet. h.). In determining whether partnership earnings retained by the partnership are separate property of a limited partner or community property of the partner and his wife, the court noted that "[p]artnership earnings are owned by the partnership prior to distribution to the partners and cannot be characterized as either separate or community property." *Id.* at *6. Rather, the limited partner's "right to receive his share of the profits is the only partnership right subject to characterization." *Id.* at *5. Other courts of appeals have likewise rejected attempts to impose an aggregate theory of partnership law, given the express language of the TRPA. . . . Allcat also argues that section 152.202(a) of the Business Organizations Code (entitled "Credits of and Charges to Partner") should control over section 152.056 (entitled "Partnership as Entity"), thereby making partnership income an exception to the separate entity concept. Section 152.202(a) provides in relevant part: "Each partner is credited with an amount equal to ... the partner's share of the partnership's profits." TEX. BUS. ORGS.CODE § 152.202(a). This provision, when read in context with section 153.206, providing how limited partnership profits and losses are allocated, merely specifies that partnership profits are credited and allocated to the partner's partnership interest according to the partnership agreement or as otherwise provided under the TRPA. TEX. BUS. ORGS.CODE § 152.202(a), 153.206; *see also id.* § 153.003 (providing that the provisions of chapter 152 apply to limited partnerships if they are not inconsistent with chapter 153 of the TRPA). The TRPA provides that partners have creditors' rights in regard to distributions of partnership profits, but it does not provide that allocations of partnership profits are property of, subject to the control of, or income to the separate partners. *See* TEX. BUS. ORGS.CODE § 153.207–.210; *see also Smith,* 2011 WL 4924073, at *5–*6; *Cleaver v. Cleaver,* 935 S.W.2d 491, 495 (Tex.App.-Tyler 1996, no writ). And the right to receive a distribution, even assuming it is authorized by the partnership, is subject to the partnership's ability to satisfy its liabilities. *See* TEX. BUS. ORGS.CODE § 153.210 (providing that distributions may not be made if, immediately after giving effect to the distribution, liabilities of the partnership will exceed the fair value of the partnership assets); *see also* TEX. BUS. ORGS.CODE § 153.105 (providing that rights of limited partners may be created only by (1) the certificate of formation; (2) the partnership agreement; (3) other sections of chapter 153; or (4) the other limited partnership provisions). Thus, under Texas law the allocation of partnership income or profits to a partner does not convert the amounts allocated into property of or income to the partner, and section 152.202(a) does not indicate a departure from the entity theory. . . . We conclude that the franchise tax constitutes a tax on Allcat as an entity; it does not constitute a tax on the net income of Allcat's natural-person limited partners within the meaning of the Bullock Amendment. We hold that Allcat's facial challenge is without merit.

Limited Partnership: Governance

Unlike a general partnership's decentralized management, the limited partnership adopts a governance structure that is more analogous to the centralized management of corporations. Like the corporate board of directors, management powers are vested in the general partner, who may choose to delegate responsibilities as he sees fit. Yet, "the relationship among partners is consensual, and requires a degree of privity which forces the general partner to seek the approval of the partners (sometimes unanimous approval) under circumstances which corporate management would find unthinkable." Brockenbrough Lamb, Jr., *Introduction, Symposium: Limited Partnership Act*, 9 ST. MARY'S L.J. 441, 441 (1978). For instance, a limited partnership agreement may provide that a general partner needs unanimous consent of the partners to encumber partnership property. Limited partners have limited rights to participate in governance. Their governance roles include voting for the admission, removal or retention of a general partner. They also have informational rights that under TBOC § 153.004(a)(3) may not be unreasonably restricted by agreement.

Bradford Partners II, L.P. v. Fahning
231 S.W.3d 513 (Tex. App. Dallas 2007)

Appellants Bradford Partners II, L.P. ("Bradford"), Wilson James Harris, and Bradford Custom Homes by Jim Harris, Inc. ("BCH") appeal a summary judgment in favor of Craig Fahning, Joann W. Fahning, and Airchaud, Inc. In nine issues, appellants contend generally that the trial court erred in: (1) granting summary judgment on the counterclaims because the Fahnings are not subrogated to the rights of the lender and BCH did not breach the partnership agreement; (2) in granting summary judgment on the appellants' claims because an adequate time for discovery had not passed and the no-evidence motion for summary judgment was deficient; and (3) striking certain portions of Harris's affidavit, the appellants' amended response to the motion for summary judgment, and exhibits attached thereto. We overrule appellants' issues and affirm the trial court's judgment.

Background

On January 1, 2002, the Fahnings, as limited partners, and BCH, as general partner, entered into a limited partnership agreement. They formed a limited partnership called Bradford Partners II, L.P. The purpose of Bradford Partners was to purchase residential real estate lots and build and market homes on those lots.

On March 26, 2002, Bradford Partners borrowed $251,440.00 from YYP Funds, Inc. as evidenced by a promissory note. The note was secured by a deed of trust on six lots. The Fahnings and Harris executed personal guarantees on the notes.

Bradford Partners became delinquent on the YYP note. YYP made demand on the guarantors. When the guarantors failed to pay, YYP sued and obtained a judgment in November

2004. YYP filed an abstract of judgment in the records of Collin County, Texas. To collect on the judgment, YYP garnished several of the Fahnings bank accounts. The Fahnings voluntarily made a payment in the amount of $28,013.75. In all total, the Fahnings paid $119,949.16 as guarantors on the note. Harris paid a total of $199,039.46 as guarantor on the note.

A second abstract of judgment was filed in the records of Collin County, Texas against Bradford Partners on January 24, 2005. On January 27, 2005, Bradford Partners executed a deed of trust in favor of C 1 Capital Markets LP and C One Capital Markets LP on lots it owned. A homeowners association filed liens against lots owned by Bradford Partners for failure to pay association dues. The Fahnings did not consent to any of the above actions and considered BCH to be in default under the partnership agreement. On July 26, 2005, the Fahnings removed BCH as the general partner of Bradford Partners and substituted Airchaud, Inc. in its place.

Appellants filed suit against the Fahnings and Airchaud on August 19, 2005 asserting claims for breach of the partnership agreement and breach of fiduciary duty. Appellants sought a declaratory judgment that the Fahnings and Airchaud were in breach of the agreement and that BCH should remain the general partner. The Fahnings and Airchaud counterclaimed. They sought a declaratory judgment that: (1) BCH, as general partner of Bradford Partners, was in default under the agreement; (2) the Fahnings, as limited partners, replaced BCH as general partner pursuant to the agreement; (3) Airchaud is the general partner of Bradford Partners; and (4) the Fahnings are subrogated to the rights of YYP. The Fahnings and Airchaud filed a motion for summary judgment and the trial court granted it. This appeal timely followed. . . .

Breach of the Partnership Agreement

In their third issue, appellants contend that the trial court erred in granting summary judgment declaring that BCH breached the agreement by allowing certain documents to be filed against Bradford. Pursuant to section 6.01(b)(ii) of the partnership agreement, the general partner, BCH, cannot, without the unanimous consent of the partners, "grant or create any mortgages, liens, easements, security interests, restrictions, restrictive covenants or other rights or interests burdening or encumbering the Partnership's real property." The summary judgment evidence shows that the following encumbrances were filed against Bradford Partners without the consent of the Fahnings, the limited partners,: (1) YYP filed an abstract of judgment on December 20, 2005; (2) Kenneth and Susan Everill filed an abstract of judgment on January 24, 2005; (3) Bradford Partners executed a deed of trust in favor of C 1 Capital Markets LP and C One Capital Markets LP against one of the lots owned by Bradford Partners on January 27, 2005; and (4) liens were filed against Bradford Partners properties on July 12, 2005 for failure to pay homeowner association dues. The Fahnings' summary judgment evidence established that BCH allowed the encumbrances to be placed against the partnership property without the unanimous consent of the limited partners. In doing so, BCH breached section 6.01(b)(ii) of the partnership agreement.

We conclude the trial court did not err in granting summary judgment and declaring that BCH breached the agreement. We overrule the appellants' third issue.

In their fourth issue, appellants contend the trial court erred in granting summary judgment and declaring that BCH was properly removed as the general partner of Bradford Partners. Appellants contend that the actions of BCH after July 26, 2005 were authorized because BCH has never been properly removed as Bradford Partners' general partner. Appellants contend that the partnership agreement provides only two grounds for removing the general partner: (1) the consent of a required interest;[FN4] and (2) an event of default by the general partner. Appellants contend that the agreement limits "default" to either the withdrawal or bankruptcy of the general partner. We disagree. The agreement does not limit the term "default." Section 9.03 addresses the replacement of a general partner who voluntarily withdraws as the general partner. That is not the situation that occurred in this case. Section 9.04 addresses the situation of a partner who becomes bankrupt. Again, that is not the situation involved in this case.

FN4. Under the partnership agreement, the term "required interest" means "the General Partner in its capacity as such and one or more Limited Partners having among them more that 75% of the Sharing Ratios of all Partners in the capacities as such."

The Fahnings removed BCH as general partner pursuant to section 9.02 of the agreement. That section provides as follows:

> 9.02 Replacement of General Partner. The General Partner may be replaced by a new General Partner with the consent of a Required Interest or in the event of a default by the General Partner hereunder, and with the unanimous consent of the Limited Partners. Any such action for replacement also must (a) select a new General Partner, (b) specify any Capital Contribution it is to make, which shall be deposited with the Partnership and its Sharing Ratio, and (c) be accompanied by an instrument executed by such new General Partner including such new General Partner's notice address, acceptance of all terms and provisions of this Agreement, an agreement to perform and discharge timely all of its obligations and liabilities hereunder. The new General Partner so selected shall be admitted to the Partnership as General Partner with the Sharing Ratio specified, and such removal shall be effective only immediately subsequent to such admission.

The agreement does not define or limit the term "default." In determining what the parties meant by "default" the court gives the word its plain, everyday meaning. *See Limestone Group, Inc. v. Sai Thong, L.L.C.*, 107 S.W.3d 793, 797 (Tex.App.-Amarillo 2003, no pet.). "Default" is defined as a failure to do an act. WEBSTER'S NINTH NEW COLLEGIATE DICTIONARY 332 (9th ed.1985). The plain meaning of the term includes breach. *See Alaniz v. Yates Ford, Inc.*, 790 S.W.2d 38, 40 (Tex.App.-San Antonio 1990, no writ). Thus, because the plain meaning of "default" includes breach we give the term in the agreement the same meaning. Under our discussion of appellant's third issue, we held that BCH breached the agreement. We conclude that BCH's breach constituted a default within the meaning of section 9.02.

Pursuant to section 9.02 of the agreement, the Fahnings, as the limited partners, had the authority to replace BCH as the general partner. The Fahnings replaced BCH with Airchaud, Inc. in accordance with the terms of section 9.02. We conclude the trial court did not err in declaring that BCH was properly removed as the general partner of Bradford Partners. We overrule the appellants' fourth issue.

Limited Partnership: Authority of General Partner

Generally, a general partner's authority is similar to the authority of a partner in a general partnership. TBOC §153.152 (a) (1) provides that a general partner in a limited partnership "has the rights and powers and is subject to the restrictions of a partner in a partnership without limited partners." A general partner acting with authority has the capacity to bring a suit in the name of the limited partnership. *See Gulf Coast Shell & Aggregate, L.P. v. Dredge La Concha*, 2008 WL 4722433 (S.D. Tex. 2008). Based on BOC § 152.209, which provides that a difference arising in a matter in the ordinary course of the partnership business may be decided by a majority-in-interest of the partners, it appears that a general partner of a limited partnership only has the authority to bring suit in the name of the limited partnership when a majority-in-interest of the general partners agree to the action.[2] Extraordinary partnership matters are decided by the unanimous consent of the general partners.

Texas Business Organization Code provisions

§ 153.152. General Powers and Liabilities of General Partner

(a) Except as provided by this chapter, the other limited partnership provisions, or a partnership agreement, a general partner of a limited partnership:

(1) has the rights and powers and is subject to the restrictions of a partner in a partnership without limited partners; and

(2) has the liabilities of a partner in a partnership without limited partners to the partnership and to the other partners.

(b) Except as provided by this chapter or the other limited partnership provisions, a general partner of a limited partnership has the liabilities of a partner in a partnership without limited partners to a person other than the partnership and the other partners.

A person may choose to be both a general partner and limited partner in the same firm. As a general partner, he has the governing rights and the exposure to personal liability that accompany that position. As a limited partner, he will be able to access any financial and voting rights that applicable law or the limited partnership agreement assigns to limited partners.

---

[2] In Gulf Coast Shell & Aggregate, L.P. v. Dredge La Concha, 2008 WL 4722433 (S.D. Tex. 2008), the court made no distinction between general partners and limited partners in stating and applying this rule to the limited partnership context, but the court's position is likely erroneous to that extent

Texas Business Organization Code provisions

§ 153.153. Powers and Liabilities of Person Who is Both General Partner and Limited Partner. A person who is both a general partner and a limited partner:

(1) has the rights and powers and is subject to the restrictions and liabilities of a general partner; and

(2) except as otherwise provided by the partnership agreement, this chapter, or the other limited partnership provisions, has the rights and powers and is subject to the restrictions and liabilities, if any, of a limited partner to the extent of the general partner's participation in the partnership as a limited partner.

Limited Partnership: Authority of Limited Partner *Daniels*

A limited partner is not an agent of the limited partnership. Therefore, he has no authority, based solely on his position as a limited partner, to bind the partnership contractually or incur tort obligations for the partnership and its partners. A limited partner may be conferred with authority to act, even if she is functioning in some other capacity, such as an agent or employee of the partnership. A limited partner also has the right and power to bring derivative claims on behalf of the partnership where the general partners fail to commence such action or where it would be futile to demand that the general partners act to protect or vindicate the partnership's interests. To be able to bring a derivative suit, the limited partner must have been a partner at the time of the transaction complained of and remain a partner through the duration of the lawsuit. A derivative suit would not be the proper course of action if the limited partner has suffered a direct injury. In that instance, a direct claim would be the proper action.

§ 153.401. Right to Bring Action. A limited partner may bring an action in a court on behalf of the limited partnership to recover a judgment in the limited partnership's favor if:

(1) all general partners with authority to bring the action have refused to bring the action; or

(2) an effort to cause those general partners to bring the action is not likely to succeed.

§ 153.402. Proper Plaintiff. In a derivative action, the plaintiff must be a limited partner when the action is brought and:

(1) the person must have been a limited partner at the time of the transaction that is the subject of the action; or

(2) the person's status as a limited partner must have arisen by operation of law or under the terms of the partnership agreement from a person who was a limited partner at the time of the transaction.

§ 153.403. Pleading. In a derivative action, the complaint must contain with particularity:
(1) the effort, if any, of the plaintiff to secure initiation of the action by a general partner; or

(2) the reasons for not making the effort.

7547 Corp. v. Parker & Parsley Development Partners, L.P.
38 F.3d 211 (Ct.App.-5th Cir., 1994)

The plaintiffs-appellants challenge the district court's summary adjudication of their claims under federal and state securities laws and under the common law for breach of fiduciary duty, waste, and conversion, based upon its conclusion that the plaintiffs lacked the requisite standing to pursue those claims. We affirm the trial court's disposition of the state law claims and the claim for violation of federal proxy laws, but reverse its judgment with respect to the remaining federal securities claims.

I. Background

The plaintiffs, 7547 Corporation ("7547 Corporation") and Sonem Partners, L.P. ("Sonem") (together referred to as the "plaintiffs"), were the beneficial owners of units in a limited partnership known as Parker & Parsley Development Partners, L.P. ("PDP"), an oil and gas master limited partnership organized under the laws of the State of Texas and listed on the American Stock Exchange. PDP established operations in December 1987 through the exchange of 3.9 million units for interests in 32 oil and gas limited partnerships. As of March 30, 1990, the number of PDP units outstanding had risen to 5.2 million. PDP was apparently managed by its sole general partner, Parker & Parsley Development Corporation ("PPDC"), which was in turn owned by Southmark Corporation ("Southmark"). PPDC sponsored several public development drilling partnerships from which it received substantial management fees and operating revenues. PPDC also received promotional interests in the partnerships in exchange for its services. In 1989, Southmark provided severance packages to its two top officers which included the option to acquire PPDC for the higher of book value or appraisal value by April 24, 1989. In the event these two officers did not exercise the purchase option, nine other PPDC officers-including the individual defendants, Scott D. Sheffield ("Sheffield"), Herbert C. Williamson, III ("Williamson"), and Timothy M. Dunn ("Dunn")-were granted an option to purchase PPDC within 80 days. These officers will be referred to collectively as the "management group." The purchase option eventually inured to the management group, but, as they were unable to obtain third-party financing for the transaction, they could not complete the purchase. The plaintiffs claim that the individual defendants consequently devised an elaborate scheme whereby they could effectively obtain the benefits of PPDC ownership-i.e., a substantial portion of its income-without personally having to purchase it. The remainder of events described below are alleged to have been conceived and precipitated by these individuals in furtherance of the scheme, and, as

noted below, we review these allegations in a light most favorable to the non-movant plaintiffs.
...

II. Analysis

Standing issues abound in this case. The defendants have raised numerous challenges to the plaintiffs' standing to bring the claims asserted, including: (i) the inability to bring state law derivative claims because the plaintiffs were never admitted as limited partners; (ii) a lack of standing under the federal securities laws because the plaintiffs were neither "purchasers" nor "sellers" of the unit interests; (iii) the failure to show injury from any alleged deceptive activities; and (iv) an inability to assert violations of the federal securities laws governing the solicitation of proxies because the plaintiffs were not eligible to vote. These standing issues are obviously quite complicated and permeate all of the plaintiffs' causes of action; however, as the district court properly determined, their resolution is jurisdictional and therefore critical to our assessment of the case. . . .

A. The Status of the Plaintiffs Under Texas Law

1. Derivative claims

The defendants argued below, and the district court agreed, that the plaintiffs had never been made limited partners of PDP and thus did not have standing under Texas law to assert derivative claims on behalf of the partnership. In the lower court's view, 7547 Corporation and Sonem, as assignees of limited partnership units, did not become "Substituted Limited Partners" as that term is defined in the PDP partnership agreement. The Texas Revised Uniform Limited Partnership Act permits a limited partner to bring a derivative action on behalf of a limited partnership, provided, among other things, that the plaintiff was a limited partner both at the time he brings the action and at the time of the transaction (or at least "had status as a limited partner aris[ing] by operation of law or under the terms of the partnership agreement from a person who was a limited partner at the time of the transaction"). Tex.Rev.Civ.Stat.Ann. Art. 6132a-1, §§ 10.01, 10.02 (West Supp.1994). The statute defines "limited partner" quite deferentially by reference to the operative partnership agreement. E.g., Tex.Rev.Civ.Stat.Ann. Art. 6132a-1, §§ 1.02(5), 3.01 & 7.04. A transferee of partnership interests can become a "limited partner":

> if and to the extent that:
>
> (1) the partnership agreement provides; or
>
> (2) all partners consent.
>
> Tex.Rev.Civ.Stat.Ann. Art. 6132a-1, § 7.04.

The PDP partnership agreement sets forth the procedure by which a transferee of limited partnership units can become a limited partner. First, the transferee must receive the units and the power to seek admission from its assignor. It must then deliver an executed transfer application to the transfer agent which includes certain requisite representations and agreements. Finally, the general partner must consent to the admission of the transferee as a "Substituted Limited Partner." That consent "may be granted or withheld in [the general partner's] sole discretion." However, the agreement also provides that consent may be "deemed" to have been given if the general partner does not expressly withhold its consent. It is undisputed that the general partner of PDP, P & P Equity, never gave its consent to the admission of Kaufmann, 7547 Corporation, or Sonem. In fact, in all three cases, it specifically withheld such consent. By letter dated September 14, 1990, P & P Equity expressly denied Kaufmann consent to be a limited partner. That "blackball" specifically extended to its affiliates and assignees, apparently including 7547 Corporation, which subsequently acquired its units from Kaufmann on December 17, 1990. Since the notice was delivered several months before Kaufmann assigned its units to 7547 Corporation, 7547 Corporation could not have become a limited partner even under the "deemed consent" provision. Moreover, the plaintiffs admit by affidavit that they never filed applications to be admitted as limited partners. The plaintiffs offer several ways around their obvious problems with standing to sue derivatively. First, they contend that they should be treated effectively as limited partners for purposes of standing. Second, they complain that summary judgment was prematurely granted before they could obtain sufficient evidence to establish their standing to sue. Finally, they contend that they are entitled to assert direct claims against the general partner and other defendants. We address each in turn.

a. Equitable status as limited partners

With regard to the first argument, the plaintiffs maintain that "standing may be granted to one who is not a limited partner where, inter alia, the wrongdoers themselves prevented the person from becoming a limited partner in order to continue in their wrongdoing without challenge." While admittedly appealing, the plaintiffs cannot cite to any authority to support this novel theory that they "should" be granted standing as limited partners as a matter of Texas law. Although the plaintiffs' allegations, if true, may amount to egregious tale of mismanagement and/or deception, for several reasons we are not persuaded that we should alter the clear language of the Texas statute to afford standing to the plaintiffs. First, the Texas statute bestows eligibility to sue derivatively only upon one who is a "limited partner," which status, as discussed above, is essentially defined by the partnership agreement. Tex.Rev.Civ.Stat.Ann. Art. 6132a-1, § 10.01. Section 10.02 makes it even clearer that the derivative plaintiff must be a " limited partner " at the time of bringing the action. Id. at § 10.02. Further, the Texas statute reflects that there are significant, attendant legal consequences to becoming a limited partner which do not affect other interest-holders. See Tex.Rev.Civ.Stat.Ann. Art. 6132a-1, § 7.02(b) (stating that an assignee of partnership interests who has not yet become a limited partner has no liability as a partner); id. at § 6.03 (setting forth the procedure by which a limited partner must withdraw from the partnership). Indeed, there are indications throughout the statute that the distinction between limited partners and mere assignees is critical to the statutory scheme. Id. at

§ 7.02 comment ("Assignability does not amount to free transferability of interest which might imperil partnership classification for federal income tax purposes; this is because the assignee does not automatically become a limited partner.... The section also prevents an assignee from becoming a partner, or exercising the rights of a partner, unless the agreement is otherwise."). We can only conclude that the Texas legislature specifically determined not to include assignees and transferees among those with derivative standing and instead deliberately chose to allow a partnership agreement to define the persons upon whom standing to sue derivatively would be conferred. E.g., Blue Chip Stamps v. Manor Drug Stores, 421 U.S. 723, 734, 95 S.Ct. 1917, 1925, 44 L.Ed.2d 539 (1975) (Where legislative body expressly includes a term in one provision of law but not in another part of the same law, it is permissible to conclude that it omitted the term intentionally.). We cannot override what we see to be the clear intent of the Texas statute in order to afford "equitable" standing to the plaintiffs in this case.

The plaintiffs nonetheless draw our attention to cases which have permitted persons who are not technically "shareholders" to assert claims on behalf of a corporation and request that we extend their holdings by analogy. The problem with doing so is that those cases do not construe the Texas law with which we are concerned. . . . T]he cases which granted a right to limited partners to sue on behalf of the partnership even before such standing was conferred by statute do not persuade us to bypass the clear language of the Texas statute. In short, we disagree with the plaintiffs that "[t]here is no good reason why [they] should not be allowed to stand in the place of the limited partner or partners whose interests" were ultimately transferred to them. . . .

2. Direct claims

The plaintiffs alternatively argue that the "near total domination and influence" of P & P Equity over the operations and assets of PDP required them to repose trust and confidence in the general partner; thus, they reason, the breach of that trust affords them a direct action against the general partner. See Texas Bank & Trust Co. v. Moore, 595 S.W.2d 502, 507-09 (Tex.1980) (holding that a fiduciary relationship exists where " 'a special confidence is reposed in another who in equity and good conscience is bound to act in good faith and with due regard to the interests of the one reposing confidence.' " (citations omitted)). The reference to Texas law is appropriate because this court has previously held that state law determines whether a shareholder may maintain a non-derivative action. See Crocker v. FDIC, 826 F.2d 347, 349 (5th Cir.1987), cert. denied, 485 U.S. 905, 108 S.Ct. 1075, 99 L.Ed.2d 235 (1988). We have no trouble in extending Crocker to the case presented, and conclude that state law is also appropriate to determine whether an action against the general partners of a limited partnership is derivative or direct. We have not been pointed to, nor have we uncovered, any Texas cases dealing with the specific issue presented, namely, whether a unitholder or limited partner can sue directly for injuries suffered by the limited partnership. As the defendants point out, the problem with using general fiduciary duty cases to find a direct cause of action in this case is that the injury here was in essence suffered by the partnership. The cases are legion that a shareholder may not sue directly for breaches of duties by officers and directors of a company because those injuries are actually suffered by the corporation. E.g., Wingate v. Hajdik, 795 S.W.2d 717, 719 (Tex.1990); see also Lewis v. Knutson, 699 F.2d 230, 237-38 (5th Cir.1983); cf. Abeloff v. Barth, 119 F.R.D. 332, 334 (D.Mass.1988) (claims for breaches of duty by general partner of limited partnership belong to the entity, not to the partners). The principle underlying this theory is that, when an injury is suffered by the corporation,

> each shareholder suffers relatively in proportion to the number of shares he owns, and each will be made whole if the corporation obtains restitution or compensation from the wrongdoer.... Such action must be brought by the corporation ... in order that the damages so recovered may be available for the payment of the corporation's creditors, and for proportional distributions to the stockholders....

Wingate, 795 S.W.2d at 719 (quoting Massachusetts v. Davis, 140 Tex. 398, 168 S.W.2d 216, 221 (1942), cert. denied, 320 U.S. 210, 63 S.Ct. 1447, 87 L.Ed. 1848 (1943)); cf. Gabrielsen v. BancTexas Group, Inc., 675 F.Supp. 367, 373 (N.D.Tex.1987) (observing that, where the entity suffers injury because of the alleged misconduct of its management, the holder of an interest has no standing to bring a direct civil action against the management). This same principle has been applied to require derivative action where an injury is in reality suffered by a limited partnership. See Attick v. Valeria Assocs., L.P., 835 F.Supp. 103, 110-11 (S.D.N.Y.1992); Abeloff, 119 F.R.D. at 334; Strain v. Seven Hills Assocs., 75 A.D.2d 360, 429 N.Y.S.2d 424, 432 (1980) ("[A] limited partner's power to vindicate a wrong done to the limited partnership and to enforce redress for the loss or diminution in value of his interest is no greater than that of a shareholder of a corporation."). We find the reasoning of these authorities instructive and predict that a Texas court would likely consider the state law claims presented to be derivative. Indeed, the fact that Texas now has a statute expressly allowing limited partners to sue derivatively on behalf of the partnership-thus making their status more equivalent to that of a shareholder-leads us to believe that a Texas court would likely be hesitant to allow a limited partner (much less a unitholder) to sue directly for wrongs suffered in reality by the partnership. Moreover, the facts of this case present an even more forceful argument for finding derivative harm only. The plaintiffs describe their damages as follows:

> [The defendants] have engaged in a complex and sophisticated scheme and common course of conduct to wrongfully misappropriate for themselves millions of dollars in fees, properties, and interests rightfully belonging to PDP and 28,000 PDP Unitholders. They also contend that, pursuant to the roll-up transaction:

> [T]he common stock of [PDP Petroleum] will be unfairly allocated between PDP and P & P Ltd. with P & P Ltd. receiving a far greater percentage of the common stock than it would have received in an arm's length transaction.

The injuries alleged by the plaintiffs are therefore collective injuries suffered by the partnership. That the disparities will eventually be passed on to the PDP unitholders upon liquidation of PDP does not commute the causes of action into direct claims on the plaintiffs' behalf; rather, the damages sought by the plaintiffs appear to be exactly like those indirect damages suffered by shareholders when a wrong is perpetrated upon the corporation. E. g., Wingate, 795 S.W.2d at 719; see generally, Leach v. FDIC, 860 F.2d 1266, 1269 (5th Cir.1988), cert. denied, 491 U.S. 905, 109 S.Ct. 3186, 105 L.Ed.2d 695 (1989); FDIC v. Howse, 802 F.Supp. 1554, 1561-62 (S.D.Tex.1992) (determination of whether claim is derivative turns on whether "all shareholders are 'wounded' or just one person has been hurt by the misconduct.").

The plaintiffs point us to two cases in which they claim a fiduciary duty was found to be owed by the general partner to a unitholder or limited partner. See Kellis v. Ring, 92 Cal.App.3d 854, 155 Cal.Rptr. 297 (1979); Eisenbaum v. Western Energy Resources, Inc., 218 Cal.App.3d 314, 267 Cal.Rptr. 5 (1990). These cases do not persuade us to permit a direct action here. Eisenbaum involved the breach of a duty owed directly to the limited partner, which has never been subject to the derivative action rule. See Wingate, 795 S.W.2d at 719 (stating that the rule requiring derivative action for corporate injuries does not prohibit a stockholder from recovering damages where wrongdoer violates duty to stockholder individually); Howse, 802 F.Supp. at 1562; Schoellkopf v. Pledger, 739 S.W.2d 914, 918-19 (Tex.App.-Dallas 1987) (recognizing that stockholder may sue for violation of his own individual rights even though corporation may also have a claim), rev'd on other grounds, 762 S.W.2d 145 (Tex.1988); cf. Crocker, 826 F.2d at 349-50 (applying analogous Mississippi rule). With respect to Kellis, the California court merely speculated that "[i]t may be that upon proper pleading" the assignee could possibly maintain an action for injunctive relief and damages. 155 Cal.Rptr. at 300 (emphasis added). The court did not determine whether this possible action need be brought derivatively or directly. The dicta in Kellis does not compel us to find a direct action here.

In conclusion, we believe that the plaintiffs' state law causes of action are properly characterized as derivative, and our finding that Texas law does not permit the plaintiffs to bring derivative actions precludes the assertion of these claims.

Limited Partnership: Admission of Partners

Subject to a partnership agreement, the admission of a new general partner or limited partner requires unanimous consent of existing partners.

Texas Business Organization Code provisions

§ 153.101. Admission of Limited Partners
(a) In connection with the formation of a limited partnership, a person acquiring a limited partnership interest becomes a limited partner on the later of:

(1) the date on which the limited partnership is formed; or

(2) the date stated in the records of the limited partnership as the date on which the person becomes a limited partner or, if that date is not stated in those records, the date on which the person's admission is first reflected in the records of the limited partnership.

(b) After a limited partnership is formed, a person who acquires a partnership interest directly from the limited partnership becomes a new limited partner on:

(1) compliance with the provisions of the partnership agreement governing admission of new limited partners; or

(2) if the partnership agreement does not contain relevant admission provisions, the written consent of all partners.

(c) After formation of a limited partnership, an assignee of a partnership interest becomes a new limited partner as provided by Section 153.253(a).

(d) A person may be a limited partner unless the person lacks capacity apart from this chapter and the other limited partnership provisions.

§ 153.253 (a) referred to above provides that "[a]n assignee of a partnership interest, including the partnership interest of a general partner, may become a limited partner if and to the extent that: (1) the partnership agreement provides; or (2) all partners consent." See also 7547 Corp. v. Parker & Parsley Development Partners, L.P., 38 F.3d 211, C.A.5 (Tex.)1994.

§ 153.151. Admission of General Partners

(a) After a limited partnership is formed, additional general partners may be admitted:

(1) in the manner provided by a written partnership agreement; or

(2) if a written partnership agreement does not provide for the admission of additional general partners, with the written consent of all partners.

(b) A person may be a general partner unless the person lacks capacity apart from this chapter.

(c) A written partnership agreement may provide that a person may be admitted as a general partner in a limited partnership, including as a sole general partner, and may acquire a partnership interest in the limited partnership without:

(1) making a contribution to the limited partnership; or

(2) assuming an obligation to make a contribution to the limited partnership.

(d) A written partnership agreement may provide that a person may be admitted as a general partner in a limited partnership, including as the sole general partner, without acquiring a partnership interest in the limited partnership.

(e) This section is not a limitation of or does not otherwise affect Section 153.152.

Limited Partnership: Right to Information

Texas Business Organization Code provisions

§ 153.552. Examination of Records and Information

(a) On written request stating a proper purpose, a partner or an assignee of a partnership interest may examine and copy, in person or through a representative, records required to be kept under Section 153.551 and other information regarding the business, affairs, and financial condition of the limited partnership as is just and reasonable for the person to examine and copy.

(b) The records requested under Subsection (a) may be examined and copied at a reasonable time and at the partner's sole expense.

(c) On written request by a partner or an assignee of a partnership interest, the partnership shall provide to the requesting partner or assignee without charge copies of:

(1) the partnership agreement and certificate of formation and all amendments or restatements; and

(2) any tax return described by Section 153.551(a)(2).

(d) A request made under Subsection (c) must be made to:

(1) the person who is designated to receive the request in the partnership agreement at the address designated in the partnership agreement; or

(2) if there is no designation, a general partner at the partnership's principal office in the United States.

Limited Partnership: Nature of a Partner's Ownership Interests

A partner's interest in the partnership is characterized as personal property.

Texas Business Organization Code provisions

§ 154.001. Nature of Partner's Partnership Interest

(a) A partner's partnership interest is personal property for all purposes.

(b) A partner's partnership interest may be community property under applicable law.

(c) A partner is not a co-owner of partnership property.

(d) Sections 9.406 and 9.408, Business & Commerce Code, do not apply to a partnership interest in a partnership, including the rights, powers, and interests arising under the governing documents of the partnership or under this code. To the extent of any conflict between this subsection and Section 9.406 or 9.408, Business & Commerce Code, this subsection controls. It is the express intent of this subsection to permit the enforcement, as a contract among the partners of a partnership, of any provision of a partnership

agreement that would otherwise be ineffective under Section 9.406 or 9.408, Business & Commerce Code.

Limited Partnership: Assignment of Ownership Interests

A partner is at liberty to assign his right to receive profits and distributions, that is, his economic rights. Such assignment does not require the consent of other partners. An assignee of the partner's interest has informational rights but not management rights.

Texas Business Organization Code provisions

§ 153.251. Assignment of Partnership Interest

(a) Except as otherwise provided by the partnership agreement, a partnership interest is assignable wholly or partly.

(b) Except as otherwise provided by the partnership agreement, an assignment of a partnership interest:

(1) does not require the winding up of a limited partnership;

(2) does not entitle the assignee to become, or to exercise rights or powers of, a partner; and

(3) entitles the assignee to be allocated income, gain, loss, deduction, credit, or similar items and to receive distributions to which the assignor was entitled to the extent those items are assigned.

§ 153.252. Rights of Assignor

(a) Except as otherwise provided by the partnership agreement, until the assignee becomes a partner, the assignor partner continues to be a partner in the limited partnership. The assignor partner may exercise any rights or powers of a partner, except to the extent those rights or powers are assigned.

(b) Except as otherwise provided by the partnership agreement, on the assignment by a general partner of all of the general partner's rights as a general partner, the general partner's status as a general partner may be terminated by the affirmative vote of a majority-in-interest of the limited partners.

§ 153.253. Rights of Assignee

(a) An assignee of a partnership interest, including the partnership interest of a general partner, may become a limited partner if and to the extent that:

(1) the partnership agreement provides; or

(2) all partners consent.

§ 153.254. Liability of Assignee

(a) Until an assignee of the partnership interest in a limited partnership becomes a partner, the assignee does not have liability as a partner solely as a result of the assignment.

(b) Unless otherwise provided by a written partnership agreement, an assignee who becomes a limited partner:

> (1) is liable for the obligations of the assignor to make contributions as provided by Sections 153.202-153.204;

> (2) is not obligated for liabilities unknown to the assignee at the time the assignee became a limited partner and that could not be ascertained from a written partnership agreement; and

> (3) is not liable for the obligations of the assignor under Sections 153.105, 153.112, and 153.162.

§ 153.255. Liability of Assignor.

Regardless of whether an assignee of a partnership interest becomes a limited partner, the assignor is not released from the assignor's liability to the limited partnership under Subchapter E and Sections 153.105, 153.112, and 153.162.

§ 153.256. Partner's Partnership Interest Subject to Charging Order

(a) On application by a judgment creditor of a partner or of any other owner of a partnership interest, a court having jurisdiction may charge the partnership interest of the judgment debtor to satisfy the judgment.

(b) To the extent that the partnership interest is charged in the manner provided by Subsection (a), the judgment creditor has only the right to receive any distribution to which the judgment debtor would otherwise be entitled in respect of the partnership interest.

(c) A charging order constitutes a lien on the judgment debtor's partnership interest. The charging order lien may not be foreclosed on under this code or any other law.

(d) The entry of a charging order is the exclusive remedy by which a judgment creditor of a partner or of any other owner of a partnership interest may satisfy a judgment out of the judgment debtor's partnership interest.

(e) This section does not deprive a partner or other owner of a partnership interest of a right under exemption laws with respect to the judgment debtor's partnership interest.

(f) A creditor of a partner or of any other owner of a partnership interest does not have the right to obtain possession of, or otherwise exercise legal or equitable remedies with respect to, the property of the limited partnership.

§ 153.552. Examination of Records and Information

(a) On written request stating a proper purpose, a partner or an assignee of a partnership interest may examine and copy, in person or through a representative, records required to be kept under Section 153.551 and other information regarding the business, affairs, and financial condition of the limited partnership as is just and reasonable for the person to examine and copy.

(b) The records requested under Subsection (a) may be examined and copied at a reasonable time and at the partner's sole expense.

(c) On written request by a partner or an assignee of a partnership interest, the partnership shall provide to the requesting partner or assignee without charge copies of:

(1) the partnership agreement and certificate of formation and all amendments or restatements; and

(2) any tax return described by Section 153.551(a)(2).

(d) A request made under Subsection (c) must be made to:

(1) the person who is designated to receive the request in the partnership agreement at the address designated in the partnership agreement; or

(2) if there is no designation, a general partner at the partnership's principal

Limited Partnership: Transfer of Partnership Property

The property of the limited partnership belongs to the partnership. A partner has no interest in any partnership property that can be voluntarily or involuntarily transferred. This is the case, even when partner contributed the property to the partnership or the limited partnership used a partner's financial contribution to purchase the property. The assertion that the partnership owns the property is consistent with the entity theory or the idea that the limited partnership is a separate entity from its partners. *See Reid Road Mun. Util. Dist. No. 2 v. Speedy Stop Food Stores, Ltd.*, 337 S.W.3d 846, 855 (Tex.2011) (noting that the general partner of a limited partnership is not an owner of the limited partnership's property).

Texas Business Organization Code provisions

§ 154.002. Transfer of Interest in Partnership Property Prohibited. A partner does not have an interest that can be transferred, voluntarily or involuntarily, in partnership property.

North Cypress Med. Ctr. Oper. Co. v. St. Laurent
296 S.W.3d 171, 175-76 (Tex.App-Houston [14th Dist.] 2009, no pet.)

This consolidated appellate proceeding, consisting of an accelerated appeal and petition for writ of mandamus, arises from a doctor's attempts to prevent the sale of his profits-only ownership interest in a hospital's limited partnership. In the accelerated appeal, the partnership challenges a temporary injunction preventing the sale or transfer of the doctor's shares. The trial court that issued the temporary injunction also ordered the partnership to deposit the doctor's future distributions into the court's registry, prompting the partnership to seek mandamus relief from this Court. The doctor has not shown he has an inadequate remedy, at law, that is, that money damages would result in inadequate compensation for the loss of his profits-only share in the partnership. Thus, the record does not support a necessary finding that the doctor would suffer an irreparable injury but for the temporary injunction. Accordingly, we reverse the trial court's order granting a temporary injunction. We further hold that the record does not support a conclusion that disputed funds are likely to be lost or depleted, a necessary finding before a trial court may order a party to deposit money into the court's registry. Therefore, we conditionally grant the petition for writ of mandamus.

I. BACKGROUND

In January 2004, Matthew St. Laurent, M.D., the appellee/real party in interest, purchased four limited partnership shares, termed "units," in North Cypress Medical Center Operating Company, Ltd. (the "partnership"). Under the terms of the limited partnership agreement (the "Agreement"), St. Laurent was permitted to share in the partnership's net income and occasional distributions but had no right to manage or control the partnership's operation, business, or activities. The Agreement also provided that the partnership, "at its sole option," could sell St. Laurent's shares without his consent for a variety of reasons, including his breach of the Agreement. In November 2007, the partnership notified St. Laurent that he had breached the Agreement's non-competition clause and that it intended to sell his shares. He responded by filing suit against North Cypress for breach of contract, conversion, breach of fiduciary duty, and conspiracy to commit breach of fiduciary duty. He sought money damages in excess of $250,000, and also asked for the equitable remedy of an injunction preventing the sale of his shares. In February 2009, the trial court granted St. Laurent's request for a temporary injunction, thereby preventing the partnership from transferring or selling his shares. . . . In addition, the trial court ordered North Cypress to pay into the court's registry St. Laurent's portion of any future partnership distributions. . . .

II. TEMPORARY INJUNCTION

In the accelerated appeal, which we address first, North Cypress contends St. Laurent was not entitled to a temporary injunction because he failed to show that he would suffer an irreparable injury in the absence of injunctive relief. We agree. . . .

Here, St. Laurent contends that his partnership shares are "unique" such that money damages cannot fully compensate him for their loss. In the alternative, he suggests that the amount of such damages cannot be adequately measured. We will address each of these contentions, in turn.

"Uniqueness" of Profits–Only Limited Partnership Share

Generally, money damages may be inadequate to compensate an injured party for the loss of property deemed to be legally "unique" or irreplaceable. *See, e.g., Patrick v. Thomas*, No. 2–07–339–CV, 2008 WL 1932104, at *3 (Tex.App.-Fort Worth May 1, 2008, no pet.) (mem. op.) (discussing owner's sentimental, nonmonetary attachment to horses). The "uniqueness" rule is most commonly applied when the disputed property involves real estate. *See Lavigne v. Holder*, 186 S.W.3d 625, 629 (Tex.App.-Fort Worth 2006, no pet.); *In re Stark*, 126 S.W.3d 635, 640 (Tex. App.-Beaumont 2004, orig. proceeding [mand. denied]) ("We agree ... that every piece of real estate is unique and that its uniqueness may, in an injunction case, constitute some evidence of an irreparable injury."). Apparently hoping to invoke this common real-estate principle, St. Laurent claims that his partnership shares should be treated as an interest in real estate because one of the purposes of the partnership is to own and maintain a hospital, North Cypress Medical Center. We disagree. First, the limited partners, including St. Laurent, do not own the hospital real estate; only the partnership does. Second, under the Agreement, St. Laurent has no right to control the management or operation of the hospital. Instead, as a limited partner, St. Laurent's only interest in the hospital real estate is confined to whatever net income may be generated from the hospital's business.

Therefore, we are not persuaded that St. Laurent's attenuated connection to the physical plant of the hospital is sufficient to constitute a "unique" interest in real estate.

Limited Partnership: Financial Matters
Contributions

Texas Business Organization Code provisions

§ 153.201. Form of Contribution. The contribution of a partner may consist of a tangible or intangible benefit to the limited partnership or other property of any kind or nature, including:

 (1) cash;

 (2) a promissory note;

 (3) services performed;

 (4) a contract for services to be performed; and

 (5) another interest in or security of the limited partnership, another domestic or foreign limited partnership, or other entity.

§ 153.202. Enforceability of Promise to Make Contribution *writing + Signed.*

(a) A promise by a limited partner to make a contribution to, or pay cash or transfer other property to, a limited partnership is not enforceable unless the promise is in writing and signed by the limited partner.

(b) Except as otherwise provided by the partnership agreement, a partner or the partner's legal representative or successor is obligated to the limited partnership to perform an enforceable promise to make a contribution to or pay cash or transfer other property to a limited partnership, notwithstanding the partner's death, disability, or other change in circumstances.

Debt must be paid!!

(c) If a partner or a partner's legal representative or successor does not make a contribution or other payment of cash or transfer of other property required by the enforceable promise, whether as a contribution or with respect to a contribution previously made, that partner or the partner's legal representative or successor is obligated, at the option of the limited partnership, to pay to the partnership an amount of cash equal to the portion of the agreed value, as stated in the partnership agreement or in the partnership records required to be kept under Sections 153.551 and 153.552, of the contribution represented by the amount of cash that has not been paid or the value of the property that has not been transferred.

(d) A partnership agreement may provide that the partnership interest of a partner who fails to make a payment of cash or transfer of other property to the partnership, whether as a contribution or with respect to a contribution previously made, required by an enforceable promise is subject to specified consequences, which may include:

(1) a reduction of the defaulting partner's percentage or other interest in the limited partnership;

(2) subordination of the partner's partnership interest to the interest of non defaulting partners;

(3) a forced sale of the partner's partnership interest;

(4) forfeiture of the partner's partnership interest;

(5) the lending of money to the defaulting partner by other partners of the amount necessary to meet the defaulting partner's commitment;

(6) a determination of the value of the defaulting partner's partnership interest by appraisal or by formula and redemption or sale of the partnership interest at that value; or

(7) another penalty or consequence.

§ 153.203. Release of Obligation to Partnership. Unless otherwise provided by the partnership agreement, the obligation of a partner or the legal representative or successor of a partner to make a contribution, pay cash, transfer other property, or return cash or property paid or distributed to the partner in violation of this chapter or the partnership agreement may be compromised or released only by consent of all of the partners.

§ 153.204. Enforceability of Obligation

(a) Notwithstanding a compromise or release under Section 153.203, a creditor of a limited partnership who extends credit or otherwise acts in reasonable reliance on an obligation described by Section 153.203 may enforce the original obligation if:

(1) the obligation is reflected in a document signed by the partner; and

(2) the document is not amended or canceled to reflect the compromise or release.

(b) Notwithstanding the compromise or release, a general partner remains liable to persons other than the partnership and the other partners, as provided by Sections 153.152(a)(2) and (b).

Limited Partnership: Allocation of Profits and Losses

Unless otherwise agreed, profits and losses are allocated *pro rata*, that is, on the basis of the partners' contributions or percentage of holdings. This approach differs from the equal sharing rule or *per capita* approach of general partnerships. The approach is justifiable on the basis that since only the general partner in a limited partnership bears unlimited liability, it is appropriate for the investors to take this into account in allocating a larger portion of the profits to the general partner. Treating everybody the same makes better sense in the general partnership context where the partners are similarly situated in terms of liability. This default rule may be changed in either form of partnership where partners decide that their particular circumstances dictate a departure from the rule.

Texas Business Organization Code provisions

§ 153.206. Allocation of Profits and Losses

(a) The profits and losses of a limited partnership shall be allocated among the partners in the manner provided by a written partnership agreement.

(b) If a written partnership agreement does not provide for the allocation of profits and losses, the profits and losses shall be allocated:

(1) in accordance with the current percentage or other interest in the partnership stated in partnership records of the kind described by Section 153.551(a); or

(2) if the allocation of profits and losses is not provided for in partnership records of the kind described by Section 153.551(a), in proportion to capital accounts.

§ 153.154. Contributions by and Distributions to General Partner. *A general partner of a limited partnership may make a contribution to, be allocated profits and losses of, and receive a distribution from the limited partnership as a general partner, a limited partner, or both.*

§ 154.203. Distributions in Kind

(a) Except as provided by the partnership agreement, a partner, regardless of the nature of the partner's contribution, is not entitled to demand or receive from a partnership a distribution in any form other than cash.

(b) Except as provided by the partnership agreement, a partner may not be compelled to accept a disproportionate distribution of an asset in kind from a partnership to the extent that the percentage portion of assets distributed to the partner exceeds the percentage of those assets that equals the percentage in which the partner shares in distributions from the partnership.

Limited Partnership: Pass-through Taxation

Under federal law, a limited partnership is a pass-through entity for purposes of income taxation. Thus, like a general partnership, limited liability partnership, limited liability company, and S corporation, the entity does not pay a federal income tax. Instead, profits and losses flow through to the members who pay taxes on the portion of the profits allocated to them. Partners are also able to take advantage of business losses by deducting the losses when filing their tax returns. That way, the limited partnership's losses is used to shelter other income earned by partners from employment, another business or other sources. In a nutshell, limited partnerships are not subject to the double taxation that corporations generally face.

Limited Partnership: Imposition of Franchise Tax

For decades, limited partnerships operated in Texas without being assessed a franchise tax. This situation changed in 2008, when the limited partnership (except a limited partnership that meets the definition of a passive entity) was included in the list of business entities that are subject to the franchise tax in Texas. This development was unsuccessfully challenged in *In re Allcat Claims Serv., L.P.*, 356 S.W.3d 455 (Tex. 2011).

Limited Partnership: Liability

Liability of General Partners

The liability of a general partner in a limited partnership is similar to the liability of partners in a general partnership. [BOC §153.152 (a) (2); (b)]. The general partner is unlimitedly liable for the firm's obligations, including the tort of other general partners, employees or agents of the firm committed in the ordinary course of business. The liability of the general partner and the limited partnership is joint and several.

Texas Business Organization Code provisions

§ 153.152. General Powers and Liabilities of General Partner

(a) Except as provided by this chapter, the other limited partnership provisions, or a partnership agreement, a general partner of a limited partnership:

(1) has the rights and powers and is subject to the restrictions of a partner in a partnership without limited partners; and

(2) has the liabilities of a partner in a partnership without limited partners to the partnership and to the other partners.

(b) Except as provided by this chapter or the other limited partnership provisions, a general partner of a limited partnership has the liabilities of a partner in a partnership without limited partners to a person other than the partnership and the other partners.

The law permits a person to simultaneously occupy the positions of a general partner and limited partner in the same firm. As a general partner, he has the governing rights and the exposure to personal liability that are ascribed to that position. As a limited partner, he will be able to access any financial and voting rights that applicable law or the limited partnership agreement assigns to limited partners.

Texas Business Organization Code provisions

§ 153.153. Powers and Liabilities of Person Who is Both General Partner and Limited Partner. A person who is both a general partner and a limited partner:

(1) has the rights and powers and is subject to the restrictions and liabilities of a general partner; and

(2) except as otherwise provided by the partnership agreement, this chapter, or the other limited partnership provisions, has the rights and powers and is subject to the restrictions and liabilities, if any, of a limited partner to the extent of the general partner's participation in the partnership as a limited partner.

Shawell v. Pend Oreille Oil & Gas Co.
823 S.W.2d 336 (Tex.App.–Texarkana, 1991)

Randall Shawell sued Pend Oreille Oil & Gas Company for the breach of oil, gas and mineral contracts. Pend Oreille brought third-party actions against Amoco Production Company and CT Corporation System, Inc. and filed a cross-claim against Shawell, and Amoco filed counterclaims against Pend Oreille and Shawell. The trial court rendered summary judgment in favor of Pend Oreille against Shawell's claims and a take-nothing judgment on the third-party actions.

We must determine whether a general partner, who is sued individually and not in the capacity as a partner, can be held liable for partnership acts and whether there was a material issue of fact raised by the evidence. We conclude that the trial court did not err in granting the motion for summary judgment and therefore affirm.

Shawell and Pend Oreille, Ltd. entered into an agreement on July 15, 1976, whereby Shawell would obtain oil and gas leases and assign them to Pend Oreille, Ltd. An amendment to this agreement required Pend Oreille, Ltd. or its assigns to notify Shawell forty-five days before any expiration date for an oil and gas lease, if it elected not to maintain any lease acquired under the agreement. Amoco Production Company received mineral rights from Pend Oreille, Ltd. When the leases lapsed after Pend Oreille, Ltd. neglected to notify Shawell, Shawell filed this suit. Shawell sued Pend Oreille Oil & Gas Company based on the breach of the contract between Shawell and Pend Oreille, Ltd. Pend Oreille Oil & Gas Company was the general partner of Pend Oreille, Ltd. No allegations were made against Pend Oreille Oil & Gas Company in its capacity as the general partner of Pend Oreille, Ltd. Shawell did not attempt to amend his pleading, even when Pend Oreille Oil & Gas Company specially excepted to Shawell's pleadings, asserting that it signed no agreement. Shawell continued to name only Pend Oreille Oil & Gas Company as defendant. Shawell's pleadings do not refer to the partnership and do not allege that Pend Oreille Oil & Gas Company was being sued in its representative capacity as general partner. In an appeal from a summary judgment, we view the summary judgment evidence in the light most favorable to the nonmovant. Every fact which tends to oppose a summary judgment is taken is true, and every reasonable inference is indulged in favor of the nonmovant. *Wilcox v. St. Mary's Univ. of San Antonio*, 531 S.W.2d 589, 592–93 (Tex.1975). The moving party has the burden of establishing that there is no genuine issue of material fact concerning its claim and that it is entitled to judgment as a matter of law. *Town North Nat'l Bank v. Broaddus*, 569 S.W.2d 489, 494 (Tex.1978). With these guidelines in mind, we turn to the summary judgment evidence. . . .

A general partner is also personally liable for the debts and obligations of a limited partnership. TEX.REV.CIV.STAT.ANN. art. 6132a, § 10(a) (Vernon 1970). In pursuing such an action, the partners generally may be sued separately, or the partnership can be sued in its partnership name alone. *Martin v. First Republic Bank, Fort Worth*, 799 S.W.2d 482 (Tex.App.–Fort Worth 1990, writ denied). However, this presumes that suit has been brought against the partnership, or against a partner. In *Texaco, Inc. v. Wolfe*, Wolfe was sued for payment for products purchased by credit cards which had been issued to Wolfe Construction Company. *Texaco, Inc. v. Wolfe*, 601 S.W.2d 737 (Tex.Civ.App.—Houston [1st Dist.] 1980, writ ref'd n.r.e.). Wolfe had formerly been a partner with the company, but had dissolved the partnership. The court held that it was necessary for Texaco to have alleged that Wolfe was a partner before it could recover from him for action taken by the partnership. There, Texaco knew that Wolfe was a partner, but chose not to plead that. *Texaco, Inc. v. Wolfe*, 601 S.W.2d at 741–42.

Shawell chose to sue Pend Oreille Oil & Gas Company and not Pend Oreille, Ltd. Because Shawell's pleadings do not mention the partnership and do not allege that Pend Oreille Oil & Gas Company was being sued in its representative capacity, judgment could not have been rendered in Shawell's favor because the named defendant was not the other party to the contract. When an individual or business entity is sued under a contract in a different capacity from that under which he signed the contract, he cannot be held liable because there is no evidence that the particular individual or entity was liable for the debt. *Texaco, Inc. v. Wolfe*, 601 S.W.2d at 740;

West Texas Util. v. Pirtle, 444 S.W.2d 202 (Tex.Civ.App.—Eastland 1969, no writ). A defendant must complain about a defect in the parties before the case is called to trial. *Sunbelt Constr. Corp. v. S & D Mechanical Contractors, Inc.,* 668 S.W.2d 415, 418 (Tex.App.—Corpus Christi 1983, writ ref'd n.r.e.); *Allright, Inc. v. Burgard,* 666 S.W.2d 515 (Tex.App.—Houston [14th Dist.] 1983, writ ref'd n.r.e.); *Butler v. Joseph's Wine Shop, Inc.,* 633 S.W.2d 926, 929 (Tex.App.—Houston [14th Dist.] 1982, writ ref'd n.r.e.). Pend Oreille timely raised the defect in the parties both by special exceptions and by the motion for summary judgment. Shawell made no effort to amend his pleadings to include the correct company or to name the company actually sued in its capacity as general partner. The posture of the summary judgment evidence can be illustrated in the following manner. A sues B on a written contract. A produces a contract between A and C. In such a situation, B may successfully pursue a summary judgment. We conclude that the trial court properly granted summary judgment in favor of Pend Oreille Oil & Gas Company. Because of our disposition of Shawell's appeal, it is unnecessary for us to determine whether Pend Oreille Oil & Gas Company properly appealed from the trial court's disposition of its cross-actions against Amoco Production Company and CT Corporation System, Inc. Those questions are moot.

The judgment of the trial court is affirmed.

****

Shaw v. Kennedy, Ltd.
879 S.W.2d 240 (Tex.App.–Amarillo,1994)

Aggrieved by the take-nothing summary judgment rendered in his action to recover contract damages from Kennedy, Ltd., Jerbo/Kennedy Corp., and Jerry M. Reinsdorf, and to foreclose mechanic's and materialman's liens, M.A. Shaw, individually, and d/b/a Contractors Co-op. Co. and d/b/a 3–C Roofing Company, contends, by four points of error, that issues of material fact exist to vitiate the summary judgment. Disagreeing, we will affirm.

In the spring of 1989, storms damaged apartment complexes in Dallas, Texas, owned by Kennedy, Ltd., an Illinois limited partnership (Kennedy). Acting as "Director of Operations" for Kennedy, David R. Weinreb executed written contracts for repair of the complexes with Shaw, doing business as 3–C Roofing Company and as Contractors Co-op. Co., hereinafter referred to as Shaw. By the contract, Shaw would repair the complexes, and Kennedy would pay for the labor and materials. Shaw filed mechanic's and materialman's liens on the complexes repaired. When the balances owing on the contracts remained unpaid by Kennedy, Shaw filed a verified action, alleging breach of contract and quantum meruit, and seeking the monies alleged to be owed, foreclosure of the liens, and recovery of attorney's fees incurred. By its amended answer, Kennedy denied Shaw's allegations and asserted affirmative defenses and counterclaims against Shaw. Subsequently, Kennedy interpleaded, and counterclaimed against, Richard C. Christopher, citing his partnership with Shaw in 3–C Roofing, and alleging, as the basis for the necessity of joining him as a third-party defendant, that the claims asserted by him were the same as those asserted by Shaw.. . . By supplemental petition, Shaw included, and claimed against, Jerbo/Kennedy Corp., an Illinois corporation, and Jerry M. Reinsdorf, an individual, as general partners of Kennedy. In so doing, he alleged the identical claims of breach of contract and quantum meruit contained in his live petition against Kennedy, but he did not allege any separate causes of action against Jerbo and Reinsdorf individually. . . .

The court rendered partial summary judgment by granting Kennedy's motion. The order was rendered in accordance with the terms and provisions of the memorandums of settlement, and included an award of $5,000 to Kennedy as attorney's fees related to enforcing the agreements made. The order disposed of all claims and issues pertaining to Kennedy, Christopher, Shaw, 3-C Roofing, and Contractors. Reinsdorf and Jerbo likewise moved for summary judgment. By their live motion, they alleged that the partial summary judgment disposing of all their partner's (Kennedy's) interest effectually disposed of Shaw's claims, leaving no cognizable claims against them individually. This was so, they submitted, because the causes of action against them arose from the same transaction as the claims against Kennedy simply by virtue of their general partnership with Kennedy rather than from any personal involvement in the transactions. The trial court granted Jerbo and Reinsdorf's motion, ordering that Shaw take nothing against them. The court also determined that the memorandums of settlement were enforceable as provided in the partial summary judgment, which was incorporated into the judgment, thereby disposing of all parties and issues and rendering final judgment. *See Teer v. Duddlesten,* 664 S.W.2d 702, 703 (Tex.1984). In appealing from the summary judgment, Shaw contends that it was improper because questions of fact exist whether (1 & 2) conditions precedent were met, (3) Weinreb had authority to act for Kennedy, and (4) the summary judgment in favor of Jerbo and Reinsdorf was dependent upon the disposition made of Shaw's claims against Kennedy. We will address the contentions of error in logical consecution.

A movant is entitled to summary judgment if he establishes the absence of genuine issues of material fact and the right to judgment under those undisputed material facts, as a matter of law, on grounds expressly stated in the motion. *Delgado v. Burns,* 656 S.W.2d 428, 429 (Tex.1983). The movant, against whom all doubts are resolved, has the burden of establishing both elements. *City of Houston v. Clear Creek Basin Authority,* 589 S.W.2d 671, 678 (Tex.1979). The foundation of the summary judgment is attacked by Shaw's third-point-of-error contention that a question of fact exists whether Weinreb had authority to execute the memorandums of settlement and legally bind Kennedy. We do not agree.

Shaw had no quarrel with Weinreb's execution of the contracts obligating Kennedy to pay for repairs to the damaged complexes. Indeed, Shaw's original petition recites that service of process for Kennedy "may be had by serving Mr. David L. Weinreb, Director of Operations, Kennedy, Ltd," and states that demands for payment pursuant to the repair contracts were made on Weinreb. Moreover, Shaw not only sought to hold Kennedy liable through the agency of Weinreb, but he relied upon the authority of Weinreb during the mediation to effect a settlement of the controversy, never once contesting Weinreb's authority to act on behalf of Kennedy. Contrasting Shaw's unsupported statement that the "only entity authorized to execute documents on behalf of a limited partnership is the General Partner," we observe that the law of agency applies to limited partnerships such as Kennedy. Tex.Rev.Civ.Stat.Ann. art. 6132b § 4(3) (Vernon 1970).

It is well settled that a principal is liable for the acts of its agent; what a principal does through an agent, he does himself. *Nahm v. J.R. Fleming & Co.*, 116 S.W.2d 1174, 1176 (Tex.Civ.App.—Eastland 1938, no writ). Kennedy has not disputed Weinreb's authority to act on its behalf and, by the Heyden affidavit, Kennedy asserts Weinreb's actual authority to act as its agent. By holding himself out as Kennedy's agent, Weinreb may act for Kennedy so long as it is lawful, usual, and reasonably necessary for Kennedy to request him to act. *Megert v. Collard*, 266 S.W.2d 543, 545 (Tex.Civ.App.—Amarillo 1953, writ ref'd n.r.e.). Additionally, Shaw did not controvert Heyden's affidavit. Shaw's only response to Heyden's affidavit was his unsupported statement that Weinreb was not authorized to act for Kennedy because he was not a general partner of Kennedy. Such is insufficient to controvert Heyden's affidavit. *See City of Houston v. Clear Creek Basin Authority*, 589 S.W.2d at 677. By his final point of error, Shaw contends the final summary judgment was improper, because there were questions of fact whether the partial summary judgment disposed of all claims asserted against Jerbo and Reinsdorf. This is so, he submits, because a judgment against a partnership does not presume a judgment against the individual partners. *Cissne v. Robertson*, 782 S.W.2d 912, 927 (Tex.App.—Dallas 1989, writ denied); *Amarillo–Panhandle Development Corp. v. Ellis*, 10 S.W.2d 733, 735 (Tex.Civ.App.—Amarillo 1928, no writ). As general partners of Kennedy, Jerbo's and Reinsdorf's liability is governed by the Texas Uniform Partnership Act (the Act). Tex.Rev.Civ.Stat.Ann. art. 6132a–1 § 4.03 (Vernon Supp.1994). Under the Act, Jerbo and Reinsdorf are jointly and severally liable with each other and with Kennedy for obligations of the limited partnership. *Shawell v. Pend Oreille Oil & Gas Co.*, 823 S.W.2d 336, 337 (Tex.App.—Texarkana 1991, writ denied). However, the allegations against Jerbo and Reinsdorf, as general partners of Kennedy, were derivative of the liability pursued against Kennedy, and no allegations of individual liability by Jerbo and Reinsdorf were made. Thus, the take-nothing summary judgment rendered in favor of the partnership extinguished Shaw's claims against Jerbo and Reinsdorf as general partners. *Hammonds v. Holmes*, 559 S.W.2d 345, 347 (Tex.1977). Shaw's fourth point of error is overruled.

Accordingly, the judgment is affirmed.

Limited Partnership: Indemnification

Subject to the provisions of the certificate or formation or limited partnership agreement, the limited partnership may be required, and in some circumstances be permitted, to indemnify a general partner, or other qualifying person, for expenses incurred in defending himself in a lawsuit or other legal proceeding. Indemnification is mandatory if the general partner is wholly successful in defending the suit. Permissive indemnification occurs where the partner's defense was not wholly successful but the partner acted in good faith and for conduct that was in an official capacity, reasonably believed that the conduct was in the best interest of the partnership. In cases of conduct not in an official capacity, indemnification is permissible if the partner's conduct was not opposed to the partnership's best interest and in the case of a criminal proceeding, the partner had no reasonable cause to believe that the conduct was unlawful. Indemnification is prohibited if the general partner is found liable for willful or intentional misconduct in the performance of his duty to the partnership, breach of his duty of loyalty to the partnership, or an act or omission not committed in good faith that constitutes a breach of duty owed to the partnership.

Texas Business Organizations Code provisions

§ 8.003. Limitations in Governing Documents

(a) The certificate of formation of an enterprise may restrict the circumstances under which the enterprise must or may indemnify or may advance expenses to a person under this chapter.

(b) The written partnership agreement of a limited partnership may restrict the circumstances in the same manner as the certificate of formation under Subsection (a).

§ 8.051. Mandatory Indemnification

(a) An enterprise shall indemnify a governing person, former governing person, or delegate against reasonable expenses actually incurred by the person in connection with a proceeding in which the person is a respondent because the person is or was a governing person or delegate if the person is wholly successful, on the merits or otherwise, in the defense of the proceeding.

(b) A court that determines, in a suit for indemnification, that a governing person, former governing person, or delegate is entitled to indemnification under this section shall order indemnification and award to the person the expenses incurred in securing the indemnification.

§ 8.101. Permissive Indemnification

(a) An enterprise may indemnify a governing person, former governing person, or delegate who was, is, or is threatened to be made a respondent in a proceeding to the extent permitted by Section 8.102 if it is determined in accordance with Section 8.103 that:

(1) the person:

(A) acted in good faith;

(B) reasonably believed:

(i) in the case of conduct in the person's official capacity, that the person's conduct was in the enterprise's best interests; and

(ii) in any other case, that the person's conduct was not opposed to the enterprise's best interests; and

(C) in the case of a criminal proceeding, did not have a reasonable cause to believe the person's conduct was unlawful;

(2) with respect to expenses, the amount of expenses other than a judgment is reasonable; and

(3) indemnification should be paid.

(b) Action taken or omitted by a governing person or delegate with respect to an employee benefit plan in the performance of the person's duties for a purpose reasonably believed by the person to be in the interest of the participants and beneficiaries of the plan is for a purpose that is not opposed to the best interests of the enterprise.

(c) Action taken or omitted by a delegate to another enterprise for a purpose reasonably believed by the delegate to be in the interest of the other enterprise or its owners or members is for a purpose that is not opposed to the best interests of the enterprise.

(d) A person does not fail to meet the standard under Subsection (a)(1) solely because of the termination of a proceeding by:

(1) judgment;

(2) order;

(3) settlement;

(4) conviction; or

(5) a plea of nolo contendere or its equivalent.

§ 8.102. General Scope of Permissive Indemnification

(a) Subject to Subsection (b), an enterprise may indemnify a governing person, former governing person, or delegate against:

(1) a judgment; and

(2) expenses, other than a judgment, that are reasonable and actually incurred by the person in connection with a proceeding.

(b) Indemnification under this subchapter of a person who is found liable to the enterprise or is found liable because the person improperly received a personal benefit:

(1) is limited to reasonable expenses actually incurred by the person in connection with the proceeding;

(2) does not include a judgment, a penalty, a fine, and an excise or similar tax, including an excise tax assessed against the person with respect to an employee benefit plan; and

(3) may not be made in relation to a proceeding in which the person has been found liable for:

(A) *wilful or intentional misconduct in the performance of the person's duty to the enterprise;*

(B) *breach of the person's duty of loyalty owed to the enterprise; or*

(C) *an act or omission not committed in good faith that constitutes a breach of a duty owed by the person to the enterprise.*

(c) *A governing person, former governing person, or delegate is considered to have been found liable in relation to a claim, issue, or matter only if the liability is established by an order, including a judgment or decree of a court, and all appeals of the order are exhausted or foreclosed by law.*

Limited Partnership: Liability of Limited Partners
Control Rule

The limited partner is not liable for firm obligations beyond her investment. This limited liability protection is lost if the limited partner participates in the control of the business and a third party detrimentally relies on the limited partner's conduct, reasonably believing that the limited partner was a general partner. Section 153 contains the traditional version of the control rule and the reliance requirement that was introduced in later statutory amendments across the country to ameliorate the effects of the control rule and thereby engender an appreciable measure of certainty in business relations.

Texas Business Organization Code provisions

§ 153.102. Liability to Third Parties

(a) *A limited partner is not liable for the obligations of a limited partnership unless:*

(1) *the limited partner is also a general partner; or*

(2) *in addition to the exercise of the limited partner's rights and powers as a limited partner, the limited partner participates in the control of the business.*

(c) *If the limited partner participates in the control of the business, the limited partner is liable only to a person who transacts business with the limited partnership reasonably believing, based on the limited partner's conduct, that the limited partner is a general partner.*

Safe Harbor

Texas Limited Partnership Law contains a non-exclusive list of activities which are excluded from the definition of participation in control. These activities are referred to as "safe harbors." Humphreys v. Medical Towers, Ltd., 893 F.Supp. 672, 688 (S.D. Tex. 1995), *aff'd*, 100 F.3d 952 (5th Cir. 1996). A prominent and somewhat contentious safe harbor provision pertains to the absence of liability for the directing minds and active hands behind entities such as corporations, limited liability companies or general partnerships that occupy the position of general partner of a limited partnership. Limited partners may simultaneously participate in control (albeit indirectly) and enjoy limited liability protection by serving as directors, officers or shareholders of a corporate general partner. Assume that 2 investors want to establish Elite, L.P. The partners do not want to be personally liable for the debts and obligations of the business. They decide to designate their existing corporation (or form a new one) as the general partner. The partners occupy leadership positions in the corporation. Through the corporation, they indirectly run the limited partnership, since the general partner, being a corporate entity would need to act through human beings.

Texas Business Organization Code provisions

§ 153.103. Actions Not Constituting Participation in Business for Liability Purposes. For purposes of this section and Sections 153.102, 153.104, and 153.105, a limited partner does not participate in the control of the business because the limited partner has or has acted in one or more of the following capacities or possesses or exercises one or more of the following powers:

(1) acting as:

(A) a contractor for or an officer or other agent or employee of the limited partnership;

(B) a contractor for or an agent or employee of a general partner;

(C) an officer, director, or stockholder of a corporate general partner;

(D) a partner of a partnership that is a general partner of the limited partnership; or

(E) a member or manager of a limited liability company that is a general partner of the limited partnership;

(2) acting in a capacity similar to that described in Subdivision (1) with any other person that is a general partner of the limited partnership;

(3) consulting with or advising a general partner on any matter, including the business of the limited partnership;

(4) acting as surety, guarantor, or endorser for the limited partnership, guaranteeing or assuming one or more specific obligations of the limited partnership, or providing collateral for borrowings of the limited partnership;

(5) calling, requesting, attending, or participating in a meeting of the partners or the limited partners;

(6) winding up the business of a limited partnership under Chapter 11 and Subchapter K of this chapter;

(7) taking an action required or permitted by law to bring, pursue, settle, or otherwise terminate a derivative action in the right of the limited partnership;

(8) serving on a committee of the limited partnership or the limited partners; or

(9) proposing, approving, or disapproving, by vote or otherwise, one or more of the following matters:

(A) the winding up or termination of the limited partnership;

(B) an election to reconstitute the limited partnership or continue the business of the limited partnership;

(C) the sale, exchange, lease, mortgage, assignment, pledge, or other transfer of, or granting of a security interest in, an asset of the limited partnership;

(D) the incurring, renewal, refinancing, or payment or other discharge of indebtedness by the limited partnership;

(E) a change in the nature of the business of the limited partnership;

(F) the admission, removal, or retention of a general partner;

(G) the admission, removal, or retention of a limited partner;

(H) a transaction or other matter involving an actual or potential conflict of interest;

(I) an amendment to the partnership agreement or certificate of formation;

(J) if the limited partnership is qualified as an investment company under the federal Investment Company Act of 1940, as amended, any matter required by that Act or the rules and regulations of the Securities and Exchange Commission under that Act, to be approved by the holders of beneficial interests in an investment company, including:

(i) electing directors or trustees of the investment company;

(ii) approving or terminating an investment advisory or underwriting contract;

(iii) approving an auditor; and

(iv) acting on another matter that that Act requires to be approved by the holders of beneficial interests in the investment company;

(K) indemnification of a general partner under Chapter 8 or otherwise;

(L) any other matter stated in the partnership agreement;

(M) the exercising of a right or power granted or permitted to limited partners under this code and not specifically enumerated in this section; or

(N) the merger, conversion, or interest exchange with respect to a limited partnership.

§ 153.104. Enumeration of Actions Not Exclusive. The enumeration in Section 153.103 does not mean that a limited partner who has acted or acts in another capacity or possesses or exercises another power constitutes participation by that limited partner in the control of the business of the limited partnership.

§ 153.105. Creation of Rights. Sections 153.103 and 153.104 do not create rights of limited partners. Rights of limited partners may be created only by:

    (1) the certificate of formation;

    (2) the partnership agreement;

    (3) other sections of this chapter; or

    (4) the other limited partnership provisions.

Delaney v. Fidelity Lease Limited
517 S.W.2d 420 (Tex.Civ.App. 1974)

This is a suit by a landlord for damages for breach of a lease contract with the defendants being the lessee, Fidelity Lease Limited, a limited partnership, Interlease Corporation, which is a corporation and the only general partner of Fidelity Lease Limited, and the twenty-two limited partners of Fidelity Lease Limited. The suit also seeks to hold certain of the limited partners personally liable as general partners. The trial Court granted summary judgment in favor of the limited partners in a severed cause in which all limited partners appear only as to their personal liability. The appeal concerns the question whether a limited partner in a limited partnership becomes liable as a general partner when he also participates as an active officer, director and shareholder of a corporation which is the sole general partner of the limited partnership. We affirm the judgment of the trial Court which held that the limited partner did not become liable as a general partner solely because of his participating in the affairs of the corporation as an officer, director or stockholder.

Fidelity Lease Limited is a limited partnership organized under the Statutes of the State of Texas. The general partner within Fidelity Lease Limited is Interlease Corporation, a Texas corporation. Among the limited partners of Fidelity Lease Limited were W. S. Crombie, Jr., William Sanders and Alan Kahn, who were also respectively the active President, Vice-President and Treasurer, as well as directors and stockholders of Interlease Corporation, the general partner of the limited partnership. In February of 1969, the plaintiffs, as lessor, entered into the lease with 'FIDELITY LEASE, LTD., a limited partnership acting by and through INTERLEASE CORPORATION, General Partner, * * * hereinafter called 'LESSEE,' * * *.' The lease was executed by the lessee, Fidelity Lease, Ltd., by the General Partner, Interlease Corporation, by W. S. Crombie, Jr., President. The acknowledgment to the lease is by W. S. Crombie, Jr., as President of Interlease Corporation, who acknowledged to the notary that the same was the act of said Interlease Corporation and that he executed the same as the act of the corporation and in the capacity therein stated. The lessors proceeded to erect on the premises a fast food service restaurant as called for by the lease and it is the plaintiffs' contention that thereafter Fidelity

Lease Limited failed to take possession of the premises as required and has paid none of the rental thereon. The suit for the breach of the lease joins as defendants the limited partnership of Fidelity Lease Limited, its general partner Interlease Corporation, and all of its limited partners among whom appear W. S. Crombie, Jr., Alan Kahn and William Sanders. ...It is alleged that these three limited partners have become liable as general partners because they had participated in the management and control of the business of the limited partnership. . . . This one point presented to us on this appeal is to the effect that the trial Court erred in granting the motion for summary judgment 'because there exists a genuine material issue of mixed fact and law as to whether the limited partners W. S. Crombie, Jr., William Sanders and Alan Kahn participated in the management and control of the business of Fidelity Lease Limited to the extent necessary to impose personal liability upon them, and the ruling of the trial court constituted an incorrect conclusion of law to the effect that such participation in the management and control of the business of the limited partnership by Appellees in their respective capacities within the corporate general partner does not subject them individually to liability*as general partners * * *.' An examination of the entire record reveals that the trial Court granted the summary judgment only upon the matter contained in the Appellants' one point. . . . It is permissible in this State to form a limited partnership where a corporation is the only general partner, provided that the purpose to be carried out by the limited partnership is lawful. Port Arthur Trust Company v. Muldrow, 155 Tex. 612, 291 S.W.2d 312 (1956); 19 Hamilton, Texas Business Organizations s 212, p. 196. While the Port Arthur Trust Company case had before it only the question of the corporation entering the limited partnership as a limited partner, the Court in no uncertain language decided that a corporation was a 'person' within the meaning of Texas law and placed no restriction as to a corporation entering the limited partnership as a general partner. There is no logical reason why it can not, and since that opinion the Secretary of State has accepted the corporate general partner in the limited partnership. 24 Sw.L.J . 285.

The Texas Uniform Limited Partnership Act, Art. 6132a, Tex.Rev.Civ.Stat.Ann., provides for the formation and operation of limited partnerships. Generally, the limited partnership is a business form intermediate between a partnership and a corporation. It consists of general partners who have all the rights, duties and obligations of partners in an ordinary partnership and limited partners whose positions are somewhat akin to shareholders in a corporation. The general partners conduct the business and are personally liable to creditors. The liability of limited partners on the partnership obligations is limited to the amount of their contributions. They do not participate in management of the limited partnership on pain of losing their limited liability. 19 Hamilton, Texas Business Organizations s 211. It is the extent of the reach of the prohibition contained in the Statute that determines this appeal. Art. 6132a, Sec. 8, states 'A limited partner shall not become liable as a general partner unless, in addition to the exercise of his rights and powers as a limited partner, he takes part in the control of the business.' If the language of this Statute is all controlling in importance then the Appellants are correct and the three questioned limited partners have become personally liable to the creditors of the limited partnership. On the other hand, if this dispute is approached from our basic notions of corporations, then no liability exists. In corporate law, it is fundamental that the shareholder, officer or director is ordinarily protected from personal liability arising from the activities of the corporation. 'This insulation from personal liability is said to be the natural consequence of the incorporation process, and is supported by the theory or 'fiction' that incorporation results in the creation of an 'entity' separate and distinct from the individual shareholders.' Sutton v. Reagan &

Gee, 405 S.W.2d 828 (Tex.Civ.App.—San Antonio 1966, writ ref'd n.r.e.). From this corporate viewpoint, limited liability is the rule rather than the exception. It is only in the exceptional situation where a court will 'pierce the corporate veil' or where some of the other well-known adjectives are used to describe the process calling for the creation of personal liability. Some six exceptions are described in Pacific American Gasoline Co. of Texas v. Miller, 76 S.W.2d 833 (Tex.Civ.App.—Amarillo 1934, writ ref'd), and one of the exceptions might be urged here, i.e., the corporate structure is being used as a vehicle for circumventing the terms of Art. 6132a, Sec. 8. Professor Hamilton, in his work at s 234, makes an analysis of the problem and he argues strongly against the creation of any personal liability where the facts are similar to those that are now before us. Where there has been a voluntary dealing between businessmen which has resulted in the execution of a contract, the plaintiff has dealt in some way with the corporation and should be aware that the corporation lacks substance. In the absence of some sort of deception, the creditor more or less assumes the risk of loss when he deals with the corporate 'shell.' If he were concerned, he should have insisted that some solvent third person guarantee the performance by the corporation. 'In contract cases the separate existence of a minimally capitalized corporation should usually be recognized. * * * if a person knowingly deals with an undercapitalized corporation he is, in effect, assuming the risk of loss if the transaction does not work out. If the person does not wish to take this risk, he should insist that the shareholders themselves enter into the contract or personally guarantee performance by the corporation. Indeed, transactions are often entered into in the name of a shell corporation precisely because the shareholders do not wish to assume personal liability. * * * When the parties themselves are apportioning the risk of loss through their relative bargaining power, there is no reason for a court to disturb this allocation of risk.' Hamilton, supra, pp. 228—229. The leading Texas Supreme Court case that reflects this attitude is Bell Oil & Gas Company v. Allied Chemical Corporation, 431 S.W.2d 336 (Tex.1968). As far as we or the parties have determined the point before us is of first impression. Certain cases in other jurisdictions have passed on statutes identical to our §8 of our Limited Partnership Act. The case of Holzman v. DeEscamilla, 86 Cal.App.2d 858, 195 P.2d 833 (4th Dist., 1948), is the leading case where a court imposed general liability on limited partners because of their participation in the control of the business of truck farming. The limited partners directed which crops were to be planted, signed the partnership checks without the consent of the general partner, required the general partner to resign as manager, and secured his successor. The Court held that the activities clearly showed that they took part in the control of the business and became liable as general partners. In certain other cases, the courts have refused to impose general liability on the limited partners merely because they had an interest and did participate to a limited extent in the affairs of the partnership. In Silvola v. Rowlett, 129 Colo. 522, 272 P.2d 287 (1954), the limited partner, as foreman in the repair shop of an automobile sales company, merely by making suggestions and expressing opinions as to the advisability of transactions, did not become liable as a general partner. In Rathke v. Griffith, 36 Wash.2d 394, 218 P.2d 757 (1950), the limited partner was named to the board of directors of the limited partnership. He never functioned as a director and because of his lack of actual participation and control was held not liable as a general partner. Two other cases have held that the lack of actual participation in the management and control did not create any general liability regardless of certain limited activities in the partnership. Plasteel Products Corporation v. Helman, 271 F.2d 354 (1st Cir. 1950); Grainger v. Antoyan, 48 Cal.2d 805, 313 P.2d 848 (1957). One case does touch somewhat upon the problem. That is, Bergeson v. Life Insurance Corporation of America, 170 F.Supp. 150 (D.Utah 1958), modified 265 F.2d

227 (10th Cir. 1959), cert. denied, 360 U.S .932, 79 S.Ct. 1452, 3 L.Ed.2d 1545. There the limited partnership was formed for the sole purpose of organizing and owning a corporation and the limited partners became directors of the corporation and therefore participated in the management. One alternative reason advanced by the trial Court for holding general liability was the terms of the statute on control. That case can well be limited to its facts as there was considerable evidence of fraudulent conduct on the part of the participants in the business. Regardless, the point was not passed on by the Circuit Court of Appeals. These cases do not attempt to state a general standard for determining when the control test is met and are limited to their specific facts. One writer points out that no satisfactory standard of 'control' has ever been enunciated though the Uniform Limited Partnership Act is over fifty years old. He suggests that the Act itself is due for an overhaul which would clarify the meaning of the control test. Alan Feldt, 82 Harvard L.Rev. 1471. Admittedly, the decision in the case before us is not free from doubt. The logical reason to hold a limited partner to general liability under the control prohibition of the Statute is to prevent third parties from mistakenly assuming that the limited partner is a general partner and to rely on his general liability. However, it is hard to believe that a creditor would be deceived where he knowingly deals with a general partner which is a corporation. That in itself is a creature specifically devised to limit liability. The fact that certain limited partners are stockholders, directors or officers of the corporation is beside the point where the creditor is not deceived. The evidence is that the three limited partners did not control Fidelity Lease Limited. It was controlled by its sole general partner, the corporate entity of Interlease Corporation. . . .

In *Delaney v. Fidelity Lease Ltd.*, 526 S.W.2d 543 (Tex. 1975), the Texas Supreme Court rejected the lower court's position and the idea of limited liability for limited partners that are also officers, directors or shareholders of the corporate general partner, viewing it as a circumvention of the law. The State Legislature disagreed with the Supreme Court and opted to approve the approach as part of the safe harbor. *See Isaminger v. Gibbs*, 2000 WL 89886 (Tex.App.2000).

Erroneous Belief

A limited partner also faces liability if she is listed as a general partner in the certificate of formation, even if her intention was to invest in the firm as a limited partner only. TBOC mitigates such harsh result by allowing the limited partner to effect an amendment of the certification to reflect her real interest within a reasonable time or to withdraw from the limited partnership entirely. Prior to corrective action being taken, the erroneously identified limited partner is liable to a third party who transacts business with the limited partnership if the "limited partner" had knowledge or notice that no certificate has been filed or that the certificate inaccurately referred to her as a general partner; and the third party reasonably believed, based on the "limited partner's" conduct, that she was a general partner at the time of the transaction and extended credit to the partnership in reasonable reliance on her credit.

Texas Business Organization Code provisions

§ 153.106. Erroneous Belief of Contributor Being Limited Partner. Except as provided by Section 153.109, a person who erroneously but in good faith believes that the person has made a contribution to and has become a limited partner in a limited partnership is not liable as a general partner or otherwise obligated because of making or attempting to make the contribution, receiving distributions from the partnership, or exercising the rights of a limited partner if, within a reasonable time after ascertaining the mistake, the person:

(1) causes an appropriate certificate of formation or certificate of amendment to be signed and filed;

(2) files or causes to be filed with the secretary of state a written statement in accordance with Section 153.107; or

(3) withdraws from participation in future profits of the enterprise by executing and filing with the secretary of state a certificate declaring the person's withdrawal under this section.

§ 153.107. Statement Required for Liability Protection

(a) A written statement filed under Section 153.106(2) must be entitled "Filing under Section 153.106(2), Business Organizations Code," and contain:

(1) the name of the partnership;

(2) the name and mailing address of the person signing the written statement; and

(3) a statement that:

(A) the person signing the written statement acquired a limited partnership interest in the partnership;

(B) the person signing the written statement has made an effort to cause a general partner of the partnership to file an accurate certificate of formation required by the code and the general partner has failed or refused to file the certificate; and

(C) the statement is being filed under Section 153.106(2) and the person signing the written statement is claiming status as a limited partner of the partnership named in the document.

(b) The statement is effective for 180 days.

(c) A statement filed under Section 153.106(2) may be signed by more than one person claiming limited partnership status under this section and Sections 153.106, 153.108, and 153.109.

§ 153.108. Requirements for Liability Protection Following Expiration of Statement

(a) If a certificate described by Section 153.106(1) has not been filed before the expiration of the 180-day period described by Section 153.107(b), the person filing the *statement has no further protection from liability under Section 153.106(2) unless the person complies with this section. To be protected under Section 153.106 the person must, not later than the 10th day after the date of expiration of the 180-day period:*

(1) withdraw under Section 153.106(3); or

(2) bring an action under Section 153.554 to compel the execution and filing of a certificate of formation or amendment.

(b) If an action is brought within the applicable period and is diligently prosecuted to conclusion, the person bringing the action continues to be protected from liability under Section 153.106(2) until the action is finally decided adversely to that person.

(c) This section and Sections 153.106, 153.107, and 153.109 do not protect a person from liability that arises under Sections 153.102-153.105.

§ 153.109. Liability of Erroneous Contributor. *Regardless of whether Sections 153.106, 153.107, and 153.108 apply, a person who makes a contribution in the circumstances described by Section 153.106 is liable as a general partner to a third party who transacts business with the partnership before an action taken under Section 153.106 if:*

(1) the contributor has knowledge or notice that no certificate has been filed or that the certificate inaccurately referred to the contributor as a general partner; and

(2) the third party reasonably believed, based on the contributor's conduct, that the contributor was a general partner at the time of the transaction and extended credit to the partnership in reasonable reliance on the credit of the contributor.

Limited Partnership: Fiduciary Duties

General Partner

A general partner owes the duties of care and loyalty to the limited partnership and the limited partners. *See Graham Mortg. Corp. v. Hall*, 307 S.W.3d 472, 479 (Tex. App. Dallas 2010) (holding that a general partner of a limited partnership owes a fiduciary duty to the limited partners). The TBOC omits the word "fiduciary" from the duties owed by general partners. *See Red Sea Gaming, Inc. v. Block Investments (Nevada) Co.*, 2010 WL 108155 (Tex. App. El Paso 2010), review denied, (Apr. 1, 2011) (noting that Texas Uniform Partnership Act does not use the word "fiduciary" in describing duties). However, there is good indication that the courts will continue to view and refer to these duties as fiduciary in nature. *See e.g. Wilson v. Cantwell*, 2007 WL 2285947 (N.D. Tex. 2007). It is a breach of the duty of loyalty, for instance, for a partner to engage in self-dealing. Self-dealing or conflict of transactions are those in which a partner is on both sides of the same deal – acting on behalf of the partnership while also acting for himself or another entity in which he has an interest. Examples include being a landlord of a building of which the partnership is a tenant or lending money to the partnership. Where there is conflict of interest, the general partner is required to resolve the conflict in favor of the partnership. It is arguable that fair self-dealing by a general partner is permissible where the

partnership comes first.

limited partnership or its partners are not harmed. Under pre-BOC case law, the duty against self-dealing subsists even when the general partner's self-dealing did not harm the limited partners. *See* Crenshaw v. Swenson, 611 S.W.2d 886, 890–91 (Tex. App.—Austin 1980, writ ref'd n.r.e.). Self-dealing is usually permissible if disclosed to other partners and they consent to it. The duty of loyalty also encompasses an obligation to refrain from competing with the partnership, appropriating or usurping business opportunities that belong to the partnership, or using partnership property for nonpartnership purposes. The general partner also owes a duty of care, which is a duty to act with the care that an ordinarily prudent person would exercise in similar circumstances. The duty of care is breached if the conduct in question is grossly negligent, reckless or intentional. The general partners' duties do not exist at the formation stage but exist only during the conduct and winding up of the partnership business. *See* TBOC §§ 152.205, 152.206. Partners may not eliminate the duties of loyalty and care by agreement. However, the duties of loyalty and care may be contractually varied by the partners, provided the variation is not manifestly unreasonable. In addition to the duties of care and loyalty, a general partner also has an obligation to discharge the duties imposed under the statute or the partnership agreement and exercise any rights and powers in the conduct or winding up of the business in good faith and in a manner reasonably believed to be in the best interest of the partnership. This obligation is not necessarily a separate duty but speaks to a standard for discharging a partner's statutory or contractual duties. The obligation to discharge duties in good faith may not be completely eliminated contractually. Further, partners have a right to information regarding the partnership's records but there is no clear provision on whether there is a duty on a partner to disclose information without request. Such a duty may be found and sustained under the common law. In *Zinda v. McCann St., Ltd.*, 178 S.W.3d 883 (Tex. App.—Texarkana 2005, pet. denied), the court held that partners in a general partnership owed each other a duty to make full disclosure of all matters relating to the partnership. The partner's right of access to partnership's books and records may not be unreasonably restricted.

A United States Bankruptcy Court has observed that Texas partnership law was changed to specify fiduciary duties in precise terms and to reject the idea of a partner being analogous to a trustee but added that changes in partnership law "expunging the fiduciary concept as to partners in their capacities as mere partners" do not appear to have "expunged the concept of a managing general partner being a fiduciary." That being the case, a managing general partner's control creates an "express trust." Accordingly, a chapter 7 bankruptcy proceeding did not discharge liability under Bankruptcy Code § 523(a)(4). *In re Jones*, 445 B.R. 677 (Bankr. N.D. Tex. 2011).

Limited Partnership: Officers or Managers of Entity General Partner
By extension, the president and chief operating officer of a corporate general partner also owes a fiduciary duty to the limited partnership. In general, under Texas law, a fiduciary is not permitted to place herself in a position where it would be for her own benefit to violate her duty

to administer the affairs of the partnership solely for the benefit of the partnership. *See In re Harwood*, 637 F.3d 615 (5th Cir. 2011).

Huges v. St. David's Support Corp.
944 S.W.2d 423, (Tex. App.- Austin, 1997)

This appeal presents us with the question of whether a general partner owes a fiduciary duty of notice to its limited partners when it sells assets under its control. Because we conclude that such a duty exists, we will reverse the trial court's summary judgment and remand the cause for a trial on the merits.

BACKGROUND

The St. David's Health Care System, Inc., (the "System") is a nonprofit corporation that operates St. David's Medical Center in Austin, a complex that includes St. David's Hospital. The System is the sole shareholder of appellee, St. David's Support Corporation ("St. David's"), another nonprofit corporation. In the early 1980's, the Board of Trustees of the System began considering an expansion of the hospital's facilities and services, known as the East Campus Project. Included in this project were plans for the construction of two new hospitals—a psychiatric hospital and a nursing and rehabilitation hospital. Upon learning of the East Campus project, Alfred Hughes approached the St. David's System proposing to arrange financing for the construction and operation of the new East Campus facilities. Under his proposal, Hughes and his affiliates would form (1) a master limited partnership, interests of which would be sold to the public, and (2) operating partnerships, interests of which would be sold to physicians. The master partnership would fund the construction of the East Campus facilities and then lease them to the operating partnerships, which would actually operate the two East Campus hospitals. In 1986, the System's Board of Trustees accepted Hughes's proposal, and Hughes began implementing it. By September of 1987, however, the System had become dissatisfied with Hughes's financing efforts. Therefore, it decided to take over the development of the East Campus Project.

Although the System retained Hughes's proposed organizational structure of master and operating partnerships, it financed the construction of the East Campus facilities through the sale of bonds. To compensate Hughes for his endeavors, the System paid Hughes $425,000. As additional compensation, it gave Hughes and his affiliates (the "Hughes appellants") what it described at oral argument as a "royalty interest" in the operating partnerships of the two new East Campus hospitals. We find this description fitting. The Hughes appellants obtained this "royalty interest" through the creation of an intricate series of interlocking partnerships. The main controlling partnership was called St. David's East Campus, Ltd. ("East Campus, Ltd."). The Hughes appellants owned forty-nine percent of this partnership and were limited partners; conversely, St. David's owned fifty-one percent of the partnership and served as its general partner. The two East Campus hospitals were each, in turn, operated by limited partnerships—St. David's Psychiatric Center, Ltd., and St. David's Rehabilitation and Nursing Center, Ltd. (collectively the "operating partnerships"). Physicians were to be the limited partners of both of these partnerships. East Campus, Ltd., served as general partner of the operating partnerships and retained a one percent interest in each of them. Thus, the Hughes appellants owned an infinitesimal part—less than one-half of one percent—but a part nonetheless, of the operating partnerships.

In 1991, a problem arose concerning the operation of the two East Campus hospitals. New Medicare regulations restricted physicians' ability to participate in entities that own hospital facilities to which those physicians refer patients. St. David's, as general partner of East Campus, Ltd., determined that the operating partnerships were potentially in violation of these regulations and devised a solution to this problem: it would sell all operating partnership assets and then dissolve both operating partnerships. St. David's discussed this solution in a series of meetings with the physician limited partners of the operating partnerships and decided to follow this course of action. It is undisputed in the record, however, that St. David's did not give the Hughes appellants notice of the impending sale or dissolutions. St. David's candidly admitted at oral argument that the reason it did not give the Hughes appellants prior notice was because it was concerned they might impede or possibly stop the sale and dissolution of operating partnerships.

St. David's did not want anything to interfere with this sale because it was convinced that continuing to operate the hospitals with physician partners was a violation of Medicare regulations. From the record, it appears St. David's did not hold the assets out for public bid; instead, it bought the assets itself through private sale. Following the sale, St. David's dissolved the operating partnerships. It then dissolved the master partnership, East Campus, Ltd., and paid the Hughes appellants $19,765, which comprised their approximate one-half of one percent share of the sale proceeds. The Hughes appellants were of the opinion that St. David's should have notified them of the sale and dissolution and given them an opportunity to participate in the sale. Accordingly, they sued St. David's for breach of fiduciary duty. St. David's claimed it was not required to give notice and, therefore, breached no duty. Both parties moved for summary judgment, and the trial court's final judgment granted St. David's motion. The Hughes appellants bring this appeal, challenging the trial court's summary judgment in seven points of error.

DISCUSSION

The touchstone issue in this appeal is whether St. David's owed the Hughes appellants a fiduciary duty that would have included a duty to notify them of the proposed sale of the operating partnerships' assets. We conclude it did. It is well established that partners are charged with a fiduciary duty. Furthermore, in a limited partnership, the general partner stands in the same fiduciary capacity to the limited partners as a trustee stands to the beneficiaries of a trust. Based on this authority, it is clear St. David's, the general partner of East Campus, Ltd., owed the Hughes appellants, limited partners of East Campus, Ltd., a fiduciary duty. St. David's contends, however, that even if it owed the Hughes appellants a fiduciary duty, it had no duty to notify them of the asset sale because they were limited partners in East Campus, Ltd., and their ownership interest in the operating partnerships was infinitesimal.

While we agree that the Hughes appellants' ownership interest was small, we conclude that they were at least entitled to notice before the operating partnership assets were sold. Among the duties that a partner owes its co-partners is the duty of "full disclosure of all matters affecting the partnership." In a limited partnership, the general partner owes the same duty of full disclosure to the limited partners. Accordingly, St. David's as general partner was required to disclose all material facts affecting East Campus, Ltd., to its limited partners, the Hughes appellants. As noted above, the Hughes appellants' interest in the operating partnerships was similar to a royalty interest. We believe this analogy is significant because a limited partner holding a royalty interest is certainly entitled to notice *before* the general partner sells the underlying assets that generate the royalty interest. We also believe that it is highly significant that the Hughes appellants were the only party involved in the sale and dissolutions that did not receive prior notice. Even the limited partners of the operating partnerships were given such notice. Further, all partnerships involved in the sale of operating partnership assets, including East Campus, Ltd., executed the sale documents. The Hughes appellants, however, did not sign any of these documents. St. David's argues that, as general partner, it was empowered to execute these documents on behalf of East Campus, Ltd. Unquestionably, St. David's did have this power. However, based upon the foregoing authority and discussion, we hold that the Hughes appellants were entitled to notice before St. David's exercised this power.

CONCLUSION

Because St. David's owed the Hughes appellants a fiduciary duty and because it breached that duty by failing to give them prior notice of the sale of the operating partnerships' assets, we reverse the trial court's summary judgment and remand the cause to the district court for a trial on the merits.

****

In Re Harwood
637 F.3D 615 (5th Cir. 2011)

David S. Harwood, a Chapter 7 debtor, appeals the district court's order affirming the bankruptcy court's ruling that certain of his debts are nondischargeable under 11 U.S.C. § 523(a)(4). He challenges the bankruptcy court's determination that his debts—loans obtained from a limited partnership that Harwood managed in his capacity as officer and director of the partnership's corporate general partner—were incurred through defalcation while acting as a fiduciary to the partnership. Because we agree that Harwood wilfully neglected a duty owed to the partnership in connection with the loans, we affirm the judgment of the district court affirming the judgment of the bankruptcy court.

I. BACKGROUND

We summarize the relevant facts here, providing greater detail as relevant to our analysis of the issues presented in this appeal. In 1991, Harwood, along with Wayne McKinney, purchased B & W Finance, a consumer lending business. In 1996, B & W Finance reorganized into a Texas limited partnership, FNFS, Ltd. ("FNFS"). All consumer lending operations were transferred into FNFS. A newly-created subchapter S corporation, B & W Finance Co., Inc. ("B & W"), served as the sole general partner of FNFS. McKinney and Harwood each owned 50% of the issued and outstanding stock of B & W, which in turn owned a 51% partnership interest in FNFS. Twenty-five limited partners owned the remaining 49% percent of partnership interests in FNFS. Harwood served as president, chief operating officer, and a director of B & W, and

McKinney served as its chief executive officer and chairman of the board. While McKinney brought substantial financial resources to the enterprise, but no particular banking expertise, Harwood brought his extensive experience in the banking and lending industry. Harwood managed the day-to-day business affairs of B & W, which provided executive and managerial support to FNFS and which, pursuant to FNFS's partnership agreement, exercised "full, sole, exclusive, and complete discretion in the management and control of the business, operations, and affairs of [FNFS]." Based on evidence adduced at trial, the bankruptcy court found that Harwood "exercised virtually all executive power over FNFS operations on a daily basis" in what the court described as "an almost autocratic fashion."

Early on in his tenure as president of B & W, Harwood began withdrawing funds from FNFS for his personal use, including a $200,000 loan in 1997 to finance construction of a large steel-frame gymnasium on his property in Arp, Texas (the "Arp property"). In 1998, Harwood memorialized these loans in two promissory notes to FNFS—a $700,000 "Master Note" accompanied by a deed of trust in favor of FNFS on the Arp property, and a $125,000 note (the "Frazier Note") secured by a second-lien deed of trust in favor of FNFS on a residential rental property on East Frazier Street in Tyler, Texas (the "Frazier property"). Harwood prepared and signed the Notes and security documents, which he kept in a personal "loan file" in a desk drawer in his office. He never filed the deeds of trust with the county clerk.

Between 1998 and 2005, Harwood received a total of seventy-three advances on the Notes, using the funds for various personal expenditures, including a down payment on a family home and a new car. Harwood made only intermittent interest payments to FNFS, which were due quarterly under the terms of the Notes. On several occasions he borrowed funds from FNFS for the purpose of making interest payments on the Notes. The bankruptcy court found that, although the FNFS employee handbook outlined policies and procedures governing employee loans, Harwood followed no formal procedure for borrowing funds from FNFS. According to the bankruptcy court, Harwood exceeded any purported debt ceiling "with impunity," issuing additional notes to FNFS when the aggregate amount of his indebtedness exceeded the amount of the Master Note. The Master Note was then "extended and renewed" to incorporate the additional advances. . . .

Harwood challenges the bankruptcy and district courts' conclusions that he "acted in a fiduciary capacity" toward FNFS within the meaning of Section 523(a)(4), and that his failure to record the deeds of trust amounted to defalcation. We address these challenges in turn.

A. "Acting in a Fiduciary Capacity" under Section 523(a)(4)

Harwood first challenges the bankruptcy court's holding that he was "acting in a fiduciary capacity" within the meaning of Section 523(a)(4). The term "fiduciary" in this context is construed narrowly, limited to "technical trusts" and to traditional fiduciary relationships involving "trust-type" obligations imposed by statute or common law. *Bennett,* 989 F.2d at 784–85. "The scope of the concept of fiduciary under [Section 523(a)(4)] is a question of federal law; however, state law is important in determining whether or not a trust obligation exists." *Id.* at 784 (citation omitted). Harwood readily concedes that, as an officer and director of B & W, he owed a fiduciary duty to B & W. Under Texas law, corporate officers and directors owe fiduciary duties to the corporations they serve and must not allow their personal interests to prevail over the interests of the corporation. *See, e.g., Pinnacle Data Servs., Inc. v. Gillen*, 104 S.W.3d 188, 198 (Tex.App.—Texarkana 2003, no pet.) (citations omitted); *see also Moreno v. Ashworth*, 892 F.2d 417, 421 (5th Cir.1990) (officer owed a fiduciary duty to the corporation he served that satisfied Section 523(a)(4)). Nor is it disputed that, under Texas law, B & W, as general partner of FNFS, owes a fiduciary duty to FNFS and to the limited partners. *See, e.g., Grierson v. Parker Energy Partners*, 737 S.W.2d 375, 377 (Tex.App.—Houston [14th Dist.] 1987) (citation omitted); *see also Bennett*, 989 F.2d at 787 ("Texas law clearly and expressly imposes trust obligations on managing partners of limited partnerships and these obligations are sufficient to meet the narrow requirements of section 523(a)(4).").

Harwood contends, however, that although he owed a fiduciary duty to B & W, which in turn owed a duty to FNFS, *he* owed no fiduciary duty to FNFS because he was not a partner of the limited partnership and did not exercise a level of control over the affairs of the partnership to justify the recognition of fiduciary obligations owing to FNFS. Thus, we consider whether Texas law imposes a "trust-type obligation" on Harwood to the limited partnership, where Harwood was an officer and director, as well as 50% shareholder, of the corporate general partner of the limited partnership. In *LSP Investment Partnership v. Bennett (In re Bennett)*, we considered an analogous issue: whether a debtor—the managing partner of a general partner of a Texas limited partnership—owed a fiduciary duty to the limited partners within the meaning of Bankruptcy Code Section 523(a)(4).

To determine whether Texas law recognizes a fiduciary duty owed by a second-tier managing partner in a two-tiered partnership structure, we relied largely on *Crenshaw v. Swenson*, 611 S.W.2d 886 (Tex.Civ.App.—Austin 1980, writ ref'd n.r.e.). In *Crenshaw*, the Texas court held that a managing partner of a partnership's general partner owed to the underlying partners "the highest fiduciary duty recognized in the law." 611 S.W.2d at 890 (citing *Huffington v. Upchurch*, 532 S.W.2d 576 (Tex.1976)). We found significant that the *Crenshaw* court "focused on the nature of the business relationship as a whole, in which one person ... in her various roles ... exercised almost complete control over" the business of the partnership in concluding that the second-tier managing partner owed a duty to the underlying partners. *Bennett*, 989 F.2d at 789.

We noted that, under Texas law, "the issue of control has always been the critical fact looked to by the courts" in determining whether to impose fiduciary responsibilities on individuals whose actions directly determine the conduct of a general partner of a limited partnership. *Id.* In *Bennett*, the debtor was the sole general partner of a general partner charged with the exclusive authority to manage and make all decisions relating to the underlying partnership. *See id.* at 781. As a result, Bennett, individually, and through a corporation that he owned which he hired to manage the partnership, had the exclusive power and authority to manage the affairs of both the general partner and the limited partnership. *Id.* We concluded that by virtue of this control, Bennett was a fiduciary of the underlying partnership under Texas law, overturning the bankruptcy court's ruling that the partnership's multi-tiered partnership structure shielded Bennett from personal liability to the partnership for misapplication of partnership funds. *Id.* at 790. We further held that Bennett's fiduciary obligations to the partnership sufficed to make Bennett a "fiduciary" within the meaning of Section 523(a)(4), finding that Texas law imposes on managing partners in a position of control over the partnership a duty analogous to that owed by a trustee to the beneficiaries of the trust. *Id.* (citations omitted). The bankruptcy court in the instant case noted that it found no controlling authority precisely on point concerning the duty of an operational officer of a corporate general partner toward a limited partnership. However, it found the *Bennett* court's analysis—that the actual degree of authority exercised over the limited partnership is relevant to determining whether a second-tier manager owes a duty to the limited partnership—equally applicable to a corporate officer who controls a limited partnership by virtue of his control over the corporate general partner. "The relevant issue should not be the choice of organizational form ... but rather an analysis of whether the degree of control actually exercised by a corporate officer over the actions of a corporate general partner warrants a corresponding recognition" that the officer has assumed responsibilities to the limited partnership. *Harwood*, 404 B.R. at 397; *see also Park v. Moorad*, 132 B.R. 58, 63 (Bankr.N.D.Okl.1991) (officer and sole shareholder of a general partner was a fiduciary of the underlying partnership for purposes of Section 523(a)(4), stating that the court would "not allow the Debtor to hide beneath a corporate shell when he so completely controlled the corporate actions, representations and decisions that in effect it had no life without him").

We have since decided *McBeth v. Carpenter*, 565 F.3d 171 (5th Cir.2009), in which we addressed, in a non-bankruptcy context, the duties owed by an officer to a subsidiary entity that the officer controlled. In *McBeth*, we noted as a general principle that "managing partners owe trust obligations to the partnership, having a duty of loyalty and due care as well as being under an obligation to discharge their duties in good faith and in the reasonable belief that they are acting in the best interest of the partnership." *Id.* at 177 (citing Tex.Rev.Civ. Stat. Ann. art. 6132b–4.04(b)–(d)). We held that Texas law imposes the same fiduciary obligations on the president of a corporate general partner to the limited partners, where the president, Carpenter, was in a position of control over the partnership by virtue of his control over the partnership's corporate general partner. *Id.* at 178. The partnership agreement entrusted in the president the "exclusive rights to manage all contracts and agreements" relating to the purchase and development of land, the purpose for which the partnership was created. *Id.* Carpenter was described as "the man in control" and the one "heading the efforts" of the partnership, and acted as—and indeed held himself out to others as being—the general partner of the partnership. *Id.* Carpenter also controlled two of the partnership's limited partners. *Id.* at 175. Citing to *Bennett* and *Crenshaw*, we held that his control over the direction of the partnership sufficed to find him a fiduciary of the partnership under Texas law. *Id.* at 178. We conclude that an officer of a corporate general partner who is entrusted with the management of the limited partnership and who exercises control over the limited partnership in a fashion analogous to *Bennett* and *McBeth* owes a fiduciary duty to the partnership that satisfies Section 523(a)(4).

We emphasize that it is not only the control that the officer actually exerts over the partnership, but also the confidence and trust placed in the hands of the controlling officer, that leads us to find that a fiduciary relationship exists sufficient for the purposes of Section 523(a)(4). With this background, we focus our analysis on whether Harwood exercised a similar degree of control over FNFS as was sufficient to find a fiduciary duty in *McBeth* and *Bennett*. . . . Harwood, as president and chief operating officer of B & W, planned and supervised the growth and expansion of the FNFS lending locations. He controlled the hiring, evaluation, promotion, and termination of FNFS employees, the number of which soon exceeded 100 at 25

B & W Finance locations. No one with daily involvement in the company's affairs could challenge Harwood's authority or decision-making. He managed all FNFS operations from the central office in Tyler, [Texas]. *Id.* The bankruptcy court also found that Harwood held himself out as the "president" of FNFS, "which, while not technically accurate, was practically true in every sense." *Id.* Moreover, Harwood exercised substantial control over B & W and partnership funds. Harwood made oral demands for advances on the Master Note, as well as for reimbursements for undocumented business expenses, which Harwood's subordinates processed without question. "The only governing policy was to do what Harwood directed." *Id.* at 380 n. 23. We agree with the bankruptcy and district courts that the board's entrustment in Harwood of the management of the partnership's affairs and the partners' investments, when combined with the practically complete control that Harwood actually exercised over the partnership's management, compels a conclusion that Harwood stood "in the same fiduciary capacity to the limited partners as a trustee stands to the beneficiaries of the trust." *McBeth*, 565 F.3d at 177 (quoting *Crenshaw*, 611 S.W.2d at 890). In the circumstances of this case, we find that Harwood acted "in a fiduciary capacity" to FNFS within the meaning of Section 523(a)(4).

****

Crenshaw v. Swenson
611 S.W.2d 886, 890 (Tex.Civ.App.—Austin 1980, writ ref'd n.r.e.).

This is an appeal from judgment entered in the 261st District Court of Travis County. Appellants, David Crenshaw and Robert Brown, and three others who do not join in this appeal, sued appellees, Elizabeth Swenson and Swenson Corporation, for breach of fiduciary duty, commingling of partnership funds, violations of the Texas Real Estate License Act, and negligent construction of partnership property. The trial court entered judgment that appellants take nothing with the exception of $3,886.00 awarded David Crenshaw for payment of sums lent to the partnership. It is from this take nothing judgment that appellants have duly perfected their appeal to this Court. In November, 1972, a limited partnership known as Rolling Hills Majestic Homes (Group I), Ltd., was formed for the purpose of building four homes for ultimate sale in the ordinary course of business. The general partner of the limited partnership was Occidental Syndicated Investments, a partnership originally consisting of Elizabeth Swenson, Robert Johnson and James Cooper. Subsequent to the execution of the partnership agreement, both Robert Johnson and James Cooper resigned as general partners. The limited partners were Elizabeth Swenson and her husband, Verner Swenson, Martin Cooper, Robert Brown, Laurence Cranberg, David Crenshaw and Gaylon Stewart. Crenshaw contributed $16,000, while Brown contributed $2,000. Under the partnership agreement, the limited partners were to invest $40,000.00 capital contributions. Of this capital contribution, $28,000.00 was used to purchase four lots owned by appellees, Swenson Corporation, a corporation solely owned by Elizabeth and Verner Swenson. After the lots were purchased, it was contemplated the partnership would obtain a construction loan to finance the building of houses on the lots. The prospective interim

294

lender, however, refused to lend money to the limited partnership, but agreed to lend money to the Swenson Corporation. As a result, the general partners transferred title to the lots back to the Swenson Corporation so that the property could be used as security for the construction loan. At this point, Elizabeth Swenson decided to have Swenson Corporation act as the general contractor and build the four houses. . . .

Following the accounting, appellants brought suit against appellees, Elizabeth Swenson and Swenson Corporation, alleging breach of fiduciary duty on the part of Elizabeth Swenson. . . . . . .

Appellants contend that the trial court erred in failing to find that appellee, Elizabeth Swenson, breached her fiduciary duty of loyalty to the partnership and to the limited partners. In this regard, appellants assert that they are entitled to equitable restitution of their capital investment. It is axiomatic that a managing partner in a general partnership, owes his co-partners the highest fiduciary duty recognized in the law. Huffington v. Upchurch, 532 S.W.2d 576 (Tex.1976). In a limited partnership, the general partner acting in complete control stands in the same fiduciary capacity to the limited partners as a trustee stands to the beneficiaries of the trust. Watson v. Limited Partners of WCKT, Ltd., 570 S.W.2d 179 (Tex.Civ.App. Austin 1978, writ ref'd n. r. e.). We must then, in deciding this case, do so under the laws applicable to trusts.

Included in the fiduciary duty which the trustee (general partner) owes to the beneficiaries (limited partners) is the duty of loyalty. Not only is it his duty to administer the partnership affairs solely for the benefit of the partnership, he is not permitted to place himself in a position where it would be for his own benefit to violate this duty. Scott, Trusts (3d Ed.) Sec. 170; Southern Trust & Mortgage Co. v. Daniel, 143 Tex. 321, 184 S.W.2d 465 (1944). The finding of fact by the trial court that appellants suffered no harm as a result of Elizabeth Swenson conveying the partnership property to the Swenson Corporation fails to address the issue of appellants' complaint and is immaterial . . . .

Texas cases have treated a trustee guilty of self-dealing as a wrongdoer whether he was or not and have applied strict liability in such cases as a matter of law. . . . Courts of necessity must exact this high standard of fiduciary fidelity. Not only are the unequal positions of the parties inconsistent with any other standard, courts are ill-equipped to discern the extent a conflict of interest may have affected the outcome of any given transaction. . . .

Applying these equitable principles, we have no difficulty in concluding that, under the facts of the present case, appellee, Elizabeth Swenson has breached her fiduciary duty to the limited partners as a matter of law and that appellants are entitled to equitable restitution to the extent of their respective partnership contribution. In reaching this decision, we realize that the conveyance of the partnership property to the Swenson Corporation is atypical of the sales in the cases herein cited. We also accept the trial court's finding that there was no commingling of partnership funds as that term is commonly applied in the cases. The undisputed facts, however, show that such a conveyance of partnership property was made and the proceeds from the sale of partnership property were deposited in the Swenson Corporation account, both without the knowledge or consent of appellants. When these two facts are considered along with the additional facts that the Swenson Corporation was the general contractor in absolute control of the partnership's destiny and that Elizabeth Swenson had the right to the exclusive listing when the finished product was sold, the case takes on an aura of self-dealing which this Court is unable to condone.

****

Limited Partner

As a general rule, a limited partner does not owe any fiduciary duty to the partnership or its partners. However, a fiduciary duty may exist when a limited partner, acting in a different capacity, exerts operating control over the affairs of the limited partnership. *Daniels v. Empty Eye, Inc.*, 368 S.W.3d 743, 2012 WL 1604837 (Tex. App.—Houston [14th Dist.] 2012, no pet. h.). Apart from fiduciary duties, the limited partner also owes a duty to discharge his or her obligations in good faith.

Strebel v. Wimberly
371 S.W.3d 267 (Tex. App.- Houston[1 Dist.], 2012).

This is an appeal from a judgment following a jury trial. Plaintiff John Wimberly sued defendant Douglas Strebel to recover profit distributions from their business ventures that Wimberly alleges Strebel wrongfully withheld. The trial court entered judgment on the jury's finding that Strebel breached his fiduciary duties to Wimberly and awarded to Wimberly actual damages and attorneys' fees. We reverse the trial court's judgment on Wimberly's breach of fiduciary duty claims because we conclude that the parties contractually disclaimed the fiduciary duties related to profit distributions to Wimberly. . . .

In seven issues, Strebel requests that the Court reverse the trial court's judgment and render judgment in his favor or, alternatively, reverse the trial court's judgment and remand the case for a new trial. In his first issue, Strebel argues that the trial court erred by entering judgment in Wimberly's favor because (a) Strebel did not owe Wimberly any fiduciary duties at the LLC level and, in any event, Wimberly's "loss of distributions" stemming from any breach of fiduciary duty was at the LP—rather than the LLC—level, (b) Strebel did not owe a fiduciary duty to Wimberly at the LP level because, as a matter of law, limited partners in Texas do not owe fiduciary duties to other limited partners, and (c) Wimberly did not sue the LP's general partner, "which took the actions that allegedly caused Wimberly to lose distributions, and the trial court did not instruct the jury ... that Strebel, as the managing manager of the [LP]'s general partner, owned a fiduciary duty to Wimberly as a limited partner.". . .

ANALYSIS

A. Fiduciary Duties

The Court instructed the jury that a fiduciary duty existed by virtue of two relationships between Strebel and Wimberly—their relationship at the LLC level (Strebel as Managing Member and Wimberly as a Member) and their relationship at the LP level (both as limited partners). Neither party argues that the question of whether a fiduciary duty existed was a question for the jury in this case. Rather, both parties appear to agree that it was a question for the court to decide as a matter of law. Specifically, they both agree that (1) whether Strebel owed Wimberly a fiduciary duty at the LLC level turns on interpretation of language in the Black River LLC agreement, and (2) whether Strebel owed Wimberly a fiduciary duty at the LP level turns on whether limited partners owe other limited partners fiduciary duties under Texas law.

2. Fiduciary duties related to Black River LP

The Black River LP Agreement was entered pursuant to the Texas Revised Limited Partner Act (TRLPA) and is governed by Texas law. The agreement is silent as to any fiduciary duties owed between and among the limited partners—i.e., Strebel, Wimberly, Manley, and Lee. In Question No. 1, the trial court instructed the jury that "because of the relationship of Douglas Strebel and John Wimberly as partners in Black River Capital Partner, LP," Strebel owed to Wimberly a fiduciary duty. Strebel argues that this instruction was erroneous because, under Texas law, "a person's mere status as a limited partner is insufficient to create fiduciary duties," and the LP agreement expressly disclaims any fiduciary duty owed by the general partner. In support, he cites two unpublished cases— Crawford v. Ancira, No. 04–96–00078–CV, 1997 WL 214835, at *5 (Tex.App.-San Antonio, April 30, 1997, no writ) (not designated for publication) and AON Props. Inc. v. Riveraine Corp., No. 14–96–00229–CV, 1999 WL 12739, at *23 (Tex.App.-Houston [14th Dist.] Jan. 14, 1999, no pet.) (not designated for publication)—and an article positing that limited partners should not owe fiduciary duties because they are passive investors. Miller, Fiduciary Duties, Exculpation, and Indemnification in Texas Business Organizations, at 11–12, 15–16, in State Bar of Tex. Prof. Dev. Program, Essentials of Business Law Course (2010).

Strebel also argues that, because a shareholder in a closely held corporation does not "as a matter of law owe a fiduciary duties to his co-shareholder [s], ... it follows with even more force that limited partners in a Texas limited partnership do not as a matter of law owe fiduciary duties to each other." For these reasons, Strebel argues that his relationship with Wimberly as a limited partner cannot support the jury's finding of a breach of fiduciary duty. Wimberly disagrees, noting that the TRLPA, which Strebel agrees governs, provides that "[i]n any case not provided for by this Act," the Texas Revised Partnership Act (TRPA) "and the rules of law and equity" govern. Tex.Rev.Civ. Stat. Ann.. art. 6132a–1 § 13.03(a)(c) (Vernon 2002). Because TRLPA contains no provisions about duties owed by limited partners to each other, Wimberly argues that the "TRPA therefore determines what fiduciary duty Strebel owed Wimberly," and it expressly provides that "[a] partner owes to the partnership and the other partners: (1) a duty of loyalty; and (2) a duty of care." Tex.Rev.Civ. Stat. Ann.. art. 6132b–4.04(a) (Vernon 2002 & Supp. 2010).

Finally, Wimberly notes that that Strebel relies only on two non-precedential, unpublished cases that are distinguishable on their facts and that do not cite or acknowledge— much less explain—why the express duties provided for by the TRPA do not apply through the TRLPA. Wimberly also points out that both the Fifth Circuit and the Texarkana Court of Appeals have, in more recently decided cases, expressly recognized that fiduciary obligations exist between limited partners. See McBeth v. Carpenter, 565 F.3d 171, 177 (5th Cir.2009) ("With respect to fiduciary duties owed by ... [defendant] limited partners to the Plaintiffs, Texas law recognizes such obligations between limited partners, applying the same partnership principles that govern the relationship between a general partner and limited partners."); Zinda v. McCann St., Ltd., 178 S.W.3d 883, 890–91 (Tex.App.-Texarkana 2005, pet. denied) (recognizing limited partners owe fiduciary duties to one another, including the duty to fully disclose all matters affecting the partnership and account for all profits and property, as well as a strict duty of good faith and candor).

As a recent commentator aptly observed, the relevant question is more nuanced than simply whether limited partners, as a matter of law, do or do not owe fiduciary duties to other limited partners. See Colin P. Marks, Limited Partnership Status and the Imposition of Fiduciary Duties in Texas, 63 Baylor L.Rev. 126, 132 (2010). A look at the facts presented in these seemingly conflicting cases demonstrates that they are reconcilable with the rule that status as a passive investor does not give rise to fiduciary duties, but that a party's status as a limited partner does not insulate that party from the imposition of fiduciary duties that arise when a limited partner also takes on a nonpassive role by exercising control over the partnership in a way that justifies the recognition of such duties or by contract. See id. at *128

("[T]hough Texas jurisprudence has failed to articulate a clear rule, it is consistent with the cases decided thus far and the nature of a limited partnership to only create a fiduciary duty in certain equitable circumstances, such as when the limited partner is exercising control over the limited partnership or is also acting in the role of general partner."). When a person serves in a dual capacity as a limited partner and as a person controlling or managing the affairs of a limited partnership, it is not the party's status as a limited partner that gives rise to fiduciary duties; rather those duties exist by virtue of the additional relationship, such as agent or employee, in which capacity that person controls or manages the business of the partnership or by contract. In Crawford v. Ancira, the first case Strebel cites, a limited partner plaintiff brought fraud claims against another limited partner in an attempt to avoid certain contractual obligations, claiming that limited partner had made misrepresentations to her that were contrary to the contractual terms. 1997 WL 214835, at *4. Recognizing that the plaintiff's fraud claim was only viable if a fiduciary or confidential relationship existed between the parties, the San Antonio Court of

Appeals rejected her claim. Id. The court reasoned that limited partners do not have the broad managerial powers enjoyed by general partners and, thus, "a person's mere status as a limited partner is insufficient to create fiduciary duties." Id. at *5. Notably, the defendant in Crawford was not also the general partner, nor was there any indication that the defendant exercised any management or control over the limited partnership affairs.

The second case Strebel cites, AON Properties v. Riveraine Corporation, involved a suit by one limited partner against another limited partner for breach of fiduciary duty, complaining about the defendant limited partner's actions in (1) voting down an agreement to sell the limited partnership to a third party, and (2) voting to remove a corporation as general partner after that corporation lost its charter. 1999 WL 12739, at *1, *23. The trial court instructed the jury that the limited partners "owe[d] each other fiduciary duties as a matter of law." Id. at *7. On appeal, the Fourteenth Court of Appeals in Houston held that this instruction was erroneous, relying on cases from other jurisdictions holding that "a limited partner does not owe a fiduciary duty unless it actively engages in control over the operation of the business so as to create duties that otherwise would not exist." Id. at *23 (emphasis added).

Because the TRLPA provisions applicable at the time provided that "a limited partner does not participate in the control of the business" by voting on the sale of "an asset or assets of the limited partnership" or by voting on the "admission, removal or retention of the general partner," the court concluded that the actions complained of by the plaintiff did not amount to the types of control that could given rise to a duty to the other limited partners.

Thus, consistent with Crawford, the AON Properties court looked to the issue of management and control by the limited partner in assessing what duty, if any, existed. In support of his argument that limited partners do owe each other fiduciary duties, Wimberly cites Zinda v. McCann Street, Ltd., a case in which one limited partner sued a general partner and other limited partners for breach of fiduciary duty. 178 S.W.3d at 890. The jury returned a verdict in favor of the general partner and the two limited partners that owned the general partner. Id. On appeal, the Texarkana Court of Appeals made no distinction between the general partner defendant and the two limited partner defendants in observing that the "relationship among the various parties was a partnership; thus the [defendants] owed fiduciary duties to" the plaintiff. Id. at 890. The court concluded, however, that the evidence supported the jury's finding that no duties had been breached, rendering its broad pronouncement about the relationships giving rise to the fiduciary duties dicta. Id. While not part of the Zinda court's analysis, it is noteworthy that the limited partners at issue there also controlled the general partner. It was thus not their status as limited partners but, rather, their operating control over the partnership through the general partner that could give rise to fiduciary duties. Id.

Finally, Wimberly cites McBeth v. Carpenter, a Fifth Circuit case in which the court, "[a]fter careful review of the record and Texas law," affirmed a judgment against limited partners for breaching fiduciary duties to other limited partners. 565 F.3d at 177. McBeth and

Reynold, the limited partner plaintiffs in McBeth, obtained a verdict against three parties: James Carpenter, Texas Water Solutions (TWS) and Texas Water Management (TWM). Id. at 174. TWS and TWM were limited partners. Id. at 174–75. Both TWS and TWM were entities controlled by Carpenter, and Carpenter further controlled the general partnership entity (not a party to the suit). Id. On appeal, in discussing Texas law the court did not distinguish between the fiduciary obligations of general partners and limited partners. Id. at 177–78. The court did, however, explain why—on the facts presented— Crawford and AON Properties would not compel a different result even if they had precedential value . . . .

We reconcile these cases by holding that status as a limited partner alone does not give rise to a fiduciary duty to other limited partners. That is not to say, however, that a party who is a limited partner does not owe fiduciary duties to other limited partners when that party, wearing a different hat, exerts operating control over the affairs of the limited partnership. For example, when a limited partner also serves as an officer of the limited partnership, as in McBeth, that partner may owe fiduciary duties based on his agency relationship to the partnership and the other limited partners, without regard for his limited partner role. The existence and scope of that duty will be defined not by the law governing limited partners, but rather by the relevant laws and contracts governing the role under which the party is exercising the authority. In this case, Strebel complains about the trial court's instruction to the jury that "because of the relationship of Douglas Strebel and John Wimberly as partners in Black River Capital Partners LP," Strebel owed Wimberly "a fiduciary duty of due care, good faith, and loyalty in managing the business of the Black River Entities." The relationship between Strebel and Wimberly as limited partners in Black River Capital Partners LP did not give rise to a direct fiduciary duty to each other.

****

Side Bar

The court also addressed the ability of partners to restrict their fiduciary duties through contract by holding as follows at pp. 284-285:

> While courts have recognized that general partners in a limited partnership owe fiduciary duties to the limited partners, e.g., Graham Mortg. Corp., 307 S.W.3d at 479, the supreme court has emphasized the importance of honoring parties' contractual terms defining the scope of their obligations and agreements, including limiting fiduciary duties that might otherwise exist. E.g., Nat'l Plan Adm'rs, Inc. v. Nat'l Health Ins. Co., 235 S.W.3d 695, 703 (Tex.2007) (recognizing parties' agreement to limit the fiduciary duties that would otherwise exist between agent and principal). This is especially true in arms-length business transactions in which the parties are sophisticated businessmen represented by counsel, as the parties were here. Id. When Strebel and Wimberly first began their consulting work, Strebel clearly owed Wimberly fiduciary duties that were expressly provided for in their LLC Agreement. But later the parties—after much negotiation and while represented by counsel—entered into a limited partnership

agreement expressly providing that all the assets of their LLC would be transferred to the LP, and that the Strebel-controlled general partner would owe no fiduciary duties to the limited partners, including Wimberly. Because Strebel's actions that Wimberly complains of were all taken in his capacity as Managing Manager of the general partner, we hold that the waiver of fiduciary duties in the Black River LP Agreement forecloses those claims. E.g., Jochec v. Clayburne, 863 S.W.2d 516, 520 (Tex.App.-Austin 1993, writ denied) (holding trial court erred by refusing to recognize that trustee's fiduciary duties had been contractually limited); Kline v. O'Quinn, 874 S.W.2d 776, 787 (Tex.App.-Houston [14th Dist.] 1994, writ denied) (holding that contract between lawyers defined scope of their duties to each other, and refusing to impose fiduciary duties in addition to the duties expressly provided for in contract).

The court appears to conflate the parties' ability to limit their fiduciary duties by contract and the ability to eliminate these duties contractually. The former is clearly permissible while current Texas law does not seem to support the latter. While the court was obviously correct in emphasizing contractual freedom, which Texas Limited Partnership Law recognizes, the court could have supported its position by reference to this statutory recognition in section 4.03(b) of the Texas Revised Limited Partnership Act (recodified in TBOC § 153.152(a)). More importantly, this freedom of contract is limited by statute to the effect that partners may not eliminate fiduciary duties but may restrict them by contract, if the restriction is not manifestly unreasonable. *See* subsections 1.03(b)(2) and (3) of the Texas Revised Partnership Act (recodified in TBOC § 152.002(b)(2) and (3)) which apply in the limited partnership context by virtue of section 13.03(a) of the Texas Revised Limited Partnership Act (recodified in TBOC §153.003(a)). Delving into the statutory provisions would have helped in assuring that the court's decision is completely consistent with the legislature's intention.

A. DISSOLUTION AND FORFEITURE

Limited partnerships do not dissolve by the change in composition of the partnership. This solidifies the entity status of the limited partnership and further marks a departure from the general partnership. Until relatively recently, all general partnerships dissolved upon the exit or addition of a partner, after which the partnership's affairs went through the winding up process. Limited partnership law has approached the issue differently allowing the limited partnership to continue in existence where a limited partner departs. The withdrawal of a general partner also does not lead to automatic dissolution. The Texas Business Organizations Code consciously avoids the use of term "dissolution" and instead approaches the question of the continued existence of the partnership from the angle of events requiring the winding up of the partnership. Unless the partnership agreement provides otherwise, the withdrawal of a general partner is an event that requires winding up. Winding up may be cancelled if there is at least one remaining general partner who would carry on the business of the partnership in accordance with the partnership agreement or if the remaining partners or a percentage specified in the partnership agreement vote to continue the business within one year of the withdrawal and, if necessary or desired, appoint one or more new general partners. A general partner that withdraws from the limited partnership is not liable for obligations of the business incurred after his departure except to creditors that extended credit to the limited partnership reasonably believing that the departing partner was still a general partner.

The limited partnership's existence may also end through a court order directing the winding up and termination of the partnership upon application of a partner if the court makes the determination that: (i) the economic purpose of the limited partnership is likely to be unreasonably frustrated, (ii) another partner has engaged in conduct relating to the limited partnership business that makes it not reasonably practicable to carry on the business in partnership with that partner, or (iii) it is not reasonably practicable to carry on the business of the limited partnership in conformity with the partnership agreement.

In a nutshell, the TBOC specifies that winding up of a limited partnership is required on: (1) the expiration of a period of duration specified in the certificate of formation or partnership agreement; (2) a voluntary decision of the partners to wind up the limited partnership (which requires written consent of all partners unless otherwise provided by the partnership agreement); (3) occurrence of an event specified in the certificate of formation or partnership agreement to cause winding up; (4) unless otherwise provided by the partnership agreement, an event of withdrawal of a general partner; (5) the absence of any remaining limited partners; or (6) entry of a judicial decree requiring winding up, dissolution, or termination of the limited partnership.

Texas Business Organization Code provisions

§ 11.051. Event Requiring Winding Up of Domestic Entity. Winding up of a domestic entity is required on:

(1) the expiration of any period of duration specified in the domestic entity's governing documents;

(2) a voluntary decision to wind up the domestic entity;

(3) an event specified in the governing documents of the domestic entity requiring the winding up, dissolution, or termination of the domestic entity, other than an event specified in another subdivision of this section;

(4) an event specified in other sections of this code requiring the winding up or termination of the domestic entity, other than an event specified in another subdivision of this section; or

(5) a decree by a court requiring the winding up, dissolution, or termination of the domestic entity, rendered under this code or other law.

§ 11.058. Supplemental Provision for Limited Partnership

(a) A voluntary decision to wind up a domestic limited partnership requires the written consent of all partners in the limited partnership unless otherwise provided by the partnership agreement. The voluntary decision to wind up may be revoked in accordance with Sections 11.151 and 153.501(d).

(b) An event of withdrawal of a general partner of a domestic limited partnership is an event requiring winding up under Section 11.051(4) unless otherwise provided by the partnership agreement. The event requiring winding up specified in this subsection may be canceled in accordance with Sections 11.152(a) and 153.501(b).

(c) An event requiring winding up of a limited partnership under Section 11.051(4) includes when there are no limited partners in the limited partnership. The event requiring winding up specified in this subsection may be canceled in accordance with Sections 11.152(a) and 153.501(e).

§ 11.314. Involuntary Winding Up and Termination of Partnership or Limited Liability Company. A district court in the county in which the registered office or principal place of business in this state of a domestic partnership or limited liability company is located has jurisdiction to order the winding up and termination of the domestic partnership or limited liability company on application by:

(1) a partner in the partnership if the court determines that:

(A) the economic purpose of the partnership is likely to be unreasonably frustrated; or

(B) another partner has engaged in conduct relating to the partnership's business that makes it not reasonably practicable to carry on the business in partnership with that partner; or

(2) an owner of the partnership or limited liability company if the court determines that it is not reasonably practicable to carry on the entity's business in conformity with its governing documents.

<u>Withdrawal of General Partner</u>

The general partner has the power, but not always the right to withdraw from the limited partnership.

Texas Business Organization Code provisions

§ 153.155. Withdrawal of General Partner

(a) A person ceases to be a general partner of a limited partnership on the occurrence of one or more of the following events of withdrawal:

(1) the general partner withdraws as a general partner from the limited partnership as provided by Subsection (b);

(2) the general partner ceases to be a general partner of the limited partnership as provided by Section 153.252(b);

(3) the general partner is removed as a general partner in accordance with the partnership agreement;

(4) unless otherwise provided by a written partnership agreement, or with the written consent of all partners, the general partner:

>*(A) makes a general assignment for the benefit of creditors;*
>
>*(B) files a voluntary bankruptcy petition;*
>
>*(C) becomes the subject of an order for relief or is declared insolvent in a federal or state bankruptcy or insolvency proceeding;*
>
>*(D) files a petition or answer seeking for the general partner a reorganization, arrangement, composition, readjustment, liquidation, winding up, termination, dissolution, or similar relief under law;*

§ 153.156. Notice of Event of Withdrawal. *A general partner who is subject to an event that with the passage of the specified period becomes an event of withdrawal under Section 153.155(a)(4) or (5) shall notify the other partners of the event not later than the 30th day after the date on which the event occurred.*

§ 153.157. Withdrawal of General Partner in Violation of Partnership Agreement. *Unless otherwise provided by the partnership agreement, a withdrawal by a general partner of a partnership having a period of duration or for a particular undertaking before the expiration of that period or completion of that undertaking is a breach of the partnership agreement.*

§ 153.158. Effect of Withdrawal

(a) Unless otherwise provided by a written partnership agreement and subject to the liability created under Section 153.162, if a general partner ceases to be a general partner under Section 153.155, the remaining general partner or partners, or, if there are no remaining general partners, a majority-in-interest of the limited partners in a vote that excludes any limited partnership interest held by the withdrawing general partner, may:

>*(1) convert that general partner's partnership interest to that of a limited partner; or*
>
>*(2) pay to the withdrawn general partner in cash, or secure by bond approved by a court of competent jurisdiction, the value of that partner's partnership interest minus the damages caused if the withdrawal constituted a breach of the partnership agreement.*

(b) Until an action described by Subsection (a) is taken, the owner of the partnership interest of the withdrawn general partner has the status of an assignee under Subchapter F.

(c) If there are no remaining general partners following the withdrawal of a general partner, the partnership may be reconstituted.

§ 11.058. Supplemental Provision for Limited Partnership

(a) A voluntary decision to wind up a domestic limited partnership requires the written consent of all partners in the limited partnership unless otherwise provided by the partnership agreement. The voluntary decision to wind up may be revoked in accordance with Sections 11.151 and 153.501(d).

(b) An event of withdrawal of a general partner of a domestic limited partnership is an event requiring winding up under Section 11.051(4) unless otherwise provided by the partnership agreement. The event requiring winding up specified in this subsection may be canceled in accordance with Sections 11.152(a) and 153.501(b).

(c) An event requiring winding up of a limited partnership under Section 11.051(4) includes when there are no limited partners in the limited partnership. The event requiring winding up specified in this subsection may be canceled in accordance with Sections 11.152(a) and 153.501(e).

§ 11.152. Continuation of Business Without Winding Up

(a) Subject to Subsections (c) and (d), a domestic entity to which an event requiring the winding up of the entity occurs as specified by Section 11.051(3) or (4) may cancel the event requiring winding up in the manner specified in the title of this code governing the domestic entity not later than the first anniversary of the date of the event requiring winding up or an earlier period prescribed by the title of this code governing the domestic entity.

(b) A domestic entity whose specified period of duration has expired may cancel that event requiring winding up by amending its governing documents in the manner provided by this code, not later than the third anniversary of the date the period expired or an earlier date prescribed by the title of this code governing the domestic entity, to extend its period of duration. The expiration of its period of duration does not by itself create a vested right on the part of an owner, member, or creditor of the entity to prevent the extension of that period. An act undertaken or a contract entered into by the domestic entity during a period in which the entity could have extended its period of duration as provided by this subsection is not invalidated by the expiration of that period, regardless of whether the entity has taken any action to extend its period of duration.

(c) A domestic entity may not cancel an event requiring winding up specified in Section 11.051(3) and continue its business if the action is prohibited by the entity's governing documents or the title of this code governing the entity.

(d) A domestic entity may cancel an event requiring winding up specified in Section 11.051(4) and continue its business only if the action:

    (1) is not prohibited by the entity's governing documents; and

    (2) is expressly authorized by the title of this code governing the entity.

(e) On cancellation of an event requiring winding up under this section, the domestic entity may continue its business.

§ 153.501. Cancellation or Revocation of Event Requiring Winding Up; Continuation of Business

(a) The limited partnership may cancel under Section 11.152 an event requiring winding up arising from the expiration of its period of duration as specified in Section 11.051(1) or from the occurrence of an event specified in its governing documents as specified in Section 11.051(3) if, not later than the 90th day after the event, all remaining partners, or another group or percentage of partners as specified by the partnership agreement, agree in writing to continue the business of the limited partnership.

(b) The limited partnership may cancel under Section 11.152 an event requiring winding up arising from an event of withdrawal of a general partner as specified in Section 11.058(b) if:

    (1) there remains at least one general partner and the partnership agreement permits the business of the limited partnership to be carried on by the remaining general partners and those remaining general partners carry on the business; or

    (2) not later than one year after the event, all remaining partners, or another group or percentage of partners specified in the partnership agreement:

        (A) agree in writing to continue the business of the limited partnership; and

        (B) to the extent that they desire or if there are no remaining general partners, agree to the appointment of one or more new general partners.

(c) The appointment of one or more new general partners under Subsection (b)(2)(B) is effective from the date of withdrawal.

(d) To approve a revocation under Section 11.151 by a limited partnership of a voluntary decision to wind up as specified in Section 11.058(a), prior to filing the certificate of termination required by Section 11.101, all remaining partners, or another group or percentage of partners as specified by the partnership agreement, must agree in writing to revoke the voluntary decision to wind up and continue the business of the limited partnership.

(e) The limited partnership may cancel under Section 11.152 an event requiring winding up arising when there are no limited partners in the limited partnership, as specified in Section 11.058(c), if, not later than the first anniversary of the date of the event requiring winding up:

(1) the legal representative or successor of the last remaining limited partner and all of the general partners agree to:

(A) continue the business of the limited partnership; and

(B) admit the legal representative or successor of the last remaining limited partner, or the person's nominee or designee, to the limited partnership as a limited partner, effective as of the date the event that caused the last remaining limited partner to cease to be a limited partner occurred; or

(2) a limited partner is admitted to the limited partnership in the manner provided by the partnership agreement, effective as of the date the event that caused the last remaining limited partner to cease to be a limited partner occurred.

§ 153.161. Liability of General Partner for Debt Incurred After Event of Withdrawal

(a) Unless otherwise provided by a written partnership agreement and subject to the liability created under Section 153.162, a general partner who ceases to be a general partner under Section 153.155 is not personally liable in the partner's capacity as a general partner for partnership debt incurred after that partner ceases to be a general partner unless the applicable creditor at the time the debt was incurred reasonably believed that the partner remained a general partner.

(b) A creditor of the partnership has reason to believe that a partner remains a general partner if:

(1) the creditor had no knowledge or notice of the general partner's withdrawal and:

(A) was a creditor of the partnership at the time of the general partner's withdrawal; or

(B) had extended credit to the partnership within two years before the date of withdrawal; or

(2) the creditor had known that the partner was a general partner in the partnership before the general partner's withdrawal and had no knowledge or notice of the withdrawal and the general partner's withdrawal had not been advertised in a newspaper of general circulation in each place at which the partnership business was regularly conducted.

§ 153.162. Liability for Wrongful Withdrawal

(a) If a general partner's withdrawal from a limited partnership violates the partnership agreement, the partnership may recover damages from the withdrawing general partner for breach of the partnership agreement, including the reasonable cost of obtaining replacement of the services the withdrawn partner was obligated to perform.

(b) In addition to pursuing any remedy available under applicable law, the partnership may effect the recovery of damages under Subsection (a) by offsetting those damages against the amount otherwise distributable to the withdrawing general partner, reducing the limited partner interest into which the withdrawing general partner's interest may be converted under Section 153.158(a)(1), or both.

Withdrawal of Limited Partner

A limited partner has neither the right nor the power to voluntarily withdraw from the partnership, absent a provision in a written partnership agreement permitting such withdrawal. Subject to any contrary agreement, a limited partner is entitled to receive, within a reasonable time after withdrawal, the fair value of her partnership interest as of the date of withdrawal.

Texas Business Organization Code provisions

§ 153.110. Withdrawal of Limited Partner. A limited partner may withdraw from a limited partnership only at the time or on the occurrence of an event specified in a written partnership agreement. The withdrawal of the partner must be made in accordance with that agreement.

§ 153.111. Distribution on Withdrawal. Except as otherwise provided by Section 153.210 or the partnership agreement, on withdrawal a withdrawing limited partner is entitled to receive, not later than a reasonable time after withdrawal, the fair value of that limited partner's interest in the limited partnership as of the date of withdrawal.

Forfeiture

Limited partnerships are required to file periodic reports. Failure to file such reports may lead to forfeiture of the right to operate within the State.

Texas Business Organization Code provisions

§ 153.301. Periodic Report. The secretary of state may require a domestic limited partnership or a foreign limited partnership registered to transact business in this state to file a report not more than once every four years as required by this subchapter.

§ 153.307. Effect of Failure to File Report

(a) A domestic or foreign limited partnership that fails to file a report under Section 153.301 when the report is due forfeits the limited partnership's right to transact business in this state. A forfeiture under this section takes effect without judicial ascertainment.

(b) When the right to transact business has been forfeited under this section, the secretary of state shall note that the right to transact business has been forfeited and the

date of forfeiture on the record kept in the secretary's office relating to the limited partnership.

§ 153.309. Effect of Forfeiture of Right to Transact Business

(a) Unless the right of the limited partnership to transact business is revived in accordance with Section 153.310:

(1) the limited partnership may not maintain an action, suit, or proceeding in a court of this state; and

(2) a successor or assignee of the limited partnership may not maintain an action, suit, or proceeding in a court of this state on a right, claim, or demand arising from the transaction of business by the limited partnership in this state.

(b) The forfeiture of the right to transact business in this state does not:

(1) impair the validity of a contract or act of the limited partnership; or

(2) prevent the limited partnership from defending an action, suit, or proceeding in a court of this state.

(c) This section and Sections 153.307 and 153.308 do not affect the liability of a limited partner.

§ 153.310. Revival of Right to Transact Business

(a) A limited partnership that forfeits the right to transact business in this state as provided by Section 153.309 may be relieved from the forfeiture by filing the required report not later than the 120th day after the date of mailing of the notice of forfeiture under Section 153.308, accompanied by the filing fees as provided by Chapter 4.

(b) If a limited partnership complies with Subsection (a), the secretary of state shall:

(1) revive the right of the limited partnership to transact business in this state;

(2) cancel the note regarding the forfeiture; and

(3) note the revival and the date of revival on the record kept in the secretary's office relating to the limited partnership.

§ 153.311. Termination of Certificate or Revocation of Registration After Forfeiture

(a) The secretary of state may terminate the certificate of formation of a domestic limited partnership, or revoke the registration of a foreign limited partnership, if the limited partnership:

(1) forfeits its right to transact business in this state under Section 153.307; and

(2) fails to revive that right under Section 153.310.

(b) Termination of the certificate or revocation of registration takes effect without judicial ascertainment.

(c) The secretary of state shall note the termination or revocation and the date on the record kept in the secretary's office relating to the limited partnership.

(d) On termination or revocation, the status of the limited partnership is changed to inactive according to the records of the secretary of state. The change to inactive status does not affect the liability of a limited partner.

§ 153.312. Reinstatement of Certificate of Formation or Registration

(a) A limited partnership the certificate of formation or registration of which has been terminated or revoked as provided by Section 153.311 may be relieved of the termination or revocation by filing the report required by Section 153.301, accompanied by the filing fees provided by Chapter 4.

(b) If the limited partnership pays the fees required by Subsection (a) and all taxes, penalties, and interest due and accruing before termination or revocation, the secretary of state shall:

(1) reinstate the certificate or registration of the limited partnership without judicial ascertainment;

(2) change the status of the limited partnership to active; and

(3) note the reinstatement on the record kept in the secretary's office relating to the limited partnership.

(c) If the name of the limited partnership is not available at the time of reinstatement, the secretary of state shall require the limited partnership as a precondition to reinstatement to:

(1) file an amendment to the partnership's certificate of formation; or

(2) in the case of a foreign limited partnership, amend its application for registration to adopt an assumed name for use in this state.

Table 3

TBOC DECONSTRUCTED	
LIMITED PARTNERSHIPS	
TOPIC	RULE
GOVERNANCE	
must keep and maintain records	3.151; 153.551
need not keep minutes (unless)	3.151
must comply with tboc chapters 4,5,10, 11 or 12	153.004
may alter/waive einding up/withdrawal	11.058
when amendment to certificate of formation required	153.051
when amendment to certificate of formation permitted	153.052
GOVERNING DOCUMENTS	
class or group of partners	154.001
applicability of general partnership statute	153.003
authority to restate certificate of formation	153.053
admitting new general partner	153.151
admitting limited partners	153.101
rights of assignee	153.253
fiing periodic reports and filing fee	153.301--.305
effect of filing report	153.306
effect of failing to file report	153.307-.309
reviving right to conduct business	153.310-.312
executinb filing instruments	153.533
judicial orders	153.554
GOVERNING PERSONS	
general partner(s) as decision makers	153.152-.153
general partner rights and duties generally	153.152
partner access to books and records	153.552
records to be kept and maintained	153.551
voting rights	154.102
action by consent without meeting	154.103
partner right ot transact business with partnership	154.201
LIABILITY	

PARTNERSHIP LIABILITY	
must keep and maintain records	3.151; 153.551
need not keep minutes (unless)	3.151
must comply with tboc chapters 4,5,10, 11 or 12	153.004
may alter/waive winding up/withdrawal	11.058
when amendment to certificate of formation required	153.051
when amendment to certificate of formation permitted	153.052
PARTNER LIABILITY	
limited partner does not have same liability as general partner	153.003
authority to make guarantees	153.004
general partner generally liable	153.152-.153
limited partner not liable	153.102
limited partner not liable even when participated in control	153.103
limited partner acting in separate capacity does not create liability as limited partner	153.104
limited partner may not be liable when erroneously believes enjoys lp status	153.106
how limited partner claims liability protection when defect in status	153.107-.109
limited partner not liable for receiving wrongful distribution	153.112
general partner liable for debt incurred after withdrawal	153.161
generl partner liable for wrongful withdrawal	153.162
assignee liability	153.254
assignor liability	153.255
charging order	153.256
DERIVATIVE PROCEEDINGS ALLOWED	153.401-.405
FINANCING	
general partner contributions	153.154
what constitutes contribution	153.201
enforceability of promise to make contribution	153.202-.205
PARTNER INTEREST IN PARTNERSHIP	
generally	154.001
assignment/transferring partnership interests	153.251-.252
allocation of profits and losses	153.206

right to distribution	153.207; .210-.209
rights of assignee	152.253
limitation on interest in specific partnership property	154.002
distribution in kind	154.203
TERMINATION	
WITHDRAWAL	
events of withdrawal	153.110; .155
effect of withdrawal	153.158
wrongful withdrawal	153.157
withdrawal of limited partner	153.110
limited partner right to distribution on withdrawal	153.111
notice of withdrawal of general partner	153.156
conversion of general partner interest after withdrawal	153.159; .160
WINDING UP	
cancellation of event requiring winding up/continuation of business	153.501; .505
rights and duties of person winding up	153.503
liquidation	153.504
limited partner estate	153.113
winding up procedures	153.502

Limited Partnerships Problem Set

1. Two experienced hair stylists, Hugo and Castro, formed Publican, LP primarily to provide children's hair care services. Hugo was the general partner while Castro was the limited partner. In March 2011, Castro approached Allied Bank and informed the manager that he was seeking a loan to pay for the purchase of a sophisticated hair styling equipment and an upgrade of Publican's beauty parlor. Castro obtained the loan for $30,000, signing a promissory note that named Publican, LP as the borrower and Allied Bank as the lender. Castro deposited the proceeds of the loan into his personal bank account and used it to purchase a timeshare in Palm Beach, Florida. Castro continued to make regular monthly payments on the loan from his personal funds, but never informed Hugo about the loan. He defaulted on the loan and Allied Bank sued to have the entire outstanding loan amount repaid immediately by the partnership and its partners. The court agreed and ruled in the bank's favor.

    Do you agree with the court's decision?

2. Barnard & Company Ltd, a Texas limited partnership has 5 limited partners and one general partner, Manny. Barnard & Company Ltd focuses on building mobile homes. One of the limited partners, Jeff, is a reputable builder but has not been interested in mobile homes. Recently, Jeff was contacted by the Lakeside Homeowners Association to build some mobile homes in its subdivision. Jeff did not present the opportunity to Barnard & Company Ltd. Instead, he gave the business opportunity to Adonai Construction, L.C., a company in which he has a 50 percent ownership interest. Adonai proceeded to construct the mobile homes with the assistance of a few day laborers, earning almost a million dollars in profit. Manny wants to recover Jeff's share of the profit on behalf of the LLC, saying that Jeff is not entitled to keep it.

    Does Manny have a sound legal argument?

3. Shannon is a limited partner of Intelligentsia, LP. Upon learning that the business school at the local university was offering a weekend course for small business owners, she decided to attend. On her way to the training program, she momentarily lost control of her vehicle and ran into Victor's SUV. After the drivers exchanged information, Shannon continued to the university. She found the course useful and registered for a 3-day companion course on behalf of Intelligentsia. The course fee is non-refundable if registrants do not withdraw within one week of registration. There was no withdrawal and Intelligentsia did not know of the registration until a few days ago when the university sent a letter demanding payment. The firm is unable to pay and the university is considering a lawsuit against the firm and its partners to recover the course fee. Victor is also suing for the cost of repairing his vehicle.

    Will Intelligentsia and the partners lose the two suits?

4. Peter, Carol and Abel inherited $250,000 from their parents, which they invested in the purchase of a children's toys franchise under a limited partnership, Portmanteau LP. Peter is the general partner while Carol and Abel are limited partners. They need additional capital infusion of $250,000 to lease and remodel an existing building which they plan to use to conduct their business. Since they do not have any money on their own after the purchase, they approached a family friend for a loan. However, the friend would rather own a part of the business, instead of lending the money. He also wants his exposure limited to the capital invested in the business while at the same time having an equal voice in management. Peter does not want to go through the trouble of forming another type of business and sought advice from local legal counsel on whether they can retain the current LP form but structure an arrangement (valid as to third parties) that limits the liability of the friend while giving him an equal voice in management. The local lawyer has written a brief legal opinion which she clearly stated that it was not possible to accommodate the two goals under an LP structure. Her legal opinion reads in part: "The whole point of utilizing the vehicle of the limited partnership is to have a general partner who makes all the decisions and is responsible for them and limited partners who contribute capital and stay away from management. Limited partners cannot legally be part of management decision-making without losing their limited liability protection." She concluded, therefore, that they should change the type of entity with which they are conducting their business.

   Do you agree with the lawyer?

5. The Ice Creamery, LP is a properly formed limited partnership. Allison is the general partner while Barrera, Choi and Tiffany are the limited partners. Barrera recently opened an ice cream shop in a new part of town and strongly believes that he is not taking customers away from the partnership, since his customers are elderly residents of a nearby nursing home who cannot drive 15 miles to the Partnership's location. In a suit by other partners for disgorgement of profits earned from Barrera's competing business, the court agreed with and adopted Barrera's arguments, adding that it is common practice today for partnerships to permit competition by its partners. The partners have filed an appeal.

   How will the appeal fare?

6. Apollo, LP was properly formed as a limited partnership in 1999 to plan weddings and other social events. Dora is named the general partner while Boot and Sharon are the limited partners. Dora took a short vacation after a busy spring last year. Within that period, a lot of orders were coming in. Sharon called Party Supplies, Inc., a long-standing customer of Apollo, LP, introduced herself as a partner and placed orders totaling $15,000 in the usual way the partnership had ordered materials through Dora. As it has

often done in the past, Party Supplies, Inc. delivered the materials to Dora's home. Dora and her family were vacationing out of state and the materials got damaged because of heavy rainfall during the period they were away. Apollo, LP has refused to pay for the damaged materials and Party Supplies, Inc. is suing.

Who wins?

7. Buffett Group, LP is a thriving limited partnership in Houston. Steve is the general partner while Emil and Belinda are the limited partners. The firm entertained proposals for building a shopping center in Pearland. On June 1, 2010 all the partners voted to apply for financing from Citizens Bank to construct the building. In signing one of the partnership documents in support of the loan application, Emil innocently misidentified himself as a general partner. The bank approved a loan of $10 million and released $1 million immediately to the firm. Construction work at the shopping center stopped because the firm failed to pay the construction company more than $1.5 million on work already completed, even though Buffet Group has collected the remaining the loan amount from the bank. Buffett Group defaulted on the loan and Citizens Bank sued to hold personally liable the partners it identified as general partners namely, Steve and Emil. Emil is challenging the suit on the grounds of his status as a limited partner and his entitlement to protection from liability under the safe harbor protection.

Is Emil liable as a general partner?

8. In 2005, 3 former employees of Dell Computers organized XD Technologies Ltd as a limited partnership to design and sell computer hardware. Two of them, Derrick and Bell are the general partners while Bryant is the limited partner. The partners agreed that only Derrick may make purchases or sign contracts on behalf of the partnership. Last year, while vacationing in Galveston, Bell ran into Perry, who owns a number of office buildings. Bell signed a lease for an office space on behalf of XD because the current lease was expiring and Perry offered very attractive terms that Bell felt anybody would find irresistible. That same day, Bell also purchased some souvenirs that he believed would be good gift items to customers and friends of the business. He did not mention the vendor that he was a partner in XD or that he was purchasing it for any company. He also paid with a personal check, which the vendor could not cash because the bank on which it was drawn failed the following week. XD partners were not interested in either of these transactions. Both Perry and the vendor sued XD and its partners seeking payment or performance of their obligations under the transactions. The court held that as a general partner, Bell had authority to bind the partnership, regardless of the objections of or contrary agreement among the partners. XD and the other partners are appealing the decision.

Who wins?

9. Danny, a limited partner of Peak, L.P. was hired by the partnership as the chief financial officer. While driving to the bank to open a line of credit for Peak, L.P., Danny negligently ran into a car in front of him. The owner of the damaged vehicle brought a civil suit, claiming thousands of dollars, for the property damage. On the defendants' motion, the court dismissed the suit against Danny, holding that a limited partner is not personally liable when his activities are covered by the safe harbor provisions of the Limited Partnership Law. The owner of the vehicle is considering an appeal.

   Would you advise him to proceed?

10. Zillion Ltd is a Texas limited partnership. It has three individual partners – Dannye, Kim, and Kourtney. Affinity, Inc., a corporation solely owned and controlled by Kim is the general partner. Accordingly, Affinity performs its functions through Kim. Kim has been using Zillion's SUV to run private errands, including dropping her daughter at daycare and driving to the mall to shop with friends. Dannye and Kourtney are upset and accuse Kim of breach of fiduciary duty. Kim contacted a lawyer who laughed off the concern, noting that limited partners do not owe fiduciary duties.

    Do you agree with the lawyer's conclusion?

LIMITED LIABILITY LIMITED PARTNERSHIPS

Although similar in name, the limited liability partnership (LLP) and the limited liability limited partnership (LLLP) have different origins. Limited liability limited partnership is a variation of a limited partnership, while limited liability partnership is a variation of a general partnership. Beyond that there is no great difference between the two partnerships as far as liability is concerned.

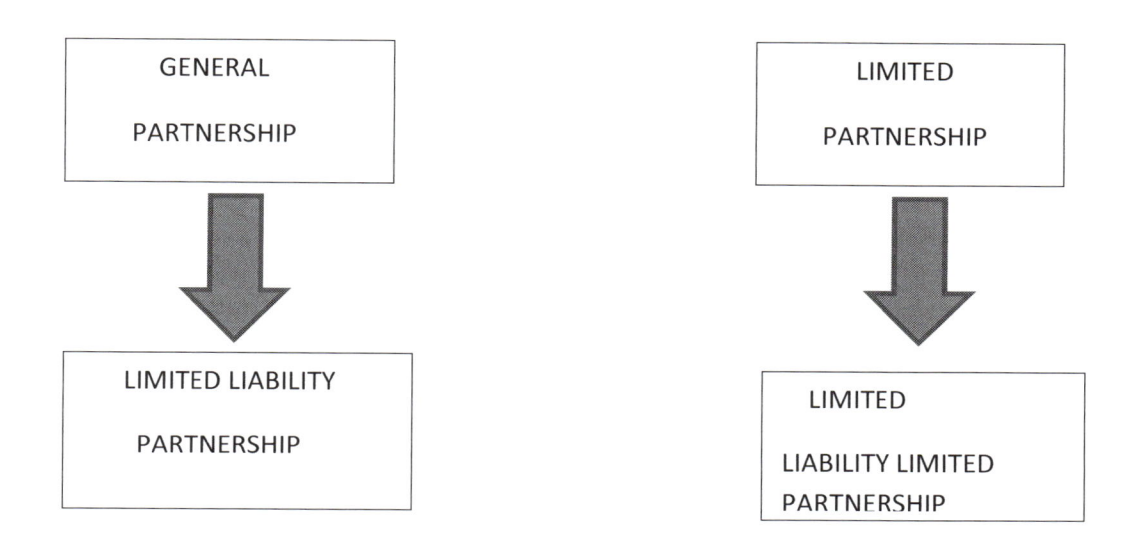

```
GENERAL PARTNERSHIP          LIMITED PARTNERSHIP
        ↓                            ↓
LIMITED LIABILITY            LIMITED LIABILITY
PARTNERSHIP                  LIMITED PARTNERSHIP
```

The LLLP was established to limit the liability of the general partners in a limited partnership. Limited partners in a limited partnership traditionally enjoyed limited liability and that does not change with the LLLP. Despite its relatively new status, major businesses (ex. CNN) are beginning to use this form. Additionally, LLLPs are particularly popular designations in real estate.

Formation

Like the limited partnership, the limited liability limited partnership (LLLP) is a filing entity. Thus all filing requirements are the same including placing the designation "LLLP" at the end of the business name. Sometimes the filing fees for this entity are higher than those for LP.

LLLP is governed by state statute and is expressly recognized in a few states including Arkansas, Arizona, Colorado, Delaware, Kentucky, Maryland, Nevada, and Texas. In states where LLLP is not expressly recognized, if the LLP is a possible entity form it is likely a business will be able to register with a designation of LLP and be granted authority to operate as such. This is because of the similarity in personal liability protection between the two.

Governance Voting

Recall that limited partners by definition are those who invest in the business but do not participate in the management of the daily affairs. In contrast, the general partners are responsible for managing the daily operations. Although they do not commonly participate in management, the limited partners do participate in governance through their right to vote in fundamental business affairs. In this way, the power of the limited partners to participate in governance is comparable to their ownership in shares of the business. Limited partners also have the right to call for resignation of general partners, which is a form of control over the affairs of the business.

The governance of the LLLP does not differ from the governance of the LP.

Liability

The LLLP like the LLP affords general partners relief from other partner's liability for the debts, and obligations of the entity. Tex. Bus. Orgs. Code § 152.801(a).

Liability protection does not protect partners from their own malpractice, tort, or contractual suits. Tex. Bus. Orgs. Code § 152.801(e)(2). Additionally, limitation of partner liability does not affect the liability of the partnership to pay its obligations out of partnership property or the manner in which service of citation or other civil process may be served in an action against a partnership. Tex. Bus. Orgs. Code § 152.801(e)(1). Recall, each general partner is an agent of the limited partnership on whom may be served any process, notice, or demand required or permitted by law to be served on the limited partnership.

Because very little case law exists regarding LLLP, it is difficult to determine if limited partners will escape liability where they also substantially participate in the management of the business as general partners. However, the scope of personal liability protection provided under the law appears broad enough to protect the LP, even when acting substantially as a general partner.

General partners do still owe a fiduciary duty to the business. On the other hand absent an agreement that states otherwise, the limited partners owe no such duty.

Finance

The financial structure of the LLLP remains governed by the rules regarding the LP.

Termination

The termination of an LLLP is the same as the termination of an LP.

Table 4

TBOC DECONSTRUCTED	
LIMITED LIABILITY PARTNERSHIPS	
TOPIC	RULE
FORMATION	
registration required	152.802
name	152.803
GOVERNANCE	
GOVERNING DOCUMENT(S)	
partnership agreement is governance document	152.208
amending governance document	152.208
when TBOC controls	
GOVERNING PERSONS	
decisionmakers	152.209
binding effect of partner action generally	152.302
binding effect of partner action after event of winding up	152.704
who qualified to wind up	152.702
withdrawing partner's power to bind partnership	152.504
rights and duties generally	152.203
partner as agent	152.301
access to books and records	152.213
rights and duties of person winding up	152.703
standards of partner conduct	152.204
FIDUCIARY DUTIES and PARTNER OBLIGATIONS	
duty of loyalty	152.205
duty of care	152.206
duties on winding up	152.207
obligation to maintain books and records	152.212
PARTNER RIGHT TO TRANSFER INTEREST	
right to transfer	152.401
effect of transfer generally	152.402
effect of transfer on transferor	152.403
rights and duties of transferee	152.404
partnership not bound by prohibited transfer	152.405
effect of death or divorce	152.406

PARTNER RIGHT TO CONTINUE PARTNERSHIP	
canceling revocation	152.709
reinstatement	152.71
LIABILITY	
PARTNERSHIP LIABILITY	
generally	152.203
not bound by prohibited transfer	152.405
withdrawing partner's power to bind partnership	152.504
redemption upon withdrawal	152.601 et.seq.
redemption to transferee	152.611
binding effect of partner act after winding up	152.704
PARTNER LIABILITY	
generally	152.801
effect of withdrawing partner's existing liability	152.505
liability of withdrawing partner to third party	152.506
partner liability to other partners; event requiring winding up	152.705
contributions to discharge obligations	152.708
REMEDIES	
remedies of partnership and partners generally	152.211
remedy	152.305
enforcement of remedy	152.306
creditor's rights	152.307
charging order	152.308
FINANCING	
GENERAL RULE	152.202
PARTNERSHIP INTERESTS	
generally	1.002(68)
transfering pship interests	152.401
effect of partner death or divorce	152.406
WINDING UP/TERMINATION	
liquidation	152.706
settlement of accounts	152.707
contributions to discharge obligations	152.708
TERMINATION	

WITHDRAWAL	
events of withdrawal	152.501
effect of withdrawal	152.502
wrongful withdrawal	152.503
withdrawing partners power to bind partnership	152.504
withdrawing partners existing liability	152.505
liability of withdrawing partner to third parties	152.506
redemption	152.601
redemption price	152.602
contribution from wrongful withdrawer	152.603
set off	152.604
interest accrual	152.605
indemnification	152.606
demand of payment	152.607
deferring payment to wrongful withdrawer	152.608
civil action to determine redemption terms	152.609
effect of partner's death or divorce	152.406
WINDING UP	
events requiring winding up	152.701
deferring payment	152.610-
rights and duties of transferee	152.404
redemption to transferee	152.611
civil action to determine transferee's redemption price	152.612
who qualified to wind up	152.702
rights and duties of person winding up	152.703
binding effect of partner acts after winding up	152.704
partner liability to other partners; event of winding up	152.705
liquidation	152.706
settlement of accounts	152.707
contributions to discharge obligations	152.708
CONTINUING PARTNERSHIP	
canceling revocation	152.709
reinstatement	152.710-

THE CORPORATION

The corporation is a popularly recognized legal entity for conducting business. Once formed, this entity has rights similar to those of a natural person. It can own property, enter into contracts, and sue or be sued in court.

Yet despite its natural person-like characterization, it doesn't have a physical existence. Instead, it is a legal construct, created by statutes and refined by case law. In Texas, the statutes governing corporations are contained in Texas Business Organizations Code ("TBOC"). In 2010, the Code replaced the Texas Business Corporations Act. Though the Code changed some statutory terms used with corporations, it did not replace the case law that had developed under the Act. As such, when answering questions about corporations in Texas, the Code, the Act, and the case law should be reviewed.

The corporation entity offers economic, governance, and risk values that are different from other entities. The economic values include various tax reducing benefits, flexibility in tax rate, increased capital raising opportunities and free transferability of rights and interest. The primary governance value is centralized management and the risk values include limiting liability to third parties and limiting director and officer liability for the consequences of their decision making. The parties to the corporation are the people who directly realize those values who include the organizer; the director(s); the officer(s); the shareholder(s); and the employee(s). This chapter will address choosing and forming the for-profit corporation, the liability and exceptions to the limited liability protections afforded corporate parties through the principle of piercing the corporate veil and challenges to the corporate authority under the ultra vires doctrine. The chapter also reviews the corporation's governance and capital structures. Finally, it will discuss winding up and terminating the corporation.

Choosing the for-profit corporation entity

Deciding whether to incorporate rather than to create a partnership or other business entity requires a careful analysis of many factors. Unlike a partnership, which may be formed informally, and without filing anything with the secretary of state's office, a corporation is a filing entity created in conformance with statutory mandates.

Nature of the Corporation

The corporation is a separate legal entity with most of the same rights as a natural person, including being entitled to be a party at court, to incur liability, and to purchase property. §2.101. Moreover, corporations are recognized as 'persons' with constitutionally protected rights as was articulated in the United States Supreme Court decision in Citizens United v. Federal Election Commission, excerpted below.

Citizens United v. Federal Election Commission
558 U.S. 310, 130 S.Ct. 876, 175 L.Ed.2d 753 (2010)

Citizens United has an annual budget of about $12 million. Most of its funds are from donations by individuals; but, in addition, it accepts a small portion of its funds from for-profit corporations.

In January 2008, Citizens United released a film entitled *Hillary: The Movie*. We refer to the film as Hillary. It is a 90–minute documentary about then-Senator Hillary Clinton, who was a candidate in the Democratic Party's 2008 Presidential primary elections. Hillary mentions Senator Clinton by name and depicts interviews with political commentators and other persons, most of them quite critical of Senator Clinton. Hillary was released in theaters and on DVD, but Citizens United wanted to increase distribution by making it available through video-on-demand.

Video-on-demand allows digital cable subscribers to select programming from various menus, including movies, television shows, sports, news, and music. The viewer can watch the program at any time and can elect to rewind or pause the program. In December 2007, a cable company offered, for a payment of $1.2 million, to make Hillary available on a video-on-demand channel called "Elections '08." Some video-on-demand services require viewers to pay a small fee to view a selected program, but here the proposal was to make Hillary available to viewers free of charge.

To implement the proposal, Citizens United was prepared to pay for the video-on-demand; and to promote the film, it produced two 10–second ads and one 30–second ad for Hillary. Each ad includes a short (and, in our view, pejorative) statement about Senator Clinton, followed by the name of the movie and the movie's Website address Citizens United desired to promote the video-on-demand offering by running advertisements on broadcast and cable television.

Before the Bipartisan Campaign Reform Act of 2002 ("BCRA"), federal law prohibited—and still does prohibit—corporations and unions from using general treasury funds to make direct contributions to candidates or independent expenditures that expressly advocate the election or defeat of a candidate, through any form of media, in connection with certain qualified federal elections. 2 U.S.C. § 441b (2000 ed.).

Citizens United wanted to make Hillary available through video-on-demand within 30 days of the 2008 primary elections. It feared, however, that both the film and the ads would be covered by §441b's ban on corporate-funded independent expenditures, thus subjecting the corporation to civil and criminal penalties under §437g. In December 2007, Citizens United sought declaratory and injunctive relief against the FEC. It argued that (1) §441b is unconstitutional as applied to Hillary; and (2) BCRA's disclaimer and disclosure requirements, BCRA §§201 and 311, are unconstitutional as applied to Hillary and to the three ads for the movie.

As the District Court found, there is no reasonable interpretation of Hillary other than as an appeal to vote against Senator Clinton. Under the standard stated in McConnell and further elaborated in WRTL, the film qualifies as the functional equivalent of express advocacy.

Courts are bound by the First Amendment. We must decline to draw, and then redraw, constitutional lines based on the particular media or technology used to disseminate political speech from a particular speaker.

When the statute now at issue came before the Court in McConnell, both the majority and the dissenting opinions considered the question of its facial validity. The holding and validity of Austin were essential to the reasoning of the McConnell majority opinion, which upheld BCRA's extension of §441b. See 540 U.S., at 205, 124 S.Ct. 619 (quoting Austin, 494 U.S., at 660, 110 S.Ct. 1391). McConnell permitted federal felony punishment for speech by all corporations, including nonprofit ones, that speak on prohibited subjects shortly before federal elections. See 540 U.S., at 203–209, 124 S.Ct. 619. Four Members of the McConnell Court would have overruled Austin.

The First Amendment provides that "Congress shall make no law ... abridging the freedom of speech." Laws enacted to control or suppress speech may operate at different points in the speech process. ... The law before us is an outright ban, backed by criminal sanctions. Section 441b makes it a felony for all corporations—including nonprofit advocacy corporations—either to expressly advocate the election or defeat of candidates or to broadcast electioneering communications within 30 days of a primary election and 60 days of a general election. Thus, the following acts would all be felonies under § 441b: The Sierra Club runs an ad, within the crucial phase of 60 days before the general election, that exhorts the public to disapprove of a Congressman who favors logging in national forests; the National Rifle Association publishes a book urging the public to vote for the challenger because the incumbent U.S. Senator supports a handgun ban; and the American Civil Liberties Union creates a Web site telling the public to vote for a Presidential candidate in light of that candidate's defense of free speech. These prohibitions are classic examples of censorship.

Section 441b is a ban on corporate speech notwithstanding the fact that a PAC created by a corporation can still speak. See McConnell, 540 U.S., at 330–333, 124 S.Ct. 619 (opinion of KENNEDY, J.). A PAC is a separate association from the corporation. So the PAC exemption from §441b's expenditure ban, §441b(b)(2), does not allow corporations to speak. Even if a PAC could somehow allow a corporation to speak—and it does not—the option to form PACs does not alleviate the First Amendment problems with §441b. PACs are burdensome alternatives; they are expensive to administer and subject to extensive regulations. For example, every PAC must appoint a treasurer, forward donations to the treasurer promptly, keep detailed records of the identities of the persons making donations, preserve receipts for three years, and file an organization statement and report changes to this information within 10 days. See id., at 330–332, 124 S.Ct. 619 (quoting MCFL, 479 U.S., at 253–254, 107 S.Ct. 616).

And that is just the beginning. PACs must file detailed monthly reports with the FEC, which are due at different times depending on the type of election that is about to occur. PACs have to comply with these regulations just to speak. This might explain why fewer than 2,000 of the millions of corporations in this country have PACs. PACs, furthermore, must exist before they can speak. Given the onerous restrictions, a corporation may not be able to establish a PAC in time to make its views known regarding candidates and issues in a current campaign.

Section 441b's prohibition on corporate independent expenditures is thus a ban on speech. As a "restriction on the amount of money a person or group can spend on political communication during a campaign," that statute "necessarily reduces the quantity of expression by restricting the number of issues discussed, the depth of their exploration, and the size of the audience reached."

Quite apart from the purpose or effect of regulating content, moreover, the Government may commit a constitutional wrong when by law it identifies certain preferred speakers. By taking the right to speak from some and giving it to others, the Government deprives the disadvantaged person or class of the right to use speech to strive to establish worth, standing, and respect for the speaker's voice. The Government may not by these means deprive the public of the right and privilege to determine for itself what speech and speakers are worthy of consideration. The First Amendment protects speech and speaker, and the ideas that flow from each.

The Court has recognized that First Amendment protection extends to corporations. *Citations omitted.* This protection has been extended by explicit holdings to the context of political speech. See, e.g., Button, 371 U.S., at 428–429, 83 S.Ct. 328; Grosjean v. American Press Co., 297 U.S. 233, 244, 56 S.Ct. 444, 80 L.Ed. 660 (1936). Under the rationale of these precedents, political speech does not lose First Amendment protection "simply because its source is a corporation." Bellotti, supra, at 784, 98 S.Ct. 1407; see Pacific Gas & Elec. Co. v. Public Util. Comm'n of Cal., 475 U.S. 1, 8, 106 S.Ct. 903, 89 L.Ed.2d 1 (1986) (plurality opinion) ("The identity of the speaker is not decisive in determining whether speech is protected. Corporations and other associations, like individuals, contribute to the 'discussion, debate, and the dissemination of information and ideas' that the First Amendment seeks to foster". The Court has thus rejected the argument that political speech of corporations or other associations should be treated differently under the First Amendment simply because such associations are not "natural persons."

Bellotti, 435 U.S. 765, 98 S.Ct. 1407, 55 L.Ed.2d 707, reaffirmed the First Amendment principle that the Government cannot restrict political speech based on the speaker's corporate identity. Bellotti could not have been clearer when it struck down a state-law prohibition on corporate independent expenditures related to referenda issues:

> "We thus find no support in the First ... Amendment, or in the decisions of this Court, for the proposition that speech that otherwise would be within the protection of the First Amendment loses that protection simply because its source is a corporation...."

It is important to note that the reasoning and holding of Bellotti did not rest on the existence of a viewpoint-discriminatory statute. It rested on the principle that the Government lacks the power to ban corporations from speaking.

Thus the law stood until Austin. Austin "upheld a direct restriction on the independent expenditure of funds for political speech for the first time in [this Court's] history." 494 U.S., at 695, 110 S.Ct. 1391 (KENNEDY, J., dissenting). There, the Michigan Chamber of Commerce sought to use general treasury funds to run a newspaper ad supporting a specific candidate. Michigan law, however, prohibited corporate independent expenditures that supported or opposed any candidate for state office. A violation of the law was punishable as a felony. The Court sustained the speech prohibition.

To bypass Buckley and Bellotti, the Austin Court identified a new governmental interest in limiting political speech: an antidistortion interest. Austin found a compelling governmental interest in preventing "the corrosive and distorting effects of immense aggregations of wealth that are accumulated with the help of the corporate form and that have little or no correlation to the public's support for the corporation's political ideas."

The Court is thus confronted with conflicting lines of precedent: a pre- Austin line that forbids restrictions on political speech based on the speaker's corporate identity and a post- Austin line that permits them. No case before Austin had held that Congress could prohibit independent expenditures for political speech based on the speaker's corporate identity. If the First Amendment has any force, it prohibits Congress from fining or jailing citizens, or associations of citizens, for simply engaging in political speech.

It is irrelevant for purposes of the First Amendment that corporate funds may "have little or no correlation to the public's support for the corporation's political ideas." Id., at 660, 110 S.Ct. 1391 (majority opinion). All speakers, including individuals and the media, use money amassed from the economic marketplace to fund their speech. The First Amendment protects the resulting speech, even if it was enabled by economic transactions with persons or entities who disagree with the speaker's ideas. See id., at 707, 110 S.Ct. 1391 (KENNEDY, J., dissenting) ("Many persons can trace their funds to corporations, if not in the form of donations, then in the form of dividends, interest, or salary").

Due consideration leads to this conclusion: Austin, 494 U.S. 652, 110 S.Ct. 1391, 108 L.Ed.2d 652, should be and now is overruled. We return to the principle established in Buckley and Bellotti that the Government may not suppress political speech on the basis of the speaker's corporate identity. No sufficient governmental interest justifies limits on the political speech of nonprofit or for-profit corporations.

****

Side Bar on Citizen's United

The U.S. Supreme Court's ruling in Citizens United changes the way corporations may spend money to support or oppose federal candidates during elections. Much of the controversy surrounding the opinion is its impact on our collective notion of democracy as being the power of the individual. It is suggested that the Citizen's United ruling paves the way for dramatically changing that democratic landscape from the power of the individual to the power of the corporation. This ruling suggests that the long held view of a corporation's personhood was unconstitutionally limited by recognizing corporate first amendment right to free speech. This could arguably change the democratic landscape from one person, one vote, a philosophy embodying "we the people" to a corporate-dominated political structure.

However, the court's ruling did not change (1) federal restrictions on tax-exempt groups and which are permitted to engage in political activity, (2) certain tax rules relating to nondeductibility of dues payments made to trade or membership organizations because of those organizations' lobbying expenses, (3) Nonprofit corporations are still prohibited from making contributions from organization funds directly to federal candidates, political committees, PACs, and national political parties and (4) federal PACs can continue to makle contributions directly to federal candidates.

The ruling does (1) give corporations, including associations, the ability to make unlimited independent expenditures and participate in electioneering communications using corporate funds. (2) Corporate funds can also be used to communicate to the public, organization employees, and members about federal candidates subject to all applicable disclaimer requirements.

Whether the ruling will dramatically change how the corporation's personhood is manifested remains to be seen.

Perpetual existence

Commonly, a corporation has a perpetual existence until and unless it chooses to be dissolved. TBOC§§ 3.003, 11.051(2), (3), 21.501.

The corporation's perpetual existence is a beneficial quality for publicly held corporations (corporations traded on stock exchanges). Because of the corporation's perpetual existence changes in the board of managers including death has no impact on the corporation's mortality.

Centralized management

While partnerships are often informally managed, public corporations are typically managed by a board of directors. TBOC provides

§21.401. MANAGEMENT BY BOARD OF DIRECTORS.

(a) Except as provided by Section 21.101 or Subchapter O, the board of directors of a corporation shall:

(1) exercise or authorize the exercise of the powers of the corporation; and

(2) direct the management of the business and affairs of the corporation.

(b) In discharging the duties of director under this code or otherwise and in considering the best interests of the corporation, a director may consider the long-term and short-term interests of the corporation and the shareholders of the corporation, including the possibility that those interests may be best served by the continued independence of the corporation.

TBOC §21.101 permits corporations to elect alternate management schemes.

§21.101. SHAREHOLDERS' AGREEMENT.

(a) The shareholders of a corporation may enter into an agreement that:

(1) restricts the discretion or powers of the board of directors;

(2) eliminates the board of directors and authorizes the business and affairs of the corporation to be managed, wholly or partly, by one or more of its shareholders or other persons;

(3) establishes the individuals who shall serve as directors or officers of the corporation;

(4) determines the term of office, manner of selection or removal, or terms or conditions of employment of a director, officer, or other employee of the corporation, regardless of the length of employment;

(5) governs the authorization or making of distributions whether in proportion to ownership of shares, subject to Section 21.303;

(6) determines the manner in which profits and losses will be apportioned;

(7) governs, in general or with regard to specific matters, the exercise or division of voting power by and between the shareholders, directors, or other persons, including use of disproportionate voting rights or director proxies;

(8) establishes the terms of an agreement for the transfer or use of property or for the provision of services between the corporation and another person, including a shareholder, director, officer, or employee of the corporation;

(9) authorizes arbitration or grants authority to a shareholder or other person to resolve any issue about which there is a deadlock among the directors, shareholders, or other persons authorized to manage the corporation;

(10) requires winding up and termination of the corporation at the request of one or more shareholders or on the occurrence of a specified event or contingency, in which case the winding up and termination of the corporation will proceed as if all of the shareholders had consented in writing to the winding up and termination as provided by Subchapter K; or

(11) otherwise governs the exercise of corporate powers, the management of the business and affairs of the corporation, or the relationship among the shareholders, the directors, and the corporation as if the corporation were a partnership or in a manner that would otherwise be appropriate only among partners and not contrary to public policy.

(b) A shareholders' agreement authorized by this section must be:

(1) contained in:

(A) the certificate of formation or bylaws if approved by all of the shareholders at the time of the agreement; or

(B) a written agreement that is:

(i) signed by all of the shareholders at the time of the agreement; and

(ii) made known to the corporation; and

(2) amended only by all of the shareholders at the time of the amendment, unless the agreement provides otherwise.

Limited liability

As an entity separate from its parties, a corporation itself is liable for its liabilities. Unless a claimant can show a basis for piercing the corporate veil of protection, the individual parties of the corporation are not liable for its debts and obligations.

§21.223. LIMITATION OF LIABILITY FOR OBLIGATIONS.

(a) A holder of shares, an owner of any beneficial interest in shares, or a subscriber for shares whose subscription has been accepted, or any affiliate of such a holder, owner, or subscriber or of the corporation, may not be held liable to the corporation or its obligees with respect to:

(1) the shares, other than the obligation to pay to the corporation the full amount of consideration, fixed in compliance with Sections 21.157-21.162, for which the shares were or are to be issued;

(2) any contractual obligation of the corporation or any matter relating to or arising from the obligation on the basis that the holder, beneficial owner, subscriber, or affiliate is or was the alter ego of the corporation or on the basis of actual or constructive fraud, a sham to perpetrate a fraud, or other similar theory; or

(3) any obligation of the corporation on the basis of the failure of the corporation to observe any corporate formality, including the failure to:

(A) comply with this code or the certificate of formation or bylaws of the corporation; or

(B) observe any requirement prescribed by this code or the certificate of formation or bylaws of the corporation for acts to be taken by the corporation or its directors or shareholders.

(b) Subsection (a)(2) does not prevent or limit the liability of a holder, beneficial owner, subscriber, or affiliate if the obligee demonstrates that the holder, beneficial owner, subscriber, or affiliate caused the corporation to be used for the purpose of perpetrating

Exception: and did perpetrate *an actual fraud on the obligee primarily for the direct personal benefit of the holder, beneficial owner, subscriber, or affiliate.*

§7.001. LIMITATION OF LIABILITY OF GOVERNING PERSON.

(a) Subsections (b) and (c) apply to:

(1) a domestic entity other than a partnership or limited liability company;

(2) another organization incorporated or organized under another law of this state; and

(3) to the extent permitted by federal law, a federally chartered bank, savings and loan association, or credit union.

(b) The certificate of formation or similar instrument of an organization to which this section applies may provide that a governing person of the organization *is not liable, or is liable only to the extent provided by the certificate of formation or similar instrument,* to the organization or its owners or members for monetary damages for an act or omission by the person in the person's capacity as a governing person.

(c) Subsection (b) does not authorize the elimination or limitation of the liability of a governing person to the extent the person is found liable under applicable law for:

Exceptions:

(1) a breach of the person's *duty of loyalty,* if any, to the organization or its owners or members;

(2) an act or omission *not in good faith that:*

(A) constitutes *a breach of duty of the* person to the organization; or

(B) involves *intentional misconduct* or a *knowing violation of law;*

(3) a transaction from which the person received an *improper benefit, regardless* of whether the benefit resulted from an action taken within the scope of the person's duties; or

(4) an act or omission for which the liability of a governing person is *expressly provided by an applicable* statute.

(d) The liability of a governing person may be limited or restricted:

(1) in a general partnership to the extent permitted under Chapter 152;

(2) in a limited partnership to the extent permitted under Chapter 153 and, to the extent applicable to limited partnerships, Chapter 152; and

(3) in a limited liability company to the extent permitted under Section 101.401.

Free transferability of rights and ownership interests

Shareholders may sell their ownership rights and interests in the corporation with minimal interference. This free transferability of ownership allows the shareholder maximum flexibility as long as there is a market for the shares.

When free transferability of shares is not preferred, the corporation may restrict the transferability in accordance with the applicable statute.

§21.209. TRANSFER OF SHARES AND OTHER SECURITIES. *Except as otherwise provided by this code, the shares and other securities of a corporation are transferable in accordance with Chapter 8, Business & Commerce Code.*

§21.210. RESTRICTION ON TRANSFER OF SHARES AND OTHER SECURITIES. *(a) A restriction on the transfer or registration of transfer of a security, or on the amount of a corporation's securities that may be owned by a person or group of persons, may be imposed by:*

(1) the corporation's certificate of formation;

(2) the corporation's bylaws;

(3) a written agreement among two or more holders of the securities; or

(4) a written agreement among one or more holders of the securities and the corporation if:

    (A) the corporation files a copy of the agreement at the principal place of business or registered office of the corporation; and

    (B) the copy of the agreement is subject to the same right of examination by a shareholder of the corporation, in person or by agent, attorney, or accountant, as the books and records of the corporation.

(b) A restriction imposed under Subsection (a) is not valid with respect to a security issued before the restriction has been adopted, unless the holder of the security voted in favor of the restriction or is a party to the agreement imposing the restriction.

§21.211. VALID RESTRICTIONS ON TRANSFER.

(a) Without limiting the general powers granted by Sections 21.210 and 21.213 to impose and enforce reasonable restrictions, a restriction placed on the transfer or registration of transfer of a security of a corporation is valid if the restriction reasonably:

    (1) obligates the holder of the restricted security to offer a person, including the corporation or other holders of securities of the corporation, an opportunity to acquire the restricted security within a reasonable time before the transfer;

(2) obligates the corporation, to the extent provided by this code, or another person to purchase securities that are the subject of an agreement relating to the purchase and sale of the restricted security;

(3) requires the corporation or the holders of a class of the corporation's securities to consent to a proposed transfer of the restricted security or to approve the proposed transferee of the restricted security for the purpose of preventing a violation of law;

(4) prohibits the transfer of the restricted security to a designated person or group of persons and the designation is not manifestly unreasonable;

(5) maintains the status of the corporation as an electing small business corporation under Subchapter S of the Internal Revenue Code;

(6) maintains a tax advantage to the corporation;

(7) maintains the status of the corporation as a close corporation under Subchapter O;

(8) obligates the holder of the restricted securities to sell or transfer an amount of restricted securities to a person or group of persons, including the corporation or other holders of securities of the corporation; or

(9) causes or results in the automatic sale or transfer of an amount of restricted securities to a person or group of persons, including the corporation or other holders of securities of the corporation.

(b) A restriction placed on the transfer or registration of transfer of a security of a corporation, on the amount of the corporation's securities, or on the amount of the corporation's securities that may be owned by a person or group of persons is conclusively presumed to be for a reasonable purpose if the restriction:

(1) maintains a local, state, federal, or foreign tax advantage to the corporation or its shareholders, including:

(A) maintaining the corporation's status as an electing small business corporation under Subchapter S of the Internal Revenue Code;

(B) maintaining or preserving any tax attribute, including net operating losses; or

(C) qualifying or maintaining the qualification of the corporation as a real estate investment trust under the Internal Revenue Code or regulations adopted under the Internal Revenue Code; or

(2) maintains a statutory or regulatory advantage or complies with a statutory or regulatory requirement under applicable local, state, federal, or foreign law.

§ 21.212. BYLAW OR AGREEMENT RESTRICTING TRANSFER OF SHARES OR OTHER SECURITIES.

(a) A corporation that has adopted a bylaw or is a party to an agreement that restricts the transfer of the shares or other securities of the corporation may file with the secretary of state, in accordance with Chapter 4, a copy of the bylaw or agreement and a statement attached to the copy that:

(1) contains the name of the corporation;

(2) states that the attached copy of the bylaw or agreement is a true and correct copy of the bylaw or agreement; and

(3) states that the filing has been authorized by the board of directors or, in the case of a corporation that is managed in some other manner under a shareholders' agreement, by the person empowered by the agreement to manage the corporation's business and affairs.

(b) After a statement described by Subsection (a) is filed with the secretary of state, the bylaws or agreement restricting the transfer of shares or other securities is a public record, and the fact that the statement has been filed may be stated on a certificate representing the restricted shares or securities if required by Section 3.202.

(c) A corporation that is a party to an agreement restricting the transfer of the shares or other securities of the corporation may make the agreement part of the corporation's certificate of formation without restating the provisions of the agreement in the certificate of formation by amending the certificate of formation. If the agreement alters any provision of the certificate of formation, the certificate of amendment shall identify the altered provision by reference or description. If the agreement is an addition to the certificate of formation, the certificate of amendment must state that fact.

(d) The certificate of amendment must:

(1) include a copy of the agreement restricting the transfer of shares or other securities;

(2) state that the attached copy of the agreement is a true and correct copy of the agreement; and

(3) state that inclusion of the certificate of amendment as part of the certificate of formation has been authorized in the manner required by this code to amend the certificate of formation

§ 21.213. ENFORCEABILITY OF RESTRICTION ON TRANSFER OF CERTAIN SECURITIES.

(a) A restriction placed on the transfer or registration of the transfer of a security of a corporation is specifically enforceable against the holder, or a successor or transferee of the holder, if:

(1) the restriction is reasonable and noted conspicuously on the certificate or other instrument representing the security; or

(2) with respect to an uncertificated security, the restriction is reasonable and a notation of the restriction is contained in the notice sent with respect to the security under Section 3.205.

(b) Unless noted in the manner specified by Subsection (a) with respect to a certificate or other instrument or an uncertificated security, an otherwise enforceable restriction is ineffective against a transferee for value without actual knowledge of the restriction at the time of the transfer or against a subsequent transferee, regardless of whether the transfer is for value. A restriction is specifically enforceable against a person other than a transferee for value from the time the person acquires actual knowledge of the restriction's existence.

Prior to forming the for-profit corporation

Prior to forming a corporation, a few steps will typically occur. First, one or more people will agree to form a corporation. These persons may serve as organizers or promoters for the to-be-formed corporation or may hire someone to serve in that capacity. The organizer helps turn their desire to form a corporation into a reality. Commonly, the organizer may "bring together the persons who become interested in the enterprise, aids in procuring subscribers [people interested in investing in the corporation] and sets in motion the machinery" leading to the corporation being formed. 2 HILDEBRAND, TEXAS CORPORATIONS, § 411. Organizers may be personally liable for their actions during the creating stage of the corporation.

The Corporation's Name

Selecting a name

Before the state will recognize a corporation to conduct business, the corporation must select a name that is neither the same nor deceptively similar to an existing corporation. TBOC §5.053. *See also Texas Administrative Code §79.39*

Sometimes an organizer may reserve a corporate name with the secretary of state to prevent another entity usurping that name prior to the filing of the certificate of formation.

Reserving a name

Any person may reserve the exclusive use of name by filing an application with the state. TBOC§ 5.101. After the State approves the name, the reservation lasts for 120 days. TBOC§ 5.104. That period may be extended by filing a renewal within the last 30 days of the original registration. TBOC§5.105.

Forming the Corporation

Texas requires all domestic corporations that operate within its borders to file a certificate of formation with the secretary of state. (TBOC §§ 4.001; 21.052- 21.055) Texas is a dejure state. Some jurisdictions recognize defacto corporation and corporations by estoppel.

Where a corporation is formed in accordance with the applicable laws, it is a de jure corporation. Once it has been formed in accordance with the applicable law, the corporate owners are shielded from personal liability for the corporation's obligations. When the corporation fails to form in accordance with the statutory requirements, its owners could be personally liable for the corporation's obligations. In those jurisdictions that recognize defacto corporations or corporations by estoppel, corporate owners may be shielded from liability.

Generally, the defacto corporation may exist in those instances where

1. There exists a statute enabling the existence of a defacto corporation and the corporation could have been legally incorporated;
2. Where the organizer made a colorable attempt (*i.e.*, good faith) to comply with the incorporation laws; and
3. The corporation has conducted its business in its corporate name and exercised corporate privileges
4. With a good faith reliance that the corporation did exist.

Where the defacto corporation is authorized to exist, the doctrine generally shields owners from personal liability – much like a de jure corporation. This doctrine has its limit. Where a person purports to act as or on behalf of a corporation knowing that either the formation document was defective, or it was never filed, then that person is liable for all liabilities resulting from his or her acts. *See In re Hausman, 13 N.Y. 3d 408, 921 N.E. 2d 191 (N.Y. 2009).*

In some cases, even though a corporation has not been created, courts of equity will treat the entity as a corporation in equity. This equitable fiction is referred to as a corporation by estoppel.

<u>The corporation by estoppel</u>

The corporation by estoppel is an equitable vehicle that estops a person who treats an entity as a corporation from later claiming that the entity was not a corporation. This doctrine works in two ways. First, it estops an outsider seeking to avoid liability on a contract with the purported corporation. Second, it estops the purported corporation from trying to avoid liability on a contract with an outsider.

In Texas, neither the defacto corporation nor the corporation by estoppel is recognized. To be recognized as a corporate entity in Texas, the corporation must have been established in accordance with the Texas Business Organizations Code.

Thus, in Texas, a failure to properly file the certificate of formation may result in the entity being treated as a sole proprietorship or a partnership. In the event of a defective filing, the entity must timely amend the certificate or otherwise correct the deficiency to be recognized as a corporation. TBOC §4.101

§4.101. CORRECTION OF FILINGS.

(a) A filing instrument that has been filed with the secretary of state that is an inaccurate record of the event or transaction evidenced in the instrument, that contains an inaccurate or erroneous statement, or that was defectively or erroneously signed, sealed, acknowledged, or verified may be corrected by filing a certificate of correction.

(b) A certificate of correction must be signed by the person authorized by this code to sign the filing instrument to be corrected.

American Vending Services, Inc., v. Durbano et.al.
881 P. 2d 917 (Utah App, 1994)

Trustees for family trust to which promissory note was conveyed brought action against promoters of corporation and against corporation on behalf of which note was issued. The Third District Court entered judgment against corporation but not against promoters, and trustees appealed. The Court of Appeals held that promoters were personally liable.

Appellants, Wayne L. and Dianne L. Morse, individually and as Trustees of the Wayne L. Morse Irrevocable Family Trusts (Morses), appeal the trial court's ruling in their favor, asserting error in the court's legal conclusions regarding de facto corporations and corporations by estoppel as well as the court's decision regarding attorney fees. Appellee and Cross-appellant, American Vending Services, Inc. (AVSI) appeals the trial court's ruling against it, asserting that the trial court erred in finding that there was insufficient evidence to support AVSI's claims of fraudulent and negligent misrepresentation, breach of contract, and mutual mistake. We reverse in part and affirm in part.

The plethora of issues in this case arise from the relatively straightforward transaction of a car wash sale. Wayne L. and Dianne L. Morse built the car wash in 1984 and operated it for approximately eleven months. Thereafter, they entered into a contract with Douglas M. Durbano and Kevin S. Garn, both licensed attorneys acting as officers of AVSI, to purchase the car wash. Mr. Durbano and Mr. Garn claim that they represented to the Morses that the corporate entity, AVSI, would purchase and operate the car wash. At the time the parties executed the contract on July 10, 1985, Mr. Durbano had not filed the Articles of Incorporation for AVSI, although he had received permission from the Utah Division of Corporations to use the name American Vending Services, Inc. Mr. Durbano claims that he had twice tried to file Articles of Incorporation for this corporate entity before the contract was executed. In both cases, however, the Articles of

Incorporation were returned because of a name conflict. The Articles of Incorporation for AVSI were finally executed on August 1, 1985 and subsequently filed on August 19, 1985. Mr. Durbano's explanation for not filing the Articles of Incorporation before the parties executed the contract on July 10, 1985 was that he was "moving offices and was too busy and distracted to file the articles." The Morses asserted personal liability of Mr. Durbano and Mr. Garn based on the fact that the corporation did not legally exist when the parties executed the contract. The trial court dismissed the Morses' claims against Mr. Durbano and Mr. Garn, finding that Mr. Durbano's efforts to twice file Articles of Incorporation "constitute[d] a bona fide attempt to organize the corporation."

AVSI operated the car wash for approximately three years. It experienced financial difficulty, however, almost from the beginning and failed to make any payments to the Morses on the balance owing under the sales contract. Mr. Durbano and Mr. Garn claim that Mr. Morse provided them with projected income figures that were padded and false. Mr. Morse claims that the numbers were based on usage meters from the car wash which had been verified by another party. Mr. Morse also explains that the figures supplied to Mr. Durbano and Mr. Garn covered the best operating months of the year and thus were not tempered by the three or four slow months of operation. Finally, Mr. Morse claims that the car wash's financial troubles stemmed more from the inexperience of Mr. Durbano and Mr. Garn in operating a car wash than from incorrect income projections. Unable to profitably operate the car wash, AVSI eventually allowed the bank to foreclose on it. At trial, Mr. Garn's accountant, who prepared the books and tax returns for all of Mr. Garn's businesses, including AVSI, testified that the business income and expense from AVSI was reported by Mr. Garn and Mr. Durbano as if they were operating a partnership. The corporate tax returns for AVSI were filed, but with the notation written across the front of the returns that the corporation was inactive.

At the conclusion of trial, the court entered its Findings of Fact. Those relevant to the issues on appeal are summarized as follows: (1) The Morses knew throughout the negotiations that Mr. Durbano and Mr. Garn intended to form a corporation to purchase the car wash; (2) Mr. Durbano and Mr. Garn's efforts to file Articles of Incorporation and obtain preapproval for the name American Vending Services, Inc. constituted a bona fide attempt to organize the corporation; (3) the Morses admitted AVSI's corporate existence in their initial answer to AVSI's complaint; (4) the Morses intended to contract with AVSI rather than with Mr. Durbano and Mr. Garn individually; and (5) AVSI's evidence concerning fraudulent and negligent misrepresentation, breach of contract, and mutual mistake was insufficient to allow AVSI the right to rescind the contract.

Based on these Findings of Fact, the trial court entered the following relevant Conclusions of Law: (1) AVSI was a de facto corporation when it purchased the car wash; (2) AVSI was a corporation by estoppel when it purchased the car wash; (3) the Morses are estopped from denying the corporate existence of AVSI; and (4) AVSI failed to establish the elements of its claims for fraud, misrepresentation, breach of contract, and mutual mistake.

The trial court awarded damages to the Morses against AVSI in the amount of $76,832.30, plus costs, interest, and reasonable attorney fees. The Morses now appeal the trial court's ruling because, although favorable to them in most respects, it was apparently a hollow victory; AVSI has no assets or income from which it can satisfy the judgment. Thus, the Morses appeal the trial court's ruling that Mr. Durbano and Mr. Garn are not personally liable on the contract. In response, Mr. Garn and Mr. Durbano filed a cross-appeal, arguing principally that the trial court erred in concluding that the evidence regarding AVSI's claims of fraudulent and negligent misrepresentation, breach of contract, and mutual mistake was insufficient to permit AVSI to rescind the contract.

We address the following issues on appeal: (1) Whether the trial court erroneously concluded that AVSI was a de facto corporation; [and] (2) Whether the trial court erred by concluding as a matter of law that AVSI was a corporation by estoppel, and thereby precluding the Morses from denying its corporate existence. [other bases for appeal are not discussed]

DeFacto Corporations in Utah. At common law, corporations could be either de jure, de facto, or by estoppel.

A de jure corporation is ordinarily thought of as one which has been created as the result of compliance with all of the constitutional or statutory requirements of a particular governmental entity. A de facto corporation, on the other hand, can be brought into being when it can be shown that a bona fide and colorable attempt has been made to create a corporation, even though the efforts at incorporation can be shown to be irregular, informal or even defective.

Corporations by estoppel come about when the parties thereto are estopped from denying a corporate existence. In other words, the parties may, by their agreements or conduct, estop themselves from denying the existence of the corporation. *Harris v. Stephens Wholesale Bldg. Supply Co.*, 54 Ala.App. 405, 309 So.2d 115, 117-18 (Ala.Civ.App.1975) (citations omitted).

In Utah, corporate formation and all its attendant formalities are governed by the Business Corporation Act. Two sections of that act are relevant to the issues raised in this appeal. Section 16-10-51 indicates that a corporation's existence begins when the State issues the certificate of incorporation.

"Upon the issuance of the certificate of incorporation, the corporate existence shall begin, and the certificate of incorporation shall be conclusive evidence that all conditions precedent required of the incorporators have been complied with and that the corporation has been incorporated under this act, except as against this state in a proceeding to cancel or revoke the certificate of incorporation or for involuntary dissolution of the corporation." Utah Code Ann. § 16-10-51 (1991). Additionally, section 16-10-139 provides: "All persons who assume to act as a corporation without authority so to do shall be jointly and severally liable for all debts and liabilities incurred or arising as a result thereof." *Id.* § 16-10-139.

At common law, the doctrine of de facto corporations was created to protect individuals from personal liability when they were legitimately conducting corporate business before the corporate formalities were complete. Under this doctrine, the corporation, rather than the individual incorporators, was held liable for preincorporation obligations if several factors were present: (1) A valid law existed under which such a corporation could be lawfully organized; (2) an attempt had been made to organize thereunder; and (3) the defective corporation was an actual user of the corporate franchise. *Robertson v. Levy,* 197 A.2d 443, 445 (D.C.App.1964) (citing *Tulare Irrigation Dist. v. Shepard,* 185 U.S. 1, 13, 22 S.Ct. 531, 536, 46 L.Ed. 773 (1902)). Often added to this list of requirements was a fourth one-"[g]ood faith in claiming to be and in doing business as a corporation." *Id.* Over time, the doctrine of de facto corporations has been "roundly criticized." *Id.*

This criticism provided partial impetus for the emergence of the Model Business Corporation Act (MBCA). The MBCA strove to codify a uniform set of laws regarding corporations and to provide some clarity and bright-line tests to previously clouded areas. Many states, including Utah, adopted the MBCA in whole or in part.

Under the Model Act, de jure incorporation is complete upon the issuance of the certificate of incorporation.... Under the unequivocal provisions of the Model Act, any steps short of securing a certificate of incorporation would not constitute apparent compliance. Therefore a de facto corporation cannot exist under the Model Act. Model Business Corporation Act Ann., § 56 cmt., at 205 (1971). Similarly, the comment to section 146 states:

[S]ection [146] is designed to prohibit the application of any theory of de facto incorporation. The only authority to act as a corporation under the Model Act arises from completion of the procedures prescribed in section 53 to 55 inclusive. The consequences of those procedures are specified in section 56 as being the creation of a corporation. No other means being authorized, the effect of section 146 is to negate the possibility of a de facto corporation.

Abolition of the concept of de facto incorporation, which at best was fuzzy, is a sound result. No reason exists for its continuance under general corporate laws, where the process of acquiring de jure incorporation is both simple and clear. The vestigial appendage should be removed. *Id.* § 146 cmt., at 908-09.

The 1977 Utah Supreme Court case of *Gillham Advertising Agency, Inc. v. Ipson,* 567 P.2d 163 (Utah 1977) impacts the present case in two important ways. First, *Gillham* is factually similar to the present case in that an individual signed an agreement as president of a corporation that did not exist in Utah at the time of signing. The agreement imposed liability on the nonexistent corporation. The supreme court held that the individual was personally liable on the debt because there was no novation of the agreement by which the corporation agreed to pay the debt and the creditor did not release the individual who signed the agreement from liability. *Id.* at 164. Furthermore, the court also justified the imposition of personal liability on the individual because no corporation existed at the time the parties executed the agreement. *Gillham*, 567 P.2d at 164-65. Second, *Gillham* is important because it cited with approval the comments from section 146 of the MBCA demonstrating the MBCA's intent to extinguish de facto corporations. *Id.* at 166

We believe that the Legislature intended to extinguish the doctrine of de facto corporations when it adopted the Business Corporation Act because the relevant portions of the Act, sections 51 and 139, were taken verbatim from the MBCA. The Legislature's word-for-word adoption of these sections can be reasonably construed as an implicit acceptance of the comments attached thereto which express the underlying intent of the MBCA generally and these sections specifically to abolish de facto corporations.

Accordingly, the trial court erred when it concluded as a matter of law that AVSI was a de facto corporation when the car wash was purchased. It is undisputed that the State of Utah had not issued a certificate of incorporation to AVSI before the car wash was sold and transferred. Hence, pursuant to section 16-10-51, AVSI's corporate existence had not yet begun. Furthermore, section 16-10-139 imposes joint and several liability on Mr. Durbano and Mr. Garn for all the debts and liabilities that they incurred or that arose as a result of their actions before the corporation legally existed. In the present case, that liability is for the judgment amount entered against AVSI by the trial court.

Corporation by Estoppel in Utah

AVSI argues next that the Morses are estopped from arguing that it was not a corporation because the Morses knew all along that Mr. Durbano and Mr. Garn intended to have AVSI purchase and run the car wash. The question of whether the doctrine of corporation by estoppel remains viable in this State after adoption of the Business Corporation Act is an issue of first impression. The Utah Supreme Court has not specifically addressed whether the doctrine of corporation by estoppel still exists after adoption of the Business Corporation Act.

The doctrine developed in the courts of equity to prevent unfairness. As one court has stated, "Corporation by estoppel is a difficult concept to grasp and courts and writers have 'gone all over the lot' in attempting to define and apply the doctrine." Timberline Equipment Co. v. Davenport, 267 Or. 64, 514 P.2d 1109, 1111 (1973). A treatise on corporations defines the doctrine as follows:

The so-called estoppel that arises to deny corporate capacity does not depend on the presence of the technical elements of equitable estoppel, viz., misrepresentations and change of position in reliance thereon, but on the nature of the relations contemplated, that one who has recognized the organization as a corporation in business dealings should not be allowed to quibble or raise immaterial issues on matters which do not concern him in the slightest degree or affect his substantial rights. *Id.* 514 P.2d at 1111-12 (quoting Ballantine, *Manual of Corporation Law and Practice* §§ 28-30 (1930)). Generally, courts apply this doctrine according to who is being charged with estoppel. Usually the courts are willing to apply corporation by estoppel when the case involves a defendant seeking to escape liability to a corporation by complaining that the corporation's existence is flawed. *Id.* at 1112. On the other hand, courts are typically more reluctant to apply the doctrine when individuals, usually incorporators, seek to escape liability by contending that the debtor is a corporation rather than the individuals who purported to act as a corporation. *Id.*

A review of jurisdictions that have addressed this issue reveals a divergence of views. For example, Oklahoma, and apparently Georgia, have adopted the position that the doctrine of corporation by estoppel cannot be invoked to deny corporate existence unless the corporation has at least a de facto existence. *Don Swann Sales Corp. v. Echols,* 160 Ga.App. 539, 287 S.E.2d 577, 579-80 (1981); *James v. Unknown Trustees,* 203 Okla. 312, 220 P.2d 831, 835 (1950). The District of Columbia and Tennessee have taken the position that the MBCA eliminated estoppel corporations altogether. *Robertson v. Levy,* 197 A.2d 443, 446 (D.C.App.1964); *Thompson & Green Mach. v. Music City Lumber Co.,* 683 S.W.2d 340, 344-45 (Tenn.App.1984). Another view, taken by Alaska, allows corporations by estoppel even when the corporation has not achieved de facto existence. *Willis v. City of Valdez,* 546 P.2d 570, 574 (Alaska 1976). Still another jurisdiction, Arkansas, has stated that corporation by estoppel rests "wholly upon equitable principles ... and should be applied only where there are equitable grounds for doing so." *Childs v. Philpot,* 253 Ark. 589, 487 S.W.2d 637, 641 (1972). Finally, Florida has adopted the position that the doctrine of corporation by estoppel cannot be invoked where the individual seeking to avoid liability had constructive or actual knowledge that the corporation did not exist. *Harry Rich Corp. v. Feinberg,* 518 So.2d 377, 381 (Fla.App.1987).

In addition, the holding in *Levy* that the MBCA eliminated both de facto and estoppel corporations is unsupported by the comments to the MBCA. The comments to §§ 56 and 146 specifically address de facto corporations, but except for several annotations to cases discussing estoppel corporations, are silent as to whether the MBCA eliminated corporations by estoppel.

I am unpersuaded by the argument that the adoption of the Utah Business Corporation Act extinguished the doctrine of corporation by estoppel in addition to de facto corporations. While some jurisdictions have adopted this position, I find no basis in the comments to the MBCA for such a stance. Likewise, I find unconvincing those cases holding that a de facto corporation must exist before the theory of corporation by estoppel has viability. The theories of de facto and estoppel corporations are separate and distinct; the former is grounded in law while the latter is based on equity.

The fact that directors, officers, and shareholders in Utah generally enjoy limited liability is a benefit conferred by the Legislature and is the result of a public policy decision aimed at encouraging Utah's citizens to engage in private enterprise with all its attendant risks. To make this limited liability available with relative ease, the Business Corporation Act, and its successor, the Revised Business Corporation Act, make the act of incorporation fairly painless-both in terms of the financial cost and effort required to incorporate. Given the ease of incorporating, I am hesitant to carve out exceptions to the general rule found in section 16-10-139 that individuals who assume to act as a corporation before that corporation exists are jointly and severally liable.

Notwithstanding my reluctance to make an exception, I am persuaded by the reasoning of the Florida Court of Appeals that the doctrine of corporation by estoppel should be viable in the narrow situation when those individuals acting on behalf of the corporation have no actual or constructive knowledge that the corporation does not exist. In *Harry Rich Corp.*, the appeals court focused on the language in Florida's statute that imposed joint and several liability on individuals who "assume to act" as a corporation. 518 So.2d at 381. Florida's statute, § 607.397, is derived from the 1969 version of the Model Business Corporation Act and does not differ materially from Utah's § 139. The court found significant that the statute does not impose liability on all those who "act," but only on those who "assume to act." Based on this distinction, the Florida court concluded that "the use of this language reflects an intent to limit the statute's application to those persons who knew or, because of their position, should have known" that the corporation did not exist. The court further noted that where corporation by estoppel (which allows recovery from the corporation) is retained alongside a statute imposing liability on an individual who assumes to act as a corporation, recovery from the individual should be permitted only where the individual acts with actual or constructive knowledge that no corporation exists. This slight windfall to the creditor can be justified on the ground that the individual has not been completely forthcoming to the creditor and should suffer the consequences. *Id.* I agree with this reasoning and would hold that the doctrine of corporation by estoppel, because it coexists with section 16-10-139, can be invoked only where both parties reasonably believe they are dealing with a corporation and neither party has actual or constructive knowledge that the corporation does not exist.

In the present case, the parties dispute whether both sides knew that a corporation was involved. Mr. Garn and Mr. Durbano claim that the Morses knew from the beginning that AVSI was to purchase the car wash. Conversely, the Morses claim that they only discovered the involvement of AVSI when they signed the papers at closing. Despite the parties' conflicting accounts, it is undisputed that at the time the Morses signed the contract, Mr. Durbano and Mr. Garn had actual or constructive knowledge that AVSI did not legally exist under the laws of Utah. Accordingly, neither Mr. Durbano nor Mr. Garn can invoke the doctrine of corporation by estoppel to shield them from personal liability for the debts that they incurred while assuming to act on behalf of the nonexistent corporation.

CONCLUSION

We reverse the trial court's conclusions that AVSI was a de facto corporation and a corporation by estoppel at the time the car wash sale was consummated and hold that Mr. Durbano and Mr. Garn are personally liable, pursuant to Utah Code Ann. § 16-10-139 (1991), for the judgment entered by the trial court against AVSI. The doctrines of de facto corporation and corporation by estoppel were both eliminated with enactment of the Business Corporation Act.

Forming the Texas Corporation

Certificate of Formation

The certificate of formation constitutes a contract between the state and the corporation. A defect in the filing of the certificate may result in the non-existence of the corporation because Texas does not recognize the defacto corporation.

§3.001. FORMATION AND EXISTENCE OF FILING ENTITIES.

(a) Subject to the other provisions of this code, to form a filing entity, a certificate of formation complying with Sections 3.003, 3.004, and 3.005 must be filed in accordance with Chapter 4.

(b) The filing of a certificate of formation described by Subsection (a) may be included in a filing under Chapter 10.

(c) The existence of a filing entity commences when the filing of the certificate of formation takes effect as provided by Chapter 4.

(d) Except in a proceeding by the state to terminate the existence of a filing entity, an acknowledgment of the filing of a certificate of formation issued by the filing officer is conclusive evidence of:

    (1) the formation and existence of the filing entity;

    (2) the satisfaction of all conditions precedent to the formation of the filing entity; and

    (3) the authority of the filing entity to transact business in this state.

Texas requires certain information to be included in the certificate of formation for filing including:

1. The corporation's name, which name cannot be the same or deceptively similar to another corporation already registered with the state. In addition, the name must include one of these words: "company," "corporation," "incorporated," or "limited"; or an abbreviated form of one of those words. § 5.054.

2. The corporation's purpose which may be specific or generally state that it is incorporated "for any lawful purpose" TBOC §§ 2.001, 3.005(a)(3).;

3. The corporation's duration, if not perpetual;

4. The name and street address of the registered agent for the corporation. The agent may be a natural person who is a resident of Texas or a juridical person authorized to do business in Texas. TBOC § 5.201(a)(2). The agent's address must be a physical address – not a post office box – because the agent must be able to be personally served by a process server. The corporation may elect to have its attorney serve as its registered agent;

5. The organizer's name(s) and address(es); The certificate must be signed by at least one organizer. who, if a natural person, must be at least 18 years of age. In addition to providing his signature, similar to the filing agent, the organizer must provide an address at which he may be served by process. This information is required for much the same reasons as is the case for the registered agent;

6. The number of shares authorized to issue. The corporation's aggregate number of shares authorized for issue must be included in the certificate. TBOC §3.007(a)(1). If the corporation is authorized to issue only one class of shares, then the par value of each share or the lack of par value must be stated as well. TBOC § 3.007(a)(2). But if more than one class is authorized for issuance then the certificate must state:

   - the designation of each class of shares;
   - the number of shares in each class;
   - the preferences, limitations, and relative rights of the shares; and
   - a statement about the par value of each share or its lack of par value.

   TBOC § 3.007(b). *See also* TBOC § 21.151.

7. The corporation's authorized capital;

8. The event requiring winding up, dissolution, or termination of the corporation; TBOC § 11.059(a)

9. The number, names and addresses of the initial board of directors, if any. The corporation's board of directors is responsible for directing the management of the corporation's business and affairs. TBOC § 21.401. The certificate must state if the corporation will be managed by a board of directors and, if so, the number of directors. TBOC§ 21.404. The board may consist of one or more directors. TBOC § 21.403(a). Additionally, consistent with the corporation's certificate or bylaws, any person – resident or alien – may be a director. TBOC § 21.402. If the corporation elects to be managed by its shareholders in lieu of a board of directors, then the certificate of formation must include the name and address of the shareholder(s) who will perform the initial board functions. The shareholder agreement approved by all shareholders may be included in the certificate of formation. TBOC§ 21.101(b)(1)(A). Unless the agreement provides otherwise, the shareholder agreement is valid for 10 years. TBOC § 21.102. Once effectively in

place, the agreement is effective among the shareholders and between the shareholders and the corporation. TBOC§ 21.104.

TBOC §§ 3.005(a), 3.007(a). Section 3.007 lists supplemental provisions that may be required for a for-profit corporation. Also, if the shareholders will have preemptive or cumulative voting rights, Texas requires that information to be included in the certificate of formation. TBOC §§ 21.203 and 21.360 If the corporation is to operate as a close corporation that election must also be reflected in the certificate of formation. A corporation is presumed to exist in perpetuity unless the certificate of formation or bylaws state otherwise. TBOC § 3.003. The statement must specify what the event is that triggers the winding up. TBOC § 11.051(3); 11.059(1), (2).

Filing the Certificate

Once the certificate is complete the organizer or incorporator must sign it and deliver it to the secretary of state with the requisite filing fee. TBOC §§ 4.001, 4.151-2. If the state finds that the certificate of formation conforms to the Code, then the certificate is effective – unless specified for some other time – at the filing date. TBOC § 4.051.

At times, corrections may be necessary. The procedure for filing a corrected certificate is similar to filing the original certificate. The Texas Business Organizations Code requires that the mistake be identified and corrected, the certificate be signed, and the fee be paid. TBOC § 4.103.

Normally, the corrected certificate is effective retroactively to the original filing date. TBOC § 4.105(a). However, if a party has been adversely affected during the period of the defect and or by the correction, then as to that party and or the affected transaction, the certificate is considered filed on the date the correction was filed. TBOC § 4.105(b).

After the certificate is filed, the Secretary of State's office will generally issue a certificate of filing that acknowledges receipt of the certificate of formation and finds that it meets the requirements for filing. However, failure of the SOS's office to issue such a certificate of filing will not impact the corporation unless the failure to issue is due to a defect in the filing. TBOC §4.002; 4.101

§4.002. ACTION BY SECRETARY OF STATE.

(a) If the secretary of state finds that a filing instrument delivered under Section 4.001 conforms to the provisions of this code that apply to the entity and to applicable rules adopted under Section 12.001 and that all required fees have been paid, the secretary of state shall:

(1) file the instrument by accepting it into the filing system adopted by the secretary of state and assigning the instrument a date of filing; and

(2) deliver a written acknowledgment of filing to the entity or its representative.

(b) If a duplicate copy of the filing instrument is delivered to the secretary of state, on accepting the filing instrument, the secretary of state shall return the duplicate copy, endorsed with the word "Filed" and the month, day, and year of filing, to the entity or its representative with the acknowledgment of filing.

§4.101. CORRECTION OF FILINGS.

(a) A filing instrument that has been filed with the secretary of state that is an inaccurate record of the event or transaction evidenced in the instrument, that contains an inaccurate or erroneous statement, or that was defectively or erroneously signed, sealed, acknowledged, or verified may be corrected by filing a certificate of correction.

(b) A certificate of correction must be signed by the person authorized by this code to sign the filing instrument to be corrected.

CORPORATE GOVERNANCE

Corporate governance is the system, principles, and processes by which a corporation is governed. Governance provides the guidelines for how the corporation may be directed and controlled so that it can fulfill its purpose, which is found in the certificate of formation. Implicit in fulfilling the corporation's purpose is the idea that the interests of the corporation's stakeholders -- directors, officers, shareholders, and third-persons -- are protected by the corporation's governance. That governance is found in a corporation's certificate of formation, its bylaws, and in state statutes.

The Organizational Meeting

Generally, the first action of the newly created corporation is to conduct an organizational meeting.

The organizational meeting occurs at the call of the majority of the board of directors named in the certificate of formation. TBOC§ 21.059(b). The purpose of the meeting is to adopt bylaws, elect officers, and transact other business. *Id.*

If the directors are not named in the certificate of formation, then at the organizational meeting, the shareholders elect directors to serve until the first annual meeting of shareholders. TBOC § 21.101(a)(3).

At least three days before the organizational meeting date, the directors who called the meeting shall notify each person named in the certificate of formation of the meeting's time and place. TBOC § 21.059(b). The meeting may be located in or outside the state, by conference telephone, or by videoconferencing. TBOC § 6.001, 2(a). These Code provisions are applicable to the initial meeting and all subsequent meetings.

Note: If the shareholders have elected not to have a board of directors but to manage the affairs of the corporation themselves pursuant to a shareholder's agreement, then at the organizational meeting, they may adopt the shareholder agreement and conduct such business of the corporation that would be handled in a traditional board-managed corporation.

The Corporation's Bylaws

The corporation's board of directors usually adopts the initial bylaws during the organizational meeting. TBOC § 21.057(a). The bylaws are a set of rules that govern the corporation's internal affairs and operations; they are only binding on intra-corporate members. Once adopted, the bylaws may be changed by amendment pursuant to the procedures contained in the bylaws. Generally, neither the bylaws nor any subsequent amendments are filed with the State.

Appointing the Corporation's Directors

It is the responsibility of the shareholders to elect the members of the board of directors. Typically, such elections are conducted during the annual shareholders meeting. Only shareholders with voting privileges are entitled to vote to elect the directors who will serve for the next term. § 21.405(a). The length of the directors' term is typically provided in the corporate by laws. If the by-laws are silent, then the director's term will last until his/her successor is elected and qualified at the next annual shareholders meeting. § 21.407.

Introducing the parties to a corporation

Shareholders

Shareholders are the owners of the corporation. They provide finance to a company by purchasing shares in it but have limited participation in the management and control of the corporation. They exercise their limited control by voting. The right to vote does not accompany all classes or series of shares. Shareholders who own shares without the right to vote are said to own non-voting shares. If voting is accomplished by shares, these shareholders are called non-voting shareholders. Corporate shareholders are generally protected from liability for corporate debts and obligations. Some shareholders may also serve as corporate directors. The dual roles might complicate the responsibilities, duties and liabilities of a shareholder that is also a corporate director and or officer.

Duties. Absent the situation where a shareholder is also an officer or director, shareholders do not participate in the management of the corporation. The traditional roles of the corporate shareholder are to elect a board of directors during the annual meeting and to vote on significant matters affecting the corporation and major decisions which would have an effect on the shareholders' rights. In addition, they also vote on fundamental changes to the corporation such as amending the certificate of formation and the bylaws, mergers and acquisitions, and other matters including approving independent auditors and non-binding resolutions.

Aside from fundamental changes, the shareholders also vote on self-interested transactions. An example of these types of transactions are incentive compensation plans and corporate indemnification of directors and officers. Both types of transactions are self-interested because they serve the interest of the group offering it - directors and its appointed officers.

Another way the shareholders can influence the board is by exercising their right to shareholder resolutions, which recommend particular actions to the board.

While generally, shareholders have little power over the directors and how they run the company, they are responsible for attending shareholder meetings and ensuring the directors and officers do not act beyond their powers.

Fiduciary Duties. Generally, shareholders in Texas corporations do not owe each other fiduciary duties. See Hoggett v. Brown, 971 S.W.2d 472, 488 (Tex.App.–Houston [14th Dist.] 1997, pet. denied) However, there are recognized exceptions to this general rule. The relationship between specific shareholders may give rise to fiduciary duties when one shareholder justifiably relies on another shareholder to act in his or her best interest. Under certain circumstances a majority shareholder owes a limited duty to the corporation and may also owe a duty directly to a minority shareholder. A majority shareholder may have a duty to a minority shareholder not to perform any act that substantially defeats the minority's reasonable expectations or is burdensome, harsh or wrongful. [See Davis v. Sheerin, 754 S.W.2d 375, 381-82 (Tex.App.—Houston [1st Dist.] 1988, writ denied) where the court found that the majority shareholder's actions were oppressive and ordered a buy out of the minority shareholder's shares.]

Shareholder Rights. The shareholder has the right to inspect the corporate records. TBOC §21.218 There are two limitations on this right: First, the shareholder must request the record for a proper purpose. What constitutes "proper purpose" is fluid, but if a shareholder requests a record to either evaluate his investment or to gain access to the shareholder list so that he can contact other shareholders to legally influence their vote, then his purpose is likely proper. But where the shareholder's purpose is to pursue unrelated personal goals e.g., to gain access to trade secrets or to pursue social or political goals then the shareholder's purpose is likely to be considered not proper.

Second, assuming the purpose is proper, then the record the shareholder requests must have a reasonable bearing upon his/her/its investment. Records that could have a reasonable bearing on an investment include contracts, emails, and accounting records. If the shareholder has a proper purpose for requesting the record and the record has a reasonable bearing upon his investment, then he will likely gain access to the record.

Distributions

When a corporation transfers value to its shareholders, it constitutes a distribution. Distributions may be paid in money, in stock or other property. Generally distributions paid to the shareholder as a return on his or her investment in the corporation are called dividends. Distributions by a corporation of its own stock are commonly known as stock dividends. Stock rights (also known as "stock options") are distributions by a corporation of rights to acquire its stock. Distributions of stock dividends and stock rights are generally tax-free to shareholders. However, stock and stock rights are treated as property and therefore constitue distribution.

> Constructive stock distributions. Certain transactions that increase a shareholder's proportionate interest in the earnings and profits or assets of a corporation are treated as distributions of stock or stock rights.
>
> Other constructive distributions include:
>
> Below-market loans. If a corporation gives a shareholder a loan on which no interest is charged or on which interest is charged at a rate below the applicable federal rate, the interest not charged may be treated as a distribution to the shareholder.
>
> Corporation cancels shareholder's debt. If a corporation cancels a shareholder's debt without repayment by the shareholder, the amount canceled is treated as a distribution to the shareholder.
>
> Transfers of property to shareholders for less than Fair Market Value (FMV). A sale or exchange of property by a corporation to a shareholder may be treated as a distribution to the shareholder. For a shareholder who is not a corporation, if the FMV of the property on the date of the sale or exchange exceeds the price paid by the shareholder, the excess may be treated as a distribution to the shareholder.
>
> Unreasonable rents. If a corporation rents property from a shareholder and the rent is unreasonably more than the shareholder would charge to a stranger for use of the same property, the excessive part of the rent may be treated as a distribution to the shareholder.
>
> Unreasonable salaries. If a corporation pays an employee who is also a shareholder a salary that is unreasonably high considering the services actually performed by the shareholder-employee, the excessive part of the salary may be treated as a distribution to the shareholder-employee.

See IRS publication 542, Corporations (Rev. March 2012) discussing the general tax laws that apply to ordinary domestic corporations. Available at http://www.irs.gov/pub/irs-pdf/p542.pdf.

Shareholder agreements

A corporation's shareholders may enter into an agreement that is effective among themselves and between them and the corporation. § 21.101; 21.104. And this is true even if the terms of agreement are inconsistent with the Code. § 21.104. In the agreement, the shareholders may agree to:

- Purpose.
- Financial interests.
- Power.
- Restrict the board of directors' discretion or powers;
- Eliminate the directors and authorize one or more shareholders to manage the corporation's business and affairs;
- Establish the persons who shall serve as the corporation's directors or officers;
- Authorize how distributions will be made;
- Designate the manner in which profits and losses will be apportioned;
- Govern the voting process for shareholders, directors, or other persons; and
- Set when winding up and terminating the organization are required.

§ 21.101(a). After the agreement is formed, it must either be contained in the corporation's certificate or be contained in the bylaws if approved by all of the shareholders at the time of the agreement. § 21.101(b)(1)(A). The agreement may also be placed in a written agreement signed by all of the shareholders at the time of the agreement. § 21.101(b)(1)(B). After the signatures are had, the agreement must be made known to the corporation. Unless otherwise provided, this agreement may only be amended by all of the shareholders at time of the amendment. *Id.*

While the agreement itself must be placed in the certificate, bylaws, or a written agreement, its existence must be conspicuously noted on either the front or back of each outstanding share's certificate. § 21.103(a). This disclosure must include specific language alerting the shareholder that the shareholder's agreement may allow for unique management policies. § 21.103(b).

The agreement, unless otherwise provided, is valid for ten years. § 21.102. It ceases to be effective when the corporation's shares are either (1) listed on a national securities exchange or (2) regularly traded in a market maintained by a member of a nation or affiliated securities association. § 21.109. Where the agreement does become ineffective, the corporation's directors may adopt an amendment to the certificate or bylaws. This amendment – done without shareholder action – may delete the ineffective agreement and any reference to it. § 21.109(c).

Directors

A director is a person who is either appointed to or elected to sit on a corporation's board that manages the corporation's affairs by electing and exercising control over the corporation's officers.

Role/Operational duties

A director's role is to serve as a fiduciary to the corporation and to the shareholders as a group but generally not to an individual shareholder. As such, shareholders traditionally cannot order a director to take any particular action. In serving as a fiduciary, the director must manage the corporation, including determining and executing corporate policy. In making such determinations, a director is required to use his best judgment and independent discretion.

The board of directors also has ultimate legal responsibility for the actions of the corporation and its subsidiaries, officers, employees, and agents. A corporate director's duties and responsibilities typically include:

- Acting on behalf of the corporation;
- Participating in regular meetings of the board of directors;
- Making corporate policy
- Providing oversight over operations
- Hiring the CEO and fixing executive compensation;
- Amending or otherwise affecting corporate bylaws
- Declaring dividends; making distribution

§21.302. AUTHORITY FOR DISTRIBUTIONS. The board of directors of a corporation may authorize a distribution and the corporation may make a distribution, subject to Section 21.303.

§21.303. LIMITATIONS ON DISTRIBUTIONS.

(a) A corporation may not make a distribution that violates the corporation's certificate of formation.

(b) Unless the distribution is made in compliance with Chapter 11, a corporation may not make a distribution:

(1) if the corporation would be insolvent after the distribution; or

(2) that exceeds the distribution limit.

§21.316. LIABILITY OF DIRECTORS FOR WRONGFUL DISTRIBUTIONS.

(a) Subject to Subsection (c), the directors of a corporation who vote for or assent to a distribution by the corporation that is prohibited by Section 21.303 are jointly and severally liable to the corporation for the amount by which the distribution exceeds the amount permitted by that section to be distributed.

(b) A director is not liable for all or part of the excess amount if a distribution of that amount would have been permitted by Section 21.303 after the date the director authorized the distribution.

(c) A director is not jointly and severally liable under Subsection (a) if, in voting for or assenting to the distribution, the director:

> *(1) relies in good faith and with ordinary care on:*
>
>> *(A) the statements, valuations, or information described by Section 21.314; or*
>>
>> *(B) other information, opinions, reports, or statements, including financial statements and other financial data, concerning the corporation or another person that are prepared or presented by:*
>>
>>> *(i) one or more officers or employees of the corporation;*
>>>
>>> *(ii) a legal counsel, public accountant, investment banker, or other person relating to a matter the director reasonably believes is within the person's professional or expert competence; or*
>>>
>>> *(iii) a committee of the board of directors of which the director is not a member;*
>
> *(2) acting in good faith and with ordinary care, considers the assets of the corporation to be valued at least at their book value; or*
>
> *(3) in determining whether the corporation made adequate provision for payment, satisfaction, or discharge of all of the corporation's liabilities and obligations, as provided by Sections 11.053 and 11.356, relies in good faith and with ordinary care on financial statements of, or other information concerning, a person who was or became contractually obligated to pay, satisfy, or discharge some or all of the corporation's liabilities or obligations.*

(d) The liability imposed under Subsection (a) is the only liability of a director to the corporation or its creditors for authorizing a distribution that is prohibited by Section 21.303.

(e) This section and Sections 21.317 and 21.318 do not limit any liability imposed under Chapter 24, Business & Commerce Code, or the United States Bankruptcy Code.

In exercising those functions the director must exercise the duties of loyalty and care.

Fiduciary Duties and the Business Judgment Rule

Generally, corporate directors and officers owe a duty of loyalty and duty of care (which incorporates the duty of obedience) to the corporation and to the shareholders as a group. The directors/officers are required to exercise their duties in good faith and in the best interest of the corporation.

Generally, the standard of care a director/officer must use is that of a reasonably prudent person. In applying this standard, courts sometimes add subjective factors, including: whether the director was part- or full-time; whether the director received compensation; and, whether the director has a special background.

Regardless of these subjective factors, a director/officer is still required to act carefully in light of her actual knowledge and that knowledge as she should have gained by reasonable care and skill. A director may show that she acted carefully by showing that she reasonably relied on the advice of others.

Even if a director/officer fails to do any or all of these things, a director/officer is only liable for the loss that her negligence caused the corporation. So if there is no damage, then there is no liability.

Duty of Loyalty

The duty of loyalty includes a requirement that the fiduciary place the corporation's interest above his, her or its own personal interest, avoid any conflict of interest, avoid self-dealing, act with honesty and full disclosure in performing his duties and avoid usurping the corporate opportunity. In most jurisdictions, including Texas, when a fiduciary acts in accordance with its duty of loyalty, the acts will be protected by the business judgment rule even if the act results in injury to the corporation. The standard by which the actions are tested are whether the actions were done in good faith and in the best interest of the corporation.

The director/officer's duty of loyalty demands that there shall be no conflict between their duty to the corporation and self interest. Imperial Group (Texas), Inc. v. Scholnick, 709 S.W. 2d 358 (Tex.App.-Tyler 1986). The duty of loyalty inquiry is commonly implicated in self-dealing cases and where the director/officer is accused of usurping a corporate opportunity. Self dealing occurs when the director/officer has a personal interest in the transaction.

A fiduciary's obligation to act with absolute loyalty will not necessarily result in personal liability if the fiduciary can show that the acts were fair. For example a fiduciary that usurps a corporate opportunity is not liable for that act when full disclosure is properly made prior to seizing the opportunity and the corporation rejected the opportunity for itself, gave permission to the fiduciary to seize the opportunity or by its actions permitted the act. Transactions where the director or officer has an interest are called interested transactions and the director or officer is referred to as an interested director or interested officer. TBOC§§ 2.101(21); An officer or director is "interested" if he or she (1) makes a personal profit from a transaction by dealing with the corporation or usurps a corporate opportunity, (2) buys or sells assets of a corporation, (3) transacts business in his or her officer's or director's capacity with a second corporation of which he or she is also an officer or director or is significantly financially associated, or (4) transacts corporate business in his or her officer's or director's capacity with a family member. *See Gearhart Indus., 741 F.2d at 719-20; Assurance Sys. Corp. v. Jackson (In re Jackson), 141 Bankr. 909 (Bankr. N.D. Tex. 1992). And see Ritchie v. Rupe, 339 S.W.3d 275 (Tex.App.-Dallas 2011, pet. filed)*

Texas statutes provide that a transaction or contract between a director and the director's corporation is presumed to be valid and will not be voidable solely by reason of the director's interest if the transaction is approved by the shareholders or disinterested directors after disclosure of the interest, or if the transaction is otherwise fair. TBOC §21.418 A director is considered disinterested if the director is not a party to the contract or transaction or does not otherwise have a material financial interest in the outcome of the contract. TBOC § 1.003.

§21.418. CONTRACTS OR TRANSACTIONS INVOLVING INTERESTED DIRECTORS AND OFFICERS.

(a) This section applies to a contract or transaction between a corporation and:

(1) one or more directors or officers, or one or more affiliates or associates of one or more directors or officers, of the corporation; or

(2) an entity or other organization in which one or more directors or officers, or one or more affiliates or associates of one or more directors or officers, of the corporation:

(A) is a managerial official; or

(B) has a financial interest.

(b) An otherwise valid and enforceable contract or transaction described by Subsection (a) is valid and enforceable, and is not void or voidable, notwithstanding any relationship or interest described by Subsection (a), if any one of the following conditions is satisfied:

(1) the material facts as to the relationship or interest described by Subsection (a) and as to the contract or transaction are disclosed to or known by:

(A) the corporation's board of directors or a committee of the board of directors, and the board of directors or committee in good faith authorizes the contract or transaction by the approval of the majority of the disinterested directors or committee members, regardless of whether the disinterested directors or committee members constitute a quorum; or

(B) the shareholders entitled to vote on the authorization of the contract or transaction, and the contract or transaction is specifically approved in good faith by a vote of the shareholders; or

(2) the contract or transaction is fair to the corporation when the contract or transaction is authorized, approved, or ratified by the board of directors, a committee of the board of directors, or the shareholders.

(c) Common or interested directors of a corporation may be included in determining the presence of a quorum at a meeting of the corporation's board of directors, or a committee of the board of directors, that authorizes the contract or transaction.

(d) A person who has the relationship or interest described by Subsection (a) may:

(1) be present at or participate in and, if the person is a director or committee member, may vote at a meeting of the board of directors or of a committee of the board that authorizes the contract or transaction; or

(2) sign, in the person's capacity as a director or committee member, a unanimous written consent of the directors or committee members to authorize the contract or transaction.

(e) If at least one of the conditions of Subsection (b) is satisfied, neither the corporation nor any of the corporation's shareholders will have a cause of action against any of the persons described by Subsection (a) for breach of duty with respect to the making, authorization, or performance of the contract or transaction because the person had the relationship or interest described by Subsection (a) or took any of the actions authorized by Subsection (d).

The standard for fairness may vary with the facts presented. In some cases, the transaction must meet the ordinary fairness test, however, where the transaction is tainted by self-dealing the transaction must be intrinsically fair. The fairness test usually consists of fair price and fair dealing.

The fairness test applies in those cases where there is potential fiduciary misconduct.

Texas does not permit a corporation to eliminate director liability for the breach of the duty of loyalty. TBOC §7.001

Duty of Care

A director's duty of care requires the director to avoid negligence in the performance of her corporate duties. A director may be negligent in either acting or failing to act.

Though the board is charged with managing the corporation, the reality is that day-to-day management is carried out by the officers, whom, of course, the board is responsible for supervising.

The duty of care requires the director and officer to conduct reasonable due diligence in managing the corporation's affairs. Reasonable due diligence generally requires the fiduciaries to inform themselves of all material information reasonably available to them before making a decision. Moreover, in Texas, a fiduciary may meet the requirement of due diligence by relying in good faith and with ordinary care on information, opinions, reports, or statements prepared or presented by officers or employees of the corporation, by a committee of the board of which the director is not a member, or by legal counsel, accountants, investment bankers, or others with professional or other expertise. TBOC §3.102; §3.105. Generally, the standard applied to determining whether the duty has been met is the "ordinarily prudent person under similar circumstances".

§ 3.102. RIGHTS OF GOVERNING PERSONS IN CERTAIN CASES.

(a) In discharging a duty or exercising a power, a governing person, including a governing person who is a member of a committee, may, in good faith and with ordinary care, rely on information, opinions, reports, or statements, including financial statements

and other financial data, concerning a domestic entity or another person and prepared or presented by:

(1) an officer or employee of the entity;

(2) legal counsel;

(3) a certified public accountant;

(4) an investment banker;

(5) a person who the governing person reasonably believes possesses professional expertise in the matter; or

(6) a committee of the governing authority of which the governing person is not a member.

(b) A governing person may not in good faith rely on the information described by Subsection (a) if the governing person has knowledge of a matter that makes the reliance unwarranted.

To exercise the duty of care a director, among other things, should:

- Attend the board of directors meetings;
- Stay well-informed on corporate matters;
- Familiarize herself with the corporation's financial health; and
- Resign when she is unable to carry out the requirements of her role.

When a corporate director or officer exercises his/her duty of loyalty and or care in good faith and in the best interest of the corporation, he or she is protected from personal liability for his or her act under the business judgment rule. This protection is afforded even when the decision results in damage to the corporation.

In Texas, despite the standard of ordinary care, courts will honor the business judgment rule as a shield from liability to a director or officer even to protect grossly negligent conduct so long as it was done in good faith and motivated by the best interest of the corporation. However, Texas will not permit the business judgment rule to protect the fiduciary who acts with fraud or an abdication of responsibility altogether.

It is also noteworthy that in Texas, a corporation may eliminate the director's liability for breach of the duty of care by stating same in the certificate of formation. TBOC§ 7.001.

§7.001. LIMITATION OF LIABILITY OF GOVERNING PERSON.

(a) Subsections (b) and (c) apply to:

(1) a domestic entity other than a partnership or limited liability company;

(2) another organization incorporated or organized under another law of this state; and

(3) to the extent permitted by federal law, a federally chartered bank, savings and loan association, or credit union.

(b) The certificate of formation or similar instrument of an organization to which this section applies may provide that a governing person of the organization is not liable, or is liable only to the extent provided by the certificate of formation or similar instrument, to the organization or its owners or members for monetary damages for an act or omission by the person in the person's capacity as a governing person.

(c) Subsection (b) does not authorize the elimination or limitation of the liability of a governing person to the extent the person is found liable under applicable law for:

(1) a breach of the person's duty of loyalty, if any, to the organization or its owners or members;

(2) an act or omission not in good faith that:

(A) constitutes a breach of duty of the person to the organization; or

(B) involves intentional misconduct or a knowing violation of law;

(3) a transaction from which the person received an improper benefit, regardless of whether the benefit resulted from an action taken within the scope of the person's duties; or

(4) an act or omission for which the liability of a governing person is expressly provided by an applicable statute.

(d) The liability of a governing person may be limited or restricted:

(1) in a general partnership to the extent permitted under Chapter 152;

(2) in a limited partnership to the extent permitted under Chapter 153 and, to the extent applicable to limited partnerships, Chapter 152; and

(3) in a limited liability company to the extent permitted under Section 101.401.

Good faith

Directors and officers are expected to conduct their responsibilities to the corporation exercising good faith. Good faith is established when it is shown that the actor had no malice or fraudulent intent and had a sincere belief that the action was for the benefit of the corporation. The business judgment rule insulates directors and officers from shareholder attack when they have acted in good faith.

Traditionally, a director manages the corporation only during a meeting of the board that has been duly convened and where a quorum is present. No one board member has the right to make decisions for the board unless that responsibility has been properly delegated.

Board decisions must be within the corporation's powers (*intra vires*) and the board's authority. The board duty to act within the powers of the corporation and their own authority were historically described as a duty of obedience. However, in light of TBOC §20.002 Texas courts generally reject demands to hold corporate officials personally liable or illegal or ultra vires acts unless the directors participated in the ace or had knowledge of the fact or unless a specific law provides for such.

§20.002. ULTRA VIRES ACTS.

(a) Lack of capacity of a corporation may not be the basis of any claim or defense at law or in equity.

(b) An act of a corporation or a transfer of property by or to a corporation is not invalid because the act or transfer was:

    (1) beyond the scope of the purpose or purposes of the corporation as expressed in the corporation's certificate of formation; or

    (2) inconsistent with a limitation on the authority of an officer or director to exercise a statutory power of the corporation, as that limitation is expressed in the corporation's certificate of formation.

(c) The fact that an act or transfer is beyond the scope of the expressed purpose or purposes of the corporation or is inconsistent with an expressed limitation on the authority of an officer or director may be asserted in a proceeding:

    (1) by a shareholder or member against the corporation to enjoin the performance of an act or the transfer of property by or to the corporation;

    (2) by the corporation, acting directly or through a receiver, trustee, or other legal representative, or through members in a representative suit, against an officer or director or former officer or director of the corporation for exceeding that person's authority; or

    (3) by the attorney general to:

        (A) terminate the corporation;

        (B) enjoin the corporation from performing an unauthorized act; or

        (C) enforce divestment of real property acquired or held contrary to the laws of this state.

(d) If the unauthorized act or transfer sought to be enjoined under Subsection (c)(1) is being or is to be performed or made under a contract to which the corporation is a party and if each party to the contract is a party to the proceeding, the court may set aside and enjoin the performance of the contract. The court may award to the corporation or to another party to the contract, as appropriate, compensation for loss or damage resulting from the action of the court in setting aside and enjoining the performance of the contract, excluding loss of anticipated profits.

Generally, the business judgment rule supports leaving board/officer decisions undisturbed if four conditions were present when the decision was made:

1. The director/officer had a reasonable basis;
2. The director/officer acted in good faith;
3. The director/officer exercised independent discretion and judgment; and
4. The director/officer believed that their decision was in the best interest of the corporation.

The business judgment rule protects the board and the corporation's officers from personal liability for decisions that are either unprofitable or harmful to the corporation. Such protection covers negligent and in Texas, grossly negligent acts that meet the four conditions. Nevertheless not all decisions by directors and officers are insulated from shareholder challenges. Shareholders seek remedy from a director or officer when their decision fails to meet the four conditions and their action harms the corporation. In this circumstance a qualified shareholder may file a derivative action against the wrongdoers for the benefit of the corporation. If the shareholder seeks individual or personal relief, she cannot use the derivative action but must file a direct action instead.

Derivative proceedings

A derivative proceeding is a civil suit brought by a shareholder on behalf of the corporation against corporate directors, officers, or employees or against a third-party who has incurred liability to the corporation. To bring or maintain this suit, the shareholder must have standing, he must submit a demand letter, and he must overcome the business judgment rule.

Standing

A shareholder has standing to bring a derivative suit if he was a shareholder at the time of the act or omission complained of TBOC § 21.552(1)(A) or if he "became a shareholder by operation of law from a person that was a shareholder at the time of the act or omission complained of." § 21.552(1)(B) AND the shareholder is able to fairly and adequately represent the corporation's interest in enforcing the corporation's right. TBOC § 21.552(2).

Demand letter

The qualified shareholder must file a demand letter on the corporation and must wait until ninety-one days after filing the letter prior to filing a derivative suit. TBOC§ 21.553(a). The demand letter must do two things. First, it must state with particularity the act, omission, or other matter that is the subject of the claim or challenge. *Id.* Second, it must request that the corporation take suitable action. *Id.*

The ninety-one day period may be avoided if: (1) the corporation previously notified the shareholder that it rejected his demand; (2) the corporation is suffering irreparable injury; or (3) the corporation will suffer irreparable injury if the shareholder is forced to wait for the ninety-first day to arrive. TBOC § 21.553(b)(1)-(3). This waiver of the 90 day waiting period will not excuse the demand which must be made.

Some jurisdictions will permit shareholders to avoid making demand if it would be futile. Texas is a demand required state and does not recognize demand futility.

Overcoming the business judgment rule

To prosecute a successful derivative suit, a shareholder must overcome the directors' protection from the business judgment rule. This will generally require that the shareholder show that the transaction is tainted by illegality, fraud, ultra vires or outside the scope of the officials' authority. Common claims include improper or unlawful distributions or declarations of dividends, misappropriation of corporate assets, self dealing, and usurping corporate opportunity.

Pace v. Houston Industries, Inc. et.al.
999 S.W.2d 615, Tex.App.-Hous. (1 Dist.), (1999)

This case involves shareholder derivative litigation. Appellants, Pace and Fuentez, are shareholders of Houston Industries, Inc. ("HII") and former employees of Houston Lighting & Power ("HL & P"), a wholly owned subsidiary of HII. In April 1992, appellants lost their jobs because of a company-wide reduction in force.

On October 5, 1992, Pace, as a shareholder, sent a "demand letter" to HII, demanding that the board of directors terminate the corporate officers and commence legal action to recover damages suffered by HII. Pace claimed that the corporate officers, including appellees Don D. Jordan and Don D. Sykora, were liable for breaches of fiduciary duty because of bad investment strategies, legal malpractice, and misappropriated lumber.

After considering Pace's allegations and management's responses, the HII directors referred the charges to the board's audit committee for investigation. The audit committee, with the assistance of HII's internal auditing department, the Deloitte & Touche accounting firm, and outside counsel, investigated the charges and found they were unsupported by the facts. The audit committee reported its findings, and the board concluded that Pace's claims did not warrant further action. In November 1992, the board notified Pace that it had considered and refused his demands.

Pace sent a second demand letter to the board in March 1993. He reasserted his initial charges and raised new claims, but did not make claims against the remaining directors. The board again referred the charges to the audit committee, which again sought the assistance of Deloitte & Touche and outside counsel for investigation. After reviewing the charges, management's responses, and the outside consultants' reports, the audit committee again recommended against further action. After the board adopted the finding, it notified Pace that his claims were without merit and that litigation would not serve HII's interest.

Pace sent a third demand letter to the board on July 21, 1993. This letter contained the allegations from the first two letters, including the request to sue appellees Jordan and Sykora, and the letter added allegations about the South Texas Nuclear Project (STP). Specifically, Pace claimed that the officers' mismanagement led to the facility's shutdown in February 1993 and increasing regulatory activity. Again, Pace charged only Jordan and Sykora, not the remaining directors.

After the STP shutdown, the board studied the causes and the regulators' concerns about the facility's operation. In the months before the vote on Pace's third demand, the board met with regulators to discuss the STP issues. In September 1993, the board considered Pace's STP claims. The disinterested directors, based on their familiarity of the events and their discussions with federal regulators, voted to refuse Pace's demand. The board notified Pace of its decision.

In response, Pace and Fuentez filed a shareholder's derivative suit, purportedly on HII's behalf. They sued not only appellees Jordan and Sykora, but also the remaining directors. HII and the individual defendants (collectively referred to as "the HII parties") counterclaimed for attorneys' fees.

The HII parties moved for summary judgment, contending that the suit, which belonged to the corporation, was barred because the directors had previously decided that the suit was not in HII's best interest. The trial court rendered an interlocutory summary judgment in favor of the HII parties. Pace and Fuentez prematurely appealed to this Court, and later withdrew their appeal because the interlocutory summary judgment was not a final judgment. On June 1, 1998, the trial court rendered final judgment. Pace and Fuentez and the HII parties have filed separate appeals.

Which Law Applies?

In their first point of error, Pace and Fuentez contend that the 1997 amendments to the applicable statute should be retroactively applied to this case. Texas law militates strongly against the retroactive application of laws. TEX. CONST. art. I, § 16. In Texas, a statute is "presumed to be prospective in its operation unless expressly made retrospective." TEX. GOV'T CODE ANN. § 311.022 (Vernon 1988). Amendments are also presumed not to apply retroactively. *Houston Indep. Sch. Dist. v. Houston Chronicle Publ'g Co.*, 798 S.W.2d 580, 585 (Tex.App.—Houston [1st Dist.] 1990, writ denied). Doubts as to retroactivity are resolved against the retroactive application of a statute. *Ex parte Abell*, 613 S.W.2d 255, 258 (Tex.1981).

Both sides agree that Texas Business Corporation Act article 5.14 governs. The article was amended effective September 1, 1997. The HII parties' interlocutory summary judgment was signed about 7 months earlier on January 28, 1997. Pace and Fuentez urge this Court to retroactively apply the 1997 amendments to the interlocutory summary judgment. They argue that the amendments to article 5.14 were procedural changes, and, therefore, should apply retroactively because the case was still pending below. *Holder v. Wood*, 714 S.W.2d 318, 319 (Tex.1986) (holding that changes in statutes affecting remedies or procedure may be applied retroactively). On the other hand, the HII parties argue that, regardless of whether the amendments were substantive or procedural, the trial court correctly rendered judgment under the old rules, and this Court should not reverse the judgment by applying new rules which did not exist at the time of the interlocutory summary judgment.

The trial court did not render a final judgment until nine months after the amendments became effective. Because the trial court had jurisdiction to reconsider its ruling on the interlocutory summary judgment during those nine months, Pace and Fuentez should have made the argument to the trial court. Because they did not do so, they did not preserve error. Accordingly, we will not apply the 1997 amendments. We overrule point of error one.

Analysis Under the Pre–1997 Law

In their third point of error, Pace and Fuentez contend that under the pre–1997 law, this is a "demand futile" case, not a "demand refused" case, because: (a) Pace's letters were not demands; (b) Fuentez was not bound by Pace's demands; (c) the trial court restricted discovery; (d) the board was not independent and disinterested; and (e) the board's investigation was inadequate.

Pace's Letters Are Considered a Demand

Pace contends that this is a demand futile case because his letters were inadequate to be considered a demand. Under the prior version of article 5.14, a shareholder had to either make a demand on the board of directors or show that such a demand would have been futile. Under the amended article, demand futility is no longer an option. TEX. BUS. CORP. ACT ANN. art. 5.14(d) (Vernon Supp.1999). A demand must (1) identify the alleged wrongdoer, (2) describe the factual basis of the claim, (3) describe the corporation's injury, and (4) request remedial action. *See Allright Mo., Inc. v. Billeter*, 829 F.2d 631, 638 (8th Cir.1987). Pace contends that his letters did not meet the second element. We disagree.

A demand is sufficient if the board of directors had a fair opportunity to consider the shareholder's claims. *See Lewis v. Sporck*, 646 F.Supp. 574, 577–78 (N.D.Cal.1986). Pace argues that his March 1993 letter was deficient because it neither specifically named the "whistleblowers" who were fired at STP nor identified "the subject matter of their complaints beyond a reference to 'security problems and other problems' at STP." He also contends that his July 1993 letter was deficient because it "refers summarily to maintenance problems, management incompetence, failure to comply with NRC 'requisites,' and intimidation of employees raising complaints at STP."

363

The allegations by Pace and Fuentez in their fourth amended petition track the allegations in Pace's letters. The fact that the petition is more detailed does not render the letters inadequate. Further, the remedy for an inadequate demand is dismissal. *See Renfro v. FDIC,* 773 F.2d 657 (5th Cir.1985). Pace provides no authority for his propositions that an inadequate demand is not a demand; therefore, this is a demand futile case. We find these arguments without merit.

Fuentez Is Bound by Pace's Demand

Fuentez contends that the trial court erred in dismissing her cause of action because she never made a demand, as required by article 5.14.

To bring a derivative suit, a shareholder must show that he or she "fairly and adequately represents the interests of the shareholders similarly situated in enforcing the right of the corporation." TEX.R. CIV. P. 42(a). Fuentez brought claims identical to Pace's claims. Either Pace or Fuentez had to prove that he or she fairly and adequately represented the remaining shareholders. We discern no logical reason why a board's decision should not bind similarly situated shareholders making identical claims. Judicial economy demands that identical claims, which in actuality belong to the corporation, be simultaneously disposed of by one demand.

Opportunity for Discovery

Pace and Fuentez contend that the trial court restricted their discovery. Specifically, they complain that the only witness the HII parties presented for deposition, Mr. Milton Carroll, was not adequately informed about the board's decisions. Three additional depositions were therefore necessary.

Pace and Fuentez issued deposition notices for the three additional witnesses, and the HII parties moved for a protective order to quash the depositions. In response, Pace and Fuentez did not file a "motion to compel." Instead, they filed a "Response to [HII's] Motion for Protective Order Prohibiting the Taking of Oral Depositions." Their "response" appears to be similar in substance to a motion to compel.

Pace and Fuentez admit that the motion for protective order and the response were not ruled on. Instead, Pace and Fuentez argue that the trial court, by not ruling on the pending motions, "in effect prevented" the depositions. We disagree.

Pace and Fuentez should have filed a motion to compel instead of a "response" to the HII parties' motion for protective order. *See* TEX.R. CIV. P. 215.1. Then, they should have either obtained a ruling on the motion to compel, or objected if the trial court refused to rule. *See* TEX.R.APP. P. 33.1(a)(2). Pace and Fuentez did neither. There is nothing in the record to demonstrate that the trial court prevented the discovery sought by appellants. Moreover, on the record before us, appellants have not shown they were harmed. *See* TEX.R.APP. P. 33.1.

Independent and Disinterested Board

Pace and Fuentez contend that this is a demand futile case because fact issues exist as to whether the board was independent and disinterested.

A corporation's directors, not its shareholders, have the right to control litigation of corporate causes of action. TEX. BUS. CORP. ACT ANN. arts. 2.02(A)(2), 2.31 (Vernon Supp.1999). A shareholder's derivative cause of action is based on a corporate cause of action. *Hajdik v. Wingate*, 753 S.W.2d 199, 201 (Tex.App.—Houston [1st Dist.] 1988), *aff'd*, 795 S.W.2d 717 (Tex.1990). Thus, the corporation, through its board of directors, determines whether the chances for a successful suit, the costs of maintaining a suit, and other factors militate in favor of instituting such an action. *Cates v. Sparkman*, 73 Tex. 619, 11 S.W. 846, 848 (1889); *Zauber v. Murray Sav. Ass'n*, 591 S.W.2d 932, 936 (Tex.Civ.App.—Dallas 1979), *writ ref'd n.r.e.*, 601 S.W.2d 940 (Tex.1980).

To bring a derivative suit in the right of a corporation, a shareholder must show that the board of directors' refusal to act was governed by something beyond unsound business judgment. *Langston v. Eagle Publ'g Co.*, 719 S.W.2d 612, 616 (Tex.App.—Waco 1986, writ ref'd n.r.e.); *Zauber*, 591 S.W.2d at 936. Under the business judgment rule, a shareholder cannot institute a derivative suit on the corporation's behalf by merely showing that the board's refusal to act was unwise, inexpedient, negligent, or imprudent. *Cates*, 11 S.W. at 849; *Langston*, 719 S.W.2d at 616–17.

Pace made a demand on the board of directors through his three letters. He invoked article 5.14 of the Texas Business Corporation Act, set forth his complaints, named the officers and directors that allegedly had harmed HII and HL & P, requested that those individuals be fired, and requested that the board sue the officers for mismanagement. The board discussed Pace's claims, and the outside directors decided that litigation was not in HII's best interest. To show that the decision was governed by something other than sound business judgment, appellants had to prove that the board's refusal to act was characterized by an ultra vires, fraudulent, and injurious practice, an abuse of power, and an oppression on the part of the company or its controlling agency clearly subversive of the rights of the minority, or of a shareholder, and which, without such interference, would leave the latter remediless. *Cates*, 11 S.W. at 849; *Langston*, 719 S.W.2d at 617.

Directors are "interested" if they have such a personal interest in the controversy or are so controlled by the alleged wrongdoers that they could not reasonably be expected to diligently pursue the action. *Zauber*, 591 S.W.2d at 937. Pace and Fuentez cite a litany of cases in which courts have found that the directors were interested, and therefore, could not act on behalf of the corporation because they were either potential litigants or controlled by potential litigants. All of these cases, however, address allegations of self-dealing or fraud by a majority of the directors. Appellant produced no evidence to show that the HII directors committed fraud or engaged in self-dealing. Thus, under the traditional notions of self-interest, Pace and Fuentez did not raise a fact issue that the refusal of the demand was improper.

Pace and Fuentez further argue that the directors could not be disinterested because they might have had to sue themselves. Therefore, they contend that a demand would have been futile. [However] Pace's demand letters complained about only appellees Jordan and Sykora. No allegations were raised against the remaining directors. Pace and Fuentez did not name the remaining directors until they filed suit.

Several jurisdictions have held that merely naming disinterested directors as defendants does not avoid the duty to make a demand. *See e.g., Lewis v. Graves*, 701 F.2d 245, 248 (2d Cir.1983); *Heit v. Baird*, 567 F.2d 1157, 1162 (1st Cir.1977); *Cottle v. Hilton Hotels Corp.*, 635 F.Supp. 1094, 1098–99 (N.D.Ill.1986). The mere fact that directors participated in and authorized the disputed transactions underlying the derivative suit is not enough by itself to excuse a demand. *See Graves*, 701 F.2d at 248. We agree with this reasoning. The mere fact that Pace and Fuentez made claims against all of the directors does not create a genuine issue of material fact as to the disinterestedness and independence of the board.

In *Lewis v. Curtis*, 671 F.2d 779, 785 (3d Cir.1982), the court held that "to allow one shareholder to incapacitate an entire board of directors merely by leveling charges against them gives too much leverage to dissident shareholders." Similarly, in *Aronson v. Lewis*, 473 A.2d 805, 815 (Del.1984), the court held that the "mere threat of personal liability for approving a questioned transaction, standing alone, is insufficient to challenge either the independence or disinterestedness of directors." We agree with the reasoning in both *Curtis* and *Aronson*.

Adequate Investigation

As set forth above, Pace and Fuentez had to prove that the board's refusal was motivated by something beyond unsound business judgment. Yet Pace and Fuentez merely contend that the board's investigation before the vote on Pace's demands was inadequate because the board was not fully informed about all of the allegations surrounding STP, Jordan, and Sykora.

A board may invoke the business judgment rule's protection only if the directors are informed before making a decision, "of all material information reasonably available to them." *Aronson*, 473 A.2d at 812. In assessing whether the board was informed, pertinent matters include the information considered, the use of experts or consultants, the notice given to the board, and its independence. *Grobow v. Perot*, 539 A.2d 180, 191 (Del.1988).

Director Milton Carroll stated that he and other voting directors had at times served on the personnel committee and were familiar with the management abilities of corporate officers, including appellees Jordan and Sykora. The board had obtained outside assessments of Pace's earlier claims, heard management's responses, and was unable to substantiate the claims.

Throughout the ongoing assessment of STP, the directors had received regular reports from the Vice President, Nuclear, and from the board's own Nuclear Committee. Before considering Pace's claims, the directors knew of the management initiatives that had been and were being implemented to address the problems at STP. The directors had met with regulatory authorities only weeks before voting on Pace's demands and were satisfied that the regulators' concerns were being addressed. Based on this information, it was the directors' judgment that Pace's claims did not justify litigation. There was no genuine issue of material fact regarding whether appellees Jordan and Sykora carried out the corporate objectives set by the board, or whether they wavered in their loyalty to HII, HL & P, or the shareholders.

In their response to the interlocutory summary judgment motion, Pace and Fuentez acknowledge that the board, before its meeting to discuss Pace's demands, had reviewed the executive summary of the diagnostic evaluation team report. This summary outlined the regulatory authority's assessment of the causes of the outage at STP. Appellants point to no authority to support that information is insufficient to support a board's decision merely because the information is obtained before a demand is received. Carroll's affidavit succinctly sets forth the information known by the board about the problems at STP before it voted on Pace's demands.

We overrule the third point of error.

Inapplicability of 1997 Amendments

The underlying thesis of appellants' second point of error is that the 1997 amendments to article 5.14 control. They contend that under the amended law, the trial court erred because: (a) the board's procedures were improper; (b) the board was not independent and disinterested when it rejected Pace's claims; and (c) Pace and Fuentez were not given an appropriate opportunity for discovery.

We have already decided that pre–1997 law applies to this case. The 1997 amendments do not apply because appellants did not preserve error. TEX.R.APP. P. 33.1(a). We therefore need not address the second point of error.

We overrule the second point of error.

Conclusion

We grant the motion for rehearing by Pace and Fuentez. We affirm the judgment of the trial court.

Elloway, et.al. v. Pate, et.al.
238 S.W.3d 882, Court of Appeals of Texas, Houston (14th Dist.), 2007

... Shareholder brought class action against chief executive officer (CEO), chairman and board of directors of oil corporation for alleged breach of fiduciary duties in connection with sale of corporation. After a jury... entered judgment in favor of defendants, ... shareholder appealed. We affirm.

BACKGROUND

James Postl was president and chief executive officer of Pennzoil and a director of Pennzoil. James Pate was chairman of Pennzoil's Board of Directors and chairman of the executive committee. Terry Savage, John Greeniaus, Brent Scowcroft, Lorne Waxlax, Forrest Haselton, Berdon Lawrence, and Gerald Smith were members of Pennzoil's Board of Directors (the "Directors").

On February 22, 2002, Rob Routs, President of Shell Oil Products US, approached Jim Postl with a cash offer for Shell to purchase Pennzoil for the price of $18.50 per share. Postl informed Routs Pennzoil was not for sale and it was committed to, and confident in, its five-year strategic plan. However, Postl told Routs he would take the offer to Pennzoil's board. On March 5, 2002, Postl took the offer to board, which agreed that the price was not adequate, but authorized Postl to have further discussions with Shell "to see if a transaction could be negotiated that would be in the best interests of the Company's stockholders."

Postl also informed the board that he would engage the investment banking company Morgan Stanley. On March 7, 2002, Postl entered into an agreement for Morgan Stanley to provide Pennzoil with financial advice and assistance in connection with the proposed Shell/Pennzoil merger. In the event the sale did not go through, Morgan Stanley would receive an advisory fee of $100,000. If the sale of the company was accomplished, Morgan Stanley would receive a transaction fee to be calculated as "0.40 % of the transaction's Aggregate Value."

Also, on March 5, 2002, a compensation committee meeting was held. The committee members were Forrest Haselton, Terry Savage, and John Greeniaus. The compensation committee approved several amendments of the company's benefits in the event of a change in control:[FN1]

> amend the company's executive severance plan with regard to a change in control of the company;

FN1. Companies often enter into agreements with their executives in anticipation of a change in control to retain key employees during the uncertainty of a potential merger or acquisition. Such agreements are referred to as change-in-control agreements or so-called "golden parachute" agreements. LINDA E. RAPPAPORT, ACHIEVING SYNERGIES IN HIGH TECH TRANSACTIONS: THE PEOPLE FACTOR, 985 PLI/Corp 73, at 76 (Apr.1997).

amend Pate's agreement to provide for coverage under Pennzoil's senior executive severance plan so that if a change in control of the company occurred, Pate would be entitled to, in addition to the continuation of his annual consulting fee, three times his annual consulting fee upon the date of such change in control (the "Pate agreement");

enter into an agreement with Postl providing that Postl would provide consulting and advisory services to the company for the three-year period following his termination and a consulting fee of $500,000 per year (the "Postl agreement"); amend the company's annual incentive plan (to provide a full year of benefits in the event of a change in control) and long-term incentive plan (payout of benefits upon a change in control); and

modify the definition of "change-in-control."

On March 7, 2002, Routs and Ron Blakely, Shell's chief financial officer, met with Postl and Tom Kellagher, Pennzoil's chief financial officer. Postl reviewed Pennzoil's publicly available information with Routs and Blakely. On March 8, 2002, Pennzoil and Shell entered into a confidentiality agreement. On March 13, 2002, Shell and Pennzoil had a due diligence meeting. On March 15, 2002, Routs called Postl to tell him Shell was increasing its offer to $20 per share. Postl responded that he was not prepared to recommend $20 per share to the Pennzoil board.

On March 18, 2002, Pennzoil's board had a telephonic meeting. The board addressed the indictment of its independent public accountants, Arthur Andersen, and the need to appoint other independent public accountants. Postl also informed the board Shell had indicated it was prepared to increase its proposed price to $20 per share, the companies had entered into a confidentiality agreement, and Pennzoil had retained Morgan Stanley to assist in advising Pennzoil in connection with any potential transaction. Also, on March 18, 2002, a telephonic compensation committee meeting was held, during which the committee approved recommending the granting of stock options.

On March 19, 2002, Routs and Postl met and agreed Shell's and Pennzoil's chief financial officers would meet to go over the financial assumptions Shell would use to prepare its final proposal. Blakely and Kellagher met the afternoon of March 19. On March 22, 2002, Routs and Postl met. They agreed this would be the last attempt at negotiating an agreeable sales prices. Routs offered $21.50, which Postl rejected. Routs left the room for awhile and conferred with Blakely. Routs returned with a $22 per share offer, which Postl said he would recommend to the Pennzoil board.

Over the weekend, Shell learned of the change-in-control benefits. Routs was angry when he learned about the cost of the change-in-control benefits. The final cost of the change-in-control benefits was substantially more than the amount Shell had estimated. On the morning of

369

March 25, Routs called Postl, asking him to rescind the change-in-control benefits. Postl refused. Routs considered terminating the transaction or reducing the price, but Shell did neither. On March 25, 2002, the Pennzoil board met and voted to recommend to the shareholders the sale of the company to Shell for $22 per share. Shell issued a press release announcing the merger agreement.

On August 1, 2002, a shareholders meeting was held, at which time 99% of Pennzoil's voting shareholders approved the sale of Pennzoil to Shell. *[footnote omitted]* On October 1, 2002, Shell and Pennzoil completed the merger.

Elloway alleges the price of $22 per share paid to the shareholders was grossly inadequate and unfair. Elloway asserts each of the Directors breached their fiduciary duties of due care and loyalty under Delaware law by failing to maximize shareholder value in connection with the sale of Pennzoil. *[footnote omitted]* The crux of Elloway's complaint is the Directors agreed to the unfair sale price to insure Shell would not walk away from the deal when it learned of the cost of the increased benefits. Elloway alleges the fact that Shell was ready and willing to pay the additional amount for the change-in-control benefits is evidence of the "cushion" the Directors had built into the $22 per share sale price, and the Directors should have obtained the additional amount in the form of an increased price per share.

Specifically, Elloway alleges the Directors breached their fiduciary duties by:

(1) failing to inform themselves of all information reasonably available to them;

(2) granting to themselves, during negotiations, substantial change in-control-benefits, which improperly motivated them to push through the acquisition regardless of whether the price was fair, and low-balling the sale price in order to build in a "cushion" to cover the increased acquisition cost resulting from the additional grants of change in control benefits;

(3) failing to take steps to maximize the value of Pennzoil by taking steps to avoid competitive bidding, and failing to make good faith attempts to solicit other potential buyers;

(4) failing to properly value Pennzoil;

(5) failing to protect against the numerous conflicts of interest resulting from their own interrelationships with the transaction; and

(6) failing to disclose all material information that would permit Pennzoil's shareholders to cast a fully informed vote.

After Elloway rested, the trial court granted the Directors' motion for a directed verdict on Elloway's due care claim. The jury rejected Elloway's claims for breach of the duty of disclosure and duty of loyalty. The jury further found the Pennzoil shareholders' vote approving the merger with Shell was fully and fairly informed. On December 15, 2005, the trial court entered a take nothing judgment on Elloway's claims against the Directors. ...

The Directors argue Elloway's due care claims were negated by the exculpatory provision in Pennzoil's certificate of incorporation. Under Delaware law, a certificate of incorporation may contain:

> A provision eliminating or limiting the personal liability of a director to the corporation or its stockholders for monetary damages for breach of fiduciary duty as a director, provided that such provision shall not eliminate or limit the liability of a director: (i) For any breach of the director's duty of loyalty to the corporation or its stockholders; (ii) for acts or omissions not in good faith or which involve intentional misconduct or a knowing violation of law; ... or (iv) for any transaction from which the director derived an improper personal benefit.... 8 DEL.CODE § 102(b)(7).

With respect to the limitation of the Directors' liability, Article IX of Pennzoil's certificate of incorporation provides, in relevant part:

> A director of this Corporation shall not be liable to the Corporation or its stockholders for monetary damages for breach of fiduciary duty as a director, except to the extent such exemption from liability or limitation thereof is not permitted under the General Corporation Law as the same exists or may hereafter be amended.

The adoption of a charter provision, in accordance with Section 102(b)(7), bars the recovery of monetary damages from directors for a successful shareholder claim that is based on violations of the duty of care, but not for violations of the fiduciary duties of loyalty or good faith. *Emerald Partners v. Berlin*, 787 A.2d 85, 90 (Del.2001). An exculpation clause authorized by section 102(b)(7) is in the nature of an affirmative defense and, therefore, the directors bear the burden to show they are entitled to its protection. *In re Walt Disney Co. Deriv. Litig.*, 907 A.2d 693, 752 (Del.Ch.2005), *aff'd*, 906 A.2d 27 (Del.2006).

In their answer, the Directors pleaded that Elloway's claim for monetary damages for any alleged breaches of the duty of care were barred by the limitation of liability provision in Pennzoil's certificate of incorporation. At the hearing on their motion for a directed verdict, the Directors argued there was no evidence of gross negligence to support Elloway's due care claim, and the trial court granted the directed verdict on that basis. ...

A director's duty in conducting a sale of the company is to seek out, in a manner consistent with his or her fiduciary duties, "the best value reasonably available to the stockholders." *In re Lukens, Inc. S'holders Litig.*, 757 A.2d 720, 731 (Del.Ch.1999). *aff'd sub nom, Walker v. Lukens*, 757 A.2d 1278 (Del.2000). In a merger or sale, the director's duty of care requires the director, before voting on a proposed plan of merger or sale, to inform himself and his fellow directors of all material information that is reasonably available to them. *Cede & Co. v. Technicolor, Inc.*, 634 A.2d 345, 368 (Del.1993), *modified on other grounds*, 636 A.2d 956 (Del.1994).

With respect to his due care claim, Elloway alleged the Directors failed to properly inform themselves of all information, i.e., the value of the change-in-control benefits and the financial health of the company, available to them, which, in turn, tainted the negotiation process, thus, preventing them from seeking the highest price reasonably obtainable. Because the elements of Elloway's due care claim were submitted in instructions accompanying the loyalty question and the jury's negative answer to the loyalty question, Elloway's due care claim was also necessarily rejected. ...

Moreover, Elloway did not present sufficient evidence. Director liability for breaching the duty of care is predicated on a showing of gross negligence. *Aronson v. Lewis*, 473 A.2d 805, 812 (Del.1984), *overruled on other grounds by Brehm v. Eisner*, 746 A.2d 244 (Del.2000). To overcome the presumption that the Directors acted on an informed basis, Elloway must show gross negligence. *Crescent/Mach I Partners, L.P. v. Turner*, 846 A.2d 963, 985 (Del.Ch.2000). Gross negligence is a reckless indifference to or a deliberate disregard of the whole body of stockholders or actions which are without the bounds of reason. *Benihana of Tokyo, Inc. v. Benihana, Inc.*, 891 A.2d 150, 192 (Del.Ch.2005), *aff'd*, 906 A.2d 114 (Del.2006).

Elloway contends he produced substantial evidence the Pennzoil board was recklessly informed about critical issues and acted outside the bounds of reason. Elloway first asserts the Directors, with the exception of Pate and Postl, "wholly ignored the issue" of synergies. Synergies are the aspects of a merger that allow the acquiring company to enhance its earnings, for example, by eliminating overlapping areas. Elloway alleges Pate, Postl, and Morgan Stanley concealed the value of the merger synergies from the rest of the board. Director Greeniaus testified that someone said synergies were not relevant to the seller in the transaction.

[However] Morgan Stanley calculated the synergies of the merger ... and Postl testified synergies were reviewed with the board in terms of what Shell was prepared to pay.

Elloway also asserts Postl and Pate concealed from the remaining Directors how well Pennzoil was performing financially at the time of the proposed transaction, and further that those Directors made no effort to determine for themselves the company's then current performance. According to one of Elloway's expert witnesses, Prof. Bernand Black, it was Pate's and Postl's responsibility to give updated financials or projections to the other board members, but the other board members still should, and could, have asked for that information.

Again, contrary to Elloway's assertion, the minutes of the March 5, 2002 board meeting state Postl "provided a projection of first quarter earnings and financial performance by each business." Director Gerald Smith testified the board, at the March 5 meeting, was told the first quarter looked promising, but two key areas—consumer business and international business—were not doing as well. Also, Prof. Black further stated, "I did not mean to convey the impression that [the Directors] were unaware of how the company was doing."

Elloway further contends the Directors did not exercise "an extra level of care and attention" in choosing a sales process to insure they obtained "the highest price ... for the shareholders." Prof. Black opined the board "should take overall charge ... of the major decisions that are going to be made; ..." such as conducting an auction or looking for alternative buyers. In documents prepared for Pennzoil management for negotiation purposes, Morgan Stanley advised Pennzoil management it had a fiduciary duty to shop the company to other potential buyers in the absence of a public auction.

Once the merger was announced, by definition, Pennzoil was available and on the market. No other companies approached Pennzoil interested in a merger, and in the months following the announcement, Pennzoil's stock never traded at $22, but just below. Postl testified the issue of other potential buyers was discussed with the board, but it was concluded there were no other credible buyers. An auction is held when there is confidence that there is a lot of interest and competition. Here, with no other credible buyers, holding an auction would not make sense. *[footnote omitted]* ... The duty to take reasonable steps to secure the highest immediately available price does not invariably require the board to conduct an auction process or a targeted market canvass because there is no single blueprint for fulfilling the duty to maximize value. *In re Toys "R" Us, Inc.*, 877 A.2d 975, 1000 (Del.Ch.2005); *see also Crescent/Mach I Partners, L.P.*, 846 A.2d at 985–86 (citations omitted) ("Generally, when a board of directors is considering a single offer [,] fairness requires a canvass of the market to determine if higher bids can be elicited. However, if the directors possess a body of reliable evidence with which to evaluate the fairness of the transaction[,] they are permitted to approve the transaction without conducting a canvass of the market."). ...

The Directors testified they believed $22 per share was a very good price for the company. It represented a 55.5 percent premium over Pennzoil's stock's trading price four weeks prior to the announcement of the merger, a 42 percent premium over Pennzoil's trading price on March 22—the day Routs and Postl agreed to the $22 per share price, and a 33 percent premium over Pennzoil's all-time high trading price of $16.50 per share. *[footnote omitted]*

Elloway also alleges the Directors failed to disclose certain information in the Proxy so the shareholders could make an informed vote on the merger. Elloway asserts the Directors failed to disclose (1) Morgan Stanley's estimated synergies were not part of its presentation to the board; (2) Pennzoil's internal earnings estimates exceeded those of Wall Street analysts; (3) management requested, in March, and received additional change-in-control benefits totaling $84.9 million; (4) additional change-in-control benefits were not disclosed to Shell until after the $22 price had been agreed upon; and (5) stock options were granted when Shell's $20–offer was pending. Elloway also complains the Proxy misrepresented that executive benefits were vetted by Towers Perrin, and understated the total change-in-control benefits received by top executives by $4 million.

The Proxy informed shareholders that Pennzoil's directors had been named in two lawsuits filed on March 28, 2002, and April 4, 2002, seeking class certification on behalf of Pennzoil shareholders. The Proxy explained the petitions alleged the directors had breached their fiduciary duties in connection with the proposed sale of Pennzoil to Shell at a price alleged to be grossly inadequate and unfair. The petitions further alleged the directors derived unspecified personal financial benefits from the acquisition at the expense of Pennzoil's shareholders. Finally, the Proxy gave the styles and cause numbers of the two lawsuits, which sought to enjoin the sale of Pennzoil to Shell.

Moreover, these are essentially the same complaints Elloway raises with regard to either the concealment of information from the Directors or the Directors' failure to inform themselves which are without merit. We conclude Elloway has not presented evidence that the Directors' conduct constitutes gross negligence. ...

As the Directors point out, this case does not involve any directors who had an interest in, or stood to acquire an interest in, the acquiring company by virtue of the merger, i.e., there is no evidence Pate or Postl stood on both sides of the transaction. Instead, Pate's and Postl's alleged interests were the change-in-control benefits and stock option grants. Simply because a director stands to gain financially through change-in-control benefits does not mean the director has a financial interest in the merger so that the board may not delegate negotiating authority to that director. *Cf. Wisconsin Inv. Bd. v. Bartlett*, No. C.A. 17727, 2000 WL 238026, at *6 (Del.Ch. Feb.24, 2000) (holding, unlike *Mills*, it was within board's business judgment to delegate authority to director to negotiate the merger, incentivized by a fee tied to the best result he could obtain for all shareholders).

It was within the board's business judgment to delegate authority to Postl to negotiate with Shell. There is no evidence (1) the Directors completely abdicated their responsibility of oversight of the negotiations to Postl and Morgan Stanley; (2) Pate or Postl controlled the rest of the Directors; or (3) Pate and Postl concealed certain information such as merger-related synergies or Pennzoil's financial status for the first quarter of 2002 from the rest of the Directors....

Accordingly, the judgment of the trial court is affirmed.

Sinclair Oil Corporation v. Levien
332 A.2d 139 (Del.Supr., 1975)

This is an appeal by the defendant, Sinclair Oil Corporation (hereafter Sinclair), from an order of the Court of Chancery, 261 A.2d 911 in a derivative action requiring Sinclair to account for damages sustained by its subsidiary, Sinclair Venezuelan Oil Company (hereafter Sinven), organized by Sinclair for the purpose of operating in Venezuela, as a result of dividends paid by Sinven, the denial to Sinven of industrial development, and a breach of contract between Sinclair's wholly-owned subsidiary, Sinclair International Oil Company, and Sinven.

Sinclair, operating primarily as a holding company, is in the business of exploring for oil and of producing and marketing crude oil and oil products. At all times relevant to this litigation, it owned about 97% Of Sinven's stock. The plaintiff owns about 3000 of 120,000 publicly held shares of Sinven. Sinven, incorporated in 1922, has been engaged in petroleum operations primarily in Venezuela and since 1959 has operated exclusively in Venezuela.

Sinclair nominates all members of Sinven's board of directors. The Chancellor found as a fact that the directors were not independent of Sinclair. Almost without exception, they were officers, directors, or employees of corporations in the Sinclair complex. By reason of Sinclair's domination, it is clear that Sinclair owed Sinven a fiduciary duty. Getty Oil Company v. Skelly Oil Co., 267 A.2d 883 (Del.Supr.1970); Cottrell v. Pawcatuck Co., 35 Del.Ch. 309, 116 A.2d 787 (1955). Sinclair concedes this.

The Chancellor held that because of Sinclair's fiduciary duty and its control over Sinven, its relationship with Sinven must meet the test of intrinsic fairness. The standard of intrinsic fairness involves both a high degree of fairness and a shift in the burden of proof. Under this standard the burden is on Sinclair to prove, subject to careful judicial scrutiny, that its transactions with Sinven were objectively fair. Guth v. Loft, Inc., 23 Del.Ch. 255, 5 A.2d 503 (1939); Sterling v. Mayflower Hotel Corp., 33 Del.Ch. 293, 93 A.2d 107, 38 A.L.R.2d 425 (Del.Supr.1952); Getty Oil Co. v. Skelly Oil Co., supra.

Sinclair argues that the transactions between it and Sinven should be tested, not by the test of intrinsic fairness with the accompanying shift of the burden of proof, but by the business judgment rule under which a court will not interfere with the judgment of a board of directors unless there is a showing of gross and palpable overreaching. Meyerson v. El Paso Natural Gas Co., 246 A.2d 789 (Del.Ch.1967). A board of directors enjoys a presumption of sound business judgment, and its decisions will not be disturbed if they can be attributed to any rational business purpose. A court under such circumstances will not substitute its own notions of what is or is not sound business judgment.

We think, however, that Sinclair's argument in this respect is misconceived. When the situation involves a parent and a subsidiary, with the parent controlling the transaction and fixing the terms, the test of intrinsic fairness, with its resulting shifting of the burden of proof, is applied. Sterling v. Mayflower Hotel Corp., supra. The basic situation for the application of the rule is the one in which the parent has received a benefit to the exclusion and at the expense of the subsidiary.

Recently, this court dealt with the question of fairness in parent-subsidiary dealings in Getty Oil Co. v. Skelly Oil Co., supra. In that case, both parent and subsidiary were in the business of refining and marketing crude oil and crude oil products. The Oil Import Board ruled that the subsidiary, because it was controlled by the parent, was no longer entitled to a separate allocation of imported crude oil. The subsidiary then contended that it had a right to share the quota of crude oil allotted to the parent. We ruled that the business judgment standard should be applied to determine this contention. Although the subsidiary suffered a loss through the administration of the oil import quotas, the parent gained nothing. The parent's quota was derived solely from its own past use. The past use of the subsidiary did not cause an increase in the parent's quota. Nor did the parent usurp a quota of the subsidiary. Since the parent received nothing from the subsidiary to the exclusion of the minority stockholders of the subsidiary, there was no self-dealing. Therefore, the business judgment standard was properly applied.

A parent does indeed owe a fiduciary duty to its subsidiary when there are parent-subsidiary dealings. However, this alone will not evoke the intrinsic fairness standard. This standard will be applied only when the fiduciary duty is accompanied by self-dealing-the situation when a parent is on both sides of a transaction with its subsidiary. Self-dealing occurs when the parent, by virtue of its domination of the subsidiary, causes the subsidiary to act in such a way that the parent receives something from the subsidiary to the exclusion of, and detriment to, the minority stockholders of the subsidiary.

We turn now to the facts. The plaintiff argues that, from 1960 through 1966, Sinclair caused Sinven to pay out such excessive dividends that the industrial development of Sinven was effectively prevented, and it became in reality a corporation in dissolution. From 1960 through 1966, Sinven paid out $108,000,000 in dividends ($38,000,000) in excess of Sinven's earnings during the same period). The Chancellor held that Sinclair caused these dividends to be paid during a period when it had a need for large amounts of cash. Although the dividends paid exceeded earnings, the plaintiff concedes that the payments were made in compliance with 8 Del.C. s 170, authorizing payment of dividends out of surplus or net profits. However, the plaintiff attacks these dividends on the ground that they resulted from an improper motive-Sinclair's need for cash. The Chancellor, applying the intrinsic fairness standard, held that Sinclair did not sustain its burden of proving that these dividends were intrinsically fair to the minority stockholders of Sinven.

Since it is admitted that the dividends were paid in strict compliance with 8 Del.C. s 170, the alleged excessiveness of the payments alone would not state a cause of action. Nevertheless, compliance with the applicable statute may not, under all circumstances, justify all dividend payments. If a plaintiff can meet his burden of proving that a dividend cannot be grounded on any reasonable business objective, then the courts can and will interfere with the board's decision to pay the dividend.

Sinclair contends that it is improper to apply the intrinsic fairness standard to dividend payments even when the board which voted for the dividends is completely dominated. In support of this contention, Sinclair relies heavily on American District Telegraph Co. (ADT) v. Grinnell Corp., (N.Y.Sup.Ct.1969) aff'd. 33 A.D.2d 769, 306 N.Y.S.2d 209 (1969). Plaintiffs were minority stockholders of ADT, a subsidiary of Grinnell. The plaintiffs alleged that Grinnell, realizing that it would soon have to sell its ADT stock because of a pending anti-trust action, caused ADT to pay excessive dividends. Because the dividend payments conformed with applicable statutory law, and the plaintiffs could not prove an abuse of discretion, the court ruled that the complaint did not state a cause of action. Other decisions seem to support Sinclair's contention. In Metropolitan Casualty Ins. Co. v. First State Bank of Temple, 54 S.W.2d 358 (Tex.Civ.App.1932), rev'd. on other grounds, 79 S.W.2d 835 (Sup.Ct.1935), the court held that a majority of interested directors does not void a declaration of dividends because all directors, by necessity, are interested in and benefited by a dividend declaration. See, also, Schwartz v. Kahn, 183 Misc. 252, 50 N.Y.S.2d 931 (1944); Weinberger v. Quinn, 264 A.D. 405, 35 N.Y.S.2d 567 (1942).

We do not accept the argument that the intrinsic fairness test can never be applied to a dividend declaration by a dominated board, although a dividend declaration by a dominated board will not inevitably demand the application of the intrinsic fairness standard. Moskowitz v. Bantrell, 41 Del.Ch. 177, 190 A.2d 749 (Del.Supr.1963). If such a dividend is in essence self-dealing by the parent, then the intrinsic fairness standard is the proper standard. For example, suppose a parent dominates a subsidiary and its board of directors. The subsidiary has outstanding two classes of stock, X and Y. Class X is owned by the parent and Class Y is owned by minority stockholders of the subsidiary. If the subsidiary, at the direction of the parent, declares a dividend on its Class X stock only, this might well be self-dealing by the parent. It would be receiving something from the subsidiary to the exclusion of and detrimental to its minority stockholders. This self-dealing, coupled with the parent's fiduciary duty, would make intrinsic fairness the proper standard by which to evaluate the dividend payments.

Consequently it must be determined whether the dividend payments by Sinven were, in essence, self-dealing by Sinclair. The dividends resulted in great sums of money being transferred from Sinven to Sinclair. However, a proportionate share of this money was received by the minority shareholders of Sinven. Sinclair received nothing from Sinven to the exclusion of its minority stockholders. As such, these dividends were not self-dealing. We hold therefore that the Chancellor erred in applying the intrinsic fairness test as to these dividend payments. The business judgment standard should have been applied.

We conclude that the facts demonstrate that the dividend payments complied with the business judgment standard and with 8 Del.C. s 170. The motives for causing the declaration of dividends are immaterial unless the plaintiff can show that the dividend payments resulted from improper motives and amounted to waste. The plaintiff contends only that the dividend payments drained Sinven of cash to such an extent that it was prevented from expanding.

The plaintiff proved no business opportunities which came to Sinven independently and which Sinclair either took to itself or denied to Sinven. As a matter of fact, with two minor exceptions which resulted in losses, all of Sinven's operations have been conducted in Venezuela, and Sinclair had a policy of exploiting its oil properties located in different countries by subsidiaries located in the particular countries.

From 1960 to 1966 Sinclair purchased or developed oil fields in Alaska, Canada, Paraguay, and other places around the world. The plaintiff contends that these were all opportunities which could have been taken by Sinven. The Chancellor concluded that Sinclair had not proved that its denial of expansion opportunities to Sinven was intrinsically fair. He based this conclusion on the following findings of fact. Sinclair made no real effort to expand Sinven. The excessive dividends paid by Sinven resulted in so great a cash drain as to effectively deny to Sinven any ability to expand. During this same period Sinclair actively pursued a company-wide policy of developing through its subsidiaries new sources of revenue, but Sinven was not permitted to participate and was confined in its activities to Venezuela.

However, the plaintiff could point to no opportunities which came to Sinven. Therefore, Sinclair usurped no business opportunity belonging to Sinven. Since Sinclair received nothing from Sinven to the exclusion of and detriment to Sinven's minority stockholders, there was no self-dealing. Therefore, business judgment is the proper standard by which to evaluate Sinclair's expansion policies.

Since there is no proof of self-dealing on the part of Sinclair, it follows that the expansion policy of Sinclair and the methods used to achieve the desired result must, as far as Sinclair's treatment of Sinven is concerned, be tested by the standards of the business judgment rule. Accordingly, Sinclair's decision, absent fraud or gross overreaching, to achieve expansion through the medium of its subsidiaries, other than Sinven, must be upheld.

Even if Sinclair was wrong in developing these opportunities as it did, the question arises, with which subsidiaries should these opportunities have been shared? No evidence indicates a unique need or ability of Sinven to develop these opportunities. The decision of which subsidiaries would be used to implement Sinclair's expansion policy was one of business judgment with which a court will not interfere absent a showing of gross and palpable overreaching. Meyerson v. El Paso Natural Gas Co., 246 A.2d 789 (Del.Ch.1967). No such showing has been made here.

Next, Sinclair argues that the Chancellor committed error when he held it liable to Sinven for breach of contract.

In 1961 Sinclair created Sinclair International Oil Company (hereafter International), a wholly owned subsidiary used for the purpose of coordinating all of Sinclair's foreign operations. All crude purchases by Sinclair were made thereafter through International. On September 28, 1961, Sinclair caused Sinven to contract with International whereby Sinven agreed to sell all of its crude oil and refined products to International at specified prices. The contract provided for minimum and maximum quantities and prices. The plaintiff contends that Sinclair caused this contract to be breached in two respects. Although the contract called for payment on receipt, International's payments lagged as much as 30 days after receipt. Also, the contract required International to purchase at least a fixed minimum amount of crude and refined products from Sinven. International did not comply with this requirement.

Clearly, Sinclair's act of contracting with its dominated subsidiary was self-dealing. Under the contract Sinclair received the products produced by Sinven, and of course the minority shareholders of Sinven were not able to share in the receipt of these products. If the contract was breached, then Sinclair received these products to the detriment of Sinven's minority shareholders. We agree with the Chancellor's finding that the contract was breached by Sinclair, both as to the time of payments and the amounts purchased.

Although a parent need not bind itself by a contract with its dominated subsidiary, Sinclair chose to operate in this manner. As Sinclair has received the benefits of this contract, so must it comply with the contractual duties.

Under the intrinsic fairness standard, Sinclair must prove that its causing Sinven not to enforce the contract was intrinsically fair to the minority shareholders of Sinven. Sinclair has failed to meet this burden. Late payments were clearly breaches for which Sinven should have sought and received adequate damages. As to the quantities purchased, Sinclair argues that it purchased all the products produced by Sinven. This, however, does not satisfy the standard of intrinsic fairness. Sinclair has failed to prove that Sinven could not possibly have produced or someway have obtained the contract minimums. As such, Sinclair must account on this claim.

Finally, Sinclair argues that the Chancellor committed error in refusing to allow it a credit or setoff of all benefits provided by it to Sinven with respect to all the alleged damages. The Chancellor held that setoff should be allowed on specific transactions, e.g., benefits to Sinven under the contract with International, but denied an over all setoff against all damages claimed. We agree with the Chancellor, although the point may well be moot in view of our holding that Sinclair is not required to account for the alleged excessiveness of the dividend payments.

We will therefore reverse that part of the Chancellor's order that requires Sinclair to account to Sinven for damages sustained as a result of dividends paid between 1960 and 1966, and by reason of the denial to Sinven of expansion during that period. We will affirm the remaining portion of that order and remand the cause for further proceedings.

Corporate Officers

The corporation's officers oversee the business' daily operations, and in their different roles they are given legal authority to act on the corporation's behalf in almost all lawful business-related activities. Officers are usually appointed by the corporation's board of directors, and while specific positions may vary from one corporation to another, typical corporate officers include:

- **Chief Executive Officer (CEO) or President.** The CEO has ultimate responsibility for the corporation's activities, and signs off on contracts and other legally-binding action on behalf of the corporation. The CEO reports to the corporation's board of directors.

- **Chief Operating Officer (COO).** Charged with managing the corporation's day-to-day affairs, the COO usually reports directly to the CEO.

- **Chief Financial Officer (CFO)** or Treasurer. The CFO is responsible (directly or indirectly) for almost all of the corporation's financial matters.

- **General Counsel (GC).** The GC is the chief legal officer for the corporation.

- **Secretary**. The corporation's Secretary is in charge of maintaining and keeping corporation's records, documents, and "minutes" from shareholder meetings.

In some corporations, one person may serve as the business's sole director, officer, and shareholder.

In general, a corporate officer's role is to serve at the will of the board of directors in carrying out the corporation's day-to-day operations. Essentially, an officer is an "agent" of the board of directors, who serves as the "principal." As such, many of the same agency concepts -- duties of care and loyalty, and express and implied authorized power -- discussed earlier apply to the officer/board relationship. A corporate officer can bind a corporation in one of four ways: express actual authority; implied actual authority; apparent authority; and ratification.

Express actual authority

An officer has the express authority to bind a corporation by an explicit grant of authority generally provided for in the corporation's bylaws.

Implied actual authority

Aside from his express actual authority, an officer also has the implied authority to do those things necessary to satisfy his role. For instance, although it may not be one of the president's enumerated powers, it is generally understood that a corporation's president has the implied authority to sign contracts binding the corporation for non-extraordinary contracts.

Also, an officer's implied authority is triggered when the board, by its own act or failure to act, implicitly grants an officer actual authority. For example, although a vice-president does not ordinarily have the authority to sign contracts binding the corporation, if the board has allowed the V.P. to do so in the past without objection, then in the event the V.P. signs a contract in the future it can be said that he is acting with implied authority.

Apparent authority

This authority is derived from actions of the board that give the appearance to a reasonable person that the officer is authorized to perform the acts at issue.

Ratification

One way that an officer can bind a corporation is through ratification. If a corporation ratifies an officer's action, then the corporation will bind itself to that act.

Templeton v. Nocona Hills Owners Association, Inc.
555 S.W.2d 534, Tex.Civ.App.-Texarkana, August 30, 1977

In suit for wrongful discharge from employment in violation of a written contract, the 97th Judicial District Court of Montague County, Marvin F. London, J., entered judgment in favor of the corporate defendant, and plaintiff appealed. The Court of Civil Appeals, Cornelius, J., held that (1) plaintiff failed to carry her burden of establishing that the corporate defendant's president was invested with actual authority to make the contract sued upon, (2) plaintiff also failed to carry her burden of establishing that the president had apparent authority to make the contract, and (3) partial performance is effective in some cases to establish ratification of an otherwise invalid contract, or to take a contract out of the operation of the statute of frauds, but the performance of work under a month-to-month employment arrangement will not bind an employer to an otherwise invalid contract for a specific term of employment unless circumstances amounting to ratification or estoppel are present. Affirmed.

Appellant Hildegard Halley Templeton instituted this action complaining that she had been wrongfully discharged from employment in violation of her written contract with appellee Nocona Hills Owners Association, Inc. She alleged that appellee's president had signed the contract which agreed to employ her as club manager for a period of one year beginning July 1, 1975. Appellee defended on grounds that the instrument upon which the suit was brought was not a valid contract because it did not contain a date when it would become effective, Nocona Hills Country Club was named as employer rather than Nocona Hills Owners Association, Inc., and because the president did not have authority to act for the corporation in that instance and the corporation had not accepted or ratified his act in doing so.

The case was tried to a jury. In response to special issues the jury found that (1) appellant and appellee entered into the employment contract; (2) the commencement date for the employment was July 1, 1975; (3) appellee discharged appellant without cause; and, (4) appellant was damaged in the sum of $7,450.00. The district court, however, sustained appellee's motion for judgment non obstante veredicto and entered a take nothing judgment. Appellant has presented six points of error which contend generally that the court erred in rendering judgment non obstante veredicto because the instrument in question had all the necessary attributes of a valid contract and was binding upon the appellee Owners Association.

To sustain the action of the district court in granting judgment non obstante veredicto we must find there was no evidence of probative force upon which the jury could have made one or more of its findings. Burt v. Lochausen, 151 Tex. 289, 249 S.W.2d 194 (1952); Tex.R.Civ.P. 301. It therefore becomes necessary to review the evidence.

The Nocona Hills Owners Association, Inc. is a corporation whose shareholders are persons who have purchased lots or homes in a twenty-seven hundred acre tract of land known as Nocona Hills Subdivision. The corporation also maintains and operates a country club at the subdivision. The facilities were initially constructed and operated by the land developer who conducted business under the name of Lake Nocona Acres, Inc. The appellee Owners Association took ownership and control of the common facilities from the developer on July 1, 1975. In June, prior to the take over, elections were held for officers and directors of the Owners Association. Seven directors were elected to take office on July 1, 1975. One of them was Preston Jameson, who was also elected president of the board. Eugene Frank Jones was appointed by the board of directors to serve as General Manager. Appellant was serving as manager of the country club at the time of the change in ownership. In June, shortly prior to the effective date of the take over, President Jameson approached appellant about remaining in her position. She consented but stated that she wanted a contract. Jameson replied that he would bring the matter before the board of directors. Subsequent conversation and negotiations occurred between Jameson and appellant. They had talked of a $1,000.00 per month salary, but after consulting the board of directors Jameson told appellant that the board would not agree to more than $850.00 per month. When appellant kept insisting upon a written contract, Jameson suggested that she "draw one up". On June 20, 1975, appellant had a secretary type the agreement, following a standard form which had been used by the country club for another employee.

At appellant's request, Jameson signed the contract on June 20th and requested Mr. Leon Jones to witness it. The testimony conflicts from this point on. Jameson testified he agreed to sign the contract to indicate his consent but that he told appellant that the contract would not be binding unless and until it was authorized by the board of directors. Appellant denied that she was so advised. On June 22, 1975, Jameson submitted the contract to the board of directors but it refused to authorize or accept it, voting only to give appellant a vote of confidence and inform her that her job (which had been on a month to month basis) was secure at her present salary of

$750.00. The appellant had continued to work as club manager during the negotiations and she continued to do so after the change in ownership. Jameson testified that he told appellant of the board's refusal to agree to the contract. Appellant denied the fact. Nine days after the change over, appellant was discharged by the general manager for disloyalty. She was paid for her work from July 1 through July 9 at the rate of $750.00 per month. She brought suit to recover the amount she would have received had the written contract been honored.

The appellee denied under oath that the contract sued upon had been executed by its authority. See Tex.R.Civ.P. 93(h). Appellant therefore had the burden to establish the authority of the officer to make the contract on behalf of the corporation. [citations omitted]

The authority of an officer to contract for a corporation may be actual or apparent. In Texas, by statute, the board of directors of a corporation, not its president, is charged generally with the duty of managing the corporation's affairs. Tex.Bus.Corp.Act Ann. art. 2.31. Consequently, actual authority of the president to contract on behalf of the corporation must be found either in specific statutes, in the organic law of the corporation, or in a delegation of authority from the board of directors formally expressed, or must be implied from the nature of his position or from custom or habit of doing business. Manufacturers' Equipment Co. v. Cisco Clay & Coal Co., 118 Tex. 370, 15 S.W.2d 609 (1929); Ennis v. Todd, supra; Tex.Bus.Corp.Act Ann. art. 2.42; Hildebrand, Texas Corporations, Vol. 2, Sec. 640, p. 597; 14 Tex.Jur.2d, Corporations, Sec. 330, p. 429, et seq. As to express authority, there was no proof in this case of any of the provisions of the corporate charter or by-laws, and there was no attempt to prove that the board of directors or the shareholders had invested the president with any authority to make contracts on its behalf. See In Re Westec Corporation, supra. In fact, the only evidence concerning contracts on behalf of the corporation was Jameson's testimony that only the board could authorize them, and that the board refused to approve the one in question here. As to implied authority, the settled rule in Texas is that a corporation president, merely by virtue of his office, has no inherent power to bind the corporation except as to routine matters arising in the ordinary course of business. [citations omitted] The execution of an employment contract binding the corporation to employ a person in a managerial position for a period of one year could not be considered a matter in the ordinary and usual course of appellee's business. Compare Leak v. Halaby Galleries, supra. Especially is this true since the power to hire and discharge employees for appellee was vested in a general manager rather than in the president. Indeed, Jameson had not even taken office as president on June 20 when the contract was executed. Under the record in this case, we are impelled to the conclusion that appellant failed in her burden to establish that Mr. Jameson was invested with actual authority to make the contract sued upon.

There was likewise a failure to produce any evidence that Jameson had apparent authority to make the contract. The doctrine of apparent authority is based on estoppel, and one seeking to charge a principal through the apparent authority of an agent must prove such conduct on the part of the principal as would lead a reasonably prudent person, using diligence and discretion, to suppose that the agent had the authority he purported to exercise. [citations omitted] The declaration or actions of the agent are not sufficient. Great American Casualty Co. v. Eichelberger, supra. The record here contains no evidence of any act on the part of the corporation's board of directors or other authorized person which would lead any reasonable person to believe that Mr. Jameson was invested with the power to execute, without approval of the board of directors, a year's employment contract.

Appellant contends, however, that if the contract was not binding upon the corporation because not executed by its authority, either actual or apparent, it should nevertheless be held to have become enforceable by reason of the parties' partial performance thereof. Aside from the fact that such a ground of recovery was neither pleaded nor submitted to the jury, we cannot agree that partial performance will authorize a recovery for appellant. A partial performance is effective in some cases to establish ratification of an otherwise invalid contract, or to take a contract out of the operation of the statute of frauds, but the performance of work under a month to month employment arrangement will not bind an employer to an otherwise invalid contract for a specific term of employment unless circumstances amounting to ratification or estoppel are present. Such circumstances are not present here. Appellant was employed on a month to month basis. The evidence shows only that when her contract was refused by the board she continued her usual employment until discharged. She was paid for the number of days she actually worked in July. No claim has been made for the additional days in that month. Under the circumstances, no further recovery was authorized.

Concerning the date of the contract, we agree with appellant that parol evidence was admissible to supply the date when the employment was to begin, and that there was evidence from which the jury could find that such date was July 1, 1975. See 17 C.J.S. Contracts s 61, p. 731. However, because of the lack of proof as to the authority of Mr. Jameson to make the contract on behalf of the corporation, the trial court was correct in rendering judgment non obstante veredicto, and his judgment must be affirmed. Great American Casualty Co. v. Eichelberger, supra.

IT IS SO ORDERED

****

Almar-York Company, Inc., v. The Fort Worth National Bank
374 S.W.2d 940 (Tex.Civ.App.-Fort Worth, 1964)

On August 9, 1960, The Fort Worth National Bank, Trustee of the Estate of Francis H. Sparrow, deceased, sued the Almar–York Company, Inc., for delinquent monthly rental payments on parts of Lots 23 and 26, a subdivision of A. Robinson Survey in Fort Worth. The defendant, on September 6, 1960, filed an answer in which it alleged the written lease, on which suit was brought, was obtained by fraud on the part of plaintiff in that plaintiff represented it would construct a rock wall in the rear of the premises. On November 16, 1962, defendant filed an amended answer in which it plead as a defense that the lease in question was executed without authority of defendant corporation. Trial resulted in an instructed verdict and judgment in favor of plaintiff. Defendant has briefed a number of points of error, the gist of which is the court erred in rendering judgment for plaintiff because of the failure of plaintiff to prove that A. W. Stubbeman, president of defendant corporation, was authorized by the directors to execute the lease.

The evidence is undisputed.

At all pertinent times Stubbeman, his wife, Ruth F. Stubbeman, and M. L. Brown, Sr., were all the directors of defendant corporation. Defendant was in the business of manufacturing, assembling and servicing air conditioning units.

The first lease was entered into between plaintiff and defendant on November 23, 1951. The lease was executed for a five year period and signed by A. W. Stubbeman, president of defendant, and attested to by Ruth F. Stubbman, secretary. Defendant immediately moved its shop, assembly and servicing departments into the building located on the described lots and also used the building as a warehouse and continued to so use the premises throughout the initial five year period.

On October 1, 1956, a new five year lease, to become effective December 1, 1956, was signed by Stubbeman as president of defendant, and attested to by Mrs. Stubbeman. The new lease provided for a monthly rental of $300.00. The monthly rental was paid until October, 1958. From the beginning period of the new lease (December 1, 1956) until October, 1957, the premises were used as they were during the first five year lease. Defendant continued to use the premises as a warehouse until October, 1958. By correspondence Stubbeman, as president of defendant, continued to recognize the lease as valid and existent.

The two directors, Stubbeman and his wife, who attested to both leases, of course knew of the second lease contract. The third director, Brown, knew the defendant corporation was using the premises and knew the purposes for which used.

Plaintiff sold the property to the City of Fort Worth in August of 1961, thus terminating the lease with defendant. The judgment for plaintiff in the amount of $9,900.00 covers the period from the date defendant ceased to pay the monthly rental to and including the month preceding the sale of the property to the City.

The defendant, though objecting to the admissibility of some of the evidence, did not challenge the truth of the admitted evidence. Defendant moved for an instructed verdict when the plaintiff rested. The motion was overruled. Defendant offered no evidence.

Generally if a corporation accepts the benefit of a contract or acquiesces therein with knowledge, it impliedly ratifies it. If the directors had knowledge of the contract, or if the facts are such as to justify the presumption that they did have knowledge then a failure to disaffirm amounts to ratification. Miller v. Sealy Oil Mill & Mfg. Co., Tex.Civ.App., 166 S.W. 1182.

The doctrine of apparent authority is based on estoppel, and one seeking to charge a principal through the apparent authority of an agent to bind the principal must prove such conduct on the part of the principal as would lead a reasonably prudent person, using diligence and discretion, to suppose that the agent has the authority he purports to exercise. Chastain v. Cooper & Reed, 152 Tex. 322, 257 S.W.2d 422; Great American Cas. Co. v. Eichelberger, Tex.Civ.App., 37 S.W.2d 1050.

A corporation, like an individual, is bound by the acts of its agent, expressly or impliedly authorized by it. It may become bound by a ratification without any formal action for that purpose by its board of directors. It may ratify by passive acquiescence as well as by affirmative action. Its acquiescence, with knowledge, proven or which should be inferred, if continued for a considerable time, will operate as a ratification. Knowles v. Northern Texas Traction Co., Tex.Civ.App., 121 S.W. 232.

Keeping in mind the undisputed evidence heretofore mentioned, and in view of the above authorities, we are of the opinion the trial court correctly held that the lease contract was enforceable by reason of ratification and apparent authority. For two years defendant occupied and paid rent under the new lease. For the first year it used the premises for the same purposes it so used them under the original lease. During the second year it continued to use the premises for warehouse purposes. Defendant did not question Stubbeman's authority to execute the lease until six years after its execution and four years after it had ceased to pay the monthly rentals.

All of defendant's points of error have been duly considered and finding no reversible error each and all points of error are overruled. Under the principles set out in the above cited cases, we affirm the judgment of the trial court.

****

Redmon v. Griffith
202 S.W.3d 225 (Tex.App.-Tyler, 2006)

Jimmie D. Redmon and Kathy Redmon (collectively the "Redmons") appeal the trial court's summary judgment entered in favor of Valta R. Griffith, both individually and as representative of the Estate of Ralph E. Griffith, deceased ("Griffith"). The Redmons raise two issues on appeal. The Griffiths raise one issue on appeal. We affirm in part and reverse and remand in part.

BACKGROUND

G.E.M. Transportation was a trucking company started by Ralph Griffith. By prior agreement, when Ralph Griffith recouped his initial investment, the company was incorporated in Texas as G.E.M. Transportation, Inc. ("G.E.M.") and twenty-five percent of the corporation's stock was transferred to Jim Redmon, who became operations manager, vice president, and director of G.E.M. Ralph Griffith was president and director of G.E.M. and retained seventy-five percent of the stock in the corporation. Ralph Griffith's wife, Valta, was secretary, treasurer, and director of G.E.M. Jim Redmon's wife, Kathy, also participated in running the business affairs of G.E.M.

In 1999, disputes arose between the Redmons and the Griffiths, and on or about August 11, 1999, Ralph Griffith terminated Jim Redmon's positions with G.E.M. [Jim Redmon retained his position as a director of G.E.M.] Less than a month later, Kathy Redmon's position at G.E.M. was likewise terminated.

On March 17, 2000, the Redmons, both individually and derivatively on behalf of G.E.M., filed the instant lawsuit against G.E.M. and the Griffiths in various capacities. By their lawsuit, the Redmons sought an accounting and inspection of G.E.M.'s corporate books and records. The Redmons further alleged that the Griffiths, as officers and directors of G.E.M., committed fraud and breached fiduciary duties owed to the Redmons by diverting corporate opportunities, funds, and revenues and by making illegal disbursements of corporate assets for their own personal use and benefit. Moreover, the Redmons sought damages for breach of contract and made a claim for shareholder oppression.

Following Ralph Griffith's death, Valta Griffith put G.E.M. into Chapter 11 bankruptcy on February 9, 2001. The bankruptcy proceeding was converted to a Chapter 7 proceeding on February 13, 2001. Following a suggestion of bankruptcy filed in the trial court on November 7, 2001, all proceedings against G.E.M. at the state level were stayed.

On May 29, 2003, the Redmons, by their second amended petition, abandoned any claims made by them on behalf of G.E.M. derivatively and removed G.E.M. as a defendant in the lawsuit. On December 15, 2003, Griffith filed both a traditional and a no evidence motion for summary judgment. The Redmons responded. Griffith subsequently moved for summary judgment on her counterclaim for conversion. On February 18, 2004, the trial court signed a final judgment ordering that the parties take nothing on their respective claims against one another. This appeal followed.

DISCUSSION

We will consider the Redmons' first and second issues together. In their first issue, the Redmons argue that the trial court improperly granted summary judgment on the basis that they lacked standing. In their second issue, the Redmons argue that the trial court erred in granting summary judgment because they presented sufficient evidence with regard to their various theories of recovery to create a genuine issue of material fact.

Standing

Standing is a component of subject matter jurisdiction, which we consider under the same standard by which we review subject matter jurisdiction generally. The test for standing requires that there be a real controversy between the parties which will actually be determined by the judicial declaration sought. *See Nootsie, Ltd. v. Williamson County Appraisal Dist.*, 925 S.W.2d 659, 661 (Tex.1996). Without a breach of a legal right belonging to the plaintiff, no cause of action can accrue to his benefit. *See Nobles v. Marcus*, 533 S.W.2d 923, 927 (Tex.1976). Thus, it follows that a plaintiff who seeks individual redress based on allegations concerning wrongs done to a corporation lacks standing.

Traditionally, a corporate officer owes a fiduciary duty to the shareholders collectively, i.e., the corporation, but he does not occupy a fiduciary relationship with an individual shareholder unless some contract or special relationship exists between them in addition to the corporate relationship. *[citations omitted]*. Moreover, a corporate shareholder has no individual cause of action for personal damages caused solely by a wrong done to the corporation. *[citations omitted]*. The cause of action for injury to the property of a corporation or for impairment or destruction of its business is vested in the corporation, as distinguished from its shareholders, even though the harm may result indirectly in the loss of earnings to the shareholders. The individual shareholders have no separate and independent right of action for wrongs to the corporation that merely result in depreciation in the value of their stock.

As a result, to recover for wrongs done to the corporation, the shareholder must bring the suit derivatively in the name of the corporation so that each shareholder will be made whole if the corporation obtains compensation from the wrongdoer. However, a corporate shareholder may have an individual action for wrongs done to him where the wrongdoer violates a duty arising from a contract or otherwise and owing directly by him to the shareholder. Such a principle is not so much an exception to the general rule as it is a recognition that a shareholder may sue for violation of his individual rights regardless of whether the corporation also has a cause of action. It is the nature of the wrong, whether directed against the corporation only or against the shareholder personally, not the existence of injury, which determines who may sue. Appellate courts have also recognized an individual cause of action for "shareholder oppression" or "oppressive conduct." *[citations omitted]* Oppressive conduct has been defined as follows:

> 1. [M]ajority shareholders' conduct that substantially defeats the minority's expectations that, objectively viewed, were both reasonable under the circumstances and central to the minority shareholder's decision to join the venture; or

388

2. [B]urdensome, harsh, or wrongful conduct; a lack of probity and fair dealing in the company's affairs to the prejudice of some members; or a visible departure from the standards of fair dealing and a violation of fair play on which each shareholder is entitled to rely.

While oppressive conduct is more easily found in the context of a close corporation, we are aware of no case law expressly limiting it to such a context. Moreover, a claim of oppressive conduct can be independently supported by evidence of a variety of conduct.

When considering questions of standing, we review the pleadings to determine whether the plaintiff has alleged facts that affirmatively demonstrate the court's jurisdiction. We resolve any doubt in favor of the plaintiff.

Claims/Causes of Action

We will address the claims and allegations in the Redmons' pleadings one by one. We will first consider whether the Redmons have standing. If we determine that they did have standing to bring a claim, we will then address the propriety of the trial court's grant of summary judgment with regard to that claim.

Standing

As set forth above, appellate courts in Texas have recognized a cause of action for oppressive conduct. The Redmons have pleaded that they were minority shareholders in G.E.M. with the Griffiths owning a seventy-five percent share of the corporate shares. In their second amended petition, the Redmons have further alleged that certain conduct on the Griffiths' part amounts to shareholder oppression. Specifically, the Redmons allege that the Griffiths have engaged in wrongful conduct; have not dealt in the company's affairs fairly to the prejudice of the Griffiths; and have not observed the standards of fair dealing on which each shareholder is entitled to rely. The Redmons also allege that the Griffiths maliciously suppressed the payment of dividends owed to them and made improper personal loans to themselves from G.E.M. in addition to paying personal expenses from corporate funds without the approval of the board of directors. Finally, the Redmons allege that the Griffiths employed "squeeze out" techniques such as diverting corporate opportunities, excessive payment of dividends to themselves, and attempts to deprive the Redmons of the fair value of their shares and of the benefits thereof. We conclude that the Redmons have made sufficient allegations, which taken as true, would demonstrate a claim for shareholder oppression. We hold that the trial court's grant of summary judgment on the ground that the Redmons lacked standing to proceed on their claim for shareholder oppression was improper.

Summary Judgment Evidence

We next consider whether the Redmons presented sufficient summary judgment evidence to create a genuine issue of material fact with regard to their shareholder oppression claim. Our review of the summary judgment record indicates that there is some evidence that the Griffiths paid personal expenses from corporate funds without the approval of the board of directors. Specifically, in her deposition testimony, Valta Griffith stated that G.E.M. purchased a life insurance policy on Ralph Griffith using corporate funds. Valta Griffith further testified that G.E.M. paid her utility bills every month without authorization by the board of directors. She further stated that G.E.M. paid her credit card bills on at least one occasion without the authorization of the board of directors. In his affidavit, Jim Redmon testified that in Spring 1999, in spite of his efforts, Ralph and Valta Griffith refused him access to certain financial statements prepared by G.E.M.'s CPA, Bob Johnston. Jim Redmon further stated that he continued to seek access to information concerning the financial condition of the company until August 1999, when his position at G.E.M. was terminated.

We conclude that the Redmons presented sufficient evidence to overcome the Griffiths' motion for summary judgment concerning their claim of shareholder oppression. Evidence concerning the use of corporate funds to pay personal expenses combined with evidence that Jim Redmon was denied access to information concerning the financial condition of the corporation sufficiently creates a material fact issue concerning whether there was a lack of probity and fair dealing in the company's affairs to the prejudice of the Redmons or otherwise, a visible departure from the standards of fair dealing, and a violation of fair play on which minority shareholders like the Redmons were entitled to rely. We hold that the trial court incorrectly granted summary judgment on the Redmons claim for shareholder oppression.

Breach of Fiduciary Duty

Standing

We will next consider the Redmons' allegations concerning breach of fiduciary duty. In their second amended petition, the Redmons allege as follows:

Breach of Fiduciary Duties

1. [T]he Griffith defendants are fiduciaries in numerous respects. First, as officers and directors of G.E.M., charged with the exclusive handling and management of the financial affairs of the corporation, they are charged with the exercise of the utmost good faith, integrity, and fair dealing in connection with this management. The Griffiths['] actions in diverting corporate opportunities, funds, and revenues, and of making illegal disbursements of corporate assets for their own personal use and benefit, constitute not only violations of their fiduciary duties, but knowing and willful violation of those duties....

2. The acts of the individual Defendants in exercising and engaging in the oppressive and "squeeze-out" tactics outlined in paragraphs L—P of Section V., above, are further acts and omissions in violation of their fiduciary duties as controlling, majority shareholders, officers[,] and directors of G.E.M., against Defendants....

In paragraph VI.(C)(1), the Redmons distinctly allege that the Griffiths violated fiduciary duties they owed as officers and directors of G.E.M. The fiduciary duty an officer or director owes to the corporation is distinguishable from a fiduciary relationship that may exist between majority and minority shareholders or otherwise by contract or other special relationship between the individual parties.

We iterate that a cause of action for injury to the property of a corporation or for impairment or destruction of its business is vested in the corporation, as distinguished from its shareholders, and that to recover for damages to the corporation, the shareholder must bring the suit derivatively in the name of the corporation so that each shareholder will be made whole if the corporation obtains compensation from the wrongdoer. Moreover, in determining who has standing to sue, we must consider the nature of the wrong alleged, not the existence of injury.

In the instant case, the Redmons abandoned their derivative claim on behalf of G.E.M. Even though the underlying facts supporting their allegations with regard to breach of fiduciary duty may intermingle, in paragraph (C)(1), they have sought a distinct avenue of recovery from the Griffiths based on allegations that they violated their fiduciary duties as officers and directors of G.E.M. Such allegations allege a breach of duty owed to the corporation. As such, since they have not alleged the breach of a legal duty owed to them individually, no cause of action can accrue to their benefit therefrom. Thus, we conclude that the Redmons do not have standing to recover from the Griffiths individually for their alleged breach of fiduciary duty as set forth in paragraph (C)(1).

We next consider the Redmons' allegations in paragraph (C)(2). With the exception of their allegation that the Griffiths violated their fiduciary duties as officers and directors of G.E.M., which are duties owed to the corporation, the Redmons' allegations that the Griffiths violated fiduciary duties as controlling majority shareholders warrant further discussion. A co-shareholder in a closely held corporation does not as a matter of law owe a fiduciary duty to his co-shareholder. Instead, the existence of such a duty depends on the circumstances. For example, a fiduciary duty exists if a confidential relationship exists. [A confidential relationship exists where influence has been acquired and abused and confidence has been reposed and betrayed. *Navistar Int'l Transp. Corp.*, 823 S.W.2d at 594. A person is justified in placing confidence in the belief that another party will act in his or her best interest only where he or she is accustomed to being guided by the judgment or advice of the other party and there exists a long association in a business relationship, as well as personal friendship. *Dominguez v. Brackey Enters., Inc.*, 756 S.W.2d 788, 791–92 (Tex.App.-El Paso 1988, writ denied). However, the fact that the relationship has been a cordial one and of long duration does not necessarily constitute a confidential relationship. (citations omitted).

A fiduciary relationship is an extraordinary one and will not be lightly created; the mere fact that one subjectively trusts another does not alone indicate that confidence is placed in another in the sense demanded by fiduciary relationships because something apart from the transaction between the parties is required. *Kline v. O'Quinn,* 874 S.W.2d 776, 786 (Tex.App.-Houston [14th Dist.] 1994, writ denied).

Further, fiduciary relationships may be created by contract, through the repurchase of a shareholder's stock in a closely held corporation, in certain circumstances in which a majority shareholder in a closely held corporation dominates control over the business, and in closely held corporations in which the shareholders operate more as partners than in strict compliance with the corporate form. *Id* at 31–32.

In the case at hand, the Redmons' pleadings allege that a majority-minority shareholder relationship existed between the Redmons and the Griffiths. They further make reference to G.E.M. as a "closely-held corporation" in paragraph V., section P of their pleadings. The Redmons further allege facts indicating a great deal of control over the business exercised by Ralph Griffith. Such allegations combined with allegations in the Redmons' pleadings that the Griffiths engaged in wrongful conduct and a lack of fair dealing with regard to the company's affairs to the prejudice of the Redmons sufficiently alleges a breach of fiduciary duty by way of oppressive conduct.

Summary Judgment Evidence

As set forth previously, because there is some evidence creating a material fact issue concerning the Redmons' shareholder oppression claim, we do not reach the issue of whether other allegations of wrongdoing potentially underlying the Redmons' shareholder oppression claim have sufficient evidentiary support in the summary judgment record.

Breach of Contract

Standing

We next consider the Redmons' allegations concerning breach of contract. In their second amended petition, the Redmons allege as follows:

Breach of Contract

The actions of Defendants in terminating the employment contracts of Plaintiffs, under the peculiar factual circumstances presented in this case, constitute shareholder oppression and are a breach of the contract of employment which each Plaintiff had with G.E.M.

The possibility exists that the firing of an at-will employee who is a minority shareholder can constitute shareholder oppression. In *Willis,* the court elaborated as follows:

The law empowers the board of directors to manage a corporation (citation omitted). Such power obviously includes the power to discharge employees. Given the broad range of business judgment allowed by law to directors and the fact that Texas is an employment-at-will state, we hold that firing alone is simply not the sort of "burdensome, harsh, or wrongful conduct" or "visible departure from the standards of fair dealing" that may constitute shareholder oppression. Nor were the [appellants'] expectations of continued employment without a contract, "objectively reasonable," under *Davis v. Sheerin*, 754 S.W.2d at 381. Texas law does not recognize a minority shareholder's right to continued employment without an employment contract (citation omitted). All are presumed to know the law. Expectations of continued employment that are contrary to well settled law cannot be considered objectively reasonable. Therefore, we hold that the trial judge erred in rendering judgment for shareholder oppression based solely on the jury's finding of wrongful lock-out.

Here, the Redmons have pleaded that the Griffiths wrongfully terminated their employment contracts, which in light of the circumstances detailed in their pleadings amounted to shareholder oppression. We conclude that the Redmons have made sufficient allegations to demonstrate standing to proceed for wrongful termination within the confines of their shareholder oppression claim.

However, the Redmons further allege that the Griffiths are liable for breach of the contracts of employment which the Redmons had with G.E.M. Privity in contract provides a party with standing to maintain the action. *See, e.g., Interstate Contracting Corp. v. City of Dallas*, 135 S.W.3d 605, 618 (Tex.2004) (citing *Brown v. Todd*, 53 S.W.3d 297, 305 (Tex.2001) (under Texas law, standing limits subject matter jurisdiction to cases involving a distinct injury to the plaintiff and a real controversy between the parties, which will be actually determined by the judicial declaration sought)). Privity is established by proving that the defendant was a party to an enforceable contract with either the plaintiff or a party who assigned its cause of action to the plaintiff. *See Conquest Drilling Fluids v. Tri–Flo Int'l*, 137 S.W.3d 299, 308 (Tex.App.-Beaumont 2004, no pet.).

Where a corporation enters into a contract, the officer's signature on the contract, with or without a designation as to his representative capacity, does not render him personally liable under the contract. *See Robertson v. Bland*, 517 S.W.2d 676, 678 (Tex.Civ.App.-Houston [1st Dist.] 1974, writ dism'd). Thus, to the extent that the Redmons seek recovery from the Griffiths apart from their shareholder oppression claim for a contract they allege they had with G.E.M., we hold they have not pleaded sufficient facts to establish standing to maintain such an action.

Constructive Fraud

We next consider the Redmons' allegations concerning constructive fraud. In their second amended petition, the Redmons allege as follows:

> With respect to any assets determined in any accounting to properly belong to the corporation, but which are held in the name of the individual Defendants, such assets, having been obtained by Plaintiffs as a result of their breaches of duties and fiduciary duties owed to the corporation, such assets should be declared to be held by the individual Defendants as constructive trustees for the benefit of the corporation since that [is] the only remedy that will adequately compensate the corporation and Plaintiffs, derivatively, and prevent the unjust enrichment of the said Defendants in violation of their fiduciary duties.

In their brief, the Redmons concede that their claims for accounting and for inspection of corporate books and records are moot. Thus, it follows that to the extent they seek to recover "assets determined in any accounting to properly belong to the corporation, but which are held in the name of the individual Defendants," that claim is likewise moot.

However, a breach of fiduciary duty is a form of constructive fraud. *Welder v. Green*, 985 S.W.2d 170, 175 (Tex.App.-Corpus Christi 1998, pet. denied); *Stum v. Stum*, 845 S.W.2d 407, 415 (Tex.App.-Fort Worth 1992, no writ) (pleadings alleging breach of fiduciary duties were sufficient to allege fraud), *overruled on other grounds, Humphreys v. Meadows*, 938 S.W.2d 750, 752 (Tex. App.-Fort Worth 1996, pet. denied). Therefore, to the extent we have held that the Redmons have standing to raise breach of fiduciary duty, we further hold that they have standing to proceed on a claim of constructive fraud.

Fraudulent Transfer

Standing

We next consider the Redmons' allegations concerning fraudulent transfer. In their second amended petition, the Redmons allege as follows:

> The Griffiths have made numerous transfers of assets belonging to them individually to the Trust for the purpose of defrauding the Redmons, whom they believed to be their creditors. These transfers are violative of various provisions of the Texas Uniform Fraudulent Transfer Act as set forth in § 24.001, *et seq.* Texas Business and Commerce Code. The Plaintiffs Redmons request various remedies available under those acts to satisfy their claims.

A transfer made or obligation incurred by a debtor is fraudulent as to a creditor, whether the creditor's claim arose before or within a reasonable time after the transfer was made or the obligation was incurred, if the debtor made the transfer or incurred the obligation with an actual intent to hinder, delay, or defraud any creditor of the debtor. TEX. BUS. & COMM.CODE ANN. § 24.005(a)(1) (Vernon 2002). In determining actual intent, consideration may be given, among other factors, to whether before the transfer was made, the debtor had been sued or threatened with suit. *See* TEX. BUS. & COMM.CODE ANN. § 24.005(b)(4) (Vernon 2002).

In their motion for summary judgment, the Griffiths contended that the Redmons' claim for fraudulent transfer was not ripe as they were not creditors of the Griffiths. Ripeness, like standing, is a threshold issue that implicates subject matter jurisdiction. *Patterson v. Planned Parenthood of Houston & Southeast Tex., Inc.*, 971 S.W.2d 439, 442 (Tex.1998). However, tort claimants are entitled to file causes of action under the Uniform Fraudulent Transfer Act based upon pending, unliquidated tort claims. *See Blackthorne v. Bellush*, 61 S.W.3d 439, 443–44 (Tex.App.-San Antonio 2001, no pet.); *see also* TEX. BUS. & COMM.CODE ANN. § 24.002(3), (4) (Vernon 2002). In the case at hand, the Redmons have brought their claim for fraudulent transfer in conjunction with their other claims, which include a tort claim for breach of fiduciary duty. *See Douglas v. Aztec Pet. Corp.*, 695 S.W.2d 312, 318 (Tex.App.-Tyler 1985, no writ) (breach of fiduciary duty is a tort). Thus, we hold that the Redmons' fraudulent transfer claim is ripe.

In their motion for summary judgment, the Griffiths further argued that even if the claim was ripe, the Redmons lacked capacity to bring the claim because it belonged to G.E.M. Although couched in terms of capacity, because the ultimate issue concerns whether the Redmons have pleaded that they have suffered a distinct injury caused by the Griffiths, which will be actually determined by the judicial declaration sought, the issue is one of standing.

Here, the Redmons alleged that the Griffiths "have made numerous transfers of assets belonging to them individually to the Trust for the purpose of defrauding the Redmons." Based on our reading of the Redmons' second amended petition, we conclude that they have properly pleaded facts which would entitle them to standing on a claim of fraudulent transfer. They have specifically limited their claim to assets belonging to the Redmons individually that were allegedly transferred to the R.E. and Valta Griffith Living Revocable Trust, which is also a defendant in this matter.

Summary Judgment Evidence

The aforementioned arguments that relate to standing were the only ones raised in the Griffiths' motion for summary judgment with regard to fraudulent transfer. Although the Griffiths made allegations generally that no evidence existed to support the Redmons' allegations with regard to fraudulent transfer, they failed to specify which elements of fraudulent transfer lacked evidentiary support. *See* TEX.R. CIV. P. 166a(i) (a no evidence motion must state the elements as to which there is no evidence). As such, we have limited our discussion to the Griffiths' jurisdictional arguments presented to the trial court in the Griffiths' motion. For the foregoing reasons, the Redmons' first issue is sustained in part and overruled in part. Furthermore, the Redmons' second issue is sustained.

TRIAL COURT'S DENIAL OF THE GRIFFITHS' MOTION FOR SUMMARY JUDGMENT

The Griffiths have likewise appealed the trial court's judgment. In their sole issue, the Griffiths argue that the trial court erred in denying their motion for summary judgment on their counterclaim against the Redmons for conversion. In their brief, the Griffiths have not presented much in the way of cogent argument, nor have they cited to any authority in support of their sole issue. *See* TEX.R.APP. P. 38.1(h). Rather, the Griffiths have referred us to their motion for summary judgment on their counterclaims "[f]or further argument." We hold that the Griffins have waived their sole issue by their failure to adequately brief it. *See id.; Kang v. Hyundai Corp.,* 992 S.W.2d 499, 503 (Tex.App.-Dallas 1999, no pet.) (failure to cite any authority constitutes a waiver). The Griffiths' sole issue is overruled.

CONCLUSION

We have held that the Redmons, by their pleadings, have sufficiently demonstrated standing with regard to their claims for (1) shareholder oppression, (2) breach of fiduciary duty by way of shareholder oppression, (3) wrongful termination of their employment within the confines of their shareholder oppression claim, (4) constructive fraud to the extent the claim has not been rendered moot, and (5) fraudulent transfer of the Griffiths' individual assets to the R.E. and Valta Griffith Living Revocable Trust. In this regard, the Redmons' first issue is sustained. We have further held that the trial court correctly determined that the Redmons did not have standing with regard to their claims for (1) breach of fiduciary duty owed by the Griffiths to G.E.M. and (2) breach of contract that the Redmons allegedly had with G.E.M. In this regard, the Redmons' first issue is overruled. We have also held that the trial court incorrectly granted summary judgment on the Redmons' claim for shareholder oppression. Therefore, we sustained the Redmons' second issue. We have further overruled the Griffiths' sole issue.

We *reverse* the trial court's judgment in part and *remand* the portions of this cause concerning (1) shareholder oppression, (2) breach of fiduciary duty by way of shareholder oppression, (3) breach of contract within the confines of the Redmons' shareholder oppression claim, (4) constructive fraud to the extent the claim has not been rendered moot, and (5) fraudulent transfer of the Griffiths' individual assets to the R.E. and Valta Griffith Living Revocable Trust for further proceedings consistent with this opinion. We *affirm* the remainder of the trial court's judgment.

Boehringer v. Konkel
2013 WL 1341160 (Tex.App.-Hous. (1 Dist.) 2013))

Appellants, Christopher Boehringer and Enginuity Engineering, Inc. ("EEI"), challenge the trial court's judgment, entered after a jury trial, in favor of appellee, Mark A. Konkel, in Konkel's suit against Boehringer and EEI for shareholder oppression. In five issues, Boehringer and EEI contend that the evidence is legally and factually insufficient to support the jury's findings that Boehringer refused to allow Konkel to examine EEI's books, awarded himself excessive salaries and compensation, and withheld payment of dividends to Konkel; Konkel failed to "establish shareholder oppression as a matter of law;" and the evidence is factually insufficient to support the jury's finding on their claims that Konkel violated the Federal Wiretap Act. We affirm.

Background

Konkel, who Boehringer met in the late 1990s when they both worked for Fubrizol Corporation in Deer Park, Texas, became a shareholder in Boehringer's close corporation in 2001. Konkel bought 49.9% of the stock for $499, and the first shareholder meeting ended with the election of Subchapter S corporation status and salaries set at $60,000 annually for both men. Boehringer acted as president, and Konkel as vice president. Both men are chemical engineers, and the company designed industrial processes and machinery and equipment used in refineries, chemical plants, biofuel facilities, and pharmaceutical production facilities.

From 2001 to 2004, the company was a two-man operation, with both men working independently on contracts. In 2005, the company began using the name "Enginuity Engineering, Incorporated," and it acquired office space, hired employees, and earned significant revenue. The two men did not discuss compensation aside from their annual salaries and splitting the corporation's profits. Between 2005 and 2008, EEI's annual sales were in excess of $1 million compared to 2004 sales of $550,000.

Shortly after this marked success, the relationship between Konkel and Boehringer deteriorated. Konkel did not live up to Boehringer's expectations; he filed invoices late, failed to renew necessary software subscriptions, and kept irregular office hours. likewise, Boehringer did not live up to Konkel's expectations; he became verbally abusive to Konkel and other employees. Some employees quit because of the abuse; some testified at trial about the abuse that they endured from Boehringer. When Konkel drafted an employee handbook, suggested a formalized holiday schedule, and attempted to outline corporate policies, Boehringer refused to consider them as he did not want to be held to policies. And, when Konkel made between ten and twenty requests for EEF's corporate records from between 2001 and 2009, Boehringer honored none of the requests, other than providing to Konkel a one-page spreadsheet that Boehringer created.

The situation reached its boiling point at the February 2, 2009 shareholder meeting. When Boehringer personally handed notice of the meeting to Konkel, he told Konkel that he was "going to make [Konkel's] fucking life miserable." On every issue presented at the meeting, at which Boehringer's lawyer kept minutes, Boehringer voted his 501 shares against Konkel's 499, with Konkel losing every measure. With Boehringer voting his 501 shares, he made his wife vice president, replacing Konkel. Also, Boehringer voted to make EEI's Subchapter S status revocable upon his own behest, and he created restrictions on the sale of stock.

During the meeting, Konkel read from a statement, reiterating his previous requests for company records. Boehringer agreed to provide three years of EEI's tax returns, but only if Konkel signed a confidentiality agreement. And when Konkel requested his share certificates, Boehringer would not provide them.

Following the shareholder meeting, Boehringer sent a company-wide email stating that Konkel was no longer in management. Boehringer instructed Konkel, through his attorney, to work out of his house because his presence in the office made Boehringer uncomfortable. He then locked Konkel out of the company's software development computer and the office.

On March 11, 2009, Boehringer instructed Konkel to be in the office between 7:00 a.m. and 5:00 p.m. Monday through Thursday and alternating Fridays. Konkel resigned from EEI the next day, stating that his only remaining connection to the corporation was as a shareholder.

Later, Konkel learned that Boehringer had secretly awarded himself a pay raise in late 2008. In 2009, Boehringer's gross pay was increased to $240,000 annually, compared to Konkel's $48,000. Boehringer testified that he did not give Konkel a raise because he "did not deserve a raise in salary based on his actions in 2007 and 2008." Boehringer also testified that he had been advised to raise his own salary because it was too low and might trigger an Internal Revenue Service ("IRS") audit.

Despite years of splitting EEI's profits according to the share percentages owned, Boehringer did not issue dividends for 2008. Typically, in late December of each year, Boehringer would estimate yearly profits and report to Konkel that number, which Konkel would use to calculate his taxes and submit a payment to the IRS. At the close of a fiscal year, Boehringer would finalize and report official earnings for tax corrections. In December 2008, Boehringer released the preliminary earnings, and at the February 2 shareholder meeting, he released the final numbers. Although Konkel used these calculations to submit $76,500 in taxes to the IRS, Boehringer never issued to Konkel the dividends from EEI's 2008 earnings. Boehringer testified that he did not do so because he was concerned about meeting EEF's financial obligations.

Before May 29, 2007, Konkel "checked a box" on the website of EEI's e-mail provider, directing the e-mail provider to make administrative copies of Boehringer's e-mail. E-mails addressed to Boehringer were then forwarded to Konkel's e-mail account.

On February 23, 2009, Konkel filed the instant suit against Boehringer and EEI, alleging shareholder oppression. He later added causes of action for breach of contract, breach of fiduciary duty, and fraudulent transfer. He also sought a declaratory judgment regarding ownership of a computer program that he had developed, to pierce the corporate veil, and obtain attorneys' fees. Boehringer filed a counterclaim against Konkel for alleged violations of both the Texas and Federal wiretap statutes.

The jury found that Boehringer had maliciously or wrongfully refused to allow Konkel to examine EEI's books, used his position to award himself an excessive salary to Konkel's detriment, and withheld EEI dividends from Konkel in 2008. The trial court had previously entered a partial summary judgment in favor of Boehringer on his contentions against Konkel for violations of the Texas and Federal Wire Tap Acts. The question of damages for any wiretap violations was submitted to the jury, which found that Konkel violated the acts "0" times and incurred "0" damages.

In its final judgment, the trial court found that shareholder oppression occurred as a matter of law. It ordered, in equitable relief, that the corporation be liquidated, with proceeds split according the share distribution after all debts were subtracted. And it further ordered that Boehringer take nothing on his counterclaims for the alleged violations of the wiretap acts.

Legal and Factual Sufficiency

In their first, second, and third issues, Boehringer and EEI complain that the evidence is legally and factually insufficient to support the jury findings that Boehringer maliciously or wrongfully refused to allow Konkel to examine EEI's books and records, awarded himself excessive salaries and compensation, and withheld payment of dividends to Konkel.

We will sustain a legal-sufficiency or "no-evidence" challenge if the record shows one of the following: (1) a complete absence of evidence of a vital fact, (2) rules of law or evidence bar the court from giving weight to the only evidence offered to prove a vital fact, (3) the evidence offered to prove a vital fact is no more than a scintilla, or (4) the evidence establishes conclusively the opposite of the vital fact. *City of Keller v. Wilson,* 168 S.W.3d 802, 810 (Tex.2005). In conducting a legal-sufficiency review, a "court must consider evidence in the light most favorable to the verdict, and indulge every reasonable inference that would support it." *Id.* at 822. The term "inference" means,

In the law of evidence, a truth or proposition drawn from another which is supposed or admitted to be true. A process of reasoning by which a fact or proposition sought to be established is deduced as a logical consequence from other facts, or a state of facts, already proved.... *Marshall Field Stores, Inc. v. Gardiner,* 859 S.W.2d 391, 400 (Tex.App.-Houston [1st Dist.] 1993, writ dism'd w.o.j.) (citing BLACK'S LAW DICTIONARY 700 (5th ed. 1979)). For a jury to infer a fact, "it must be able to deduce that fact as a logical consequence from other proven facts." *Id.*

If there is more than a scintilla of evidence to support the challenged finding, we must uphold it. *Formosa Plastics Corp. USA v. Presidio Eng'rs & Contractors, Inc.*, 960 S.W.2d 41, 48 (Tex.1998). " '[W]hen the evidence offered to prove a vital fact is so weak as to do no more than create a mere surmise or suspicion of its existence, the evidence is no more than a scintilla and, in legal effect, is no evidence.' " *Ford Motor Co. v. Ridgway*, 135 S.W.3d 598, 601 (Tex.2004) (quoting *Kindred v. Con/Chem, Inc.*, 650 S.W.2d 61, 63 (Tex.1983)). However, if the evidence at trial would enable reasonable and fair-minded people to differ in their conclusions, then jurors must be allowed to do so. *City of Keller*, 168 S.W.3d at 822; *see also King Ranch, Inc. v. Chapman*, 118 S.W.3d 742, 751 (Tex.2003). "A reviewing court cannot substitute its judgment for that of the trier-of-fact, so long as the evidence falls within this zone of reasonable disagreement." *City of Keller*, 168 S.W.3d at 822.

In conducting a factual-sufficiency review, we must consider, weigh, and examine all of the evidence that supports or contradicts the jury's determination. *See Dow Chem. Co. v. Francis*, 46 S.W.3d 237, 242 (Tex.2001); *Plas–Tex, Inc. v. U.S. Steel Corp.*, 772 S.W.2d 442, 445 (Tex.1989). We note that the jury is the sole judge of the witnesses' credibility, and it may choose to believe one witness over another; a reviewing court may not impose its own opinion to the contrary. *See Golden Eagle Archery, Inc. v. Jackson*, 116 S.W.3d 757, 761 (Tex.2003). We may set aside the verdict only if the evidence is so weak or the finding is so against the great weight and preponderance of the evidence that it is clearly wrong or manifestly unjust. *Pool v. Ford Motor Co.*, 715 S.W.2d 629, 635 (Tex.1986).

"The doctrine of shareholder oppression protects the close corporation minority stockholder from the improper exercise of majority control." Douglas Moll, *Majority Rule Isn't What It Used To Be: Shareholder Oppression in Texas Close Corporations*, 63 TEX. B.J. 434, 435 (2000). This Court has held that there are two non-exclusive definitions of shareholder oppression:

> 1. majority shareholders' conduct that substantially defeats the minority's expectations that, objectively viewed, were both reasonable under the circumstances and central to the minority shareholder's decision to join the venture; or

> 2. burdensome, harsh, or wrongful conduct; a lack of probity and fair dealing in the company's affairs to the prejudice of some members; or a visible departure from the standards of fair dealing and a violation of fair play on which each shareholder is entitled to rely. *Willis v. Bydalek*, 997 S.W.2d 798, 801 (Tex.App.-Houston [1st Dist.] 1999, pet. denied); *see also Ritchie v. Rupe*, 339 S.W.3d 275, 289 (Tex.App.-Dallas 2011, pet. granted).

In determining whether majority shareholder conduct rises to the level of oppression, we exercise caution, balancing the minority shareholder's reasonable expectations against the corporation's need to exercise its business judgment and run its business efficiently. *Ritchie*, 339

S.W.3d at 289. As we observed in *Davis v. Sheerin,* however, "[c]ourts take an especially broad view of the application of oppressive conduct to a closely-held corporation, where oppression may more easily be found." 754 S.W.2d 375, 381 (Tex.App.-Houston [1st Dist.] 1988, writ denied). It is within the province of a jury as factfinder to determine whether certain acts occurred when those acts are disputed. *Ritchie,* 339 S.W.3d at 289. The determination of whether those facts constitute shareholder oppression toward a minority shareholder is a question of law for the trial court. *Davis,* 754 S.W.2d at 380; *See Ritchie,* 339 S.W.3d at 289. A claim of oppressive conduct can be independently supported by evidence of a variety of conduct. *Davis,* 754 S.W.2d at 380. Oppressive conduct is an independent ground for relief that does not require a showing of fraud, illegality, mismanagement, wasting of assets, or deadlock. *Id.* at 381–82.

In regard to the first definition of shareholder oppression, we note that when determining whether a minority shareholder's reasonable expectations were substantially defeated, we distinguish between those specific reasonable expectations and general reasonable expectations. *Ritchie,* 339 S.W.3d at 290. Specific expectations will require proof of specific facts giving rise to the expectations in a particular case and a showing that the expectation was reasonable under the circumstances of the case as well as central to the minority shareholder's decision to join the venture. *Id.* at 291. Examples of specific reasonable expectations are employment in the corporation or a role in management. *Id.*

General reasonable expectations are expectations that arise from the mere status of being a shareholder. *Id.* These expectations belong to all shareholders and, absent evidence to the contrary, are both reasonable and central to the decision to invest in the corporation. *Id.* Examples of general reasonable expectations are the right to proportionate participation in the earnings of the company, the right to any stock appreciation, the right, with proper purpose, to inspect corporate records, and the right to vote if the stock has voting rights. *Id.* at 291–92.

Access to EEI's Books and Records

In their first issue, Boehringer and EEI assert that the evidence is legally and factually insufficient to support the jury's finding that Boehringer maliciously and wrongfully refused to allow Konkel to examine EEI's books and records. Jury Question One asked:

> Do you find from a preponderance of the evidence that Chris Boehringer maliciously or wrongfully refused to allow Mark Konkel to examine the books and records of Enginuity Engineering, Inc.?

Boehringer and EEI do not challenge Jury Question One as defective on appeal, nor do they complain about the trial court's denial of their tendered charge on this question. Accordingly, we will not review any objection to the charge that they made at trial. Boehringer and EEI acknowledge that they did not raise a separate issue on the jury charge, but urge us to consider the correctness of Jury Question One as subsidiary to their legal- and factual-sufficiency issue. However, an appellant's brief must "state concisely all issues or points presented for review." TEX.R.APP. P. 38.1(f). Rule 38.1(f) also compels that this Court treat the statement of an issue or point "as covering every subsidiary question that is fairly included." *Id.*

Boehringer and EEI have cited no authority, nor have we found any, considering a challenge to a jury question as a subsidiary question to a legal- and factual-sufficiency issue on appeal. Accordingly, we will review the sufficiency of the evidence under the question asked and the instructions actually given. *See Osterberg v. Peca,* 12 S.W.3d 31, 33 (Tex.2000) ("[I]t is the court's charge, not some other unidentified law, that measures the sufficiency of the evidence."); *see also Cathey v. Meyer,* 115 S.W.3d 644, 659–50 (Tex.App.-Waco 2003), *aff'd in part, rev'd in part on other grounds,* 167 S.W.3d 327 (Tex.2005) (considering sufficiency issue, but concluding waiver where appellant had not raised as issue on appeal his objections to wording of jury charge).

Konkel testified that he "made more than ten, less than 20" requests for EEI's records over a period of eight and a half years, including requests in each year from 2001 to 2005. During this time, Boehringer did not provide access to bank records or tax returns or any other EEI records, with one exception: after one of Konkel's requests, Boehringer provided a one-page ledger sheet that he drafted himself.

Konkel also made a written request for EEI's financial records in 2007. In two e-mails, dated May 24 and 25, 2007, Konkel wrote to Boehringer as follows:

> I also need a complete detailed ledger report for our cash flow for all of last year, and this year as of April. I do have a vested interest in seeing where our money is being spent. A report from QuickBooks listing check number—paid to-amount—date is all I am looking for. Then every month after that. Nothing less than I would easily get from an accounting firm.

Konkel's statement that he had a vested interest in seeing how the company's money was being spent constitutes a statement of a proper purpose for which the request was made. Boehringer responded, via e-mail, "We will address this sometime next week prior to a Board Meeting." Konkel testified, however, that there was no board meeting scheduled or held and Boehringer did not offer any contrary evidence. And Boehringer admitted that he never gave Konkel any tax returns or any bank statements.

The minutes of the February 2, 2009 shareholder meeting document another request by Konkel for EEI's books and records and contain a copy of Konkel's written request made the same day:

> 1) I, Mark Konkel, need to see and to have the opportunity to copy all original banking documents available, or electronic bank documents, if originals are not available,

including, but not limited to all cancelled checks, deposit slips, bank statements, wire transfers—everything regarding any transfers of money to the corporation.

2) I need to see and be able to copy all corporate documents I have not seen.

In response, Boehringer offered access to only the last three years of tax returns provided that Konkel sign a confidentiality statement. Konkel testified that he was not provided any corporate records until they were ordered produced for this lawsuit.

Boehringer further argues there is legally- and factually-insufficient evidence to support a finding that he withheld EEI's records maliciously or wrongfully. In Jury Question One, the trial court instructed the jury that:

A person acts "maliciously" when his actions are accompanied by ill-will, bad or evil motive, or such gross indifference to the rights of others as will amount to a willful or wanton act, done without just cause or excuse.

"Wrongfully" means an act committed with evil intent, with legal malice, without reasonable ground for believing the act to be lawful, and without legal justification.

As Boehringer and EEI note, the admitted ill-will between Boehringer and Konkel does not automatically establish ill-will in regard to Konkel's requests for EEF's records. Malice can be established by direct or circumstantial evidence. *See Seber v. Union Pac. R.R. Co.,* 350 S.W.3d 640, 654 (Tex.App.-Houston [14th Dist.] 2011, no pet.).

As a shareholder, Konkel had a general and reasonable expectation to have access to review EEI's corporate records. Although there is evidence that Boehringer did provide Konkel with a ledger sheet after one of his requests to see EEI's records, Boehringer did not respond to Konkel's repeated requests for records. And there is evidence that Boehringer acted with ill-will, bad or evil motive, or gross indifference to Konkel's rights as a shareholder. When Boehringer responded to Konkel's written request in 2007, he did not provide or agree to provide the requested records, he simply said, "We will address this sometime next week prior to a Board Meeting." There is evidence that there was no actual board meeting scheduled and this was Boehringer's way of threatening Konkel, reminding him that he was the majority shareholder, and controlled Konkel as the minority shareholder. Boehringer did not offer any evidence of justification for his refusal to provide EEF's corporate records after Konkel had asked to see them. The jury could have reasonably inferred from the evidence presented that Boehringer's refusal to provide EEI's corporate records stemmed from ill-will, bad or evil motive, or gross indifference to Konkel's rights as a shareholder in the corporation.

Viewing the evidence in the light most favorable to the jury's finding and indulging every reasonable inference that would support it, we conclude that the jury could have reasonably found that Boehringer maliciously or wrongfully refused to allow Konkel to examine EEF's book and records. We further conclude that the evidence supporting this finding is not so weak as to render the jury's verdict clearly wrong and manifestly unjust. Accordingly, we hold that the evidence is legally and factually sufficient to support the jury's finding that Boehringer maliciously or wrongfully refused to allow Konkel to examine EEI's books and records.

We overrule Boehringer and EEI's first issue.

Excessive Salary and Compensation

In their second issue, Boehringer and EEI assert that the evidence is legally and factually insufficient to support the jury's finding that Boehringer maliciously or wrongfully awarded himself an excessive salary. Jury Question Two asked:

> Do you find from a preponderance of the evidence that Chris Boehringer maliciously or wrongfully used his position as the President of Enginuity Engineering, Inc. to award excessive salaries and compensation to himself to the detriment of Mark Konkel?

An expectation of annual compensation through employment cannot be said to be a general expectation held by all shareholders of a corporation. *See Argo Data Res. Corp. v. Shagrithaya,* 380 S.W.3d 249, 266(Tex.App.-Dallas 2012, pet. filed). Accordingly, if Konkel was complaining about his annual salary from EEI, he would be required to provide proof of specific facts showing that his specific expectation of a certain level of compensation was reasonable under the circumstances and central to his decision to join EEI. However, Konkel is not complaining about his own compensation, but that Boehringer's raising of his own salary was detrimental to Konkel.

The minutes of the August 4, 2001 Boehringer & Associates shareholder meeting, during which Konkel joined the company as a 49.9% shareholder, contain the board resolution declaring that Boehringer, as president, and Konkel, as vice-president, would both receive $60,000 annually as salary, "until such salary shall be changed by the Shareholders at the annual or special meeting called for that purpose." Konkel testified that he and Boehringer never discussed salaries after that time, although Boehringer would make statements to him such as, "We're going to pay ourselves 40,000 this year." And Konkel was never paid more than $70,000 a year.

In 2009, Boehringer unilaterally increased his own salary to $20,000 per month (gross), and he received that salary for at least five months despite testifying that at the beginning of 2009, "[B]usiness started to dry up, you know, drastically. And we were getting in a position where there was a cash crunch." At the same time, Boehringer did not raise Konkel's salary as vice president, stating that Konkel "didn't deserve a raise in salary." In the first two months of 2009, Konkel's net monthly salary was $1,937.28 and $1,677.00 while Boehringer's was $14,700.00. Boehringer testified that he was advised to raise his salary because a low salary might trigger an IRS audit as his low salary was so disproportionate to the annual corporate revenue of EEI as a Subchapter S corporation. Boehringer explained that this was why he then raised his own salary, despite his concerns about "running out of funds in 2009 to meet the obligations ... to our different creditors, the rent, software leases, maintenance on software utilities." Boehringer noted that that because EEI was a Subchapter S corporation, he needed to pay himself a reasonable salary and his salary was unreasonably low. There is no evidence that, in previous years, Boehringer and Konkel's salaries had been different or their corporate profit distributions had ever been different based on their 49.9%/50.1% net profit split.

Boehringer and Konkel's business relationship started with an agreement that each would receive a $60,000 yearly salary. This supports an inference that they viewed their contributions to the corporation as equal. And the near equal split in stock and split of profits based on stock ownership percentages further supports this inference. Moreover, there is no evidence of a significant shift in the nature, extent, and scope of their work that would warrant a substantial difference in the salaries of Boehringer and Konkel. Thus, the jury could have reasonably inferred that Boehringer awarded himself an excessive salary.

Boehringer next asserts that there is insufficient evidence to support the finding that Boehringer acted maliciously or wrongfully in raising his salary. After he informed Konkel that he would make Konkel's life "miserable," Boehringer did not issue yearly dividends and claimed economic hardship for EEI. Yet, despite this hardship, he increased his own salary while denying a pay raise to Konkel, claiming he "didn't deserve a raise in salary." Boehringer did not inform Konkel, an interested shareholder, of his significant pay raise, nor is there evidence of an annual or special shareholder meeting to change the corporate officers' salaries as provided in the board resolution from 2001. Prefacing his actions with an expressed intent to make Konkel's life "miserable" supplies evidence of Boehringer's bad motive. Additionally, granting himself a secret pay raise defeats Boehringer's stated motivation for denying dividends, economic hardship.

As a shareholder, Konkel had a general and reasonable expectation to have the right to proportionate participation in the earnings of the company. Based on the board resolution from the first shareholder meeting at which Konkel joined the company he had a reasonable expectation that corporate money would be divided equally between Boehringer and him as the two shareholders, based on their proportionate ownership of shares. The board resolution provided for an equal salary that would be changed only by the shareholders at an annual or special meeting. The jury could have reasonably inferred from the evidence presented that Boehringer used his position as president of EEI to award himself an excessive salary to Konkel's detriment.

Viewing the evidence in the light most favorable to the jury's finding and indulging every reasonable inference that would support it, we conclude that the jury could have reasonably found that Boehringer wrongfully awarded himself an excessive salary to Konkel's detriment. We further conclude that the evidence supporting this finding is not so weak as to render the jury's verdict clearly wrong and manifestly unjust. Accordingly, we hold that the evidence is legally and factually sufficient to support the jury's finding that Boehringer maliciously or wrongfully used his position as president of EEI to award himself excessive salaries and compensation to the detriment of Konkel.

We overrule Boehringer and EEI's second issue.

Withholding Dividend Payments

In their third issue, Boehringer and EEI assert that the evidence is legally and factually insufficient to support the jury's finding that he used his position as president of EEI to maliciously or wrongfully direct the withholding of dividend payment to Konkel in 2008. EEI was set up as a Subchapter S corporation, and the evidence shows that Boehringer and Konkel split the corporation's net profits based on their respective ownership of 50.1% and 49.9% of the shares each year between 2001 and 2007.

Konkel testified that Boehringer would disclose preliminary yearly profits in late December of each year and then provide the final numbers in January. Konkel would use these preliminary figures to file his taxes and avoid late penalties. In 2008, Konkel paid $75,000 in taxes based on Boehringer's statement to him that EEF's net profit for 2008 was $574,000 minus Konkel's expenses. After Boehringer provided final numbers at the February 2, 2009 shareholder meeting, Konkel corrected his $75,000 tax payment with an additional $1,500 in taxes to avoid a penalty. Konkel's statement that he received no payments in 2009 referred to the 2008 dividend. Boehringer testified that he did not pay himself a K–1 distribution for 2008, even though he paid the IRS $86,000 as a pre-tax payment on January 15, 2009. He stated that when the time came to pay the 2008 dividend, certain creditor accounts had not been paid, and, after those payments, there was no money left to be distributed. Boehringer explained that he did not believe that the $574,000 that he had estimated as net profits for 2008 was "cash in the bank" at the time he made the estimate.

The right to proportionate participation in the earnings of a company is a general reasonable expectation of any shareholder. *See Argo,* 380 S.W.3d at 265. A minority shareholder's rights may be impacted if he is prevented from sharing in the profits of the company. *See id.* A shareholder does not, on the other hand, have a general reasonable expectation about the compensation levels of the corporation's executives. *Id.* (citing *Ritchie,* 339 S.W.3d at 292). Therefore, Konkel needed to demonstrate that Boehringer received compensation in excess to what was reasonable for his position and level of responsibility such that he received a de facto dividend to the exclusion of Konkel. *See Argo,* 380 S.W.3d at 268; *see also Gibney v. Culver,* No. 13–06–112–CV, 2008 WL 1822767 at *16 (Tex.App.-Corpus Christi Apr. 24, 2008, pet. denied) (mem. op).

A shareholder does not have a general expectation of receiving a dividend. *Argo,* 380 S.W.3d at 270. Corporations are not required to issue dividends under Texas law. *See* current version at TEX. BUS. ORGS.CODE ANN. § 21.302 (Vernon 2012.

Here in 2009, after Boehringer had promised to make Konkel's life "miserable," Boehringer, as president of EEI, withheld the K–1 distribution of profits for the 2008 fiscal year. The jury could have reasonably inferred from the evidence about the non-payment of a corporate dividend for 2008 and 2009, and Boehringer's increase in his own salary to a $20,000 monthly gross payment, that Boehringer gave himself a de facto dividend to the exclusion of Konkel as the minority shareholder. It is true that because neither shareholder received a dividend for 2008, EEI's corporate earnings were "distributed" to Konkel to the same extent that they were "distributed" to Boehringer. However, in the context of a corresponding salary increase for Boehringer, the jury could have concluded that Boehringer withheld issuance of a dividend and used his two-fold pay increase as a means of denying Konkel his proportionate participation in the company's earnings as a shareholder.

The jury could have reasonably inferred from the evidence presented that Boehringer used his position as president of EEI to maliciously or wrongfully direct the withholding of payment of dividends from EEI to Konkel in 2008.

Viewing the evidence in the light most favorable to the jury's finding, and indulging every reasonable inference that could support it, we conclude that the jury could have reasonably found that Boehringer wrongfully withheld the payment of the 2008 corporate dividend while increasing his own salary to Konkel's detriment. We further conclude that the evidence supporting this finding is not so weak as to render the jury's verdict clearly wrong and manifestly unjust. Accordingly, we hold that the evidence is legally and factually sufficient to support the jury's findings that Boehringer maliciously or wrongfully used his position as president of EEI to direct the withholding of payment of dividends from EEI to Konkel in 2008.

We overrule Boehringer and EEI's third issue.

Shareholder Oppression

In their fourth issue, Boehringer and EEI argue that because the evidence is insufficient to support the above jury findings, the trial court erred in finding that they engaged in shareholder oppression as a matter of law. Whether certain conduct constitutes shareholder oppression is a question of law. *Willis,* 997 S.W.2d at 801. We review questions of law de novo. *J.M. Davidson, Inc. v. Webster,* 128 S.W.3d 223, 239 (Tex.2003). Specifically, we review the trial court's legal conclusions drawn from the facts to determine their correctness. *See BMC Software Belgium, N.V. v. Marchand,* 83 S.W.3d 789, 794 (Tex.2002).

"Because any one of a variety of activities or conduct can give rise to shareholder oppression, the fact that there may be a lack of evidence to support the existence of one such activity does not defeat the claim so long as there is evidence to support that another such instance of conduct occurred." *Redmon v. Griffith,* 202 S.W.3d 225, 234 n. 3 (Tex.App.-Tyler 2006, pet. denied). Denying access to company books or records, paying excessive compensation, and wrongfully withholding dividends are typical wrongdoings found in shareholder oppression cases. *Willis,* 997 S.W.2d at 801–802 (describing fact patterns in various shareholder oppression cases).

Here, all three of the above jury findings regarding certain acts by Boehringer relate to general reasonable expectations that any shareholder would have based on his mere status as a shareholder of a corporation. *See Ritchie,* 339 S.W.3d at 291–92 (explaining difference between general and specific reasonable expectations of shareholders and giving examples of both). Absent evidence to the contrary, these expectations are reasonable under the circumstances and central to the decision to invest in a corporation. *See id.*

Conduct of majority shareholders that substantially defeats the reasonable expectations of a minority shareholder will often be conduct that is "burdensome," "harsh," or "wrongful," or constitutes "a lack of probity and fair dealing in the company's affairs" or "a visible departure from the standards of fair dealing and a violation of fair play on which each shareholder is entitled to rely." *See id.* at 294. The trial court could have reasonably concluded, based on the jury's findings, that Boehringer acted oppressively toward Konkel by refusing to allow him access to EEI's corporate records and not issuing him a dividend in 2008, while at the same time granting himself an excessive salary without any shareholder vote or resolution.

In addition to the jury's findings and the evidence outlined above, there is evidence that Boehringer locked Konkel out of EEI's office and his software development computer. Boehringer also sent a company-wide e-mail stating that Konkel was no longer part of management and employees were not "to listen to Konkel anymore." As the majority shareholder, at the February 2, 2009 shareholder meeting, Boehringer also voted in restrictions on the sale of Konkel's stock. *See Ritchie,* 339 S.W.3d at 292–93 (citing *Sandor Petroleum Corp. v. Williams,* 321 S.W.2d 614, 616–17 (Tex.Civ.App.-Eastland 1959, writ ref'd n.r.e.) (noting general reasonable expectation of shareholder of being able to sell unrestricted shares of stock).

The three acts found by the jury to have occurred in this case substantially defeated Konkel's general reasonable expectations as a shareholder. Sufficient evidence supported the jury findings, and any one of the acts alone would support the trial court's finding of shareholder oppression. Accordingly, we hold that the trial court did not err in finding shareholder oppression as a matter of law.

We overrule Boehringer and EEI's fourth issue.

Federal Wiretap Act

In his fifth issue, Boehringer argues that the evidence is factually insufficient to support the jury's finding that Konkel violated the Federal Wiretap Act "0 days" because he had proved the "answer" had to be "1447 days."

Prior to trial Boehringer moved for partial summary judgment, seeking an affirmative finding that Konkel had violated the Texas and Federal Wiretap Acts, which the trial court granted.

In Jury Question Eight, the trial court informed the jury that it had previously determined that Konkel had violated the Federal Wiretap Act and it was up to the jury to determine the amount of damages that Boehringer could recover. Then, the trial court asked the jury to determine the number of days that Konkel had violated the Federal Wiretap Act. It instructed the jury that either of three separate acts could constitute a separate violation: (1) an interception of an e-mail intended for Boehringer; (2) a disclosure of such an e-mail or its contents to another person; and (3) an intentional use of such e-mail and its contents.

The jury answered that Konkel had violated the Federal Wiretap Act "0 days." Boehringer moved for a judgment notwithstanding the jury verdict in regard to the Federal Wiretap Act, which was denied by the trial court. On appeal, Boehringer does not challenge the jury question as it was submitted to the jury, he argues only that the evidence is factually insufficient to support the jury's finding.

The Federal Wiretap Act provides a private right of action against one who "intentionally intercepts, endeavors to intercept, or procures any other person to intercept or endeavor to intercept, any wire, oral, or electronic communication." 18 U.S.C. § 2511(1)(a) (2008); *see* 18 U.S.C. § 2520 (2008) (providing private right of action). The Federal Wiretap Act defines "intercept" as "the aural or other acquisition of the contents of any wire, electronic, or oral communication through the use of any electronic, mechanical, or other device." *Id.* § 2510(4) (2008). Thus, Boehringer had to establish five elements to make his claim: that Konkel (1) intentionally (2) intercepted, endeavored to intercept, or procured another person to intercept or endeavor to intercept (3) the contents of (4) an electronic communication (5) using a device.

Although the trial court granted summary judgment on liability under the Federal Wiretap Act, it further instructed the jury on acts that constituted separate violations of the act. Thus, the jury was asked to determine the number of days that Konkel violated the act based on an instruction that spoke to liability under the statute.

Boehringer's forensic computer expert, Paul Price, found in Konkel's e-mail inbox 3,118 emails addressed to Boehringer along with other emails addressed to other EEI employees. Price testified that the emails were not supposed to be in Konkel's inbox because he was not the

409

intended recipient, but he could not testify as to whether the emails were intercepted or copied. Price further testified that Boehringer's e-mails were reviewed by Konkel for 447 days based on Price's adding up the number of days that the emails were received.

Konkel testified that he directed his e-mail provider to make administrative copies of exempt employees' e-mails by checking a box on the e-mail provider's company website. And he testified that he did not "intercept" the emails.

The Federal Wiretap Act does not apply to electronic communications that are in storage. *See Steve Jackson Games, Inc. v. U.S. Secret Serv.*, 36 F.3d 457, 461–62 (5th Cir.1994). Boehringer presented no evidence that Konkel disclosed the e-mails or their contents to another person or evidence of the intentional use of the e-mails or their contents. We conclude that the jury's finding that Konkel violated the Federal Wiretap Act "0 days" is not so against the great weight and preponderance of the evidence as to be clearly wrong and unjust. Accordingly we hold that the evidence is factually sufficient to support the jury's finding.

We overrule Boehringer's fifth issue.

Conclusion

We affirm the judgment of the trial court.

Corporate Liability

Generally, the parties in a corporation are shielded from personal debts and obligations of the corporation. Only the corporation is responsible for such obligations. In some circumstances a corporation may seek to avoid responsibility or a claimant may seek to support its claim of corporate liability by asserting the ultra vires doctrine. Texas specifically precludes the use of ultra vires as either a claim or a defense at law or in equity. TBOC §20.002.³

---

³ *See* Tex. Bus. Org. Code §§ 2.001, 2.003, 2.007, 2.008, 2.101, 3.005(a)(3); *And See* "Texas courts have refused to impose personal liability on corporate directors for illegal or *ultra vires* acts of corporate agents unless the directors either participated in the act or had actual knowledge of the act." *Resolution Trust Corp. v. Norris*, 830 F.Supp. 351, 357 (S.D. Tex. 1993).

Ultra Vires Doctrine

Directors, officers and shareholders are protected from liability except in a few limited circumstances. Ultra vires is Latin for "beyond the powers of."[4] Historically the doctrine was often used by the courts. This is because early corporations were typically formed for limited purposes. Anytime a corporation engaged in activities that were beyond its limited purpose, the parties to the corporation exposed themselves to personal liability.

As with other business organizations, part of the reason people choose to form a corporation is that it shields them from personal liability. Once in place, the corporation's shield is quite protective. But it can be pierced. Plaintiffs seeking to pierce the shield to reach the personal assets of parties to the corporation do so using the ultra vires doctrine. Ultra vires is generally available to challenge a purported corporate act that was made without authority or capacity. Historically, this doctrine applied in cases where a corporation attempted to perform an activity that was outside of the authority granted to it by the state.[5] Effectively, a successful employ of the ultra vires doctrine would result in the personal liability of the actor and or corporate shareholders. The corporation would generally not be able to use the doctrine to defend against complying with an agreement that it had entered with an unwary third party.

Today, most corporations are authorized to have broad powers to act so that it is difficult to act outside the scope of the corporate authority. The Model Business Corporation Act states that: "The validity of corporate action may not be challenged on the ground that the corporation lacks or lacked power to act." Ultra vires may still arise in certain non profit corporations, public entities and charities, but no longer is viable in the typical for profit corporation.

Piercing the corporate veil

A shareholder may not be held liable to the corporation or its obligees with respect to:

- The shares fixed in compliance with other Code provisions, for which the shares were either issued or are to be issued;
- Any contractual obligation of the corporation on the basis that the shareholder was either the corporation's alter ego or on the basis of actual or constructive fraud, a sham to perpetrate a fraud, or other similar theory; or
- Any obligation of the corporation that arose because the corporation failed to observe any corporate formality. This includes the corporation's failure to comply with the Code, certificate of formation, or the corporation's bylaws. It also includes the corporation's failure to observe the same for acts to be taken by it or its directors or shareholders. § 21.223(a)(1)-(3)(A), (B).

---

[4] ultra vires adj. [Latin "beyond the powers (of)"] (18c) Unauthorized; beyond the scope of power allowed or granted by a corporate charter or by law <the officer was liable for the firm's ultra vires actions>. — Also termed extra vires. ULTRA VIRES, Black's Law Dictionary (9th ed. 2009), ultra vires

[5] See Frank A Mack, The Law on Ultra Vires Acts and Contracts of Private Corporations, 14 Marquette L. Rev. 212 (1930). (change font type and size for these footnotes)

But a shareholder may be liable if an obligee can demonstrate that the shareholder used the corporation to defraud the obligee primarily for the shareholder's benefit. § 21.223(b).

When a court holds shareholders personally liable for the debts and obligations of the corporation, this is called "piercing the corporate veil". Piercing the corporate veil generally applies in close corporations and not in publicly traded corporations. In some jurisdictions, courts might pierce the corporate veil and impose personal liability on directors, officers and or shareholders when:

- **Alter Ego:** There is no real separation between the company and its owners. If the owners fail to maintain a formal legal separation between their business and their personal financial affairs, a court could find that the corporation is the owners' alter ego (sham) and that the owners are personally operating the business as if the corporation didn't exist. For instance, if the owner pays personal bills from the business checking account a court may decide that there is no separateness between the entity and the shareholder that justifies the protection from liability. The act of diverting corporate funds for personal use and or intermingling private funds with corporate funds is called commingling assets.
- **Corporate Formalities:** In some jurisdictions, when a corporation ignores the legal formalities that a corporation must follow (for example, failure to have regular meetings or maintaining proper records), a court could decide that the owner isn't entitled to the limited liability that the corporate business structure would ordinarily provide.
- **Fraud:** If the owner(s) recklessly borrowed and lost money, made business deals knowing the business couldn't pay the invoices, or otherwise acted recklessly or dishonestly, a court could find that the limited liability protection shouldn't apply.
- **The company's creditors suffered an unjust cost.** If someone who did business with the company is left with unpaid bills or an unpaid court judgment and the above factors are present, a court could try to correct this unfairness by piercing the veil.
- **Inadequate Capitalization:** In some circumstances, a court may find that the corporation never had enough funds to operate successfully[6]

The Texas Rule
TBOC§21.223

"(a)(2)Texas limits the liability of corporate shareholders for any contractual obligation of the corporation for any matter relating to or arising from the obligation on that basis that the holder, beneficial owner, subscriber or affiliate is or was the alter ego of the corporation or on the basis of actual or constructive fraud, a sham to perpetrate a fraud, or other similar theory; or

(3) any obligation of the corporation on the basis of the failure of the corporation to observe any corporate formality…

---

[6] For a general discussion on the law of piercing the corporate veil, see Peter B. Oh, Veil-Pierciing, 89 Tx L. Rev. 81 (2010). (change font)

(b) Subsection (a)(2) does not prevent or limit the liability of a [share]holder, beneficial owner, subscriber, or affiliate if the oblige demonstrates that the [share]holder, beneficial owner, subscriber, or affiliate caused the corporation to be used for the purpose of perpetrating and did perpetrate an actual fraud on the oblige primarily for the direct personal benefit of the [share]holder, beneficial owner, subscriber, or affiliate."

Allied Chemical Carriers, Inc., v. National Biofuels LP, et al.
Not Reported in F.Supp.2d, 2011 WL 2672512, S.D.Tex., July 07, 2011
United States District Court, S.D. Texas, Houston Division

BACKGROUND

FE is the general partner of FPS, the parent of two Houston-based electricity providers. Manalac is the Executive Vice President of FE. FPS was the parent of NBF when it was operating as a biofuels trading business. NBF stopped trading biofuels in late 2007. National Biofuels, L.P. and National Biofuels LLC are no longer in business, have not been served, and have not participated in this lawsuit. NBF entered into two contracts for Allied to transport biofuels, one in January 2007 and one in March 2007. NBF subsequently failed to pay for the transportation services Allied provided under the two contracts, so Allied pursued and obtained two arbitration awards against NBF by default in October 2008. One arbitration award was for $107,623.97, and the second award was for $16,842.59. The arbitration awards were later reduced to judgment in the United States District Court for the Southern District of New York. In March 2009, Allied initiated proceedings to register the arbitration awards and the corresponding judgment in Texas where NBF was domiciled.

In April 2009, FE advised Allied that Certificates of Cancellation had been filed on behalf of NBF and its general partner, National Biofuels, L.L.C., the day after Allied initiated proceedings to register the judgment. When NBF went out of business, FPS lost approximately $11,000,000.00 in capital contributions, lost approximately $5,000,000.00 in connection with loans that FPS had guaranteed and was subsequently required to pay, and absorbed several thousand dollars in unpaid administrative services.

Allied then filed this lawsuit seeking to pierce NBF's corporate veil in order to collect from Defendants the arbitration awards and resulting judgment. After a full opportunity to complete discovery, Defendants moved for summary judgment. The Motion has been fully briefed and is ripe for decision.

Rule 56 of the Federal Rules of Civil Procedure mandates the entry of summary judgment, after adequate time for discovery and upon motion, against a party who fails to make a sufficient showing of the existence of an element essential to the party's case, and on which that party will bear the burden at trial. *Celotex Corp. v. Catrett*, 477 U.S. 317, 322 (1986); *Little v. Liquid Air Corp.*, 37 F.3d 1069, 1075 (5th Cir.1994) *(en banc); see also Baton Rouge Oil and*

Chem. Workers Union v. ExxonMobil Corp., 289 F.3d 373, 375 (5th Cir.2002). Summary judgment "should be rendered if the pleadings, the discovery and disclosure materials on file, and any affidavits show that there is no genuine issue as to any material fact and that the movant is entitled to judgment as a matter of law." FED. R. CIV. P. 56(a); *Celotex,* 477 U.S. at 322–23; *Weaver v. CCA Indus., Inc.,* 529 F.3d 335, 339 (5th Cir.2008).

For summary judgment, the initial burden falls on the movant to identify areas essential to the non-movant's claim in which there is an "absence of a genuine issue of material fact." *Lincoln Gen. Ins. Co. v. Reyna,* 401 F.3d 347, 349 (5th Cir.2005). The moving party, however, need not negate the elements of the non-movant's case. *See Boudreaux v. Swift Transp. Co.,* 402 F.3d 536, 540 (5th Cir.2005). The moving party may meet its burden by pointing out " 'the absence of evidence supporting the nonmoving party's case.' " *Dufy v. Leading Edge Prods., Inc.,* 44 F.3d 308, 312 (5th Cir.1995) (quoting *Skotak v. Tenneco Resins, Inc.,* 953 F.2d 909, 913 (5th Cir.1992)).

In deciding whether a genuine and material fact issue has been created, the court reviews the facts and inferences to be drawn from them in the light most favorable to the nonmoving party. *Reaves Brokerage Co. v. Sunbelt Fruit & Vegetable Co.,* 336 F.3d 410, 412 (5th Cir.2003).

ANALYSIS

Allied seeks to "pierce the corporate veil" in order to impose on Defendants the obligation to pay the arbitration award against NBF. Under current Texas statutory law, a shareholder "may not be held liable to the corporation or its obligees with respect to ... any contractual obligation of the corporation ... on the basis that the holder ... is or was the alter ego of the corporation or on the basis of actual or constructive fraud, a sham to perpetrate a fraud, or other similar theory...." *Willis v. Donnelly,* 199 S.W.3d 262, 272 (Tex.2006) (citing TEX. BUS. ORGS.CODE § 21.223(a)(2)). The liability of a shareholder for a corporation's contractual obligation that is limited by § 21.223 "is exclusive and preempts any other liability imposed for that obligation under common law or otherwise." *Id.* (citing TEX. BUS. ORGS.CODE § 21.224). The only exception to § 21.223's rule that a corporation's contractual debt cannot be imposed on a shareholder is where the shareholder "caused the corporation to be used for the purpose of perpetrating and did perpetrate an actual fraud on the obligee primarily for the direct personal benefit of the" shareholder. *Id.* (citing TEX. BUS. ORGS.CODE § 21.223(b)). Section 21.223(a)(3) specifically precludes piercing the corporate veil based on a failure of the corporation to observe any corporate formality. TEX. BUS. ORGS.CODE § 21.223(a)(3); *Howell v. Hilton Hotels Corp.,* 84 S.W.3d 708, 714 (Tex.App.-Houston [1 st Dist.] 2002, pet. denied).

Allied relies throughout its Response on general language regarding "alter ego" and "sham to perpetrate a fraud" theories to pierce the corporate veil. Although it is true that these are two categories that can allow piercing the corporate veil under Texas law, § 21.223(b) adds additional requirements for piercing the corporate veil in cases involving a corporation's contractual debt. *See Rimade Ltd. v. Hubbard Enters., Inc.,* 388 F.3d 138, 143 (5th Cir.2004).

The requirements of § 21.223 apply equally to attempts to pierce the corporate veil based on an alter ego theory and based on a "sham to perpetrate a fraud" theory. *See id.;* TEX. BUS. ORGS.CODE § 21.223(a). As a result, Allied's reliance on *Castleberry v. Branscum,* 721 S.W.2d 270 (Tex.1986), and its case law progeny, is misplaced. As was previously noted by this Court, the Texas Legislature enacted § 21.223 in response to the *Castleberry* decision and "now requires a showing of actual fraud in order to pierce the corporate veil" in cases involving a corporation's contractual obligations. *See Acceptance Indem. Ins. Co. v. Maltez,* 619 F.Supp.2d 289, 301 (S.D.Tex.2008); *see also Fid. & Deposit Co. of Md. v. Commercial Cas. Consultants, Inc.,* 976 F.2d 272, 275 (5th Cir.1992) (recognizing that *Castleberry* was superseded by the Texas Legislature). It accordingly is clear that current Texas law requires a showing of actual fraud perpetrated for the direct personal benefit of the shareholder in order to pierce the corporate veil to collect a corporation's contractual debts from a shareholder. *See, e.g., Willis,* 199 S.W.3d at 272.

Actual Fraud Element

To prove actual fraud for purposes of § 21.223, the plaintiff must prove "dishonesty of purpose or intent to deceive." *See Menetti v. Chavers,* 974 S.W.2d 168, 173–74 (Tex.App.-San Antonio 1998, no pet.). Additionally, the actual fraud must have related specifically to the contract at issue. *See Rutherford v. Atwood,* 2003 WL 22053687, * *4–5 (Tex.App.-Houston [1st Dist.] Aug. 29, 2003, reh'g overruled) (citing *Menetti,* 974 S.W.2d at 175); *see also Farr v. Sun World Sav. Ass'n,* 810 S.W.2d 294, 295 (Tex.App.-El Paso 1991, no pet.) (finding actual fraud to pierce the corporate veil because fraud directly related to transaction at issue).

Allied argues that Defendants' filing of Certificates of Cancellation on behalf of NBF and National Biofuels, LLC one day after Allied filed a petition to register its judgment against NBF in Texas raises an inference of actual fraud. Allied's argument is unpersuasive. Initially, even if the filing of Certificates of Cancellation raised an inference of actual fraud, which is doubtful, any such fraud would be unrelated to the contracts for Allied to transport biofuels for NBF. Moreover, it is undisputed that FPS did not file Certificates of Cancellation for NBF and National Biofuels, LLC when Allied sought to recover amounts owed on the transportation contracts, when Allied instituted arbitration proceedings, when Allied obtained arbitration awards by default against NBF, or when Allied obtained confirmation of the arbitration awards and had them reduced to judgment. Instead, the evidence shows, and the only reasonable inference raised by the evidence is, that Certificates of Cancellation for NBF and National Biofuels, LLC were filed when the winding up process was complete. Unlike the situation in *In re JNS Aviation LLC,* 376 B.R. 500 (Bankr.N.D.Tex.2007), and in *Latham v. Burgher,* 320 S.W.3d 602 (Tex.App.-Dallas 2010, no pet .), relied on by Allied, Defendants in this case did not create a new company to conduct the same biofuels business, but instead the existing NBF entities stopped conducting business and were completely dissolved. The timing of the Certificates of Cancellation does not raise a reasonable inference that Defendants "caused the corporation to be used for the purpose of perpetrating and did perpetrate an actual fraud" on

Allied in connection with the transportation contracts. The evidence, if presented at trial, would not lead the Court to rule differently. On this basis, Defendants are entitled to summary judgment.

Direct Personal Benefit Element

Even had Allied presented evidence that raised a genuine issue of material fact regarding the actual fraud element of the § 21.223 exception, Allied's effort to pierce the corporate veil would fail. Allied has not presented evidence that raises a genuine fact dispute regarding the direct personal benefit element. The statute provides that the corporate veil can be pierced only if the corporation was used to perpetrate an actual fraud "for the direct personal benefit" of the shareholder or affiliate. *See* TEX. BUS. ORGS. CODE § 21.223(b). The actual fraud must have been for the direct personal benefit of the shareholder.

Allied presents evidence that Kenmont Special Opportunities Fund, L.P. ("Kenmont") made several loans to NBF totaling over $16,000,000.00. FPS guaranteed those loans on NBF's behalf. In 2007, Kenmont called the loans and FPS was forced to buy out the remaining balance of $7.3 million. Allied argues that this evidence raises an inference that FPS, as NBF's only secured creditor, and the other Defendants perpetrated an actual fraud for their own direct personal benefit. The Court is not persuaded. Evidence that FPS, the guarantor of the loans, was required to buy out the remaining balance on those loans does not raise a reasonable inference that FPS intended to perpetrate a fraud on Allied for Defendants' personal benefit. Moreover, any inference that FPS and the other Defendants would buy out a loan balance in excess of $7,000,000.00 and knowingly give up $11,000,000.00 in capital contributions in order to defraud Allied out of less than $200,000.00 is not a reasonable one. On this basis also, Defendants are entitled to summary judgment.

CONCLUSION AND ORDER

Allied has not presented evidence that raises a genuine issue of material fact in support of its attempt to impose against Defendants the arbitration award-created debt of NBF. Specifically, Allied has not presented evidence to raise a genuine issue of material fact regarding the actual fraud and direct personal benefit requirements of § 21.223 of the Texas Business Organizations Act. Accordingly, it is hereby **ORDERED** that Defendants' Motion for Summary Judgment is **GRANTED.** The Court will issue a separate final judgment.

Walkovszky v. Carlton
18 N.Y.2d 414, 223 N.E.2d 6, 276 N.Y.S.2d 585

This case involves what appears to be a rather common practice in the taxicab industry of vesting the ownership of a taxi fleet in many corporations, each owning only one or two cabs.

The complaint alleges that the plaintiff was severely injured four years ago in New York City when he was run down by a taxicab owned by the defendant Seon Cab Corporation and negligently operated at the time by the defendant Marchese. The individual defendant, Carlton, is claimed to be a stockholder of 10 corporations, including Seon, each of which has but two cabs registered in its name, and it is implied that only the minimum automobile liability insurance required by law (in the amount of $10,000) is carried on any one cab. Although seemingly independent of one another, these corporations are alleged to be 'operated * * * as a single entity, unit and enterprise' with regard to financing, supplies, repairs, employees and garaging, and all are named as defendants. The plaintiff asserts that he is also entitled to hold their stockholders personally liable for the damages sought because the multiple corporate structure constitutes an unlawful attempt 'to defraud members of the general public' who might be injured by the cabs.

The defendant Carlton has moved, pursuant to dismiss the complaint on the ground that as to him it 'fails to state a cause of action'. The court at Special Term granted the motion but the Appellate Division, by a divided vote, reversed, holding that a valid cause of action was sufficiently stated. The defendant Carlton appeals to us, from the nonfinal order, by leave of the Appellate Division on a certified question.

The law permits the incorporation of a business for the very purpose of enabling its proprietors to escape personal liability (see, e.g., Bartle v. Home Owners Co-op., 309 N.Y. 103, 106, 127 N.E.2d 832, 833) but, manifestly, the privilege is not without its limits. Broadly speaking, the courts will disregard the corporate form, or, to use accepted terminology, 'pierce the corporate veil', whenever necessary 'to prevent fraud or to achieve equity'. (International Aircraft Trading Co. v. Manufacturers Trust Co., 297 N.Y. 285, 292, 79 N.E.2d 249, 252.) In determining whether liability should be extended to reach assets beyond those belonging to the corporation, we are guided, as Judge Cardozo noted, by 'general rules of agency'. (Berkey v. Third Ave. Ry. Co., 244 N.Y. 84, 95, 155 N.E. 58, 61, 50 A.L.R. 599.) In other words, whenever anyone uses control of the corporation to further his own rather than the corporation's business, he will be liable for the corporation's acts 'upon the principle of Respondeat superior applicable even where the agent is a natural person'. (Rapid Tr. Subway Constr. Co. v. City of New York, 259 N.Y. 472, 488, 182 N.E. 145, 150.) Such liability, moreover, extends not only to the corporation's commercial dealings but to its negligent acts as well.

In the Mangan case, the plaintiff was injured as a result of the negligent operation of a cab owned and operated by one of four corporations affiliated with the defendant Terminal.

Although the defendant was not a stockholder of any of the operating companies, both the defendant and the operating companies were owned, for the most part, by the same parties. The defendant's name (Terminal) was conspicuously displayed on the sides of all of the taxis used in the enterprise and, in point of fact, the defendant actually serviced, inspected, repaired and dispatched them. These facts were deemed to provide sufficient cause for piercing the corporate veil of the operating company—the nominal owner of the cab which injured the plaintiff—and holding the defendant liable. The operating companies were simply instrumentalities for carrying on the business of the defendant without imposing upon it financial and other liabilities incident to the actual ownership and operation of the cabs.

In the case before us, the plaintiff has explicitly alleged that none of the corporations 'had a separate existence of their own' and, as indicated above, all are named as defendants. However, it is one thing to assert that a corporation is a fragment of a larger corporate combine which actually conducts the business. (See Berle, The Theory of Enterprise Entity, 47 Col.L.Rev. 343, 348—350.) It is quite another to claim that the corporation is a 'dummy' for its individual stockholders who are in reality carrying on the business in their personal capacities for purely personal rather than corporate ends. (See African Metals Corp. v. Bullowa, 288 N.Y. 78, 85, 41 N.E.2d 366, 469.) Either circumstance would justify treating the corporation as an agent and piercing the corporate veil to reach the principal but a different result would follow in each case. In the first, only a larger Corporate entity would be held financially responsible (citations omitted) Either the stockholder is conducting the business in his individual capacity or he is not. If he is, he will be liable; if he is not, then it does not matter—insofar as his personal liability is concerned—that the enterprise is actually being carried on by a larger 'enterprise entity'. (See Berle, The Theory of Enterprise Entity, 47 Col.L.Rev. 343.)

At this stage in the present litigation, we are concerned only with the pleadings and, since CPLR 3014 permits causes of action to be stated 'alternatively or hypothetically', it is possible for the plaintiff to allege both theories as the basis for his demand for judgment. In ascertaining whether he has done so, we must consider the entire pleading, educing therefrom "whatever can be imputed from its statements by fair and reasonable intendment." (Condon v. Associated Hosp. Serv., 287 N.Y. 411, 414, 40 N.E.2d 230, 231). Reading the complaint in this case most favorably and liberally, we do not believe that there can be gathered from its averments the allegations required to spell out a valid cause of action against the defendant Carlton.

The individual defendant is charged with having 'organized, managed, dominated and controlled' a fragmented corporate entity but there are no allegations that he was conducting business in his individual capacity. Had the taxicab fleet been owned by a single corporation, it would be readily apparent that the plaintiff would face formidable barriers in attempting to establish personal liability on the part of the corporation's stockholders. The fact that the fleet ownership has been deliberately split up among many corporations does not ease the plaintiff's burden in that respect. The corporate form may not be disregarded merely because the assets of the corporation, together with the mandatory insurance coverage of the vehicle which struck the plaintiff, are insufficient to assure him the recovery sought. If Carlton were to be held individually liable on those facts alone, the decision would apply equally to the thousands of cabs which are owned by their individual drivers who conduct their businesses through corporations organized pursuant to section 401 of the Business Corporation Law, Consol.Laws, c. 4 and carry the minimum insurance required by subdivision 1 (par. (a)) of section 370 of the Vehicle and Traffic Law, Consol.Laws, c. 71. These taxi owner-operators are entitled to form such corporations (cf. Elenkrieg v. Siebrecht, 238 N.Y. 254, 144 N.E. 519, 34 A.L.R. 592), and we agree with the court at Special Term that, if the insurance coverage required by statute 'is inadequate for the protection of the public, the remedy lies not with the courts but with the Legislature.' It may very well be sound policy to require that certain corporations must take out liability insurance which will afford adequate compensation to their potential tort victims. However, the responsibility for imposing conditions on the privilege of incorporation has been committed by the Constitution to the Legislature (N.Y. Const., art. X, s 1) and it may not be fairly implied, from any statute, that the Legislature intended, without the slightest discussion or debate, to require of taxi corporations that they carry automobile liability insurance over and above that mandated by the Vehicle and Traffic Law.

This is not to say that it is impossible for the plaintiff to state a valid cause of action against the defendant Carlton. However, the simple fact is that the plaintiff has just not done so here. While the complaint alleges that the separate corporations were undercapitalized and that their assets have been intermingled, it is barren of any 'sufficiently particular(ized) statements' that the defendant Carlton and his associates are actually doing business in their individual capacities, shuttling their personal funds in and out of the corporations 'without regard to formality and to suit their immediate convenience.' Such a 'perversion of the privilege to do business in a corporate form' would justify imposing personal liability on the individual stockholders. Nothing of the sort has in fact been charged, and it cannot reasonably or logically be inferred from the happenstance that the business of Seon Cab Corporation may actually be carried on by a larger corporate entity composed of many corporations which, under general principles of agency, would be liable to each other's creditors in contract and in tort. In his affidavit in opposition to the motion to dismiss, the plaintiff's counsel claimed that corporate assets had been 'milked out' of, and 'siphoned off' from the enterprise. Quite apart from the fact that these allegations are far too vague and conclusory, the charge is premature. If the plaintiff succeeds in his action and becomes a judgment creditor of the corporation, he may then sue and attempt to hold the individual defendants accountable for any dividends and property that were wrongfully distributed.

In point of fact, the principle relied upon in the complaint to sustain the imposition of personal liability is not agency but fraud. Such a cause of action cannot withstand analysis. If it is not fraudulent for the owner-operator of a single cab corporation to take out only the minimum required liability insurance, the enterprise does not become either illicit or fraudulent merely because it consists of many such corporations. The plaintiff's injuries are the same regardless of whether the cab which strikes him is owned by a single corporation or part of a fleet with ownership fragmented among many corporations. Whatever rights he may be able to assert against parties other than the registered owner of the vehicle come into being not because he has been defrauded but because, under the principle of Respondeat superior, he is entitled to hold the whole enterprise responsible for the acts of its agents.

In sum, then, the complaint falls short of adequately stating a cause of action against the defendant Carlton in his individual capacity.

The order of the Appellate Division should be reversed, with costs in this court and in the Appellate Division, the certified question answered in the negative and the order of the Supreme Court, Richmond County, reinstated, with leave to serve an amended complaint.

KEATING, Judge (dissenting)

The defendant Carlton, the shareholder here sought to be held for the negligence of the driver of a taxicab, was a principal shareholder and organizer of the defendant corporation which owned the taxicab. The corporation was one of 10 organized by the defendant, each containing two cabs and each cab having the 'minimum liability' insurance coverage mandated by section 370 of the Vehicle and Traffic Law. The sole assets of these operating corporations are the vehicles themselves and they are apparently subject to mortgages.

From their inception these corporations were intentionally undercapitalized for the purpose of avoiding responsibility for acts which were bound to arise as a result of the operation of a large taxi fleet having cars out on the street 24 hours a day and engaged in public transportation. And during the course of the corporations' existence all income was continually drained out of the corporations for the same purpose.

The issue presented by this action is whether the policy of this State, which affords those desiring to engage in a business enterprise the privilege of limited liability through the use of the corporate device, is so strong that it will permit that privilege to continue no matter how much it is abused, no matter how irresponsibly the corporation is operated, no matter what the cost to the public. I do not believe that it is.

Under the circumstances of this case the shareholders should all be held individually liable to this plaintiff for the injuries he suffered. (See Mull v. Colt Co., D.C., 31 F.R.D. 154, 156; Teller v. Clear Serv. Co., 9 Misc.2d 495, 173 N.Y.S.2d 183.) At least, the matter should not be disposed of on the pleadings by a dismissal of the complaint. 'If a corporation is organized and carries on business without substantial capital in such a way that the corporation is likely to have no sufficient assets available to meet its debts, it is inequitable that shareholders should set up such a flimsy organization to escape personal liability. 'Limited liability', …, 'is the rule, not the exception; and on that assumption large undertakings are rested, vast enterprises are launched, and huge sums of capital attracted. But there are occasions when the limited liability sought to be obtained through the corporation will be qualified or denied. Mr. Chief Judge CARDOZO stated that a surrender of that principle of limited liability would be made 'when the sacrifice is so essential to the end that some accepted public policy may be defended or upheld.' * * * The cases of fraud make up part of that exception * * * But they do not exhaust it. An obvious inadequacy of capital, measured by the nature and magnitude of the corporate undertaking, has frequently been an important factor in cases denying stockholders their defense of limited liability. * * * That rule has been invoked even in absence of a legislative policy which undercapitalization would defeat. It has often been held that the interposition of a corporation will not be allowed to defeat a legislative policy, whether that was the aim or only the result of the arrangement. * * * 'the courts will not permit themselves to be blinded or deceived by mere forms of law' but will deal 'with the substance of the transaction involved as if the corporate agency did not exist and as the justice of the case may require.'" (321 U.S., pp. 362—363, 64 S.Ct., p. 537; emphasis added.)

The policy of this State has always been to provide and facilitate recovery for those injured through the negligence of others. The automobile, by its very nature, is capable of causing servere and costly injuries when not operated in a proper manner. The great increase in the number of automobile accidents combined with the frequent financial irresponsibility of the individual driving the car led to the adoption of section 388 of the Vehicle and Traffic Law which had the effect of imposing upon the owner of the vehicle the responsibility for its negligent operation. It is upon this very statute that the cause of action against both the corporation and the individual defendant is predicated.

In addition the Legislature, still concerned with the financial irresponsibility of those who owned and operated motor vehicles, enacted a statute requiring minimum liability coverage for all owners of automobiles. The important public policy represented by both these statutes is outlined in section 310 of the Vehicle and Traffic Law. That section provides that: 'The legislature is concerned over the rising toll of motor vehicle accidents and the suffering and loss thereby inflicted. The legislature determines that it is a matter of grave concern that motorists shall be financially able to respond in damages for their negligent acts, so that innocent victims of motor vehicle accidents may be recompensed for the injury and financial loss inflicted upon them.'

The defendant Carlton claims that, because the minimum amount of insurance required by the statute was obtained, the corporate veil cannot and should not be pierced despite the fact that the assets of the corporation which owned the cab were 'trifling compared with the business to be done and the risks of loss' which were certain to be encountered. I do not agree.

The Legislature in requiring minimum liability insurance of $10,000, no doubt, intended to provide at least some small fund for recovery against those individuals and corporations who just did not have and were not able to raise or accumulate assets sufficient to satisfy the claims of those who were injured as a result of their negligence. It certainly could not have intended to shield those individuals who organized corporations, with the specific intent of avoiding responsibility to the public, where the operation of the corporate enterprise yielded profits sufficient to purchase additional insurance.

The defendant contends that a decision holding him personally liable would discourage people from engaging in corporate enterprise.

What I would merely hold is that a participating shareholder of a corporation vested with a public interest, organized with capital insufficient to meet liabilities which are certain to arise in the ordinary course of the corporation's business, may be held personally responsible for such liabilities. Where corporate income is not sufficient to cover the cost of insurance premiums above the statutory minimum or where initially adequate finances dwindle under the pressure of competition, bad times or extraordinary and unexpected liability, obviously the shareholder will not be held liable (Henn, Corporations, p. 208, n. 7).

The only types of corporate enterprises that will be discouraged as a result of a decision allowing the individual shareholder to be sued will be those such as the one in question, designed solely to abuse the corporate privilege at the expense of the public interest.

For these reasons I would vote to affirm the order of the Appellate Division.

Indemnification

Director's limited liability
Indemnification

Generally, a director's liability for certain litigation expenses will be limited because the corporation will indemnify her from having to pay those expenses. To indemnify a person is to reimburse that person for a loss she suffered because of a third party's act or default.

A director is eligible to be indemnified if she incurred those litigation expenses because she was sued for acts occurring in her capacity as a director. The Code recognizes four ways that a director may be indemnified: by a voluntary decision of the corporation; by statutory mandate; by court order; and, by a permissive decision of the corporation. §§ 8.003; 8.051; 8.052; 8.101.

Where the decision to indemnify is at the corporation's discretion, the corporation must provide a written report to the shareholders notifying them of its decision to indemnify a director. § 8.152(a). The report must be made with or before the notice or waiver of notice of the next shareholder's meeting. § 8.152(b)(1). Or it can be made the next time the directors submit an action to the shareholders without a meeting. § 8.152(b)(2). Whichever method chosen to deliver the notice to the shareholders, the report must be made within one year from the date the director was indemnified. § 8.152(c).

Voluntary indemnification

In its certificate of formation, the corporation may decide to indemnify a director, officer, employee, shareholder, or other person. § 8.003. Their decision is valid so long as it is consistent with the chapter 8 of the Code. § 8.004.

Mandatory indemnification

If a director or former director is sued in an action because of her role with the corporation, then the corporation must indemnify her against reasonable expenses actually incurred by her in her successful defense. § 8.051.

Court-ordered indemnification

A director – who was sued because she was a director – may apply to the court to have the court order the corporation to indemnify the director. § 8.052(a). If the court decides to issue the order, the court may award her the amount the court determines is fair and reasonable in view of all the relevant circumstances. *Id.* The court's decision is not influenced by whether the director is found liable to the corporation or because she improperly received a benefit. § 8.052(b)(1)-(2). The indemnity amount awarded is reduced, however, if the director is found liable for the same. § 8.052(c)(1)-(2).

Permissive indemnification

A corporation may indemnify a director who either was or is threatened to be made a respondent in a civil or criminal proceeding for a resulting judgment and expenses. §§ 8.101, 8.102(a)(1)-(2). Generally, the decision to indemnify is made by a majority vote of the board of directors who are both disinterested and independent. § 8.103(a)(1). To vote, the disinterested and independent directors do not have to constitute a quorum. *Id.*

In civil proceedings where the director is being sued for conduct occurring in her official capacity, the director is eligible to be indemnified if she acted in good faith and reasonably believed that her conduct was in the corporation's best interests. § 8.101(a)(1)(A)-(B). The same is also true in any other civil proceeding, so long as the director's conduct was not opposed to the corporation's best interests. *Id.* In criminal proceedings, a corporation may indemnify a director if it did not have a reasonable cause to believe that the director's conduct was unlawful. § 8.101(a)(1)(C).

The corporation's capital structure

Equity and Debt

A for profit corporation's finances are generally structured around equity and debt. Equity is an investment that is attached to an ownership interest in the corporation. It is usually represented by stock which may be common or preferred.

Common stock is the only financial asset a corporation must issue because owners of the corporation own shares or stock in the company. While it is the board of directors that is charged with managing the corporation, it is commonly stated that shareholders or stockholders actually control the corporation by virtue of their right to elect the members of the board. As is typical with owners of business entities, shareholders earn dividends from surplus rather than gross income and on termination of the corporation, receive distributions only after creditors are paid.

Preferred stock is issued by the corporation to investors who desire an ownership interest in the corporation but are willing to forego control as preferred stockholders are generally non-voting owners. These non-voting shares may convert to voting shares if the corporation fails to pay dividends after an extended period of time. Preferred shareholders are often given the right to vote on fundamental structural changes to the corporation. Preferred stockholders enjoy a preference over common stockholders in their claims to dividends and distributions. Such claims however are subordinate to those of creditors.

Debt is a contractual obligation issued by the corporation to repay a lender the loan. Debt is usually memorialized in instruments known as promissory notes, bonds (secured) or debentures (unsecured). The investor is commonly referred to as a lender or creditor.

Winding up and terminating the corporation

A corporation may decide to terminate its conduct of business through unanimous shareholder action or on board resolution supported by two thirds of the voting shares.

Triggering events include: (1) the passing of a specified time period; (2) the voluntary decision by the corporation to wind up; (3) the happening of an event specified in the corporation's governing documents (*e.g.*, the certificate, the bylaws); or (4) a court decree requiring the winding up. § 11.051.

When an event triggering winding up occurs, the corporation's governing body will start to wind up the corporation's business and affairs. § 11.052(a). The windup includes:

1. Ceasing to carry on any business not necessary to the windup;
2. Sending a written notice of the winding up to known persons who have a claim against the corporation;
3. Collecting and selling property that isn't going to be distributed to the corporation's shareholders; and
4. Performing any other acts necessary to windup the corporation's business and affairs.

§ 11.052(a)(1)-(4). While the windup process is ongoing, the corporation may still participate in legal actions. § 11.052(b).

Winding up and the court's involvement

A court may supervise the corporations winding up. § 11.054. The Code grants the courts a broad supervision rights. Not only may the court appoint a person to carry out the winding up, but it may also do whatever else the circumstances may require. Id.

Voluntary winding up by the corporation

When a corporation desires to wind up its business and affairs, certain procedures must be followed. Those procedures change depending on whether the corporation has commenced business and issued shares. If it hasn't then the majority of the corporation or the board of directors identified in the certificate need adopt a winding up resolution. § 21.502(2). If, however, the corporation has commenced, then either all of the shareholders have to provide written consent to wind up; or, the board must adopt a resolution directing that the winding up be submitted to the shareholders for approval. § 21.502(1), (3)(A)(ii).

In situations where a board submits a winding up proposal to the shareholders additional two steps must be followed. First, a winding up meeting must be called. § 21.502(3)(A)(ii). The shareholders must be given written notice that the purpose or one of the purposes of the meeting is to consider winding up. § 21.503. Second, at this meeting, because winding up is a fundamental action, the shareholders must give an affirmative vote to commence the winding up. § 21.364(a)(2); § 21.503(b). Unless modified by the certificate of formation, an affirmative vote is had when at least two thirds of shareholders entitled to vote have approved. § 21.364(b). Once approved, the directors will manage the winding up process. § 21.504.

Sale of all or substantially all of corporate assets (Acquisitions)

With growing frequency businesses are acquired by new owners. Many times the underlying purpose for buying an existing business is business expansion and or growth. Buying an existing business permits the new owner to expand the existing assets in lieu of starting a new business altogether. Commonly businesses achieve these goals by mergers and/or acquisitions. In a merger, one or more companies fuse to form a single entity, while in an acquisition one company takes over another while both parties can retain their separate legal existence. However, the acquired company will often vote to terminate their business.

An acquisition occurs when a purchaser acquires all or substantially all of the assets or stock of the seller company. Typically, once the purchaser pays for the assets, the seller company winds up, liquidates and terminates. If the purchaser did not assume the seller company's liabilities, the debts are paid during liquidation and any surplus is distributed to the owners.

Corporate combinations are sometimes structured in a non-statutory way for tax reasons or to avoid dissenting shareholders' appraisal rights. Texas provides that appraisal rights accrue to shareholders in the case of any major transaction pursuant to statute. See generally, TBOC ch.10

The board of directors may determine from time to time to sell corporate assets in furtherance of the corporate business. In that instance, only board action is required. However, when a sale fundamentally impacts the corporate ownership and control of corporate assets, the sale will generally constitute a sale of all or substantially all of the corporate assets. This notwithstanding, a corporation may pledge, or execute a mortgage or deed of trust to secure the debt of the corporation without being characterized as a sale even though the control over the encumbered assets may be significantly reduced during the term of the unpaid debt. On the other hand, the transaction is likely to constitute a sale of all or substantially all assets when the assets sold represent a significant part of the corporate operations such that it affects corporate existence.

TBOC provides that when the sale is not in the regular and ordinary course of business and results in the sale of all or substantially all of the corporate assets, the directors of the corporation must authorize the sale by resolution. TBOC § 21.455 Following the corporate resolution, the all shareholders entitled to vote on the winding up must approve the sale by a two-thirds vote, regardless of the class or series of voting stock the shareholder owns. TBOC §21.457. Note that unless the certificate of formation provides otherwise, shares entitled to vote as a class are entitled to vote only as a class. Further, if the certificate of formation provides that the vote shall be other than by two-thirds, the certificate shall prevail so long as the certificate minimally provides for a majority vote. TBOC § 21.365 .

§21.364. *VOTE REQUIRED TO APPROVE FUNDAMENTAL ACTION.*

(a) In this section, a "fundamental action" means:

> *(1) an amendment of a certificate of formation, including an amendment required for cancellation of an event requiring winding up in accordance with Section 11.152(b);*
> *(2) a voluntary winding up under Chapter 11;*
> *(3) a revocation of a voluntary decision to wind up under Section 11.151;*
> *(4) a cancellation of an event requiring winding up under Section 11.152(a); or*
> *(5) a reinstatement under Section 11.202.*

(b) Except as otherwise provided by this code or the certificate of formation of a corporation in accordance with Section 21.365, the vote required for approval of a fundamental action by the shareholders is the affirmative vote of the holders of at least two-thirds of the outstanding shares entitled to vote on the fundamental action.

(c) If a class or series of shares is entitled to vote as a class or series on a fundamental action, the vote required for approval of the action by the shareholders is the affirmative vote of the holders of at least two-thirds of the outstanding shares in each class or series of shares entitled to vote on the action as a class or series and at least two-thirds of the outstanding shares otherwise entitled to vote on the action. Shares entitled to vote as a class or series shall be entitled to vote only as a class or series unless otherwise entitled to vote on each matter submitted to the shareholders generally or otherwise provided by the certificate of formation.

(d) *Unless an amendment to the certificate of formation is undertaken by the board of directors under Section 21.155, separate voting by a class or series of shares of a corporation is required for approval of an amendment to the certificate of formation that would result in:*

  (1) the increase or decrease of the aggregate number of authorized shares of the class or series;
  (2) the increase or decrease of the par value of the shares of the class or series, including changing shares with par value into shares without par value or changing shares without par value into shares with par value;
  (3) effecting an exchange, reclassification, or cancellation of all or part of the shares of the class or series;
  (4) effecting an exchange or creating a right of exchange of all or part of the shares of another class or series into the shares of the class or series;
  (5) the change of the designations, preferences, limitations, or relative rights of the shares of the class or series;
  (6) the change of the shares of the class or series, with or without par value, into the same or a different number of shares, with or without par value, of the same class or series or another class or series;
  (7) the creation of a new class or series of shares with rights and preferences equal, prior, or superior to the shares of the class or series;
  (8) increasing the rights and preferences of a class or series with rights and preferences equal, prior, or superior to the shares of the class or series;
  (9) increasing the rights and preferences of a class or series with rights or preferences later or inferior to the shares of the class or series in such a manner that the rights or preferences will be equal, prior, or superior to the shares of the class or series;
  (10) dividing the shares of the class into series and setting and determining the designation of the series and the variations in the relative rights and preferences between the shares of the series;
  (11) the limitation or denial of existing preemptive rights or cumulative voting rights of the shares of the class or series;
  (12) canceling or otherwise affecting the dividends on the shares of the class or series that have accrued but have not been declared; or
  (13) the inclusion or deletion from the certificate of formation of provisions required or permitted to be included in the certificate of formation of a close corporation under Subchapter O.

(e) *The vote required under Subsection (d) by a class or series of shares of a corporation is required notwithstanding that shares of that class or series do not otherwise have a right to vote under the certificate of formation.*

(f) *Unless otherwise provided by the certificate of formation, if the holders of the outstanding shares of a class that is divided into series are entitled to vote as a class on a proposed amendment that would affect equally all series of the class, other than a series in which no shares are outstanding or a series that is not affected by the amendment, the holders of the separate series are not entitled to separate class votes.*

(g) *Unless otherwise provided by the certificate of formation, a proposed amendment to the certificate of formation that would solely effect changes in the designations, preferences, limitations, or relative rights, including voting rights, of one or more series of shares of the corporation that have been established under the authority granted to the board of directors in the certificate of formation in accordance with Section 21.155 does not require the approval of the holders of the outstanding shares of a class or series other than the affected series if, after giving effect to the amendment:*

> (1) *the preferences, limitations, or relative rights of the affected series may be set and determined by the board of directors with respect to the establishment of a new series of shares under the authority granted to the board of directors in the certificate of formation in accordance with Section 21.155; or*

> (2) *any new series established as a result of a reclassification of the affected series are within the preferences, limitations, and relative rights that are described by Subdivision (1).*

§21.365. CHANGES IN VOTE REQUIRED FOR CERTAIN MATTERS.

(a) *With respect to a matter for which the affirmative vote of the holders of a specified portion of the shares entitled to vote is required by this code, the certificate of formation of a corporation may provide that the affirmative vote of the holders of a specified portion, but not less than the majority, of the shares entitled to vote on that matter is required for shareholder action on that matter.*

(b) *With respect to a matter for which the affirmative vote of the holders of a specified portion of the shares of a class or series is required by this code, the certificate of formation may provide that the affirmative vote of the holders of a specified portion, but not less than the majority, of the shares of that class or series is required for action of the holders of shares of that class or series on that matter.*

(c) *If a provision of the certificate of formation provides that the affirmative vote of the holders of a specified portion that is greater than the majority of the shares entitled to vote on a matter is required for shareholder action on that matter, the provision may not be amended, directly or indirectly, without the same affirmative vote unless otherwise provided by the certificate of formation.*

(d) *If a provision of the certificate of formation provides that the affirmative vote of the holders of a specified portion that is greater than the majority of the shares of a class or series is required for shareholder action on a matter, the provision may not be amended, directly or indirectly, without the same affirmative vote unless otherwise provided by the certificate of formation.*

§21.455. APPROVAL OF SALE OF ALL OR SUBSTANTIALLY ALL OF ASSETS.

(a) Except as provided by the certificate of formation of a domestic corporation, a sale, lease, pledge, mortgage, assignment, transfer, or other conveyance of an interest in real property or other assets of the corporation does not require the approval or consent of the shareholders of the corporation unless the transaction constitutes a sale of all or substantially all of the assets of the corporation.

(b) A corporation must approve the sale of all or substantially all of its assets by complying with this section.

(c) The board of directors of the corporation shall adopt a resolution that approves the sale of all or substantially all of the assets of the corporation and:

 (1) recommends that the sale of all or substantially all of the assets of the corporation be approved by the shareholders of the corporation; or

 (2) directs that the sale of all or substantially all of the assets of the corporation be submitted to the shareholders for approval without recommendation if the board of directors determines for any reason not to recommend approval of the sale.

(d) The resolution proposing the sale of all or substantially all of the assets of the corporation shall be submitted to the shareholders of the corporation for approval as provided by this subchapter. The board of directors may place conditions on the submission of the proposed sale to the shareholders.

(e) If the board of directors approves the sale of all or substantially all of the assets of the corporation but does not adopt a resolution recommending that the proposed sale be approved by the shareholders of the corporation, the board of directors shall communicate to the shareholders the reason for the board's determination to submit the proposed sale to shareholders without a recommendation.

(f) The shareholders of the corporation shall approve the sale of all or substantially all of the assets of the corporation as provided by this subchapter. After the approval of the sale by the shareholders, the board of directors may abandon the sale of all or substantially all of the assets of the corporation, subject to the rights of a third party under a contract relating to the assets, without further action or approval by the shareholders.

§ 21.456. GENERAL PROCEDURE FOR SUBMISSION TO SHAREHOLDERS OF FUNDAMENTAL BUSINESS TRANSACTION.

(a) If a fundamental business transaction involving a corporation is required to be submitted to the shareholders of the corporation under this subchapter, the corporation shall notify each shareholder of the corporation that the fundamental business transaction is being submitted to the shareholders for approval at a meeting of shareholders as required by this subchapter, regardless of whether the shareholder is entitled to vote on the matter.

(b) If the fundamental business transaction is a merger, conversion, or interest exchange, the notice required by Subsection (a) shall contain or be accompanied by a copy or summary of the plan of merger, conversion, or interest exchange, as appropriate, and the notice required by Section 10.355.

(c) The notice of the meeting must:

   (1) be given not later than the 21st day before the date of the meeting; and
   (2) state that the purpose, or one of the purposes, of the meeting is to consider the fundamental business transaction.

§21.457. GENERAL VOTE REQUIREMENT FOR APPROVAL OF FUNDAMENTAL BUSINESS TRANSACTION.

(a) Except as provided by this code or the certificate of formation of a corporation in accordance with Section 21.365, the affirmative vote of the holders of at least two-thirds of the outstanding shares of the corporation entitled to vote on a fundamental business transaction is required to approve the transaction.

(b) Unless provided by the certificate of formation or Section 21.458, shares of a class or series that are not otherwise entitled to vote on matters submitted to shareholders generally are not entitled to vote for the approval of a fundamental business transaction.

(c) Except as provided by this code, if a class or series of shares of a corporation is entitled to vote on a fundamental business transaction as a class or series, in addition to the vote required under Subsection (a), the affirmative vote of the holders of at least two-thirds of the outstanding shares in each class or series of shares entitled to vote on the fundamental business transaction as a class or series is required to approve the transaction. Shares entitled to vote as a class or series shall only be entitled to vote as a class or series on the fundamental business transaction unless that class or series is otherwise entitled to vote on each matter submitted to the shareholders generally or is otherwise entitled to vote under the certificate of formation.

(d) Unless required by the certificate of formation, approval of a merger by shareholders is not required under this code for a corporation that is a party to the plan of merger unless that corporation is also a party to the merger.

Mergers

A merger occurs when a business entity is absorbed by another resulting in the termination of the absorbed company. Statutory mergers are achieved by following the requirements of the applicable statute. Once the statutory merger is complete the surviving entity has acquired all of the defunct entity's assets and liabilities. The survivor will also be substituted for the defunct entity in litigation. Typically such mergers provide that the shareholders of the defunct company receives cash or shares of the survivor company as compensation for their interest in the former company.

Statutory mergers also provide a vehicle for companies to combine into one. The result of the combination is that neither of the combining companies survives the merger. Instead a new company is created. This newly created company acquires the assets and assumes the liabilities of the defunct companies.

The boards of directors of the merging companies initiate the statutory merger by adopting a formal "plan of merger". The plan of merger must set forth the name of the surviving corporation, the terms and conditions of the merger, including how the shareholders will vote on the merger, and how the shareholders will be compensated for their interests in the merged company. In approving the merger, the board of directors is bound by its fiduciary duties to the shareholders to act in the best interests of the company. Shareholders are generally entitled to statutory protections to avoid fraud during merger transactions including protections under federal disclosure and anti-fraud laws. See TBOC §§10.002-10.004

After the boards of directors adopt a plan of merger, the plan must usually be submitted to the shareholders of each corporation for approval. Approval of the acquired corporation's shareholders is always required because the merger fundamentally changes their interests. Texas allows shareholders to opt out of a merger, and provides that shareholders who are entitled to vote and who disapprove of the merger, have the right to cash out of the transaction and receive the appraised fair value for their shares. Texas is one of the states with this sort of provision. TBOC §§10.352-10.359

§ 10.002. PLAN OF MERGER: REQUIRED PROVISIONS.

(a) A plan of merger must be in writing and must include:

(1) the name of each organization that is a party to the merger;
(2) the name of each organization that will survive the merger;
(3) the name of each new organization that is to be created by the plan of merger;
(4) a description of the organizational form of each organization that is a party to the merger or that is to be created by the plan of merger and its jurisdiction of formation;
(5) the manner and basis of converting or exchanging any of the ownership or membership interests of each organization that is a party to the merger into:

(A) ownership interests, membership interests, obligations, rights to purchase securities, or other securities of one or more of the surviving or new organizations;
(B) cash;
(C) other property, including ownership interests, membership interests, obligations, rights to purchase securities, or other securities of any other person or entity; or
(D) any combination of the items described by Paragraphs (A)-(C);

(6) the identification of any of the ownership or membership interests of an organization that is a party to the merger that are to be canceled rather than converted or exchanged;
(7) the certificate of formation of each new domestic filing entity to be created by the plan of merger;
(8) the governing documents of each new domestic nonfiling entity to be created by the plan of merger; and
(9) the governing documents of each non-code organization that:

(A) is to survive the merger or to be created by the plan of merger; and
(B) is an entity that is not:

(i) organized under the laws of any state or the United States; or
(ii) required to file its certificate of formation or similar document under which the entity is organized with the appropriate governmental authority.

(b) An item required by Subsections (a)(7)-(9) may be included in the plan of merger by an attachment or exhibit to the plan.

(c) If the plan of merger provides for a manner and basis of converting or exchanging an ownership or membership interest that may be converted or exchanged in a manner or basis different than any other ownership or membership interest of the same class or series of the ownership or membership interest, the manner and basis of conversion or exchange must be included in the plan of merger in the same manner as provided by Subsection (a)(5). A plan of merger may provide for cancellation of an ownership or membership interest while providing for the conversion or exchange of other ownership or membership interests of the same class or series as the ownership or membership interest to be canceled.

§10.003. CONTENTS OF PLAN OF MERGER: MORE THAN ONE SUCCESSOR. *If more than one organization is to survive or to be created by the plan of merger, the plan of merger must include:*

(1) the manner and basis of allocating and vesting the property of each organization that is a party to the merger among one or more of the surviving or new organizations;

(2) the name of each surviving or new organization that is primarily obligated for the payment of the fair value of an ownership or membership interest of an owner or member of a domestic entity subject to dissenters' rights that is a party to the merger and who complies with the requirements for dissent and appraisal under this code applicable to the domestic entity; and

(3) the manner and basis of allocating each liability and obligation of each organization that is a party to the merger, or adequate provisions for the payment and discharge of each liability and obligation, among one or more of the surviving or new organizations.

§10.004. PLAN OF MERGER: PERMISSIVE PROVISIONS. *A plan of merger may include:*

(1) amendments to the governing documents of any surviving organization;

(2) provisions relating to an interest exchange, including a plan of exchange; and

(3) any other provisions relating to the merger that are not required by this chapter.

§10.352. DEFINITIONS. *In this subchapter:*

(1) "Dissenting owner" means an owner of an ownership interest in a domestic entity subject to dissenters' rights who:

    (A) provides notice under Section 10.356; and
    (B) complies with the requirements for perfecting that owner's right to dissent under this subchapter.

(2) "Responsible organization" means:

    (A) the organization responsible for:

        (i) the provision of notices under this subchapter; and
        (ii) the primary obligation of paying the fair value for an ownership interest held by a dissenting owner;

    (B) with respect to a merger or conversion:

        (i) for matters occurring before the merger or conversion, the organization that is merging or converting; and
        (ii) for matters occurring after the merger or conversion, the surviving or new organization that is primarily obligated for

the payment of the fair value of the dissenting owner's ownership interest in the merger or conversion;

(C) with respect to an interest exchange, the organization the ownership interests of which are being acquired in the interest exchange; and

(D) with respect to the sale of all or substantially all of the assets of an organization, the organization the assets of which are to be transferred by sale or in another manner.

§10.353. *FORM AND VALIDITY OF NOTICE.*

(a) Notice required under this subchapter:

(1) must be in writing; and
(2) may be mailed, hand-delivered, or delivered by courier or electronic transmission.

(a) Failure to provide notice as required by this subchapter does not invalidate any action taken.

§10.354. *RIGHTS OF DISSENT AND APPRAISAL.*

(a) Subject to Subsection (b), an owner of an ownership interest in a domestic entity subject to dissenters' rights is entitled to:

(1) dissent from:

(A) a plan of merger to which the domestic entity is a party if owner approval is required by this code and the owner owns in the domestic entity an ownership interest that was entitled to vote on the plan of merger;

(B) a sale of all or substantially all of the assets of the domestic entity if owner approval is required by this code and the owner owns in the domestic entity an ownership interest that was entitled to vote on the sale;

(C) a plan of exchange in which the ownership interest of the owner is to be acquired;

(D) a plan of conversion in which the domestic entity is the converting entity if owner approval is required by this code and the owner owns in the domestic entity an ownership interest that was entitled to vote on the plan of conversion; or

(E) a merger effected under Section 10.006 in which:

(i) the owner is entitled to vote on the merger; or

(ii) the ownership interest of the owner is converted or exchanged; and

(2) subject to compliance with the procedures set forth in this subchapter, obtain the fair value of that ownership interest through an appraisal.

(b) Notwithstanding Subsection (a), subject to Subsection (c), an owner may not dissent from a plan of merger or conversion in which there is a single surviving or new domestic entity or non-code organization, or from a plan of exchange, if:

(1) the ownership interest, or a depository receipt in respect of the ownership interest, held by the owner is part of a class or series of ownership interests, or depository receipts in respect of ownership interests, that are, on the record date set for purposes of determining which owners are entitled to vote on the plan of merger, conversion, or exchange, as appropriate:

(A) listed on a national securities exchange; or
(B) held of record by at least 2,000 owners;

(2) the owner is not required by the terms of the plan of merger, conversion, or exchange, as appropriate, to accept for the owner's ownership interest any consideration that is different from the consideration to be provided to any other holder of an ownership interest of the same class or series as the ownership interest held by the owner, other than cash instead of fractional shares or interests the owner would otherwise be entitled to receive; and

(3) the owner is not required by the terms of the plan of merger, conversion, or exchange, as appropriate, to accept for the owner's ownership interest any consideration other than:

(A) ownership interests, or depository receipts in respect of ownership interests, of a domestic entity or non-code organization of the same general organizational type that, immediately after the effective date of the merger, conversion, or exchange, as appropriate, will be part of a class or series of ownership interests, or depository receipts in respect of ownership interests, that are:

(i) listed on a national securities exchange or authorized for listing on the exchange on official notice of issuance; or
(ii) held of record by at least 2,000 owners;

(B) cash instead of fractional ownership interests the owner would otherwise be entitled to receive; or

(C) any combination of the ownership interests and cash described by Paragraphs (A) and (B).

(c) Subsection (b) shall not apply to a domestic entity that is a subsidiary with respect to a merger under Section 10.006.

§ 10.355. NOTICE OF RIGHT OF DISSENT AND APPRAISAL.

(a) A domestic entity subject to dissenters' rights that takes or proposes to take an action regarding which an owner has a right to dissent and obtain an appraisal under Section 10.354 shall notify each affected owner of the owner's rights under that section if:

(1) the action or proposed action is submitted to a vote of the owners at a meeting; or
(2) approval of the action or proposed action is obtained by written consent of the owners instead of being submitted to a vote of the owners.

(b) If a parent organization effects a merger under Section 10.006 and a subsidiary organization that is a party to the merger is a domestic entity subject to dissenters' rights, the responsible organization shall notify the owners of that subsidiary organization who have a right to dissent to the merger under Section 10.354 of their rights under this subchapter not later than the 10th day after the effective date of the merger. The notice must also include a copy of the certificate of merger and a statement that the merger has become effective.

(c) A notice required to be provided under Subsection (a) or (b) must:

(1) be accompanied by a copy of this subchapter; and
(2) advise the owner of the location of the responsible organization's principal executive offices to which a notice required under Section 10.356(b)(1) or (3) may be provided.

(d) In addition to the requirements prescribed by Subsection (c), a notice required to be provided under Subsection (a)(1) must accompany the notice of the meeting to consider the action, and a notice required under Subsection (a)(2) must be provided to:

(1) each owner who consents in writing to the action before the owner delivers the written consent; and
(2) each owner who is entitled to vote on the action and does not consent in writing to the action before the 11th day after the date the action takes effect.

(e) Not later than the 10th day after the date an action described by Subsection (a)(1) takes effect, the responsible organization shall give notice that the action has been effected to each owner who voted against the action and sent notice under Section 10.356(b)(1).

§ 10.356. PROCEDURE FOR DISSENT BY OWNERS AS TO ACTIONS; PERFECTION OF RIGHT OF DISSENT AND APPRAISAL.

(a) An owner of an ownership interest of a domestic entity subject to dissenters' rights who has the right to dissent and appraisal from any of the actions referred to in Section 10.354 may exercise that right to dissent and appraisal only by complying with the procedures specified in this subchapter. An owner's right of dissent and appraisal under Section 10.354 may be exercised by an owner only with respect to an ownership interest that is not voted in favor of the action.

(b) To perfect the owner's rights of dissent and appraisal under Section 10.354, an owner:

(1) if the proposed action is to be submitted to a vote of the owners at a meeting, must give to the domestic entity a written notice of objection to the action that:

(A) is addressed to the entity's president and secretary;
(B) states that the owner's right to dissent will be exercised if the action takes effect;
(C) provides an address to which notice of effectiveness of the action should be delivered or mailed; and
(D) is delivered to the entity's principal executive offices before the meeting;

(2) with respect to the ownership interest for which the rights of dissent and appraisal are sought:

(A) must vote against the action if the owner is entitled to vote on the action and the action is approved at a meeting of the owners; and
(B) may not consent to the action if the action is approved by written consent; and

(3) must give to the responsible organization a demand in writing that:

(A) is addressed to the president and secretary of the responsible organization;
(B) demands payment of the fair value of the ownership interests for which the rights of dissent and appraisal are sought;
(C) provides to the responsible organization an address to which a notice relating to the dissent and appraisal procedures under this subchapter may be sent;
(D) states the number and class of the ownership interests of the domestic entity owned by the owner and the fair value of the ownership interests as estimated by the owner; and
(E) is delivered to the responsible organization at its principal executive offices at the following time:

(i) not later than the 20th day after the date the responsible organization sends to the owner the notice required by Section 10.355(e) that the action has taken effect, if the action was approved by a vote of the owners at a meeting;

(ii) not later than the 20th day after the date the responsible organization sends to the owner the notice required by Section 10.355(d)(2) that the action has taken effect, if the action was approved by the written consent of the owners; or

(iii) not later than the 20th day after the date the responsible organization sends to the owner a notice that the merger was effected, if the action is a merger effected under Section 10.006.

(c) An owner who does not make a demand within the period required by Subsection (b)(3)(E) or, if Subsection (b)(1) is applicable, does not give the notice of objection before the meeting of the owners is bound by the action and is not entitled to exercise the rights of dissent and appraisal under Section 10.354.

(d) Not later than the 20th day after the date an owner makes a demand under Subsection (b)(3), the owner must submit to the responsible organization any certificates representing the ownership interest to which the demand relates for purposes of making a notation on the certificates that a demand for the payment of the fair value of an ownership interest has been made under this section. An owner's failure to submit the certificates within the required period has the effect of terminating, at the option of the responsible organization, the owner's rights to dissent and appraisal under Section 10.354 unless a court, for good cause shown, directs otherwise.

(e) If a domestic entity and responsible organization satisfy the requirements of this subchapter relating to the rights of owners of ownership interests in the entity to dissent to an action and seek appraisal of those ownership interests, an owner of an ownership interest who fails to perfect that owner's right of dissent in accordance with this subchapter may not bring suit to recover the value of the ownership interest or money damages relating to the action.

§10.357. WITHDRAWAL OF DEMAND FOR FAIR VALUE OF OWNERSHIP INTEREST.

(a) An owner may withdraw a demand for the payment of the fair value of an ownership interest made under Section 10.356 before:

(1) payment for the ownership interest has been made under Sections 10.358 and 10.361; or
(2) a petition has been filed under Section 10.361.

(b) Unless the responsible organization consents to the withdrawal of the demand, an owner may not withdraw a demand for payment under Subsection (a) after either of the events specified in Subsections (a)(1) and (2).

§ 10.358. RESPONSE BY ORGANIZATION TO NOTICE OF DISSENT AND DEMAND FOR FAIR VALUE BY DISSENTING OWNER.

(a) Not later than the 20th day after the date a responsible organization receives a demand for payment made by a dissenting owner in accordance with Section 10.356(b)(3), the responsible organization shall respond to the dissenting owner in writing by:

(1) accepting the amount claimed in the demand as the fair value of the ownership interests specified in the notice; or
(2) rejecting the demand and including in the response the requirements prescribed by Subsection (c).

(b) If the responsible organization accepts the amount claimed in the demand, the responsible organization shall pay the amount not later than the 90th day after the date the action that is the subject of the demand was effected if the owner delivers to the responsible organization:

(1) endorsed certificates representing the ownership interests if the ownership interests are certificated; or
(2) signed assignments of the ownership interests if the ownership interests are uncertificated.

(c) If the responsible organization rejects the amount claimed in the demand, the responsible organization shall provide to the owner:

(1) an estimate by the responsible organization of the fair value of the ownership interests; and
(2) an offer to pay the amount of the estimate provided under Subdivision (1).

(d) If the dissenting owner decides to accept the offer made by the responsible organization under Subsection (c)(2), the owner must provide to the responsible organization notice of the acceptance of the offer not later than the 90th day after the date the action that is the subject of the demand took effect.

(e) If, not later than the 90th day after the date the action that is the subject of the demand took effect, a dissenting owner accepts an offer made by a responsible organization under Subsection (c)(2) or a dissenting owner and a responsible organization reach an agreement on the fair value of the ownership interests, the responsible organization shall pay the agreed amount not later than the 120th day

after the date the action that is the subject of the demand took effect, if the dissenting owner delivers to the responsible organization:

(1) endorsed certificates representing the ownership interests if the ownership interests are certificated; or
(2) signed assignments of the ownership interests if the ownership interests are uncertificated.

Involuntary winding up and termination of the corporation

A corporation may be ordered to wind up and terminate if it either fails to do something proscribed by law or violates some law. Texas' legislatures and courts are reluctant to do so, however. The applicable law is replete with opportunities for the corporation to avoid being involuntarily wound up, even after an involuntary order has been entered.

Prior to an involuntary order being entered, the corporation will receive notice and an opportunity to cure its deficiency. Satisfying the deficiency leads to the corporation's corporate existence being reinstated, effective to the date it originally filed its certificate of formation. Failure to satisfy it triggers the winding up and termination process.

In addition to other reasons not discussed here, a corporation may be ordered to be wound up and terminated for four reasons: (1) administrative termination, (2) judicial termination, (3) franchise tax termination, and upon (4) shareholder or creditor request.

Administrative termination

Under TBOC the Secretary of State may terminate a corporation after notice, if the corporation fails to: (1) timely file a report; (2) timely pay a fee or penalty; (3) maintain a registered agent or registered office in Texas; or (4) pay the filing fee for its certificate of formation. § 11.251(b)(1), (2).

If, after notice, the corporation does not cure the defect and termination is required, the secretary of state shall issue a certificate of termination, and deliver the certificate to the filing entity at its registered office or principal place of business. Issuance of the certificate of termination terminates the corporation. § 11.252(c). The certificate tells the corporation that it has been involuntarily terminated and the date and cause of the termination. § 11.252(b).

TBOC also provides that the involuntarily terminated filing entity may file a certificate of reinstatement up to the third anniversary date of its involuntary termination if it has cured all defects or causes for the involuntary termination. § 11.253(a-d). If the state finds that the entity has corrected the circumstances that led to the involuntary termination or that the circumstances did not exist at the time of the termination, then it shall reinstate the entity. § 11.253(a)(1), (2). If a filing entity is reinstated before the third anniversary of the date of its involuntary termination, the entity is considered to have continued in existence without interruption from the date of termination. § 11.253(d).

Judicial termination

The Attorney General (AG) may seek an involuntary winding up and termination of a corporation §11.303 when the corporation:

1. failed to comply with a condition precedent to its formation;
2. fraudulently filed the certificate of formation or an amendment to the certificate;
3. misrepresented a material matter in any document submitted to the State; or
4. continues to transact in business beyond the scope of its purpose clause contained in its certificate of formation. § 11.301.

§11.301. INVOLUNTARY WINDING UP AND TERMINATION OF FILING ENTITY BY COURT ACTION.

(a) A court may enter a decree requiring winding up of a filing entity's business and termination of the filing entity's existence if, as the result of an action brought under Section 11.303, the court finds that one or more of the following problems exist:

(1) the filing entity or its organizers did not comply with a condition precedent to its formation;

(2) the certificate of formation of the filing entity or any amendment to the certificate of formation was fraudulently filed;

(3) a misrepresentation of a material matter has been made in an application, report, affidavit, or other document submitted by the filing entity under this code;

(4) the filing entity has continued to transact business beyond the scope of the purpose of the filing entity as expressed in its certificate of formation; or

(5) public interest requires winding up and termination of the filing entity because:

(A) the filing entity has been convicted of a felony or a high managerial agent of the filing entity has been convicted of a felony committed in the conduct of the filing entity's affairs;

(B) the filing entity or high managerial agent has engaged in a persistent course of felonious conduct; and

(C) termination is necessary to prevent future felonious conduct of the same character.

(b) Sections 11.302-11.307 do not apply to Subsection (a)(5).

§11.302. NOTIFICATION OF CAUSE BY SECRETARY OF STATE.

(a) The secretary of state shall provide to the attorney general:

(1) the name of a filing entity that has given cause under Section 11.301 for involuntary winding up of the entity's business and termination of the entity's existence; and

(2) the facts relating to the cause for the winding up and termination.

(b) When notice is provided under Subsection (a), the secretary of state shall notify the filing entity of the circumstances by writing sent to the entity at its registered office in this state. The notice must state that the secretary of state has given notice under Subsection (a) and the grounds for the notification. The secretary of state must record the date a notice required by this subsection is sent.

(c) A court shall accept a certificate issued by the secretary of state as to the facts relating to the cause for the winding up and termination and the sending of a notice under Subsection (b) as prima facie evidence of the facts stated in the certificate and the sending of the notice.

§11.303. FILING OF ACTION BY ATTORNEY GENERAL. *The attorney general shall file an action against a filing entity in the name of the state seeking termination of the entity's existence if:*

(1) the filing entity has not cured the problems for which winding up and termination is sought before the 31st day after the date the notice under Section 11.302(b) is mailed; and

(2) the attorney general determines that cause exists for the involuntary winding up of a filing entity's business and termination of the entity's existence under Section 11.301.

§11.304. CURE BEFORE FINAL JUDGMENT. *An action filed by the attorney general under Section 11.303 shall be abated if, before a district court renders judgment on the action, the filing entity:*

(1) cures the problems for which winding up and termination is sought; and

(2) pays the costs of the action.

§11.305. JUDGMENT REQUIRING WINDING UP AND TERMINATION. *If a district court finds in an action brought under this subchapter that proper grounds exist under Section 11.301(a) for a winding up of a filing entity's business and termination of the filing entity's existence, the court shall:*

(1) make findings to that effect; and

(2) subject to Section 11.306, enter a judgment not earlier than the fifth day after the date the court makes its findings."

The court's order compels the corporation to begin its process of winding up. After the corporation has completed its winding up, or whenever the court deems it necessary, the court may enter an order terminating the corporation. § 11.313 (1)(2). The corporation is terminated after the court's clerk files a certified copy of the order. § 11.313(c).

Failure to pay franchise taxes

Failure to report or make tax payments required by the Code may lead to a corporation being involuntarily wound up and terminated. Tex. Tax Code Ann. §§ 1717.51 et seq. In the event of termination of entity for failure to pay franchise taxes, the directors are subject to personal liability for corporate obligations, including franchise taxes. § 171.362(a). Failing to either file the required reports or pay the required taxes when due results in a five percent penalty. *Id.* Thirty days later, if the directors still haven't complied then another five percent penalty is levied. § 171.362(b).

A corporation's failure to meet its tax obligations has two effects. First, the corporation will forfeit its corporate privileges. Second, the corporation will forfeit its charter, either through judicial or administrative action.

When the filing entity has failed to timely pay its franchise taxes it is subject to losing its corporate privileges. Corporate privileges include the right to conduct business in Texas in the entity's name, the right to sue in the entity name, and director's and officer's protection from liability. TTC §171.255(a) provides that when the entity loses its corporate privileges "each director or officer of the corporation is liable for each debt of the corporation that is created or incurred in the state after the date on which the report, tax or penalty is due and before the corporate privileges are revived."

When the entity is in jeopardy of losing its corporate privileges, the corporation will receive written notice from the Comptroller of Public Accounts about its delinquency. Forty-five days later, if the corporation hasn't cured its delinquency then corporate privileges are forfeited. §§ 171.251, 171.256. Forfeiture does not result in the entity's termination.

To avoid forfeiture the corporation must make full payment of its delinquent franchise taxes within 120 days after the privileges were revoked. § 171.258. If the corporation fails to do so, then charter forfeiture proceedings begin.

Bringing judicial action

To obtain forfeiture from the court, the state comptroller must certify to the Attorney Genral (AG) and the Secretary of State the names of those corporations whose charters are subject to forfeiture. § 171.302. Once certified the AG is required to bring suit against the delinquent corporation if it determines that grounds exist for the forfeiture. § 171.303.

The corporation may still revive its charter even if a court orders its charter forfeited. To revive the charter, the corporation will request a bill of review to set aside the forfeiture. §171.306. If the court sets aside the forfeiture, the corporation's privileges are revived. §§171.307, 171.308.

Administrative forfeiture

Through administrative action, the Secretary of State may cause a corporation's charter to be forfeited. § 171.309(1)(2). Similar to when action by the AG's office is triggered, 120 days after the corporation's privileges were revoked the State may enter "Charter Forfeited" on the corporation's records. But the State may only do so if, during those 120 days, the corporation did not cure its defect.

As was the case with the forfeiture by court order, a corporation may have its administrative forfeiture set aside. §§ 171.312 to 171.34. The corporation may do so by satisfying all penalties and delinquent tax obligations. Once satisfied, the corporation's privileges are revived and the doors of Texas's courts are reopened.

Shareholder or creditor request for termination

There are at least two ways for a shareholder or creditor to have a corporation liquidated by court-order. The first way is immediate but sets a high bar for a creditor to reach. A court may order a corporation immediately liquidated if a creditor establishes that the corporation's unsecured creditors, as a class, will suffer irreparable harm unless assets of the corporation's property are immediately liquidated. § 11.405(a)(4).

Alternatively, a shareholder or creditor may ask the court to appoint a receiver to rehabilitate the corporation. If the shareholder makes the request, the shareholder must establish that the corporation is insolvent, the directors or shareholders are deadlocked, or the directors engaged in illegal acts. § 11.404(a)(1)(A)-(E). If the creditor makes the request, the creditor must show that the corporation is insolvent and that the creditor has a claim against the corporation. § 11.404(a)(2)(A), (B).

After receivership has been granted the court may order the corporation be liquidated. § 11.405(a). The court will enter this order if the corporation does not present a feasible plan to the receiver that would cure the defect leading to the receivership. § 11.405(a)(3). The corporation has one year from the date the court appointed the receiver to cure the defect. *Id*. If that date passes, then the court – after considering other factors listed at § 11.405(b)(1)-(3) – may enter the liquidating order.

Table 5

ORGANIZING TBOC CORPORATIONS	
TOPIC	**STATUTE**
FORMATION/CREATION TERMINOLOGY	
corporate terms	1.006
formation and existence	3.001
duration	3.003
organizers	3.004
certificate of formation	3.005
supplemental for cloase corporation	3.008
right to amend certificate of formation	3.051
procedures to amend certificate of formation	3.052
certificate of amendment	3.053
effect of filing certificate of amendment	3.056
right to restate certificate of formation	3.057
procedures to restate certificate of formation	3.058
restated certificate of formation	3.059
PURPOSES/POWERS	
generally	2.001-2.012
powers of domestic entity	2.101-2.114
CERTIFICATE OF FORMATION	
requirements	3.005
name of filing entity	5.054
type of filing entity	21.002(5)
purpose clause	3.005(3)
period of duration	3.005(4)
street address of registered agent	3.005(5)
name of registered agent	3.005(5)
name and address of organizer	3.004
signatures	1.002(82)
filing entity filings	3.001(a)(b)
amending the certificate of formation	3.051 et.seq.

restating the certificate of formation	3.057 et. seq.
supplemental provisions	3.007
amendment	3.051-3.054
FILINGS INCL FEES	
signing and delivering filings	4.001 et seq
on finding by secretary of state	4.002(a),(b)
prompt filing	4.004
effect of issuance by secretary of state	4.005(d)
liability for false filing	4.007
penalty for false filing	4.008
penalties for late filing	21.802(a)
NAMES	
entity name	5.001 et seq
name of limited liability partnership	5.063
reserving entity name	5.101--5.105
REGISTERED AGENTS/OFFICES	
generally	5.200 et.seq.
consent to serve	5.2011
duties of registered agent	5.206
registration of registered agent without consent	5.207
registered agent's immunity from liability	5.208
agent for service of process and notice	5.255
effect of failure to designate registered agent	5.251(1)
GOVERNANCE	
GOVERNING PERSONS	
directors are managers	21.401--402
certificated shares	1.002(7)
governing authority defined	1.002(35)
governing person defined	1.002(37)
officer defined	1.002(61)
ownership interest defined	1.002(64)

governance rules	3.101 et. seq.
duties of officers	3.103
uncertificated shares	3.201-3.205
restrictions on transferability	3.202 and et. seq.
signature on certificates	3.203
delivery	3.204
emergency governance	3.251--254
GOVERNING DOCUMENTS	
governing documents defined	1.002(36)
shareholder agreements	21.101 et. seq
by-laws	21.057--058
the close corporation	21.701 et.seq.
FIDUCIARY DUTIES	
limiting fiduciary duties	7.001
wrongful distributions	21.002(6)
limitations on distributions	21.303
director liability for wrongful distribution	21.316--318
property used to discharge obligations	11.053
court supervision of winding up	11.054
survival after termination	11.356
limiting governing person liability	3.102
self dealing	21.418
disinterested person	1.003
self dealing safe harbour	1.003(b)
interested contracts ok	21.418
BOOKS AND RECORDS	
requirement to keep generally	3.151
right to inspect records	3.152
right of owner or member to inspect	3.153
supplemental records required	21.173
MEETINGS	
organization	21.059
overview	6.001-.053
entity action	6.201-.205

s/h quorum	21.358
director quorum	21.413
annual	21.351
cumulative iff opt in	21.360-363
fundamental changes	21.364
VOTING	
record dates	6.101 et seq
voting of interests owned by another entity	6.153
voting of interests	6.151.-.156
voting trusts	6.251
voting agreements	6.252
inspection of voting list	21.354
voting in election of directors	21.359
proxies	21.367--371
record date for written consent to action	21.356
record date for shareholder meeting	21.357
POWERS	
ultra vires	20.002 et seq
generally	2.101
LIABILITY	
shareholder	21.223
pre-formation subscription	21.166
LIMITATION OF LIABILITY	
governing person	7.001
indemnification and insurance	8.001 et seq
SHAREHOLDER LIABILITY	
shareholder agreement	21.101 et.seq.
generally	21.107
limitation of liability for obligations	21.223(a)
piercing corp veil	21.223(b)
business enterprise theory	21.224,225
exceptions to limitations on liability	21.225

DIRECTOR/OFFICER LIABILITY	
action by directors	21.415
director liability for wrongful distributions	21.316
officer duties	3.103
DERIVATIVE PROCEEDINGS	
derivative litigation	21.551 et seq
ultra vires	20.002(c)(2)
demand required	21.553
LIABILITY DURING WINDING UP	
generally	11.052
property applied to discharge obligations	11.053
definitions	11.001
writing defined	1.002(89)
WINDING UP/TERMINATION	
certificate of termination	11.101
court action during winding up	11.055
appeals	12.004
close corporation	21.708-709; 757
defined	1.002(8)
filings generally	4.001 et.seq.
filing fees	4.152
registered agent	5.201
winding up	11.001 et.seq.
supplemental for corporations	11.059
revoking voluntary winding up	11.151
reinstatement	11.201 et.seq.
termination of filing entity	11.251-.253
judicial winding up	11.301-.308
liability of terminated filing entity	11.351
limited survival after termination	11.356
governing persons during limited survival	11.357

appointing receiver	11.401
governors not necessary parties	11.411
decree of involuntary termination	11.412
shares defined	21.202
voting fundamental changes	21.364
changes in vote	21.365
action by directors	21.415
winding up procedures	21.502
late filing penalties	21.802
statutory preemptive rights	21.204-.205

Corporations Problem Set

1. In June 2007, Acton, Blair, and Chang hired an attorney to incorporate their carpet cleaning business in Texas. The lawyer filed the Certificate of Formation for the company with the Secretary of State (SOS), along those of five other clients. On July 3, 2007, the attorney received a package from the SOS. He opened it and saw a number of Certificates stamped "Filed". He emailed Acton, Blair and Chang to inform them that their business, Mega Carpet Clean, Inc. (MCC) had been incorporated. With this information, the three investors commenced business and elected themselves as directors to fill the only 3 slots on the Board of Directors. They also solicited additional investments, leading to the addition in July 2007 of 55 new shareholders, none of whom was involved in management. In August 2007, MCC signed a 3-year cleaning contract with the Total Energy, LP and received $1 million in advance. In September 2007, the attorney returned from summer vacation to find another envelope containing the Certificate he filed in June 2007, accompanied by a letter stating that MCC's Certificate of Formation had not been approved due to some defects in the document. The attorney notified Acton, Blair and Chang, who continued to do business while working with the lawyer to rectify the errors. Due to a host of problems, MCC breached the cleaning contract in November, 2007. Total Energy sued MCC, and upon discovering the defective incorporation, amended its court papers to include the 58 shareholders as defendants. The trial and appellate courts have held that since there was no incorporation at the time the contract was entered into, the business was a general partnership; all the shareholders were liable as general partners. Acton, Blair, Chang and the other 55 shareholders have appealed to the Texas Supreme Court.

   Who wins and why?

2. Maple Leaf, Inc. was incorporated in March 2012. Prior to its incorporation, the promoter signed a 12-month lease with Hero Property Management, LLC. The lease was signed on January 1, 2012 and covered the period from January 1, 2012 till December 31, 2012 for a rent of $6,000 per month. In April 2012, Maple Leaf, Inc. started conducting business operations on the leased premises. Hero has not received any rent and in January 2013 brought a lawsuit against Maple Leaf, Inc. for the unpaid rent of $72,000. Maple Leaf, Inc. moved to dismiss the suit, arguing that since it did not sign the contract before or after its incorporation, the proper party to be sued is the promoter. The court disagreed, holding that Maple Leaf, Inc. was responsible for the entire $72,000 in overdue rent.

   Do you agree with the court?

3. Chick Fest Restaurants Corporation owns a chain of popular restaurants. The founders of the business are devoutly religious, who express their faith by keeping the business doors closed on Sundays. Recently, the Board of Directors, consisting primarily of the

founders' family members, voted to make an anonymous donation of $1 million to the Children's Art Museum of Houston. A shareholder who stopped by the corporate headquarters overheard two directors discussing the donation and was upset. He sued, seeking an order declaring the donation *ultra vires* and compelling the directors to reimburse the corporate treasury up to that amount. The directors counter-argue that the donation would benefit the corporation as children drive most of their sales. The court sided with the directors, noting that reasonable charitable contributions are within the powers of any corporation. The shareholder is appealing.

Discuss whether the appeal would fail.

4. Bloomberg Energy Corporation is a Texas corporation engaged in renewable energy trading since its formation in 2007. The early years of the company were difficult and the company was not profitable until 2012. With the national focus on alternative energy, business has experienced a boom after receiving a number of lucrative contracts awarded by the federal government. It recorded a multi-million dollar profit in 2012, but the directors have not declared any dividends. Barajas, who holds cumulative preferred shares, has brought an action in court seeking orders to (1) compel the directors to declare dividends (2) direct the directors to distribute the entire profits as dividends; and (3) pay him accumulated dividends for each year since 2008.

Is he entitled to any of the relief he seeks?

5. Pinnacle, Inc. is a real estate development company. Due to the credit freeze following the financial crisis of 2008, no bank was willing to lend to home builders. Barry, one of the directors of Pinnacle, offered to extend a loan of $5 million to the company at 8% interest annually. At the time of the loan, there was a new federal loan program aimed at reviving the construction industry. Pinnacle would have qualified for this loan, which had a maximum interest rate of 2%. The directors did not know about the existence of the loan, because it was not widely publicized. A Pinnacle shareholder sued the directors, alleging that their lack of diligence would end up costing the company thousands of dollars in avoidable interest payments. The court held that the business judgment rule protected all the directors and that none of them can be held personally liable for the loan.

Did the court get it right?

6. Kangaroo, Inc. has a 7-member board of directors. Five of the directors were present at a properly-convened board meeting on November 1, 2011 while the absent ones – Donna and Darren Shelby - gave proxies to their colleague, Alfredo to vote on their behalf. The proxies dated October 28, 2011 stated that they were irrevocable for 12 months. The meeting was called to decide on a proposal for the expansion of the business to build a factory in China. The directors who gave proxies to Alfredo wanted him to vote against the proposal. At the meeting, Alfredo was persuaded by a consultant's presentation about

the factory's prospects and decided to vote in favor of the proposal. He sent a quick text message to the absent directors about his change of mind. Unimpressed by Alfredo's *volte face* and unwilling to let him support the proposal, the Shelbys sent a reply text revoking their proxies. At the board meeting, three of the directors voted against the expansion proposal. Alfredo and the chairman of the board voted for the proposal. The chairman also ruled that the attempted revocation of the proxies by the Shelbys was improper and against the express terms of the instrument. The chairman allowed Alfredo to vote the proxies as he saw fit and Alfredo voted in favor of expanding operations to China. With four votes in favor and three against, the chairman declared that the construction of the factory would commence in earnest.

Is the board's action supported by law?

7. Jaguar Enterprises, Inc. was formed as a Texas business corporation in 2002. Jaguar is authorized to issue 5,000 common shares and 2,500 preferred shares. The company's certificate of formation, by-laws or other documents contain no provision pertaining to preemptive rights. A month after formation, the board of directors approved the issue of 1,000 common shares to the founding shareholders, each of whom received 250 common shares. The following quarter, the directors issued 50 common shares to Ibrahim in compensation for his exceptional service as a senior employee. In July 2012, the company's board of directors proposed to issue to Alicia 100 common shares for cash. Ibrahim does not want his interests diluted and files suit requesting the court order the company to issue him a proportionate amount of shares to maintain his interest. The court rejected his challenge, holding that he had no preemptive rights since Jaguar is a Texas corporation and the transaction took place in 2012. The court further held that even if preemptive rights existed, this case falls under one of the exceptions. Thus, Ibrahim had no preemptive rights "based on the well-recognized rule in all jurisdictions that shares issued to employees do not have preemptive rights."

Do you agree with the court?

8. Hibiscus Corporation is a small, family-owned business that has elected close corporation status under Texas law. To prevent the admission of new shareholders who may work against the interests of the corporation, existing shareholders included a clause in the governing Shareholder Agreement that states that the shares of the company may not be sold or transferred to another person, without first offering the company an option to purchase the shares at twice the price for which they were bought. This provision, however, is not written on the share certificates. Jermaine, a shareholder, recently transferred 25% of his shares, in contravention of the Shareholder Agreement to Tarantino for $25,000. Tarantino did not have actual knowledge of the restriction on the transferability of shares. When the company refused to recognize Tarantino as a shareholder, he (joined by Jermaine) sued arguing that in a capitalist society, the right to

own and transfer property is fundamental and that Tarantino's lack of knowledge made him a *bona fide* purchaser for value whose innocently acquired rights should not be defeated. The court agreed, noting that one of the core attributes of corporations under our free enterprise system is the free transferability of ownership interests. Hibiscus has appealed the decision.

Who wins and why?

9. Rodriguez is a director of Assent Tours, Inc., a Texas corporation that specializes in organizing tours in Manhattan, New York and Washington, DC. Rodriguez lives in Houston where he has other business interests. Last year he enrolled in two separate executive courses on hospitality and aircraft maintenance organized by the Houston Schools of Hotel Management and engineering respectively. To finance his participation, Rodriguez obtained a $30,000 loan from Citibank and the loan was guaranteed by Assent following a vote by disinterested directors. Rodriguez defaulted on the loan and Citibank wants to enforce the guarantee. Bus Lines, LLC, a valuable trade creditor of Assent, is seeking an injunction to prevent the corporation from making payment on the loan guarantee, in lieu of debt owed to it, arguing that it was beyond the corporation's powers to enter into the loan guarantees.

Will Bus Lines, LLC prevail?

10. Jonathan is a director and president of Horizon Communications Corporation, a provider of video-conferencing services. The company is a known leader of this market segment and its last audited accounts showed a business volume of $10 million in 2010. Under Horizon's by-laws, transactions with a dollar value above $50,000 require the approval of the board of directors. In January 2011, without discussing with other board members, Jonathan ordered supplies worth $55,000 from Cardinal Electronics, LLC. The order was placed in the name of Horizon but for reasons of convenience, Jonathan directed delivery to his home address. When Horizon's other directors found out about the purchase, they informed Cardinal that Horizon is not under any obligation to pay for the items. Cardinal instituted legal action against Horizon and Jonathan. The court held that Jonathan alone is responsible for the $55,000 debt in view of Horizon's by-laws as well as the inveterate and venerable corporate law principle that a single director has no agency authority to bind a corporation.

To what extent do you disagree with the court?

LIMITED LIABILITY COMPANIES

Core Concepts

Nature and Structure

The limited liability company ("LLC") is a relatively recent, innovative business form that combines some of the most attractive attributes of the corporation (separate legal personality and limited liability) and those of the partnership (structural flexibility and pass-through taxation). It should be noted that while some courts and commentators occasionally refer to the LLC as a "limited liability corporation," the LLC is not a corporation and is properly addressed as a company. The owners of the LLC are called members. A member can be an individual, partnership, corporation, trust, or any other legal entity. LLCs have been a feature of Texas law since 1991. LLCs in Texas are governed by the Texas Business Occupations Code (the "TBOC"). Section 1.008(e) of the TBOC specifies that the provisions of the code applicable to LLCs, notably the provisions of Chapter 101 and those provisions of Title 1 that apply to LLCs, may be cited as the "Texas Limited Liability Company Law." Chapter 101 applies specifically to LLCs but must be read alongside Title 1 (Chapters 1 to 12) of the TBOC, which contains provisions applicable to all types of business entities.

The core characteristics of a Texas LLC are as follows:

1. Separate Entity. The LLC has a separate legal existence from its owners. As a separate legal person, the LLC may hold property, sue and be sued in its own name. The assets of the LLC do not belong to the members.

2. Limited Liability. Owners of the LLC are clothed with a shield of limited liability and thus are not personally liable for the company's debt or other obligations. The members are only liable to the extent of their investment or on an independent legal basis, such as for tort committed in the course of business.

3. Flexible Management. Generally, unlike corporations that are characterized by centralized management and general partnerships that are characterized by decentralized management, LLCs enjoy considerable flexibility in the choice of management structure. LLCs may choose to be member-managed, manager-managed, or a variation of these governance approaches.

4. Continuity of Life. LLCs in Texas have perpetual existence unless they opt for a restricted or definite duration.

5. Transferability. Similar to the corporation, a member of a limited liability company may wholly or partly assign its interest. However, the assignment will not entitle the assignee to become a member of the company, participate in the management and affairs of the company, or exercise membership rights. §101.108 Under TBOC an assignee only becomes a member with unanimous consent of the existing members.

6. Pass-through Taxation. A Texas LLC may be taxed as a partnership or sole proprietorship for federal income tax purposes. In that case, the entity pays no tax. Instead income and losses flow through to the members, who pay taxes on their receipts or deduct the losses to reduce other personal income tax liability.

7. Member withdrawal or expulsion statutorily prohibited.

Since its emergence in the American landscape in 1977, the LLC has grown to become the favored investment vehicle for small enterprises, outpacing corporations, general partnerships, limited partnerships, and limited liability partnerships. The growing popularity of the LLC has been attributed to its hybridity and a variety of other factors causing the LLC to gain favor of bigger businesses also.

Advantages and Disadvantages of the LLC

LLCs are favored over corporations because they have pass-through taxation, instead of the double taxation that burdens corporations. Corporations in Texas are permitted to incorporate for any lawful purpose, however, this is subject to some restrictions. For example, a for-profit corporation may not be formed for a nonprofit purpose. The TBOC also prohibits for-profit corporations from combining certain cattle businesses or oil businesses within a single for-profit corporation. TBOC §§ 2.007 and 2.008. The LLC does not face any of these prohibitions. The LLC is only required to have a purpose clause that permits the company to be organized for "any lawful purpose," although a LLC may opt for a narrow or specific purpose clause. LLCs also hold a distinct advantage over the traditional general partnerships, because they provide investors with limited liability. General partners' liability is limited only if they register as a limited liability partnership (LLP). Although some other business forms, notably the S corporation, the limited partnership ("LP"), the LLP, and LLLP have stepped in to remedy the tax and liability disadvantages of earlier business forms, LLCs are still the most advantageous.

In exchange for pass-through taxation, S corporations are saddled with a host of onerous restrictions; including a limitation on the number of shareholders to a maximum of 100, restriction to only one class of stock, non-admission of non-resident aliens as shareholders, and restriction of shareholding generally to natural persons, with the exception of a few qualified estates and trusts. See 26 U.S.C.A. § 1361(b)(1). The LLC has none of these restrictions and is open to foreign investors, pension plans, and corporate joint ventures. Additionally, investors in LPs are not burdened with double taxation and they provide for limited liability. However, not all the investors can enjoy that protection as there must be a general partner who is exposed to unlimited personal liability. A corporate general partner ("CGP") may be used to circumvent the personal liability problem, however, not only is this still a more circuitous process than simply forming an LLC, the LP risks being taxed as a corporation in some situations.

The limited liability partnership ("LLP") comes closest to paralleling the combination of the advantages of the LLC. The LLP includes limited liability for all investors and an absence of double taxation, without being saddled with all the restrictions of the S corporation. However, the LLC has some advantages vis-à-vis the LLP.

LLP vs LLC

First, LLCs provide a full shield of limited liability. While LLPs in many states also provide a full shield, some former or current statutes in other states have only provided a partial shield. This partial shield protects partners from some, but not all, partnership obligations by imposing some form of limitation on the liability protection, such as supervisory liability.

Second, the LLC generally does not impose a burden of annual renewal, while the LLP requires a filing of an annual application in order to renew its certificate and maintain its limited liability status. Moreover, there is also the concern among many lawyers that the LLP's shield might be more 'porous' than the shield provided by corporations or limited liability companies. Additionally, there is concern that any change in membership in a partnership constitutes a termination of the old partnership and the creation of a new partnership, potentially exposing LLP partners to personal liability during that period the partnership is dissolved.

In the earlier years of the LLP, a number of states (including Texas until 2011) required LLPs to obtain and maintain a liability insurance policy or segregate funds in lieu thereof. This requirement could be onerous on business start-ups. In Texas, an LLP is assessed an annual fee of $200 per partner, without a similar cost imposed on LLCs. Further, unlike an LLP, one person can form an LLC in most states, thus making it possible for single entrepreneurs to adopt the form. Not only is the LLP option foreclosed to such individuals, but opting for an LLC obviates the extra hassle of searching for compatible and reliable business associates. Finally, some states restrict the use of LLPs to professional firms, while no such restriction applies to the LLC.

None of the statements above should be construed as suggesting that the LLC is devoid of disadvantages in comparison to the other business forms. The LLC is relatively new and as such, the law is still developing. This could create uncertainty and make investors uncomfortable. In addition, a merger or other reorganization between an LLC and a larger publicly held corporation will be subject to taxes. If the transaction involves corporations only, it will be completed on a tax-free basis. Furthermore, LLCs, like corporations and other entities, face franchise taxes. This is unlike general partnerships in Texas, which are owned solely by natural persons or LPs and LLPs that qualify as passive entities. *See generally* Emeka Duruigbo, *Avoiding a Limited Future for the De Facto LLC and LLC by Estoppel*, 12 U. PA. J. BUS. L. 1013, 1020-1023 (2010).

In summary, the LLC presents the following advantages and disadvantages.

LLC Advantages

- Pass-through taxation - (i.e., no double taxation).
- Limited liability - the owners of the LLC, called "members," are protected from liability for acts and debts of the LLC.
- Can be set up with just one natural person involved or, in some states, one owner which may be an entity itself.
- No requirement of an annual general meeting for members and generally less emphasis on formalities.
- May elect to operate through centralized management or decentralized management.
- LLCs may have perpetual existence.

- LLCs require less administrative paperwork and recordkeeping
- Membership interests of LLCs can be assigned without transferring management rights
- LLCs may engage in some types of businesses that are not permissible for the corporation or professional limited liability company (PLLC). While a PLLC may be formed for the purpose of providing any professional service, professionals adopting that business form may only engage in more than one purpose if the entity is expressly authorized to provide more than one type of professional service.

LLC Disadvantages

- Earnings of members of an LLC may be subject to self-employment tax.
- A limited liability company that is treated as a partnership cannot take advantage of incentive stock options, engage in tax-free reorganizations, or issue Section 1244 stock.
- LLCs are relatively new, the first having been established in 1977 in Wyoming. While all states had adopted a LLC statute by 1997, there is a lack of uniformity among limited liability company statutes. Businesses that operate in more than one state may not receive consistent treatment.
- In order to be treated as a partnership, an LLC must have at least two members. An S corporation can have one shareholder. Although all states allow single member LLCs, a single member LLC cannot elect partnership classification for federal tax purposes. It can only be treated as a sole proprietor unless it elects to file as a corporation.
- Some states do not tax partnerships but do tax limited liability companies.

Texas Business Organization Code provisions

§ 101.101. *Members Required*

(a) A limited liability company may have one or more members. Except as provided by this section, a limited liability company must have at least one member.

(b) A limited liability company that has managers is not required to have any members during a reasonable period between the date the company is formed and the date the first member is admitted to the company.

(c) A limited liability company is not required to have any members during the period between the date the continued membership of the last remaining member of the company is terminated and the date the agreement to continue the company described by Section 11.056 is executed.

Entity Status

The LLC is a separate entity from its owners. Accordingly, it is capable of suing, being sued, and of holding property in its own name. An LLC member "may be named as a party in an action by or against the [LLC] only if the action is brought to enforce the member's right against or liability to the company." TBOC § 101.113. Because members of the LLC are distinct from the LLC, certain circumstances may warrant a separate assessment of liability. Characterizing the

LLC as an entity separate from its members may sometimes lead to tension or even threaten to frustrate the objectives of other public policy initiatives, such as the workers' compensation law.

Texas Business Organization Code provisions

§ 101.113. Parties to Actions. A member of a limited liability company may be named as a party in an action by or against the limited liability company only if the action is brought to enforce the member's right against or liability to the company.

Ingalls v. Standard Gypsum, L.L.C.
70 S.W.3d 252 (Tex. App. – San Antonio 2001, pet., denied)

BACKGROUND

Temple–Inland and McQueeney formed the limited liability company, Standard Gypsum, in accordance with the Texas Limited Liability Company Act. *Tex.Rev.Civ. Stat. Ann. Art. 1528n (Vernon Supp. 2001)* Temple–Inland and McQueeney are the two members of Standard Gypsum, as defined by the Texas Limited Liability Company Act. Temple–Inland and Standard Gypsum entered into a written management agreement (the "Agreement") in which Temple–Inland agreed to "manage and operate [Standard Gypsum's plant in McQueeney, Texas] in a manner which is consistent with [Temple–Inland's] management and operation of its own gypsum wallboard manufacturing facilities." Temple–Inland also agreed to procure and maintain, at Standard Gypsum's expense, adequate workers' compensation insurance covering all plant employees. On February 2, 1997, Mitchell Ingalls was injured in the course and scope of his employment while working at Standard Gypsum's plant. Ingalls' arm became caught in a machine at the plant, requiring its amputation. Ingalls filed suit against McQueeney and Temple–Inland, alleging that they were negligent for failing to provide a guard around the machine and for failing to place the emergency button closer to the machine. McQueeney and Temple–Inland moved for summary judgment. Both parties argued that because they are members of Standard Gypsum, they are also "employers" under the Texas Workers' Compensation Act, thus, immune from suit pursuant to the exclusive-remedy provision. As an alternative theory, Temple–Inland argued that, along with Standard Gypsum, it is Ingalls' "co-employer," because it had the right to control him at the time of the accident in accordance with the written Agreement. The trial court granted summary judgment in favor of both Temple–Inland and McQueeney.

Exclusive–Remedy Provision Of The Texas Workers' Compensation Act

Under the Texas Workers' Compensation Act, "[r]ecovery of workers' compensation benefits is the exclusive remedy of an employee covered by workers' compensation insurance coverage or a legal beneficiary against the *employer or an agent or employee of the employer* for the death of or a work-related injury sustained by the employee." Tex. Labor Code Ann. § 408.001(a) (Vernon 1996) (emphasis added). The Texas Workers' Compensation Act defines an employer as "a person who makes a contract of hire, employs one or more employees, and has workers' compensation insurance coverage." Id. § 401.011(18). While an employee cannot sue his employer, he can sue a "third party" for damages incurred as a result of "an injury or death that is compensable under this subtitle." Id. § 417.001. Ingalls argues that McQueeney and Temple–Inland are third parties under the Texas Workers' Compensation Act. McQueeney and Temple–Inland argue that they should be considered employers. . . .

Members of Limited Liability Companies

McQueeney and Temple–Inland argue that, as members of a limited liability company, they should be considered "employers" of Standard Gypsum's employees for purposes of workers' compensation. This is an issue of first impression. However, there are three cases which provide guidance: *Lawler v. Dallas–Statler–Hilton Joint Venture,* 793 S.W.2d 27 (Tex.App.-Dallas 1990, writ denied), *Sims v. Western Waste Indus.,* 918 S.W.2d 682 (Tex.App.-Beaumont 1996, writ denied), and *Alice Leasing Corp. v. Castillo,* 53 S.W.3d 433 (Tex.App.-San Antonio 2001, pet. denied).

Lawler and *Alice Leasing:* Joint Ventures and Partnerships

McQueeney and Temple–Inland rely substantially on *Lawler.* In *Lawler,* the plaintiff, a maid supervisor, was injured while working at the Dallas Hilton Hotel, for which she collected workers' compensation benefits. 793 S.W.2d at 28. The Dallas Hilton Hotel was owned by Dallas Statler Hilton Joint Venture. *Id.* The joint venture, in turn, was owned by Hilton Hotel Corp. and Prudential Insurance Co. *Id.* Under a lease and management agreement, the Hilton Hotel Corp. managed the hotel on behalf of the joint venture. *Id.* The plaintiff sued Hilton Hotel Corp., Prudential Insurance Co., and the joint venture for negligence. *Id.* All three claimed that they were immune from liability under the Texas Workers' Compensation Act as the plaintiff's "employers." The Fifth Court of Appeals likened a joint venture to a partnership and noted that where a partnership is an employer, the individual partner is also an employer and not an employee as contemplated by the Texas Workers' Compensation Act. *Id.* at 31. The court also noted that some states had applied the aggregate theory to partnerships, reasoning that the partnership is an association of persons who are viewed as co-owners. *Id.* at 34. Other states have adopted an entity theory, concluding that a partnership is an entity in itself rather than an aggregate of its members. *Id.* The distinction between the two theories is that under the aggregate theory, a plaintiff is barred from bringing an action against a partner where the partnership is the employer. *Id.* at 33. In contrast, under the entity theory, "the employee of a partnership is not an employee of an individual partner and can recover against such partner, as a third party, for negligent injury incident to employment." *Id.* (citation omitted). While the court observed that Texas appears to be predominantly an entity theory state, "there are still aggregate features" to the Uniform Partnership Act. *See id.* at 34 (noting that for example, the partnership act provides for joint and several liability). Thus, the court concluded,

> the better rule in cases involving claims by employees against employers is the majority rule that the individual partners or joint venturers are also employers of the partnership's or joint venturer's employees. Although in most other areas Texas is predominantly an entity theory state, it is not inconsistent with the [Uniform Partnership Act] or case law to apply the aggregate theory to the employment

relationship. Id.Furthermore, the court emphasized that its holding was consistent with the theory and practice of workers' compensation law. Id. . . .

Recently, however, we noted in *Alice Leasing Corp. v. Castillo,* that *Lawler* had been overruled by statute. 53 S.W.3d 433, 443 (Tex.App.-San Antonio 2001, pet. denied). We emphasized that since *Lawler* issued, the Legislature unequivocally embraced the entity theory of partnership law in 1993. *Id.* The Texas Revised Partnership Act defines a partnership as "an entity distinct from its partners." *Id.* Thus, we concluded that *Lawler* had been overruled by statute and "cannot support Alice Leasing's position that the aggregate theory should be applied here." *Id.* Therefore, even if we were to conclude that a limited liability company is comparable to a partnership or joint venture, Temple–Inland and McQueeney cannot rely on *Lawler*.

Sims: Parent Corporations and Their Subsidiaries

In *Sims v. Western Waste Industries,* the plaintiff was an employee of Western Waste Industries of Texas ("WWIT"), working as a "bumper" on a garbage truck, when he injured his leg. 918 S.W.2d 682, 683 (Tex.App.-Beaumont 1996, writ denied). He sued Western Waste Indus., Inc. ("WWI"), the parent corporation of his employer. *Id.* WWI was allegedly involved in the design, manufacture, and marketing of the truck involved in the plaintiff's accident. *Id.* WWI argued that it was the "alter ego" of WWIT, the "real" employer of the plaintiff, and was entitled to assert immunity under the Texas Workers' Compensation Act. *Id.* The Ninth Court of Appeals did not agree. It noted that parent and subsidiary corporations are separate and distinct legal entities. *Id.* at 684. If they were considered to be the same entity, "would an employee be an employee of all subsidiaries and parents and would everyone under the corporate 'umbrella' be immune from suit as a third party under [w]orkers' [c]ompensation?" *Id.* at 686. Nothing in the Texas Workers' Compensation Act indicates that this was the intent of the legislature. *Id.* . . . Ingalls relies heavily on *Sims,* arguing that the limited liability shield provided to members of an LLC is the key consideration for treating members of an LLC the same as parents of a corporation with regard to the exclusive-remedy provision. We agree.

Like the Texas Business Corporation Act, the Texas Limited Liability Company Act shields its members from liability. Article 4.03 of the Texas Limited Liability Company Act provides that "[e]xcept as and to the extent the regulations specifically provide otherwise, a member or manager is not liable for the debts, obligations or liabilities of a limited liability company including under a judgment decree, or order of a court." Tex.Rev.Civ. Stat. Ann. art. 1528n, § 4.03 (Vernon Supp.2001). Moreover, "[a] member of a limited liability company is not a proper party to proceedings by or against a limited liability company, except where the object is to enforce a member's right against or liability to the limited liability company." *Id.* § 4.03(C). In *Sims,* the court of appeals emphasized that the parent corporation could not argue that it was not liable for the actions of its subsidiary and then argue that it was the same entity for purposes of workers' compensation. 918 S.W.2d at 686. McQueeney and Temple–Inland are likewise arguing that while they benefit from limited liability under the Texas Limited Liability Company Act, they should be considered "employers" for purposes of workers' compensation. The key distinction in this case, however, is that the parent corporation in *Sims* was being sued for products liability, i.e. an independent tort. The parent corporation was not being sued solely because it was the owner of the subsidiary. Implicit in the *Sims* opinion is the requirement that the parent of the corporation commit some independent tort separate and apart from the employment relationship. Even Ingalls has conceded that a passive shareholder of a corporation should not be considered a "third party" under the Texas Workers' Compensation Act solely on the basis of being an "owner" of the corporation. As the trial court granted summary judgment solely on the basis of McQueeney being a member of an LLC without considering whether it had allegedly committed an independent tort, we reverse the trial court's judgment with respect to McQueeney and remand for further proceedings consistent with this opinion.

FORMATION

Filing of Certificate

A LLC is formed by filing a certificate of formation with the Secretary of State accompanied by a filing fee. The certificate of formation was known as the Articles of Organization under previous LLC legislation. The TBOC specifies a short list of information that must be included in the certificate. Unless a later effective date is specified in the certificate, the LLC's existence commences upon the filing of the certificate of formation by the Secretary of State, that is, after the Secretary receives and accepts the certificate executed and submitted by the organizer(s) of the LLC. TBOC §4.002

Members of the LLC may also enter into an oral or written company agreement. TBOC §101.052 The company agreement, formerly known as regulations in Texas and also known by such other names as the "operating agreement" or "Limited Liability Company Agreement" is analogous to a partnership agreement, corporate by-laws or shareholders' agreement. The existence of the company agreement is not required for the formation or operation of the LLC. Without question, members are better advised to have such an agreement, preferably in written form, to ensure that their objectives regarding the governance of internal affairs of the company are properly memorialized.

Subjects typically covered by a company agreement may include the process for admission of new members, required contribution by members, definition of classes of members or managers, voting rights, allocation of profits, losses and distributions, transfer of membership interests, and dissolution. Subjects covered may also be contained in the certificate of formation, as an alternative medium. Further, the references in the LLC statute to company agreement would include those provisions in the certificate of formation. TBOC § 101.051.

Because the company agreement is not a public document, LLC members, for privacy reasons, may prefer to keep the internal governance rules within that document instead of including them in the publicly-filed certificate of formation. In the event of a conflict between the provisions of the certificate of formation and the company agreement, the certificate of formation prevails. Generally, the provisions of the company agreement prevail over the TBOC subject to the limitations imposed by TBOC §101.054 and in TBOC § 101.052(d) ("The company agreement may contain any provisions for the regulation and management of the affairs of the limited liability company not inconsistent with law or the certificate of formation.").

While an LLC eventually is required to have at least one member, an LLC may be formed without any members. Thus, TBOC makes room for the formation of "shelf" LLCs.

Texas Business Organizations Code provisions

§ 3.001. Formation and Existence of Filing Entities

(a) Subject to the other provisions of this code, to form a filing entity, a certificate of formation complying with Sections 3.003, 3.004, and 3.005 must be filed in accordance with Chapter 4.

(b) The filing of a certificate of formation described by Subsection (a) may be included in a filing under Chapter 10.

(c) The existence of a filing entity commences when the filing of the certificate of formation takes effect as provided by Chapter 4.

(d) Except in a proceeding by the state to terminate the existence of a filing entity, an acknowledgment of the filing of a certificate of formation issued by the filing officer is conclusive evidence of:

(1) the formation and existence of the filing entity;

(2) the satisfaction of all conditions precedent to the formation of the filing entity; and

(3) the authority of the filing entity to transact business in this state.

§ 3.005. Certificate of Formation

(a) The certificate of formation must state:

(1) the name of the filing entity being formed;

(2) the type of filing entity being formed;

(3) for filing entities other than limited partnerships, the purpose or purposes for which the filing entity is formed, which may be stated to be or include any lawful purpose for that type of entity;

(4) for filing entities other than limited partnerships, the period of duration, if the entity is not formed to exist perpetually and is intended to have a specific period of duration;

(5) the street address of the initial registered office of the filing entity and the name of the initial registered agent of the filing entity at the office;

(6) the name and address of each:

(A) organizer for the filing entity, unless the entity is formed under a plan of conversion or merger;

(B) general partner, if the filing entity is a limited partnership; or

(C) trust manager, if the filing entity is a real estate investment trust;

(7) if the filing entity is formed under a plan of conversion or merger, a statement to that effect and, if formed under a plan of conversion, the name, address, date of formation, prior form of organization, and jurisdiction of formation of the converting entity; and

(8) any other information required by this code to be included in the certificate of formation for the filing entity.

(b) The certificate of formation may contain other provisions not inconsistent with law relating to the organization, ownership, governance, business, or affairs of the filing entity.

(c) Except as provided by Section 3.004, Chapter 4 governs the signing and filing of a certificate of formation for a domestic entity.

§ 3.010. Supplemental Provisions Required in Certificate of Formation of Limited Liability Company. *In addition to the information required by Section 3.005, the certificate of formation of a limited liability company must state:*

(1) whether the limited liability company will or will not have managers;

(2) if the limited liability company will have managers, the name and address of each initial manager of the limited liability company; and

(3) if the limited liability company will not have managers, the name and address of each initial member of the limited liability company.

§ 4.002. Action by Secretary of State

(a) If the secretary of state finds that a filing instrument delivered under Section 4.001 conforms to the provisions of this code that apply to the entity and to applicable rules adopted under Section 12.001 and that all required fees have been paid, the secretary of state shall:

(1) file the instrument by accepting it into the filing system adopted by the secretary of state and assigning the instrument a date of filing; and

(2) deliver a written acknowledgment of filing to the entity or its representative.

(b) If a duplicate copy of the filing instrument is delivered to the secretary of state, on accepting the filing instrument, the secretary of state shall return the duplicate copy, endorsed with the word "Filed" and the month, day, and year of filing, to the entity or its representative with the acknowledgment of filing.

§ 4.051. General Rule. *A filing instrument submitted to the secretary of state takes effect on filing, except as permitted by Section 4.052 or as provided by the provisions of this code that apply to the entity making the filing or other law.*

§ 4.052. Delayed Effectiveness of Certain Filings. *Except as provided by Section 4.058, a filing instrument may take effect after the time the instrument would otherwise take effect as provided by this code for the entity filing the instrument and:*

(1) at a specified date and time; or

(2) on the occurrence of a future event or fact, including an act of any person.

§ 101.051. Certain Provisions Contained in Certificate of Formation

(a) A provision that may be contained in the company agreement of a limited liability company may alternatively be included in the certificate of formation of the company as provided by Section 3.005(b).

(b) A reference in this title to the company agreement of a limited liability company includes any provision contained in the company's certificate of formation instead of the company agreement as provided by Subsection (a).

§ 101.001. Definitions

In this title:

(1) "Company agreement" means any agreement, written or oral, of the members concerning the affairs or the conduct of the business of a limited liability company. A company agreement of a limited liability company having only one member is not unenforceable because only one person is a party to the company agreement.

§ 101.052. Company Agreement

(a) Except as provided by Section 101.054, the company agreement of a limited liability company governs:

(1) the relations among members, managers, and officers of the company, assignees of membership interests in the company, and the company itself; and

(2) other internal affairs of the company.

(b) To the extent that the company agreement of a limited liability company does not otherwise provide, this title and the provisions of Title 1 applicable to a limited liability company govern the internal affairs of the company.

(c) Except as provided by Section 101.054, a provision of this title or Title 1 that is applicable to a limited liability company may be waived or modified in the company agreement of a limited liability company.

(d) The company agreement may contain any provisions for the regulation and management of the affairs of the limited liability company not inconsistent with law or the certificate of formation.

§ 101.053. Amendment of Company Agreement. The company agreement of a limited liability company may be amended only if each member of the company consents to the amendment.

Pinnacle Data Services, Inc. v. Gillen
104 S.W.3d 188 (Tex. App.-Texarkana 2003)

Pinnacle Data Services, Inc. (PDS) brought suit against Joseph Gillen, Charles Baldridge, and MJCM, L.L.C. (collectively referred to herein as GBM). PDS claimed GBM was guilty of unjust enrichment, member oppression, breach of contract, breach of fiduciary duty, breach of duty of loyalty, and civil conspiracy. PDS also claimed it was entitled to declaratory relief, as well as reformation. GBM filed a combination traditional and no-evidence motion for summary judgment, and the trial court granted the motion, dismissing all claims. On appeal, PDS brings the following points of error: (1) the trial court erred by granting summary judgment with respect to declaratory relief, member oppression, and unjust enrichment; and (2) the trial court erred by granting more relief than GBM requested in its motion for summary judgment.

In 1997 Max Horton, Morris Horton, Joseph Gillen, and Charles Baldridge formed MJCM, L.L.C. (herein MJCM). The parties agreed that Gillen and Baldridge would each own twenty-five percent of MJCM, and PDS would own the remaining fifty percent. The Regulations were signed by Gillen and Baldridge, individually, and by Max Horton, as president of PDS. The Articles of Organization (Articles) listed the original members as Gillen, Baldridge, and PDS. According to the Regulations and the Articles, MJCM was to be managed by its members. Further, the members agreed to receive payment in the form of profit distributions instead of salaries and bonuses. The distributions were made pursuant to the terms set forth in the Articles and Regulations.

However, as MJCM became more profitable, the members began to disagree over how the company should be managed. On August 29, 2000, the members convened for a meeting. At this meeting, Gillen proposed amendments to the Articles that would convert MJCM from member managed to manager managed, and Gillen would be named as manager. The Regulations provide that the Articles can only be amended by an affirmative vote of at least sixty-six and two-thirds percent of the ownership interest, while the Articles allow for their amendment by an affirmative vote of two-thirds of the members. The Regulations also provide that, to the extent the Regulations conflict with the Articles, the Articles control. Gillen and Baldridge voted to institute the proposed changes. After being named manager, Gillen relieved Max and Morris Horton of their duties with MJCM. Gillen also increased the number of employees and began paying himself and Baldridge salaries and bonuses. PDS brought suit, and the trial court granted summary judgment in favor of GBM, and PDS brings this appeal. . . .

Declaratory Relief

PDS claimed it was entitled to the following declaratory relief:

(a) the Regulations control over the Articles with respect to member voting powers and procedures;

(b) the Amended Articles adopted on August 29, 2000 are void and of no effect;

(c) Pinnacle is a member-managed company;

(d) the election of Gillen as manager on August 29, 2000 is void and of no effect; and

(e) any amendments to the Articles and Regulations since August 29, 2000 are void.

It is undisputed that a determination of whether the Articles or the Regulations control will dispose of each claim for declaratory relief. The dispute arises from a conflict in the voting procedures set forth in the Regulations and the Articles. The Regulations provide in pertinent part:

> At any meeting of Members, presence of Members entitled to cast at least sixty-six and two-thirds percent of the total votes of all Members entitled to vote at such meeting constitutes a quorum. Action on a matter is approved if the matter receives approval by at least sixty-six and two-thirds percent of the total number of votes entitled to be cast by all Members in the Company entitled to vote at such meeting or such greater number as may be required by law or the Articles for the particular matter under consideration.

On the other hand, the Articles provide:

> Approval of 2/3 of the members is needed for (1) amending the articles of organization or the regulations; (2) changing the status of the Company from one in which management is reserved to the members to one in which management is vested in one or more managers, or vice versa....

Therefore, if the Articles control, Gillen and Baldridge had the authority to amend the Articles and change the management structure of MJCM despite not having PDS's consent. Under the Texas Limited Liability Company Act (TLLCA), the regulations of a limited liability company "may contain any provisions for the regulation and management of the affairs of the limited liability company not inconsistent with law or the articles of organization." Tex.Rev.Civ. Stat. Ann. art. 1528n, § 2.09 (Vernon Supp.2003) (emphasis added). Further, the first page of the Regulations provides:

> These Regulations are subject to, and governed by, the Texas Limited Liability Company Act and the Articles [defined as the Articles of Organization]. In the event of a conflict between the provisions of these Regulations and the mandatory provisions of the Act or the provisions of the Articles, the provisions of the Act or the Articles control.

It is undisputed that Max Horton, as president of PDS, signed the Regulations, which included the above clause concerning conflict between the Articles and the Regulations. Further, Baldridge signed and filed the Articles with the Secretary of State on March 31, 1997, making them available to the public. Despite the express terms of the TLLCA and the Regulations, PDS asserted several arguments in support of its contention that the Regulations control, none of which are supported by law or evidence. For example, PDS contended that, because the

Regulations were signed by all parties, it constituted a contract, and under rules of contract interpretation, the Regulations control over the Articles. PDS cited no statutory or case law in support of this contention, and this Court has found none. In fact, such a holding would be in direct contradiction with the express language of the TLLCA and the Regulations. See Tex. Rev. Civ. Stat. Ann. art. 1528n, § 2.09.

PDS also contended it was not given a copy of the Articles until two years after the Regulations were signed, which made the Articles unenforceable. Again, PDS failed to cite authority for its contention. PDS has also failed to produce any evidence that it sought to obtain a copy of the Articles before that time, even though it signed Regulations that were expressly subordinate to the Articles. Further, the Articles were on file with the Secretary of State beginning March 31, 1997, and Max Horton admitted in his deposition that he kept a copy of the Articles in his desk. The terms set forth in the Regulations, Articles, and the TLLCA are not rendered inoperative because PDS failed to exercise diligence in obtaining a copy of the Articles before agreeing to their terms. See Frey v. DeCordova Bend Estates Owners Ass'n, 632 S.W.2d 877, 880 (Tex. App.Fort Worth 1982), aff'd, 647 S.W.2d 246 (Tex.1983) (courts will not interfere with corporation's right of internal management provided governing body does not substitute legislation for interpretation, overstep bounds of reason, common sense, or contravene public policy). Therefore, PDS has not raised a genuine issue of fact, and the trial court did not err by granting summary judgment with respect to its claim for declaratory relief.

Formation of Series LLC

An LLC may also choose to establish one or more "series." A series LLC makes it possible to segregate assets and liabilities within the LLC umbrella. Thus, under a series LLC structure, particular debts, liabilities, obligations, and expenses may only be enforced against the assets of a particular series, and not the LLC as a whole. To utilize this option, the certificate of formation of the LLC must contain a specified notice pertaining to the limitations on enforceability of such debts, liabilities, obligations, and expenses.

Texas Business Organization Code provisions

§ 101.601. Series of Members, Managers, Membership Interests, or Assets
(a) A company agreement may establish or provide for the establishment of one or more designated series of members, managers, membership interests, or assets that:

> *(1) has separate rights, powers, or duties with respect to specified property or obligations of the limited liability company or profits and losses associated with specified property or obligations; or*
> *(2) has a separate business purpose or investment objective.*

(b) A series established in accordance with Subsection (a) may carry on any business, purpose, or activity, whether or not for profit, that is not prohibited by Section 2.003.

§ 101.602. Enforceability of Obligations and Expenses of Series Against Assets

(a) Notwithstanding any other provision of this chapter or any other law, but subject to Subsection (b) and any other provision of this subchapter:

(1) the debts, liabilities, obligations, and expenses incurred, contracted for, or otherwise existing with respect to a particular series shall be enforceable against the assets of that series only, and shall not be enforceable against the assets of the limited liability company generally or any other series; and

(2) none of the debts, liabilities, obligations, and expenses incurred, contracted for, or otherwise existing with respect to the limited liability company generally or any other series shall be enforceable against the assets of a particular series.

(b) Subsection (a) applies only if:

(1) the records maintained for that particular series account for the assets associated with that series separately from the other assets of the company or any other series;

(2) the company agreement contains a statement to the effect of the limitations provided in Subsection (a); and

(3) the company's certificate of formation contains a notice of the limitations provided in Subsection (a).

§ 101.605. General Powers of Series.
A series established under this subchapter has the power and capacity, in the series' own name, to:

(1) sue and be sued;

(2) contract;

(3) hold title to assets of the series, including real property, personal property, and intangible property; and

(4) grant liens and security interests in assets of the series.

Pre-formation Contracts

Sometimes, business owners commence business activities prior to the filing of the certificate or while awaiting the response of the Secretary of State. It could be that they do not want to miss out on an attractive deal on an office lease or want to sign an employment contract with a highly-valued potential employee who is entertaining an offer from another place. In the corporate context, such contracts are known as promoter contracts or pre-incorporation contracts and the rules are fairly clear as to how to assign liability in the event of non- or inadequate performance of the contract. It appears that these rules of corporate law have been imported into the LLC context. Accordingly, an LLC organizer (promoter) who signs a contract before the LLC acquires legal existence will be personally liable on the contract. The organizer will be exonerated only if he indicated at the time of the contract that the LLC will be the sole obligor on the contract or if there is a subsequent novation. Where there are multiple organizer s, each organizer may be liable on contracts made by other organizer s prior to formation of the company as if the organizer s were partners. Since a pre-formation agreement may be enforced against a organizer, the organizer may also make a claim under the contract. The LLC will be liable if it adopts the contract. Adoption may be express or implied through conduct, such as acceptance of benefits under the contract. Upon adoption, LLC may also enforce the pre-organization contract. *See generally In re JNS Aviation, LLC*, 376 B.R. 500, 525 (Bankr. N.D. Tex. 2007) (applying corporate promoter principles in holding that an individual who entered into and signed a purchase agreement in the name of a nonexistent LLC was personally obligated under the contract and may also make a claim under it). The court in *JNS Aviation* also observed as follows: "Texas courts have held that "a promoter can be personally liable for entering into a contract for an unformed corporation," and "[b]ecause any enforceable agreement is mutual and binding on both parties. logic dictates a promoter who is liable under an agreement may also make a claim under such a contract." Fish v. Tandy Corp., 948 S.W.2d at 897."

Lentz Engineering, L.L.C. v. Brown,
No. 14-10-00610-CV, 2011 WL 4449655 (Tex. App. – Houston [14 Dist.], 2011)

Appellant Lentz Engineering, L.L.C. sued appellee Alden Brown for breach of contract and quantum meruit. Lentz claimed that Brown was liable as a partner in a general partnership with William Wilkins, who contracted for Lentz's services. After a bench trial, the court rendered a final judgment that Lentz take nothing from Brown. In three issues, Lentz argues that Brown judicially admitted he was a partner with Wilkins, and that the evidence is legally and factually insufficient to support the trial court's judgment. We affirm.

BACKGROUND

Wilkins approached Brown in late 2004 or early 2005 with a proposal to purchase and develop a 20–acre tract of land in Manvel, Texas. Wilkins entered into a contract with a third party in January 2005 to purchase the property. Brown and Wilkins met with an attorney in February and agreed to form a Texas limited liability company (LLC). Brown gave Wilkins $400,000 in March to purchase the property, and Wilkins acquired the property for himself on April 13, 2005. One day later, the attorney filed articles of organization for Manvel Villa Development, LLC, which identified Brown and Wilkins as managers. Brown and Wilkins also established a bank account for the LLC. Brown became suspicious of Wilkins's conduct during the summer and undertook efforts to recover his money and obtain title in the property. Meanwhile, Wilkins entered into a contract with Lentz in June 2005 for Lentz to provide engineering services related to the property. Lentz performed these services but did not turn over the work product because Lentz was never paid. Lentz sued Brown and Wilkins for breach of contract and quantum meruit, and Wilkins defaulted. After a bench trial, the court rendered judgment that Lentz take nothing from Brown. The court issued findings of fact and conclusions of law, specifically finding that (1) Brown and Wilkins agreed to establish the LLC for the purpose of owning and developing the property; (2) they never were general partners; and (3) Brown could not be personally liable for the contract between Lentz and Wilkins. Lentz appealed ....

Principles of Partnership and LLC Formation and Liability

A general partnership is an association of two or more persons to carry on a business for profit as owners, regardless of whether the persons intend to create a partnership or whether the association is actually called a "partnership." Tex. Bus. Orgs.Code Ann. § 152.051(b) (Vernon 2009). Factors indicating that persons have created a partnership include:

(1) receipt or right to receive a share of profits of the business;
(2) expression of an intent to be partners in the business;
(3) participation or right to participate in control of the business;
(4) agreement to share or sharing:
    (A) losses of the business; or
    (B) liability for claims by third parties against the business; and

(5) agreement to contribute or contributing money or property to the business.

Id. § 152.052(a). Whether a partnership exists depends on the totality of the circumstances. *Ingram v. Deere*, 288 S.W.3d 886, 903–04 (Tex.2009). Although conclusive evidence of all of these factors will establish the existence of a partnership as a matter of law, *id.* at 904, evidence of all of these factors is not required to show the existence of a partnership, *id.* at 896. The absence of evidence of all of the factors will preclude the finding of a partnership. *Id.* at 904. And even conclusive evidence of only one of the factors usually will be insufficient to show the existence of a partnership. *Id.* An association or organization is not a partnership if it was created under the statute governing the formation of LLCs. *See* Tex. Bus. Orgs.Code Ann. § 152.051(c). An LLC is formed when a certificate of formation is filed with the Secretary of the State of Texas. *See id.* §§ 1.002(22), 3.001(c), 4.051. Partners in a general partnership may be held personally liable for debts or obligations of the partnership. *See id.* § 152.304. But managers or members of an LLC generally may not be held personally liable for the debts or obligations of the company. *See id.* § 101.114.

II. Legal Sufficiency

When conducting a legal sufficiency review, we view the evidence in the light most favorable to the verdict and indulge every reasonable inference that would support it. *City of Keller v. Wilson*, 168 S.W.3d 802, 822 (Tex. 2005). We credit evidence favorable to the verdict if reasonable fact finders could and disregard contrary evidence unless reasonable fact finders could not. *Id.* at 827. When an appellant challenges the legal sufficiency of an adverse finding on an issue for which the appellant had the burden of proof, the appellant must demonstrate that the evidence conclusively establishes all vital facts in support of the issue. *Dow Chem. Co. v. Francis*, 46 S.W.3d 237, 241 (Tex. 2001); *TH Invs., Inc. v. Kirby Inland Marine, L.P.*, 218 S.W.3d 173, 189 (Tex.App.Houston [14th Dist.] 2007, pet. denied). The appellant must show that there is no evidence to support the fact finder's finding and that the evidence conclusively establishes the opposite of the finding. *See Dow,* 46 S.W.3d at 241 (citing *Sterner v. Marathon Oil Co.,* 767 S.W.2d 686, 690 (Tex.1989)); *TH Invs.,* 218 S.W.3d at 189–90. The ultimate test for legal sufficiency is whether the evidence would enable a reasonable and fair-minded fact finder to reach the verdict under review. *Wilson,* 168 S.W.3d at 827. Here, Lentz had the burden to establish the existence of a partnership. *See Valero Energy Corp. v. Teco Pipeline Co.,* 2 S.W.3d 576, 585 (Tex.App.-Houston [14th Dist.] 1999, no pet.); *Negrini v. Plus Two Adver., Inc.,* 695 S.W.2d 624, 631 (Tex.App.Houston [1st Dist.] 1985, no writ). Thus, Lentz must show on appeal that there is no evidence to support the trial court's finding and that all of the evidence conclusively establishes the existence of a partnership between Brown and Wilkins when Lentz and Wilkins entered into a contract. Lentz has not done so.

First, there is some evidence to support the trial court's finding of no partnership. Both parties expressed intent to form an LLC. Wilkins testified that he and Brown established an LLC "[f]or purposes of developing the Manvel property," "[c]ontinuing on with the project," and "to finish the project." The purpose of the meeting with an attorney in February 2005 was in part to establish the LLC. Brown testified that Wilkins recommended forming an LLC "as proper business protocol." Brown also testified, "[W]e never agreed to be partners in the first place. I mean, we—we were doing the project together. We weren't planning on doing this, you know, staying together as a partnership or anything like that." Wilkins testified he opened a bank account in the name of the LLC "to do the Manvel," and "[t]he account was to finish the project." The certificate of organization for the LLC became effective on April 14, 2005—before the date on which Lentz entered into a contract with Wilkins. Although there is some evidence pointing to the existence of a partnership, all of the evidence does not conclusively establish this fact.

There is uncontroverted evidence that Brown and Wilkins agreed to split profits from the development and sale of the property "50/50" after Brown recovered his initial investment costs. There also is uncontroverted evidence that Brown and Wilkins both participated or had a right to participate in control of the business: they testified that Wilkins initially was to do all of the legwork in connection with purchasing and developing the property, but Brown later sent a cease-and-desist letter to Wilkins claiming that all expenses had to be approved by Brown in writing. Further, there is evidence of Brown's expression of intent to be partners. But the evidence of intent is controverted, as discussed above, by Brown's testimony at trial and the formation of the LLC. In July 2005, Brown filed a sworn "declaration of ownership" in an attempt to have the property put in his name; he claimed a 50 percent ownership interest in the property and stated that he had "an agreement with William Wilkins to be partners in connection with the purchase, development and/or the sale of real estate." In a later suit against Wilkins to recover the property, Brown alleged that he and Wilkins "entered into a business partnership, where Brown agreed to entrust $605,000 to Wilkins for the acquisition of certain real estate."

Thus, we are left with uncontroverted evidence of only two of the factors: splitting profits and participating in control of the business. We conclude that the totality of the circumstances does not conclusively establish the existence of a partnership in this case. *Cf. Sysco Food Servs. of Austin, Inc. v. Miller,* No. 03–03–00078–CV, 2003 WL 21940009, at 3–4 (Tex.App.-Austin Aug. 14, 2003, no pet.) (mem.op.) (holding, prior to the totality-of-the-circumstances test, the appellant failed to conclusively establish the existence of a partnership and individual liability for the appellee; although there was some evidence of sharing profits and mutual control over the business, there was no evidence of sharing losses or appellee's authorization to be liable as a partner, and the appellant did not enter into a contract with the appellee's alleged partner until after the formation of an LLC and without any representation that the appellee was a general partner). Lentz also argues that the formation of an LLC does not displace a preexisting partnership, and that Brown and Wilkins's conduct before formation of the LLC established a partnership. For example, Lentz notes that Brown transferred money to Wilkins in March 2005 and Wilkins purchased the property shortly before the LLC was formed. Although courts have held promoters of a company may be liable on contracts made by other promoters prior to formation of the company as if the promoters were partners, Lentz has not cited any authority to suggest that liability should be imposed on one promoter because of another promoter's conduct *after* the formation of the company. *See Bank of De Soto v. Reed,* 50 Tex.Civ.App. 102, 109–10, 109 S.W. 256, 260 (1908, no writ) ("It is a general principle that *until a corporation is legally organized* the co-adventures will, as to third persons, be liable as partners for all debts contracted on behalf of the aggregated body with their consent, express or implied.") (emphasis added)). The mere fact that promoters of a company engage in conduct to further the company's formation and business does not per se establish a partnership under the Texas Business Organizations Code so that partner-like liability of promoters may be extended beyond the date of the company's formation.

****

Kahn v. Imperial Airport, L.P.,
308 S.W.3D 432 (Tex. App.—Dallas 2010, no pet.)

This appeal involves a commercial lease (the Lease) for a retail store selling adult novelty items under the name "Condom Sense" in Irving, Texas. Imperial Airport, LP (Imperial), the lessor, sued Steven Kahn, Condom Sense, Inc. (CSI), and M. Stack, LLC (M. Stack) for breach of the Lease. CSI and M. Stack counterclaimed, alleging Imperial had breached a pre-Lease agreement between Kahn and Imperial's leasing agent. The trial court's judgment found Kahn liable and awarded Imperial damages for breach of the Lease, attorney's fees, and interest. The judgment ordered that Imperial take nothing on its claims against CSI and M. Stack and that CSI and M. Stack take nothing on their breach-of-Lease counterclaim. Kahn appeals; Imperial cross-appeals. We affirm the trial court's judgment in part and reverse and remand it in part.

BACKGROUND

Imperial owned the leased premises; Bradford Management Company, Inc. managed the property for Imperial. Bradford employee Michael Brashears negotiated the Lease with Kahn. Kahn signed the Lease in July 2005. The Lease term began October 1, 2005 and extended for sixty-three months. The leased premises were to be occupied by a store under the name "Condom Sense." Kahn operated four stores under the same name in Dallas. During the negotiations, Brashears visited at least one of the Dallas stores. Thus, both parties knew the nature of the store that was to occupy the premises. At trial two different versions of the Lease were introduced into evidence. . . . Other than the date, the significant difference between the two signature blocks is Kahn's inclusion on his version of the handwritten phrase "DBA Condom Sense."

With Imperial's knowledge, Kahn applied for the store's certificate of occupancy himself. He did not disclose the nature of the business in his application. In December 2005, Kahn oversaw creation of M. Stack, a limited liability corporation [sic] that Kahn claims was to be the actual lessee. During this time period, Imperial finished out the premises to Kahn's specifications at a cost of $27,000. Rent was paid for the initial months of the Lease term by an entity named SB TAZ, LLC. The Irving Condom Sense store opened on February 9, 2006. The next day, the store was raided by the Irving police, who seized some, but not all, of the store's inventory. The City of Irving did not close the store down. However, Kahn, his mother Marcia Kahn, and M. Stack (collectively designated the Applicants by the City) entered into an Agreed Order with the City. The terms of that order required the store to cease sale of "items used in conjunction with sexual activity" and to change its name. In return, the Applicants would avoid prosecution. But despite the order, the store did not re-open, and after April 2006 no more rent payments were made. Imperial locked the lessee out, seized the remaining inventory, and attempted to re-let the premises. Imperial did not find a new tenant until August 2007.

Imperial sued Steven Kahn, CSI, and M. Stack for breach of the Lease. Imperial also made claims for misrepresentation against Kahn. CSI and M. Stack counterclaimed based on the seizure of the inventory. The case was tried to the court, and the trial court issued a lengthy set of findings of fact and conclusions of law. The court's judgment denied Imperial's claims against CSI and M. Stack. It ordered Kahn to pay Imperial the finish-out costs, leasing commissions incurred, attorneys' fees, interest, and costs. Finally, the judgment ordered Imperial to return the seized inventory. Kahn appeals. Imperial cross-appeals as to certain trial-court rulings involving Kahn and CSI. M. Stack is not a party to this appeal. . . .

BREACH OF LEASE

The parties' issues are rooted in the Lease at the most fundamental level. They disagree concerning the identity of the lessee, whether there was a breach of the Lease, and the appropriate measure of damages for any breach found. We address these issues in turn.

Identifying the Lessee

The trial court concluded Kahn breached the Lease and is individually liable as the lessee. Kahn's first four issues challenge these findings. Imperial's first cross-issue, on the other hand, argues CSI should be held liable as lessee jointly and severally along with Kahn.

Two Versions of the Lease

In his first issue, Kahn challenges the trial court's ruling admitting into evidence a version of the Lease that varied from the version introduced by Kahn. Kahn argues Imperial's version of the Lease was not properly admitted because it was proved up by an untimely filed business records affidavit. . . . Kahn makes no argument at all concerning any harm purportedly caused by the shortened time period between the filing date and the start of trial. Instead, Kahn's arguments are limited to the potential harm caused by admitting a version of the Lease that does not include any assertion Kahn was signing for a "DBA." We conclude the court's admission and examination of the second version of the Lease did not probably cause rendition of an improper judgment. . . .

Kahn's Individual Liability

In his third and fourth issues, Kahn challenges the trial court's findings that he entered into the Lease in his individual capacity and should be liable in that capacity. Kahn testified he signed the Lease on July 21, 2005 as Condom Sense's president. He testified he was not president of CSI on that date, but he did not know what entities he *was* president of on that date. Kahn claimed at trial that M. Stack was really the lessee under the Lease, although he acknowledged that "M. Stack" did not appear anywhere in the Lease. He agreed that M. Stack did not exist when the Lease was signed, or when the Certificate of Occupancy was signed, and that he had no authority to sign the Lease for M. Stack. Kahn testified it was his practice to have a DBA Condom Sense enter into a lease on behalf of an entity to be formed after "everything [is] resolved." If the landlord wanted the lease signed before formation, he testified, there would be an addendum to the lease. But Kahn testified no addendum was drafted in this case, and he had never notified anyone at Bradford that M. Stack was to be the lessee for the Irving store.

Kahn's arguments have no basis in law. Initially, an individual cannot sign for and bind a DBA entity. A DBA is no more than an assumed or trade name. And it is well-settled that a trade name has no legal existence. *See Davis v. Raney Auto Co.*, 249 S.W. 878, 878 (Tex.Civ.App.- Texarkana 1923, no writ) (trade name "has no actual or legal existence"). Thus, to the extent Kahn purported to sign the Lease on behalf of Condom Sense as a DBA, he bound only himself. Likewise, one cannot sign for and bind a legal entity that does not yet exist. Kahn argues he signed the Lease as a promoter for the later-created M. Stack. But when a promoter signs a contract on behalf of an unformed entity, he is personally liable on the contract unless there is an agreement with the contracting party that the promoter is not liable. *Fish v. Tandy Corp.*, 948 S.W.2d 886, 897 (Tex.App.-Fort Worth 1997, writ denied). Our record contains no evidence Imperial agreed not to hold Kahn liable. Moreover, the Lease was not made in the name of the unformed entity; there was conflicting testimony concerning whether Brashears knew Kahn was purporting to sign for an unformed entity; and no evidence was presented indicating M. Stack adopted the Lease after its formation. *See id.* We conclude that, under the facts of this case, Kahn is personally liable on the Lease.

---

1. Defective Formation

Entrepreneurs, courts, and scholars have long grappled with the problem of defects arising in the course or process of organizing a business. Promoters' or business organizers' failure to follow all the steps designated by statute for the valid existence of their business entity of choice exposes the owners of the putative, but officially non-existent, entity to personal liability for contractual obligations incurred in its name or torts committed in the course of its business. Other pertinent questions pertain to whether the "entity" can receive or make conveyances of property, maintain a suit or be sued in its own name, and whether investors will be able to rely on a lack of formal organization to avoid obligations to innocent third parties. In the older forms of business organization, the courts stepped in to remedy the problems occasioned by defective organization by cloaking the owners with limited liability that a proper organization traditionally affords and recognizing the validity of the contracts. This investiture has been accomplished through the doctrines of de facto corporation, corporation by estoppel, and analogous concepts in general and limited partnership law. Some states have also imported these concepts into the LLC context by recognizing the doctrines of de facto LLC and LLC by estoppel. A de facto LLC would exist where there is (1) a statute authorizing organization as an LLC in the state, (2) colorable compliance or good faith effort to comply with the statute, and (3) actual use or exercise of the powers and privileges of an LLC. An LLC by estoppel may arise where parties treat a business enterprise as a valid LLC even if no attempt at formal organization has been made. It is not certain that Texas courts will recognize these concepts as part of Texas law. *See generally* Emeka Duruigbo, *Avoiding a Limited Future for the De Facto LLC and LLC by Estoppel*, 12 U. PA. J. BUS. L. 1013 (2010).

GOVERNANCE

Management Structure

A hallmark of the LLC is the flexibility of management that LLC statutes provide to investors. The LLC offers two primary forms of management structure, namely member-management and manager-management. A Texas LLC is required to choose either manager-management or member-management at the time of formation. If the LLC selects manager management, the name and address of the manager must be included on the certificate or formation. An individual, corporation, partnership, or other entity may be designated as the manager. *See* TBOC § 1.002(69-b). The certificate must contain the names and addresses of the initial members, where members choose to manage the firm. Member management is analogous to the management structure of the general partnership. In a member managed LLC, members are invested with authority to govern the affairs of the business. Thus, the members are agents of the firm with actual or apparent authority to bind the LLC and incur obligations in contracts and torts. Where member management is selected, members make decisions using the general partnership style of per capita voting, i.e., the members have an equal vote on matters pertaining to the firm. Manager management is similar to the management structure of the corporation in which governance powers reside in the board of directors. A manager-managed LLC may have one manager or a group of managers who may constitute the board of managers. The LLC's manager may be a member or someone appointed from the outside the entity without any ownership stake in the firm. In a manager managed LLC, the manager is the agent of the firm and members have no agency authority to bind the firm. Investors may also choose a combination of these forms of management. For instance, they may opt for manager management but condition certain important decisions and actions on the approval of the members. Management in a member-managed LLC may also be concentrated in some of the members, instead of in all of them. In such a situation, the members not involved in management would possess apparent authority to bind the firm, while lacking the actual authority to do so. TBOC § 101.254. Regardless of the type of management structure adopted, an LLC could also have officers if it so desires. TBOC § 3.103. Officers may possess actual or apparent authority to bind the LLC.

Texas Business Organization Code provisions

§ 3.010. Supplemental Provisions Required in Certificate of Formation of Limited Liability Company. In addition to the information required by Section 3.005, the certificate of formation of a limited liability company must state:

> *(1) whether the limited liability company will or will not have managers;*
>
> *(2) if the limited liability company will have managers, the name and address of each initial manager of the limited liability company; and*
>
> *(3) if the limited liability company will not have managers, the name and address of each initial member of the limited liability company.*

§ 1.002. Definitions
In this code:

...(35)(A) "Governing authority" means a person or group of persons who are entitled to manage and direct the affairs of an entity under this code and the governing documents of the entity, except that if the governing documents of the entity or this code divide the authority to manage and direct the affairs of the entity among different persons or groups of persons according to different matters, "governing authority" means the person or group of persons entitled to manage and direct the affairs of the entity with respect to a matter under the governing documents of the entity or this code.

§ 101.251. Governing Authority. The governing authority of a limited liability company consists of:

> *(1) the managers of the company, if the company's certificate of formation states that the company will have one or more managers; or*

(2) the members of the company, if the company's certificate of formation states that the company will not have managers.

§ 101.252. Management by Governing Authority. The governing authority of a limited liability company shall manage the business and affairs of the company as provided by:

(1) the company agreement; and

(2) this title and the provisions of Title 1 applicable to a limited liability company to the extent that the company agreement does not provide for the management of the company.

§ 101.302. Number and Qualifications

(a) The managers of a limited liability company may consist of one or more persons.

(b) Except as provided by Subsection (c), the number of managers of a limited liability company consists of the number of initial managers listed in the company's certificate of formation.

(c) The number of managers of a limited liability company may be increased or decreased by amendment to, or as provided by, the company agreement, except that a decrease in the number of managers may not shorten the term of an incumbent manager.

(d) A manager of a limited liability company is not required to be a:

(1) resident of this state; or

(2) member of the company.

§ 101.254. Designation of Agents; Binding Acts

(a) Except as provided by this title and Title 1, each governing person of a limited liability company and each officer of a limited liability company vested with actual or apparent authority by the governing authority of the company is an agent of the company for purposes of carrying out the company's business.

(b) An act committed by an agent of a limited liability company described by Subsection (a) for the purpose of apparently carrying out the ordinary course of business of the company, including the execution of an instrument, document, mortgage, or conveyance in the name of the company, binds the company unless:

(1) the agent does not have actual authority to act for the company; and

(2) the person with whom the agent is dealing has knowledge of the agent's lack of actual authority.

(c) An act committed by an agent of a limited liability company described by Subsection (a) that is not apparently for carrying out the ordinary course of business of the company binds the company only if the act is authorized in accordance with this title.

§ 3.103. Officers

(a) Officers of a domestic entity may be elected or appointed in accordance with the governing documents of the entity or by the governing authority of the entity unless prohibited by the governing documents.

(b) An officer of an entity shall perform the duties in the management of the entity and has the authority as provided by the governing documents of the entity or the governing authority that elects or appoints the officer.

(c) A person may simultaneously hold any two or more offices of an entity unless prohibited by this code or the governing documents of the entity.

EZ Auto, L.L.C. v. H.M. JR. Auto Sales,
No. 04-01-00820-CV, 2002 WL 1758315 (Tex. App.—San Antonio 2002)
Opinion On Appellant's Motion For Rehearing

Appellant's motion for rehearing is denied. . . .

FACTUAL AND PROCEDURAL BACKGROUND

EZ is a limited liability company managed under the direction of its managers. Marks was named as the initial manager in EZ's articles of organization. HM is in the wholesale automobile business. Beginning in February of 1999, HM sold four vehicles to Marks. HM's principal, H .M. Adams, Jr. ("Adams"), testified that he checked with dealers regarding EZ's reputation and verified that EZ's license was "good." The license is required to enable a dealer to transfer title without paying sales tax. The first three vehicles were purchased using an envelope draft signed by Marks on behalf of EZ. In an envelope draft, the selling dealer places the title and other documents in an envelope and deposits them with his bank which forwards the envelope and its contents to the purchasing dealer's bank. The purchasing dealer verifies the accuracy and completeness of the documents and then orders his bank to pay the selling dealer for the draft. After the third draft was returned unopened and unpaid, Marks paid HM with a personal check, explaining that he was having problems with his account. Marks also paid HM for the fourth vehicle on April 19, 1999, with his personal check in the amount of $19,600; however, the title history revealed that the vehicle was sold to EZ which transferred title to a third party. When the check was returned for insufficient funds, HM sued EZ. HM subsequently received $15,000 in payment against the amount due.

Donald E. Kirkham testified that Marks had been removed as manager at a meeting in November of 1998. Although minutes were introduced reflecting a special meeting, the documents do not reflect that notice of the meeting was sent to all members. Kirkham testified that he did not cancel EZ's license or otherwise take any action to ensure that Marks was not using EZ's license number. Kirkham explained that EZ continued to use the license to sell its remaining inventory through auction. The trial court entered findings of fact and conclusions of law. The trial court found: (1) HM sold the fourth vehicle to EZ through Marks and the vehicle was assigned to EZ on the title certificate and references EZ's license number; (2) Marks explained that he was paying by personal check due to EZ's banking difficulties and the check was in essence a loan to EZ; and (3) Marks was named as the sole manager of EZ and was never removed as manager because EZ did not give proper notice of the special meeting at which it claimed Marks was terminated as manager. The trial court concluded that Marks had actual and apparent authority to act for EZ. Based on its findings of fact and conclusions of law, the trial court rendered judgment in favor of HM for the sum of $4,600 (the balance of the purchase price that was unpaid), $1,220.45 (interest paid by HM under its line of credit because the purchase price remained unpaid), plus prejudgment interest and attorney's fees. EZ was the only party to file a notice of appeal.

Sufficiency Of The Evidence

The question of agency is generally one of fact. *Bhalli v. Methodist Hosp.*, 896 S.W.2d 207, 210 (Tex. App. –Houston [1st Dist.] 1995, writ denied); *Ross v. Texas One Partnership,);* 806 S.W.2d 222 (Tex.1991); 796 S.W.2d 206, 209–10 (Tex. App. –Dallas 1990, *writ denied)..* The question only becomes one of law if the facts are established or undisputed. *Bhalli,* 896 S.W.2d at 210; *Ross,* 796 S.W.2d at 209–10. In this case, the facts were disputed; therefore, whether Marks had actual or apparent authority is a question of fact. The trial court found that Marks had actual and apparent authority. Although the trial court mislabeled this finding of fact as a conclusion of law, "the designation is not controlling and we may treat it as a finding of fact." *Ray v. Farmers State Bank of Hart,* 576 S.W.2d 607, 608 n. 1 (Tex.1979). . . . Absent actual or apparent authority, an agent may not bind a principal. *Suarez v. Jordan,* 35 S.W.3d 268, 272–73 (Tex.App.-Houston [14th Dist.] 2000, no pet.). Both actual and apparent authority are created through conduct of the principal directed either to the agent (actual authority) or to a third person (apparent authority). *Id.* Actual authority includes authority that the principal: (1) intentionally confers upon the agent; (2) intentionally allows the agent to believe he has; or (3) by want of ordinary care allows the agent to believe himself to possess. *See, e.g., Suarez,* 35 S.W.3d at 273; *Disney Enterprises, Inc. v. Esprit Finance, Inc.,* 981 S.W.2d 25, 30 (Tex.App.-San Antonio 1998, pet. dism'd w.o.j.); *Spring Garden 79U, Inc. v. Stewart Title Co.,* 874 S.W.2d 945, 948 (Tex.App.-Houston [1st Dist.] 1994, no writ); *Currey v. Lone Star Steel Co.,* 676 S.W.2d 205, 209 (Tex.App.-Fort Worth 1984, no writ).

Article 2.21 of the Texas Limited Liability Company Act ("Act") provides that each manager of a limited liability company whose management is vested in managers is an agent of the limited liability company for purposes of its business. TEX.REV.CIV. STAT. ANN.. art. 1528n, art. 2.21B (Vernon 1997). Any act of such a manager binds the limited liability company unless: (1) the manager lacks the authority to act for the limited liability company; and (2) the person with whom the manager is dealing has knowledge of the manager's lack of authority. *Id.* EZ's articles of organization vest management in its managers and provide that "[a]ny one manager may act on behalf of" EZ. Marks is named as the initial manager. EZ's regulations provide that a manager may only be removed at a meeting of the members called expressly for that purpose, and the regulations require notice be given to each member of any such meeting. The evidence in this case conclusively established that Marks was the initial manager of EZ, vesting him with actual authority. However, the question is whether Marks continued to have actual authority to act on behalf of EZ at the time of the transaction in question. Evidence was introduced to show that Marks had been removed as manager at a special meeting held on November 1, 1998. HM contends that the removal was invalid because notice of the meeting was not properly given, and the record supports the contention that notice of the meeting was not sent. EZ correctly asserts, however, that HM does not have standing to complain about the regularity of the notice. *Swain v. Wiley College,* 74 S.W.3d 143, 148 (Tex.App.-Texarkana 2002, no pet.); *Texlite, Inc. v. Wineburgh,* 373 S.W.2d 325, 328 (Tex.Civ.App.-Dallas 1963, writ ref'd n.r.e.). Because HM was not a member of EZ, it cannot collaterally attack the legality of the actions taken at the special meeting based on any informality or irregularity in the notice. *Swain,* 74 S.W.3d at 148; *Texlite,* 373 S.W.2d at 328.

Although HM does not have standing to complain directly about the regularity of the notice, the absence of notice still is important in determining whether Marks continued to have actual authority. Marks was a member of EZ, thus entitling him to notice of any meeting at which he would be removed as manager. Our record contains no evidence that the notice of the special meeting called to remove Marks as manager was sent to Marks. Because Marks did not receive notice of the special meeting, EZ was required to exercise ordinary care to dispossess Marks of the belief that he had authority to act after his removal. In its motion for rehearing, EZ relies on testimony by its attorney at trial as evidence that Marks received notice that he no longer had actual authority. Specifically, EZ relies on its attorney's testimony that: (1) a letter was sent certified and regular mail to Marks on November 2, 1998, notifying him of his removal; (2) Marks's attorney phoned EZ's attorney upon receipt of the letter; and (3) Marks was enjoined from being within 200 feet of EZ's location. However, the trial court sustained Marks's objections to the testimony regarding the phone call from Marks's attorney and the testimony regarding the injunction; therefore, that testimony was not admitted as evidence before the trial court and cannot be considered in our sufficiency review. Furthermore, the trial court sustained a best evidence objection with regard to the letter on the grounds that the letter was the best evidence. Although EZ's attorney later testified regarding the letter, and Marks's attorney failed to re-urge the best evidence objection, the letter still was not admitted as evidence.

Under a legal sufficiency review, we are required to disregard the testimony by EZ's attorney regarding the letter because it is contrary to the trial court's finding. *See Anderson,* 806 S.W.2d at 794. Under a factual sufficiency review, in the absence of the letter, we cannot conclude that the testimony by EZ's attorney makes the trial court's finding of actual authority "so against the great weight and preponderance of the evidence as to be clearly wrong and unjust." *See Ortiz,* 917 S.W.2d at 772. The trial court, as the trier of fact, could have disbelieved the testimony by EZ's attorney in the absence of evidence that the letter was sent and received, and the trial court is the sole judge of a witness's credibility. *See Rodriguez,* 63 S.W.3d at 480. In addition, the testimony by EZ's attorney is contrary to Kirkham's testimony that he never took any action to ensure that Marks did not continue to use EZ's license number and Kirkham's testimony that he told customers, who were having trouble obtaining titles to vehicles sold to them by EZ, that Marks "apparently had taken care of it" and that "apparently you [the customers] will get your license plates," which is some evidence that Kirkham continued to represent to customers that Marks had authority to take care of EZ's business. We conclude that the evidence is legally and factually sufficient to support the trial court's finding that Marks had actual authority to bind EZ. *See Suarez,* 35 S.W.3d at 273 (actual authority includes authority that the principal by want of ordinary care allows the agent to believe himself to possess). . . .

Conclusion

Actual authority includes the authority that the principal, by want of ordinary care, allows an agent to believe himself to possess. The evidence is legally and factually sufficient to support the trial court's finding of actual authority. Accordingly, the trial court's judgment is affirmed.

Decision-Making

Decisions are made at duly constituted meetings, with a majority of the decision-makers (members or managers as the case may be) constituting a quorum, unless the certificate of formation or company provides otherwise. Meetings may be held at a physical location or by conference telephone, similar communications equipment, or another suitable electronic communications system. TBOC § 6.001 and § 6.002. A written consent as a substitute for a meeting is permitted if signed by persons having at least the minimum number of votes that would be necessary to take the action at a meeting at which all persons entitled to vote on the matter were present and voted. Voting is done on a per capita basis, i.e. one person, one vote, which is the same approach under the general partnership. A number of matters require approval of a majority of the members or managers while another category of matters requires unanimous approval of the members if not otherwise provided by the company agreement or certificate of formation. For instance, a decision to wind-up the company requires a majority vote of the members. Approval of all members is needed for the admission of new members; issuance of membership interests; amendment of the company agreement; and a cancellation of an event requiring winding-up. In all other cases, binding decisions are made by a majority of members or managers as the act of a majority of the members or managers entitled to vote at a meeting where a quorum is present is the act of the governing authority or members, as appropriate. Members and managers may vote in person or by written proxies, although in the case of managers, voting by written proxy is permissible only if authorized by the company agreement or certificate of formation. It should be noted that members or managers are not restricted to the means of decision making specified in the statute, but may provide for any means of formal or informal decision making they desire.

Texas Business Organization Code provisions

§ 101.353. Quorum. A majority of all of the governing persons, members, or committee members of a limited liability company constitutes a quorum for the purpose of transacting business at a meeting of the governing authority, members, or committee of the company, as appropriate.

§ 101.354. Equal Voting Rights. Each governing person, member, or committee member of a limited liability company has an equal vote at a meeting of the governing authority, members, or committee of the company, as appropriate.

§ 101.355. **Act of Governing Authority, Members, or Committee.** Except as provided by this title or Title 1, the affirmative vote of the majority of the governing persons, members, or committee members of a limited liability company present at a meeting at which a quorum is present constitutes an act of the governing authority, members, or committee of the company, as appropriate.

§ 101.356. **Votes Required to Approve Certain Actions**

(a) Except as provided in this section or any other section in this title, an action of a limited liability company may be approved by the company's governing authority as provided by Section 101.355.

(b) Except as provided by Subsection (c), (d), or (e) or any other section in this title, an action of a limited liability company not apparently for carrying out the ordinary course of business of the company must be approved by the affirmative vote of the majority of all of the company's governing persons.

(c) Except as provided by Subsection (d) or (e) or any other section in this title, a fundamental business transaction of a limited liability company, or an action that would make it impossible for a limited liability company to carry out the ordinary business of the company, must be approved by the affirmative vote of the majority of all of the company's members.

(d) Except as provided by Subsection (e) or any other section of this title, the company's members must approve by an affirmative vote of all the members:

(1) an amendment to the certificate of formation of a limited liability company; or

(2) a restated certificate of formation that contains an amendment to the certificate of formation of a limited liability company.

(e) A requirement that an action of a limited liability company must be approved by the company's members does not apply during the period prescribed by Section 101.101(b).

§ 101.552. **Approval of Voluntary Winding Up, Revocation, Cancellation, or Reinstatement**

(a) A majority vote of all of the members of a limited liability company or, if the limited liability company has no members, a majority vote of all of the managers of the company is required to approve:

(1) a voluntary winding up of the company under Chapter 11;

(2) a revocation of a voluntary decision to wind up the company under Section 11.151; or

(3) a reinstatement of a terminated company under Section 11.202.

(b) The consent of all of the members of the limited liability company is required to approve a cancellation under Section 11.152 of an event requiring winding up specified in Section 11.051(1) or (3).

(c) An event requiring winding up specified in Section 11.056 may be canceled in accordance with Section 11.152(a) if the legal representative or successor of the last remaining member of the domestic limited liability company agrees to:

> *(1) cancel the event requiring winding up and continue the company; and*

> *(2) become a member of the company effective as of the date of termination of the membership of the last remaining member of the company, or designate another person who agrees to become a member of the company effective as of the date of the termination.*

§ 101.053. Amendment of Company Agreement. *The company agreement of a limited liability company may be amended only if each member of the company consents to the amendment.* [100%]

§ 101.105. Issuance of Membership Interests After Formation of Company. *A limited liability company, after the formation of the company, may:*

> *(1) issue membership interests in the company to any person with the approval of all of the members of the company; and* [100%]

> *(2) if the issuance of a membership interest requires the establishment of a new class or group of members or membership interests, establish a new class or group as provided by Sections 101.104(a)(2), (b), and (c).*

§ 101.357. Manner of Voting

> *(a) A member of a limited liability company may vote:*

>> *(1) in person; or*

>> *(2) by a proxy executed in writing by the member.*

> *(b) A manager or committee member of a limited liability company may vote:*

>> *(1) in person; or*

>> *(2) if authorized by the company agreement, by a proxy executed in writing by the manager or committee member, as appropriate.*

§ 101.358. Action by Less Than Unanimous Written Consent

> *(a) This section applies only to an action required or authorized to be taken at an annual or special meeting of the governing authority, the members, or a committee of the governing authority of a limited liability company under this title, Title 1, or the governing documents of the company.*

> *(b) Notwithstanding Sections 6.201 and 6.202, an action may be taken without holding a meeting, providing notice, or taking a vote if a written consent or consents stating the action to be taken is signed by the number of governing persons, members, or committee members of a limited liability company, as appropriate, necessary to have at least the minimum number of votes that would be necessary to take the action at a meeting at*

which each governing person, member, or committee member, as appropriate, entitled to vote on the action is present and votes.

§ 101.359. Effective Action by Members or Managers With or Without Meeting. Members or managers of a limited liability company may take action at a meeting of the members or managers or without a meeting in any manner permitted by this title, Title 1, or the governing documents of the company. Unless otherwise provided by the governing documents, an action is effective if it is taken:

(1) by an affirmative vote of those persons having at least the minimum number of votes that would be necessary to take the action at a meeting at which each member or manager, as appropriate, entitled to vote on the action is present and votes; or

(2) with the consent of each member of the limited liability company, which may be established by:

(A) the member's failure to object to the action in a timely manner, if the member has full knowledge of the action;

(B) consent to the action in writing signed by the member; or

(C) any other means reasonably evidencing consent.

§ 6.052. Waiver of Notice

(a) Notice of a meeting is not required to be given to an owner, member, or governing person of a domestic entity, or a member of a committee of the owners, members, or governing persons, entitled to notice under this code or the governing documents of the entity if the person entitled to notice signs a written waiver of notice of the meeting, regardless of whether the waiver is signed before or after the time of the meeting.

(b) If a person entitled to notice of a meeting participates in or attends the meeting, the person's participation or attendance constitutes a waiver of notice of the meeting unless the person participates in or attends the meeting solely to object to the transaction of business at the meeting on the ground that the meeting was not lawfully called or convened.

(c) Unless required by the certificate of formation or the governing documents, the business to be transacted at a meeting of the owners, members, or governing persons of a domestic entity, or the members of a committee of the governing persons, or the purpose of such a meeting, is not required to be specified in a written waiver of notice of the meeting.

(d) The participation or attendance at a meeting of a person entitled to notice of the meeting constitutes a waiver by the person of notice of a particular matter at the meeting that is not included in the purposes or business of the meeting described in the notice unless the person objects to considering the matter when it is presented.

Admission

Virtually any natural person, legal entity, association, government agency, or representative may be a member of an LLC. A person is admitted as a member of the LLC upon the later to occur of (i) the formation of the LLC or (ii) the time provided in and upon compliance with the company agreement, or if the company agreement does not so provide, when the person's admission is reflected in the records of the LLC. Once an LLC has been formed, a person may be admitted as a member after a vote of the current members or pursuant to the terms of the company agreement. A person may be admitted as a member of an LLC without making or being obligated to make a contribution to the LLC. A person may also become a member of an LLC without acquiring a membership interest in the company, so long as one or more persons own a membership interest in the LLC. Acquisition of a membership interest whether directly from the LLC or from an existing member does not automatically confer member status. The acquirer of the membership interest obtains economic rights and only becomes a member with the consent of all other members, unless the company agreement contains a contrary provision. This is different from a corporation, where acquisition of shares makes one a shareholder and co-owner of the corporation. In this sense, the LLC membership interest is similar to the economic interest in a partnership which entitles the acquirer to receive profits, losses, and distributions; not governance rights or member status.

Transfer of interests

A member is free to transfer, his membership interest in the LLC, in whole or in part, subject to any prohibitions and/or limitations stated in the LLC's operating agreement. The membership interest is an economic interest and consists of the financial rights to profits and losses and the right to participate in distributions. The assignment of a membership interest does not trigger the winding up of the company. Apart from a voluntary inter vivos transfer of the membership interest, one might also become an assignee as a result of the foreclosure of a security interest in the membership interest, or by virtue of the death or divorce of a member or a member's spouse. The assignee's rights include the right to allocation of the profits and losses of the business, the right to receive distributions to which the assignor would have been entitled, and the right to require reasonable information and to reasonably inspect the books and records of the LLC. A member who has assigned his membership interest does not cease to be a member merely by assigning the interest. Until the assignee becomes a member, the assignor member retains his status as a member and have all the associated rights and powers not assigned. An assignee of an interest in an LLC shall not be admitted as a member or have any right to participate in the management of the business and affairs of the LLC, except upon either the approval of all members of the LLC or under the terms of the operating agreement. In other words, a member's full ownership interest, including governance rights (such as the right to vote for the admission of new members), can only be transferred with the consent of all members. In this regard, the LLC mirrors the general partnership, limited partnership, limited liability partnership, and limited liability limited partnership. Obviously, this is a default rule and may be modified by agreement of the members. The company agreement may also set the parameters for the transfer of a membership interest. The TBOC offers no specific guidance on this issue, but it is likely the courts would uphold such restrictions.

Texas Business Organization Code provisions

§ 101.102. Qualification for Membership

(a) A person may be a member of or acquire a membership interest in a limited liability company unless the person lacks capacity apart from this code.

(b) A person is not required, as a condition to becoming a member of or acquiring a membership interest in a limited liability company, to:

> (1) make a contribution to the company;
>
> (2) otherwise pay cash or transfer property to the company; or
>
> (3) assume an obligation to make a contribution or otherwise pay cash or transfer property to the company.

(c) If one or more persons own a membership interest in a limited liability company, the company agreement may provide for a person to be admitted to the company as a member without acquiring a membership interest in the company.

§ 101.103. Effective Date of Membership

(a) In connection with the formation of a company, a person becomes a member of the company on the date the company is formed if the person is named as an initial member in the company's certificate of formation.

(b) In connection with the formation of a company, a person being admitted as a member of the company but not named as an initial member in the company's certificate of formation becomes a member of the company on the latest of:

> (1) the date the company is formed;
>
> (2) the date stated in the company's records as the date the person becomes a member of the company; or
>
> (3) if the company's records do not state a date described by Subdivision (2), the date the person's admission to the company is first reflected in the company's records.

(c) A person who, after the formation of a limited liability company, acquires directly or is assigned a membership interest in the company or is admitted as a member of the company without acquiring a membership interest becomes a member of the company on approval or consent of all of the company's members.

§ 101.105. Issuance of Membership Interests After Formation of Company.

A limited liability company, after the formation of the company, may:

> (1) issue membership interests in the company to any person with the approval of all of the members of the company; and

(2) if the issuance of a membership interest requires the establishment of a new class or group of members or membership interests, establish a new class or group as provided by Sections 101.104(a)(2), (b), and (c).

§ 1.002. Definitions. (54) *"Membership interest"* means a member's interest in an entity. With respect to a limited liability company, the term includes a member's share of profits and losses or similar items and the right to receive distributions, but does not include a member's right to participate in management.

§ 101.106. Nature of Membership Interest

(a) A membership interest in a limited liability company is personal property.

(a-1) A membership interest may be community property under applicable law.

(a-2) A member's right to participate in the management and conduct of the business of the limited liability company is not community property.

(b) A member of a limited liability company or an assignee of a membership interest in a limited liability company does not have an interest in any specific property of the company.

(c) Sections 9.406 and 9.408, Business & Commerce Code, do not apply to a membership interest in a limited liability company, including the rights, powers, and interests arising under the company's certificate of formation or company agreement or under this code. To the extent of any conflict between this subsection and Section 9.406 or 9.408, Business & Commerce Code, this subsection controls. It is the express intent of this subsection to permit the enforcement, as a contract among the members of a limited liability company, of any provision of a company agreement that would otherwise be ineffective under Section 9.406 or 9.408, Business & Commerce Code.

§ 101.108. Assignment of Membership Interest

(a) A membership interest in a limited liability company may be wholly or partly assigned.

(b) An assignment of a membership interest in a limited liability company:

(1) is not an event requiring the winding up of the company; and

(2) does not entitle the assignee to:

(A) participate in the management and affairs of the company;

(B) become a member of the company; or

(C) exercise any rights of a member of the company.

§ 101.109. Rights and Duties of Assignee of Membership Interest Before Membership

(a) A person who is assigned a membership interest in a limited liability company is entitled to:

(1) receive any allocation of income, gain, loss, deduction, credit, or a similar item that the assignor is entitled to receive to the extent the allocation of the item is assigned;

(2) receive any distribution the assignor is entitled to receive to the extent the distribution is assigned;

(3) require, for any proper purpose, reasonable information or a reasonable account of the transactions of the company; and

(4) make, for any proper purpose, reasonable inspections of the books and records of the company.

(b) An assignee of a membership interest in a limited liability company is entitled to become a member of the company on the approval of all of the company's members.

(c) An assignee of a membership interest in a limited liability company is not liable as a member of the company until the assignee becomes a member of the company.

§ 101.110. Rights and Liabilities of Assignee of Membership Interest After Becoming Member

(a) An assignee of a membership interest in a limited liability company, after becoming a member of the company, is:

(1) entitled, to the extent assigned, to the same rights and powers granted or provided to a member of the company by the company agreement or this code;

(2) subject to the same restrictions and liabilities placed or imposed on a member of the company by the company agreement or this code; and

(3) except as provided by Subsection (b), liable for the assignor's obligation to make contributions to the company.

(b) An assignee of a membership interest in a limited liability company, after becoming a member of the company, is not obligated for a liability of the assignor that:

(1) the assignee did not have knowledge of on the date the assignee became a member of the company; and

(2) could not be ascertained from the company agreement.

§ 101.111. Rights and Duties of Assignor of Membership Interest

(a) An assignor of a membership interest in a limited liability company continues to be a member of the company and is entitled to exercise any unassigned rights or powers of a member of the company until the assignee becomes a member of the company.

(b) An assignor of a membership interest in a limited liability company is not released from the assignor's liability to the company, regardless of whether the assignee of the membership interest becomes a member of the company.

§ 101.1115. Effect of Death or Divorce on Membership Interest

(a) For purposes of this code:

(1) on the divorce of a member, the member's spouse, to the extent of the spouse's membership interest, if any, is an assignee of the membership interest;

(2) on the death of a member, the member's surviving spouse, if any, and an heir, devisee, personal representative, or other successor of the member, to the extent of their respective membership interest, are assignees of the membership interest; and

(3) on the death of a member's spouse, an heir, devisee, personal representative, or other successor of the spouse, other than the member, to the extent of their respective membership interest, if any, is an assignee of the membership interest.

(b) This chapter does not impair an agreement for the purchase or sale of a membership interest at any time, including on the death or divorce of an owner of the membership interest.

Membership Interest and Admission of Members

Faulkner v. Kornman
No. 10-301, 2012 WL 1066736 1 (Bankr. S.D. Tex. 2012)

Factual Background

Dennis S. Faulkner, Trustee of the Heritage Creditor's Trust (the "Trustee"), registered in the Southern District of Texas a final judgment issued by the Bankruptcy Court of the Northern District of Texas in Adv. Pro. No. 06–03377–bjh. The matter was referred by the District Court to this Court. This Court issued an Order for Turnover Relief and Appointment of Receiver ("Original Turnover Order") on September 16, 2010. (ECF No. 165). The Original Turnover Order required Gary M. Kornman, Steadfast Investments, L.P., GMK Family Holdings, L.L.C., Tikchick Investment Partnership, L.P., Ettman Family Trust I, Strategic Leasing, L.P., Vehicle Leasing, L.L.C., Executive Air Crews, L.L.C., Executive Aircraft Management, L.L.C., Valiant Leasing, L.L.C., The Heritage Organization Agency, Inc., Heritage Properties, L.L.C., and Financial Marketing Services, Inc. (collectively, the "Judgment Debtors") to turnover, among other things, all nonexempt property to Jeff Mims as permanent Receiver (the "Receiver"). (ECF No. 165). Thereafter, Kornman executed a Conveyance of Interest to the Receiver on behalf of himself and all Judgment Debtors. (ECF No. 537–5). The Conveyance of Interest stated that "each of the Judgment Debtors does hereby turn over, transfer, assign, and convey unto Jeff Mims, the appointed Permanent Receiver, any and all of his or its right, title, and interest in and to any property that are described in the attached Exhibits which were filed by the Judgment Debtors...." (ECF No. 537–5). In an effort to enforce the registered final judgment, the Trustee identified certain financial accounts, called Flex–Funds, owned by entities who are not Judgment Debtors. Although these entities themselves are not Judgment Debtors, many of the Judgment Debtors owned these entities outright or owned a significant interest in them (and those transferred interests are now owned by the Receiver after the Conveyance). The Receiver's ownership interest in these entities ranges from quite small to 100%. The Trustee filed a Motion to Compel Turnover of the Flex–Funds Accounts owned by these non-Judgment Debtor entities. (ECF No. 537, 634). A hearing was held on March 7, 2012, at which the Court made several rulings. The Court declined to hold that the Receiver, even if he owned 100% of an entity and had sole control over it, was entitled to use a Flex–Fund Account to satisfy a judgment. That entity, for example, may have creditors who would be first entitled to the Flex–Fund Account. The Court did, however, determine those entities in which the Receiver has a 100% ownership interest and those entities over which the Receiver has sole control. A series of rulings were made in open court, mostly without objection from the parties.

Analysis

Kornman objected to the first three series of rulings by this Court. (ECF No. 666 at 39). These three rulings comprised the first three bullet points of the Order issued after the hearing. (ECF No. 660). Kornman acquiesced to the remaining rulings. (ECF No. 666 at 39). The remaining rulings comprised the last five bullet points of the Order issued after the hearing. (ECF No. 660). This Memorandum Opinion addresses the contested rulings.

Eagle View Capital Management LLC a/k/a Flagstone Management LLC

The Court ruled that: (i) the Receiver owns 100% of Eagle View Capital Management LLC ("EVCM LLC"); and (ii) that the Receiver is the sole member and may exercise control of EVCM LLC. Kornman stipulated that the Receiver owns 100% of the membership interest in EVCM LLC. Only the second portion of this ruling is contested. Prior to the Conveyance of Interest to the Receiver, there were two members of EVCM LLC: (i) Kornman, who owned 95%, and (ii) Eagle View Capital Management, Inc., who was the managing member and owned the remaining 5%. (ECF No. 634–3). These interests were assigned to the Receiver by the Conveyance of Interest. The Receiver, even as an assignee of 100% of the membership interest may not automatically become a member. TEX. BUS. ORG.CODE § 101.108(b)(2)(B). "An assignee of a membership interest in a limited liability company is entitled to become a member of the company on the approval of all of the company's members." TEX. BUS. ORG.CODE § 101.109(b). Kornman did not merely assign his 95% membership interest in EVCM LLC. Kornman assigned all of his rights as a member of the EVCM LLC. (ECF No. 537–5). That the Texas Business Organizations Code recognizes such a distinction is ascertained from the text of § 101.111(a): "An assignor of a membership interest in a limited liability company continues to be a member of the company and is *entitled to exercise any unassigned rights or powers of a member of the company* until the assignee becomes a member of the company." TEX. BUS. ORG.CODE § 101.111(a) (emphasis added). Kornman assigned all of his rights as a member, including the ability to approve the admission of new members. This is in addition to, and separate from, the assignment of his membership interest.

The only other member was Eagle View Capital Management, Inc. Kornman was the 100% shareholder of this corporation, but assigned all his interest to the Receiver. (ECF No. 537–5). The Receiver, as the 100% shareholder, is entitled to control the actions of the corporation, either directly or through the company's board. As the sole shareholder, the Receiver could declare his control through a shareholders' agreement that "eliminates the board of directors and authorizes the business and affairs of the corporation to be managed, wholly or partly, by one or more of its shareholders...." TEX BUS. ORG.CODE § 21.101(a)(2). The Receiver may manage the business and affairs of Eagle View Capital Management, Inc. The Receiver owns 100% of the membership interest in EVCM LLC. Of the two members of EVCM LLC, one (Kornman) is no longer entitled to object to the admission of the Receiver as a member and his approval need not be sought. The other member (Eagle View Capital Management, Inc.) is 100% owned by the Receiver, who is entitled to manage its business and affairs. The Receiver, on behalf of Eagle View Capital Management, Inc., may approve the admission of himself as a member of EVCM LLC. The Receiver may exercise control over EVCM LLC. In addition to being its 100% sole owner, the Receiver manages the business and affairs of both of EVCM LLC's members (his own and those of Eagle View Capital Management, Inc.).

The Court's March 7, 2012, Order will be amended to reflect that the Receiver is the "sole owner" rather than the "sole member" of EVCM LLC. In fact, the Receiver and Eagle View Capital Management, Inc. are both members.

****

Interest Transfer Restrictions

Ramco Oil & Gas LTD. v. Anglo–Dutch (Tenge) L.L.C.
207 S.W.3d 801 (Tex. App.—Houston [14th Dist.] 2006)

This case arises out of a business dispute over interests in a foreign oil and gas field. After a lengthy trial involving complicated facts and extensive expert testimony, the trial court rendered judgment on the jury's verdict, awarding plaintiffs/appellees/cross-appellants $6.4 million in lost profits, plus attorney's fees and interest, based on their breach-of-contract claims against defendants/appellants/cross-appellees. The main issue on appeal is whether the evidence proves with reasonable certainty the profits appellees claim to have lost as a result of appellants' breaches of contract. We conclude that it does not. We also conclude that the trial court correctly granted summary judgment as to appellees' claims for breach of fiduciary duty, misappropriation, and misappropriation of trade secrets. Accordingly, we reverse the trial court's judgment and render judgment that appellees take nothing against appellants.

I. OVERVIEW

Scott Van Dyke repeatedly tried without success to realize his "dream and business plan" by purchasing the equity of a company with development rights in a potentially lucrative oil and gas field in Kazakhstan, so that he could try to profitably develop this field. After learning that another company had acquired these development rights, Van Dyke concluded that the purchaser acquired these rights by using confidential information obtained in violation of confidentiality agreements. Van Dyke's companies filed suit against the companies he believed had breached these agreements and misappropriated confidential information and trade secrets.

I. FACTUAL AND PROCEDURAL BACKGROUND

In 1992, Van Dyke and appellee/cross-appellant Anglo–Dutch Petroleum International, Inc. (hereinafter "AD International"), a Texas corporation in which he was a principal, became involved in a group of companies that sought to identify, evaluate, and determine the feasibility of oil and gas opportunities in the former Soviet Union. Sugarland Oil Company, a Delaware corporation, was also a member of this group. The group purchased geological and geophysical data on a field in Kazakhstan known as the Tenge Field. The Soviet Union had produced gas from shallow horizons in the Tenge Field, and this data showed potential oil horizons beneath the gas. After deciding that the possibilities in the Tenge Field were worth pursuing, appellee/cross-appellant Anglo–Dutch (Tenge) L.L.C. (hereinafter "AD Tenge"), a company in which Van Dyke owned a ninety-percent interest, formed a Delaware limited liability company named Tenge Development L.L.C. (hereinafter "Tenge Development"). Sugarland (Kazakhtenge) L.L.C. (hereinafter "Sugarland"), a Delaware company, also owned an interest in Tenge Development. Tenge Development, in turn, was a member of Anglo–Dutch (Kazakhtenge) L.L.C. (hereinafter "Kazakhtenge"), a Texas limited liability company. Later, N.I.R. Tenge L.P. (hereinafter the "Israeli Company"), an Israeli limited partnership, and Overseas Petroleum and Investment Corporation (hereinafter the "Taiwanese Company"), a Panamanian corporation affiliated with the government of Taiwan, both provided capital and became members of Kazakhtenge. At all material times, Tenge Development served as the administrative member of Kazakhtenge. Although Van Dyke's company AD Tenge was the administrative member of Tenge Development and thus effectively the administrative member of Kazakhtenge until May 1996, neither Van Dyke nor any of his companies owned or controlled a majority interest in Tenge Development or Kazakhtenge at any material time. Lacking this ownership and control, Van Dyke and his companies, on various occasions, attempted unsuccessfully to acquire all of the interests in Tenge Development and Kazakhtenge

In November 1993, Kazakhtenge and Mangistaumunaygaz Production Association (hereinafter the "Gas Production Association"), a Kazakhstani association affiliated with the Kazakhstan government, entered into a Foundation Agreement regarding the creation of the Tenge Joint Enterprise (the "Joint Enterprise"), a Kazakhstani joint enterprise. Under this Foundation Agreement, which had a term of twenty-five years, each party owned a fifty-percent interest . . . . The purpose of the Joint Enterprise was to develop the Tenge Field. The Foundation Agreement and the Charter creating the Joint Enterprise allowed the Joint Enterprise to develop and sell hydrocarbons produced from the Tenge Field. In May 1997, appellant/cross-appellee Ramco Energy PLC (hereinafter "Ramco Energy"), a Scottish company, signed a confidentiality agreement with Anglo–Dutch (Neftenge) L.L.C. (hereinafter "AD Neftenge") and examined the possibility of becoming involved in the development of the Tenge Field. In June 1997, Ramco Energy decided not to pursue this matter. Three months later, in August 1997, appellant/cross-appellee Ramco Oil & Gas, Ltd. (hereinafter "Ramco Oil"), a Scottish company, learned that Halliburton Energy Services, Inc. (hereinafter "Halliburton") was reviewing the Tenge Field prospect. Having worked with Halliburton in developing other opportunities in Central Asia, Ramco Oil decided to examine the possibility of becoming involved in the development of the Tenge Field with Halliburton. Ramco Oil and Halliburton signed an agreement delineating the terms of their relationship.

On November 26, 1997, Ramco Oil and Halliburton entered into a Letter of Intent with AD Tenge and Anglo–Dutch (Jersey) Limited (hereinafter "AD Jersey"), a Channel Islands company, detailing, among other things, an approach to purchasing interests in Tenge Development and Kazakhtenge. The Letter of Intent was subject to many conditions, including approvals of executive management and, if necessary, Ramco Oil's and Halliburton's boards of directors. The Letter of Intent incorporated the terms of the May 1997 confidentiality agreement signed by Ramco Energy and stated that the terms of this agreement shall apply *mutatis mutandis* ("all necessary changes having been made"), as if Ramco Oil had entered into the same agreement with AD Tenge. Pursuing development of the Tenge Field necessarily would require interface and dealings with the government of Kazakhstan. To obtain expertise and assistance in this regard, Ramco Oil and Halliburton retained as a consultant Golden Eagle Partners ("Golden Eagle"), which had experience in communications and relations with the Kazakhstan government. For business reasons unrelated to the Tenge Field, Halliburton formally withdrew from the Letter of Intent in July 1998. Ramco Oil withdrew as well in November 1998. AD Tenge and AD International (hereinafter collectively referred to as "Plaintiffs") and Van Dyke continued to seek to purchase the interests of the Tenge Development and Kazakhtenge members not affiliated with Plaintiffs. Golden Eagle and Central Asia Industrial Investments, N.V. (hereinafter "Central Asia"), a Netherlands Antilles company, also negotiated with the Tenge Development and Kazakhtenge members. On March 8, 2000, Kazakhtenge entered into a purchase agreement with Central Asia, under which it agreed to sell Central Asia all of the shares in a company to which Kazakhtenge would transfer all of its interest in the Joint Enterprise. Central Asia paid $2 million in cash at the closing of this purchase and agreed to future payments conditioned on future production. Plaintiffs filed this suit against Halliburton, Ramco Energy, Ramco Oil, and others, alleging breach of contract and various torts. Plaintiffs claimed that, in breach of their obligations to keep the information about the Tenge Field confidential, Halliburton, Ramco Energy, and Ramco Oil disclosed confidential information concerning the Tenge Field to Golden Eagle, which Golden Eagle and Central Asia then used for their own benefit. . . .

Tenge Development's Approval as a Prerequisite to Plaintiffs' Purchase of the Kazakhtenge Interest

In arguing that the evidence of lost profits is speculative and not reasonably certain, the Ramco Parties assert that, even if Central Asia had not purchased Kazakhtenge's interest in the Joint Enterprise, Tenge Development would not have approved Plaintiffs' purchase of any member's interest in Kazakhtenge. Plaintiffs argue that Tenge Development's approval was not necessary. Therefore, we examine whether Plaintiffs needed Tenge Development's approval.

First, we note that [Plaintiffs' expert John] Brickhill was inconsistent as to whose interest in Kazakhtenge the Plaintiffs would have needed to purchase. On direct examination, Brickhill testified that Plaintiffs' damage model was based on Plaintiffs' owning all of Kazakhtenge's equity. He projected that, to accomplish this acquisition of interests, Plaintiffs would purchase the interests of the "old investors" in Kazakhtenge. Although the only entity Brickhill mentioned by name as an "old investor" was the Taiwanese Company, Brickhill's calculations were based on Plaintiffs' owning all of the equity, meaning Plaintiffs would have had to acquire both the Taiwanese Company's and Tenge Development's interests in Kazakhtenge.

Tenge Development's approval obviously would have been required to purchase its interest; however, on redirect examination, Brickhill testified that part of Van Dyke's "dream and business plan" was to obtain control of Kazakhtenge by purchasing only the Taiwanese Company's interest in Kazakhtenge. Although Brickhill did not change his damage model to allow for payments of profits to Tenge Development as a continuing member of Kazakhtenge, Brickhill asserted on redirect examination that the Taiwanese Company was the only "old investor" whose interest Plaintiffs needed to acquire to obtain control over Kazakhtenge. Brickhill indicated that Plaintiffs could have obtained approval of their purchase of the Taiwanese Company's 66.5% interest by having the Taiwanese Company cast a majority vote in favor of the purchase. To evaluate this part of Brickhill's testimony regarding the purchase of only the Taiwanese Company's interest, we first determine whether Plaintiffs needed Tenge Development's approval to buy only the Taiwanese Company's interest in Kazakhtenge. The unambiguous language of the Kazakhtenge Regulations shows that Tenge Development's approval would have been required because unanimous approval of all Kazakhtenge members is necessary for the assignment of any or all of a member's interest:

11.01 Requirements Applicable to Assignment

> No assignment of all or any portion of a Member's Interest, other than those provided for in Section 4.05, shall be valid or permitted unless approved by a unanimous vote of the other Members. No assignee of any Interest of a Member shall have any rights in and under the Regulations, the Foundation Agreement and Charter, or the Tenge Field unless or until such assignment is approved and such assignee expressly undertakes in writing, in a form satisfactory to all of the non-assigning Members, to perform the obligations of the assignor, and provides any parent guarantees or other assurances, plus reimbursement of any transactional costs as all of the non-assigning Members may determine to be necessary.

Because section 4.05 would not have applied, under section 11.01 of the Kazakhtenge Regulations, Plaintiffs would have needed Tenge Development's approval before purchasing the Taiwanese Company's interest in Kazakhtenge. When confronted with the Kazakhtenge Regulations, Brickhill admitted that section 11.01 requires members' unanimous approval for assignments of interests in Kazakhtenge. However, Brickhill later testified that he believed Plaintiffs could have acquired the Taiwanese Company's interest without Tenge Development's approval by having the Taiwanese Company (1) assign all of its rights to Kazakhtenge distributions to Plaintiffs under section 11.02 of the Kazakhtenge Regulations and (2) agree to always cast its vote in Kazakhtenge matters as directed by Plaintiffs. Section 11.02 of the Kazakhtenge Regulations reads, in pertinent part, as follows:

11.02 Assignment of Rights to Distributions and Mortgage of Interest

> A Member may assign all or a portion of its rights to Distributions, and may mortgage, pledge or otherwise encumber all or part of its Interest, without having first to obtain any approvals from the other Members, provided that: (i) such Member shall continue to exercise control of the vote associated with its Interest and shall remain liable for all obligations relating to such Interest ...

Under the unambiguous language of the Kazakhtenge Regulations, the Taiwanese Company and Plaintiffs, as a matter of law, could not have used section 11.02 to avoid the need for Tenge Development's approval if, as posited by Brickhill, the Taiwanese Company would be contractually obligating itself to vote as directed by Plaintiffs. This voting agreement would violate the Taiwanese Company's obligation to "continue to exercise control of the vote associated with its Interest," as required by section 11.02. Therefore, we conclude that section 11.02 would not have provided a means by which Plaintiffs could have circumvented the requirement of Tenge Development's approval of Plaintiffs' purchase of the Taiwanese Company's interest. In sum, under the unambiguous language of the Kazakhtenge Regulations, as a matter of law, Tenge Development's approval would have been required for any sale of the Taiwanese Company's interest in Kazakhtenge to Plaintiffs. Brickhill testified that Sugarland did not mention this need for Tenge Development's approval in its correspondence; however, Sugarland's omission does not change or waive the unambiguous language of the Kazakhtenge Regulations requiring such approval. Brickhill also testified that it would make no sense for the Taiwanese Company to have agreed to a unanimous-approval requirement for such transactions and that he did not believe the Taiwanese people who run the Taiwanese Company are "stupid." Regardless of Brickhill's views and the Taiwanese Company's folly or wisdom in agreeing to the Kazakhtenge Regulations, these regulations have not been challenged or set aside, and we must give force to their unambiguous language as written. *See Schaefer,* 124 S.W.3d at 161–62. We cannot rewrite the relevant provisions under the guise of interpretation. *See id.*

****

Eikon King Street Manager, L.L.C. v. LSF King Street Manager, L.L.C.
109 S.W.3d 762 (Tex. App.—Dallas 2003)

BACKGROUND

Eikon and Lone Star were members in a limited liability company formed to develop a large condominium project in California. Eikon invested approximately $3 million plus "the business opportunity" in the project; Lone Star invested approximately $44 million.

The Buy–Sell Provision

The parties' Agreement included a buy-sell provision, which forms the substantive basis of this lawsuit. According to its terms, one member (the "Invoking Member") initiated the procedure by delivering written notice to the other member (the "Offeree Member"). That notice set forth an amount (the "Stated Amount") which represented the price at which the Invoking Member would be willing to purchase all of the properties and other assets owned by the company, as if the Invoking Member were a hypothetical third party proposing to purchase the assets of the company. The Agreement then set forth a formula whereby the Stated Amount was used to calculate the value of each member's interest in the company following such a hypothetical sale. The notice constituted a two-fold offer. By serving the notice, the Invoking Member was offering both (a) to purchase the interest of the Offeree Member for a price equal to the value of the Offeree Member's share, and (b) to sell its own (i.e., the Invoking Member's) interest to the Offeree Member for a price equal to the value of the Invoking Member's own share. The Offeree Member was thus put to an election: it could choose to sell its own interest to the Invoking Member or to purchase the Invoking Member's interest. The Offeree Member was required to give notice of its election within thirty days, or it would be deemed to have elected to sell its interest to the Invoking Member. Whichever member was going to purchase the interest of the other member was then required to deliver a cash deposit in the amount of ten percent of the Stated Amount to the selling member. At the closing, the purchasing member was required to pay the entire purchase price for the seller's interest in "cash or other immediately available funds." The seller was required to execute documents necessary for the sale; if the seller refused to do so, the purchaser was granted a power of attorney to execute the documents on the seller's behalf.

Eikon's Invocation of the Buy–Sell Provision

Eikon attempted to invoke the buy-sell provision by delivering a notice to Lone Star. That notice identified a Stated Amount of $145,432,132.00. In the notice, Eikon offered to purchase Lone Star's interest for $9,500,000.00 or to sell its own interest to Lone Star for $4,071,429.00. Lone Star accepted the Stated Amount proffered by Eikon. But Lone Star believed Eikon had miscalculated the amount of its final offer and that the correct price for Eikon's share—based upon the agreed Stated Amount—should have been $2,015,112.00. Nevertheless, with that explanation, Lone Star agreed to buy Eikon's interest. Rather than provide the required ten percent cash deposit to Eikon, Lone Star placed in escrow a cashier's check for $2,015,112.00 and a letter of credit for the remainder of the ten percent. At the closing, Lone Star tendered a cashier's check for $4,071,429.00, the full amount claimed by Eikon for its interest. However, Lone Star expressly reserved its right to the contested portion of that payment. Eikon accepted the full payment from Lone Star but refused to execute the closing documents. Lone Star exercised the power of attorney granted by the Agreement and signed the documents on Eikon's behalf.

The Litigation

Eikon brought this suit before the closing took place, alleging initially that Lone Star had breached the Agreement by failing to deliver the cash deposit required by the buy-sell provision. Eikon sought liquidated damages and attorney's fees. Lone Star answered and counterclaimed, seeking a declaratory judgment that required Eikon to sell its interest pursuant to the Agreement. Eikon generally denied the allegations of the counterclaim. As discussed above, the closing went forward despite Eikon's initiation of legal proceedings. After the closing, Eikon tendered the $4,071,429.00 check it had received from Lone Star into the registry of the trial court. Later, Eikon obtained permission from the trial court and withdrew $2,015,112.00, the uncontested amount which it was due. Thus, $2,056,317.00 remained in the registry of the court pending the outcome of the litigation. In December 2001, Lone Star filed its motion for summary judgment. The following month, Eikon filed its Third Amended Petition. That petition included claims against Lone Star based on breach of contract, conversion, fraud and fraudulent inducement, promissory estoppel, and declaratory judgment. Eikon sought actual damages, liquidated damages, exemplary damages, attorney's fees, and declaratory relief in the form of a vindication of Eikon's rights under the Agreement. Eikon also filed an amended answer to Lone Star's counterclaim, raising the affirmative defenses of waiver, ambiguity, and failure to perform conditions precedent. Lone Star sought summary judgment in its favor on all claims asserted by Eikon. The motion contained ten grounds. Eikon filed a response to Lone Star's motion and filed its own partial motion for summary judgment as well. Eventually, Eikon's motion was denied; Lone Star's motion was granted. The trial court's order did not specify reasons for the ruling. . . .

Compliance With The Buy Sell Procedure

Eikon's first point charges that the trial court erroneously granted summary judgment on its breach of contract claim because Lone Star failed to comply with the buy-sell procedures dictated by the Agreement. Specifically, Eikon argues Lone Star failed to (1) make a "mirror-image" acceptance of the offer made by Eikon, (2) provide the required ten percent cash deposit to Eikon, and (3) pay the purchase price at closing in cash or other "immediately available" funds. Accordingly, Eikon argues it is entitled to recover the $ 2,056,317.00 that was tendered conditionally at the closing and that remained in the court's registry. Interpretation of the Agreement is a question of law for this Court. See *DeWitt County Elec. Coop., Inc. v. Parks*, 1 S.W.3d 96, 100 (Tex.1999); *Coker v. Coker*, 650 S.W.2d 391, 393 (Tex.1983).

Adequacy of the Acceptance

Eikon argues at the outset that Lone Star was required to issue a "mirror-image" acceptance of the offer Eikon made in its notice. However, the Agreement does not employ "mirror-image" language. Instead, the Agreement requires the Offeree Member to elect to purchase the Invoking Member's interest "at the price at which the Invoking Member shall be deemed to have offered to sell such interest," or to sell its own interest "at the price at which the Invoking Member shall be deemed to have offered to purchase such interest." The key factor in determining the Invoking Member's offer is the Stated Amount. The value of any member's individual interest is based on a prescribed calculation from that number. Lone Star accepted the Stated Amount proposed by Eikon, but it challenged the methodology and accuracy of Eikon's calculations. The gravamen of Eikon's complaint under this issue is that Lone Star was not free to challenge Eikon's methodology or calculations. If faced with a defective notice, Lone Star could have ignored the notice or issued a notice of its own. However, Eikon argues, Lone Star could not correct errors in Eikon's notice and then treat the corrected notice as binding on the parties. We find at least three bases for rejection of this argument. First, our review of Eikon's live pleading and its response to Lone Star's motion for summary judgment establishes this "mirror image" argument was not raised below. Although Eikon urged a different purchase price from Lone Star, it did not urge that Lone Star's acceptance amounted to a breach of the Agreement. Except to attack the legal sufficiency of the movant's grounds for summary judgment, the nonmovant must expressly present to the trial court in a written answer or response any reason for avoiding the movant's entitlement to summary judgment. TEX.R. CIV. P. 166a(c); *McConnell v. Southside Indep. Sch. Dist.*, 858 S.W.2d 337, 343 (Tex.1993). Any issue not expressly presented to the trial court in a written motion or response may not be raised as grounds for reversal on appeal. *In re A.L.H.C.*, 49 S.W.3d 911, 915 (Tex.App.-Dallas 2001, pet. denied). Second, Eikon does not quarrel with Lone Star's challenges to its calculations. In its summary judgment response, Eikon argued only that the language of the buy-sell provision was "confusing and convoluted," but that it had nonetheless acted reasonably in creating its notice. On appeal, Eikon does not challenge the basis of Lone Star's calculations in any meaningful fashion. Finally, what Eikon does argue on appeal is that Lone Star ratified the "defective notice" by choosing to respond to it. We disagree with this argument as well. Ratification requires a person to adopt or confirm a prior act that did not then legally bind that person and which that person had the right to repudiate; the person must adopt or confirm with knowledge of all material facts. *Avary v. Bank of America, N.A.*, 72 S.W.3d 779, (Tex.App.-Dallas 2002, pet. denied). Like waiver, ratification is largely a matter of intent. *Id.* Lone Star's intent is clear from the record: its acceptance was specifically limited to acceptance of the Stated Amount, not of Eikon's related calculations. Indeed, those calculations were challenged immediately by Lone Star in its original acceptance letter. Lone Star did not ratify the calculations in Eikon's notice.

We reject this first argument under Eikon's first point.

Delivery of the Cash Deposit

Eikon's second complaint concerning Lone Star's performance under the buy-sell provision relates to the requirement of a cash deposit upon acceptance of Eikon's offer. The Agreement states that, within thirty days after receipt of the Invoking Member's notice, the member who will purchase the other's interest must deliver to the other member "cash in an amount equal to ten percent (10%) of the Stated Amount." This deposit would be returned to the purchaser after a successful closing. If the seller defaulted or was otherwise unable to complete the sale, then the deposit would be returned to the purchaser. On the other hand, if the purchaser defaulted, then the deposit could be kept by the seller as liquidated damages. The Stated Amount offered by Eikon and accepted by Lone Star was $145,432,132.00. Thus, Lone Star should have delivered $14,543,213.00 in cash to Eikon. Instead, Lone Star notified Eikon that it was depositing $14,543,213.00 in an escrow account, in the form of a cashier's check for $2,015,112.00 plus a letter of credit in the amount of $12,528,101.00. According to Lone Star, the funds were to be held for Eikon's benefit, but the escrow structure would ensure the return of the deposit to Lone Star if the sale did not close. We agree with Eikon that the placement of these funds in escrow for Eikon's benefit was not equivalent to delivering a cash deposit to Eikon as the Agreement contemplated. Nevertheless, we conclude this variance is not determinative of the appeal. The purpose of the deposit was to assure the sale took place once the offer had been made and accepted. In this instance, the parties did go forward and close the sale. Accordingly, had the deposit been delivered in cash to Eikon, Eikon would have been required to return it to Lone Star at the closing in any event. Eikon argues it did not waive its complaint by attending the closing. We agree, but our decision is not based on a waiver theory. Instead, we conclude that issues involving the cash deposit would only become relevant if the sale had not closed. In that event, we would need to ask whose default prevented the closing and, as a result, who would be allowed to keep the deposit. As it is, the closing took place, and those questions need not be addressed.

We reject this second argument under Eikon's first point.

Tender of Immediately Available Funds at Closing

The Agreement required Lone Star to pay the purchase price for Eikon's interest in "cash or other immediately available funds" at the closing. Appellant's final argument under this point is that Lone Star failed to comply with this provision when it delivered a cashier's check in the amount of $4,071,429.00—the price demanded by Eikon in its original notice—while expressly reserving its rights in what it consistently argued was the erroneously-calculated portion of that payment. Eikon does not argue that the cashier's check was not "immediately available funds." Instead, Eikon argues that the reservation of rights somehow rendered the funds unavailable. Eikon's argument is unavailing. In fact, by the time of the closing, Eikon itself had already filed suit over performance issues. Both parties were entitled to proceed to closing while reserving their rights to litigate the amount finally due at closing. Lone Star tendered the largest amount possibly due; it paid that amount in the form of a cashier's check, which certainly qualifies as immediately available funds. Lone Star was entitled to express its intention to pursue its rights to some of those funds, and doing so did not change the availability of the funds during the interim.

We reject this final argument under Eikon's first point. The trial court correctly entered summary judgment in favor of Lone Star on Eikon's breach of contract claim. We resolve the entire first point against Eikon.

Withdrawal of Membership

Unless an LLC agreement provides otherwise, a member may not resign from withdraw or be expelled from a Texas LLC prior to the dissolution and winding up of the LLC. TBOC §101.107

Ownership and Transfer of property

As a separate entity, the LLC owns its properties and there is a clear partition of company assets and members' personal assets. Members do not have any ownership interest in the LLC's property. Accordingly, the LLC's assets may not be used to satisfy a member's personal obligations, voluntarily or involuntarily. A creditor of an LLC member may obtain a charging order of the membership interest, entitling the creditor to receive distributions to which the debtor member would be entitled. This is an exclusive remedy for satisfying a judgment out of the judgment debtor's membership interest and does not entitle the creditor to reach the assets of the LLC or confer a right to inspect the company's books. A member of the LLC, even in a member managed LLC, lacks the right to transfer any of the property of the LLC without the authorization of other members. While the member does not have this right, he may have the power to do so in a member managed LLC under apparent authority. If he satisfies the conditions that the transaction must be in the ordinary course of the company's business and the third party is unaware of the limitation of authority.

Texas Business Organizations Code provisions

§ 101.106. Nature of Membership Interest

...(b) A member of a limited liability company or an assignee of a membership interest in a limited liability company does not have an interest in any specific property of the company.

§ 101.112. Member's Membership Interest Subject to Charging Order

(a) On application by a judgment creditor of a member of a limited liability company or of any other owner of a membership interest in a limited liability company, a court having jurisdiction may charge the membership interest of the judgment debtor to satisfy the judgment.

(b) If a court charges a membership interest with payment of a judgment as provided by Subsection (a), the judgment creditor has only the right to receive any distribution to which the judgment debtor would otherwise be entitled in respect of the membership interest.

(c) A charging order constitutes a lien on the judgment debtor's membership interest. The charging order lien may not be foreclosed on under this code or any other law.

(d) The entry of a charging order is the exclusive remedy by which a judgment creditor of a member or of any other owner of a membership interest may satisfy a judgment out of the judgment debtor's membership interest.

(e) This section may not be construed to deprive a member of a limited liability company or any other owner of a membership interest in a limited liability company of the benefit of any exemption laws applicable to the membership interest of the member or owner.

(f) A creditor of a member or of any other owner of a membership interest does not have the right to obtain possession of, or otherwise exercise legal or equitable remedies with respect to, the property of the limited liability company.

Record-keeping and Right to Information

Members of an LLC should set forth in the LLC agreement how to keep and maintain the required books and records of the LLC. Members of LLCs or assignees of membership interests have the right, subject to reasonable standards set forth in the LLC agreement or otherwise established by the manager or members of the LLC, to obtain from the LLC upon reasonable demand for any purpose reasonably related to the member's interest as a member of the LLC, certain information regarding the affairs of the LLC, as enumerated in Section 3.151 of the TBOC. It is therefore advisable that at a minimum, an LLC keep records of such information. An LLC may maintain its records in a form other than written form, provided such form is capable of conversion into written form within a reasonable time frame.

§ 3.153. Right of Examination by Owner or Member. *Each owner or member of a filing entity may examine the books and records of the filing entity maintained under Section 3.151 and other books and records of the filing entity to the extent provided by the governing documents of the entity and the title of this code governing the filing entity.*

§ 101.502. Right to Examine Records and Certain Other Information

(a) A member of a limited liability company or an assignee of a membership interest in a limited liability company, or a representative of the member or assignee, on written request and for a proper purpose, may examine and copy at any reasonable time and at the member's or assignee's expense:

(1) records required under Sections 3.151 and 101.501; and

(2) other information regarding the business, affairs, and financial condition of the company that is reasonable for the person to examine and copy.

(b) A limited liability company shall provide to a member of the company or an assignee of a membership interest in the company, on written request by the member or assignee sent to the company's principal office in the United States or, if different, the person and address designated in the company agreement, a free copy of:

(1) the company's certificate of formation, including any amendments to or restatements of the certificate of formation;

(2) if in writing, the company agreement, including any amendments to or restatements of the company agreement; and

(3) any tax returns described by Section 101.501(a)(2).

§ 101.054. Waiver or Modification of Certain Statutory Provisions Prohibited; Exceptions

(e) The company agreement may not unreasonably restrict a person's right of access to records and information under Section 101.502.

FINANCIAL MATTERS

Raising Capital

The LLC offers the same flexibility in raising capital as a for-profit corporation. An LLC may raise funds by admitting new members. A person can become a member of the LLC without owning any membership interest, provided there is at least one other member with a membership interest. Members make contributions to the LLC, although this is not a requirement for membership or acquiring of a membership interest. Because the company agreement may define or provide for the establishment of classes of members with different rights, powers, and duties, this may be a factor in the raising of capital as each potential investor may be attracted to or dissuaded from a particular class based on the investor's preferences and level of risk tolerance. The LLC may also raise capital by issuing debt securities or through loans from financial institutions and other sources that may or may not be collateralized.

Texas Business Organization Code provisions

§ 1.002. Definitions

(9) "Contribution" means a tangible or intangible benefit that a person transfers to an entity in consideration for an ownership interest in the entity or otherwise in the person's capacity as an owner or a member. The benefit includes cash, services rendered, a contract for services to be performed, a promissory note or other obligation of a person to pay cash or transfer property to the entity, or securities or other interests in or obligations of an entity, but does not include cash or property received by the entity:

>   (A) with respect to a promissory note or other obligation to the extent that the agreed value of the note or obligation has previously been included as a contribution; or

>   (B) that the person intends to be a loan to the entity.

§ 101.102. Qualification for Membership

(a) A person may be a member of or acquire a membership interest in a limited liability company unless the person lacks capacity apart from this code.

(b) A person is not required, as a condition to becoming a member of or acquiring a membership interest in a limited liability company, to:

>   (1) make a contribution to the company;

>   (2) otherwise pay cash or transfer property to the company; or

>   (3) assume an obligation to make a contribution or otherwise pay cash or transfer property to the company.

(c) If one or more persons own a membership interest in a limited liability company, the company agreement may provide for a person to be admitted to the company as a member without acquiring a membership interest in the company.

§ 101.104. Classes or Groups of Members or Membership Interests

(a) The company agreement of a limited liability company may:

>   (1) establish within the company classes or groups of one or more members or membership interests each of which has certain expressed relative rights, powers, and duties, including voting rights; and

>   (2) provide for the manner of establishing within the company additional classes or groups of one or more members or membership interests each of which has certain expressed relative rights, powers, and duties, including voting rights.

(b) The rights, powers, and duties of a class or group of members or membership interests described by Subsection (a)(2) may be stated in the company agreement or stated at the time the class or group is established.

(c) If the company agreement of a limited liability company does not provide for the manner of establishing classes or groups of members or membership interests under Subsection (a)(2), additional classes or groups of members or membership interests may be established only by the adoption of an amendment to the company agreement.

(d) The rights, powers, or duties of any class or group of members or membership interests of a limited liability company may be senior to the rights, powers, or duties of any other class or group of members or membership interests in the company, including a previously established class or group.

Pass-through Taxation

Compared to the corporation, the LLC offers advantageous tax treatment. Similarly to partnerships, LLCs enjoy pass-through taxation, if they elect to be taxed as a partnership or taxed as a disregarded entity, in the case of single-member LLCs. In such cases, there is no entity-level tax; accordingly, an LLC does not pay federal income taxes on its profits. Instead, the profits and losses flow-through to the proprietors of the business. Not only does this mean reduced tax liability or more money in the pockets of the investors, but members are also able to benefit from business losses by deducting such losses on their individual tax returns. An LLC is also free to elect to be taxed as a corporation. See 26 C.F.R. § 301.7701-3.

Franchise and other Taxes

LLCs in Texas are subject to a franchise tax. This places the LLC in the same position as most other business entities such as the corporation, LP, LLP, and LLLP. It also puts the LLC at a disadvantage vis-à-vis a general partnership comprised exclusively of natural persons, since such partnerships are not assessed a franchise tax in Texas. LLCs may also be subject to the property tax on all personal and real property within the State of Texas and owned by the LLC unless exempt by law.

Allocation of Profits and Losses

Unless otherwise provided in the LLC's operating agreement, the profits and losses of an LLC shall be allocated and distributions of cash or assets shall be made on the basis of the agreed value (as stated in the records of the LLC) of the contributions made by each member to the extent they have been received by the LLC and have not been returned. Thus, the default rule in Texas effectively is pro rata allocation of profits and losses.

Texas Business Organization Code provisions

§ 101.201. Allocation of Profits and Losses. The profits and losses of a limited liability company shall be allocated to each member of the company on the basis of the agreed value of the contributions made by each member, as stated in the company's records required under Section 101.501.

Distributions

Distributions are shared on the basis of the agreed value of the members' contributions, unless the company agreement specifies a different manner. Without a provision to that effect in the company agreement, members have no right to a distribution prior to the member's withdrawal or winding up of the LLC. A member who withdraws properly from the LLC, as specified in the company agreement, has the right to receive, within a reasonable time after the withdrawal, the fair value of the member's interest as of the date of withdrawal. Distributions may be made in cash and there is no automatic right to receive distributions in kind. Such a right must be provided for in the company agreement. It is important to distinguish between allocations and distributions. Allocations refer to the delineation and apportioning of income and losses of the business to the owners for book and tax purposes. Distributions refer to the actual transfer to the owners of the allocated amounts. As in other pass-through entities, an LLC may allocate profits without making an actual distribution of the allocated amount to the members. In such a situation, the members would have a tax liability without the actual amount to meet the obligation. To avoid that, the members may provide that allocation of profits would always be accompanied by a distribution of the allocated amount or at least a sufficient amount to meet the tax liability. Distributions are prohibited if they would render the LLC insolvent. A member may be asked to return an improperly made distribution if the member knew that the distribution was wrongly made.

Texas Business Organization Code provisions

§ 101.202. Distribution in Kind. A member of a limited liability company is entitled to receive or demand a distribution from the company only in the form of cash, regardless of the form of the member's contribution to the company.

§ 101.203. Sharing of Distributions. Distributions of cash and other assets of a limited liability company shall be made to each member of the company according to the agreed value of the member's contribution to the company as stated in the company's records required under Sections 3.151 and 101.501.

§ 101.204. Interim Distributions. A member of a limited liability company, before the winding up of the company, is not entitled to receive and may not demand a distribution from the company until the company's governing authority declares a distribution to:

(1) each member of the company; or

(2) *a class or group of members that includes the member.*

§ 101.205. Distribution on Withdrawal. *A member of a limited liability company who validly exercises the member's right to withdraw from the company granted under the company agreement is entitled to receive, within a reasonable time after the date of withdrawal, the fair value of the member's interest in the company as determined as of the date of withdrawal.*

§ 101.206. Prohibited Distribution; Duty to Return

(a) Unless the distribution is made in compliance with Chapter 11, a limited liability company may not make a distribution to a member of the company if, immediately after making the distribution, the company's total liabilities, other than liabilities described by Subsection (b), exceed the fair value of the company's total assets.

(b) For purposes of Subsection (a), the liabilities of a limited liability company do not include:

(1) a liability related to the member's membership interest; or

(2) except as provided by Subsection (c), a liability for which the recourse of creditors is limited to specified property of the company.

(c) For purposes of Subsection (a), the assets of a limited liability company include the fair value of property subject to a liability for which recourse of creditors is limited to specified property of the company only if the fair value of that property exceeds the liability.

(d) A member of a limited liability company who receives a distribution from the company in violation of this section is not required to return the distribution to the company unless the member had knowledge of the violation.

(e) This section may not be construed to affect the obligation of a member of a limited liability company to return a distribution to the company under the company agreement or other state or federal law.

(f) For purposes of this section, "distribution" does not include an amount constituting reasonable compensation for present or past services or a reasonable payment made in the ordinary course of business under a bona fide retirement plan or other benefits program.

LIABILITY

One of the advantages of the LLC is that members enjoy limited liability protection from the debts and obligations of the business. This protection also extends to managers of the LLC. The company agreement may impose personal liability on members for the company's debts, obligations, or liabilities. TBOC § 101.114. The rule of non-liability does not shield members and managers from liability for their own torts, even when committed in the course of business. In that case, both the LLC and the member or manager that committed the tort would be jointly and severally liable. An LLC member's non-liability also does not extend to situations where the

506

member is liable under some independent legal basis, such as signing a personal guarantee of the LLC's performance of an obligation under a contract. Apart from members' direct liability for their own torts or on some other independent basis, LLC members may also be held personally liable under the doctrine of piercing the veil.

The doctrine of piercing the veil in the LLC context, is based on the right in corporate law that enables the court to remove the insulation from personal liability enjoyed by LLC members under certain circumstances, such as co-mingling of personal and company funds or otherwise using the company as a personal instrumentality. Prior to 2011 when TBOC codified the doctrine and made clear that it applied to LLCs, the courts had already determined that the veil of an LLC may be pierced to hold members personally liable. See e.g., *Sanchez v. Mulvaney*, 274 S.W.3d 708, 712 (Tex.App.2008). As is the case in the corporate context, the liability shield of an LLC may be pierced if (1) the company is the alter ego of its members; the company is used for illegal purposes; or (3) the company is used as a sham to perpetrate a fraud. In piercing the veil cases based on claims for breach of contract, the plaintiff must show that the defendant used the LLC to commit actual fraud for the defendant's direct personal benefit. See *K–SOLV, LP v. Edward J. McDonald*, 2013 WL 1928798 (Tex.App.-Houston [1st Dist.]); *Shook v. Walden*, 368 S.W.3d 604 (Tex. App.–Austin 2012, no pet.) ("[W]e conclude that the courts must resolve the question the same way the Legislature eventually did – the veil of an LLC may be pierced with respect to the entity's contractual liabilities only upon proof that the defendant used the LLC to perpetrate actual fraud for the defendant's direct personal benefit.") As is the case with corporations, the company veil will not be pierced for failure to follow formalities required by TBOC or the company's governing documents. In a nutshell, LLC-member liability is subject to the same statutory limitations and exceptions as corporate-shareholder liability. TBOC § 101.002(a). *See also* TBOC §§ 21.223–.226. An LLC member is also liable to make its contributions to the LLC and other payment obligations that are provided in an LLC agreement and, under certain limited circumstances, a member may be required to return distributions wrongfully made to it. TBOC § 101.206(d).

Texas Business Organizations Code provisions

§ 101.114. Liability for Obligations. Except as and to the extent the company agreement specifically provides otherwise, a member or manager is not liable for a debt, obligation, or liability of a limited liability company, including a debt, obligation, or liability under a judgment, decree, or order of a court.

§ 101.151. Requirements for Enforceable Promise. A promise to make a contribution or otherwise pay cash or transfer property to a limited liability company is enforceable only if the promise is:

    (1) in writing; and

    (2) signed by the person making the promise.

§ 101.153. Failure to Perform Enforceable Promise; Consequences

(a) A member of a limited liability company, or the member's legal representative or successor, who does not perform an enforceable promise to make a contribution, including a previously made contribution, or to otherwise pay cash or transfer property to the company, is obligated, at the request of the company, to pay in cash the agreed value of the contribution, as stated in the company agreement or the company's records required under Sections 3.151 and 101.501, less:

(1) any amount already paid for the contribution; and

(2) the value of any property already transferred.

(b) The company agreement of a limited liability company may provide that the membership interest of a member who fails to perform an enforceable promise to make a payment of cash or transfer property to the company, whether as a contribution or in connection with a contribution already made, may be:

(1) reduced;

(2) subordinated to other membership interests of non-defaulting members;

(3) redeemed or sold at a value determined by appraisal or other formula; or

(4) made the subject of:

(A) a forced sale;

(B) forfeiture;

(C) a loan from other members of the company in an amount necessary to satisfy the enforceable promise; or

(D) another penalty or consequence.

§ 101.154. Consent Required to Release Enforceable Obligation.

The obligation of a member of a limited liability company, or of the member's legal representative or successor, to make a contribution or otherwise pay cash or transfer property to the company, or to return cash or property to the company paid or distributed to the member in violation of this code or the company agreement, may be released or settled only by consent of each member of the company.

§ 101.155. Creditor's Right to Enforce Certain Obligations.

A creditor of a limited liability company who extends credit or otherwise acts in reasonable reliance on an enforceable obligation of a member of the company that is released or settled as provided by Section 101.154 may enforce the original obligation if the obligation is stated in a document that is:

(1) signed by the member; and

(2) not amended or canceled to evidence the release or settlement of the obligation.

Limited Liability

Black v. Bruner

Not Reported in S.W.3d, 2003 WL 724312 (Tex.App.-San Antonio)

In this restricted appeal, J. Rodney Black challenges the trial court's summary judgment in favor of William R. Bruner ("Bruner"). In a restricted appeal, we review four elements: (1) notice filed within six months of the date of judgment; (2) by a party to the suit; (3) who did not participate at trial; and (4) the error complained of must be apparent from the face of the record. *Norman Communications v. Tex. Eastman Co.,* 955 S.W.2d 269, 270 (Tex.1997). In this case, notice was timely filed by Black, who was a defendant in the suit and who did not participate at trial. The sole remaining issue is whether the error complained of is apparent on the face of the record. *See Norman Communications,* 955 S.W.2d at 270. Black contends that error is apparent on the face of the record because the record demonstrates that Bruner was not entitled to summary judgment based on the evidence he presented. *See Havens v. Ayers,* 886 S.W.2d 506, 510 (Tex.App.-Houston [1st Dist.] 1994, no writ) (finding error apparent on face of record where record contained no evidence to support one of the elements essential to movant's claim); *Mora v. Southwestern Bell Media, Inc.,* 763 S.W.2d 527, 529 (Tex.App.-El Paso 1988, no writ) (failure of summary judgment proof appears on the face of the record). We agree.

Bruner sued Black for contractual indemnity under two agreements. One agreement provided for Bruner to be indemnified by WBB Enterprises, L.C., a Texas limited liability company of which Black is a member. The other agreement provided for Bruner to be indemnified by Ground Stabilizers, L.P., a Texas limited partnership of which WBB is the general partner. As a matter of law, the agreements are not ambiguous. *See Friendswood Dev. Co. v. McDade + Co.,* 926 S.W.2d 280, 282 (Tex.1996) (noting whether contract is ambiguous is question of law). Both agreements are signed by Black and others as members of WBB. As a member of WBB, Black is not individually liable for the obligations of WBB unless WBB's regulations [i.e. Company Agreement] otherwise provide. *See* TEX.REV.CIV. STAT. ANN.. art. 1528n, art. 4.03 (Vernon 1997). No summary judgment evidence was presented to prove that WBB's regulations provide that its members are individually liable for WBB's obligations. Accordingly, the agreements did not conclusively establish that Black had any contractual obligation to indemnify Bruner, and Bruner's affidavit to the contrary cannot contradict the express terms of the agreement. *See Friendswood Dev. Co.,* 926 S.W.2d at 283 (parol evidence may not be admitted for the purpose of creating an ambiguity and may not be admitted to contradict the express terms of an unambiguous agreement).

The trial court's judgment is reversed, and the cause is remanded to the trial court for further proceedings consistent with this opinion.

Phillip Alexander Hajdasz v. Chase Merritt West Loop, L.L.C.
Not Reported in S.W.3d, 2010 WL 3418268 (Tex.App.-Houston (14 Dist.))

Appellee, Chase Merritt West Loop, L.L.P. ("Chase Merrit"), sued appellant, Phillip Alexander Hajdasz, for breach of a lease agreement. At trial, Hajdasz moved for a directed verdict arguing he was not a party to the lease agreement and could not be held personally liable for the alleged breach. The court denied his motion for directed verdict on that basis and submitted the case to the jury on the theory of Hajdasz's liability as a principal. The jury returned a verdict in favor of Chase Merritt and awarded damages, interest, and attorney's fees. On appeal, Hajdasz contends (1) the evidence is legally and factually insufficient to show his personal liability on the lease, and (2) the trial court erred in submitting the case to the jury. We reverse and render judgment in favor of Hajdasz.

I. BACKGROUND

In a written Office Lease Agreement, dated July 12, 2005, Global Funding Solutions, L.L.C. ("Solutions"), identified as a "Texas Corporation," as tenant, and Property Texas SC One Corporation ("Property One"), as landlord, entered into a lease for office space. Hajdasz, the branch manager of Solutions's Houston office, signed the lease as Solutions's "Operations Manager." In the fall of 2005, the Houston office split from Solutions and reorganized under the name Medium Mind Consulting, L.L.C ("MMC"). Hajdasz apparently intended for MMC to assume the liabilities of Solutions, including the lease with Property One, though the record contains no express agreement to that effect with either Property One or its eventual successor, Chase Merritt. MMC then, via an assumed-name certificate, began doing business as "Global Funding Services." Property One explicitly acknowledged this name change, and a year later the lease was amended to name Global Funding Services, L.L.C. ("Services"), identified as a "Texas limited liability company," as the new tenant. On behalf of Services, Hajdasz signed various documents relating to this lease agreement as Services's "Operations Manager." In July of 2007, Property One deeded the property containing the office space to Chase Merritt, and Chase Merritt became the successor in interest to Property One. Subsequently, Services defaulted on the amended lease. In March of 2008, Chase Merritt filed suit on the amended lease. For reasons that are unclear, Chase Merritt sued only Hajdasz individually, but not Services, although that entity was the only tenant named in the amended lease. At trial, Hajdasz moved for a directed verdict at the close of Chase Merritt's case-in-chief, arguing he was not personally liable for Services's default. The trial court denied the motion. The jury found Hajdasz personally liable for breach of the lease agreement, and awarded Chase Merritt $82,275.32 in actual damages, plus interest and attorney's fees. On appeal, Hajdasz contends (1) the evidence is legally and factually insufficient to show he is personally liable on the lease, and (2) the court erred in denying his motion for directed verdict and submitting the case to the jury.

II. DISCUSSION

A. *Standard of Review—Legal Sufficiency*

In a legal-sufficiency review, we view the evidence in the light most favorable to the verdict and indulge every reasonable inference that supports the verdict. *City of Keller v. Wilson,* 168 S.W.3d 802, 822 (Tex.2005). We are to credit evidence in support of the judgment if reasonable jurors could and disregard contrary evidence unless reasonable jurors could not. *See id.* at 827. If the evidence falls within the zone of "reasonable disagreement," we may not substitute our judgment for the fact finder's. *Id.* at 822. We must affirm unless (1) there is no evidence supporting the judgment, (2) the evidence favoring the verdict is somehow rendered incompetent, or (3) the contrary evidence conclusively establishes the opposite proposition. *See id.* at 810–11. Simply stated, we are to consider whether the evidence at trial would have enabled reasonable and fair-minded people to reach the verdict that is under review. *Id.* at 827.

B. Lack of Personal Liability

The jury found, and Hajdasz does not dispute, that the lease agreement was breached. The issue presented here, however, requires us to decide, on the appellate record presented, whether appellant can actually be held liable for that breach. As previously stated, Chase Merritt did not sue Services, the tenant expressly named in the amended lease agreement. Instead, it sought only to hold Services's operations manager, Hajdasz, personally liable for the company's breach. Services, the defaulting tenant, is identified in the amended lease agreement as a limited liability company. That designation can be legally significant because, as a general rule, managers are not individually liable for the debts of the limited liability company. *McCarthy v. Wani Venture, AS.*, 251 S.W.3d 573, 590 (Tex.App.-Houston [1st Dist.] 2007, pet. denied.); *see* Tex. Bus. Orgs.Code Ann § 101.114 (Vernon 2009). The Texas Business Organizations Code states: "Except as and to the extent the company agreement specifically provides otherwise, a member or manager is not liable for a debt, obligation, or liability of a limited liability company, including a debt, obligation, or liability under a judgment, decree, or order of a court." § 101.114. Generally, when an agent contracts for a disclosed principal, as Hajdasz did in signing the amended lease on behalf of Services, the agent is not liable on the contracts he makes. *See Schaeffer v. O'Brien*, 39 S.W.3d 719, 721 (Tex.App.-Eastland 2001, no pet.); *Mediacomp, Inc. v. Capital Cities Commc'n, Inc.*, 698 S.W.2d 207, 211 (Tex.App.-Houston [1st Dist.] 1985, no writ) (citing *Whataburger, Inc. v. Rutherford*, 642 S.W.2d 30, 34 (Tex.App.Dallas 1982, no writ)). In the instant case, for Hajdasz to be liable under a breach-of-contract claim, Chase Merritt would have needed to prove that he agreed to individual liability on the lease. *See* § 101.114; *McCarthy*, 251 S.W.3d at 590. However, the record reveals that Hajdasz signed the original lease solely in the capacity of Solutions's "Operations Manager," and the amended lease agreement only as Services's "Operations Manager." There is no evidence that Hajdasz ever agreed to be individually liable on the lease or amended lease. *See id.; City of Keller*, 168 S.W.3d at 810–11. Accordingly, we sustain Hajdasz's first issue.

III. CONCLUSION

We conclude the evidence is legally insufficient to support a finding that Hajdasz is individually liable on the lease, and we therefore sustain Hajdasz's first issue on appeal. *City of Keller*, 168 S.W.3d at 810–11. Because of our disposition of his first issue, we need not reach his remaining issues. Therefore, we reverse the trial court's judgment and render a take-nothing judgment in favor of Hajdasz.

Direct Liability

LJ Charter, L.L.C., v. Air America Jet Charter, Inc.,

2009 WL 4794242 (Tex. App.—Houston [14th Dist.] 2009)

This case involves a commercial dispute over the use of a hangar at the City of Houston's Hobby Airport. The trial court entered a judgment in favor of appellee and cross-appellant, Air America Jet Charter, Inc. ("Air America"), which both sides challenge on appeal. We modify the trial court's judgment and affirm as modified.

FACTUAL AND PROCEDURAL BACKGROUND

Appellant and cross-appellee LJ Charter, L.L.C. ("LJ Charter") is owned by appellants and cross-appellees Charles N. "Buzzy" Schwarz, Jr. ("Buzzy Schwarz") and Charles N. "Trey" Schwarz, III ("Trey Schwarz"). LJ Charter was a private aircraft management company that held a valuable asset: a lease from the City of Houston ("City") on a "135" hangar (located on Larson Street and it will be referred to as either the "Larson Street Hangar" or just the "Hangar") located at Hobby Airport. LJ Charter's lease ran through December, 2000. Under City requirements, to lease a 135 hangar such as the Larson Street Hangar, the lessee had to hold a 135 certificate from the Federal Aviation Administration ("FAA"). A 135 certificate is the license that enables an entity to engage in the business of chartering private aircraft. A 135 certificate lists the specific types of aircraft the FAA has determined the entity has the capability to safely fly. LJ Charter owned two aircraft: a Learjet and a King Air 90, but it did not possess a 135 certificate. Prior to the events directly at issue in this litigation, LJ Charter had avoided the City's requirement that the Hangar lessee hold a 135 certificate by bringing a company into the Hangar that did have a 135 certificate.FN3 For reasons not disclosed in the record, that relationship ended and LJ Charter faced the prospect of losing the Larson Street Hangar if it did not find a replacement. After lengthy negotiations with another charter company fell through, LJ Charter approached Air America.

Air America is a small charter company owned by Blair McCarter, Jr. It held a 135 certificate from the FAA. Air America also operated two planes (a Learjet and a Navajo, both leased from another company owned by McCarter) and was operating out of another hangar at Hobby Airport operated by Fletcher Aviation. One disadvantage of operating out of the Fletcher Hangar was Air America had to pay close to retail prices for its aviation fuel. In the summer/fall of 2000, LJ Charter and Air America entered into discussions over Air America moving into the Larson Street Hangar. Aware that LJ Charter's lease ended in December 2000, McCarter expressed a lack of interest in moving into the new hangar only to face the prospect of moving again a short time later. LJ Charter convinced McCarter that the move would be a good thing for both parties because (1) the Larson Street Hangar had a tank farm and therefore Air America would be able to obtain its aviation fuel for wholesale rather than retail prices; (2) the Schwarzes represented they knew a lot of people in the "business" and could bring additional aircraft into the Larson Street Hangar, which would then be available for Air America to charter; and (3) they had connections with the City and were working on extending the lease into the future. The sales pitch was successful and ultimately, on October 14, 2000, the two companies entered into the

"Charter Aircraft Services Management Agreement" (the "Agreement"). Included in the Agreement was Exhibit "A" setting forth additional obligations under the Agreement. Paragraph 7 of Exhibit "A" provides:

> If at any time during the term of this Agreement, [LJ Charter] should (for any reason whatsoever) not want [Air America] in it's Hangar, [LJ Charter] will pay $25,000.00 to [Air America] for a relocation fee, provided there are no Hangar sales pending as stated above in Paragraph six (6).

To help get the City's approval of the new relationship and thereby keep LJ Charter in control of the valuable Larson Street Hangar, John Weatherly, LJ Charter's attorney, drafted a letter to the Houston Airport Systems' Properties Division. In that letter, Weatherly wrote: "in an effort to comply with what we believe to be the City's request, my clients have structured a business arrangement with Air America Charter, Inc. ("Air America") concerning the operation of the Leased Premises. Specifically, L.J. Charter and Air America have entered into a Joint Venture Charter Aircraft Services Management Agreement (the "Joint Venture Agreement") concerning operation of the Leased Premises."

The relationship between the two companies was rocky from the beginning. First, the LJ Charter King Air 90 was not airworthy and was unavailable for charters during the entire time period the two companies shared the Hangar. Next, LJ Charter did not live up to all of the duties it was supposed to fulfill under the terms of the Agreement. These included arranging fuel deliveries, maintaining the facility and the equipment, and paying half of the various expenses. In addition, LJ Charter did not bring additional aircraft into the Hangar. Finally, the LJ Charter Learjet began experiencing mechanical problems and eventually it also became unavailable for charters. The Schwarzes decided it was not worth the expense to make the Learjet flyable and they ultimately sold it. Therefore, starting sometime in 2002, there were no LJ Charter aircraft available for Air America to charter. At a specific time not disclosed in the record, the Schwarzes purchased a new plane, a Westwind. A large amount of trial time was spent discussing this Westwind. According to the testimony, the Westwind was a nicer aircraft than a Learjet: it had a larger, more luxurious passenger compartment, and, most important, a larger fuel capacity. There was testimony that Air America anticipated the Westwind would be added to its 135 charter certificate as a replacement for the lost Learjet. This did not occur. Instead, the Schwarzes decided to place ownership of the Westwind into another company they owned: R & S Aircraft Investments, L.L.C. ("R & S"). In addition, the Schwarzes decided to not place the R & S Westwind on Air America's 135 charter certificate but instead placed it on that of a competitor: Starflite Management Group, Inc. ("Starflite"). There was testimony this decision was made because Starflite already had Westwinds on its 135 certificate and Air America did not, and to add a Westwind to the Air America certificate would have required a significant financial investment. There was also testimony that the R & S Westwind, while not on Air America's 135 charter, was available for Air America to charter at a ten percent commission rather than the standard fifteen percent commission LJ Charter owed Air America for the chartering of its aircraft under the Agreement. Finally, despite the fact the R & S Westwind was not on Air America's charter, there was testimony it was frequently fueled and stored at the Larson Street Hangar and the bill for such services was never paid. On July 6, 2003, Trey Schwarz used Air America's Learjet to fly his father-in-law to Kansas. He specifically asked Air America to bill him for that flight, which it did. The total invoice for the flight came to $5,980.00. Trey Schwarz never paid that invoice. Ultimately, the biggest issue between Air America and LJ Charter was the Hangar lease. The original lease term ran out at the end of December 2000, and the City extended the lease on a month-to-month basis. As a result, there were periodic discussions between Air America, primarily Mike Edwards, Air America's vice president, and Trey Schwarz, regarding the status of the lease negotiations between the City and LJ Charter. Each time, Trey Schwarz reported he was taking care of it. Air America accepted those representations until August 2003, when it received notice from the City that it had to vacate the Larson Street Hangar by August 31, 2003. At that point, Trey Schwarz asked Air America to stick with LJ Charter as he was working diligently with the City to work out the lease situation. Through continuing discussions with Trey Schwarz, combined with the fact that after August 31, 2003, the City never moved to force Air America to vacate the Hangar, Edwards believed that LJ Charter had worked out a new lease with the City. This belief lasted until Air America received a Feb. 19, 2004 letter from Trey Schwarz informing Air America that LJ Charter was terminating its relationship with Air America and that Air America had to vacate the Larson Street Hangar by March 30, 2004.

This notice to vacate the Hangar was the end result of Buzzy and Trey Schwarz deciding the economics of the deal with Air America were not working out. According to Buzzy Schwarz, the discussions between father and son probably started some six months before Air America was ultimately kicked out of the Hangar. Those discussions also involved the City. A September 3, 2003 email from Jim Murff at the City to Trey Schwarz revealed that McCarter was calling the City to discuss the status of the Hangar lease and Murff did not want to discuss that situation with McCarter until he had talked to Trey Schwarz. These discussions between the City and the Schwarzes continued and on January 4, 2004, Lucy Ortiz of the City's aviation department informed Trey Schwarz that the Larson Street Hangar lessee must actually be the holder of the 135 certificate. Trey Schwarz replied that he understood and that he would work on a different plan. Trey Schwarz testified this different plan did not include Air America. In addition, Trey Schwarz testified that in January 2004 he was already in negotiations with Starflite about Starflite moving into the Hangar and that he did not inform Air America of those conversations. On February 18, 2004, Trey Schwarz told Ortiz that he wanted Starflite to be the name on the Hangar lease. In addition, Trey Schwarz told Ortiz: "I would ask that this remain confidential until I can personally meet with Blair McCarter as there is more than a business relationship with Air America." Trey Schwarz testified he did not inform Air America of this decision at that time. On March 1, 2004 Ortiz emailed the new lease, bearing the name of Starflite as the lessee, to Trey Schwarz. Ortiz asked that if he agreed with the lease, to have Starflite execute three copies and then return the lease to her. Trey Schwarz admitted that the City sent the lease to him because he was the person negotiating with the City for Starflite. Ortiz also wrote that, "in accordance with your instructions, [she] changed the name of the Lessee and are now copying you on any notices required to be given under the lease." Ortiz testified during trial by video deposition. She testified the City requires the lessee of a 135 hangar to actually hold the FAA 135 certificate. According to Ortiz, during a meeting sometime in 2000 involving the City, LJ Charter, and Air America over the Larson Street Hangar, the City informed LJ Charter and Air America that they could enter into some kind of joint venture and form a company and that company would have to hold the 135 certificate. Ortiz also testified as to how Trey Schwarz had such influence on the transfer of the Larson Street Hangar from LJ Charter to Starflite. She explained that the City works with the current lessee when it is time to enter into a new lease for a hangar. According to Ortiz, for the Hangar to not revert back to the control of the City and then be put out for lease according to the City's preferred order of leasing,FN8 the same entity has to remain in control of the lease. So, according to Ortiz, the City would have been willing to put the lease in Air America's name as long as the Schwarzes, or a company owned by the Schwarzes, owned an interest in Air America. However, Trey Schwarz never asked for the lease to be put in Air America's name, but instead he asked that Starflite be the named lessee and he represented to the City that CNS Ventures, L.L.C. ("CNS"), another company owned by Buzzy Schwarz and Trey Schwarz, owned an interest in Starflite. Finally, Ortiz testified that Trey Schwarz conducted all of the negotiations for Starflite to move into the Larson Street Hangar.

After Air America was evicted from the Larson Street Hangar, Air America filed suit against several people and entities: LJ Charter, CNS, Starflite, Buzzy Schwarz, Trey Schwarz, Jeff Ware, and David Trigg. Air America asserted numerous causes of action including breach of contract, quantum meruit, breach of fiduciary duty, fraud, tortious interference with contract, and conspiracy. LJ Charter filed a counterclaim asserting causes of action for breach of contract, fraud, tortious interference with contract, conversion, the placement of an improper lien on an aircraft, and conspiracy. In addition, LJ Charter sought to pierce the corporate veil and hold McCarter personally liable. . . .

DISCUSSION

On appeal, the parties bring multiple issues challenging the trial court's judgment. We initially address those issues raised by appellants, we then address Air America's issues. . . .

Air America's Cross-Appeal

Are Trey Schwarz and Buzzy Schwarz directly liable for fraud damages imposed against LJ Charter?

In its second cross-point, Air America contends the trial court should have held Trey Schwarz and Buzzy Schwarz jointly and severally liable for the fraud damages imposed against LJ Charter. Air America makes two arguments in support of its argument [that] Trey and Buzzy Schwarz should be held jointly and severally liable. First, Air America asserts Buzzy and Trey Schwarz are directly liable for the fraud. Second, Air America argues that since, in answer to Question 23, the jury found that both Trey and Buzzy Schwarz were part of a civil conspiracy to commit fraud, they must be held jointly and severally liable for the fraud damages. We need only address Air America's direct liability argument. It is the general rule in Texas that company agents are individually liable for fraudulent or tortious acts committed while in the service of their limited liability company. Sanchez v. Mulvaney, 274 S.W.3d 708, 712 (Tex.App.-San Antonio 2008, no pet.). The jury, in response to Question 21, found that both Trey Schwarz and Buzzy Schwarz committed fraud against Air America. Therefore, since Trey Schwarz and Buzzy Schwarz committed fraud, the judgment should have held them, along with LJ Charter, jointly and severally liable for the fraud damages. Accordingly, we sustain Air America's second cross-point on appeal.

CONCLUSION

We affirm the trial court's judgment in favor of Air America on Air America's breach of contract cause of action based on the Agreement. Having sustained part of appellants' first issue on appeal and Air America's second and third cross-points on appeal, we modify the judgment as follows: (1) Air America's recovery for breach of joint venture fiduciary duty is deleted as a violation of the One Satisfaction Rule; (2) Air America shall recover $5,980.00 from Charles N. "Trey" Schwarz, III for breach of the oral agreement to pay for air charter services; and (3) LJ Charter, L.L.C., Charles N. "Buzzy" Schwarz, Jr., and Charles N. "Trey" Schwarz, III, shall be jointly and severally liable for Air America's common law fraud damages. Having modified the judgment, we affirm the judgment as modified.

****

Sanchez v. Mulvaney D/B/A Freestone Equipment Co. and Hypersonic Construction, LLC
274 S.W.3d 708 (Tex.App.–San Antonio, 2008)

Appellants, Henry Sanchez, Jr. and Josefina Sanchez, are the co-owners of real property on which they intended to construct a Sonic Drive-in restaurant. The Sanchezes hired appellee Hypersonic Construction, LLC ("Hypersonic") as the general contractor. Appellee, Ryan Mulvaney, was one of the member-owners of Hypersonic. Ryan Mulvaney d/b/a Freestone Equipment Co. ("Mulvaney") was also one of the subcontractors on the project. Alamo Concrete Products, Ltd. ("Alamo") supplied the concrete. At some point during construction, Alamo was not paid for all the concrete it supplied to the project, and it filed a mechanic's and materialman's lien encumbering the Sanchezes' property. To avoid foreclosure and obtain permanent financing for the project, the Sanchezes paid Alamo the amount owed, plus attorney's fees and interest. The Sanchezes then sued Hypersonic; Ryan Mulvaney individually, in his capacity as an owner of Hypersonic, and in his capacity as owner/operator of Freestone Equipment Co.; and four other individuals who were either owners or managers of Hypersonic on the following causes of action: violation of the Construction Trust Fund Act, DTPA violations, breach of contract, conversion, and common law contribution and equitable subrogation. In their petition, the Sanchezes asserted they paid to Hypersonic sufficient funds earmarked for payment to Alamo, but that neither Hypersonic nor Mulvaney ensured that the money was tendered to Alamo. The Sanchezes sought reimbursement for the monies paid by them to Alamo. During mediation, the Sanchezes settled their claims against the four other individuals. Also, by this time, Hypersonic was defunct and insolvent. Eventually, the trial court rendered summary judgment in favor of Mulvaney on all of the Sanchezes' claims, and this appeal ensued.

MULVANEY'S MOTION FOR SUMMARY JUDGMENT

As a preliminary matter, we first address the parties' disagreement over the type of summary judgment sought by Mulvaney and the grounds on which he sought summary judgment. Mulvaney's motion states he sought both a traditional and no-evidence summary judgment. However, we determine the standard of proof on a summary judgment motion after considering the substance of the motion, rather than categorizing the motion strictly by its form or title. *See Rodgers v. Weatherspoon*, 141 S.W.3d 342, 344 (Tex.App.–Dallas 2004, no pet.). A motion for summary judgment must state the specific grounds upon which judgment is sought.

See TEX.R. CIV. P. 166a(c). Under traditional summary judgment standards, a party moving for summary judgment has the burden of establishing as a matter of law that no genuine issue of material fact exists as to one or more essential elements of the plaintiff's cause of action. *Casso v. Brand*, 776 S.W.2d 551, 556 (Tex.1989); *Nixon v. Mr. Prop. Mgmt. Co.*, 690 S.W.2d 546, 548–49 (Tex.1985). On the other hand, a no-evidence motion for summary judgment "must state the elements as to which there is no evidence." *See* TEX.R. CIV. P. 166a(i). A no-evidence motion for summary judgment is legally insufficient as a matter of law if it is not specific in challenging a particular element or is conclusory. *See McConnell v. Southside Ind. Sch. Dist.*, 858 S.W.2d 337, 342 (Tex.1993); *Callaghan Ranch, Ltd. v. Killam*, 53 S.W.3d 1, 3 (Tex.App.–San Antonio 2000, pet. denied). The Sanchezes assert that, to the extent Mulvaney's motion seeks a no-evidence summary judgment, it was insufficient because it failed to identify any elements of their causes of action upon which Mulvaney moved for summary judgment. Mulvaney contends his reply to the Sanchezes' response set out the elements of the Sanchezes' claims as to which there was no evidence. For the first time in his reply, Mulvaney specifically challenged the Sanchezes' causes of action under the Texas Construction Trust Fund Act, and for DTPA violations, breach of contract, conversion, and common law contribution and equitable subrogation. However, a movant may not use a reply brief to meet the specificity requirement or to assert new grounds for summary judgment. *Community Initiatives, Inc. v. Chase Bank of Texas*, 153 S.W.3d 270, 280 (Tex.App.–El Paso 2004, no pet.); *see also Callaghan Ranch*, 53 S.W.3d at 4; *Sams v. N.L. Indus.*, 735 S.W.2d 486, 487–88 (Tex.App.–Houston [1st Dist.] 1987, no writ). Therefore, we do not consider any arguments raised in Mulvaney's reply and we will consider only those grounds specifically raised in Mulvaney's motion for summary judgment in order to determine the basis on which he moved for judgment. In his motion for summary judgment, Mulvaney argued all of the liability the Sanchezes sought to impose on him was related to or arose from the contract between Hypersonic and the Sanchezes; therefore, personal liability could be imposed on him only if the Sanchezes could pierce Hypersonic's corporate veil. Mulvaney argued the corporate veil could not be pierced because there was no evidence he committed any actual fraud or that he used Hypersonic as a sham to perpetrate a fraud. Mulvaney also argued that the Sanchezes could not impose individual liability on him based upon Hypersonic's forfeiture of its charter because all causes of action arose before Hypersonic forfeited its charter in December 2006. Mulvaney did not seek to establish his entitlement to a traditional summary judgment by arguing that there existed no genuine issue of material fact as to one or more essential elements of each of the Sanchezes' causes of action. Instead, he sought a no-evidence summary judgment only on the grounds that he was shielded from personal liability because there was no evidence of actual fraud on his part. Therefore, we construe Mulvaney's motion as seeking a no-evidence summary judgment, and we apply the appropriate standard of review. A no-evidence summary judgment motion is improperly granted when the non-movant brings forth more than a scintilla of probative evidence that raises a genuine issue of material fact. TEX.R. CIV. P. 166a(i); *Gomez v. Tri City Cmty. Hosp., Ltd.*, 4 S.W.3d 281, 283 (Tex.App.–San Antonio 1999, no pet.). More than a scintilla of evidence exists if the evidence would allow reasonable and fair-minded people to differ in their conclusions. *Forbes, Inc. v. Granada Biosciences, Inc.*, 124 S.W.3d 167, 172 (Tex.2003). Less than a scintilla of evidence exists if the evidence is so weak as to do no more than create a mere surmise or suspicion of a fact. *Id.*

BREACH OF CONTRACT CLAIM

There is no dispute that the only contract in this case is the one entered into between the Sanchezes and Hypersonic. In their petition, the Sanchezes alleged Hypersonic "and its individual owners" breached the construction contract because "[Hypersonic] ... failed to perform numerous obligations under said contract." The Sanchezes sought recovery against Mulvaney and the other individual defendants "as a result of [Hypersonic's] forfeited status as a Texas Limited Liability Company." Thus, the Sanchezes sought to hold Mulvaney individually liable for *Hypersonic* 's breach of its contractual obligations. Generally, members are not individually liable for the debts of a limited liability company. *McCarthy v. Wani Venture, A.S.*, 251 S.W.3d 573, 590 (Tex.App.–Houston [1st Dist.] 2007, pet. denied). Hypersonic is a limited liability corporation [sic] to which state law principles for piercing the corporate veil apply. *Id.* Therefore, the Sanchezes could hold Mulvaney individually liable for Hypersonic's alleged breach of its contractual obligations only to the extent they pierced the corporate veil. *See Willis v. Donnelly*, 199 S.W.3d 262, 271 (Tex.2006). Accordingly, the burden shifted to the Sanchezes to bring forth more than a scintilla of probative evidence that raises a genuine issue of material fact on the issue of actual fraud on Mulvaney's part. In their response to Mulvaney's motion for summary judgment, the Sanchezes alleged only that section 171.252 of the Texas Tax Code applies exclusively to corporations, Hypersonic is a limited liability corporation, and, therefore, they "may seek recovery from [Mulvaney] for [Hypersonic's] breach of contract." The Sanchezes brought forth no evidence of fraud on Mulvaney's part that would entitle them to hold him individually liable for any breach by Hypersonic of its contractual obligations. Therefore, the trial court properly rendered summary judgment in favor of Mulvaney on the Sanchezes' breach of contract claim.

NON–CONTRACT CLAIMS

We believe Mulvaney's argument that liability could be imposed on him only if the Sanchezes pierced Hypersonic's corporate veil misconstrues the non-contract claims brought against him. In their petition, the Sanchezes alleged Mulvaney "intentionally or knowingly or with intent to defraud, directly or indirectly retained, used, disbursed, or otherwise diverted [construction payments] without first fully paying obligations then owed ... to [Alamo]." The Sanchezes also alleged Mulvaney violated the DTPA by making certain misrepresentations, breaching certain warranties, and engaging in an unconscionable action or course of action. It is therefore clear that the Sanchezes sought to hold Mulvaney individually liable for his *own* allegedly tortious or fraudulent actions. The issue of a defendant's liability in his individual capacity is distinct from that of his liability under an alter ego theory. A corporation's agent is personally liable for his own fraudulent or tortious acts, even when acting within the course and scope of his employment. *See Miller v. Keyser,* 90 S.W.3d 712, 717 (Tex.2002); *Cimarron Hydrocarbons Corp. v. Carpenter,* 143 S.W.3d 560, 564 (Tex.App.–Dallas 2004, pet. denied); *Gore v. Scotland Golf, Inc.,* 136 S.W.3d 26, 32 (Tex.App.–San Antonio 2003, pet. denied). In an action seeking to hold an agent individually liable for his tortious or fraudulent acts, the corporate veil is not required to be pierced. *Gore,* 136 S.W.3d at 32; *Kingston v. Helm,* 82 S.W.3d 755, 761 (Tex.App.–Corpus Christi 2002, pet. denied). Therefore, the trial court erred in rendering summary judgment in favor of Mulvaney on the Sanchezes' non-contract claims on the grounds that the Sanchezes were required to pierce the corporate veil. *See Cimarron*

Hydrocarbons, 143 S.W.3d at 564 ("Our review of [movant's] summary judgment motion reveals he failed to show or even allege that no evidence exists to support one or more elements of [non-movant's] negligence, DTPA, and breach of warranty claims against [movant] *in his individual capacity.*") (emphasis added).

CONCLUSION

We affirm the trial court's summary judgment in favor of Mulvaney on the Sanchezes' breach of contract claim and we reverse the summary judgment in all other respects and remand for further proceedings.

****

Piercing the Company Veil

McCarthy v. Wani Venture, A.S.,
251 S.W.3d 573, (Tex.App.-Houston [1st Dist.] 2007).

Appellee, Wani Venture, A.S., successor in interest to Norgips USA, Inc. (collectively "Norgips") filed a suit on a sworn account against several defendants, alleging fraud and seeking to pierce the corporate veil. As of the time of trial, all of the original defendants had filed bankruptcy, had been severed out of the case, or had been non-suited, with the exception of appellant, Marcie McCarthy. Following a jury trial, the trial court rendered judgment against McCarthy for $669,957. In six issues, McCarthy argues that (1) the trial court erred in submitting an incorrect definition of "actual fraud" in the jury charge; (2) there is no evidence that her company, Triple M Supply LLC, committed an actual fraud; (3) there is no evidence to support the damages and attorney's fees award; (4) there is no evidence or insufficient evidence that McCarthy caused Triple M Supply to be used to perpetrate an actual fraud and did perpetrate an actual fraud upon Norgips, primarily for her own direct personal benefit; and (5) the trial court erred in finding McCarthy individually liable for the amounts that the jury found that Triple M Supply owed Norgips. We affirm.

Background
Triple M Supply's Purchase Order

Norgips, a Florida corporation, manufactures and sells wallboard, also known as drywall or sheetrock. John Kingston, Norgips's president, testified that, in 2000, there was a severe shortage of wallboard in the marketplace, and "people were scrambling to try to find drywall any place in the world that they could in order to supply the U.S. production." Kingston hired Steven Klubak to be Norgips's general manager and to monitor the Texas and Florida markets. Kingston explained that part of the reason that he hired Klubak was because Klubak told him that "he had this customer in Texas that was a big player that could help [Norgips] be a major factor in the Texas market." The "big player" was Triple M Supply, LLC. Triple M Supply was a wallboard distributor owned, in three equal parts, by Anthony Moschella, Michael Moschella (Anthony's brother), and Marcie McCarthy (Michael's girlfriend). Triple M Supply completed Norgips's confidential credit application, and it was agreed that Triple M Supply would be Norgips's sole distributor in the east Texas market. Triple M Supply prepared a purchase order for Norgips to ship approximately $1.3 milion of wallboard from Poland to the Port of Houston. Once the shipment arrived, it was stored in a warehouse in the Port of Houston, and Norgips would deliver the wallboard incrementally, in response to individual invoices from Triple M Supply. Kingston testified that it was Norgips's intention to hold Triple M Supply liable for the full amount of the purchase order. The first delivery was placed in April 2000. Triple M Supply was slow in making payments and, in October 2000, its $108,000 check was returned for insufficient funds. Kingston testified that, after the check bounced, "the red flag went up and we started having serious concerns as to whether or not we were going to get the money that was due to us." Kingston testified that there was "constant communication" between Klubak and Anthony Moschella regarding Norgips's outstanding bills. After Norgips received a $66,000 check from Triple M Supply in late October—$42,000 less than the amount owed from the bounced check, Kingston asked Klubak to meet with Triple M Supply to review its accounts receivables. Kingston wanted Klubak to determine what payments were due to Triple M Supply from its customers and to explore the likelihood of whether it could satisfy its debt to Norgips.

In December 2000, Anthony Moschella provided Klubak with bookkeeping records of Triple M Supply's accounts receivables. From these records, Kingston discovered that there were outstanding receivables for more than $500,000. He saw that Triple M Supply's largest customer was JTMM Construction Company. Based on his review of these records, Kingston learned that Anthony Moschella, Michael Moschella, and Marcie McCarthy had another business, Triple M Operating. Triple M Supply had apparently stopped "invoicing" customers in July 2000, and Triple M Operating had begun invoicing the customers who purchased Norgips's wallboard. Kingston testified that he was alarmed to discover that "the people that we had our contractual relationship with, Triple M Supply, was no longer distributing our board." Instead, Triple M Operating was distributing the board. From the accounting records provided to Norgips, there appeared to be no distinction between the various companies. Kingston testified that this discovery "immediately raised a flag" because it seemed as though Triple M Supply, which "owed a lot of money to a lot of people," was setting up new corporations in order to continue doing business. Kingston was concerned because handwritten notes on the accounts receivables records led him to believe that these were old debts that were not going to be paid. Kingston also discovered that, during the time that it was Norgips's exclusive distributor, Triple M Supply was actually selling a competitor's board, while Norgips's board sat in the warehouse. In January 2001, Kingston and Klubak met with Anthony and Michael Moschella in an attempt to determine whether Norgips was ever going to be paid. Anthony Moschella again provided a copy of Triple M Supply's bookkeeping records of its accounts receivables. This second set of records showed that, in the month since the previous accounts receivables records had been provided to Norgips, Triple M Supply had collected more than $50,000—none of which had been used to pay the outstanding balance it owed to Norgips. Kingston testified that Anthony Moschella reassured him and explained that "he had $470,000 of good receivables there that he would expect to receive payment on." Anthony Moschella "pledged" the receivables to Norgips. At that point, Triple M Supply owed Norgips $504,000. Kingston was surprised to learn from Anthony Moschella at the meeting, however, that Triple M Supply had collected $150,000 from sales of Norgips's wallboard but had diverted those funds to Mexico to another of Anthony Moschella's business ventures. Within a week of the meeting, a $71,170.87 check made out to Norgips from Triple M Supply was returned for insufficient funds. Norgips's last delivery of wallboard to Triple M Supply occurred in December 2000. Kingston testified that Norgips sold $1,047,000 of wallboard to Triple M Supply. However, Triple M Supply had paid Norgips only $504,800, and still owed Norgips $541,850. In February 2001, Kingston was contacted by Leeland Dykes, a stock broker. Dykes explained that he had hired a private detective and had learned that Norgips was owed a lot of money by Triple M Supply. Kingston flew to Houston to meet with Dykes, and he was told that Klubak, who still worked for Norgips, and Anthony Moschella had been trying to corner the wallboard market and drive up the price so that they could sell it at a premium. Kingston learned that Klubak had been brokering other companies' wallboard and had sold more than $500,000 of wallboard from Shamrock, a Norgips competitor, while he was Norgips's general manager. Kingston was told that Shamrock had been "stiffed" for $105,000 and had obtained a judgment against Klubak for that amount. As soon as he returned from his meeting with Dykes, Kingston fired Klubak. Shortly thereafter, Kingston discovered that there were three UCC filings reflecting that all of the assets of Triple M Supply, Triple M Operating, and JTMM had been pledged to creditors other than Norgips. These pledges were contrary to Anthony Moschella's representations that the receivables were pledged to Norgips and that he would formalize the assignment with a creditor's lien. . . .

Piercing the LLC Veil

In issue four, McCarthy argues that there was legally and factually insufficient evidence to support the jury's finding that she caused Triple M Supply to be used to perpetrate an actual fraud and did perpetrate an actual fraud upon Norgips, primarily for her own direct personal benefit. As a result of this finding, Norgips was able to pierce the LLC veil around Triple M Supply and recover damages from McCarthy, individually. The evidence showed that McCarthy had contributed $391,000 to Triple M Supply as a start-up business. McCarthy was aware of the fraudulent business practices of Anthony Moschella, including using one entity to pay another's bills. She did nothing to stop these practices. Furthermore, she accepted interest payments on her loan and ultimately received repayment in full, at the expense of Norgips and other creditors. The evidence presented at trial showed that the fraudulent operation of Triple M Supply simply would not have been possible without McCarthy's contributions. McCarthy testified that her involvement in the daily affairs of Triple M Supply stopped in late 1999 or early 2000. She did not regularly attend board meetings and claimed to be unaware of Triple M Supply's purchase agreement with Norgips and the existence of Triple M Operating until after this suit was instituted. She received her last officer's check in April 2000, shortly before Triple M Supply took delivery of Norgips's wallboard. McCarthy was an equal participant and director in most of the entities that participated in defrauding Norgips. The fraudulent conduct would not have been possible without McCarthy's infusion of capital into Triple M Supply. Triple M Supply was organized as a Texas Limited Liability Company ("LLC") about six weeks after McCarthy's contribution of "seed money." There was no evidence that Triple M Supply executed a promissory note or that this was, in fact, a capital contribution. Triple M Operating borrowed $600,000–$391,000 of which was used to repay McCarthy's "loan." Even though the repayment to McCarthy was diverted through another entity, McCarthy was made whole at the expense of Norgips, who was owed more than $540,000 by Triple M Supply. McCarthy received health insurance, a salary, officers' draws, and interest payments as compensation for being an owner of Triple M Supply. Furthermore, McCarthy was aware of the fraudulent manner in which Triple M Supply was being managed. She admitted that she knew Triple M Supply was paying the debts of other companies. McCarthy willingly received substantial interest payments on her loans despite her knowledge of Anthony Moschella's fraudulent business practices.

Because there was legally and factually sufficient evidence to support the jury's finding, we overrule issue four.

Individual Liability

In issue five, McCarthy argues that the trial court erred in finding her liable for Triple M Supply's debt because, pursuant to the Texas Limited Liability Company Act ("TLLCA"), a member of a Texas limited liability company ("LLC") is liable in very limited circumstances and, specifically, not for a debt. TEX.REV.CIV. STAT. ANN.. art. 1528n, § 4.03(A) (Vernon 2006). McCarthy argues that because the TLLCA does not address whether or under what circumstances a litigant may "pierce" the veil of an LLC for corporate debt, the veil is impenetrable. We disagree. Generally, members are not individually liable for the debts of the LLC The TLLCA provides in pertinent part that: "Except as and to the extent the regulations specifically provide otherwise, a member or manager is not liable for the debts, obligations or liabilities of a limited liability company including under a judgment decree, or order of a court." TEX.REV.CIV. STAT. ANN.. art. 1528n, § 4.03(A) (Vernon 2006). The TLLCA does not address whether or under what circumstances a litigant may "pierce" the corporate veil of an LLC in order to hold a member liable for a debt of the LLC. *Id.* However, Texas courts and other jurisdictions, have applied to LLCs the same state law principles for piercing the corporate veil that they have applied to corporations. *See e.g. Pinebrook Props., Ltd. v. Brookhaven Lake Prop. Owners' Ass'n,* 77 S.W.3d 487, 499 (Tex.App.-Texarkana 2002, pet. denied) (applying corporate alter ego veil piercing precedent in analyzing plaintiff's attempts to pierce veil of LLC); *In re Secs. Inv. Prot. Corp. v. R.D. Kushnir & Co.,* 274 B.R. 768, 775–76 (Bankr.N.D.Ill.2002) (concluding that, while Illinois LLC Act precludes piercing on basis of failure to follow formalities, nothing in statute bars piercing LLC veil on other grounds applicable to corporations); *Hamilton v. AAI Ventures, L.L.C.,* 768 So.2d 298, 302 (La.App.2000) (applying corporate veil piercing principles in upholding trial court's piercing of LLC veil to hold member liable on LLC contract); *Kaycee Land & Livestock v. Flahive,* 46 P.3d 323, 327 (Wyo.2002) (holding that, while Wyoming LLC Act was silent as to veil piercing, there was no policy or legal reason to treat LLCs different from corporations in this regard; when LLC has caused damage and has inadequate capitalization, co-mingled funds, diverted assets, or used LLC as a mere shell, individual members are immune from liability. Legislative silence cannot be stretched to condone such an illogical result.). McCarthy has not offered, nor can we find, any judicial support for the proposition that existing state law doctrines of piercing the corporate veil should not be applied to LLCs.

Texas courts have disregarded the corporate fiction and pierced the corporate veil when the corporate form has been used as part of an unfair device to achieve an inequitable result. *See Castleberry v. Branscum,* 721 S.W.2d 270, 272 (Tex.1986), *superseded in part by statute,* TEX.

BUS. CORP. ACT ANN. art. 2.21(Vernon Supp.2005). Specifically, courts have disregarded the corporate form when it is used as a sham for perpetrating a fraud. *Id.* Here, the trial court did not err in its application of law. The jury found that McCarthy used an LLC as a sham to perpetrate a fraud, and the trial court applied this finding to pierce the corporate veil of the LLC. The jury found that McCarthy used Triple M Supply LLC to perpetrate actual fraud and did perpetrate actual fraud upon Norgips primarily for McCarthy's own direct personal benefit. As shown above, there was evidence presented at trial that McCarthy and her two partners (1) used Triple M Supply as a front to borrow funds and order wallboard on credit from Norgips and others; (2) diverted to themselves and to entities in which McCarthy had either an ownership and/or financial interest, proceeds due to Triple M Supply through the use of complex and undocumented financial transactions and the commingling of inventory and bank accounts; and (3) left Triple M Supply undercapitalized and unable to pay its creditors. McCarthy had a direct ownership and/or financial interest in each of the entities that benefited from sums due to Triple M Supply: JTMM, M Global, Triple M Operating, and Woodpal. Funds and inventory of these companies were intermingled without documentation, as evidenced by Anthony Moschella's frequent financial transfers among the various entities. Funds from Triple M Supply were being used to pay the debt of JTMM. Triple M Operating was paying the debts of Triple M Supply. After a checking account for Triple M Supply was opened, large sums of money were transferred out of Triple M Supply's bank account to several related businesses including K–Cor Supply and JTMM. Additionally, over $500,000 of inventory was switched "on the books" from JTMM Supply to Triple M Supply without any further documentation between the two companies. Triple M Supply was then loaded with debt and subsequent creditors, including Norgips, were not paid back. McCarthy, however, was paid. This was the case even though significant deposits were made to Triple M Supply from customer payments from the sale of Norgips's wallboard. As a result of these acts, Triple M Supply was left undercapitalized and without sufficient funding to pay its debts. Accordingly, we hold that the trial court did not err in finding McCarthy liable on Triple M Supply's debt. As such, we overrule issue five. . . .

Justice JENNINGS, dissenting.

Because the majority errs in concluding that the evidence is legally sufficient to support the jury's finding that appellant, Marcie McCarthy, primarily for her own direct personal benefit, caused Triple M Supply, LLC ("TMS") to be used to perpetrate an actual fraud, and did perpetrate an actual fraud upon appellee, Wani Venture, A.S., as successor in interest to Norgips USA, Inc. (collectively "Norgips"), I respectfully dissent. In her fourth issue, McCarthy argues that the trial court erred in entering judgment against her because there is no evidence that she was a substantial factor in causing Norgips's injury, that she caused TMS to be used to perpetrate a fraud, and that a fraud was committed "primarily for her own direct personal benefit." In sum, she contends that there is no evidence that she "knew of any alleged 'fraudulent scheme,' much less being a substantial factor, in bringing about the injury to Norgips, or that money [she] received was related to any fraudulent scheme."

Standard of Review

We must sustain a legal sufficiency or "no-evidence" challenge if the record shows one of the following: (1) a complete absence of evidence of a vital fact, (2) rules of law or evidence bar the court from giving weight to the only evidence offered to prove a vital fact, (3) the evidence offered to prove a vital fact is no more than a scintilla, or (4) the evidence establishes conclusively the opposite of the vital fact. *City of Keller v. Wilson,* 168 S.W.3d 802, 810 (Tex.2005). Evidence does not exceed a scintilla if it does no more than create a mere surmise or suspicion that a fact exists. *Ford Motor Co. v. Ridgway,* 135 S.W.3d 598, 601 (Tex.2004). If the evidence at trial would enable reasonable and fair-minded people to differ in their conclusions, then jurors must be allowed to do so. *City of Keller,* 168 S.W.3d at 822. In conducting a legal sufficiency review of the evidence, a court must consider all of the evidence in the light most favorable to the verdict and indulge every reasonable inference that would support it. *Id.*

As further explained by the Texas Supreme Court,

> The evidence presented, viewed in the light most favorable to the prevailing party, must be such as to permit the logical inference [that the jury must reach]. There must necessarily be a logical connection, direct or inferential, between the evidence offered and the fact to be proved. However, we must also bear in mind the difference between materiality of the evidence and the issue of evidentiary sufficiency. Simply because a piece or pieces of evidence are material in the sense that they make a "fact that is of consequence to the determination of the action more ... or less probable," does not render the evidence legally sufficient.

Transp. Ins. Co. v. Moriel, 879 S.W.2d 10, 24–25 (Tex.1994) (citations omitted). As Professor McCormick emphasized, "a brick is not a wall." *Id.* (quoting Charles T. McCormick, HANDBOOK OF THE LAW OF EVIDENCE § 152 (West ed.1954)).

Actual Fraud

Generally, under Texas law, shareholders are not liable for the debts of a corporation; however, Texas courts will pierce the corporate veil to prevent fraud or to achieve equity. *Castleberry v. Branscum,* 721 S.W.2d 270, 271–72 (Tex.1987). In particular, courts will disregard the corporate fiction when individuals exploit the **593* corporate form as a sham to perpetrate a fraud. *Id.* at 272. In response to *Castleberry,* the Texas Legislature amended article 2.21 of the Texas Business Corporations Act in 1989 to establish "a clear legislative standard under which the liability of a shareholder for the obligations of a corporation is to be determined in the context of contractual obligations and all matters relating thereto." TEX. BUS. CORP. ACT ANN. art 2.21, Comment of Bar Committee–1996 (Vernon 2003).

Under article 2.21A, a shareholder has no obligation to the obligees of a corporation regarding any contractual obligation of the corporation on the basis of actual or constructive fraud or a sham to perpetrate a fraud, "unless the obligee demonstrates that the [shareholder] ... *caused* the corporation to be used for the purpose of perpetuating and did perpetrate an actual fraud on the obligee primarily for the direct personal benefit of the [shareholder]...." *Id.* art. 2.21A(2) (emphasis added). Actual fraud occurs when:

> a. a party conceals or fails to disclose a material fact within the knowledge of that party,
>
> b. the party knows that the other party is ignorant of the fact and does not have an equal opportunity to discover the truth,

c. the party intends to induce the other party to take some action by concealing or failing to disclose the fact, and

d. the other party suffers injury as a result of acting without knowledge of the undisclosed fact.

Bradford v. Vento, 48 S.W.3d 749, 754–55 (Tex.2001). The test for cause in fact is whether an "act or omission was a substantial factor in bringing about injury," without which the harm would not have occurred. *Doe v. Boys Clubs of Greater Dallas, Inc.*, 907 S.W.2d 472, 477 (Tex.1995). In accordance with article 2.21A(2) and case law, the trial court instructed the jury on actual fraud and to answer the following question:

> Did Marcella McCarthy cause Triple M Supply, LLC to be used to perpetrate an actual fraud, and did perpetrate an actual fraud upon Norgips, primarily for her own direct personal benefit?
>
> For purposes of this question, you are instructed that to "cause" is to be a substantial factor in bringing about an injury that would otherwise not have occurred. There can be more than one cause.

The jury answered this question, "Yes."

Thus, Norgips had the burden to prove that McCarthy actually did in fact cause TMS to be used to defraud Norgips primarily for her own direct personal benefit. Here, however, there is no evidence that McCarthy did anything or omitted to do anything to actually cause TMS to be used to perpetrate an actual fraud, and did perpetrate an actual fraud, upon Norgips. Nor is there any evidence that she did any such thing "primarily for her own direct personal benefit." Norgips argues that the evidence is legally sufficient to support the jury's finding essentially because McCarthy (1) provided $391,000 as seed money to start up TMS as proposed by her boyfriend, Michael Moschella, and his brother, Anthony Moschella; (2) admitted that "[d]uring the maiden year for [TMS]," she took an active role in the business," was vice president, and, held a one-third interest in it; (3) accepted "both pay checks and benefits from the third party employee leasing company as salary" and checks from JTM Supply and TMS as her "director's fee" or "officer's draw"; (4) "went to dinner with Michael and Steve Klubak in Florida"; (5) knew that TMS was paying the debts of other companies; (6) accepted checks from TMS "as payment on secured debt owed by JTM"; (7) claimed that Anthony Moschella stated that "he could do whatever he wanted with the money in any of the companies' accounts"; (8) although she "reduced her hands-on activities," she "condoned through her silence and inaction, Anthony's total disregard of his representation to the State of Texas and Norgips that [TMS] had been organized to conduct 'lawful business' "; (9) "did not combine the power of her third ownership with the third ownership of her boyfriend Michael, to take control of the company and conduct its business lawfully"; (10) did not hire an accountant, invoke her rights to see a complete set of company books and records, resign as vice president, or assign or give away her interest in TMS; and (11) she "got her money back" and was made whole at the expense of TMS. In sum, "she took the route that she thought was the best way to protect her own initial contribution of $391,000, her fees, her salary, and her benefits."

However, none of this evidence, taken separately or together, supports a logical inference that McCarthy in fact caused TMS to be used to perpetrate an actual fraud, and did perpetrate an actual fraud, upon Norgips, primarily for her own direct personal benefit. In fact, Norgips concedes in its briefing to this Court that McCarthy "would not admit that she knew anything about Norgips or TMS's transfer of funds in the year 2000." Although Norgips asserts that the jury was free to disbelieve her denial of knowledge, it directs us to no evidence in the record that supports an inference that she in fact had knowledge of Anthony Moschella's dealings with Norgips. The majority acknowledges that McCarthy testified that her involvement in the daily affairs of TMS actually ceased in late 1999 or early 2000, she did not regularly attend board meetings, and was unaware of TMS's purchase agreement with Norgips until Norgips filed the instant suit. It also notes that she received her last officer's check in April 2000, before TMS received delivery of Norgips's wallboard. Nevertheless, the majority holds that the evidence is legally sufficient to support the jury's finding. It notes that McCarthy had contributed $391,000 to TMS as a start-up business; accepted interest payments on her loan and was ultimately fully repaid, at the expense of Norgips and other creditors; was an "equal participant and director in most of the entities that participated in defrauding Norgips"; received health insurance, a salary, officers' draws, and interest payments as compensation from TMS; and knew that TMS "was paying the debts of other companies." Most importantly, the majority asserts that McCarthy was "aware of the fraudulent business practices of Anthony Moschella, including using one entity to pay another's bills." The majority concludes that the fraudulent operation of TMS "simply would not have been possible without McCarthy's contributions" and faults her for doing nothing to stop the practices of Anthony Moschella.

When the majority makes the conclusory statement that McCarthy "was aware of the fraudulent business practices of Anthony Moschella," the only evidence in the record of her knowledge of his activities is that, as testified to by McCarthy herself, she "[d]idn't like the way Tony did things." She was asked, "what was the source of the clash between you that led to your leaving the office?" McCarthy answered, "the interest checks were paid to me and I would question him about why one company was paying interest that another company owed the debt and he would just shrug me off. He wouldn't give me answers and stuff like that." She did know that TMS was paying JTM's debt; however, McCarthy also testified that she took issue with the fact that Anthony Moschella said he could run the business the way he wanted to and "[n]o matter what I said or did I couldn't get results from him for anything." However, although the majority characterizes this testimony as knowledge of "the fraudulent business practices of Anthony Moschella," McCarthy actually testified that she was not even aware of the fact that TMS placed an order with Norgips for sheet rock until after this lawsuit was filed. Nothing in the record contradicts her testimony or otherwise shows that she had any knowledge of the Moschella brothers' actions in regard to Norgips. The bottom line is that none of the evidence relied upon by Norgips and the majority supports an inference that McCarthy actually did anything whatsoever to intentionally or knowingly cause TMS to be used to perpetrate an actual fraud, and did perpetrate an actual fraud upon Norgips, primarily for her own direct personal benefit. As argued by McCarthy, there is simply no evidence that she caused TMS to be used to perpetrate a fraud, that a fraud was committed "primarily for her own direct personal benefit," or that any omission by her was a substantial factor in bringing about Norgips's injury. Simply because Norgips presented many pieces of evidence that might be considered material does not mean that the evidence is legally sufficient to support the jury's findings. *See Moriel*, 879 S.W.2d at 24–25. There is simply no evidence in the record that McCarthy actually exploited the corporate form of TMS as a sham to perpetrate a fraud upon Norgips for her own personal gain. Thus, although the majority has a lot of scattered bricks, it has no wall. *See id.*

Accordingly, I would sustain McCarthy's fourth issue, reverse the judgment of the trial court, and render judgment in favor of McCarthy.

****

Ward Family Foundation V. Arnette (In re Arnette)
454 B.R. 663, 680 (Bankr.N.D.Tex.2011)

Plaintiff, The Ward Family Foundation (the "Foundation"), is a non-profit corporation that uses the income earned on its investments to support a number of charitable causes. Defendant, Christopher Adam Arnette ("Arnette"), is an individual resident of Dallas, Texas, who filed for relief under chapter 7 of the Bankruptcy Code on December 22, 2009. In the Adversary, Plaintiff seeks to (i) liquidate its claim against Arnette, (ii) have its claim determined to be nondischargeable in Arnette's bankruptcy case, and/or (iii) have Arnette's discharge denied.

I. FACTUAL AND PROCEDURAL BACKGROUND

A. The "Investment Opportunity" As Presented to the Foundation

Arnette met John Winslow ("Winslow"), an employee of the Foundation, at church in the fall of 2006. As they became acquainted, Winslow learned that Arnette was in the real estate business. Specifically, Arnette had two companies, HomeQwest HomeBuyers, Inc. a/k/a HomeBuyers of Texas, Inc. ("HomeQwest") and Autopilot Property, LLC ("Autopilot"), through which he, in general terms, purchased residential real estate, rehabilitated the properties, and then either sold or leased them to a third party with an option to own. Winslow, a financial advisor and the Foundation's Chief Operating Officer, was always looking for new investments for the Foundation and the Ward family generally. As a result, Winslow suggested to Arnette that they have lunch to discuss potential business opportunities. The lunch occurred on or about October 25, 2006. There, Arnette talked about his track record of buying and selling houses, saying that he (i) had completed over $10 million in residential transactions, (ii) had completed 30–40 deals in the previous year, and (iii) was "on track" to complete more than 50 transactions in 2006. The premise of Arnette's business as explained to Winslow was that Arnette, acting through one of his companies, would buy a house, fix it up to be "the nicest in the neighborhood," and then resell it for a profit. Arnette told Winslow that he had existing investors but that he needed to expand his group of private investors. Arnette said he preferred to use private investors because banks take too long to approve and close loans, and most of his deals involved highly motivated sellers who needed to sell their homes quickly. On October 27, 2006, Arnette followed up by sending Winslow an email to which he attached "an informational piece for you to look over. It is a pdf that explains our basic process of how the business is done (in general). This should give you a clear understanding of the investment opportunity." Plaintiff's Exhibit 1. Winslow brought his boss William Ward ("Ward"), the patriarch of the Ward family, into the discussions because he thought an investment with Arnette might be a fit for the Ward family or the Foundation. The Foundation ultimately decided to invest with Arnette, through his companies, HomeQwest and Autopilot. Though the documentation supporting the Foundation's investments is not extensive, in general terms, the Foundation agreed to lend either HomeQwest or Autopilot enough funds to purchase a particular piece of real property and to repair it for resale (based upon an estimate of repair costs provided by Arnette). The Foundation would be repaid on the earlier of the sale or refinancing of the rehabbed property, or the one-year anniversary of the property's acquisition. With two exceptions, the parties agreed that the Foundation would earn eighteen percent (18%) interest on the principal amounts loaned. If a property sold for more than the original principal amount of the loan (plus accrued interest), the surplus would belong to HomeQwest or Autopilot as its profit on the transaction. The Foundation understood that the funds it was advancing would be used solely for financing the costs to acquire each property and covering the estimated out-of-pocket repair costs for each property. . . . Initially, the Foundation agreed to loan HomeQwest the funds to purchase and repair the . . . "Initial Properties." . . . The "deal" worked as it was supposed to regarding the Initial Properties. Each property was purchased and either sold or refinanced timely, allowing the Foundation to be repaid for its loans as required by the promissory notes secured by the Initial Properties. From April 2007 through January 2008, Arnette solicited investments from the Foundation for eight more properties (collectively, the "Subsequent Properties," or individually, a "Subsequent Property") on behalf of HomeQwest and Autopilot . . . . Overall, the Foundation loaned HomeQwest and Autopilot a total of $1,743,400 for the purchase and repair of the Subsequent Properties.

B. The Investment Opportunity Sours

In mid-December 2008, Autopilot and the Foundation, among others, were sued by various Dallas taxing authorities in connection with unpaid property taxes . . . . In their subsequent meetings, and according to the testimony of Winslow and Ward, Arnette "confessed" to, among other things: (i) misusing the proceeds from the Foundation's loans— *i.e.,* not using them to make the repairs, (ii) having personal and business financial problems, and (iii) not being able to repay the notes, which were secured by liens on the Subsequent Properties. While Arnette denies having "confessed" to anything, he agrees that (i) the loan proceeds were not used to repair all of the Subsequent Properties, (ii) there were no funds remaining in HomeQwest (or otherwise) from which to repair the Subsequent Properties, and (iii) the notes were in default and could not be repaid. As of January 2009, all of the notes evidencing the Foundation's loans had matured. However, HomeQwest had failed to sell any of the Subsequent Properties and had failed to repay any amounts due under those notes. On February 2, 2009, the Foundation, acting through a special purpose vehicle it created for this purpose—The Ward Family Foundation Holdings, LLC—accepted deeds in lieu of foreclosure on each of the Subsequent Properties. . . .

II. LEGAL ANALYSIS

As noted previously, the Foundation seeks a money judgment against Arnette for fraud, breach of contract, suit on a note, unjust enrichment, promissory estoppel, money had and received, and to recover the reasonable attorneys' fees and costs it has incurred in obtaining that judgment. In addition, the Foundation seeks an award of exemplary damages where applicable. Finally, the Foundation seeks a determination that the amounts owed to it, together with any other damages awarded to it, are nondischargeable under section 523(a)(2)(A), (a)(4), and/or (a)(6) of the Bankruptcy Code and that Arnette is not entitled to a discharge under section 727(a)(5) of the Bankruptcy Code. From the Court's perspective, the Court must first determine if the Foundation is entitled to a judgment against its borrowers, HomeQwest and Autopilot. If the Court concludes that Arnette's companies can be held liable, the Court will next consider whether Arnette can also be held liable for the Foundation's damages. Then, if the Court concludes that Arnette can be held liable for the Foundation's damages, the Court will consider the nondischargeability and objection to discharge issues. . . .

Can Arnette be held Personally Liable?

(1) Piercing the Corporate and Limited Liability Shield

There are "three broad categories in which a court may pierce the corporate veil: (1) the corporation is the alter ego of its owners and/or shareholders; (2) the corporation is used for illegal purposes; and (3) the corporation is used [as a sham] to perpetrate a fraud." *Rimade Ltd. v. Hubbard Enterprises, Inc.,* 388 F.3d 138, 143 (5th Cir.2004) (citing *W. Horizontal Drilling, Inc. v. Jonnet Energy Corp.,* 11 F.3d 65, 67 (5th Cir.1994)). The Foundation argues that the Court should disregard HomeQwest's and Autopilot's corporate and limited liability shields under the alter ego and sham theories. But before the Court analyzes those theories, it will consider whether the Foundation must satisfy section 21.223 of the Texas Business Organizations Code, which "sets forth additional requirements for piercing the corporate veil in cases based on claims for *breach of contract.*" *Rimade,* 388 F.3d at 143 (emphasis added).

a. Section 21.223 of the Texas Business Organizations Code

The Foundation contends that section 21.223 does not apply to its veil piercing claims because they sound in tort, not contract. The Court's research reveals some inconsistency among the decisions dealing with the scope of section 21.223 and its predecessor statute. Some courts have found that "[g]iven its broad scope, [section] 21.223 applies to both contractual claims and ancillary torts," including fraud. *In re Antone's Records, Inc.,* 08–12292–CAG (Adv. No 09–01010), 2011 WL 309146, at 24 (Bankr.W.D.Tex. Jan. 25, 2011) (collecting state and federal court cases so stating). Other courts, however, have said that courts should not "be too liberal in determining that a cause of action 'relates to or arises from a corporation's contractual obligation.' To define fraud [and] fraudulent inducement ... claims as 'matters relating to or arising from a corporation's contractual obligation,' and thus require plaintiffs to meet [section 21.223]'s requirements in order to hold the individual tortfeasor liable extends the statute beyond its intended and logical reach." *Kingston v. Helm,* 82 S.W.3d 755, 766 (Tex.App.2002). In *Kingston,* the court found that the statute "seeks to protect shareholders— *i.e.,* persons having some kind of ownership interest in the corporation—from being held personally liable for corporate obligations." *Id.* The *Kingston* court believed "that identifying shareholders or owners as the only class of persons protected by the statute indicates that the kind of liability it protects them from is liability that would exist by virtue of the mere status as an owner of or shareholder in the corporation." But the court did "not believe that this article was intended to shield a corporate officer or agent who commits tortious conduct merely because the officer or agent also possesses an ownership interest in the corporation." *Id.; but see Texas–Ohio Gas, Inc. v. Mecom,* 28 S.W.3d 129, 133–34 (Tex.App.2000) (holding that suit against vice-president and manager of corporation for fraud, fraudulent inducement, negligent misrepresentation, and tortious interference with a contract was subject to requirements of section 21.223, which provides the "exclusive means for recovery against shareholders of a corporation for such claims" because such claims "attempt[ ] to hold shareholders personally liable for a 'matter relating to or arising from' a contractual obligation of the corporation").

While the disagreement over the precise scope of section 21.223 is interesting, this Court need not resolve it here because, even assuming section 21.223 applies, the Foundation has satisfied the statute's requirements. Under section 21.223, merely proving alter ego or sham to perpetrate a fraud "is not enough; in order to pierce the corporate veil, the [Foundation] must also demonstrate fraud by and direct personal benefit to the obligor." *Thrift v. Estate of Hubbard,* 44 F.3d 348, 353 (5th Cir.1995); *see* Tex. Bus. Orgs. Code Ann. § 21.223 (West 2010) (the veil may be pierced where the defendant shareholder "caused the corporation to be used for purposes of perpetrating and did perpetrate an actual fraud on the obligee primarily for the direct personal benefit of the holder"). "Where actual fraud primarily for the benefit of the perpetrating shareholder or shareholders can be shown, the various doctrines for disregarding the corporate entity, including alter ego and a sham to perpetrate a fraud, are still very much alive." *Farr v. Sun World Sav. Ass'n,* 810 S.W.2d 294, 296 (Tex.App.1991).

i. Actual Fraud

In the context of piercing the corporate veil, the concept of "actual fraud" contained in section 21.223 is not the same as the common law tort of fraud discussed above. *Latham v. Burgher,* 320 S.W.3d 602, 607 (Tex.App.2010). The plaintiff need not prove each element of common law fraud; rather, actual fraud under section 21.223 simply requires proof of "dishonesty of purpose or intent to deceive." *Id.* at 607; *see also Dick's Last Resort of W. End, Inc. v. Market/Ross, Ltd.,* 273 S.W.3d 905, 908 (Tex.App.2008) (rejecting the argument that an actual fraud jury instruction should include elements of the tort of common law fraud because it was enough for the instruction to provide that "actual fraud means actions involving dishonesty of purpose or intent to deceive"); *Castleberry v. Branscum,* 721 S.W.2d 270, 273 (Tex.1986), *superceded by statute as recognized in W. Horizontal Drilling, Inc. v. Jonnet Energy Corp.,* 11 F.3d 65, 68 (5th Cir.1994); *Priddy v. Rawson,* 282 S.W.3d 588, 600 (Tex.App.2009); *Solutioneers Consulting, Ltd. v. Gulf Greyhound Partners, Ltd.,* 237 S.W.3d 379, 387 (Tex.App.2007). Here, the Court concludes that the Foundation has proven actual fraud for the purposes of section 21.223. HomeQwest and Autopilot, acting through Arnette, made material misrepresentations to the Foundation from the outset. Arnette overstated his prior successes (through HomeQwest and Autopilot) in order to induce the Foundation to invest with them. And by the time HomeQwest and Autopilot, acting through Arnette, began dealing with the Foundation, Arnette knew (or should have known), at a minimum, that the investors believed that the proformas he prepared included at least an implicit promise to use their loan proceeds solely for the purchase and repair of the targeted property. Otherwise, the "deal" proposed by HomeQwest and Autopilot could not work as represented. In other words, without the repair funds actually being spent on repairs, the 70–75% loan-to-value ratio represented by them to their investors could not be achieved. In fact, this misuse of repair funds was at least one of the reasons for [an earlier investor's] threatened lawsuit.

Notwithstanding [the earlier investor's] allegations of theft and misuse of funds being made immediately prior to the commencement of his business dealings with the Foundation, Arnette did nothing to clarify this issue with his next investor, the Foundation. In other words, Arnette continued to use the same types of documents and failed to disclose to the Foundation that he believed that he could use its loan proceeds for purposes other than the repair of the properties on which the Foundation would have a lien. Of course, had Arnette so stated— through clarifying the documents or otherwise—the entire premise of the "safe investment" would have crumbled, as the touted loan-to-value ratio that made the investment "safe" would no longer exist. *See* P–1 at p. WFF 00591 (Arnette's explanation of why the investment was safe).

It is clear from the evidence that HomeQwest and Autopilot, acting through Arnette, never intended to comply with the terms of the agreement that were so critical to the Foundation's decision to invest with them. When the Foundation demanded explanations from Arnette regarding the disposition of hundreds of thousands of dollars of the Foundation's money, Arnette continued his fraudulent ways by lying about the status of the repairs to the properties, the outstanding tax obligations against the properties, and the status of insurance on the properties. Sadly, based upon the credible trial evidence, there is no doubt that Arnette was dishonest in his dealings with the Foundation and intended to mislead the Foundation from the outset.

ii. Primarily for Arnette's Personal Benefit

The evidence also showed that HomeQwest and Autopilot perpetrated the actual fraud primarily for Arnette's direct personal benefit. Tex. Bus. Orgs. Code Ann. § 21.223(b) (West 2010). After reviewing the evidence in light of the considerable case law on this issue, the Court concludes that the fraud here did primarily serve to directly benefit Arnette. . . . Here, there is no doubt that Arnette used HomeQwest and Autopilot to perpetrate a fraud that primarily served to directly benefit him. . . . HomeQwest and Autopilot were wholly owned and controlled by Arnette. He was the only one who stood to benefit from the companies' continued operations. And he knew that if his companies failed, he would lose his livelihood. Obtaining the Foundation's investments was therefore critically important to Arnette personally, and he directly benefitted from that investment. Moreover, Arnette used Foundation loan proceeds to make distributions and advances to himself, thereby enabling him to continue to support his family and lifestyle. Had Arnette not defrauded the Foundation into investing with his companies, he would not have received the benefit of the Foundation's funds for these advances and distributions.

b. Sham to Perpetrate a Fraud

The "sham to perpetuate injustice" or "sham to perpetrate a fraud" theory has been recognized in Texas as a distinct method by which to pierce the corporate veil. *See Castleberry*, 721 S.W.2d at 273. Under Texas law, the sham theory "is an equitable doctrine, and Texas courts take a 'flexible fact-specific approach focusing on equity.' The Texas Supreme Court has also noted that the variety of shams is infinite, and that the purpose of the doctrine should not be thwarted by adherence to any particular theory of liability." *Permian Petroleum Co. v. Petroleos Mexicanos,* 934 F.2d 635, 643–44 (5th Cir.1991) (internal citations and quotations omitted). The focus of the analysis under this theory "is on some inequitable result for the claimant, because of abuses of the corporate form." *Gibraltar Sav. v. LDBrinkman Corp.,* 860 F.2d 1275, 1289 (5th Cir.1988). The question of injustice or inequity is a question of fact. *Id.*

After reviewing Texas case law, the Court does not find that the sham to perpetrate a fraud theory applies in this case. In general, the theory most frequently applies "where the corporate fiction is resorted to as a means of evading an existing legal obligation." *Id.* For example, in *Castleberry* the court found a sham to perpetrate a fraud when two shareholders created a new corporation and transferred all of the assets of the original corporation to it to avoid the original corporation's obligation to pay the third shareholder for the buy-back of his shares. 721 S.W.2d at 274–75; *see also JNS,* 418 B.R. at 907–08 (owners transferred company assets to a newly formed entity intending to leave liabilities behind in a "worthless shell"). Neither HomeQwest nor Autopilot were "resorted to as a means of evading an existing legal obligation." Both companies existed before the Foundation invested with Arnette. Moreover, Arnette did not transfer assets among his companies with the purpose of using the corporate form to shield those assets from creditors. The Court thus finds the sham to perpetrate a fraud theory inapplicable here.

c. Alter Ego

Texas courts recognize the alter ego doctrine as another theory to pierce the corporate veil. *Sparks v. Booth,* 232 S.W.3d 853, 868 (Tex.App.2007) (citing *Castleberry,* 721 S.W.2d at 272). Under this theory, liability follows if there exists such unity between the corporation and the individual that the corporation ceases to be separate, and holding only the corporation liable would promote injustice. *See Mancorp, Inc. v. Culpepper,* 802 S.W.2d 226, 228 (Tex.1990) (citing *Castleberry,* 721 S.W.2d at 272). As proof of alter ego, a court may consider: (1) the payment of alleged corporate debts with personal checks or other commingling of funds; (2) representations that the individual will financially back the corporation; (3) the diversion of company profits to the individual for his personal use; (4) inadequate capitalization; and (5) other failure to keep corporate and personal assets separate. *See Mancorp,* 802 S.W.2d at 228; *Morris v. Powell,* 150 S.W.3d 212, 220 (Tex.App.2004), *overruled on other grounds Michiana Easy Livin' Country, Inc. v. Holten,* 168 S.W.3d 777, 788–89 (Tex.2005). However, the failure of a corporation to observe any corporate formality is no longer a factor in considering whether alter ego exists. *See* Tex. Bus. Orgs. Code Ann. § 21.223(a)(3) (West 2010). In sum, the plaintiff must prove it is necessary to hold the individual liable, as opposed to the corporate form, in order to avoid a substantial injustice to the plaintiff. *Mancorp,* 802 S.W.2d at 228. Based upon the facts . . . . the evidence supports a finding of alter ego. Moreover, the Foundation has proven that Arnette, acting through HomeQwest and Autopilot, defrauded the Foundation; yet, HomeQwest and Autopilot are out of business and have no assets to satisfy a judgment in the Foundation's favor. *See Stewart & Stevenson Servs., Inc. v. Serv–Tech Inc.,* 879 S.W.2d 89, 110 (Tex.App.1994) (In a tort case "the financial strength or weakness of the corporate tortfeasor is an important consideration" in the alter ego analysis). For these reasons, the Court concludes that Arnette should be held personally liable for the debts of both HomeQwest and Autopilot under the alter ego theory.

Pinebrook Properties, LTD. v Brookhaven Lake Property Owners Association
77 S.W.3d 487 (Tex.App.–Texarkana,2002)

Pinebrook Properties, Ltd., Pinebrook Properties Management, L.L.C., and A.C. Musgrave, Jr. (Pinebrook) appeal the trial court's judgment providing various relief for the different parties. The conflict embodied in this litigation is the culmination of a long and complicated history, including two prior suits resulting in appeals to this Court. The case currently before us (Musgrave III) is the result of the consolidation by the trial court of a suit filed in the year 2000 by Pinebrook Properties against Brookhaven Lake Property Owners Association and counterclaims by the Association and various lot owners (Owners) remaining after they were severed from a 1997 lawsuit. The other claims from the 1997 lawsuit were the subject of a recent appeal to this Court, which were decided in *Musgrave v. Owen,* 67 S.W.3d 513 (Tex.App.-Texarkana 2002, no pet.) (*Musgrave* II). Pinebrook brings eight issues in this appeal: 1) whether the trial court erred by denying, on grounds of res judicata and collateral estoppel, claims for injunctive relief sought by Pinebrook Properties against the Association; 2) whether the trial court erred in finding Pinebrook Properties and Pinebrook Management are the alter egos of Musgrave . . . .

Musgrave succeeded three other owners as the owner of certain real property in the Brookhaven in the Pines Addition. He purchased the lake, the roadways serving the lots, and some forested recreational property in the addition. The lot owners enjoy exclusive rights to hunt, fish, and recreate on the recreational property and the lake, and to use the roadways for ingress and egress. *Anderson v. McRae,* 495 S.W.2d 351, 355 (Tex.Civ.App.-Texarkana 1973, no writ). In December 1998, Pinebrook Properties, a Texas limited partnership, succeeded Musgrave's interest in the lake, roadways, and recreational property. Pinebrook Management, a Texas limited liability company, is the general partner of Pinebrook Properties. In this case (Musgrave III), Pinebrook Properties filed suit seeking injunctive relief from the trial court to stop the Association from working on the roadways and lake, and then billing Pinebrook. The Owners, the appellees in Musgrave III, include a number of people who were not parties to the first suit involving the Brookhaven in the Pines Addition, which we decided in *Musgrave v. Brookhaven Lake Prop. Owners Ass'n,* 990 S.W.2d 386 (Tex.App.-Texarkana 1999, pet. denied) (*Musgrave* I). As counterplaintiffs in Musgrave III, the Owners sought injunctive relief, declaratory judgment, and monetary relief against Pinebrook Properties, Pinebrook Management, and Musgrave. They contend Pinebrook Properties and Pinebrook Management are merely alter egos of Musgrave, who transferred his interest in the property to Pinebrook Properties in December 1998. . . .

Pinebrook contends in its second point of error that the trial court erred in finding Pinebrook Properties and Pinebrook Management are alter egos of Musgrave, and judgment should not have been granted against Musgrave individually. Pinebrook contends the standard of review for all its remaining points of error is abuse of discretion. However, in this second point of error, Pinebrook is challenging the trial court's finding of fact that Pinebrook Properties and Pinebrook Management are the alter egos of Musgrave. . . . Alter ego is a basis for disregarding the corporate fiction. *Castleberry v. Branscum,* 721 S.W.2d 270, 272 (Tex.1986). It applies "when there is such unity between corporation and individual that the separateness of the corporation has ceased and holding only the corporation liable would result in injustice." *Id.* (citing *First Nat'l Bank v. Gamble,* 134 Tex. 112, 132 S.W.2d 100, 103 (1939)). Alter ego "is shown from the total dealings of the corporation and the individual, including the degree to which ... corporate and individual property have been kept separately, the amount of financial interest, ownership and control the individual maintains over the corporation, and whether the corporation has been used for personal purposes." *Castleberry,* 721 S.W.2d at 272; *Hall v. Timmons,* 987 S.W.2d 248, 250 (Tex.App.-Beaumont 1999, no pet.). Failure to comply with corporate formalities is no longer a factor in considering whether alter ego exists. TEX. BUS. CORP. ACT ANN. art. 2.21(A)(3) (Vernon Supp.2002); *see Aluminum Chems. (Bolivia), Inc. v. Bechtel Corp.,* 28 S.W.3d 64, 67 (Tex.App.-Texarkana 2000, no pet.). Pinebrook Properties, Ltd., a Texas limited partnership, owns the lake, dam, roadways, and recreational areas at issue in this case. Pinebrook Properties Management, L.L.C., a Texas limited liability company, is the general partner of Pinebrook Properties. Musgrave is the president and general managing partner of Pinebrook Management. The trial court erred in its application of law. The theory of alter ego, or piercing the corporate veil, is inapplicable to partnerships. Under traditional general partnership law, each partner is liable jointly and severally for the liabilities of the partnership. . .

Under corporation law, officers and shareholders are not liable for the actions of the corporation absent an independent duty. *Leitch v. Hornsby,* 935 S.W.2d 114, 117 (Tex.1996). Because officers and shareholders may not be held liable for the actions of the corporation, the theory of alter ego is used to pierce the corporate veil so the injured party might recover from an officer or shareholder who is otherwise protected by the corporate structure. Alter ego is inapplicable with regard to a partnership because there is no veil that needs piercing, even when dealing with a limited partnership, because the general partner is always liable for the debts and obligations of the partnership to third parties. The trial court erred in finding Pinebrook Properties is the alter ego of Musgrave.

Having determined Pinebrook Properties cannot be the alter ego of Musgrave, we now turn to the trial court's finding that Pinebrook Management, which is a limited liability company, is the alter ego of Musgrave. A limited liability company is any company organized and in existence in conformity with the Texas Limited Liability Company Act (TLLCA). TEX.REV.CIV. STAT. ANN.. Art. 1528n, art. 1.02(A)(3) (Vernon 1997). The Texas Legislature's enactment of the TLLCA created a new business entity, the limited liability company. A limited liability company is a separate and distinct entity from other types of business entities already in existence in Texas, such as the corporation or the limited partnership. "Except as and to the extent the regulations specifically provide otherwise, a member or manager is not liable for the debts, obligations or liabilities of a limited liability company including under a judgment decree, or order of a court." TEX.REV.CIV. STAT. ANN.. Art. 1528n, art. 4.03(A) (Vernon 1997). In determining if there is evidence legally sufficient to support the trial court's finding, we look to see if there is such unity between Musgrave and Pinebrook Management that the separateness has ceased to exist, and whether holding only Pinebrook Management liable, as the general partner of Pinebrook Properties, would result in injustice. *See Castleberry,* 721 S.W.2d at 272. We must look to the relationship between Musgrave and Pinebrook Management to see if alter ego is shown from the total dealings of Musgrave and Pinebrook Management—for example, if the corporate and individual properties have been kept separate; the amount of financial interest, ownership, and control the individual maintains over the corporation; and whether the corporation has been used for personal purposes. *See id.* The evidence of alter ego between Musgrave and Pinebrook Management presented by the Owners is that Pinebrook Management had no checking account, had not filed a tax return, and that Musgrave sent a letter to the lot owners, signing his own name and not designating that he signed it in any other capacity. However, the Owners failed to cite any authority holding that failure to have a checking account, or failure to file tax returns, establishes alter ego. There is no evidence provided that Musgrave commingled funds or that his assets and those of Pinebrook Management were not kept separate. The evidence clearly shows Pinebrook Management has never had the need, or been required, to file a tax return. This is no evidence that Pinebrook is the alter ego of Musgrave.

The Owners also rely on a letter signed by Musgrave after he transferred the property to Pinebrook Properties which denied reimbursement for expenditures. They contend this letter shows alter ego and Musgrave's disregard for the corporate structure. However, failing to sign the letter with "president," or putting the corporate name on the letter, is a corporate formality. Failure to comply with corporate formalities is no longer considered in determining alter ego and is therefore no evidence of alter ego. TEX. BUS. CORP. ACT ANN. art. 2.21(A)(3); *Aluminum Chems. (Bolivia), Inc.,* 28 S.W.3d at 67. The Owners contend Musgrave testified that Pinebrook Properties' and Pinebrook Management's only sources of income are derived from contributions or loans made by Musgrave. A review of Musgrave's testimony reveals neither Pinebrook Properties nor Pinebrook Management have any sources of income. Musgrave specifically testified there has never been any money flowing through Pinebrook Management. The only money expended on Pinebrook Management by Musgrave shown by the evidence is that he paid to have it incorporated. Musgrave has never received any funds from Pinebrook Properties or Pinebrook Management. There is evidence that Musgrave lent money to Pinebrook Properties via written open notes payable on demand. However, this is no evidence of the relationship between Musgrave and Pinebrook Management, or that their funds are commingled, or that Musgrave has disregarded the corporate structure of Pinebrook Management in any way. The final evidence on which the Owners rely is Musgrave's testimony at trial: "Well, I own the property. I pay taxes on the property." The Owners contend this statement shows Musgrave disregarded the separation of the corporate enterprise. The context of this statement is as follows:

Q. You are objecting to the property owners association making any rules or regulations regarding that lake, correct?
A. Not any.

Q. Well, what does the word "exclusive" mean to you?

A. Well, I own the property. I pay taxes on the property. Their exclusive rights are for use of the lake and the recreational property for hunting and fishing. Beyond that, they don't have the rights to set rules and regulations.

Although Musgrave did make the statement on which the Owners rely, based on the context in which it was made, we conclude it is no more than a scintilla of evidence that Musgrave disregarded the corporate structure or enterprise. The evidence reveals Musgrave is not the sole manager of Pinebrook Management. There are two other managers involved, Bill Ragsdale and Billy Boles. Finally, there is no evidence that Musgrave used Pinebrook Management for personal purposes. The Owners stated at oral argument that Musgrave transferred the land to Pinebrook Properties after suit was filed against him, suggesting that Pinebrook Properties and Pinebrook Management were created fraudulently. However, the Owners did not plead fraud or that Pinebrook Properties or Pinebrook Management were created in violation of law. The Owners, in their pleadings, rely solely on alter ego as the basis for Musgrave's liability. The trial court erred in finding that Pinebrook Properties, a limited partnership, is the alter ego of Musgrave, and there is no evidence to support the trial court's finding that Pinebrook Management is the alter ego of Musgrave. Because the Owners, in their pleadings and trial strategy, relied on attaching individual liability to Musgrave solely on the theory of alter ego, we reverse the judgment as to Musgrave and render judgment that the Owners take nothing against him.

Derivative Suits

A member may also bring a derivative lawsuit to remedy a wrong done to the LLC by managers, managing members or officers, such as a breach of duty of care or duty of loyalty. The TBOC makes most of the provisions that generally apply to derivative proceedings, such as the contemporaneous ownership requirement and the demand requirement, inapplicable to closely held LLCs which are LLCs that have less than 35 members and have no membership interests listed on a national securities exchange or quoted on an over-the-counter market. A court also has the option to treat the claim involving a closely held LLC as either a derivative or direct claim and to determine whether the recovery should be paid to the plaintiff member or the LLC. This set of provisions is identical with the TBOC provisions dealing with derivative claims involving closely-held corporations.

Texas Business Organization Code provisions

§ 101.452. Standing to Bring Proceeding. A member may not institute or maintain a derivative proceeding unless:

(1) the member:

(A) was a member of the limited liability company at the time of the act or omission complained of; or

(B) became a member by operation of law from a person that was a member at the time of the act or omission complained of; and

(2) the member fairly and adequately represents the interests of the limited liability company in enforcing the right of the limited liability company.

§ 101.453. Demand

(a) A member may not institute a derivative proceeding until the 91st day after the date a written demand is filed with the limited liability company stating with particularity the act, omission, or other matter that is the subject of the claim or challenge and requesting that the limited liability company take suitable action.

(b) The waiting period required by Subsection (a) before a derivative proceeding may be instituted is not required if:

(1) the member has been previously notified that the demand has been rejected by the limited liability company;

(2) the limited liability company is suffering irreparable injury; or

(3) irreparable injury to the limited liability company would result by waiting for the expiration of the 90-day period.

§ 101.454. Determination by Governing or Independent Persons

(a) The determination of how to proceed on allegations made in a demand or petition relating to a derivative proceeding must be made by an affirmative vote of the majority of:

100%

(1) the independent and disinterested governing persons present at a meeting of the governing authority at which interested governing persons are not present at the time of the vote if the independent and disinterested governing persons constitute a quorum of the governing authority;

(2) a committee consisting of two or more independent and disinterested governing persons appointed by the majority of one or more independent and disinterested governing persons present at a meeting of the governing authority, regardless of whether the independent and disinterested governing persons constitute a quorum of the governing authority; or

(3) a panel of one or more independent and disinterested persons appointed by the court on a motion by the limited liability company listing the names of the persons to be appointed and stating that, to the best of the limited liability company's knowledge, the persons to be appointed are disinterested and qualified to make the determinations contemplated by Section 101.458.

(b) The court shall appoint a panel under Subsection (a)(3) if the court finds that the persons recommended by the limited liability company are independent and disinterested and are otherwise qualified with respect to expertise, experience, independent judgment, and other factors considered appropriate by the court under the circumstances to make the determinations. A person appointed by the court to a panel under this section may not be held liable to the limited liability company or the limited liability company's members for an action taken or omission made by the person in that capacity, except for acts or omissions constituting fraud or wilful misconduct.

§ 101.455. Stay of Proceeding

(a) If the domestic or foreign limited liability company that is the subject of a derivative proceeding commences an inquiry into the allegations made in a demand or petition and the person or group of persons described by Section 101.454 is conducting an active review of the allegations in good faith, the court shall stay a derivative proceeding until the review is completed and a determination is made by the person or group regarding what further action, if any, should be taken.

(b) To obtain a stay, the domestic or foreign limited liability company shall provide the court with a written statement agreeing to advise the court and the member making the demand of the determination promptly on the completion of the review of the matter. A stay, on motion, may be reviewed every 60 days for the continued necessity of the stay.

(c) If the review and determination made by the person or group is not completed before the 61st day after the date on which the court orders the stay, the stay may be renewed for one or more additional 60-day periods if the domestic or foreign limited liability company provides the court and the member with a written statement of the status of the review and the reasons why a continued extension of the stay is necessary.

§ 101.458. Dismissal of Derivative Proceeding

(a) A court shall dismiss a derivative proceeding on a motion by the limited liability company if the person or group of persons described by Section 101.454 determines in good faith, after conducting a reasonable inquiry and based on factors the person or group considers appropriate under the circumstances, that continuation of the derivative proceeding is not in the best interests of the limited liability company.

(b) In determining whether the requirements of Subsection (a) have been met, the burden of proof shall be on:

(1) the plaintiff member if:

(A) the majority of the governing authority consists of independent and disinterested persons at the time the determination is made;

(B) the determination is made by a panel of one or more independent and disinterested persons appointed under Section 101.454(a)(3); or

(C) the limited liability company presents prima facie evidence that demonstrates that the persons appointed under Section 101.454(a)(2) are independent and disinterested; or

(2) the limited liability company in any other circumstance.

§ 101.461. Payment of Expenses

(a) In this section, "expenses" means reasonable expenses incurred by a party in a derivative proceeding, including:

(1) attorney's fees;

(2) costs of pursuing an investigation of the matter that was the subject of the derivative proceeding; or

(3) expenses for which the domestic or foreign limited liability company may be required to indemnify another person.

(b) On termination of a derivative proceeding, the court may order:

(1) the domestic or foreign limited liability company to pay the expenses the plaintiff incurred in the proceeding if the court finds the proceeding has resulted in a substantial benefit to the domestic or foreign limited liability company;

(2) the plaintiff to pay the expenses the domestic or foreign limited liability company or other defendant incurred in investigating and defending the proceeding if the court finds the proceeding has been instituted or maintained without reasonable cause or for an improper purpose; or

(3) a party to pay the expenses incurred by another party relating to the filing of a pleading, motion, or other paper if the court finds the pleading, motion, or other paper:

(A) was not well grounded in fact after reasonable inquiry;

(B) was not warranted by existing law or a good faith argument for the extension, modification, or reversal of existing law; or

(C) was interposed for an improper purpose, such as to harass, cause unnecessary delay, or cause a needless increase in the cost of litigation.

§ 101.463. Closely Held Limited Liability Company

(a) In this section, "closely held limited liability company" means a limited liability company that has:

(1) fewer than 35 members; and

(2) no membership interests listed on a national securities exchange or regularly quoted in an over-the-counter market by one or more members of a national securities association.

(b) Sections 101.452-101.459 do not apply to a closely held limited liability company.

(c) If justice requires:

(1) a derivative proceeding brought by a member of a closely held limited liability company may be treated by a court as a direct action brought by the member for the member's own benefit; and

(2) a recovery in a direct or derivative proceeding by a member may be paid directly to the plaintiff or to the limited liability company if necessary to protect the interests of creditors or other members of the limited liability company.

Rogers v. Alexander
244 S.W.3d 370, 388 (Tex. App.—Dallas 2007)

James O. Rogers, William M. Burmeister, Conservative Care, Inc., and Care Affiliates, Inc., appeal the trial court's judgment, following a jury trial, in favor of Daniel Alexander, Leslie Alexander, and Judith Pucci. In nineteen issues, appellants argue (1) there is no evidence to support an award of damages on any of appellees' claims; (2) appellees' expert witness was unqualified, unreliable, and used faulty damage models; (3) appellees have no standing to recover damages, even if they presented some evidence of damages; (4) appellees are not entitled to declaratory relief; (5) the contract between the parties was not illusory, unconscionable, or unenforceable; (6) there is no evidence of fraud, civil theft, fraudulent inducement, breach of contract, or civil conspiracy; (7) there is no clear and convincing evidence to support the award of punitive damages, (8) the admission of certain irrelevant and prejudicial evidence entitles appellants to a new trial; (9) the damages awarded are excessive, and (10) the judgment violates the election-of-remedies doctrine. We affirm the trial court's judgment.

In March 2002, Daniel Alexander, his wife, Leslie Alexander, and Judith Pucci formed Alexander & Pucci, L.L.C. d/b/a Accent Home Health (Accent). Daniel served as chief financial officer, Leslie became Accent's administrator, and Judith was Accent's director of nursing. Accent hired an accounting firm and obtained a state license and a Medicare certification in August 2002 so that it could both see patients in Texas and accept Medicare insurance money. Other than the funds Leslie, Daniel, and Judith had put into Accent, Accent had received no outside funds between March 2002 and August 2002. Nevertheless, money from pending Medicare claims was "building in an account" until Accent was approved to accept Medicare patients. Daniel and Leslie took more money out of their savings, Judith took a loan from her mother, and Leslie "started hopping on the phone calling Medicare trying to get this connection put in place." Leslie succeeded in speeding up the approval process, and Accent began receiving its Medicare payments in September 2002. With the Medicare payments, Accent had "more money coming in than [it was] spending." By the end of 2002, Accent showed a profit of almost $36,000, and Daniel, Leslie, and Judith were able to pay themselves salaries and give a bonus to themselves and all of their employees. In December 2002, Rogers contacted Daniel to "talk about home health." Rogers was a neighbor of a friend of Daniel's. Daniel and Leslie met with Rogers at a restaurant and discussed Accent's startup and operations. Leslie "walked away [from the meeting] not quite sure exactly what Mr. Rogers did." Nevertheless, Rogers scheduled another meeting where Leslie got the impression Rogers was involved in outpatient therapy and felt that he and Accent could work together. Rogers represented that he was a certified public accountant and had a master's degree in accounting. It appears from the record that Rogers is not a certified public accountant.

On January 6, 2003, Daniel and Leslie met with Rogers again and Rogers represented that he had outpatient clinics and could help Accent with staffing as it grew. Rogers also reiterated his status as a C.P.A. and indicated he had personal contacts with "between fifty and a hundred doctors," had been in the health care industry for many years, and had helpful connections throughout the metroplex. Rogers said that he could also help with day-to-day accounting. The next meeting, which also included Judith, occurred at Rogers' outpatient therapy clinic where Rogers made a business proposal that he wrote out on a "scratch sheet." Leslie had already described to Rogers her plans to expand Accent's operations by opening another office in August or September. Rogers stated that they were losing $40,000 to $60,000 per week in referrals he could bring to Accent because he did not have a license to provide home health care. Under the deal Rogers presented, Daniel, Leslie, and Judith would keep one hundred percent of the business Accent already had. As to the "vast amount of business" that Rogers would bring to Accent, Rogers would keep eighty percent with the remaining twenty percent split between Daniel, Leslie, and Judith. "[T]he biggest benefit" of Rogers' proposal was that he would provide money to enable Accent to "start expanding immediately," open another agency, and take all of Daniel's Leslie's and Judith's money out of the bank. Rogers said he was an "accredited investor," which "meant that he could walk into a bank and get a loan for at least seven figures." Rogers asked what Leslie thought it would cost to start expanding right away, and she indicated it would take about $150,000 to start another agency and get the necessary license and another $100,000 to cover expenses once they took their money out of Accent. Rogers stated he would be "hands off in the day-to-day operations of the company," but he would help with the accounting. Rogers said he would write up a "term sheet" and meet at Accent's office to review it. . . .

Rogers sent his attorneys to Accent's office to question employees, and Leslie and Daniel contacted attorneys of their own, ultimately filing suit in late July 2003. In their original petition, Daniel, Leslie, and Judith sought a declaratory judgment that the investment agreement was void, and they also brought claims for fraudulent inducement, breach of fiduciary duty, and, if the investment agreement was held to be enforceable, claims for breach of the investment agreement. In his original answer and counterclaim, Rogers maintained that Leslie, Daniel, and Judith owed an ongoing duty of loyalty to Accent and were subject to agreements not to compete with Accent, solicit any of Accent's clients, or reveal any of Accent's confidential information. Rogers alleged Leslie, Daniel, and Judith had breached these duties under the parties' agreement and this threatened to disrupt or destroy Accent's business. In particular, Rogers complained of Leslie, Daniel, and Judith's refusal to sign a formal change of ownership form that would allow Accent to continue its operations and receive payments, including payments for services already rendered. As a result, Rogers sought damages, interest, and attorney's fees. . . . A jury subsequently entered a verdict in which it found Rogers committed fraud in the inducement and fraud against Leslie, Daniel, and Judith as to the signing of the investment agreement; Burmeister, Care Affiliates, and Conservative Care knowingly participated or knowingly accepted benefits of Rogers' fraud . . . .The trial court entered judgment that recounted the jury's verdict and awarded Leslie, Daniel, and Judith $883,259.75 each, representing "actual damages in the amount of $831,203.89 and pre-judgment interest at the rate of five percent...." The judgment also awarded exemplary damages and attorney's fees. In addition, the judgment declared the investment agreement void for a variety of reasons and declared Leslie, Daniel, and Judith to be the "sole and rightful Members" of Accent. This appeal followed.

Here, the record shows Rogers approached Leslie, Daniel, and Judith and indicated he was a C.P.A., had a master's degree in accounting, and had personal contacts with "between fifty and a hundred doctors." Rogers stated Accent was losing $40,000 to $60,000 per week in referrals that he could bring to Accent. Rogers brought forth a term sheet and investment agreement purported to give Rogers eighty percent of the business he brought to Accent and effectively gave Rogers control over when or if to disburse funds to Accent after closing up to $250,000. Rogers delayed the closing on the agreement because he "didn't have all the financials," and he brought [Appellant William M.] Burmeister in to take over Accent's accounts payable. Leslie added Rogers to the signature card at Accent's bank, and Rogers transferred $95,000 and $34,000 into a Bank One account. However, Rogers did not put Leslie, Daniel, or Judith on the signature card of the Bank One account or give them any access to the Bank One account. Apparently, the Bank One account had $100,000 in it when Rogers transferred the $95,000 from Accent. Rogers withdrew his $100,000 after the transfer and began operating off Accent's funds. After several months of excuses, Rogers provided a balance sheet showing a "Bank One Funding" of $100,000 and a $150,000 "Line for expansion," but the record shows the $100,000 never left Rogers' control, and the $150,000 was never made available to Accent. The balance sheet also, without explanation, showed a $152,181.26 allowance for doubtful accounts. Leslie, Daniel, and Judith ultimately left Accent and undertook the lengthy underlying litigation to recover damages from Rogers and Burmeister. Viewing all the evidence, it appears Rogers and Burmeister knowingly made false representations to Leslie, Daniel and Judith intending that they would act upon the misrepresentations, and Leslie, Daniel and Judith acted on the misrepresentations and thereby suffered injury. See Formosa, 960 S.W.2d at 47. Accordingly, we overrule Rogers' and Burmeister's argument that no evidence supported the jury's finding that they committed fraud. See City of Keller, 168 S.W.3d at 827. Because evidence supported the jury's finding of fraud and all relief granted was justified by the finding of fraud, we need not address whether Rogers and Burmeister were also liable for civil theft, fraudulent inducement, breach of contract, or civil conspiracy. Thus, we will not further address Rogers' and Burmeister's twelfth, thirteenth, fourteenth, and fifteenth issues. . . .

In Rogers' and Burmeister's first and fifth issues, they argue no evidence supported the award of damages on any of Leslie, Daniel, and Judith's claims, and even if there was competent evidence of damages, Leslie, Daniel, and Judith lacked standing to recover damages recovered by a corporation. . . . Rogers and Burmeister argue that, even if there was competent evidence of damages, Leslie, Daniel, and Judith lacked standing to recover damages recovered by a corporation. Article 5.14(L) of the business corporation act provides that a derivative proceeding by a shareholder of a closely held corporation may be treated by a court as a direct action brought by the shareholder for his own benefit, and a recovery in a direct or derivative proceeding by a shareholder may be paid either directly to the plaintiff or to the corporation. Tex. Bus. Corp. Act Ann. art. 5.14(L) (Vernon 2003). A closely held corporation means a corporation with less than thirty-five shareholders that has no shares listed on a national securities exchange or regularly quoted in an over-the-counter market by one or more members of a national securities association. Id. At trial, Rogers' counsel argued that Leslie, Daniel, and Judith lacked "standing to assert the damages alleged in this case and said damages belong to Accent Home Health who has been severed." The parties had previously discussed at length the applicability of article 5.14(L), and the trial court overruled the objection that Leslie, Daniel, and Judith lacked standing. The court's charge asked the jury to determine fair compensation to Leslie, Daniel, and Judith for Rogers' and Burmeister's fraud, and the trial court entered its final judgment awarding damages the jury determined were out-of-pocket damages resulting from Rogers' and Burmeister's fraud. The record shows Accent's shareholders were Leslie, Daniel, and Judith. There is no evidence in the record that Accent had shares listed on a national securities exchange or regularly quoted in an over-the-counter market by one or more members of a national securities association. Under these circumstances, we conclude the trial court did not err in allowing Leslie, Daniel, and Judith to proceed under article 5.14(L).

****

Holly v. Deason
2005 WL 770595 (N.D. Tex. 2005).

All four motions (collectively referred to herein as the "Current Motions") seek to dismiss claims brought by the Defendants/Third Party Plaintiffs Robert Holly ("Holly") and Anthony Alcedo ("Alcedo"). The Court held a hearing on these four motions on December 14, 2004. Because all four of the above listed motions involve the same issues of law, the discussion of the four motions is combined, with each issue of law being addressed in turn. After considering the parties' arguments and briefing, and the applicable law, the Court hereby GRANTS in PART and DENIES in PART the Current Motions.

I. Background

The history of this case is rather complex and involves over twenty parties and countless claims, counter claims, and third party claims. The parties and legal questions at issue in the Current Motions, however, are significantly more limited.

a. Cast of Characters

A summary of the main cast of characters involved in the Current Motions may be most helpful. The following eight parties, two businesses, and six individuals are at issue in the motions now before this Court:

> 1. DDH Aviation, LLC, f/k/a DDH Aviation, Inc. ("DDH"). DDH is an airplane brokerage company that was founded in 1997 by Deason, Debo, and Holly wherein Deason supplied the capital to start the business and Debo and Holly supplied the labor (i.e., Debo and Holly were the brokers working for DDH). Initially, DDH was formed as a corporation but later altered its business form to become a limited liability company;

> 2. Darwin Deason ("Deason"). Deason is a financially wealthy business man who supplied the capital to allow Debo and Holly to start their airplane brokerage firm, DDH. Deason became the Board Chair upon the founding of the company. Deason at all times has been a shareholder/owner of DDH. Deason is also the founder and a shareholder of ACS, a Fortune 500 company headquartered in Dallas;

> 3. Dennis Debo ("Debo"). An aircraft salesman, Debo was approached by Holly in connection to Holly's idea for a new business. Debo connected Holly with Deason as a potential investor for Holly's business idea, an airplane brokerage endeavor. Debo and Holly invested their labor and expertise in buying/selling

aircraft while Deason invested capital, and together, the three men founded DDH. Debo and Holly were paid under a commission structure that changed a few times throughout the relationship and is, in part, at issue in the pending motions;

4. Robert Holly ("Holly"). The man who had the initial idea for starting an airplane brokerage business, which with Debo's and Deason's assistance was born (DDH). Debo and Holly invested their labor and expertise in buying/selling aircraft while Deason invested capital. Together, the three men founded DDH. Debo and Holly were paid under a commission structure that changed a few times throughout the relationship and is, in part, at issue in the pending motions;

5. Anthony Alcedo ("Alcedo"). DDH hired Alcedo as an additional sales person upon recommendation from Holly. Alcedo acquired a small amount of stock in DDH and was paid under a commission structure;

6. Affiliated Computer Services, Inc. ("ACS"). ACS is a Fortune 500 company headquartered in Dallas that was founded by Deason. ACS is known as a business outsourcing company;

7. Star Chen ("Chen"). Chen was an Officer and Director of both ACS and DDH at times relevant to this case. Chen served as Senior Financial Advisor to ACS and as a financial advisor to DDH. At no point was Chen a shareholder or guarantor of DDH; and,

8. William Deckelman, Jr. ("Deckelman"). Deckelman was an Officer and Director of both ACS and DDH at times relevant to this case. Deckelman is General Counsel for ACS and has also served as an Officer and General Counsel for DDH. At no point, however was Deckelman a shareholder or guarantor of DDH.

b. Procedural History

This case began when DDH filed suit against Holly and Alcedo, as well as several foreign corporations, for claims arising primarily out of Holly's and Alcedo's alleged wrongdoings as DDH employees. The substance of the wrongdoings alleged in this initial complaint ("DDH's Complaint") is that Holly and Alcedo participated in side dealings wherein they pocketed full profits rather than reporting their sales to DDH and receiving a commission from the sales.

Simultaneous with the filing of their Answers to DDH's Complaint, Holly and Alcedo (collectively referred to herein as the "Third Party Plaintiffs") filed counterclaims against DDH as well as third party complaints against Deason, Deckelman, Chen, and ACS. The counterclaims and third party complaints (collectively referred to as the "Third Party Complaints") allege a barrage of claims including, among others, claims for breach of contract, fraud, breach of fiduciary duty, conversion, fraudulent transfer, and shareholder oppression.

c. Facts Related to Third Party Complaints

In a fair attempt to summarize the heart of the Third Party Complaints, Third Party Plaintiffs' claims seem to arise from Deason's alleged pillaging of DDH to pay for his lavish lifestyle. Holly and Alcedo, in their Third Party Complaints, accuse Deason of pillaging DDH's resources to provide for his personal yachts, personal jet service, and personal limousine service. Third Party Plaintiffs claim Deason went so far in using his power and influence as to cause ACS to partake in a questionable dealing with DDH so to extend DDH's credit allowing Deason access to a greater line of credit (DDH's) to use in providing for his self-pampering. Third Party Plaintiffs allege further that Debo, Chen, and Deckelman aided Deason in covering up his misuse of DDH's resources and credit line. They assert that these three Officers/Directors of DDH were aware of Deason's pillaging, and permitted, or in some cases directly aided, Deason to continue to pillage DDH. Third Party Plaintiffs argue the tying up of resources prevented DDH from operating productively because the shortened line of available credit prevented DDH's brokers from entering deals they would otherwise have been able to make. As Holly and Alcedo were paid through a commission structure, this halt in brokering opportunities directly limited their ability to earn money. According to Holly and Alcedo, once they questioned and brought attention to Deason's alleged abuse of DDH's resources, Deason used his power and influence to control the other members of the DDH Board of Directors to change the corporate form of DDH, thereby eliminating all of Holly's and Alcedo's ownership interest in the company without paying them for their shares in DDH. . . .

III. Movants' Arguments

In sum, all four of the pending motions are based in three general arguments: (1) Third Party Plaintiffs lack standing to bring derivative claims, (2) Third Party Plaintiffs fail to establish a basis for Alter Ego, Joint Enterprise, and/or Single Business Enterprise theories of liability, and (3) Third Party Plaintiffs fail to state a claim for fraud, let alone with particularity. It should be noted that in making these three arguments, the specific claims in large part are not discussed. Several claims, in fact, would survive even if Movants are to succeed on all three of these arguments.

a. Standing

Movants challenge Third Party Plaintiffs' standing to assert any derivative claims on behalf of DDH. Two main issues arise regarding this argument. The first and preliminary issue is whether Third Party Plaintiffs have asserted any derivative claims whatsoever. The second issue is whether Third Party Plaintiffs are exempt from the typical demand requirements that are prerequisite to the filing of a derivative suit.

1. Derivative Claims

The preliminary issue regarding the standing argument is whether or not Third Party Plaintiffs have asserted any derivative claims in this action whatsoever. The nature of the actions and the styling of the Third Party Complaints strongly suggest that some portion of Third Party Plaintiffs' claims are derivative in nature. Many of the claims Third Party Plaintiffs make, most obviously those claims for breach of fiduciary duties, regard duties owed to DDH-not duties owed directly to Holly or Alcedo. Regarding the styling of the Third Party Complaints, Third Party Plaintiffs include in the title "DDH Aviation, L.L.C. f/k/a DDH Aviation, Inc.'s Supplemental Complaint Against Darwin Deason, Dennis Debo, Star Chen, William Deckelman, Jr. and ACS, Inc." While it is hard to imagine how such claims made in a complaint with such a title could reflect anything other than an initial intent to bring claims in the form of a derivative proceeding, Third Party Plaintiffs adamantly deny that any of the claims they assert are derivative claims. However, in explaining that all claims are "direct" claims as opposed to derivative claims, Third Party Plaintiffs point to DDH's status as a closely held corporation and the laws that apply to derivative suits brought on behalf of closely held corporations. Specifically, Third Party Plaintiffs state that to the extent their claims. . . are construed to be derivative it was unintentional. Alcedo/Holly brought his shareholder claims based on the fiduciary responsibilities of Deason, Debo, Deckelman, and Chen as a direct action as allowed per Texas Business Corporation Act Article 5.14(L). Holly and Alcedo Responses ¶ 6. Thus, even though Third Party Plaintiffs maintain they are "directly" suing officers/directors of DDH, they clearly appear to be doing so in a derivative fashion.

Third Party Plaintiffs' insistence on referring to these claims as direct claims may, in part, be due to a mis-reading of Tex. Bus. Corp. Act Ann. art. 5.14(L). In relevant part, that law reads, "a derivative proceeding brought by a shareholder of a closely held corporation *may be treated* by a court *as a direct action* brought by the shareholder for his own benefit." Tex. Bus. Corp. Act Ann. art. 5.14(L)(1)(a) (emphasis added). In other words, the court may *treat* such an action as a direct action so to allow recovery to be paid directly to the plaintiff (as opposed to the corporation) if justice requires; however, this does not mean the action is no longer a derivative proceeding. *See* Tex. Bus. Corp. Act Ann. art. 5.14(L)(1)(b). What is clear (or better said, clear enough) is that some of Third Party Plaintiffs' claims are derivative in nature, and accordingly, article 5.14 applies to those claims. The question then becomes whether DDH is a closely held corporation such that article 5.14(L) exempts Third Party Plaintiffs from the typical demand requirements.

2. Exemption from Demand Requirements

Movants argue that Third Party Plaintiffs' derivative claims should be dismissed for failure to meet the prerequisite demand requirements. *See* Tex. Bus. Corp. Act Ann. art. 5.14(C). The law requires that a shareholder file a written demand stating "the act, omission, or other matter that is the subject of the claim or challenge and requesting that the corporation take suitable action" prior to bringing a derivative action in the courts. Tex. Bus. Corp. Act Ann. art. 5.14(C)(1). In the case of closely held corporations, however, there is an exception to the demand requirement. *See* Tex. Bus. Corp. Act Ann. art. 5.14(L). Movants argue that this exception should not apply because Third Party Plaintiffs failed to plead in the Third Party Complaints that DDH is a closely held corporation. Under Texas Law, a closely held corporation is a corporation with less than 35 shareholders that has no shares listed on a national securities exchange or regularly quoted in an over-the-counter market by one or more of a national securities association. Tex. Bus. Corp. Act. Ann. art. 5.15(L)(2). Although Third Party Plaintiffs may claim that DDH is a closely held corporation in their briefing, they *do not allege* so in their pleadings. As stated earlier, in considering the Current Motions (Motions to Dismiss), this Court must accept all *well-pleaded* facts as true and view the facts in the light most favorable to the Third Party Plaintiffs. *See Campbell v. City of San Antonio,* 43 F.3d 973, 975 (5th Cir.1995). As Third Party Plaintiffs did not *plead* DDH to be a closely held corporation, this Court cannot accept it as such. In sum, in order to qualify for the exceptions of art. 5.14(L), *the pleadings* must allege sufficient facts. Moreover, because some of Third Party Plaintiffs' claims are derivative in nature, Fed.R.Civ.P. 23.1 applies to those claims as well. That rule states in pertinent part that *"[i]n a derivative action* brought by one or more shareholders or members to enforce a right of a corporation or of an unincorporated association ... *the complaint shall be verified* ...." Fed.R.Civ.P. 23.1 (emphasis added). Plaintiffs have failed to comply with this requirement. Accordingly, Movants motion to dismiss Third Party Plaintiffs' derivative claims is GRANTED. Under Fed.R.Civ.P. 15(a), however, this Court grants Third Party Plaintiffs leave to file an amended complaint that comports with both Tex. Bus. Corp. Act Ann. art. 5.14(L), as well as Fed.R.Civ.P. 23.1, within 20 days of the date of this Order.

Indemnification

The TBOC provides that an LLC may indemnify and hold harmless any member or manager against any and all claims. The TBOC does not outline any circumstances under which indemnity would be required and does not place any limits on the types of liabilities that may be indemnified by an LLC. The approach here is flexible and leaves a lot of room for each company and the court to determine the appropriate course of action in a given situation.

Texas Business Organization Code provisions

§ 101.402. Permissive Indemnification, Advancement of Expenses, and Insurance or Other Arrangements

    (a) A limited liability company may:

        (1) indemnify a person;

        (2) pay in advance or reimburse expenses incurred by a person; and

        (3) purchase or procure or establish and maintain insurance or another arrangement to indemnify or hold harmless a person.

    (b) In this section, "person" includes a member, manager, or officer of a limited liability company or an assignee of a membership interest in the company.

FIDUCIARY DUTIES

The TBOC is silent as to the precise duties owed by members and managers of an LLC. However, the TBOC recognizes that such duties may exist and provides that the company agreement may expand or restrict any such duties. Based on principles of agency law, members in a member managed LLC and managers in a manager managed LLC owe duties to the LLC. *See* Restatement (Third) of Agency §§ 8.01 to 8.06; Restatement (Third) of Agency § 8.08. These duties are probably also owed to the individual members of the LLC, especially where the company agreement so provides. See *Strebel v. Wimberly*, 2012 WL 112253 (Tex. App.—Houston [1st Dist.] 2012, no pet. h.) (holding, based on the operating agreement, that managers of Delaware LLC owed individual members fiduciary duties). The core duties owed are the fiduciary duty of loyalty, the fiduciary duty of care and the contractual obligation of good faith and fair dealing. A manager, or a member in a member-managed LLC, owes a duty to exercise care in carrying out the management of the LLC, although the specific contours of this duty await precise definition by Texas courts. The company agreement may also set forth the standards for what constitutes acceptable discharge of this duty. It is likely that the business judgment rule applies to protect the substantive business decisions of disinterested managers and managing members that go wrong, including negligent ones, absent egregiousness. The duty of loyalty requires that duty-holders refrain from competing with the firm, usurping business opportunities that belong to the company or engaging in self-dealing or conflict of interest transactions. Self-dealing is permissible if the transaction is fair to the company or approved or ratified by disinterested managers or members. Members may also contractually limit the scope of the fiduciary duties, although they may not completely eliminate the duties. For instance, members may agree to allow competition with the core business of the firm or eliminate conflict of interest as a breach of duty of loyalty. It should be noted that members in a manager managed LLC do not owe fiduciary duties. Thus, in terms of authority, liability and fiduciary duties, members of a manager managed LLC are in an analogous position to limited partners and shareholders of a corporation run by directors.

Texas Business Organizations Code provisions

§ 101.255. Contracts or Transactions Involving Interested Governing Persons or Officers

(a) This section applies to a contract or transaction between a limited liability company and:

(1) one or more governing persons or officers, or one or more affiliates or associates of one or more governing persons or officers, of the company; or

(2) an entity or other organization in which one or more governing persons or officers, or one or more affiliates or associates of one or more governing persons or officers, of the company:

(A) is a managerial official; or

(B) has a financial interest.

(b) An otherwise valid and enforceable contract or transaction described by Subsection (a) is valid and enforceable, and is not void or voidable, notwithstanding any relationship or interest described by Subsection (a), if any one of the following conditions is satisfied:

    (1) the material facts as to the relationship or interest described by Subsection (a) and as to the contract or transaction are disclosed to or known by:

        (A) the company's governing authority or a committee of the governing authority and the governing authority or committee in good faith authorizes the contract or transaction by the approval of the majority of the disinterested governing persons or committee members, regardless of whether the disinterested governing persons or committee members constitute a quorum; or

        (B) the members of the company, and the members in good faith approve the contract or transaction by vote of the members; or

    (2) the contract or transaction is fair to the company when the contract or transaction is authorized, approved, or ratified by the governing authority, a committee of the governing authority, or the members of the company.

(c) Common or interested governing persons of a limited liability company may be included in determining the presence of a quorum at a meeting of the company's governing authority or of a committee of the governing authority that authorizes the contract or transaction.

(d) A person who has the relationship or interest described by Subsection (a) may:

    (1) be present at or participate in and, if the person is a governing person or committee member, may vote at a meeting of the governing authority or of a committee of the governing authority that authorizes the contract or transaction; or

    (2) sign, in the person's capacity as a governing person or committee member, a written consent of the governing persons or committee members to authorize the contract or transaction.

(e) If at least one of the conditions of Subsection (b) is satisfied, neither the company nor any of the company's members will have a cause of action against any of the persons described by Subsection (a) for breach of duty with respect to the making, authorization, or performance of the contract or transaction because the person had the relationship or interest described by Subsection (a) or took any of the actions authorized by Subsection (d).

§ 101.401. Expansion or Restriction of Duties and Liabilities.

The company agreement of a limited liability company may expand or restrict any duties, including fiduciary duties, and related liabilities that a member, manager, officer, or other person has to the company or to a member or manager of the company.

Gadin v. Societe Captrade
2009 WL 1704049 (S.D. Tex. 2009)

For the following reasons, Defendant's Motion must be denied.

I. BACKGROUND

This case arises out of a failed business venture between Plaintiff, a citizen of Texas, and Captrade, a French company whose majority owners and/or investors are Defendants Francois Soulier and Olivier Romary. In 2005, Defendants approached Plaintiff to form a limited liability company in Texas to supply industrial materials for the oil and gas industry. (Pl.Compl.¶ 8.) The company, ABO Supply, LLC ("ABO") was formed with Plaintiff holding 35 percent of the membership shares and Captrade, 65 percent. (*Id* .) From 2005 to 2008, Plaintiff managed the day-to-day operations of ABO, including paying bills, making sales calls, hiring employees, and marketing the company; he did not, however, collect a salary in compensation for his services. (*Id.* at ¶ 10.) Plaintiff contends that relations were so cordial with Defendants that they "often disregard[ed] the company formalities and deal[t] directly with each other." (*Id.* at ¶ 11.) Sometime near June 2008, Defendants, acting on behalf of Captrade, threatened Plaintiff that he would not be receiving compensation or distribution for his services and hired, without Plaintiff's involvement, an outside manager to run ABO. (*Id.* at ¶ 12.) Plaintiff avers that the new manager manipulated ABO's books to de-value the company so that Plaintiff would have to accept a lower than market price for his membership share. (*Id.* at ¶ 13.) In July 2008, Plaintiff was coerced into signing a "non-binding Memorandum of Understanding" in which he agreed to sell his membership interest for an under-valued price. (*Id.* at ¶ 14.) Plaintiff was also coerced into resigning from ABO. (*Id.*) After Plaintiff's departure, Captrade began taking clients from ABO, and Captrade, Soulier, and Romary began moving company records and financial information to a different location. (*Id.* at ¶ 15.) Finally, in October 2008, Captrade called a special meeting to dissolve ABO, but Plaintiff voted against it. Plaintiff now brings claims of breach of fiduciary duty, minority member oppression, alter ego, and seeks a full and complete accounting and attorneys' fees. This Court has jurisdiction pursuant to 28 U.S.C. § 1332.

II. MOTION TO DISMISS

A. Standard

A court may dismiss a complaint for "failure to state a claim upon which relief can be granted." FED. R. CIV. P. 12(b)(6) (2008). When considering a Rule 12(b)(6) motion to dismiss, a court must "accept the complaint's well-pleaded facts as true and view them in the light most favorable to the plaintiff." *Johnson v. Johnson,* 385 F.3d 503, 529 (5th Cir.2004). "To survive a Rule 12(b)(6) motion to dismiss, a complaint 'does not need detailed factual allegations,' but must provide the plaintiff's grounds for entitlement to relief—including factual allegations that when assumed to be true 'raise a right to relief above the speculative level.' " *Cuvillier v. Taylor,* 503 F.3d 397, 401 (5th Cir.2007) (citing *Bell Atl. Corp. v. Twombly,* 550 U.S. 544, 555, 127 S.Ct. 1955, 167 L.Ed.2d 929 (2007)). That is, "a complaint must contain sufficient factual matter, accepted as true, to 'state a claim to relief that is plausible on its face.' " *Ashcroft v. Iqbal,* ——U.S. ——, ——, 129 S.Ct. 1937, 1949, 173 L.Ed.2d 868, —— (May 18, 2009) (quoting *Twombly,* 550 U.S. at 570). Although the Court generally considers a motion to dismiss for failure to state a claim based on the face of the Complaint, the Court may also take notice of matters of public record when considering a 12(b)(6) motion. *See Davis v. Bayless,* 70 F.3d 367, 372 n. 3 (5th Cir.1995); *Cinel v. Connick,* 15 F.3d 1338, 1343 n. 6 (5th Cir.1994).

B. Analysis

1. Breach of Fiduciary Duty

Captrade contends that Plaintiff's breach of fiduciary duty claim must be dismissed because Plaintiff has failed to state facts that show that one member of a limited liability corporation [sic] has a fiduciary duty to another member; thus, he and Captrade are not in a fiduciary relationship. Captrade explains that, to demonstrate an informal fiduciary relationship, Plaintiff must show that a fiduciary relationship existed before and apart from Plaintiff and Captrade's involvement with ABO. Captrade contends that the subjective trust Plaintiff placed in Captrade does not automatically establish a fiduciary relationship. Plaintiff responds that Plaintiff used his personal credit, business contacts, and name in order to fund the start-up and business operations. In addition, Plaintiff argues that he relied upon Defendants' representations that investments of time and resources would make his stake in the company profitable. The elements of a breach of fiduciary duty claim are: (1) a fiduciary relationship between the plaintiff and defendant; (2) the defendant must have breached his fiduciary duty to the plaintiff; and (3) the defendant's breach must result in injury to the plaintiff or benefit to the defendant. *Navigant Consulting, In. v. Wilkinson,* 508 F.3d 277, 283 (5th Cir.2007).

Texas recognizes two types of relationships that give rise to fiduciary duties: formal and informal. Formal relationships are those for which fiduciary duties are owed as a matter of law. They include, for example, the relationship between attorney and client, between principal and agent, or between directors of a corporation and the corporation and its stockholders. *Four Bros. Boat Works, Inc. v. Tesoro Petroleum Companies, Inc.,* 217 S.W.3d 653, 668 (Tex.App.-Houston [14 Dist.] 2006, pet. denied); *Pinnacle Data Services, Inc. v. Gillen,* 104 S.W.3d 188, 198 (Tex.App.-Texarkana 2003, no pet.) (internal citations omitted). A common law duty of good faith and fair dealing does not exist in all contractual relationships. *See Subaru of America, Inc. v. David McDavid Nissan, Inc.,* 84 S.W.3d 212, 225 (Tex.2002); *Schlumberger Tech. Corp. v. Swanson,* 959 S.W.2d 171, 177 (Tex.1997) (citing *Crim Truck & Tractor Co. v. Navistar Int'l Transp. Corp.,* 823 S.W.2d 591, 594 (Tex.1992), *superceded by statute on other grounds*); *English v. Fischer,* 660 S.W.2d 521, 522 (Tex.1983). An informal relationship may give rise to a fiduciary duty when one person trusts in and relies on another, whether the relationship is moral, social, domestic, or purely personal. *Schlumberger Tech. Corp.,* 959 S.W.2d at 176. "[T]o impose such a relationship in a business transaction, the relationship must exist prior to, and apart from, the agreement made the basis of the suit." *See Willis v. Donnelly,* 199 S.W.3d 262 (Tex.2006) (quoting *Schlumberger Tech. Corp.,* 959 S.W.2d at 177); *Meyer v. Cathey,* 167 S.W.3d 327, 330 (Tex.2005) (affirming a take-nothing judgment after a jury trial on a breach of fiduciary duty claim because the agreement between the parties disavowed the creation of fiduciary duties relationship between them even though they had entered previous arms-length transactions, they were friends, and they were frequent dinner partners). *Cf. Lee v. Hasson,*—S.W.3d—, 2007 WL 236899 (Tex.App.-Houston [14 Dist.] 2007, pet. denied) (upholding jury verdict based on breach of fiduciary duty when the defendant was a close personal friend of the plaintiff, she depended on the defendant for personal and moral support, she shared confidential information with him, and she relied on him for financial guidance). Moreover, subjective trust does not transform an arms-length business transaction into a fiduciary relationship. *Schlumberger Tech. Corp.,* 959 S.W.2d at 177 (citing *Crim Truck & Tractor Co.,* 823 S.W.2d at 595); *Playboy Enterprises, Inc. v. Editorial Caballero, S.A. de C.V.,* 202 S.W.3d 250, 266 (Tex.App.-Corpus Christi 2006, pet. denied).

The Texas Limited Liability Company Act does not directly address the duties owed by manager and members. It provides:

> To the extent that at law or in equity, a member, manager, officer, or other person has duties (including fiduciary duties) and liabilities relating thereto to a limited liability company or to another member or manager, such duties and liabilities may be expanded or restricted by provisions in the regulations.

TEX.REV.CIV. STAT. ANN. Art. 1528n, art. 2.20B (Vernon Supp.2009). Texas courts have not yet held that a fiduciary duty exists as a matter of law among members in a limited liability company. *See, e.g., Pinnacle Data Services, Inc. v. Gillen,* 104 S.W.3d at 198 (remanding the lower court's finding of summary judgment and suggesting that fiduciary duties exist in the LLC context by analogy to corporate duties of loyalty); *Suntech Processing Systems, LLC v. Sun Communications, Inc.,* 2000 WL 1780236, at 6–7 (Tex.App.-Dallas 2000, pet. denied) (remanding the issue to the district court for further fact-finding consistent with an informal fiduciary relationship). Other states that find fiduciary duties among members in an LLC derive them from state-specific statutes. *See, e.g., Lynes v. Helm,* 339 Mont. 120, 168 P.3d 651 (Mont.2007); *Gottsacker v. Monnier,* 281 Wis.2d 361, 697 N.W.2d 436 (Wis.2005). Because the existence of a fiduciary duty is a fact-specific inquiry that takes into account the contract governing the relationship as well as the particularities of the relationships between the parties, the Court will deny Captrade's Motion to Dismiss.

****

Entertainment Merchandising Technology, L.L.C. v. Houchin
720 F. Supp. 2d 792 (N.D. Tex. 2010)

Came on for consideration the motion of defendant, Robert E. Houchin, for summary judgment as to all claims and causes of action brought by plaintiffs, Entertainment Merchandising Technology, L.L.C. ("EMT"), Mark Olmstead ("Olmstead"), Johnny R. Weaver ("Weaver"), Earl D. Morris ("Morris"), and Michael J. Dietz ("Dietz") (Olmstead, Weaver, Morris, and Dietz collectively the "Individual Plaintiffs"). Having considered the motion and all related filings by the parties, the summary judgment record, and applicable legal authorities, the court concludes that the motion should be granted in part and denied in part.

I.

Plaintiffs' Claims

This case is before the court as a declaratory judgment action pursuant to 28 U.S.C. §§ 2201-2202, wherein the Individual Plaintiffs seek a declaration that they are co-inventors and co-owners of the invention the subject of United States Patent No. 7,316,614 B2 ("'614 Patent"). Plaintiffs also assert state law causes of action for breach of contract, breach of fiduciary duty, fraud, and conversion. Plaintiffs seek exemplary damages, attorney's fees, and forfeiture by defendant of all right, title, and interest in the patented invention, and in whatever interest defendant may have in EMT. . . .

III.
Undisputed Facts

Although the parties appear to agree on very little concerning the facts underlying plaintiffs' claims, the following facts are undisputed in the summary judgment record:

At some time between 2000 and 2002, defendant and some of the Individual Plaintiffs began to work on a gaming system, referred to by the Individual Plaintiffs as a "sweepstakes invention" and identified in the application for the '614 Patent as a "Method and Apparatus for Conducting a Sweepstakes." Pls.' App. Vol. I, at 55; Def.'s App. Vol. II, at 204. At some point discussions ensued among the parties as to the formation of an entity, EMT, that would have some involvement with the sweepstakes invention. On December 16, 2002, Olmstead filed Articles of Organization with the Texas Secretary of State for the formation of EMT. On at least two occasions defendant signed letters purportedly as a representative of EMT. Pls.' App. Vol. II at 339, 543.

In June 2003, defendant contacted James Walton ("Walton"), a patent attorney, concerning the filing of a patent application for the sweepstakes invention. Sometime later that month defendant signed a letter of engagement with Walton; the signature block is as follows:

"Entertainment Merchandising Technologies

_____
By: Robert E. Houchin, Manager."

Pls.' App. Vol. II, at 338. Defendant signed on the designated line.

On or about November 4, 2003, Walton filed the application for the '614 Patent, naming defendant as the sole inventor. Some time in November 2003, Olmstead contacted Walton and informed him that defendant was not the sole inventor of the invention which was the subject of the patent application. Walton subsequently prepared assignments for the Individual Plaintiffs, which they signed, assigning any interest they might have in the invention, the patent application, and in any patent that might issue, to EMT. Walton prepared a patent application assignment for defendant, which he sent to defendant in December 2004. Defendant never returned the assignment form to Walton. On January 11, 2005, defendant filed a substitute power of attorney, revoking Walton's power of attorney and naming new counsel. On January 21, 2005,

Walton filed a Request to Correct Inventorship with the United States Patent Office, including with the request separate Statement of Added Inventor forms signed by Olmstead, Weaver, and Morris, and a Declaration for Patent Application signed by the Individual Plaintiffs. When Walton learned from the Patent Office that defendant had revoked his power of attorney, he filed in May 2005 a Petition to Correct Inventorship, which the Patent Office denied in March 2006. On January 8, 2008, the Patent Office issued the '614 Patent, naming defendant and the Individual Plaintiffs as inventors. Defendant's attorney filed a request for correction, and on January 29, 2008, the Patent Office issued a Certificate of Correction naming defendant as the sole inventor. . . .

V.
Analysis

B. *Breach of Fiduciary Duty*

To prevail on their claim for breach of fiduciary duty plaintiffs must establish (1) the existence of a fiduciary relationship between the plaintiffs and defendant; (2) a breach by the defendant of his fiduciary duty to the plaintiffs; and (3) the defendant's breach resulted in injury to the plaintiffs or benefit to the defendant. *Navigant Consulting, Inc. v. Wilkinson*, 508 F.3d 277, 283 (5th Cir.2007). Texas recognizes both formal and informal fiduciary relationships. Formal relationships are those for which fiduciary duties are owed as a matter of law, including the relationship between attorney and client, partners, in trustee relationships, or between directors of a corporation and the corporation and its stockholders. *Id.*; *Ins. Co. of N. Am. v. Morris*, 981 S.W.2d 667, 674 (Tex.1998); *Dunagan v. Bushey*, 152 Tex. 630, 263 S.W.2d 148, 152 (1953).

"An informal relationship may give rise to a fiduciary duty where one person trusts in and relies on another, whether the relation is a moral, social, domestic, or purely personal one." *Schlumberger Tech. Corp. v. Swanson*, 959 S.W.2d 171, 176 (Tex.1997) (internal citations omitted). However, a fiduciary relationship does not arise in every relationship involving a high degree of trust and confidence. *Id.* at 176-77. "[T]o impose such a relationship in a business transaction, the relationship must exist prior to, and apart from, the agreement made the basis of the suit." *Id.* at 177.

Here, defendant contends, and plaintiffs do not dispute, that no relationship existed between the parties prior to or apart from the alleged underlying agreement as would give rise to a fiduciary duty based on an informal relationship. Plaintiffs instead urge the court to find the existence of a fiduciary duty on two grounds: (1) defendant's capacity as an officer of EMT, analogous to the fiduciary relationship between partners or corporate officers and shareholders; or, (2) between he and the Individual Plaintiffs as co-inventors. As to their second ground, plaintiffs acknowledge that 35 U.S.C. § 262 does not establish a fiduciary relationship between co-inventors, and the court sees no reason to create such a duty out of thin air, especially in light of the Texas Supreme Court's caution not to "create a [fiduciary] relationship lightly." *Id.* As to plaintiffs' first ground, that a fiduciary duty existed by virtue of defendant's position as an officer of EMT, Title 3 of the Texas Business Organizations Code, concerning limited liability companies, states:

> The company agreement of a limited liability company *may expand or restrict any duties, including fiduciary duties,* and related liabilities that a member, manager, officer, or other person has to the company or to a member or manager of the company.

Tex. Bus. Orgs. Code Ann. § 101.401 (Vernon Supp.2009) (emphasis added). No Texas court has held that fiduciary duties exist between members of a limited liability company as a matter of law. *See, e.g., Gadin v. Societe Captrade,* 2009 WL 1704049 (S.D.Tex. June 17, 2009); *Suntech Processing Sys., L.L.C. v. Sun Comm., Inc.,* 2000 WL 1780236 (Tex.App.-Dallas 2000, pet. denied). Whether such a fiduciary relationship exists is typically a question of fact. *Kaspar v. Thorne,* 755 S.W.2d 151, 155 (Tex.App.-Dallas 1988, no writ).

Whether or not a fiduciary duty arose out of any position defendant may have held with EMT, the court agrees that the breach of fiduciary duty claim is barred by the four-year statute of limitations. Tex. Civ. Prac. & Rem.Code § 16.004(a)(5). Even where a person is owed a fiduciary duty, "when the fact of misconduct becomes apparent it can no longer be ignored, regardless of the nature of the relationship." *S.V. v. R.V.,* 933 S.W.2d 1, 8 (Tex.1996). Defendant contends that plaintiffs knew or should have known that he breached any alleged fiduciary duty when they discovered he filed the patent application naming himself as sole inventor on November 4, 2003, or by at least January 21, 2005, the date plaintiffs submitted a Petition to Correct Inventorship to the Patent Office with the blank assignment of interest form defendant failed or refused to sign. Here, plaintiffs do not specifically identify the act or acts of defendant that allegedly constitute a breach of fiduciary duty. Plaintiffs do not dispute defendant's assertions as to the dates they knew or should have known he failed or refused to assign his interest in the patent application to EMT, or that they knew such a failure to act would have been a breach of any fiduciary duty owed to them. Thus, to the extent plaintiffs contend defendant breached a fiduciary duty by naming himself as sole inventor on the patent application or by refusing or failing to sign the assignment, plaintiffs knew or should have known of those acts by January 21, 2005, at the latest. To the extent plaintiffs contend the breach occurred when the corrected patent issued on January 29, 2008, the parties have directed the court to no summary judgment evidence showing that defendant was still a member, officer, or otherwise affiliated with EMT on that date. It appears the opposite is true, as plaintiffs argue in their response:

> *Had* [defendant] been President of EMT, Inc. and failed to transfer his interest in the Patent to EMT, Inc. under the facts and circumstances in this case, he would not [sic] doubt have breached a fiduciary duty as of the issuance of the patent on January 8, 2008. Pls.' Br. in Opp'n to Def.'s Mot. for Summ. J. at 25 (emphasis added). No breach of fiduciary duty can arise when no relationship exists between the parties, as evidently was the case on January 29, 2008. Thus, at the latest, it appears plaintiffs' claim of breach of fiduciary duty accrued on January 21, 2005. The instant claim for breach of fiduciary duty, filed March 30, 2009, is therefore barred by limitations.

MERGER, DISSOLUTION AND TERM OF EXISTENCE

The TBOC permits any entity or organization to merge or consolidate with any other entity or organization. Organization and entity are defined to include a corporation, limited or general partnership, limited liability company, business trust, real estate investment trust, joint venture, joint stock company, cooperative, association, bank, insurance company, credit union, savings and loan association, or other organization, regardless of whether the organization is for-profit, nonprofit, domestic, or foreign. To merge an LLC must enter into a plan of merger. Unless the LLC agreement requires a different vote or consent, such merger or consolidation must be approved by a majority of members or by the members of each class or group, as appropriate.

In a terminological shift, the TBOC dispenses with the term "dissolution" and settles for "events requiring winding up" of an LLC. The TBOC provides that an LLC will have perpetual existence unless a time is otherwise specified in the certificate of formation or the LLC agreement. The TBOC further provides that an LLC is required to wind up its business (1) upon the happening of events specified in the LLC agreement, (2) unless otherwise provided in the LLC agreement, upon the affirmative vote or written consent of the members of the LLC, or if there is more than one class or group of members, in either case, by members who own more than one half of the then current percentage or other interest in the LLC or by the members in each class or group, as appropriate, (3) at any time there are no members, provided however that the LLC is not dissolved and is not required to be wound up if a new member is admitted and the LLC is continued in accordance with the provisions of Section 11.056(a)(1) or (2) of the TBOC, or (4) upon decree of court requiring the winding up and dissolution of the LLC.

If an event requiring winding up has occurred and has not been revoked or canceled, an LLC must proceed to wind up its affairs as soon as reasonably practicable. During the winding up stage, the assets of the company are applied toward paying or satisfying creditors and distributing any remaining assets to the members. Section 11.053 of the TBOC provides that the assets of the LLC shall first be distributed to creditors of the LLC, whether by payment or the making of reasonable provision for payment thereof, and then, unless otherwise provided in the LLC agreement, to members in satisfaction of liabilities for distributions, for return of their contributions and with respect to their interests in the LLC in the proportions in which the members share in distributions. The LLC is not permitted to carry on its business, except to the extent necessary to wind up, although the business of the LLC may continue, wholly or partly, including delaying the disposition of property, for the limited period necessary to avoid unreasonable loss. Alternatively, under certain circumstances, there may be a revocation or cancellation of the events requiring a winding up. The existence of the LLC terminates with the filing of a "certificate of termination" but this is subject to a three-year survival period for limited purposes. Under certain circumstances, the existence of the LLC can be "reinstated" after termination during the three-year survival period.

Texas Business Organizations Code provisions

§ 11.051. Event Requiring Winding Up of Domestic Entity. Winding up of a domestic entity is required on:

(1) the expiration of any period of duration specified in the domestic entity's governing documents;

(2) a voluntary decision to wind up the domestic entity;

(3) an event specified in the governing documents of the domestic entity requiring the winding up, dissolution, or termination of the domestic entity, other than an event specified in another subdivision of this section;

(4) an event specified in other sections of this code requiring the winding up or termination of the domestic entity, other than an event specified in another subdivision of this section; or

(5) a decree by a court requiring the winding up, dissolution, or termination of the domestic entity, rendered under this code or other law.

§ 11.056. Supplemental Provisions for Limited Liability Company

(a) The termination of the continued membership of the last remaining member of a domestic limited liability company is an event requiring winding up under Section 11.051(4) unless, not later than the 90th day after the date of the termination, the legal representative or successor of the last remaining member agrees:

(1) to continue the company; and

(2) to become a member of the company effective as of the date of the termination or to designate another person who agrees to become a member of the company effective as of the date of the termination.

(b) The event requiring winding up specified in Subsection (a) may be canceled in accordance with Sections 11.152(a) and 101.552(c).

§ 11.052. Winding Up Procedures

(a) Except as provided by the title of this code governing the domestic entity, on the occurrence of an event requiring winding up of a domestic entity, unless the event requiring winding up is revoked under Section 11.151 or canceled under Section 11.152, the owners, members, managerial officials, or other persons specified in the title of this code governing the domestic entity shall, as soon as reasonably practicable, wind up the business and affairs of the domestic entity. The domestic entity shall:

(1) cease to carry on its business, except to the extent necessary to wind up its business;

(2) if the domestic entity is not a partnership, send a written notice of the winding up to each known claimant against the domestic entity;

(3) collect and sell its property to the extent the property is not to be distributed in kind to the domestic entity's owners or members; and

(4) perform any other act required to wind up its business and affairs.

(b) During the winding up process, the domestic entity may prosecute or defend a civil, criminal, or administrative action.

§ 11.053. Property Applied to Discharge Liabilities and Obligations

(a) Except as provided by Subsection (b) and the title of this code governing the domestic entity, a domestic entity in the process of winding up shall apply and distribute its property to discharge, or make adequate provision for the discharge of, all of the domestic entity's liabilities and obligations.

(b) Except as provided by the title of this code governing the domestic entity, if the property of a domestic entity is not sufficient to discharge all of the domestic entity's liabilities and obligations, the domestic entity shall:

(1) apply its property, to the extent possible, to the just and equitable discharge of its liabilities and obligations, including liabilities and obligations owed to owners or members, other than for distributions; or

(2) make adequate provision for the application of the property described by Subdivision (1).

(c) Except as provided by the title of this code governing the domestic entity, after a domestic entity has discharged, or made adequate provision for the discharge of, all of its liabilities and obligations, the domestic entity shall distribute the remainder of its property, in cash or in kind, to the domestic entity's owners according to their respective rights and interests.

(d) A domestic entity may continue its business wholly or partly, including delaying the disposition of property of the domestic entity, for the limited period necessary to avoid unreasonable loss of the entity's property or business.

§ 11.055. Court Action or Proceeding During Winding Up.
During the winding up process, a domestic entity may continue prosecuting or defending a court action or proceeding by or against the domestic entity.

§ 11.314. Involuntary Winding Up and Termination of Partnership or Limited Liability Company.
A district court in the county in which the registered office or principal place of business in this state of a domestic partnership or limited liability company is located has jurisdiction to order the winding up and termination of the domestic partnership or limited liability company on application by:

(1) a partner in the partnership if the court determines that:

(A) the economic purpose of the partnership is likely to be unreasonably frustrated; or

(B) another partner has engaged in conduct relating to the partnership's business that makes it not reasonably practicable to carry on the business in partnership with that partner; or

(2) an owner of the partnership or limited liability company if the court determines that it is not reasonably practicable to carry on the entity's business in conformity with its governing documents.

§ 11.151. Revocation of Voluntary Winding Up

(a) Before the termination of the existence of a domestic entity takes effect, the domestic entity may revoke a voluntary decision to wind up the entity by approval of the revocation in the manner specified in the title of this code governing the entity.

(b) A domestic entity may continue its business following the revocation of a voluntary decision to wind up under Subsection (a).

§ 11.152. Continuation of Business Without Winding Up

(a) Subject to Subsections (c) and (d), a domestic entity to which an event requiring the winding up of the entity occurs as specified by Section 11.051(3) or (4) may cancel the event requiring winding up in the manner specified in the title of this code governing the domestic entity not later than the first anniversary of the date of the event requiring winding up or an earlier period prescribed by the title of this code governing the domestic entity.

(b) A domestic entity whose specified period of duration has expired may cancel that event requiring winding up by amending its governing documents in the manner provided by this code, not later than the third anniversary of the date the period expired or an earlier date prescribed by the title of this code governing the domestic entity, to extend its period of duration. The expiration of its period of duration does not by itself create a vested right on the part of an owner, member, or creditor of the entity to prevent the extension of that period. An act undertaken or a contract entered into by the domestic entity during a period in which the entity could have extended its period of duration as provided by this subsection is not invalidated by the expiration of that period, regardless of whether the entity has taken any action to extend its period of duration.

(c) A domestic entity may not cancel an event requiring winding up specified in Section 11.051(3) and continue its business if the action is prohibited by the entity's governing documents or the title of this code governing the entity.

(d) A domestic entity may cancel an event requiring winding up specified in Section 11.051(4) and continue its business only if the action:

(1) is not prohibited by the entity's governing documents; and

(2) is expressly authorized by the title of this code governing the entity.

(e) On cancellation of an event requiring winding up under this section, the domestic entity may continue its business.

§ 101.552. Approval of Voluntary Winding Up, Revocation, Cancellation, or Reinstatement

(a) A majority vote of all of the members of a limited liability company or, if the limited liability company has no members, a majority vote of all of the managers of the company is required to approve:

(1) a voluntary winding up of the company under Chapter 11;

(2) a revocation of a voluntary decision to wind up the company under Section 11.151; or

(3) a reinstatement of a terminated company under Section 11.202.

(b) The consent of all of the members of the limited liability company is required to approve a cancellation under Section 11.152 of an event requiring winding up specified in Section 11.051(1) or (3).

(c) An event requiring winding up specified in Section 11.056 may be canceled in accordance with Section 11.152(a) if the legal representative or successor of the last remaining member of the domestic limited liability company agrees to:

(1) cancel the event requiring winding up and continue the company; and

(2) become a member of the company effective as of the date of termination of the membership of the last remaining member of the company, or designate another person who agrees to become a member of the company effective as of the date of the termination.

§ 11.102. Effectiveness of Termination of Filing Entity.
Except as otherwise provided by this chapter, the existence of a filing entity terminates on the filing of a certificate of termination with the filing officer.

§ 11.356. Limited Survival After Termination

(a) Notwithstanding the termination of a domestic filing entity under this chapter, the terminated filing entity continues in existence until the third anniversary of the effective date of the entity's termination only for purposes of:

(1) prosecuting or defending in the terminated filing entity's name an action or proceeding brought by or against the terminated entity;

(2) permitting the survival of an existing claim by or against the terminated filing entity;

(3) holding title to and liquidating property that remained with the terminated filing entity at the time of termination or property that is collected by the terminated filing entity after termination;

(4) applying or distributing property, or its proceeds, as provided by Section 11.053; and

(5) settling affairs not completed before termination.

(b) A terminated filing entity may not continue its existence for the purpose of continuing the business or affairs for which the terminated filing entity was formed unless the terminated filing entity is reinstated under Subchapter E.

(c) If an action on an existing claim by or against a terminated filing entity has been brought before the expiration of the three-year period after the date of the entity's termination and the claim was not extinguished under Section 11.359, the terminated filing entity continues to survive for purposes of:

(1) the action until all judgments, orders, and decrees have been fully executed; and

(2) the application or distribution of any property of the terminated filing entity as provided by Section 11.053 until the property has been applied or distributed.

§ 11.201. Conditions for Reinstatement

(a) A terminated entity may be reinstated under this subchapter if:

(1) the termination was by mistake or inadvertent;

(2) the termination occurred without the approval of the entity's governing persons when their approval is required by the title of this code governing the terminated entity;

(3) the process of winding up before termination had not been completed by the entity; or

(4) the legal existence of the entity is necessary to:

(A) convey or assign property;

(B) settle or release a claim or liability;

(C) take an action; or

(D) sign an instrument or agreement.

(b) A terminated entity may not be reinstated under this section if the termination occurred as a result of:

(1) an order of a court or the secretary of state;

(2) an event requiring winding up that is specified in the title of this code governing the terminated entity, if that title prohibits reinstatement; or

(3) forfeiture under the Tax Code.

§ 11.202. Procedures for Reinstatement

(a) To the extent applicable, a terminated entity, to be reinstated, must complete the requirements of this section not later than the third anniversary of the date the termination of the terminated entity's existence took effect.

(b) The owners, members, governing persons, or other persons must approve the reinstatement of the domestic entity in the manner provided by the title of this code governing the domestic entity.

(c) After approval of the reinstatement of a filing entity that was terminated, and not later than the third anniversary of the date of the filing of the entity's certificate of termination, the filing entity shall file a certificate of reinstatement in accordance with Chapter 4.

(d) A certificate of reinstatement filed under Subsection (c) must contain:

(1) the name of the filing entity;

(2) the filing number the filing officer assigned to the entity;

(3) the effective date of the entity's termination;

(4) a statement that the reinstatement of the filing entity has been approved in the manner required by this code; and

(5) the name of the entity's registered agent and the address of the entity's registered office.

(e) A tax clearance letter from the comptroller stating that the filing entity has satisfied all franchise tax liabilities and may be reinstated must be filed with the certificate of reinstatement if the filing entity is a taxable entity under Chapter 171, Tax Code, other than a nonprofit corporation.

§ 11.205. Effectiveness of Reinstatement of Filing Entity.
The reinstatement of a terminated filing entity that previously filed a certificate of termination takes effect on the filing of the entity's certificate of reinstatement.

§ 11.206. Effect of Reinstatement.
When the reinstatement of a terminated entity takes effect:

(1) the existence of the terminated entity is considered to have continued without interruption from the date of termination; and

(2) the terminated entity may carry on its business as if the termination of its existence had not occurred.

Table 6

DECONSTRUCTING TBOC LIMITED LIABILITY COMPANY	
TOPIC	**STATUTE**
Series LLC	101.601-101.621
FORMATION	
definitions	101.001
applicability of other laws	101.002
Purposes of entity	2.001
Prohibited purposes	2.003; 2.007
General powers	2.101; 2.103-.105
certificate of formation	3.005
organizers	3.004
Formation/existence of filing entities	3.001
Amending certificate of formation	3.051-3.054
Effect of filing certificate of amendment	3.056
restatements	3.057-3.059; 3.061
specific provisions	101.051-101.054
Signature and delivery	4.001(a),(b)
Time for filing	4.004
Liability for false filing	4.007
Penalties for false filing	4.008; 21.802
filing fees	4.154
filing takes effect	4.051-4.059
filing amendment	4.101-4.106
general	5.001-5.053
llc names	5.059
reservation	5.101-5.106
registration	5.151-5.155
definition	5.2
designation & consent	5.201-5.2011

change	5.202-5.203
resignation	5.204
duties	5.206
designation w/o consent	5.207-5.208
failue to designate	5.251-5.253
agent for service	5.255
GOVERNANCE	
general	3.101-3.102
officers	3.103-3.105
general	3.152
owner/member	3.153
uncertificated shares	3.201-3.205
emergency governance	3.251--254
restrictions on transferability	3.202 and et. seq.
signature on certificates	3.203-3.204
members	101.101-101.103
classes of members	101.104
memebership interest	101.105-101.106
withdrawal or expulsion	101.107
assignment of interest	101.108-101.1115
managers	101.301-101.307
modification	101.401
supplemental	101.501
right to examine	101.502
location	6.001
forms	6.002
notice	6.051-6.053; 101.352
general	101.351
quorum	101.353
record dates	6.101 et seq
voting of interests	6.151 et.seq.
voting trusts	6.251
voting agreements	6.252
equal voting rights	101.354
governing authority	101.355
votes required	101.356
manner	101.357

Keep and maintain records	3.151
Supplemental records required	101.501
LIABILITY	
Limitation of liability for governing person	7.001
member/manager obligations	101.114
modification	101.401
indemnification	101.402
definitions	101.451
derivative proceedings	101.452-101461
WINDING UP/TERMINATION	
definitions	11.001
eligible persons	101.551
approval	101.552
events requiring	11.051
procedures	11.052
property applied to discharge obligations	11.053
court action	11.054-11.055
supplemental LLC	11.056
certificate of termination	11.101-11.102
action of SOS	11.104
revocation	11.151
continuation w/o winding up	11.152
reinstatement	11.201-11.203
involuntary termination	11.251-11.254
judicial winding up	11.301-11.315

Limited Liability Company Problem Set

1. Julie Hayes submitted a certificate of formation with the Secretary of State (SOS) on behalf of Julie Ventures, LLC, and enclosed a check for the filing fee. Because Julie's co-investors had not signed an operating agreement at that point, Julie did not file an operating agreement with the SOS until three months later when the company agreement was concluded. Meanwhile, the SOS' office filed the certificate of formation a week after its submission and notified Julie accordingly. On the day she received the letter from the SOS, Julie, acting on behalf of the LLC, entered into a three-year lease for an office space for the business. The landlord, upon reneging on the contract, argues that there was no valid contract with Julie Ventures because the company, having not adopted its operating agreement at the time of the lease, had not fully come into existence and was therefore without contractual capacity. The court agreed with the landlord, holding that an operating agreement is a vital formation document that should have been filed concurrently with the other formation document, the certificate of formation, failing which no LLC had been properly formed. Julie Ventures, LLC is appealing the decision.

    Will the company prevail on appeal?

2. Michael Real Estate Brokers, LLC has 55 members. The members opted for manager-management, and constituted a board of managers consisting of 30 of the members. The operating agreement stated that the board of managers would operate as a body and that similarly to a board of directors, no manager acting alone could bind the company to any contractual obligation. In February 2011, 5 of the managers, while playing tennis with some friends learned of a potentially lucrative business opportunity. Immediately, they signed a confidentiality agreement and commenced negotiations on behalf of the LLC. Interpreting the confidentiality agreement as forbidding them from mentioning the negotiations to anybody, including the other managers and members, they did not discuss the matter with anybody until the deal was finalized and the resulting contract signed. The contract obligated the LLC to purchase some apartment complexes owned by a retiring developer at bargain prices. The contract further provided that if payment was not received within 30 days, the deal would terminate and the LLC would be obligated to pay a termination fee of $100,000. The other managers did not like the proposal and voted not to approve any funds to effectuate the deal. After 30 days, the developer sued to enforce the obligation to pay $100,000. His principal argument was that he negotiated in good faith and did not know that the LLC had more than 5 managers. The court ruled in favor of the developer and upheld the deal, noting that having up to 30 managers was excessive and therefore, left room for innocent third parties to be misled.

    Do you agree with the court?

3. Geraldine is the sole manager of Caption Masters, LLC. The LLC was organized to conduct "any lawful business." However, the company has concentrated, since formation, on providing graphic designs for the entertainment industry. Last year, Geraldine signed a contract with Pavilion Energy, Inc. whereby Caption agreed to purchase and take delivery of natural gas from Pavilion's processing facility in Baytown and distribute to end users in the Houston area. Geraldine signed the long-term contract because the gas business was booming and she did not want Caption to miss out on the good times. Three months after signing the contract, natural gas prices dropped sharply as a result of increased production driven by hydraulic fracturing and horizontal drilling of shale gas formations across Texas. Thus, Caption was no longer able to perform on the contract. Pavilion sued Caption, Geraldine and all the members of Caption Masters, LLC for breach of contract. The members were surprised when they were served with the complaint, as they had never been briefed on the deal.

Which, if any, of the defendants are liable for breach of contract?

4. Bell is a member of Prima, LLC, a member-managed LLC that has earned a deserved reputation as a leading general services company that does business with integrity. The company agreement provides that only Cory, a founding member, would negotiate and sign contracts spanning more than a year. In January 2010, Bell approached ABC Stores, Inc., for the supply of office materials. ABC's president is a lawyer and was comfortable with signing a 5-year multi-million dollar contract with Bell under which ABC would be Prima's exclusive supplier of office equipment and stationery. Prima repudiated the contract because of its length and onerous terms. ABC sought to enforce the contract, considering that it lost an alternate customer while negotiating with Bell. The trial court ruled in favor of ABC holding that since an LLC is structured in some respects as a partnership, LLC members are analogous to partners and therefore have apparent authority to bind the firm in the ordinary course of business. Prima is appealing the decision.

Will the appeal fail?

5. Dex and Ritz agreed to form Dritzy L.L.C. Two weeks after drawing up and mailing all the necessary papers to the Texas secretary of state, Dex entered into a contract on behalf of Dritzy L.L.C. with Mercantile Products and Services Group, Inc. Twelve days after the execution of the contract, Dex and Ritz received a letter from the secretary of state informing them that the certificate of formation was not filed because two of the organizers' signatures were missing. Unfortunately, the letter had inadvertently been misfiled among other papers for eighteen months, before Dex opened it and read it. Dex and Ritz had operated the business during the eighteen months period, using office stationery that bears the name Dritzy L.L.C. and transacting business with individuals and legal persons as an LLC. When Dex and Ritz stopped performing on the Mercantile

contract, Mercantile filed a lawsuit against them individually, claiming that the business was not an LLC and that the individuals behind the purported LLC are therefore personally liable.

Discuss fully whether Dex and Ritz formed an LLC, if not what type of entity was formed.

6. RSVP, L.L.C. is a manager-managed LLC that specializes in organizing upscale social events and high-level conferences in Houston, Texas. In February 2012, Radd a founding member of the company received a telephone call from Jerry, the manager of Hiltonix Hotels. The phone call led to Radd entering into an oral agreement with Hiltonix that RSVP would coordinate events at a major convention that the hotel was hosting that year, an activity within the scope of RSVP, L.L.C.'s business. Neither RSVP L.L.C. nor Radd fulfilled the terms of the contract and the hotel, which sustained a heavy loss, is suing Radd and RSVP, L.L.C.

What is the likely outcome?

7. Lakesha is one of two members of Excellence, LLC, a member-managed LLC that provides tax advisory services. Lakesha wanted some fishing gear for her family but did not want her name to show on the purchase, which would be the case if she used a personal credit card or check. Last year, Lakesha ordered fishing gear from Aqua, Inc. on behalf of the LLC, signing the purchase agreement, "Lakesha, as a member of Excellence, LLC." The vendor accepted the order, sent an invoice to the LLC's address, and in due course received a check drawn on the LLC's bank account. The LLC made the payment with the understanding that Lakesha would reimburse the firm and refrain from ordering personal supplies through the LLC. Early this year, Lakesha placed an order with the same vendor, who proceeded to ship the fishing supplies to the LLC's address. Lakesha took delivery of the supplies. The LLC refused to make any payment to Aqua, Inc. The vendor sued the LLC but the court held that since fishing supplies were not in the ordinary course of business of a tax advisory firm, there was no conceivable basis to hold the LLC liable.

Do you agree?

8. Beset with serious financial difficulties, Omni a member and senior manager of OKD Ventures, L.L.C. transferred his membership interest to Kero. The LLC has 9 other members. Six of them support the transfer and have voted to admit Kero as a new member. The remaining 3 members insist that Kero cannot validly be admitted to membership or share in the profits regardless of the vote of the other members. Kero responded by seeking a declaration that he is a member of OKD, with all the accompanying rights and obligations. The trial court granted the prayer, noting that membership interests in an LLC is analogous to shares of corporations and that when a shareholder sells his shares, the purchaser becomes a shareholder in the corporation. The appellate court reversed the trial court's ruling, holding that a transferee of a membership

interest does not become a member or receive a portion of the profits without the unanimous vote of the current members.

Which ruling is correct and why?

9. Mustapha is a successful venture capitalist. He resides in Istanbul and is in fact a Turkish national who visits the United States occasionally. He invested in a new biotechnology start-up in Austin that holds a few patents on some processes for improving care for cancer patients. The business was registered as an LLC in 1999. The business has experienced exponential growth and the in-house counsel is advising the management to convert the firm to an S Corporation, touting its numerous advantages, especially when the enterprise chooses to go public as expected. Mustapha has contacted an outside law firm to seek a second opinion on the conversion proposal. An associate in the firm concluded that the conversion would be in the best interest of the company. A senior partner walked into the associate's office yesterday and lectured him for 10 minutes about the strengths and weaknesses of the two investment vehicles and concluded that the associate's choice of vehicle posed insurmountable problems for their client, Mustapha.

Why is the proposed conversion problematic for Mustapha?

10. Joel, Smith, and Austin are brothers. They are also the only members of ThreeBros L.L.C. They chose the LLC as a business form because they were informed that it allowed more flexibility than corporations for investors to conduct their business the way they felt most comfortable, instead of being burdened with a lot of formalities and procedural requirements with which they would have to comply if they chose to incorporate. They did not retain the services of a book keeper and easily co-mingled business and personal funds. As a result, they have not been able to pay Maya, who supplied all the office equipment for the business. There is also a pending lawsuit by Delia who was injured as a result of negligent driving by Austin on his way to conduct business for the company. The company is now insolvent and the three brothers claim that they are shielded from personal liability. Thus, only the assets of the LLC should be available for dealing with the company's debts. The assets are woefully insufficient.

Do Maya and Delia have any legal bases on which to hold the three brothers personally liable?

APPENDIX

Sample Certificate of Formation*

CERTIFICATE OF FORMATION
OF
BPZ RESOURCES, INC.

The undersigned natural person of the age of at least eighteen years acting as incorporator of a corporation under the Texas Business Organizations Code ("TBOC") does hereby adopt the following Certificate of Formation for such corporation. This document becomes effective when the document is filed by the Secretary of State of the State of Texas.

ARTICLE I
NAME

The name of the entity is BPZ RESOURCES, INC. (the "Corporation").

ARTICLE II
TYPE OF ENTITY

The type of filing entity being formed is a Texas for-profit corporation.

ARTICLE III
DURATION

The period of its duration is perpetual.

ARTICLE IV
PURPOSE

The entity is being formed to:

(a) transact any and all lawful business or businesses;
(b) undertake any lawful purpose or purposes; and
(c) have and exercise all the powers conferred by the TBOC;

as the same may be undertaken by an entity organized under the TBOC, as the same may be amended from time to time and of the type set out in Article II of this Certification of Formation.

ARTICLE V
INITIAL REGISTERED OFFICE AND AGENT

The street address of the entity's initial registered office is 580 Westlake Park Blvd., Suite 525 Houston, TX 77079, and the name of its initial registered agent at such address is Manuel Pablo Zúñiga-Pflücker.

ARTICLE VI
ORGANIZER

The name and address of the organizer is:

Manuel Pablo Zúñiga-Pflücker   Two Westlake
580 Westlake Park Blvd., Suite 525
Houston, TX 77079

ARTICLE VII
AUTHORIZED SHARES

The aggregate number of shares which the Corporation shall have authority to issue is two hundred seventy-five million (275,000,000) shares, of which two hundred fifty million (250,000,000) shares shall be designated as common stock, no par value, and twenty-five million (25,000,000) shares shall be designated as preferred stock, no par value.

The following is a statement fixing certain of the designations and rights, voting rights, preferences, and relative, participating, optional or other rights of the preferred stock and the common stock of the Corporation, and the qualifications, limitations or restrictions thereof, and the authority with respect thereto expressly granted to the board of directors of the Corporation to fix and such provisions not fixed by this Certificate of Formation.

(a)   Preferred Stock

The board of directors is hereby expressly vested with the authority to adopt a resolution or resolutions providing for the issuance of authorized but unissued shares of preferred stock, which shares may be issued from time to time in one or more series and in such amounts as may be determined by the board of directors in such resolution or resolutions. The rights, voting rights, designations, preferences, and relative, participating, optional or other rights, if any, of each series of preferred stock and the qualifications, limitations or restrictions, if any, of such preferences and/or rights (collectively the "Series Terms"), shall be such as are stated and expressed in a resolution or resolutions providing for the creation or revision of such Series Terms (a "Preferred Stock Series Resolution") adopted by the board of directors. The board shall have the power and authority, to the fullest extent permissible under the TBOC, as currently in effect or as amended, to determine and establish by a Preferred Stock Series Resolution, the Series Terms of a particular series, including, without limitation, determination of the following:

(1)   The number of shares constituting that series and the distinctive designation of that series, or any increase or decrease (but not below the number of shares thereof then outstanding) in such number;

(2)   The dividend rate on the shares of that series; whether such dividends, if any, shall be cumulative, noncumulative, or partially cumulative and, if cumulative or partially cumulative, the date or dates from which dividends payable on such shares shall accumulate; and the relative rights of priority, if any, of payment of dividends on shares of that series;

(3)   Whether that series shall have voting rights, in addition to the voting rights provided by law, and, if so, the terms of such voting rights;

(4)   Whether that series shall have conversion privileges with respect to shares of any other class or classes of stock or of any other series of any class of stock, and, if so, the terms and conditions of such conversion, including provision for adjustment of the conversion rate upon occurrence of such events as the board of directors shall determine;

(5)   Whether the shares of that series shall be redeemable at the option of either the Corporation or the holder, and, if so, the terms and conditions of such redemption, including relative rights of priority, if any, of redemption, the date or dates upon or after which they shall be redeemable, provisions regarding redemption notices, and the amount per share payable in case of redemption, which amount may vary under different conditions and at different redemption dates;

(6)   Whether the Corporation shall have any repurchase obligation with respect to the shares of that series and, if so, the terms and conditions of such obligation, subject, however, to the limitations of the TBOC;

(7)   Whether that series shall have a sinking fund for the redemption or purchase of shares of that series, and, if so, the terms and amount of such sinking fund;

(8)   The rights of the shares of that series in the event of voluntary or involuntary liquidation, dissolution or winding up of the Corporation, and the relative rights of priority, if any, of payment of shares of that series;

(9)   The conditions or restrictions upon the creation of indebtedness of the Corporation or upon the issuance of additional preferred stock or other capital stock ranking on a parity therewith, or prior thereto, with respect to dividends or distribution of assets upon liquidation;

(10)   The conditions or restrictions with respect to the issuance of, payment of dividends upon, or the making of other distributions to, or the acquisition or redemption of, shares ranking junior to the preferred stock or to any series thereof with respect to dividends or distribution of assets upon liquidation;

(11)   The relative priority of each series of preferred stock in relation to other series of preferred stock with respect to dividends or distribution of assets upon liquidation; and

(12)   Any other designations, powers, preferences and rights, including, without limitation, any qualifications, limitations or restrictions thereof.

Any of the Series Terms, including voting rights, of any series may be made dependent upon facts ascertainable outside the Certificate of Formation and the Preferred Stock Series Resolution, provided that the manner in which such facts shall operate upon such Series Terms is clearly and expressly set forth in the Certificate of Formation or in the Preferred Stock Series Resolution.

Subject to the provisions of this Article VII, shares of one or more series of preferred stock may be authorized or issued from time to time as shall be determined by and for such consideration as shall be fixed by the board of directors, in an aggregate amount not exceeding the total number of shares of preferred stock authorized by the Certificate of Formation. All shares of any one series of preferred stock so designated by the board of directors shall be alike in every particular, except that shares of any one series issued at different times may differ as to the dates from which dividends thereon shall be cumulative.

(b)   Common Stock

(1)   *Dividends. Subject to the provisions of any Preferred Stock Series Resolution, the board of directors may, in its discretion, out of funds legally available for the payment of dividends and at such times and in such manner as determined by the board of directors, declare and pay dividends on the common stock of the Corporation.*

No dividend (other than a dividend in capital stock ranking on a parity with the common stock or cash in lieu of fractional shares with respect to such stock dividend) shall be declared or paid on any share or shares of any class of stock or series thereof ranking on a parity with the common stock in respect of payment of dividends for any dividend period unless there shall have been declared, for the same dividend period, like proportionate dividends on all shares of common stock then outstanding.

(2)   *Liquidation. In the event of any liquidation, dissolution or winding up of the Corporation, whether voluntary or involuntary (each, a "Liquidation Event"), after payment or provision for payment of the debts and other liabilities of the Corporation and payment or setting aside for payment of any preferential amount due to the holders of any other class or series of stock, the holders of the common stock shall be entitled to receive ratably any or all assets remaining to be paid or distributed.*

(3)   *Voting Rights. Subject to any special voting rights set forth in any Preferred Stock Series Resolution, the holders of the common shares of the Corporation shall be entitled at all meetings of shareholders to one vote for each share of such stock held by them.*

(c)   Prior, Parity or Junior Rank

Whenever reference is made in this Article VII to shares "ranking prior to" another class of stock or "on a parity with" another class of stock, such reference shall mean and include all other shares of the Corporation in respect of which the rights of the holders thereof as to the payment of dividends or as to distributions upon a Liquidation Event, as the case may be, are given preference over, or rank on an equality with, as the case may be, the rights of the holders of such other class of stock. Whenever reference is made to shares "ranking junior to" another class of stock, such reference shall mean and include all shares of the Corporation in respect of which the rights of the holders thereof as to the payment of dividends or as to distributions upon a Liquidation Event, as the case may be, are junior and subordinate to the rights of the holders of such class of stock.

Except as otherwise provided herein or in any Preferred Stock Series Resolution, each series of preferred stock ranks on a parity with each other with respect to the payment of dividends and distributions upon a Liquidation Event, and each ranks prior to the common stock with respect to the payment of dividends and distributions upon a Liquidation Event. Common stock ranks junior to the preferred stock with respect to the payment of dividends and distributions upon a Liquidation Event.

(d)   Liquidation

For the purposes of Section (b)(2) of this Article VII and for the purpose of the comparable sections of any Preferred Stock Series Resolution, the merger or consolidation of the Corporation into or with any other corporation, or the merger of any other corporation into it, or the sale, lease, or conveyance of all or substantially all the assets, property or business of the Corporation, shall not be deemed to be a liquidation, dissolution or winding up of the Corporation.

(e)   Reservation and Retirement of Shares

The Corporation shall at all times reserve and keep available, out of its authorized but unissued shares of common stock or out of shares of common stock held in its treasury, the full number of shares of common stock into which all shares of any series of preferred stock having conversion privileges from time to time outstanding are convertible.

Unless otherwise provided in a Preferred Stock Series Resolution with respect to a particular series of preferred stock, all shares of preferred stock redeemed or acquired (as a result of conversion or otherwise) shall be retired and restored to the status of authorized but unissued shares.

ARTICLE VIII
INITIAL DIRECTORS

The number of persons constituting the initial board of directors is six (6) and the names and addresses of the persons who are to serve as directors until the first annual meeting of shareholders or until (their) successor(s) are elected and qualified are:

[All names with street addresses listed here]

By lot, the initial directors named above shall designate two directors to serve one (1) year terms, two directors to serve two (2) year terms, and two directors to serve three (3) year terms. Thereafter, the term of each director shall be one (1) year, resulting in a staggered board of directors. The terms expiring in any given year shall expire at the end of the regular meeting of the directors. Elections for successor directors shall be held at such meeting, and all directors present shall be entitled to vote during the election for successor directors. At the first annual meeting of shareholders and at each annual meeting thereafter, the holders of shares entitled to vote in the election of directors shall elect directors to hold office until the next succeeding annual meeting.

ARTICLE IX
NO PREEMPTIVE RIGHTS

No holder of any shares of the Corporation shall be entitled as a matter of right to purchase or subscribe for any part of any shares of the Corporation authorized by this Certificate of Formation or of any additional stock of any class to be issued by reason of any increase of the authorized shares of the Corporation or of any bonds, certificates of indebtedness, debentures, warrants, options or other securities convertible into any class of shares of the Corporation, but any shares authorized by this Certificate of Formation or any such additional authorized issue of any shares or securities convertible into any shares may be issued and disposed of by the board of directors to such persons, firms, corporations or associations for such consideration and upon such terms and in such manner as the board of directors may in its discretion determine without offering any thereof on the same terms or on any terms to the shareholders then of record or to any class of shareholders, provided only that such issuance may not be inconsistent with any provision of law or with any of the provisions of this Certificate of Formation.

ARTICLE X
BYLAWS

The board of directors is expressly authorized to adopt, amend and repeal the bylaws. The Corporation's shareholders are hereby expressly prohibited from amending or repealing the bylaws.

ARTICLE XI
MEETINGS OF SHAREHOLDERS

An annual meeting of the shareholders shall be held at such times as may be stated or fixed in accordance with the bylaws. Special meetings may only be called by (i) the chairman of the board (if any), the president, the board of directors, or such other person or persons as may be authorized in this Certificate of Formation or the bylaws, or (ii) by the holders of not less than thirty (30%) percent of all the shares entitled to vote at the proposed special meeting. No action of the shareholders may be taken by written consent or consents of the shareholders.

ARTICLE XII
LIMITATION OF DIRECTOR'S LIABILITY

To the fullest extent permitted by applicable law, a governing person of the Corporation shall not be liable to the Corporation or its shareholders for monetary damages for an act or omission in such governing person's capacity as a director. This Article XII does not eliminate or limit the liability of a governing person to the extent such governing person is found liable under applicable law for (i) a breach of such governing person's duty of loyalty to the Corporation or its shareholders; (ii) an act or omission not in good faith that (A) constitutes a breach of the duty of loyalty of the governing person to the organization, or (B) involves intentional misconduct or a knowing violation of the law; (iii) a transaction from which the *governing person received an improper benefit, regardless of whether the benefit resulted from an action taken within the scope of the person's duties; or (iv) an act or omission for which the liability of a person is expressly provided for by statute. If the Texas Business Organizations Code or any other statute is amended subsequently to the effective date of this Certificate of Formation to authorize corporate action further eliminating or limiting the personal liability of governing person, then the liability of a governing person of the Corporation shall be eliminated or limited to the full extent permitted by such statute, as so amended.*

Any repeal or modification of the foregoing paragraph by the shareholders of the Corporation shall not adversely affect any right or protection of a governing person of the Corporation existing at the time of such repeal or modification.

ARTICLE XIII
INDEMNIFICATION

(a)   The Corporation shall indemnify and hold harmless the Directors (each, and "Indemnified Person") to the fullest extent permitted by law from and against any and all losses, claims, demands, costs, damages, liabilities, joint or several, expenses of any nature (including reasonable attorneys' fees and disbursements), judgments, fines, settlements and other amounts arising from any and all claims, demands, actions, suits or proceedings, whether civil, criminal, the Indemnified Person may be involved or threatened to be involved, as a party or otherwise, arising out of or incidental to the business or activities of or relating to the Corporation regardless of whether the Indemnified Person continues to be a director at the time any such liability or expense is paid or incurred. The indemnification provided in this Article XIII may not be made to or on behalf of any director if a final adjudication establishes that the Indemnified Person's acts or omissions involved intentional misconduct, fraud or a knowing violation of the law.

(b)   Expenses (including reasonable attorneys' fees and disbursements) incurred by an Indemnified Person in defending any claim, demand, action, suit, or proceeding subject to this Article XIII shall, from time to time, upon request by this Indemnified Person, be advanced by the Corporation prior to the final disposition of such claim, demand, action, suit or proceeding upon receipt by the Corporation if (i) a written affirmation by such Indemnified Person of his, her or its good faith belief that he, she or it has met the standard of conduct necessary for indemnification under this Article XIII, and (ii) a written undertaking, by or on behalf of such Indemnified Person, to repay such amount if it shall ultimately be determined, by a court of competent jurisdiction that such indemnified person is not entitled to be indemnified as authorized by this Article XIII or otherwise.

(c)   Any indemnification hereunder shall be satisfied only out of the assets of the Corporation, and the shareholders shall not be subject to personal liability by reason of these indemnification provisions.

(d)   An Indemnified Person shall not be denied indemnification in whole or in part under this Article XIII or otherwise by reason of the fact that the Indemnified Person had an interest in the transaction with respect to which the indemnification applies if the

transaction was otherwise permitted or not expressly prohibited by the terms of this Certificate of Formation.

(e)   The provisions of this Article XIII are for the benefit of the Indemnified Persons, their heirs, successors, assigns and administrators and shall not be deemed to create any rights for the benefit of any other person(s) or entity(ies).

ARTICLE XIV
NO CUMULATIVE VOTING

Cumulative voting is expressly prohibited. At each election of directors, every shareholder entitled to vote at such election shall have the right to vote, in person or by proxy, the number of shares owned by him with respect to each of the persons nominated for election as a director and for whose election he has a right to vote; no shareholder shall be entitled to cumulate his votes by giving one candidate a number of votes equal to the number of directors to be elected, multiplied by the number of shares owned by such shareholder, or by distributing such votes on the same principle among any number of candidates.

ARTICLE XV
CREATION PURSUANT TO CONVERSION

The Corporation was incorporated pursuant to a plan of conversion whereby BPZ Energy, Inc., a Colorado corporation (the "converting entity"), was converting into BPZ Resources, Inc., a Texas corporation (the "converted entity"). The converting entity was incorporated in Colorado on June 17, 1993. The address of the converting entity is 580 Westlake Park Boulevard, Suite 525, Houston, Texas 77079, which remained the address of the converted entity.

[Signature Page to Follow]

Dated as of the 17th day of August, 2007.

BPZ RESOURCES, INC.

By:/s/
Name here
Chief Executive Officer and President

- *available at http://www.sec.gov/Archives/edgar/data/1023734/000110465907064919/a07-22681_1ex3d1.htm*

TABLE OF CASES	PAGE

7547 Corp. v. Parker & Parsley Development Partners, L.P.
38 F.3d 211 (Ct.App.-5th Cir. ,1994 — 255

Allied Chemical Carriers, Inc., v. National Biofuels LP, et al.
Not Reported in F.Supp.2d, 2011 WL 2672512, S.D.Tex., July 07, 2011
United States District Court, S.D. Texas, Houston Division — 413

Almar-York Company, Inc., v. The Fort Worth National Bank
374 S.W.2d 940 (Tex.Civ.App.-Fort Worth, 1964) — 384

American Vending Services, Inc., v. Durbano et.al.
881 P. 2d 917 (Utah App, 1994) — 337

Apcar Investment Partners VI, Ltd. v. Gaus
161 S.W.3d 137 (Tex.App.-Eastland, 2005) — 220

Baptist Mem'l Hosp. Sys. v. Sampson
969 S.W.2d 945 (Tex. 1998) — 52

Biggs v. U.S. Fire Ins. Co.
611 S.W.2d 624, Tex., 1981 — 36

Black v. Bruner
Not Reported in S.W.3d, 2003 WL 724312 (Tex.App.-San Antonio) — 509

Boehringer v. Konkel
2013 WL 1341160 (Tex.App.-Hous. (1 Dist.) 2013)) — 396

Bohatch v. Butler & Binion
977 S.W.2d 543, 41 Tex. Sup. Ct. J. 308 — 166

Boyd v. Eikenberry
132 Tex. 408, 122 S.W.2d 1045 (1939) — 4

Bradford Partners II, L.P. v. Fahning
231 S.W.3d 513 (Tex. App. Dallas 2007) — 250

CCR, INC., et al., v. Chamberlain, et al.,
Number 13-97-312-CV, Tex.Ct.App.-Corpus Christi (13th Dist) — 115

Champion v. Mizell
904 S.W.2d 617 (Texas) 1995 — 162

Citizens United v. Federal Election Commission
558 U.S. 310, 130 S.Ct. 876, 175 L.Ed.2d 753 (2010) — 324

Coleman v. Coleman
170 S.W.3d 231(Tex.App.-Dallas, 2005) 196

Coleman v. Klöckner & Co. et.al.
180 S.W.3d 577 (Tex. App.— Houston [14th Dist.] 2005) 10

Crenshaw v. Swenson
611 S.W.2d 886, 890 (Tex.Civ.App.—Austin 1980, writ ref'd n.r.e.) 294

Del Carmen Flores v. Summit Hotel Group
492 F. Supp. 2d 640 (W.D. Tex. 2006) 7

Delaney v. Fidelity Lease Limited
517 S.W.2d 420 (Tex.Civ.App. 1974) 281

Destec Energy, Inc., v. Houston Lighting & Power Company
966 S.W.2d 792 (Tex.App.-Austin, 1998) 127

Disney Enterprises, Inc. v. Esprit Finance, Inc.,
981 S.W.2d 25 (Tex. App. – San Antonio 1998) 58

EZ Auto, L.L.C. v. H.M. JR. Auto Sales,
No. 04-01-00820-CV, 2002 WL 1758315 (Tex. App.—San Antonio 2002)
Opinion On Appellant's Motion For Rehearing 479

Eikon King Street Manager, L.L.C. v. LSF King Street Manager, L.L.C.
109 S.W.3d 762 (Tex. App.—Dallas 2003) 496

Elloway, et.al. v. Pate, et.al.
238 S.W.3d 882, Court of Appeals of Texas, Houston (14th Dist.), 2007 368

Entertainment Merchandising Technology, L.L.C. v. Houchin
720 F. Supp. 2d 792 (N.D. Tex. 2010) 552

Evanston Insurance Company v. Dillard Department Stores, Inc., v. Chargois et.al.
602 F.3d 610 (U.S.Ct.App-5th—2010) 225

Exxon Corporation v. Breezevale Ltd
82 S.W.3d 429 (TexApp-Dallas, 2002) 99

Farnsworth v. Deaver
147 S.W.3d 662, Tex. App., Amarillo, 2004 202

Faulkner v. Kornman
No. 10-301, 2012 WL 1066736 1 (Bankr. S.D. Tex. 2012) 490

Gadin v. Societe Captrade
2009 WL 1704049 (S.D. Tex. 2009) — 550

Hartford v. McGillicuddy
103 Me. 224, 68 A. 860 (1907) — 88

Holly v. Deason
2005 WL 770595 (N.D. Tex. 2005) — 543

Howell v. Hilton Hotels Corp.
84 S.W.3d 708 Court of Appeals of Texas, Houston (1st Dist.), 2002 — 156

Hughes v. St. David's Support Corp.
944 S.W.2d 423, (Tex. App.- Austin, 1997) — 288

In Re Allcat Claims Serv., L.P.
356 S.W.3d 455 (Tex. 2011) — 247

In Re Harwood
637 F.3D 615 (5th Cir. 2011) — 290

In re Leal v. Mokhabery
360 B.R. 231, 2007 — 187

Ingalls v. Standard Gypsum, L.L.C.
70 S.W.3d 252 (Tex. App. – San Antonio 2001, pet., denied) — 459

Ingram and Behavioral Psychology Clinic, P.C. v. Deere et.al.
288 S.W.3d 886 (Tex, 2009) — 105

Kahn v. Imperial Airport, L.P.,
308 S.W.3D 432 (Tex. App.—Dallas 2010, no pet.) — 473

LJ Charter, L.L.C., v. Air America Jet Charter, Inc.,
2009 WL 4794242 (Tex. App.—Houston [14th Dist.] 2009) — 512

Laredo Med. Grp. v. Lightner
153 S.W.3d 70 (Tex. App. — San Antonio 2004) — 70

Lentz Engineering, L.L.C. v. Brown,
No. 14-10-00610-CV, 2011 WL 4449655 (Tex. App. – Houston [14 Dist.], 2011) — 470

Long v. Lopez
115 S.W.3d 221 (Tex.Civ.App.-Ft. Worth, 2003) — 137

May v. Ken-Rad Corporation, Inc.
279 Ky. 601, 131 S.W.2d 490 (1939)   22

McCarthy v. Wani Venture, A.S.,
251 S.W.3d 573, (Tex.App.-Houston [1st Dist.] 2007)   519

Nationsbank v. Dilling
922 S.W.2d 950 (Tex. 1996)   33

New Terminal Warehouse Corp. v. Wilson
589 S.W.2d 465 (Tex. App. – Houston [14th Dist.] 1979)   19

North Cypress Med. Ctr. Oper. Co. v. St. Laurent
296 S.W.3d 171, 175-76 (Tex.App-Houston [14th Dist.] 2009, no pet.)   266

Pace v. Houston Industries, Inc. et.al.
999 S.W.2d 615, Tex.App.-Hous. (1 Dist.), (1999)   361

Phillip Alexander Hajdasz v. Chase Merritt West Loop, L.L.C.
Not Reported in S.W.3d, 2010 WL 3418268 (Tex.App.-Houston (14 Dist.))   509

Pinebrook Properties, LTD. v Brookhaven Lake Property Owners Association
77 S.W.3d 487 (Tex.App.–Texarkana, 2002)   533

Pinnacle Data Services, Inc. v. Gillen
104 S.W.3d 188 (Tex. App.-Texarkana 2003)   466

Ramco Oil & Gas LTD. v. Anglo–Dutch (Tenge) L.L.C.
207 S.W.3d 801 (Tex. App.—Houston [14th Dist.] 2006)   492

Redmon v. Griffith
202 S.W.3d 225 (Tex.App.-Tyler, 2006)   386

Rogers v. Alexander
244 S.W.3d 370, 388 (Tex. App.—Dallas 2007)   540

Sanchez v. Mulvaney D/B/A Freestone Equipment Co. and Hypersonic Construction, LLC
274 S.W.3d 708 (Tex.App.–San Antonio, 2008)   516

Shaw v. Kennedy, Ltd.
879 S.W.2d 240 (Tex.App.–Amarillo,1994)   273

Shawell v. Pend Oreille Oil & Gas Co.
823 S.W.2d 336 (Tex.App.-Texarkana, 1991)   271

Siller v. LPP Mortgage Ltd.
Court of Appeals of Texas, San Antonio
Not Reported in S.W.3d, 2008 WL 5170251   131

Sinclair Oil Corporation v. Levien
332 A.2d 139 (Del.Supr., 1975) — 375

Sociedad De Solaridad Social "El Estillero" v. J.S. Mcmanus Produce Co.
964 S.W.2d 332 (Tex. App. – Corpus Christi 1998) — 27

Southwestern Bell Media, Inc. v. Trepper
784 S.W.2d 68 (Tex. App. — Dallas 1989) — 81

Strebel v. Wimberly
371S.W.3d 267 (Tex. App.- Houston[1 Dist.], 2012) — 296

Streetman v. Benchmark Bank
890 S.W.2d 212 (Tex. App. – Eastland 1994) — 29

Suarez v. Jordan
35 S.W.3d 268 (Tex. App. — Houston [14 Dist.] 2000) — 40

Templeton v. Nocona Hills Owners Association, Inc.
555 S.W.2d 534, Tex.Civ.App.-Texarkana, August 30, 1977 — 381

United States of America, Ex Rel., v. Integrated Coast Guard Systems, et.al.
705 F.Supp.2d 519 (2010) U S Dist Ct, N.D. Texas, Dallas Division — 121

Von Hohn, and in the Interest of H.B.V.H. and A.S.V.H., Minor Children
260 S.W.3d 631(Tex App-Tyler, 2008) — 146

Walkovszky v. Carlton
18 N.Y.2d 414, 223 N.E.2d 6, 276 N.Y.S.2d 585 — 416

Ward Family Foundation V. Arnette (In re Arnette)
454 B.R. 663, 680 (Bankr.N.D.Tex.2011) — 527

West v. Touchstone
620 S.W.2d 687 (Tex. App. — Dallas 1981) — 66

Wilson v. Contwell
2007 WL 2285947 N.D.Tex., 2007 — 164

Wyndham Hotel Co. v. Self
893 S.W.2d 630 (Tex. App. — Corpus Christi 1994) — 42

TABLE OF STATUTES

Restatement of Agency 3d — Page

§1.01 Agency Defined — *1*
§1.02 Parties' Labeling and Popular Usage Not Controlling — *1*

§ 2.01 Actual Authority — *25*
§ 2.02 Scope of Actual Authority — *25*
§ 2.03 Apparent Authority — *26*
§ 2.04 Respondeat Superior — *80*
§ 2.05 Estoppel To Deny Existence Of Agency Relationship — *45*

§ 3.02 Formal Requirements — *80*
§ 3.04 Capacity To Act As Principal — *22*
§ 3.05 Capacity To Act As Agent — *22*
§ 3.06 Termination Of Actual Authority--In General — *86*
§ 3.07 Death, Cessation Of Existence, & Suspension Of Powers — *85*
§ 3.08 Loss Of Capacity — *86*
§ 3.09 Termination By Agreement Or By Occurrence Of changed Circumstances — *86*
§ 3.10 Manifestation Terminating Actual Authority — *87*
§ 3.11 Termination Of Apparent Authority — *87*
§ 3.12 Power Given As Security; Irrevocable Proxy — *87*
§ 3.13 Termination Of Power Given As Security Or Irrevocable Proxy — *87*

§ 4.01 Ratification Defined — *57*
§ 4.02 Effect Of Ratification — *57*
§ 4.03 Acts That May Be Ratified — *57*
§ 4.04 Capacity To Ratify — *57*
§ 4.05 Timing Of Ratification — *57*
§ 4.06 Knowledge Requisite To Ratification — *57*
§ 4.07 No Partial Ratification — *57*
§ 4.08 Estoppel To Deny Ratification — *57*

§ 6.01 Agent For Disclosed Principal — *75*
§ 6.02 Agent For Unidentified Principal — *76*
§ 6.03 Agent For Undisclosed Principal — *76*
§ 6.04 Principal Does Not Exist Or Lacks Capacity — *77*
§ 6.06 Setoff — *76*
§ 6.07 Settlement With Agent By Principal Or Third Party — *77*
§ 6.08 Other Subsequent Dealings Between Third Party And Agent — *75*
§ 6.09 Effect Of Judgment Against Agent Or Principal — *80*
§ 6.10 Agent's Implied Warranty Of Authority — *80*
§ 6.11 Agent's Representations — *75*

§ 7.01 Agent's Liability To Third Party — *76*

§ 7.02 Duty To Principal; Duty To Third Party	76
§ 7.03 Principal's Liability--In General	78
§ 7.04 Agent Acts With Actual Authority	79
§ 7.05 Principal's Negligence In Conducting Activity Through Agent; Principal's Special Relationship With Another Person	79
§ 7.06 Failure In Performance Of Principal's Duty Of Protection	79
§ 7.07 Employee Acting Within Scope Of Employment	79
§7.07(3)(a)	3
§ 7.08 Agent Acts With Apparent Authority	79
§ 8.01 General Fiduciary Principle	64
§ 8.02 Material Benefit Arising Out Of Position	64
§ 8.03 Acting As Or On Behalf Of An Adverse Party	64
§ 8.04 Competition	64
§ 8.05 Use Of Principal's Property; Use Of Confidential Information	64
§ 8.06 Principal's Consent	65
§ 8.07 Duty Created By Contract	65
§ 8.08 Duties Of Care, Competence, And Diligence	65
§ 8.09 Duty To Act Only Within Scope Of Actual Authority And To Comply With Principal's Lawful Instructions	66
§ 8.10 Duty Of Good Conduct	66
§ 8.11 Duty To Provide Information	66
§ 8.12 Duties Regarding Principal's Property--Segregation, Record-Keeping, And Accounting	66
§ 8.13 Duty Created By Contract	63;66
§ 8.14 Duty To Indemnify	63
§ 8.15 Principal's Duty To Deal Fairly And In Good Faith	63

Texas Business Organization Code	**Page**
§ 1.002. Definitions	477;488;503
§ 2.003. General Prohibited Purposes	246
§3.001. Formation And Existence Of Filing Entities.	344;463
§ 3.005. Certificate of Formation	245;463
§ 3.010. Supplemental Provisions Required in Certificate of Formation of Limited Liability Company	464;477
§ 3.011. Supplemental Provisions Regarding Certificate of Formation of Limited Partnership	246
§ 3.102. Rights Of Governing Persons In Certain Cases.	356
§ 3.103. Officers	479
§ 3.153. Right of Examination by Owner or Member	502
§4.002. Action By Secretary Of State	346;464
§ 4.051. General Rule	464
§ 4.052. Delayed Effectiveness of Certain Filings	465

Section	Page
§4.101. Correction Of Filings	337;347
§ 5.055. Name of Limited Partnership or Foreign Limited Partnership	246
§ 6.052. Waiver of Notice	485
§ 7.001. Limitation Of Liability Of Governing Person.	331;357
§ 8.003. Limitations in Governing Documents	276
§ 8.051. Mandatory Indemnification	276
§ 8.101. Permissive Indemnification	276
§ 8.102. General Scope of Permissive Indemnification	277
§ 10.002. Plan Of Merger: Required Provisions	431
§10.003. Contents Of Plan Of Merger: More Than One Successor	432
§10.004. Plan Of Merger: Permissive Provisions	433
§10.352. Definitions	433
§10.353. Form And Validity Of Notice	434
§10.354. Rights Of Dissent And Appraisal	435
§ 10.355. Notice Of Right Of Dissent And Appraisal	436
§ 10.356. Procedure For Dissent By Owners As To Actions; Perfection Of Right Of Dissent And Appraisal	437
§10.357. Withdrawal Of Demand For Fair Value Of Ownership Interest	438
§ 10.358. Response By Organization To Notice Of Dissent And Demand For Fair Value By Dissenting Owner	439
§ 11.051. Events requiring winding up	302;557
§ 11.052. Winding Up Procedures	557
§ 11.053. Property Applied to Discharge Liabilities and Obligations	558
§ 11.055. Court Action or Proceeding During Winding Up	558
§ 11.056. Supplemental Provisions for Limited Liability Company	557
§ 11.058. Supplemental Provision for Limited Partnership	303;305
§ 11.102. Effectiveness of Termination of Filing Entity	560
§ 11.151. Revocation of Voluntary Winding Up	559
§ 11.152. Continuation of Business Without Winding Up	305;559
§ 11.201. Conditions for Reinstatement	561
§ 11.202. Procedures for Reinstatement	562
§ 11.205. Effectiveness of Reinstatement of Filing Entity	562
§ 11.206. Effect of Reinstatement	562
§ 11.301. Involuntary Winding Up And Termination Of Filing Entity By Court Action.	441
§ 11.302. Notification Of Cause By Secretary Of State.	441
§ 11.303. Filing Of Action By Attorney General.	442
§ 11.304. Cure Before Final Judgment.	442
§ 11.305. Judgment Requiring Winding Up And Termination.	442
§ 11.314. Involuntary Winding Up and Termination of Partnership or Limited Liability Company	303;558
§ 11.356. Limited Survival After Termination	560
§20.002. Ultra Vires Acts	359

§21.101. Shareholders' Agreement	*329*
§21.209. Transfer Of Shares And Other Securities	*332*
§21.210. Restriction On Transfer Of Shares And Other Securities	*332*
§21.211. Valid Restrictions On Transfer	*332*
§ 21.212. Bylaw Or Agreement Restricting Transfer Of Shares Or Other Securities	*334*
§ 21.213. Enforceability Of Restriction On Transfer Of Certain Securities	*334*
§21.223 Limitation Of Liability For Obligations	*330;412*
§ 21.302. Authority For Distributions.	*352*
§ 21.303. Limitations On Distributions.	*352*
§ 21.316. Liability Of Directors For Wrongful Distributions.	*352*
§21.364. Vote Required To Approve Fundamental Action	*426*
§21.365. Changes In Vote Required For Certain Matters	*428*
§21.401. Management By Board Of Directors	*328*
§ 21.418. Contracts Or Transactions Involving Interested Directors And Officers.	*355*
§21.455. Approval Of Sale Of All Or Substantially All Of Assets	*429*
§ 21.456. General Procedure For Submission To Shareholders Of Fundamental Business Transaction	*429*
§21.457. General Vote Requirement For Approval Of Fundamental Business Transaction	*430*
§ 101.001. Definitions	*465*
§ 101.051. Certain Provisions Contained In Certificate Of Formation.	*465*
§ 101.052. Company Agreement.	*465*
§ 101.053. Amendment Of Company Agreement.	*466;484*
§ 101.054. Waiver Or Modification Of Certain Statutory Provisions Prohibited; Exceptions.	
§ 101.101. Members Required	*458*
§ 101.102. Qualification for Membership	*487;503*
§ 101.103. Effective Date of Membership	*487*
§ 101.104. Classes or Groups of Members or Membership Interests	*503*
§ 101.105. Issuance of Membership Interests After Formation of Company	*484;487*
§ 101.106. Nature of Membership Interest	*488;501*
§ 101.108. Assignment of Membership Interest	*488*
§ 101.109. Rights and Duties of Assignee of Membership Interest Before Membership	*489*
§ 101.110. Rights and Liabilities of Assignee of Membership Interest After Becoming Member	*489*
§ 101.111. Rights and Duties of Assignor of Membership Interest	*489*
§ 101.112. Member's Membership Interest Subject to Charging Order	*501*
§ 101.1115. Effect of Death or Divorce on Membership Interest	*490*
§ 101.113. Parties to Actions	*459*
§ 101.114. Liability for Obligations	*506*

§	Title	Page
§ 101.151.	Requirements for Enforceable Promise	507
§ 101.153.	Failure to Perform Enforceable Promise; Consequences	508
§ 101.154.	Consent Required to Release Enforceable Obligation	508
§ 101.155.	Creditor's Right to Enforce Certain Obligations	508
§ 101.201.	Allocation of Profits and Losses	505
§ 101.202.	Distribution in Kind	505
§ 101.203.	Sharing of Distributions	505
§ 101.204.	Interim Distributions	505
§ 101.205.	Distribution on Withdrawal	506
§ 101.206.	Prohibited Distribution; Duty to Return	506
§ 101.251.	Governing Authority.	477
§ 101.252.	Management by Governing Authority	478
§ 101.254.	Designation of Agents; Binding Acts	478
§ 101.255.	Contracts or Transactions Involving Interested Governing Persons or Officers	548
§ 101.302.	Number and Qualifications	478
§ 101.353.	Quorum	482
§ 101.354.	Equal Voting Rights	482
§ 101.355.	Act of Governing Authority, Members, or Committee	483
§ 101.356.	Votes Required to Approve Certain Actions	483
§ 101.357.	Manner of Voting	484
§ 101.358.	Action by Less Than Unanimous Written Consent	484
§ 101.359.	Effective Action by Members or Managers With or Without Meeting	485
§ 101.401.	Expansion or Restriction of Duties and Liabilities	549
§ 101.402.	Permissive Indemnification, Advancement of Expenses, and Insurance or Other Arrangements	547
§ 101.452.	Standing to Bring Proceeding	536
§ 101.453.	Demand	537
§ 101.454.	Determination by Governing or Independent Persons	537
§ 101.455.	Stay of Proceeding	538
§ 101.458.	Dismissal of Derivative Proceeding	538
§ 101.461.	Payment of Expenses	539
§ 101.463.	Closely Held Limited Liability Company	539
§ 101.502.	Right to Examine Records and Certain Other Information	502
§ 101.551.	Persons Eligible To Wind Up Company.	
§ 101.552.	Approval Of Voluntary Winding Up, Revocation, Cancellation, Or Reinstatement.	483;560
§ 101.054.	Waiver or Modification of Certain Statutory Provisions Prohibited; Exceptions	502
§ 101.601.	Series of Members, Managers, Membership Interests, or Assets	468
§ 101.602.	Enforceability of Obligations and Expenses of Series Against Assets	469
§ 101.605.	General Powers of Series	469
§ 152.001.	Definitions.	176
§ 152.002.	Effect Of Partnership Agreement; Nonwaivable And Variable Provisions.	103;161

§ 152.051.	Partnership Defined.	98
§ 152.052.	Rules For Determining If Partnership Is Created.	104
§ 152.053.	Qualifications To Be Partner; Nonpartner's Liability To Third Person.	126;153
§ 152.054.	False Representation Of Partnership Or Partner.	114; 126;153
§ 152.056.	Partnership As Entity.	125
§ 152.101.	Nature Of Partnership Property.	125
§ 152.102.	Classification As Partnership Property.	125
§ 152.201.	Admission As Partner.	134
§ 152.202.	Credits Of And Charges To Partner.	144
§ 152.203.	Rights And Duties Of Partner.	134
§ 152.204.	General Standards Of Partner's Conduct.	134; 155;160
§ 152.205.	Partner's Duty Of Loyalty.	135;160
§ 152.206.	Partner's Duty Of Care.	135;160
§ 152.207.	Standards Of Conduct Applicable To Person Winding Up Partnership Business.	135;155;161;176
§ 152.208.	Amendment To Partnership Agreement.	104;135
§ 152.209.	Decision-Making Requirement.	136
§ 152.210.	Partner's Liability To Partnership And Other Partners.	153
§ 152.211.	Remedies Of Partnership And Partners.	136
§ 152.212.	Books And Records Of Partnership.	136
§ 152.213.	Information Regarding Partnership.	137;161
§ 152.214.	Certain Third-Party Obligations Not Affected.	137
§ 152.301.	Partner As Agent.	137
§ 152.302.	Binding Effect Of Partner's Action.	137
§ 152.303.	Liability Of Partnership For Conduct Of Partner.	156
§ 152.304.	Nature Of Partner's Liability.	154
§ 152.305.	Remedy.	154
§ 152.306.	Enforcement Of Remedy.	154
§ 152.307.	Extension Of Credit In Reliance On False Representation.	114; 155
§ 152.308.	Partner's Partnership Interest Subject To Charging Order.	144
§ 152.401.	Transfer Of Partnership Interest.	145
§ 152.402.	General Effect Of Transfer.	145
§ 152.403.	Effect Of Transfer On Transferor.	145
§ 152.404.	Rights And Duties Of Transferee.	145
§ 152.405.	Power To Effect Transfer Or Grant Of Security Interest.	146
§ 152.406.	Effect Of Death Or Divorce On Partnership Interest.	146
§ 152.501.	Events Of Withdrawal.	176
§ 152.502.	Effect Of Event Of Withdrawal On Partnership And Other Partners.	178
§ 152.503.	Wrongful Withdrawal; Liability.	178
§ 152.504.	Withdrawn Partner's Power To Bind Partnership.	179
§ 152.505.	Effect Of Withdrawal On Partner's Existing Liability.	179
§ 152.506.	Liability Of Withdrawn Partner To Third Party.	179
§ 152.601.	Redemption If Partnership Not Wound Up.	180
§ 152.602.	Redemption Price.	180
§ 152.603.	Contribution Obligation.	180

§ 152.604. Setoff For Certain Damages.	180
§ 152.605. Accrual Of Interest.	180
§ 152.606. Indemnification For Certain Liability.	180
§ 152.607. Demand Or Payment Of Estimated Redemption.	181
§ 152.608. Deferred Payment On Wrongful Withdrawal.	182
§ 152.609. Action To Determine Terms Of Redemption.	182
§ 152.610. Deferred Payment On Winding Up Partnership.	182
§ 152.611. Redemption Of Transferee's Partnership Interest.	183
§ 152.612. Action To Determine Transferee's Redemption Price.	183
§ 152.701. Effect Of Event Requiring Winding Up.	184
§ 152.702. Persons Eligible To Wind Up Partnership Business.	184
§ 152.703. Rights And Duties Of Person Winding Up Partnership Business.	184
§ 152.704. Binding Effect Of Partner's Action After Event Requiring Winding Up.	185
§ 152.705. Partner's Liability To Other Partners After Event Requiring Winding Up.	185
§ 152.706. Disposition Of Assets.	185
§ 152.707. Settlement Of Accounts.	185
§ 152.708. Contributions To Discharge Obligations.	186
§ 152.709. Cancellation Or Revocation Of Event Requiring Winding Up; Continuation Of Partnership.	186
§ 152.710. Reinstatement.	187
§ 152.801. Liability Of Partner.	224
§ 152.802. Registration	218
§ 152.803. Name.	218
§ 152.805. Limited Partnership.	218
§ 153.002. Construction	242
§ 153.003. Applicability of Other Laws	242
§ 153.004. Nonwaivable Title 1 Provisions	242
§ 153.005. Waiver or Modification of Rights of Third Parties	243
§ 153.101. Admission of Limited Partners	260
§ 153.102. Liability to Third Parties	278
§ 153.103. Actions Not Constituting Participation in Business for Liability Purposes	279
§ 153.104. Enumeration of Actions Not Exclusive	281
§ 153.105. Creation of Rights	281
§ 153.106. Erroneous Belief of Contributor Being Limited Partner	285
§ 153.107. Statement Required for Liability Protection	285
§ 153.108. Requirements for Liability Protection Following Expiration of Statement	285
§ 153.109. Liability of Erroneous Contributor	286
§ 153.110. Withdrawal of Limited Partner	308
§ 153.111. Distribution on Withdrawal	308
§ 153.151. Admission of General Partners	261
§ 153.152. General Powers and Liabilities of General Partner	253;271

§	Title	Page
§ 153.153.	Powers and Liabilities of Person Who is Both General Partner and Limited Partner	254;271
§ 153.154.	Contributions by and Distributions to General Partner	270
§ 153.155.	Withdrawal of General Partner	303
§ 153.156.	Notice of Event of Withdrawal	304
§ 153.157.	Withdrawal of General Partner in Violation of Partnership Agreement	304
§ 153.158.	Effect of Withdrawal	304
§ 153.161.	Liability of General Partner for Debt Incurred After Event of Withdrawal	307
§ 153.162.	Liability for Wrongful Withdrawal	307
§ 153.201.	Form of Contribution	267
§ 153.202.	Enforceability of Promise to Make Contribution	268
§ 153.203.	Release of Obligation to Partnership	269
§ 153.204.	Enforceability of Obligation	269
§ 153.206.	Allocation of Profits and Losses	269
§ 153.251.	Assignment of Partnership Interest	263
§ 153.252.	Rights of Assignor	263
§ 153.253.	Rights of Assignee	261;263
§ 153.254.	Liability of Assignee	264
§ 153.255.	Liability of Assignor	264
§ 153.256.	Partner's Partnership Interest Subject to Charging Order	264
§ 153.301.	Periodic Report	308
§ 153.307.	Effect of Failure to File Report	308
§ 153.309.	Effect of Forfeiture of Right to Transact Business	309
§ 153.310.	Revival of Right to Transact Business	309
§ 153.311.	Termination of Certificate or Revocation of Registration After Forfeiture	309
§ 153.312.	Reinstatement of Certificate of Formation or Registration	310
§ 153.401.	Right to Bring Action	254
§ 153.402.	Proper Plaintiff	254
§ 153.403.	Pleading	255
§ 153.501.	Cancellation or Revocation of Event Requiring Winding Up; Continuation of Business	306
§ 153.552.	Examination of Records and Information	262;265
§ 154.001.	Nature of Partner's Partnership Interest	262
§ 154.002.	Transfer of Interest in Partnership Property Prohibited	265
§ 154.201.	Business Transactions Between Partner and Partnership.	161
§ 154.203.	Distributions in Kind	270

Made in the USA
Charleston, SC
04 August 2013